Cisco Router Configuration Handbook

Second Edition

M000238746

Dave Hucaby, CCIE No. 4594

Steve McQuerry, CCIE No. 6108

Andrew Whitaker

Cisco Press

800 East 96th Street

Indianapolis, IN 46240

Cisco Router Configuration Handbook, Second Edition

Dave Hucaby, Steve McQuerry, Andrew Whitaker

Copyright © 2010 Cisco Systems, Inc.

Published by:
Cisco Press
800 East 96th Street
Indianapolis, IN 46240 USA

Printed in the United States of America

First Printing June 2010

Library of Congress Cataloging-in-Publication data is on file.

ISBN-13: 978-1-58714-116-4

ISBN-10: 1-58714-116-7

Warning and Disclaimer

This book is designed to provide information about configuring Cisco routers. Every effort has been made to make this book as complete and as accurate as possible, but no warranty or fitness is implied.

The information is provided on an "as is" basis. The authors, Cisco Press, and Cisco Systems, Inc. shall have neither liability nor responsibility to any person or entity with respect to any loss or damages arising from the information contained in this book or from the use of the discs or programs that may accompany it.

The opinions expressed in this book belong to the author and are not necessarily those of Cisco Systems, Inc.

Trademark Acknowledgments

All terms mentioned in this book that are known to be trademarks or service marks have been appropriately capitalized. Cisco Press or Cisco Systems, Inc., cannot attest to the accuracy of this information. Use of a term in this book should not be regarded as affecting the validity of any trademark or service mark.

Corporate and Government Sales

The publisher offers excellent discounts on this book when ordered in quantity for bulk purchases or special sales, which may include electronic versions and/or custom covers and content particular to your business, training goals, marketing focus, and branding interests. For more information, please contact: **U.S. Corporate and Government Sales 1-800-382-3419** corpsales@pearsontechgroup.com

For sales outside the United States, please contact: **International Sales** international@pearsoned.com

Feedback Information

At Cisco Press, our goal is to create in-depth technical books of the highest quality and value. Each book is crafted with care and precision, undergoing rigorous development that involves the unique expertise of members from the professional technical community.

Readers' feedback is a natural continuation of this process. If you have any comments regarding how we could improve the quality of this book, or otherwise alter it to better suit your needs, you can contact us through e-mail at feedback@ciscopress.com. Please make sure to include the book title and ISBN in your message.

We greatly appreciate your assistance.

Publisher: Paul Boger	**Manager, Global Certification:** Erik Ullanderson
Associate Publisher: Dave Dusthimer	**Business Operation Manager, Cisco Press:** Anand Sundaram
Executive Editor: Brett Bartow	**Senior Development Editor:** Christopher Cleveland
Managing Editor: Sandra Schroeder	**Project Editor:** Seth Kerney
Copy Editor: Apostrophe Editing Services	**Technical Editors:** Steve Kalman, Joe Harris
Editorial Assistant: Vanessa Evans	**Indexer:** WordWise Publishing Services
Book Designer: Louisa Adair	**Proofreaders:** Sheri Cain and Water Crest Publishing
Composition: Mark Shirar	

CISCO

Americas Headquarters	Asia Pacific Headquarters	Europe Headquarters
Cisco Systems, Inc.	Cisco Systems (USA) Pte. Ltd.	Cisco Systems International BV
San Jose, CA	Singapore	Amsterdam, The Netherlands

Cisco has more than 200 offices worldwide. Addresses, phone numbers, and fax numbers are listed on the Cisco Website at **www.cisco.com/go/offices.**

CCDE, CCENT, Cisco Eos, Cisco HealthPresence, the Cisco logo, Cisco Lumin, Cisco Nexus, Cisco StadiumVision, Cisco TelePresence, Cisco WebEx, DCE, and Welcome to the Human Network are trademarks; Changing the Way We Work, Live, Play, and Learn and Cisco Store are service marks; and Access Registrar, Aironet, AsyncOS, Bringing the Meeting To You, Catalyst, CCDA, CCDP, CCIE, CCIP, CCNA, CCNP, CCSP, CCVP, Cisco, the Cisco Certified Internetwork Expert logo, Cisco IOS, Cisco Press, Cisco Systems, Cisco Systems Capital, the Cisco Systems logo, Cisco Unity, Collaboration Without Limitation, EtherFast, EtherSwitch, Event Center, Fast Step, Follow Me Browsing, FormShare, GigaDrive, HomeLink, Internet Quotient, IOS, iPhone, iQuick Study, IronPort, the IronPort logo, LightStream, Linksys, MediaTone, MeetingPlace, MeetingPlace Chime Sound, MGX, Networkers, Networking Academy, Network Registrar, PCNow, PIX, PowerPanels, ProConnect, ScriptShare, SenderBase, SMARTnet, Spectrum Expert, StackWise, The Fastest Way to Increase Your Internet Quotient, TransPath, WebEx, and the WebEx logo are registered trademarks of Cisco Systems, Inc. and/or its affiliates in the United States and certain other countries.

All other trademarks mentioned in this document or website are the property of their respective owners. The use of the word partner does not imply a partnership relationship between Cisco and any other company. (0812R)

Dedications

Dave Hucaby: This book is dedicated to my wife, Marci, and my daughters, Lauren and Kara. I am blessed to have three wonderful girls in the house; their love, encouragement, and support carry me along. God is good!

Steve McQuerry: I dedicate this work to my beautiful wife and love of my life, Becky. Also, to my wonderful children, Katie, Logan, and Cameron. You are all my inspiration. Your patience, love, and support give me the courage and strength needed to spend the required time and energy on a project like this. Even through the long hours, I want you to know I love you all very much.

About the Authors

David Hucaby, CCIE #4594, is a lead network engineer for the University of Kentucky, where he designs, implements, and maintains campus networks using Cisco products. Prior to his current position, he was a senior network consultant, providing design and implementation consulting, focusing on Cisco-based VPN and IP telephony solutions. Hucaby has bachelor of science and master of science degrees in electrical engineering from the University of Kentucky. He is also the author of *CCNP Switching Exam Certification Guide* by Cisco Press.

Stephen McQuerry, CCIE #6108, is an instructor and consultant with more than ten years of networking industry experience. He is a certified Cisco Systems instructor (CCSI) and a course director/developer, teaching routing and switching concepts for Global Knowledge. McQuerry regularly teaches Cisco Enterprise courses. Additionally, he has developed and taught custom Cisco switching courses. McQuerry holds a bachelor of science degree in engineering physics from Eastern Kentucky University. He is also the author of *Interconnecting Cisco Network Devices* by Cisco Press.

Andrew Whitaker has been teaching and developing Cisco courses for more than seven years and holds the following certifications: CCNP, CCVP, CCSP, CCDP, CCNA:Security, MCT, CEI, CISSP, LPT, CEH, ECSA, MCTS, MCSE, CNE, A+, Network+, Security+, Convergence+, CTP, CICP, CHFI, EMCPA. He is the author of several books, including *Penetration Testing and Network Defense* by Cisco Press.

About the Technical Reviewers

Steven Kalman is the principal officer at Esquire Micro Consultants, which offers lecturing, writing, and consulting services. He has more than 30 years of experience in data processing, with strengths in network design and implementation. Kalman is an instructor and author for Learning Tree International. He has written and reviewed many networking-related titles. He holds CCNA, CCDA, ECNE, CEN, and CNI certifications.

Joe Harris, CCIE No. 6200 (R/S, Security & SP), is a Triple CCIE working for Cisco as a systems engineer within the Wireline and Emerging Providers organization, where he specializes in security and MPLS-related technologies. With more than 16 years of extensive experience focusing on advance technologies within the IT arena, Joe has been primarily focused on supporting various enterprise-sized networks revolving around all aspects of Cisco technology. He has also provided high-end consulting for both large and small corporations, as well as local government and federal agencies. Joe holds a bachelor of science degree from Louisiana Tech University and resides with his wife and two children in Frisco, Texas.

Acknowledgments

Dave Hucaby: I am very grateful for another opportunity to work on a Cisco Press project. Getting to dabble in technical writing has been great fun, a highlight in my career, and a lot of work, too! Naturally, these good folks at Cisco Press have gone the extra mile to make writing enjoyable and achievable: Brett Bartow, who kindly accepted my idea for a book like this and kindly prodded us along to meet deadlines we didn't think we could, and Chris Cleveland, who is a superb development editor. As a matter of fact, every Cisco Press person I have met along the way has been so nice, encouraging, and excited about their work!

Thanks to our technical reviewers: Steve Kalman and Joe Harris. Working on a book of this nature has been challenging. The sheer volume and scope of the Cisco IOS Software commands and features are a little overwhelming. I truly appreciate reviewers who can help us see a bigger picture of better organization and accuracy while we're writing in the depths of configuration commands. This book is also a testimony to the great number of things you can do with a router, thanks to the Cisco IOS Software. I don't know how many hundreds of commands we have covered in this book, but we had to leave out many more lesser-used commands just to keep a handle on the book's size and scope. I'm amazed at the robustness of the software and its dynamic nature.

I would like to express my thanks to my friend and coauthor Steve McQuerry. We've followed each other around for many years, and it has been great to work on this project with him. Hopefully, we Kentucky boys can work on more things like this.

Lastly, I would like to acknowledge the person who stole my laptop computer halfway through the first edition of this book project. Whoever you are, you left me a victim of my own lack of current backups. I made up a silly joke many years ago: "A backup is worth a million bytes, especially if you have to type them all back in." Indeed.

Steve McQuerry: About 20 years ago, the late Rodger Yockey gave me an opportunity as a field engineer in the computer industry. Since then, several people have been there at key moments to help my career go in certain directions. I owe a great debt to these people, as they have helped me reach the level I am at today. It is not often that one has the opportunity to thank those who have been instrumental in molding his career. In addition to Rodger, I would like to take a moment to also thank Ted Banner for his guidance and mentoring. I would also like to thank Chuck Terrien for giving me the opportunity to work as an instructor in the Cisco product line. I would like to thank Brett Bartow for the opportunity to begin sharing my experiences with the network community by writing for Cisco Press. Last but not least, I have to thank my friend and coauthor, Dave Hucaby. This book was his concept, and I thank him for the opportunity work with him once again. I hope we will always find a way to continue working together in the future.

Since I began working on book and course projects a couple of years ago, I have a newfound respect for what it takes to edit, coordinate, publish, and basically keep authors on track. Behind every Cisco Press book is an incredible staff, and I would be remiss if I did not acknowledge their work. Chris Cleveland, again it has been great working with you. I hope that we can work together again in the future.

Without the following individuals behind the book, it would be no more than a collection of jumbled notes and napkin sketches of networking configurations:

The sharp eyes of all our technical editors on the first and this edition: Joe Harris, Steve Kalman, Alexander Marhold, and Kevin Turek.

All my students and fellow instructors at Global Knowledge. Your challenges and questions provide me with the drive to have a better understanding.

My wife and children for their never-ending patience and understanding during this and all of my projects.

Most important, God, for giving me the skills, talents, and opportunity to work in such a challenging and exciting profession.

Andrew Whitaker: I would like to express my thanks to both Dave Hucaby and Steve McQuerry for this opportunity. Brett Bartow and Chris Cleveland, it is great to work with both of you again. Finally, to Steve Kalman and Joe Harris, I appreciate how diligently you worked to ensure a quality book.

Contents at a Glance

Contents

Icons Used in This Book

Throughout this book, you see the following icons used for networking devices:

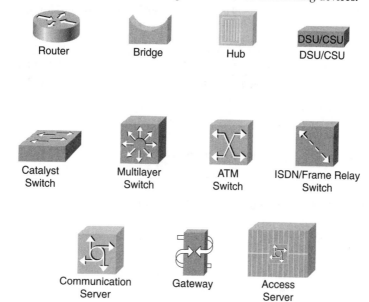

Router   Bridge   Hub   DSU/CSU

Catalyst Switch   Multilayer Switch   ATM Switch   ISDN/Frame Relay Switch

Communication Server   Gateway   Access Server

The following icons are used for peripherals and other devices:

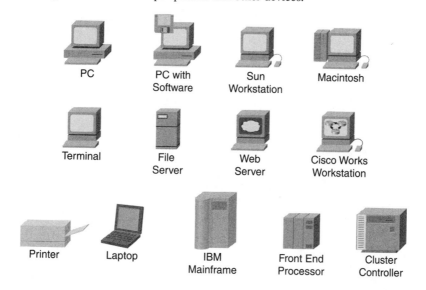

PC   PC with Software   Sun Workstation   Macintosh

Terminal   File Server   Web Server   Cisco Works Workstation

Printer   Laptop   IBM Mainframe   Front End Processor   Cluster Controller

Command Syntax Conventions

The conventions used to present command syntax in this book are the same conventions used in the IOS Command Reference. The Command Reference describes these conventions as follows:

- **Boldface** indicates commands and keywords that are entered literally as shown. In actual configuration examples and output (not general command syntax), boldface indicates commands that are manually input by the user (such as a **show** command).

- *Italic* indicates arguments for which you supply actual values.

- Vertical bars (|) separate alternative, mutually exclusive elements.

- Square brackets ([ ]) indicate an optional element.

- Braces ({ }) indicate a required choice.

- Braces within brackets () indicate a required choice within an optional element.

Introduction

There are many sources of information and documentation for configuring Cisco networking devices, but few provide a quick and portable solution for networking professionals. This book is designed to provide a quick-and-easy reference guide for a wide range of commonly used features that can be configured on Cisco routers. In essence, the subject matter from an entire bookshelf of Cisco IOS Software documentation, along with other networking reference material, has been "squashed" into one handy volume that you can take with you.

This idea for this book began with my study habits for the CCIE written and lab exam. Over time, I found that I had put together a whole notebook of handwritten notes about how to configure a variety of Cisco router features. I also found that I began carrying this notebook with me into the field as a network consultant. When you're on the job and someone requires you to configure a feature you're not too familiar with, it's nice to have your handy reference notebook in your bag! Hopefully, this book will be that handy reference for you.

Features and Organization

This book is meant to be used as a tool in your day-to-day tasks as a network administrator or engineer. As such, we have avoided presenting a large amount of instructional informa-tion or theory on the operation of protocols or commands. That is better handled in other textbooks dedicated to a more limited subject matter.

Instead, this book is divided into parts that present quick facts, configuration steps, and explanations of configuration options for each feature in the Cisco IOS Software.

How to Use This Book

All the information in this book has been designed to follow a quick-reference format. If you know what feature or technology you want to use, you can turn right to the section that deals with it. Sections are numbered with a quick-reference index, showing both chapter and section number. For example, 13-3 is Chapter 13, Section 3. You'll also find shaded index tabs on each page, listing the section number, the chapter subject, and the topic dealt with in that section.

Facts About a Feature

Each section in a chapter includes a bulleted list of quick facts about the feature, technol-ogy, or protocol. Refer to these lists to quickly learn or review how the feature works. Immediately following, we have placed a note that details what protocol or port number the feature uses. If you are configuring filters or firewalls and you need to know how to al-low or block traffic from the feature, look for these notes.

Configuration Steps

Each feature covered in a section includes the required and optional commands used for common configuration. The difference is that the configuration steps are presented in an outline format. If you follow the outline, you can configure a complex feature or technol-ogy. If you find that you don't need a certain feature option, skip over that level in the out-line.

Sample Configurations

Each section includes an example of how to implement the commands and their options. We have tried to present the examples with the commands listed in the order you would actually enter them to follow the outline. Many times, it is more difficult to study and un-derstand a configuration example from an actual router, because the commands are dis-played in a prede-fined order, not in the order you entered them. Where possible, the ex-amples have also been trimmed to show only the commands presented in the section.

Further Reading

Each chapter ends with a recommended reading list to help you find more in-depth sources of information for the topics discussed.

Chapter 1

Configuration Basics

This chapter presents background and configuration information for the following configuration basics:

- 1-1: User Interfaces
- 1-2: File Management
- 1-3: Cisco Discovery Protocol (CDP)
- 1-4: System Time
- 1-5: Logging
- 1-6: System Monitoring
- 1-7: Service Assurance Agent (SAA)
- 1-8: Buffer Management
- 1-9: Some Troubleshooting Tools

1-1: User Interfaces

A router supports user access by command-line interface (CLI), a web browser, or by GUI device management tools. A router also provides a user interface to the ROM monitor bootstrap code.

Users can execute IOS commands from a user level or from a privileged level. User level offers basic system information and remote connectivity commands. Privileged level offers complete access to all router information, configuration editing, and debugging commands.

A router offers many levels of configuration modes, allowing the configuration to be changed for a variety of router resources.

A context-sensitive help system offers command syntax and command choices at any user prompt.

A history of IOS commands executed can be kept. Command lines can also be edited and reused.

The output from a command can be searched and filtered so that useful information can be found quickly.

Parameters for the CLI connection to the router can be set to preferred values.

Asynchronous ports on a router can be connected to other serial devices. You can open reverse-Telnet connections to the external devices for remote access.

Banners can be defined and displayed at various points in the login process.

Menus can be defined to give terminal session users easy access to other functions or remote systems.

Role Based Access Control (RBAC) enables you to define the rules for an assigned role that restricts the authorization that the user has to access for management and configuration.

Access to the router can be configured for Secure Shell (SSH) version 1 or version 2.

Configuration

1. User interface modes.

    a. User EXEC mode: Users can connect to a router via the console port, auxiliary port, Telnet session, SSH session, or the Security Device Manager (SDM). By default, the initial access to a router places the user in user EXEC mode and offers a limited set of commands. When connecting to the router, a user-level password might or might not be required.

    b. Privileged EXEC mode:

    ```
    (exec) enable
        password: [password]
    ```

    As soon as a user gains access in user EXEC mode, the **enable** command can be used to enter *privileged EXEC* or *enable* mode. Full access to all commands is available. To leave privileged EXEC mode, use the **disable** or **exit** commands.

    c. Configuration mode:

    ```
    (exec) configure terminal
    ```

    From privileged EXEC mode, configuration mode can be entered. Router commands can be given to configure any router feature that is available in the IOS software image. When you are in configuration mode, you are managing the router's active memory. Anytime you enter a valid command in any configuration mode and press Enter, the memory is immediately changed. Configuration mode is organized in a hierarchical fashion. Global configuration mode allows commands that affect the router as a whole. Interface configuration mode allows commands that configure router interfaces. There are many other configuration modes that you can move into and out of, depending on what is being configured. To move from a lower-level configuration mode to a higher level, type **exit**. To leave global configuration mode and return to privileged EXEC mode, type **exit** at the global configuration prompt. To leave any configuration mode and return to privileged EXEC mode, type **end** or press **Ctrl-z**.

2. User interface features.

   a. Entering commands:

   ```
   (any mode) command
   (any mode) no command
   ```

   Commands can be entered from any mode (EXEC, global, interface, subinterface, and so on). To enable a feature or parameter, type the command and its options normally, as in *command*. To disable a command that is in effect, begin the command with **no**, followed by the command. You can see the commands that are in effect by using the **show running-config** command. Note that some commands and parameters are set by default and are not shown as literal command lines in the configuration listing.

   Commands and their options can also be abbreviated with as few letters as possible without becoming ambiguous. For example, to enter the interface configuration mode for ethernet 0, the command **interface ethernet 0** can be abbreviated as **int e 0**.

   A command line may be edited using the left and right arrow keys to move within the line. If additional characters are typed, the remainder of the line to the right is spaced over. The Backspace and Delete keys may be used to make corrections.

   Note   If the router displays a console informational or error message while you are typing a command line, you can press Ctrl-l or Ctrl-r to redisplay the line and continue editing. You can also configure the lines (console, vty, or aux) to use logging synchronous. This causes the router to automatically refresh the lines after the router output. If you issue debug commands with logging synchronous enabled, you might have to wait for the router to finish the command (such as a ping) before you see the output.

   b. Context-sensitive help.

   You can enter a question mark (**?**) anywhere in a command line to get additional information from the router. If the question mark is typed alone, all available commands for that mode are displayed. Question marks can also be typed at any place after a command, keyword, or option. If the question mark follows a space, all available keywords or options are displayed. If the question mark follows another word without a space, a list of all available commands beginning with that substring is displayed. This can be helpful when an abbreviated command is ambiguous and flagged with an error.

   An abbreviated command may also be typed, followed by pressing the Tab key. The command name is expanded to its full form if it is not ambiguous.

If a command line is entered but doesn't have the correct syntax, the error "% Invalid input detected at '^' marker" is returned. A caret (^) appears below the command character where the syntax error was detected.

c. Command history.

(Optional) Set the number of commands to save (default 10). To set the history size for the current terminal session, enter

`(exec) `**`terminal history `**`[`**`size`**` lines]`

To set the history size for all sessions on a line, enter

`(line) history [size lines]`

Recall commands to use again.

From any input mode, each press of the up arrow (q) or **Ctrl-p** recalls the next older command. Each press of the down arrow (Q) or **Ctrl-n** recalls the next most recent command. When commands are recalled from history, they can be edited as if you just typed them. The **show history** command displays the recorded command history.

Note   The up- and down-arrow keys require the use of an ANSI-compatible terminal emulator (such as VT100).

d. Search and filter command output.

Sift through output from a **show** command:

`(exec) show command ... | {begin | include | exclude} reg-expression`

A **show** command can generate a long output listing. If the listing contains more lines than the terminal session can display (set using the *length* parameter), the output is displayed a screenful at a time with a *--More--* prompt at the bottom. To see the next screen, press the spacebar. To advance one line, press the Enter key. To exit to the command line, press **Ctrl-c**, **q**, or any key other than Enter or the spacebar.

To search for a specific regular expression and start the output listing there, use the **begin** keyword. This can be useful if your router has many interfaces in its configuration. Rather than using the spacebar to eventually find a certain configuration line, you can use **begin** to jump right to the desired line. To display only the lines that include a regular expression, use the **include** keyword. To display all lines that don't include a regular expression, use the **exclude** keyword.

Sift through output from a more command:

`(exec) more file-url | {begin | include | exclude} reg-expression`

The **more** command displays the contents of a file on the router. A typical use is to display the startup (**more nvram:startup-config**) or running (**more system:running-config**) configuration file. By default, the file is displayed one screen at a time with a *--More--* prompt at the bottom.

To search for a specific regular expression and start the output listing there, use the **begin** keyword. To display only the lines that include a regular expression, use the **include** keyword. To display all lines that don't include a regular expression, use the **exclude** keyword.

Search through the output at a *--More--* prompt:

`(--More--) {/ | + | -}regular-expression`

At a *--More--* prompt, you can search the output by typing a slash (/) followed by a regular expression. To display only lines that include the regular expression, type a plus (**+**). To display only lines that don't include the regular expression, type a minus (-).

What is a regular expression?

A regular expression can be used to match lines of output. Regular expressions are made up of patterns—either simple text strings (such as ethernet or ospf) or more-complex matching patterns. Typically, regular expressions are regular text words that offer a hint to a location in the output of a **show** command.

A more-complex regular expression is made up of patterns and operators. Table 1-1 lists the characters that are used as operators.

Table 1-1 *Operator Characters*

Character	Meaning
.	Matches a single character.
*	Matches zero or more sequences of the preceding pattern.
+	Matches one or more sequences of the preceding pattern.
?	Matches zero or one occurrence of the preceding pattern.
^	Matches at the beginning of the string.
$	Matches at the end of the string.
_	Matches a comma, braces, parentheses, beginning or end of a string, or a space.
[ ]	Defines a range of characters as a pattern.
( )	Groups characters as a pattern. If this is used around a pattern, the patterncan be recalled later in the expression using a backslash (\) and the patternoccurrence number.

3. Terminal sessions.

a. Start a new session:

`(exec) telnet host`

This initiates a Telnet connection to *host* (either an IP address or a host name). Then, from the router CLI, you can continue communicating with the remote host.

b. Name a session:

`(exec) name-connection`
>   `(exec) Connection number: number`
>   `(exec) Enter logical name: name`

An active session can be assigned a text string name to make the session easier to identify with the **show sessions** or **where** command.

c. Suspend a session to do something else.

During an active Telnet session to a host, press the escape sequence **Ctrl-Shift-6, x**, also written as **Ctrl-^, x. Ctrl-^** is the IOS escape sequence, and the additional **x** tells the router to suspend a session. This suspends the Telnet session and returns you to the local router command-line prompt.

Note   It is possible to have nested Telnet sessions open. For example, from the local router, you can Telnet to another router A, then Telnet to another router B, and so forth. To suspend one of these sessions, you must also nest your escape sequences. Pressing a single **Ctrl-^x** suspends the session to router A and returns you to the local router. Pressing **Ctrl-^ Ctrl-^x** suspends the session to router B and returns you to router A's prompt. (Press the **x** only at the final escape sequence.)

d. Show all active sessions:

`(exec) show sessions`

All open sessions from your connection to the local router are listed, along with connection numbers. You can also use the where command to get the same information.

e. Return to a specific session.

First, use the **show sessions** command to get the connection number of the desired session. Then, just type the connection number by itself on the command line. The session is reactivated. You can also just press Return or Enter at the command-line prompt, and the last active connection in the list is reactivated. The last active connection in the list is denoted by an asterisk (*). This makes toggling between the local router and a single remote session easier.

Note   When you resume the connection, you are prompted with the message "[Resuming connection 2 to Router ...]". You must press Enter again to actually resume the connection.

f. End an active session:

```
(remote session) Ctrl-^ x
        (exec) disconnect connection-number
```

As soon as the remote session is suspended, you can use the **disconnect** command to end the session and close the Telnet connection. Otherwise, your session remains open until the remote host times out the connection (if at all).

g. Terminal screen format.

Set the screen size for the current session only:

```
(exec) terminal length lines
(exec) terminal width characters
```
Set the screen size for all sessions:
```
        (line) length lines
(line) width characters
```

The screen is formatted to *characters* wide by *lines* high. When the number of lines of output from a command exceeds *lines*, the *--More--* prompt appears. If you don't want the output displayed by page with *--More--*, use **length 0**. The default length for sessions is 24 lines, and the default width for settings is 80 characters.

h. Allow for temporary locking of your terminal session.

```
(line)lockable
```

You can prevent access to your session while still keeping the session open by setting a temporary password. To enable this feature, first configure the **lockable** line configuration command. Then, to temporarily lock your session, enter the **lock** command in either user or privileged EXEC mode. You will be prompted for a password that you can use later when resuming your session.

i. Reverse Telnet connections.

Connect an asynchronous serial router line.

Any asynchronous line on a router can be used to support remote connections to external devices (that is, console ports on other Cisco routers or switches). Using a console "rollover" cable or a high-density access server cable, connect an async line on the local router to an asynchronous serial port on the external device. The AUX port or any async serial line on a Cisco access server can be used for this purpose.

Enable the Telnet protocol on a line:

```
(line) transport input telnet
(line) no login
(line) no exec
```

To choose the appropriate line, use either **line aux 0** or **line** *number,* where *number* is the async line number. Because this line is used as a transparent connection between the external device and a remote user, no interactive process should be running on the local router that would interfere. Therefore, the **no login** command should be used to stop any local login prompting process, and **no exec** should be used to stop the executive process from interacting with any local character interpretation from devices attached to the line.

Set the async serial parameters:

```
(line) speed baud
(line) databits {5 | 6 | 7 | 8}
(line) stopbits {1 | 1.5 | 2}
(line) parity {none | even | odd | space | mark}
```

The async line should be set to match the characteristics of the remote device. **speed** sets both receive and transmit baud rates, baud. Common values are 300, 1200, 2400, 4800, 9600, 19200, 38400, and 115200. To view the default or current line settings, use the **show line** line command.

Open a reverse Telnet connection to the line:

```
(exec) telnet ip-address port
```

From a remote location (or from the local router if desired), open a Telnet session to the IP address of the local router. In addition, a TCP port number must be given, as *port*. Reverse Telnet connections to async lines use TCP port numbers, beginning with 2000. You determine the port number by adding the line number (in decimal) to 2000 (also in decimal). For example, line 1 is port 2001, and line 15 is port 2015.

Note   You will be Telnetting to an active IP address on the router. Although this can be any address on the router, it is a common practice to configure a loopback address on the router. See Chapter 2, "Interface Configuration," for more information on loopback addresses.

If you have a router with many async lines, it might be difficult to determine the correct line number for a specific line. Use **show users all** to display all available lines on the router, including the console, AUX line, and vty or Telnet lines. The physical line number is displayed in the leftmost column of the output, under the heading "Line." Usually, the console is line 0 (but it can't be used for reverse Telnet), and the AUX line is line 1, followed by other async lines and/or vty lines.

Also, you might sometimes receive a response that the port is unavailable. In this case, either another user has an active Telnet session open on that port, or the physical line needs to be reset. To reset the line, use the **clear line** line-number command on the local router.

Close the reverse-Telnet session:

```
(session) Ctrl-^ x
(exec) disconnect session
```

To suspend the current reverse-Telnet session and return to the local router prompt, press the escape sequence (the default is **Ctrl-^ x** or **Ctrl-Shift-6 x**). To end the reverse-Telnet session, use the **disconnect** command along with the session number. If you forget the session number of the reverse-Telnet session, use the **show sessions** or **where** command.

j. Send a message to another terminal session:

```
(exec) send {line-number | * | aux number | console number | tty number |
vty number}
```

Sometimes it is convenient to send quick messages to users who are Telnetted into a router. For example, you and a colleague might be logged into the same router but be located in different cities. A text message can be sent to either a specific line number (*line-number*), all lines (*), the AUX line (**aux** *number*), the router console (**console** *number*), a specific tty line (**tty** *number*), or a specific vty line (**vty** *number*). To find a user on a specific line, use the **show users** command. The router prompts for a text message to send. After typing the message, end with **Ctrl-z.**

k. Configure session timeout values.

Define an absolute timeout for a line:

```
(line) absolute-timeout minutes
```

All active sessions on the line are terminated after *minutes* have elapsed. (The default is 0 minutes, or an indefinite session timeout.)

Define an idle timeout for a line:

```
(line) session-timeout minutes [output]
```

All active sessions on the line are terminated only if they have been idle for *minutes*. (The default is 0 minutes, or an indefinite idle timeout.) The **output** keyword causes the idle timer to be reset by outbound traffic on the line, keeping the connection up.

Define an idle timeout for all EXEC-mode sessions:

`(line) exec-timeout minutes [seconds]`

Active EXEC mode sessions are automatically closed after an idle period of *minutes* and *seconds* (the default is 10 minutes). To disable idle EXEC timeouts on the line, use the **no exec-timeout** or **exec-timeout 0 0** command.

Enable session timeout warnings:

`(line) logout-warning [seconds]`

Users are warned of an impending logout *seconds* before it occurs. By default, no warning is given. If the *seconds* field is left off, it defaults to 20 seconds.

4. Secure Shell connections.

Note   Cisco IOS supports only SSH version 1, with User ID and Password authentication. To use SSH, you must have an IPSec encryption software image. A DES (56-bit) image supports only DES encryption, and a 3DES (168-bit) image supports either DES or 3DES. (See Appendix A, "Cisco IOS Software Releases and Filename Conventions," for details on determining what feature sets your software image supports.) SSH uses UDP and TCP port number 22.

a. Configure a host name and a domain name for the router:

`(global) hostname hostname`
`(global) ip domain-name domain`

The router must have both a host name and an IP domain name assigned, although the router does not have to be entered in a domain name server. The host name and domain name are used during encryption key computation.

b. Generate the RSA key pair for authentication:

`(global) crypto key generate rsa`

A public and private key pair is generated for authentication to a remote session. This command is executed once at the time it is entered. Neither the command nor the keys are shown as part of the router configuration, although the keys are stored in a private NVRAM area for security. This command prompts for a modulus length (360 to 2048 bits; the default is 512). The higher the modulus, the better the encryption and the longer the computation time. Cisco recommends a minimum modulus of 1024 bits. You can view your public key by executing the **show cry key mypubkey rsa** privileged EXEC command. You can delete the RSA key pair with the **crypto key zeroize rsa** privileged EXEC command.

c. Enable Authentication, Authorization, and Accounting (AAA) authentication:

```
(global)aaa new-model
```

or

```
(line)login local
```

The **aaa new-model** command causes the local username and pasword to be used on the router in the absence of other AAA statements. Alternatively, you can use the **login local** line command to accomplish the same task.

AAA user authentication:

Users can be authenticated by a remote AAA server. For more information on configuring an AAA server, see Section 12-2.

d. Configure user authentication.

Local user authentication:

```
(global) username username password password
```

Users can be authenticated locally on the router, provided that both a username and password are configured. The password is entered as a cleartext string containing up to 80 alphanumeric characters, including embedded spaces. Passwords are case-sensitive.

e. Configure SSH parameters:

```
(global) ip ssh {[timeout seconds] | [authentication-retries retries]}
```

The **timeout** keyword defines the maximum time for SSH negotiation with the remote device (the default is 120 seconds). The number of authentication retries can be defined with the **authentication-retries** keyword (the maximum is 5 retries; the default is 3).

f. Enable the SSH protocol on a line:

```
(line)#transport input ssh
```

By default, all input protocols are allowed on lines. Enter the **no transport input all** command to disable all inbound connections on a line. Then enter the **transport input ssh** command to allow only inbound SSH connections on a line.

g. Configure the SSH version:

```
(config)#ip ssh version [1 | 2]
```

Starting with IOS 12.1(19)E, you can use SSH version 2. To support both versions 1 and 2, enter the **no ip ssh version** global configuration command. This IOS version also introduced the capability to display a login banner prior to connecting to a router unless the router is configured to use only SSH version 1.

h. Telnet to the router from an SSH-capable device.

All inbound SSH sessions to the router are opened to the VTY (Telnet) lines. The number of concurrent Telnet sessions (both non-SSH and SSH) is limited by the number of VTY lines that are configured.

i. (Optional) Open an outbound SSH session from the router:

```
(exec) ssh [-v 2][-l userid] [-c {des | 3des | aes192-cbc | aes256-cbc}]
[-m hmac-md5

| hmac-md5-96 | hmac -sha1 | hmac-sha1-96 ][-o numberofpasswdprompts

prompts] [-p port] {ip-address | hostname} [command]
```

An SSH session is opened to the host given by *ip-address* or *hostname*. Starting with IOS 12.1(19)E, you can specify SSH 2 with the **–v 2** keyword. By default, the current username on the local router is used for authentication on the remote device. This can be overridden by the -l *userid* keyword. The type of encryption is specified as either DES, 3DES, AES192-cbc, or AES256-cbc using the -c keyword. The **–m** keyword sets the hashing algorithm used for authentication if configured on the SSH router. The number of prompts for a password can be set by the -o *numberofpasswdprompts* keyword. (1 to 5; the default is 3.) The port number used for the SSH session can be set using the **-p** *port* keyword. (The default is 22.) The *command* field specifies the command to be run on the remote device, assuming that the authenticated user has access to that command. If embedded spaces are needed, enclose the command string in double quotation marks.

5. Configuring access to the router.

a. (Optional) Set up authentication for users.

Define a username and password:

```
(global) username name {password password | password encrypt-type

  encrypted-password}
```

Enable authentication for a specific username name. The password keyword can define a text string password to be used at login time. An encrypted password from a previous router configuration can be copied and pasted into this command using the encrypt-type encrypted-password fields. An encrypt-type of 0 means that the password is unencrypted and is in clear text, and 7 means that the password is already encrypted.

Define a username to run a command automatically:

```
(global) username name nopassword autocommand command
```

The username *name* is defined as a login name. When it is used, no password is required, and the router command *command* is run automatically. Afterward, the user is logged out and disconnected.

Alter a user's access privileges:

```
(global) username name [access-class acc-list] [noescape] [nohangup]
 [privilege level]
```

The **access-class** keyword specifies an access list for the username that overrides one used in a line's **access-class** command. The **noescape** keyword prevents the user from using the escape sequence to suspend the session. The **nohangup** keyword returns the user to EXEC mode after an automatic command completes. A user's default privilege level (1) can be set using the **privilege** keyword.

b. Configure login authentication.

First, you must choose a line for incoming users.

For an asynchronous port (line), enter the following command:

```
(global) line {console 0 | aux 0 | number}
```

Asynchronous ports are called *lines* in the router configuration. Lines are identified by number. If you aren't sure of the line number on an async port, use the **show users all** command to display all lines and their numbers. You can configure the following lines: console port (**line console 0**), auxiliary port (**line aux 0**), and async lines on an access server (**line** *number*).

For a virtual terminal line (vty) for Telnet access, enter the following command:

```
(global) line vty first [last]
```

vty ports are also called *lines* in the router configuration. Several vty lines can be configured so that more than one Telnet session can be active to the router. A range of vty lines can be configured at one time by using both *first* and *last* vty numbers.

Note VTY lines require a password to be configured before user access is enabled. Otherwise, the router closes any incoming Telnet sessions immediately.

To enable login authentication without a username, enter the following command sequence:

```
(line) login
```

```
(line) password password
```

Users are prompted for a password on the specified line. The *password* text string can be up to 80 alphanumeric characters with embedded spaces. The first character cannot be a number.

To enable login authentication with a router-defined username, enter the following command:

```
(line) login local
```

Individual usernames must first be configured as shown in Step 5a. The router then authenticates users on the specified line against the locally defined usernames and passwords.

To enable logins with TACACS authentication, enter the following command:

```
(line) login tacacs
```

The router authenticates users by interacting with a standard or extended TACACS (not TACACS+) server.

To enable logins with AAA/TACACS+, enter the following command:

```
(line) login authentication
```

The router authenticates users by interacting with an external AAA server. Refer to Section 13-2 for more information on configuring AAA features.

c. Privileged mode (enable mode):

```
(global) enable secret enable-password
```

To access privileged mode, you must enter the enable password. This password can be set to *enable-password*. The password is encrypted using a strong nonreversible encryption algorithm and is then stored in a special secure location in NVRAM. The password must have 1 to 25 alphanumeric characters. The first character cannot be a number, and embedded spaces are accepted.

The enable password can also be set using the **enable password** command. Cisco recommends using the **enable secret** command instead, because the password has a stronger encryption and is not stored in the router configuration.

The **enable secret** [**level** *level*] enable-password command can be used to set the password required for entering the privilege level specified. Levels range from 0 to 15, where 1 is the normal EXEC level and 15 is enable mode.

Note   An **enable** or **enable secret** password is not required for the router. If you don't have one configured, you are not prompted for the password when you issue the **enable** command from the console. If you do not have an **enable** or **enable secret** password, however, you can't access privileged EXEC mode from any Telnet or other line into the router.

Access to specific IOS commands can be granted to privilege levels so that you can create user communities with varying capabilities. For example, you might want to allow a group of users to access the **show cdp neighbors** command without being in enable mode at level 15. Use the following command to allow a privilege level to run a command:

```
(global) privilege mode [level level command | reset command]
```

Here, *mode* is the basic mode of the user-level interface. There are many modes to choose from, but the most common ones are **configure** (global configuration mode) and **exec** (EXEC mode). The desired privilege level is given as *level* and the IOS command as *command*. The **reset** keyword can be used to reset the command's privilege level to the default.

d. Encrypt passwords displayed in the router configuration:

```
(global) service password-encryption
```

By default, passwords on lines and usernames, as well as the enable password, are displayed as clear text (not encrypted) in the router configuration. This command can be used to cause the passwords to be displayed in a basic encrypted form. (The passwords themselves are not stored encrypted; rather, they are only displayed encrypted with commands such as **show running-config**.)

6. (Optional) Configure system banners:

```
(global) banner {motd | login | exec | incoming} delimiter
```

```
(global) ... text ...
```

```
(global) delimiter
```

The message-of-the-day banner is defined with the **motd** keyword. It displays *before* the router login prompt when connecting via Telnet and *after* a user logs into the router when connecting via SSH. The login banner, defined with the **login** keyword, displays after the message of the day and just before the login prompt. The login banner does not display when a router is configured to use only SSHv1. The exec banner, defined with the **exec** keyword, displays just after a user logs into the router. The reverse-Telnet banner, defined with the **incoming** keyword, displays after the message-of-the-day banner when a user connects to the router using reverse Telnet.

The banner text can be one or more lines. It is bounded by the delimiter character. Choose an uncommon character as the delimiter (such as ~ or %). The message-of-the-day banner is useful when important network news or an access policy or legal warnings must be presented to potential users. The remaining banners can relay specific information about the system, such as the name, location, or access parameters.

The following built-in tokens can be used to include other configured information in a banner:

$(hostname)—The host name of the router (from **hostname**)

$(domain)—The domain name of the router (from **ip domain-name**)

$(line)—The line number of the async or vty line

$(line-desc)—The line description (from the **description** command on the async interface associated with the line)

$(peer-ip)—The IP address of the peer machine

$(gate-ip)—The IP address of the gateway machine

$(encap)—The encapsulation type (SLIP or PPP)

$(encap-alt)—Displays the encapsulation type as SL/IP instead of SLIP

$(mtu)— The maximum transmission unit size

7. (Optional) Configure session menus.

    a. (Optional) Configure a title message:

```
(global) menu name title delimiter

(global) ...text...

(global) delimiter
```

A title or banner can be defined and displayed prior to menu options. The title can be used to display a welcome message and instructions on making menu choices. All commands pertaining to a menu must be linked to the menu name. Title text can be one or more lines, bounded by the delimiter character. To clear the screen prior to the menu title, use the **menu** *name* **clear-screen** command.

    b. Configure a prompt:

```
(global) menu name prompt delimiter

(global) ...text...

(global) delimiter
```

The menu prompt displays a text message after the menu items, as the user is being prompted for a response.

    c. Configure menu items.

Next, you configure your menu items. You can have up to 18 menu items. To create them, repeat Steps d through f that follow for each item.

    d. Define an item title:

```
(global) menu name text item text
```

Each item in the menu named *name* has a key that the user must press to select the item. This is defined as *item*. It can be a character, number, or word. The item key is displayed to the left of the item text in the menu.

    e. Define an item command:

```
(global) menu name command item command
```

When a menu item is selected by the *item* key, the *command* string is executed. For example, the command could open a Telnet session to a remote system. A command can also be defined as a "hidden" command such that no item text is displayed for the user to see. To do this, configure the menu command but don't configure the companion menu text.

Menus can also be nested so that a menu selection can invoke an entirely different menu of choices. To do this, use the keyword **menu** as the *command* string (such as **menu** *name* **command** item **menu** *name2*). Then define the new nested menu with the **menu text** and **menu command** lines.

> **Note**   You can also define a menu item that allows the user to return to a command prompt or a higher-level menu and end the current menu. Define a menu item with **menu-exit** as the command (that is, **menu** *name* **command** *item* **menu-exit**).

   f. Define a default menu item:

```
(global) menu name default item
```

If the user presses the Enter key without specifying an item, the item is selectedby default.

   g. Execute a menu.

Execute from the command line:

```
(exec) menu name
```

The menu called *name* is executed at the command-line prompt. In this case, remember to include a menu item that allows the menu to terminate (**menu** *name* **command** *item* **menu-exit**). Otherwise, you will be caught in an endless loop of menu choices.

Execute automatically on a line:

```
(line) autocommand menu name
```

The menu *name* is executed automatically as soon as a user accesses the line with a terminal session. In this case, it would be wise to keep the user in a menu loop so that he or she won't end up in an unknown or potentially dangerous state, such as the command-line prompt.

Execute automatically for a user:

```
(global) username user autocommand menu name
```

The menu *name* is executed automatically as soon as the user named *user* successfully logs into the router.

h. (Optional) Configure the menu to operate in line mode:

(global) **menu** *name* **line-mode**

You can configure the menu to have users enter a line # instead of a key. This command is automatically enabled with menus that contain more than nine menu items.

i. (Optional) Configure single-spaced menus:

(global) **menu** *name* **single-space**

Menus are double-spaced by default when there are fewer than nine items. They are single-spaced when there are a nine or more items. This command causes menus with fewer than nine items to display as single-spaced.

j. (Optional) Display informational status:

(global) **menu** *name* **status-line**

An informational status line can be displayed before the menu title. This line indicates the router hostname, user line number, and the current terminal type.

8. Web browser interface.

a. Enable the web interface:

(global) ip http server

The web interface server is started, allowing users to monitor or configure the router through a web browser.

> **Note** The router web interface should not be used, especially for access from a public (Internet) network, due to a major vulnerability with the HTTP server service. This vulnerability is documented as Cisco Bug ID CSCdt93862. To disable the HTTP server, use the **no ip http-server** command. In addition to this bug, the default authentication uses cleartext passwords. If you must use the web interface, be sure to configure a stronger authentication method and limit access in Steps c and d, which follow.

b. (Optional) Set the web browser port number:

(global) ip http port number

HTTP traffic for the web interface can be set to use TCP port *number* (default 80).

c. (Optional) Limit access to the web interface:

(global) ip http access-class access-list

A standard IP access list (specified by either number or name) can be used to limit the source IP addresses of hosts accessing the web interface. This should be used to narrow the range of potential users accessing the router's web interface.

d. (Optional) Choose a method for user authentication:

```
(global) ip http authentication {aaa | enable | local | tacacs}
```

Users attempting to access the router's web interface can be challenged and authenticated with several different mechanisms. By default, the **enable** method (the cleartext enable password must be entered) is used for authentication. You should use one of the stronger authentication methods: **aaa** (AAA/TACACS+; see Section 13-2 for more information), **local** (authentication is performed locally on the router, using usernames and passwords), and **tacacs** (standard or extended TACACS authentication).

e. View the router's home page.

From a web browser, use the URL **http://**_router_**/** where _router_ can be the router's IP address or host name. The default router home page is available to users with a privilege level of 15. Only IOS commands available to lesser privilege levels are available to users who are limited to a privilege level less than 15.

1-2: File Management

Cisco IOS has many files and file systems that require management.

File management consists of managing configuration files and operating system files.

Cisco routers use a file system known as IFS (IOS File System).

IFS commands replace many older file-management commands.

IFS commands allow for viewing and classification of all files, including fileson remote servers.

With IFS, there are no longer any differences for management of files on different platforms.

With IFS, you can copy files with complete path information to eliminate the need for system prompting.

Three Flash file system types are supported on Cisco platforms—Class A, Class B, and Class C.

Note   IFS is an extremely powerful way of managing files within the router file systems and on remote systems. In order to provide backward compatibility, many aliases map to older commands for file management. See Table 1-4 at the end of this section for a listing of the older commands and the IFS equivalents.

Navigating File Systems

1. Viewing the available file systems:

```
(privileged) show file systems
```

This command gives you a detailed listing of all the file systems available on the router. This command lists the total size and the amount of free space on the file system in bytes, the type of file system, the flags for the file system, and the alias name used to access the file system. File system types include Flash, NVRAM, and network, as well as some others, such as ROM file systems, which contain microcode. Table 1-2 lists some of the file systems that are available. Note that not all file systems are available on all platforms.

Table 1-2 *Cisco File Systems*

Prefix	File System
system:	Contains the system memory, including the running configuration.
Prefix	File System
nvram:	Nonvolatile Random-Access Memory. This contains the startup configuration.
flash:	Flash memory typically is the location of the IOS. This is the default or starting file system for file system navigation. The prefix flash: is available on all platforms. For platforms that do not have a device named flash:, the prefix flash: is aliased to slot0:. Therefore, you can use the prefix flash: to refer to the main Flash memory storage area on all platforms.
bootflash:	Boot Flash memory typical location for Rxboot IOS image.
slot0:	First PCMCIA Flash memory card.
slot1:	Second PCMCIA Flash memory card.
tftp:	Trivial File Transfer Protocol (TFTP) network server.
ftp:	File Transfer Protocol (FTP) network server.
slavenvram:	NVRAM on a slave RSP card of a high-end router, such as a 7513, configured for redundancy.
slavebootflash:	Internal Flash memory on a slave RSP card of a high-end router, such as a 7513, configured for redundancy.
slaveslot0:	First PCMCIA card on a slave RSP card of a high-end router, such as a 7513, configured for redundancy.
slaveslot1:	Second PCMCIA card on a slave RSP card of a high-end router, such as a 7513, configured for redundancy.
flh:	Flash load helper log files.
null:	Null destination for copies. You can copy a remote file to null to determine its size.
rcp:	Remote copy protocol (rcp) network server.
disk0:	Rotating media.
xmodem:	Obtain the file from a network machine using the Xmodem protocol.
ymodem:	Obtain the file from a network machine using the Ymodem protocol.

2. Change the default file system directory:

    `(privileged) cd [filesystem:]`

    Use this command to move to a specific file system or directory within that file system. By moving to a specific file location, you can use file system commands without having to specify the filesystem: option. For example, if you do a dir command without specifying the filesystem:, it uses the directory that was specified by the default directory or the cd command. The default file system directory is flash.

3. List the current directory:

    `(privileged) pwd`

    This command prints the working directory. By using this command, you can determine the default file system directory. Use this command to verify that you have moved into the appropriate directory when using the cd command.

4. Display information about the files:

    `(privileged) dir [/all] [filesystem:][path/filename]`

    This command displays a directory of the default directory structure as specified by the **cd** command. By using the option **/all**, you see files that have been deleted but not permanently removed from a file system. You can also specify a **file system** by using the filesystem: option. If you want to view a single file, provide the path and filename also. You can use an asterisk (*) as a wildcard to display a group of files with common starting characters. You can use this command to get a list of files on any available local file system.

    `(privileged) show filesystem:`

    This command displays the contents of a file system. It is similar to the **dir** command, but the output is formatted differently. This command does not allow individual files or remote file systems to be displayed.

5. View the information about a local or remote file:

    `(privileged) show file information filesystem:path`

    This command allows you to view information about a file on a remote or local file system. The output displays the image type and size.

6. View the contents of a local or remote file:

    `(privileged) more [/ascii | /binary | /ebcdic] filesystem:path`

    Use this command to view the contents of a remote or local file. The options **ascii**, **binary**, and ebcdic allow you to specify the type of format in which you would like to see the file presented. The *filesystem:path* options allow you to specify a particular file on a valid file system. For example, **more /ascii tftp://172.16.3.1/myconfig.txt** displays the file myconfig.txt located on TFTP server 172.16.3.1 in ASCII format.

Deleting Files from Flash

Cisco hardware platforms have three different classifications of file systems. Each of these file systems deals differently with deleting and permanently removing files from the Flash file system. Table 1-3 lists these three types of file systems and the platforms that use them.

Table 1-3   *File System Types*

File System Type	Platforms
Class A	Cisco 7000 family, C12000, LS1010, Catalyst 6500 series, 12000 Gigabit Switch Router (GSR), LS1010
Class B	Cisco 1003, Cisco 1004, Cisco 1005, Cisco 1600 series, Cisco 1700 series, Cisco 2500 series, Cisco 2600 series, Cisco 3600 series, Cisco 4000 series, Cisco AS5200
Class C	Cisco MC3810, disk0 of SC3640

1. Delete a file from Flash memory:

   (privileged) **delete** [**filesystem:**]*filename*

   This command deletes a file from Flash on any of the three classifications of file systems. For Type A and B file systems, the file is marked as deleted and shows up only if the command **dir /all** is used. Files that are marked as deleted can be restored using the undelete command. For type C file systems, the delete command permanently removes the file from the system. The file system must be a Flash file system.

2. Restore a deleted file:

   (privileged) undelete index [filesystem:]

   For type A and B file systems, if a file has been deleted, you can restore it using the **undelete** command. You must provide the **index** number of the file listed by the **dir/all** command. If the file is not located in your working directory, determined by the **pwd** command, you can specify the **filesystem:** option.

3. Permanently remove a file from Class A Flash memory:

   (privileged) squeeze filesystem:

   If you want to permanently remove a file that has been deleted from a Class A file system, you must **squeeze** the file system. This command removes any file on the file system that has been marked as deleted.

4. Permanently remove a file from Class B Flash memory or NVRAM:

   (privileged) erase [flash: | bootflash: | nvram:filename]

To permanently remove a file from a Class B file system, you must **erase** the file system device. This command removes all the files in the device. By using the command **erase nvram:filename**, you can delete a file from NVRAM.

5. Reformat the file system:

    (privileged) `format filesystem:`

    For Class A and Class C devices, you can remove all the files and reformat the device using the **format** command.

Moving System Files

With most computer systems, it is important to be able to move files from one location to another. To move system files, you use the **copy** command. This command, along with path parameters, moves system files. The results of some file-system moves are unique. For example, when a file is copied to the system:running-configuration file, the result is a file merge. This section discusses some common copy commands and the results, but on the whole, files can be moved to file systems that allow you to write to the system. The command structure for **copy** commands is **copy [/erase]** *source-location destination-location*. The source and destination locations can be any writeable file system and path. By using the **/erase** option, you can always erase the destination of a writeable file system before the file is copied. The source location can be any file system that contains files that need to be moved. With all these commands, you can specify the address and filename, or you can leave them out, and the system will prompt you for the information.

1. Save the active configuration file to be used for startup:

    (privileged) `copy system:running-config nvram:startup-config`

    This command copies the system's current active configuration into the startup configuration file. When anything is copied to the location **nvram:**startup-config,it is a complete overwrite. In other words, any information that was in that file is completely lost and is overwritten with the source file. The startup configuration file is loaded at startup.

2. Copy a file into the active configuration:

    (privileged) `copy source system:running-config`

    This command copies a file into the current running configuration. The source can be any location that contains a text file that has configuration parameters framed in the appropriate syntax. When files are copied to the running configuration, they are merged with the current configuration. In other words, if a configuration parameter such as an address exists in both places—running and source—the running is changed by the parameter that is being copied from the source location. If the configuration parameter exists only in the source location, it is added to the running configuration. If a parameter exists in the running configuration but is not modified in the source configuration, there is no change to the running configuration. The source location can be a file in any location, including a file on a TFTP server or FTP server or a text file that has been written to Flash memory.

3. Save a file to a TFTP server:

`(privileged)` **`copy`** *`source`* **`tftp://`***`address`***`/filename`**

This command allows you to save any readable file from an IFS source location to a TFTP server specified in the address of the destination parameter. If you do not supply a filename and address, you are prompted by the system for this information.

4. Save a file to an FTP server with anonymous login:

`(privileged)` **`copy`** *`source`* **`ftp://`***`directory`*`/`*`filename`*

You can also save files to an FTP server. FTP offers a more reliable and robust method of file transfer. As with TFTP, you can copy from any source location to an FTP server. Any readable file can be copied. The main difference is that FTP requires a username and password for the transfer of traffic. The username and password can be specified in global configuration or on the command line. If you don't specify a username in the command or globally for the router, the router uses an anonymous login. The username is anonymous, and the e-mail type password is formed by the router using the current session as the username, the router name as the host name, and the IP domain as the domain name (session@hostname.domain).

5. Save a file to an FTP server using the username and password specified in global configuration:

`(global)` **`ip ftp username`** *`username`*

`(global)` **`ip ftp password`** *`password`*

`(privileged)` **`copy`** *`source`* **`ftp://`***`address`*`/`*`directory`*`/`*`filename`*

If you have configured an IP FTP username and password, and you do not specify a password in the command line, the configured username and password are used when you copy files to and from an FTP server.

6. Save a file to an FTP server using the username and password specified in the command line:

`(privileged)` **`copy`** *`source`* **`ftp://`***`username:password@address`*`/`*`directory`*`/`*`filename`*

If you want to specify the password in the command line, you can do so with the format *username:password@address.* The username and password are separated by a colon (:), and the address of the FTP server follows the at (@) symbol.

7. Save a file to Flash memory:

`(privileged)` **`copy`** *`source`* *`flash-filesystem:`*`//`*`path`*`/`*`filename`*

You can copy a file to any Flash file system of a router with the **copy** command. Some writeable file systems, such as a Class A file system, allow you to create and write to directories as well as files. This **copy** command allows you to move files into a Flash file system. Files that are moved into Flash are usually IOS files, but Flash can be used to store any file as long as you have room to place it. If fact, as soon as a file has been placed in Flash memory, the router can be configured as a TFTP server and can then serve that file to other devices. See the following subsection for more information about configuring your router to act as a TFTP server.

8. Save a file to an RCP server:

```
(privileged) copy source rcp://directory/filename
```

You can also transfer files using the RCP protocol. Like FTP, RCP requires a username and password that can be configured in either global configuration or on the command line.

9. Save a file to an RCP server using the username and password in global configuration:

```
(global) ip rcmd remote-username username
(global) ip ftp username password
(privileged) copy source rcp://address/directory/filename
```

If you configure an IP RCMD username and password and you do not specify a password in the command line, the configured username and password are used when you copy files to and from an FTP server.

10. Save a file to an RCP server using the username and password specified in the command line:

```
(privileged) copy source rcp://username:password@address/directory/filename
```

If you want to specify the password in the command line, you can do so with the format *username:password@address*. The username and password are separated by a colon (:), and the address of the RCP server follows the at (@) symbol.

Configuration Rollback

The configruation rollback feature enables you to archive IOS configuration files if you need to rollback to a previous configuration file. Only the differences between the current configuration and the archived configuration file are applied when performing rollback.

1. Enter arcchive configuration mode:

```
(global) archive
```

2. Specify the location and filename prefix for the archived file:

```
(config-archive) path disk0:myconfig
```

If your platform has a disk0, you can save the archive in disk0:, disk1:, ftp:, pram:, rcp:, slavedisk0:, slavedisk1:, or tftp:. If your platform does not have disk0, you can save the archive to ftp:, http:, pram:, rcp:, or tftp:.

3. Optionally, configure the maximum number of archived files to be saved:

```
(config-archive) maximum number
```

The *number* of maximum archive files can be set to any value between 1 to 14. The default is 10.

4. Optionally, set the time increment for automatically saving an archive of the current running configuration:

   `(config-archive)` **`time-period`** `minutes`

5. Optionally, replace a current configuration file with a saved configuration file:

   `(privileged)` **`configure replace`** `path:configuration-file [list]`

   The *list* keyword lists the lines applied during the configuration rollback.

Related File Management Commands

1. Compress the configuration file:

   `(global)` **`service compress-config`**

   This command allows you to compress your configuration file. Because NVRAM is limited on a router, a very large configuration file might need to be compressed before being stored in NVRAM. The **service compress-config** command compresses the file to one-third of its normal size.

   > **Note**   Configuration compression is supported only on routers that have Release 10 or later of boot ROM. If your router does not have this version or a later version, you need to perform a ROM upgrade to compress your configuration file. Check your device's documentation to find out how to perform a ROM upgrade.

2. Specify an IOS image to boot from in a Flash file system:

   `(global)` **`boot system flash`** `flash-filesystem:/directory/filename`

   By default, routers boot the first valid image in the default Flash location. If you have more than one file in Flash memory and you do not want to boot the first file, you must specify which file is to be used as the IOS image. The **boot system flash** command specifies which file to use.

3. Change the config-file environment parameter for Class A file systems:

   `(global)` **`boot config`** `flash-filesystem:directory/filename`

For a Class A file system, you can copy configuration files to the Flash filesystem. You can also specify to the router that it is to load a configuration from Flash instead of the startup-config file located in NVRAM. To do this, you must first copy the active configuration to the Flash file system. Then, in global configuration mode, use the **boot config** parameter followed by the file system name and file location and name. After you save this configuration, the router attempts to load the configuration from the specified location.

4. Configure the router to act as the TFTP server for files in Flash memory:

    (global) **tftp-server flash** *flash-filesystem*:/*directory*/*filename*

5. The command in step 4 specifies a file to be served out of the Flash memory file system by the router acting as a TFTP server. You can serve multiple files out of Flash using the following command to disable the parser cache:

    (global) **no parser cache**

    Starting with IOS 12.1(5)T, Cisco routers enable the parser cache feature by default. This feature enables the rapid recognition and translation of configuration lines in the configuration file that differ slightly from previously used lines. This improves performance and is especially useful if you have a large number of access-list statements or virtual circuits. You can disable this feature to free up resources.

6. Enable exclusive configuration change access:

    (global) **configuration mode exclusive** {auto | manual}

    The configuration lock prevents multiple users from modifying the running configuration file at the same time. This feature can be set to **auto** to enable this feature any time someone enters the **configure terminal** command, or it can be set to **manual** to enable this feature any time the **configure terminal lock** command is entered.

Alias Commands

Because the IFS is the third-generation file-management system for Cisco IOS, alias commands have been established to provide backward compatibility for commands that existed in previous operating systems. This allows you to use file-management commands that you might have learned in previous releases without having to learn the new command structure. Table 1-4 shows the alias commands and the IFS equivalent commands.

Table 1-4 *File Management Alias Commands*

Release 10.2 and Earlier Command	Release 10.3 to 11.3 Command	Release 12.0 and Later (IFS) Command
write terminal	show running-config	show system:running-config or more system:running-config
show config	show startup-config	show system:startup-config or more system:startup-config
write memory	copy running-config startup-config	copy system:running-config nvram:startup-config
write erase	erase startup-config	erase nvram:
write network	copy running-config tftp:	copy system:running-config tftp://address/filename
config memory	copy startup-config running-config	copy nvram:startup-config system:running-config
config network	copy tftp running-config	copy tftp://address/filename system:running-config
config overwrite	copy tftp startup-config	copy tftp://address/filename nvram:startup-config

Cisco's official stance on older commands is that they might not be supported in future releases, so it is conceivable that commands that existed before Release 12.0 might not be supported in future releases of Cisco IOS.

1-3: Cisco Discovery Protocol (CDP)

Cisco Discovery Protocol allows for dynamic discovery of directly connected Cisco devices across SNAP-supported media.

CDP runs on all Cisco hardware running Cisco IOS 10.2 or later.

CDP provides information on neighboring platform, operating system, and Layer 3 addressing.

CDP version 2 supports information about duplex and VLAN settings.

CDP is enabled by default on all interfaces and can be disabled on a global or per-interface basis.

CDP is media- and protocol-independent. CDP operates as a Layer 2 SNAP frame and requires only that the media support SNAP frames.

Configuration

CDP is enabled by default. Step 1 is not required, because it is a default setting. The steps listed here are designed to help you manage CDP on your router.

1. Enable CDP globally (the default is on):

   ```
   (global) cdp run
   ```

   This enables the CDP process. This is the default setting. To disable CDP for the whole router, use the no cdp run command.

2. (Optional) Set the update time for CDP advertisements:

   ```
   (global) cdp timer seconds
   ```

   This command sets the update interval in seconds. This is a global command, so you can specify only a single time interval, and all interfaces will use the same update interval. The default setting is 60 seconds.

3. (Optional) Specify the holdtime of the CDP information:

   ```
   (global) cdp holdtime seconds
   ```

   This command specifies the holdtime that is to be sent with the CDP update. This holdtime tells the neighboring router how long to keep the CDP information. If no update is received by the neighboring router at the end of the holdtime, that router discards the cdp information.

4. Change the CDP send parameters for a given interface (this is on by default):

   ```
   (global) cdp advertise-v2
   ```

   This command allows the router to send out Version 2 updates for CDP. CDP Version 2 supports three new type length values (TLVs)—VTP management domain, native VLAN, and duplex mode. If a router does not support V2 updates, the new TLVs are ignored, and CDP continues operating normally.

5. (Optional) Enable CDP on an interface:

   ```
   (interface) cdp enable
   ```

   This command lets CDP updates be sent out a particular interface. The default configuration is on for all interfaces. To disable CDP on a particular interface, use the no cdp enable command. Disabling CDP can be useful for conserving bandwidth or if the device on the other side of the link is not a Cisco device.

   Use the show cdp and show cdp interface commands to verify the configuration of CDP.

Example

This example alters CDP's operational parameters by changing the holdtime to 480 seconds and the update time to 120 seconds. The Ethernet interface is operating normally, but we are assuming that the serial interface is connected to a non-Cisco router. Therefore, to conserve bandwidth, CDP is disabled on that interface.

```
cdp holdtime 480
cdp timer 120
```

```
interface ethernet 0
        ip address 1.2.2.1 255.255.255.0

interface serial 0
        ip address 1.4.4.1 255.255.255.0
        encapsulation ppp
        no cdp enable
```

1-4: System Time

System time is maintained by the IOS software. When a router is initialized, the system time is set from a hardware time clock (system calendar) in the router.

An accurate system clock is important to maintain for logging and debugging time stamps, various **show** commands, and timed access lists.

System time is maintained as Coordinated Universal Time (UTC or GMT). The format of time as it is displayed can be configured with IOS commands.

System time can be set manually or by Network Time Protocol (NTP). In addition, a router's hardware time clock can be updated by NTP if desired.

NTP uses the concept of *stratum* to determine how close an NTP speaker is to an authoritative time source (an atomic or radio clock). Stratum 1 means that an NTP server is directly connected to an authoritative time source. NTP also compares the times reported from all configured NTP peers. It doesn't listen to a peer that has a significantly different time.

NTP associations with other NTP peers can be protected through access lists and through an encrypted authentication.

For an authoritative time source, NTP can be configured to listen to public NTP servers on the Internet. Alternatively, NTP can be contained within an enterprise network by configuring one router to act as if it has an authoritative time source. Other NTP peers within the organization then synchronize their time with that router.

NTP version 3 is based on RFC 1305 and uses UDP port 123 and TCP port 123. Information about public NTP servers and other NTP subjects can be found at www.eecis.udel.edu/~ntp/.

Configuration

You can set the system time either manually or using the Network Time Protocol (NTP).

With manual configuration, you set the time and date on the router, along with the time zone and whether to observe daylight saving time. With manual configuration, the router has no way to preserve the time settings and cannot ensure that the time remains accurate. NTP is defined by RFC 1305. It provides a mechanism for the devices in the network to get their time from an NTP server. With NTP, all the devices are synchronized and keep very accurate time.

Setting the System Time Manually

1. Set the time zone:

    ```
    (global) clock timezone zone hrs-offset min-offset
    ```

    The time zone is set to the abbreviated name zone (such as EST, PST, or CET). This name is used only for display purposes. It can be any common zone name. The actual displayed time is defined by an offset in hours (*hrs-offset*) and minutes (*min-offset*) from UTC.

2. (Optional) Configure daylight saving time:

    ```
    (global) clock summer-time zone recurring [week day month hh:mm week day
      month hh:mm [offset]]
    (global) clock summer-time zone date [date month | month date] year hh:mm
      [date month | month date] year hh:mm [offset]
    ```

    If daylight saving time begins and ends on a certain day and week of a month, use the command with the **recurring** keyword. The week number *week* (including the words "first" and "last"), the name of the *day,* the name of the *month*, and the time *hh:mm* in 24-hour format can all be given to start and stop daylight saving time. The *offset* value gives the number of minutes to add during daylight saving time (the default is 60).

    Otherwise, the **date** keyword can be used to specify the exact date and time that daylight saving time begins and ends in a given year.

3. (Optional) Set the system clock (IOS clock):

    ```
    (exec) clock set hh:mm:ss [day month | month day] year
    ```

    The time is given in 24-hour format. *day* is the day number, *month* is the name of the month, and *year* is the full four-digit year.

    The system clock is set from the hardware calendar when the router is restarted. It also can be set manually from the hardware calendar using the (exec) **clock read-calendar** command.

4. (Optional) Set the system calendar (hardware clock):

    ```
    (exec) calendar set hh:mm:ss [day month | month day] year
    ```

    The hardware clock is set to the given time (24-hour format) and date. The *month* is the name of the month, *day* is the day number, and *year* is the full four-digit year. As an alternative, the system calendar can also be set from the system clock using the (exec) **clock update-calendar** command.

Setting the System Time Through NTP

1. Define one or more NTP peer associations:

    ```
    (global) ntp peer ip-address [version number] [key keyid]
      [source interface] [prefer]
    ```

The NTP peer is identified at *ip-address*. The NTP version can be given with the **version** keyword (1 to 3; the default is version 3). If NTP authentication will be used, the key keyword identifies the authentication key to use (see Step 3b). If desired, the source address used in NTP packets can be taken from an interface using the source keyword. Otherwise, the router uses the **source** address from the outbound interface. The **preferred** keyword forces the local router to provide time synchronization if there is contention between peers.

2. (Optional) Configure NTP delivery.

   a. Configure NTP broadcast service:

   ```
   (global) ntp broadcast [version number]
   ```

   (global) ntp broadcast client

   (global) ntp broadcastdelay microseconds

   By default, NTP sends and receives unicast packets with peers. Broadcasts can be used instead if several NTP peers are located on a common network. The **ntp broadcast** command enables the sending of broadcast packets. The **ntp broadcast client** command enables the reception of broadcast packets. The **ntp broadcastdelay** command sets the round-trip delay for receiving client broadcasts (1 to 999999 microseconds; the default is 3000).

   b. Set the NTP source IP address:

   (global) ntp source interface

   The source address used for all NTP packets is taken from *interface*. This address can be overridden for specific NTP peers with the **ntp peer** command.

   c. Disable NTP on an interface:

   (interface) ntp disable

   By default, NTP is enabled on all interfaces. This command disables the reception and processing of NTP packets on a single interface.

3. (Optional) Restrict access to NTP.

   a. Restrict by access list:

   (global) ntp access-group {query-only | serve-only | serve | peer} acc-list

   A standard IP access list can be used to limit NTP communication to only those addresses permitted by the list. A specific NTP transaction can be applied to the access list using the following keywords: **query-only** (allow only control queries), **serve-only** (allow only time requests), **serve** (allow requests and queries, but *don't* synchronize to a remote peer), and **peer** (allow requests and queries, and allow synchronization to a remote peer).

   More than one **ntp access-group** command can be given, each with different transactions and access lists. The first match found in sequential order is granted.

b. Restrict by NTP authentication.

Enable NTP authentication:

`(global) ntp authenticate`

Define an authentication key:

`(global) ntp authentication-key key-number md5 value`

An MD5 authentication key numbered *key-number* is created. The key is given a text-string *value* of up to eight cleartext characters. As soon as the configuration is written to NVRAM, the key value is displayed in its encrypted form.

Apply one or more key numbers to NTP:

`(global) ntp trusted-key key-number`

Remote NTP peers must authenticate themselves using the authentication key numbered *key-number*. This command can be used multiple times to apply all desired keys to NTP.

4. (Optional) Make the router an authoritative NTP source.

a. Use the hardware calendar as an authoritative source:

`(global) clock calendar-valid`

If no outside authoritative NTP time source is available or desirable, the local router can be configured to use its hardware system calendar as an authoritative source. The calendar time can then be forwarded by NTP to other peer routers.

b. Enable NTP authoritative source service:

`(global) ntp master [stratum]`

The local router is configured as an authoritative source at stratum level *stratum* (1 to 15; the default is 8). If no NTP peers at a lower stratum level can be found, the router advertises itself at the configured stratum and can begin synchronizing clocks on other peers.

Example

The router is configured for the U.S. Eastern time zone and daylight saving time. The hardware clock is set, and the system clock is then set from the hardware clock.

```
clock timezone EST -5
clock summer-time EST recurring 1 sunday april 2:00 last sunday october 2:00
exit

calendar set 12:52:00 august 6 2001
clock read-calendar
```

NTP is configured for authentication. One key, sourceA, authenticates a peer at 172.17.76.247, and another key, sourceB, authenticates a peer at 172.31.31.1.

```
ntp authenticate
ntp authentication-key 1 md5 sourceA
ntp authentication-key 2 md5 sourceB
ntp trusted-key 1
ntp trusted-key 2
ntp peer 172.17.76.247 key 1
ntp peer 172.31.31.1 key 2
```

1-5: Logging

Logging is used by the router to send system messages to a logging facility.

Logging messages can be logged to four different facilities: system console, system buffers, terminal lines, or syslog server.

Logging history can be maintained to ensure that messages being sent to SNMP servers are not dropped.

Logging displays all error and debug messages by default. The level can be set to determine which messages should be sent to the facilities.

Logging messages displayed to the console can interrupt input on the console. The command **logging synchronous** can alleviate this problem.

Time-stamping logging messages or setting the syslog source address can help in real-time debugging and management.

Note Logging to a syslog server uses UDP port 514.

Configuration

Logging is enabled by default. Step 1 is not required, because it is a default setting. The steps listed here are designed to help you manage logging on your router.

1. Enable logging globally (the default is on):

   (global) logging on

   This is the default setting. To disable logging the router, use the **no logging on** command. If you disable logging, messages are logged only to the console port. None of the other facilities are used.

2. (Optional) Log messages to a syslog server:

   (global) **logging** *hostaddress*

   This command enables routing to a host running the syslog daemon. Syslog listens on UDP port 514 for text messages to log to a file. By logging to a syslog server, you have the system messages in a file to review.

3. (Optional) Log messages to the router buffer:

`(global)` **`logging buffered`**

Logging buffered stores all messages to system memory. These messages are stored in memory and remain there until the device is powered off or the buffer is cleared. The default setting for buffering varies from platform to platform and might or might not be enabled. Buffering can be set from 4096 to 4294967295 bytes.

Caution By setting up buffering, you use system resources that can be used for operational aspects of routing. If you set up buffering, be sure not to waste system memory.

4. (Optional) Log messages to a terminal line:

`(privileged on a TTY or VTY line )` **`terminal monitor`**

Logging automatically sends messages to the console port. In order to have messages sent to any other TTY or a vty (Telnet) line, you must use the command terminal logging while logged into that line from privileged exec mode. As soon as you type this command, logging as specified by the logging monitor command (see Step 7) is displayed until you log out.

5. (Optional) Log messages to an SNMP station:

`(global)` **`snmp-server enable trap`**

This command allows the syslog message traps to be sent to an SNMP management station. In order to use this option, you also have to set up SNMP management on the device. Section 1-6 describes the configuration of SNMP.

6. (Optional) Adjust the history of messages:

`(global)` **`logging history size`**

The router keeps a history of logged messages to ensure that an important SNMP message isn't lost. This command keeps the number of messages specified by the size in the router history table. The table is circular in nature so that as it fills up, it overwrites the first entry in the table. The history size can be set from 1 to 500 entries. The default size is 1.

Note The history file is different from the buffer. History stores a cyclic list of the logging information from 1 to 500 entries. It was designed to keep the last few messages in the event that they were not logged to an SNMP device. Buffering syslog messages is a way of storing the messages to memory instead of to a syslog or SNMP device.

7. (Optional) Specify which types of messages should be displayed:

`(global)` **`logging {console | monitor | trap | history}`** *`level`*

This command allows you to decide which messages should be logged to a particular facility. For example, with the **logging monitor** command, you can choose to send to terminal lines only messages that are warnings or below by setting the level to 4. The level can be set for each output facility. The **console** option specifies what is displayed on the console. The **trap** option specifies what is sent to the syslog server. The **history** option specifies what level is kept in the local history table if you have enabled the syslog message traps to be sent to an SNMP management station. When you set a level, that level and any lower level are displayed to the facility. Table 1-5 lists the error message levels and keywords.

The default of all facilities is to log at the debug level. This means that all messages at debugging level and below are sent to the logging facility.

8. (Optional) Specify the source address of the syslog packets:

`(global) logging source-interface type number`

This command allows you to specify which interface address is used as the source IP address for the syslog packets. The default address is the address of the sending interface. But if you always wanted to use a particular address, such as the loopback address, to be able to easily identify or filter on a particular device, this command would specify an address to be used for all packets.

9. (Optional, recommended) Enable time stamps for messages:

`(global) service timestamps log datetime`

This command configures the router to time-stamp any log message with the date and time as it is set on the router. This gives the person viewing the logged messages more detailed information about when the messages occurred. This can also be useful in determining what other factors might be involved in problems or symptoms.

Table 1-5   *Error Message Logging Levels*

Level	Keyword	Description
0	Emergency	The system is unusable.
1	Alert	Immediate action is needed.
2	Critical	Critical condition
3	Error	Error condition
4	Warning	Warning condition
5	Notification	Normal but significant condition
6	Informational	Informational message only
7	Debugging	Debugging message

10. Control the output of logging messages to terminal or console lines (optional):

`(line configuration)` **`logging synchronous`**

The **logging synchronous** command specifies to the router that logging output should be presented in a synchronous fashion. In other words, if someone is typing, the output should refresh the prompt so that the command line is synchronized with the user input.

Verifying Logging

1. View the logging configuration and buffer:

`(privileged)` **`show logging`**

This command is used to verify logging information and configuration, as well as to view the contents of the logging buffer.

2. Clear logging information:

`(privileged)` **`clear logging`**

This command clears logging messages from the logging buffer.

Example

In this example, we want to increase the buffers used for logging to 4096 and configure the device to buffer only messages that are at the warning level and below. For all other logging information (console and Telnet), we want to log messages that are at the informational level and below. Time stamps have been enabled to give us information about when the message was logged. The console and Telnet lines have been configured for synchronous logging to prevent annoying interruptions for users of these lines. Finally, the device has been configured to log messages to the syslog server 172.16.12.201 for notification-level messages and below using a source address of the loopback 1 interface.

```
logging buffered 4096 warnings
logging monitor informational
!
interface Loopback0
      ip address 191.255.255.254 255.255.255.255
      no ip directed-broadcast
!
logging trap notifications
logging source-interface Loopback0
logging 172.16.12.101
line con 0
      login
      password cisco
```

```
      logging synchronous
line aux 0
      login
      password cisco
      logging synchronous
line vty 0 4
      login
      password cisco
      logging synchronous
```

1-6: System Monitoring

Simple Network Management Protocol (SNMP) allows you to monitor information about and manage a network device.

A Management Information Base (MIB) is a collection of variables stored on a network device. The variables can be updated by the device or queried from an external source.

MIBs are structured according to the SNMP MIB module language, which is based on the Abstract Syntax Notation 1 (ASN.1) language.

An SNMP agent runs on a network device and maintains the various MIB variables. Any update or query of the variables must be handled through the agent.

An SNMP agent can also send unsolicited messages, or *traps*, to an SNMP manager. Traps are used to alert the manager to changing conditions on the network device.

An SNMP manager is usually a network management system that queries MIB variables, can set MIB variables, and receives traps from a collection of network devices.

SNMP agents can send either *traps* or *inform requests*. Traps are sent in one direction and are unreliable. Inform requests are reliable in the sense that they must be acknowledged or be resent.

SNMP version 1 (SNMPv1) is the original version. It is based on RFC 1157 and has only basic cleartext community strings for security. Access can be limited to the IP address of the SNMP manager.

SNMP Version 2 (SNMPv2c) is an enhanced version based on RFCs 1901, 1905, and 1906. It improves on bulk information retrieval and error reporting but uses the cleartext community strings and IP addresses to provide security.

SNMP Version 3 (SNMPv3) is based on RFCs 2273 to 2275 and offers robust security. Data integrity and authentication can be provided through usernames, MD5, and SHA algorithms. Encryption can be provided through DES.

Remote Monitoring (RMON) provides a view of traffic flowing through a router. By default, IOS can provide RMON alarms and events. An IOS with full RMON support provides nine management groups—statistics, history, alarms, hosts, hostTopN, matrix, filter, capture, and event.

Full RMON also allows packet capture, although only packet headers are captured. This minimizes the security risk of revealing the payload information. (Packet capture is supported only on Cisco 2500 and AS5200 Ethernet interfaces.)

> **Note**   SNMP requests and responses are sent using UDP port 161. Notifications or traps are sent using UDP port 162.

Configuration

1. Configure SNMP identity.

    a. Define the contact information:

    ```
    (global) snmp-server contact contact-string
    ```

    The *contact-string* contains text information that the router can provide about the network administrator.

    b. Define the device location:

    ```
    (global) snmp-server location location-string
    ```

    The *location-string* is text information that the router can provide about its physical location.

    c. Define the device serial number:

    ```
    (global) snmp-server chassis-id id-string
    ```

    The *id-string* is text information that the router can provide about its own serial number. If the hardware serial number can be read by the IOS software, this number is the default chassis ID.

2. Configure SNMP access.

    a. (Optional) Define SNMP views to restrict access to MIB objects:

    ```
    (global) snmp-server view view-name oid-tree {included | excluded}
    ```

    If necessary, an SNMP manager can be limited to view only specific parts of the router's MIB tree. A view can be defined with the name *view-name*. The *oid-tree* value is the object identifier of the MIB subtree in ASN.1 format. This value is a text string with numbers or words representing the subtree, separated by periods (such as *system*, *cisco*, *system.4*, and *1.*.2.3*). Any component of the subtree can be wildcarded with an asterisk. Viewing access of the subtree is either permitted or denied with the **included** and **excluded** keywords.

    Multiple views can be defined, each applied to a different set of users or SNMP managers.

> **Note**   For more information about the MIB tree structure and MIBs in general, see Appendix C, "SNMP MIB Structure."

    b. Define access methods for remote users.

(SNMPv1 or SNMPv2c only) Define community strings to allow access:

(global) **snmp-server community** *string* [**view** *view*] [**ro** | **rw**] *acc-list*

A community string value *string* is used to permit access to SNMP information on the router. Any SNMP manager that presents a matching community string is permitted access. An optional view can be specified with the **view** keyword. Access is then limited to only the MIB objects permitted by the view definition. Access is granted as read-only or read-write with the **ro** and **rw** keywords. An optional standard IP access list *acc-list* can be given to further limit access to only SNMP managers with permitted IP addresses.

(SNMPv3 only) Define names for the engine IDs.

To specify the local engine ID name, enter the following command:

(global) **snmp-server** *engineID* [**local** *id-string*] | [**remote** *ip-address* **udp-port** *port id-string*]

SNMPv3 uses authentication and encryption based on several parameters. Each end of the SNMP trust relationship must be defined, in the form of engine ID text strings, id-string. These values are 24-character strings, but they can be specified with shorter strings that will be filled to the right with 0s. The local router running SNMP must be defined with the **local** keyword and id-string.

To specify the remote SNMP engine ID name, enter the following command:

(global) **snmp-server** *engineID* **remote** *ip-address* [**udp-port** *port*]*id-string*

The remote SNMP engine (an SNMP instance on a remote host or management station) is defined with an *ip-address* and a text string named *id-string*. An optional UDP port to use for the remote host can be given with the **udp-port** keyword (the default is 161).

> **Note**   If either local or remote engine ID names change after these commands are used, the authentication keys become invalid, and users have to be reconfigured. MD5 and SHA keys are based on user passwords and the engine IDs.

(Optional) Define a group access template for SNMP users:

(global) **snmp-server group** [*groupname* {**v1** | **v2c** | **v3** {**auth** | **noauth** | **priv**}}] [**read** *readview*] [**write** *writeview*] [**notify** *notifyview*] [**access** *acc-list*]

The template *groupname* defines the security policy to be used for groups of SNMP users. The SNMP version used by the group is set by the **v1**, **v2c**, and **v3** keywords. For SNMPv3, the security level must also be specified as **auth** (packet authentication, no encryption), **noauth** (no packet authentication), or **priv** (packet authentication with encryption).

SNMP views can also be specified to limit MIB access for the group, using the keywords **read** (view *readview* defines readable objects; it defaults to all Internet 1.3.6.1 OID space), **write** (view *writeview* defines writable objects; there is no default write access), and **notify** (view *notifyview* defines notifications that can be sent to the group; there is no default). An optional standard IP access list *acc-list* can be used to further limit SNMP access for the group.

(Optional) Define SNMP users and access methods.

For SNMPv1 or SNMPv2c, apply a user to a group:

```
(global) snmp-server user username groupname [remote ip-address]
   {v1 | v2c} [access acc-list]
```

A user username is defined as belonging to the group template groupname. The IP address of the remote SNMP manager where the user belongs can be specified with the **remote** keyword. The version of SNMP must be specified with the **v1** or **v2c** keywords. A standard IP access list can be used with the **access** keyword to allow only specific source addresses for the SNMP user.

For SNMPv3, apply a user to a group and security policies:

```
(global) snmp-server user username groupname [remote ip-address] v3  [en-
crypted] [auth {md5 | sha} auth-password [priv des56 priv-password]]
[access
acc-list]
```

A user username is defined as belonging to the group template groupname. The IP address of the remote SNMP manager where the user belongs can be specified with the **remote** keyword. SNMP Version 3 must be specified with the **v3** keyword. A standard IP access list can be used with the **access** keyword to allow only specific source addresses for the SNMP user.

By default, passwords for the user are input as text strings. If the **encrypted** keyword is given, passwords must be input as MD5 digests (already encrypted). An authentication password for the user is specified with the **auth** keyword, the type of authentication as keywords **md5** (HMAC-MD5-96 Message Digest 5) or **sha** (HMAC-SHA-96), and a text string as auth-password (up to 64 characters). A password that enables privacy or encryption of SNMP packets for the user is defined with the **priv des56** keyword and a text string priv-password (up to 64 characters).

Note   In order to use des56 and SHA encryption, you must have the cryptographic software image for your router.

c. (Optional) Limit the router operations controlled by SNMP.

Enable the use of the SNMP reload operation:

```
(global) snmp-server system-shutdown
```

By default, SNMP cannot be used to issue a reload operation to the router. If this function is desired, this command can be used to enable reload control.

Specify the TFTP server operations controlled by SNMP:

`(global) snmp-server tftp-server-list acc-list`

SNMP can be used to cause the router to save or load its configuration file to a TFTP server. The standard IP access list *acc-list* can be used to permit only a limited set of TFTP server IP addresses.

3. (Optional) Configure SNMP notifications.

   a. Define a global list of notifications to send:

   `(global) snmp-server `**`enable traps`**` [type] [option]`

   Notifications (both traps and informs) are enabled for the types specified. Because only one type can be given with this command, the command can be issued as many times as necessary. If the *type* keyword is not specified, all available notifications are enabled. In addition, if this command is not issued at least once, none of the notifications it controls are enabled.

   Here are possible notifications:

   aaa-server—AAA server state changes (AS5300 and AS5800).

   bgp—BGP state changes.

   calltracker—Call setup or teardown.

   config—Router configuration changes.

   dial—Dialing state changes.

   dlsw—DLSw state changes. The *option* keyword can be **circuit** (circuit state changes) or **tconn** (peer transport connections).

   ds0-busyout—Busyout state of DS0 interfaces (AS5300).

   ds1-loopback—DS1 in loopback mode (AS5300).

   dsp—DSPU state changes with PU or LU.

   entity—Configuration changes (entity MIB).

   envmon—Environmental conditions have been exceeded. The *option* keyword can be **voltage** (line voltage), **shutdown** (a shutdown condition is pending), **supply** (redundant power supply), **fan** (fan failure), or **temperature**. If no option is given, all options are enabled.

   frame-relay—DLCI status changes.

   hsrp—HSRP state changes.

isdn—Status of ISDN calls. The *option* keyword can be **call-information, chan-not-avail** (D channel unavailable), **layer2** (layer 2 status changes), or **u-interface**.

msdp—Multicast Source Discovery Protocol (MSDP) status changes.

repeater—Ethernet hub repeater status. The *option* keyword can be **health** (RFC 1516 health information) or **reset** (RFC 1516 hub reset).

snmp—Basic router status changes. The *option* keyword can be **authentication** (authentication failures), **linkup** (the interface has come up), **linkdown** (the interface has gone down), or **coldstart** (the router is reinitializing). If none of these keywords is given, all of them are enabled.

b. Define recipients of notifications:

```
(global) snmp-server host host [traps | informs] [version {1 | 2c | 3 [auth |
    noauth | priv]}] community-string [udp-port port] [type]
```

A single host (*host* is either IP address or host name) is specified to receive SNMP notifications (either **traps** or **informs**). The SNMP version can optionally be given as SNMPv1 (**1**, the default), SNMPv2c (**2c**), or SNMPv3 (**3**). With SNMPv3, a keyword can be given to select the type of security: **auth** (use MD5 and SHA authentication), **noauth** (no authentication or privacy, the default), or **priv** (DES encryption for privacy).

The *community-string* keyword is used to specify a "password" that is shared between the SNMP agent and SNMP manager. The UDP port used can be given as *port* (the default is 162).

The notification *type* can be given as one of the following keywords. If no keyword is specified, all available notifications are enabled for the host.

aaa-server—AAA server state changes (AS5300 and AS5800).

bgp—BGP state changes.

bstun—Block Serial Tunneling (BSTUN) state changes.

calltracker—Call setup or teardown.

casa—MultiNode Load Balancing (MNLB) forwarding agent state changes.

channel—Channel Interface Processor (CIP) state changes.

config—Router configuration changes.

dlsw—DLSw state changes. The *option* keyword can be **circuit** (circuit state changes) or **tconn** (peer transport connections).

ds0-busyout—Busyout state of DS0 interfaces (AS5300).

ds1-loopback—DS1 in loopback mode (AS5300).

dsp—Domain-Specific Part (DSP).

dspu—DSPU state changes with PU or LU.

entity—Configuration changes (entity MIB).

envmon—Environmental conditions have been exceeded. The *option* keyword can be **voltage** (line voltage), **shutdown** (a shutdown condition is pending), **supply** (redundant power supply), **fan** (fan failure), or **temperature**. If no option is given, all options are enabled.

frame-relay—DLCI status changes.

hsrp—HSRP state changes.

isdn—Status of ISDN calls. The *option* keyword can be **call-information, chan-not-avail** (the D channel is unavailable), **layer2** (layer 2 status changes), or **u-interface**.

llc2—Logical Link Control type 2 (LLC2) state changes.

msdp—Multicast Source Discovery Protocol (MSDP) status changes.

repeater—Ethernet hub repeater status. The *option* keyword can be **health** (RFC 1516 health information) or **reset** (RFC 1516 hub reset).

rsrb—Remote Source-Route Bridging (RSRB) state changes.

rsvp—Resource Reservation Protocol (RSVP).

rtr—Service Assurance Agent (SAA or RTR).

sdlc—Synchronous Data Link Control (SDLC).

sdllc—SDLC Logical Link Control (SDLLC).

snmp—Basic router status changes. The *option* keyword can be **authentication** (authentication failures), **linkup** (the interface has come up), **linkdown** (the interface has gone down), or **coldstart** (the router is reinitializing). If none of these keywords is given, all of them are enabled.

stun—Serial Tunnel (STUN).

syslog—Logging messages. The syslog level is defined with the **logging history level** command.

tty—TCP connection closing.

voice—Voice port state changes.

x25—X.25 events.

xgcp—External Media Gateway Control Protocol (XGCP).

c. (Optional) Tune notification parameters.

Specify inform request options:

```
(global) snmp-server informs [retries retries] [timeout seconds]
  [pending pending]
```

Informs are sent in a reliable fashion, requiring acknowledgment from the inform recipient. The maximum number of inform retries can be set with the **retries** keyword (the default is 3). The **timeout** keyword sets the number of seconds to wait for an acknowledgment before resending (the default is 30 seconds). Pending informs must also be kept in router memory until they are acknowledged. The **pending** keyword sets the maximum number of pending requests kept in memory at any one time (the default is 25). As soon as the maximum is reached, the oldest request is removed from memory.

Specify trap options:

```
      (global) snmp-server trap-timeout seconds
```

```
(global) snmp-server queue-length length
```

SNMP traps are not sent reliably, because no acknowledgment is required. Traps can be queued and re-sent only when there is no route to the trap recipient. In that case, the router waits *seconds* (the default is 30) before retransmitting the trap. In addition, ten traps can be queued for each recipient by default. The **queue-length** command can be used to set the queue size to *length* traps each.

Specify the source address to use for notifications:

```
(global) snmp-server trap-source interface
```

SNMP traps can be sent from any available router interface. To have the router send all traps using a single source IP address, specify the *interface* to use. In this way, traps can easily be associated with the source router.

d. (Optional) Enable SNMP link traps on specific interfaces:

```
(interface) snmp trap link-status
```

By default, all interfaces generate SNMP link traps when they go up or down. If this is not desired, use the **no snmp trap link-status** command on specific interfaces.

4. (Optional) Enable SNMP manager:

```
(global) snmp-server manager
```

Allow the router to send SNMP requests and to receive SNMP responses and SNMP notifications from another device.

5. (Optional) Enable RMON support.

a. Configure the type of analysis:

```
(interface) rmon {native | promiscuous}
```

The **native** keyword causes RMON to examine only packets destined for the router interface. Otherwise, **promiscuous** examines all packets on the LAN segment.

> **Note**   RMON analysis is CPU-intensive. Enable RMON only after you have determined that it will not adversely affect the router's performance. Obviously, promiscuous mode causes more CPU overhead, because more packets are examined.

b. (Optional) Define the size of the RMON queue:

`(global) rmon queuesize packets`

The size of the RMON analysis queue can be set to the number of *packets* (the default is 64).

c. Define an RMON alarm:

`(global) rmon alarm number object interval {delta | absolute} rising-threshold rise [event] falling-threshold fall [event] [owner string]`

An alarm indexed by *number* is configured to monitor a specific MIB variable *object*. The object is given as a dotted-decimal value in the form of *entry.integer.instance*. The *interval* field specifies the number of seconds that the alarm monitors the object. The **delta** keyword watches a change between MIB variables, and **absolute** watches a MIB variable directly. The alarm can be configured to test the object against a **rising-threshold** and a **falling-threshold**, where *rise* and *fall* are the threshold values that trigger the alarm. The *event* fields specify an event number in an event table to trigger for the rising and falling thresholds. An optional **owner** text string can be given as the owner of the alarm.

d. Define the type of data to collect.

Collect history statistics:

`(interface) rmon collection history {controlEntry number} [owner name]`

`[buckets nbuckets] [interval seconds]`

The history group of statistics is assigned an index *number*. An optional **owner** can be assigned for the collection. The **buckets** keyword defines the number of collection buckets to be used. The **interval** keyword specifies the number of seconds during the polling cycle.

Collect other statistics:

`(interface) rmon collection {host | matrix | rmon1} {controlEntry number}`

`[owner name]`

Statistics can be gathered based on host devices (**host**), on conversations between devices (**matrix**), or on all possible RMON collections (**rmon1**). The history group of statistics is assigned an index *number*. An optional **owner** can be assigned for the collection.

Example

A router is configured for SNMP, using community *public* for read-only access and community *noc_team* for read-write access. SNMP access is limited to any host in the 172.30.0.0 network for read-only and to network management hosts 172.30.5.91 and 172.30.5.95 for read-write access. SNMP traps are sent to an SNMP agent machine at 172.30.5.93 using community string *nms*. All possible traps are sent, except for router configuration change traps.

```
snmp-server contact John Doe, Network Operations
snmp-server location Building A, closet 415
snmp-server community public ro 5
snmp-server community noc_team rw 6

snmp-server host 172.30.5.93 traps nms
snmp-server enable traps
no snmp-server enable config

access-list 5 permit 172.30.0.0 0.0.255.255
access-list 6 permit host 172.30.5.91
access-list 6 permit host 172.30.5.95
```

1-7: Service Assurance Agent (SAA)

SAA performs various measurements of network performance, either through operations configured and scheduled manually from the IOS command line or through an SNMP manager with the Cisco round-trip time monitoring (RTTMON) MIB.

SAA can measure the following types of response times: DHCP, DLSw+, DNS, ICMP Echo, SNA Echo, FTP, HTTP, UDP jitter, traceroute, TCP Connect, and UDP Echo.

Some SAA measurements can be made using only the local router and a remote host. Other measurements require a remote Cisco router running the SAA responder.

SAA measurements are collected and stored as statistical distributions. They can be collected in a historic fashion if desired.

The jitter operation measures the variance in delay between successive packets. This is especially useful for voice traffic, where a low jitter is required for good voice quality.

The TCP Connect operation measures the time required to request and open a TCP connection. This is useful for simulating the response of Telnet connections.

Configuration

1. Define global SAA parameters.

    a. (Optional) Set the amount of SAA memory:

    (global) rtr low-memory bytes

    The amount of router memory available to SAA operations is set to *bytes* (the default is 25% of available memory). The amount of memory should always be set to a value less than the amount of free memory, as reported by the **show memory** command. Memory is actually allocated when an SAA operation is scheduled.

    b. (Optional) Use a key chain for MD5 authentication between the SAA collector and responder.

    Define a key chain:

    (global) key chain keychain-name

    A key chain contains one or more authentication keys that can be used.

    Configure a numbered key in the key chain:

    (keychain) key number

    Keys can be numbered from 0 to 2147483647.

    Define the text string for the key:

    (keychain-key) key-string text

    The authentication string *text* is used as an authentication key. The string is from 1 to 80 characters (uppercase and lowercase alphanumerics; the first character must be alphabetic).

    Apply the key chain to SAA on *both* collector and responder routers:

    (global) rtr key-chain name

2. Define an SAA operation to perform:

    (global) **rtr** *number*

    An SAA operation identified by *number* is defined, and the router is placed in **rtr** configuration mode.

3. Define the type of operation to perform.

    a. DHCP operation:

    (rtr) type dhcp [source-ipaddr source-addr] [dest-ipaddr dest-addr]

    [option option]

    By default, the broadcast address 255.255.255.255 is used on all available interfaces to detect answering DHCP servers. The round-trip time to detect a server and obtain a lease is measured. If desired, you can target specific DHCP servers by adding the **ip dhcp-server** *ip-address* command or by using the **dest-ipaddr** keyword with the server address *dest-addr*. If the **source-ipaddr** keyword is used, the DHCP request has a source address of *source-addr*. The **option** keyword is used to specify a DHCP option, which must be 82.

b. DLSw+ operation:

```
(rtr) type dlsw peer-ipaddr ip-addr
```

The response time between the local router and the DLSw+ peer at *ip-addr* is measured. DLSw+ must first be configured on both the local and remote routers. (See Section 5-3 for more information.) The SAA operation is required only on the local router.

c. DNS operation:

```
(rtr) type dns target-addr target-addr name-server dns-addr
```

The round-trip time between a DNS request and a reply is measured. The request is for a host at IP address *target-addr*. It is aimed at a DNS server at IP address *dns-addr*. In addition, the *target-addr* can be a host name so that a reverse lookup time is measured.

d. Echo operation.

ICMP echo:

```
(rtr) type echo protocol ipicmpecho {ip-addr | hostname}[source-ipaddr

  ip-addr]

(optional) (rtr) lsr-path {name | ip-addr}  ...
```

An end-to-end ICMP echo response time is measured between the local router and an end device. The end device can be identified by IP address *ip-addr* or by *hostname*. You can use the **source-ipaddr** keyword to specify an IP address *ip-addr* to be used as the source address. If desired, you can specify a loose source route path by adding the **lsr-path** command. The path is formed by the string *name* or the *ip-addr* values.

The ICMP echo has a default payload size of 28 bytes, making a total packet size of 64 bytes. The **request-data-size** command can be used to increase the size of the echo request packet.

SNA RU echo:

```
(rtr) type echo protocol snaruecho sna-hostname
```

An end-to-end SNA SSCP native echo response time is measured between the local router and an SNA device. The SNA host name defined for the PU in VTAM is given as *sna-hostname*.

SNA LU echo:

```
              (rtr) type echo protocol {snalu0echoappl | snalu2echoappl}
sna-hostname
 [application-name sna-application] [mode-name sna-mode]
```

An end-to-end SNA LU0 connection from the local router to the NSPECHO host application (Cisco-supplied) is measured. The SNA host name defined for the PU in VTAM is given as *sna-hostname*. The SNA application can be given with the **application-name** keyword, as *sna-application* (the default is NSPECHO). The **mode-name** keyword specifies the SNA mode as *sna-mode*.

e. FTP operation:

```
(rtr) type ftp operation operation-type url url [source-ipaddr  source-
ipaddr] [mode {passive | active}]
```

The FTP file download response time is measured. The only FTP operation that is supported is "get," specified as *operation-type*. The file to be downloaded is specified using the **url** keyword. The URL is given as *url*, and it must be in the form of a typical URL. If the user and password are specified, the form is *ftp://user:password@host/filename*. Otherwise, the default username **anonymous** and password **test** can be used with the form *ftp://host/filename*. If desired, you can give the source address of the FTP request (that is, the router) using the **source-ipaddr** keyword. The FTP mode is specified with the **mode** keyword. It can be **passive** (the default) or **active**.

f. HTTP operation.

Define the operation:

```
(rtr) type http operation {get | raw} url url [name-server dns-addr] [ver-
sion version] [source-addr {name | src-addr}] [source-port port] [cache
{enable | disable}] [proxy proxy-url]
```

The round-trip response time is measured to request a base HTML page from a server and receive a response. To configure a standard HTTP "get" operation, use the **get** keyword. An HTTP raw request must have the **raw** keyword, followed by the **http-raw-request** command (discussed next). The URL to get is given as url. The address of a name server can be given as dns-addr with the **name-server** keyword. The source address of the HTTP request can be given as name or src-addr with the **source-addr** keyword. In addition, the HTTP port can be specified as port (the default is 80) using the **source-port** keyword. The HTTP version is given with the **version** keyword. You can download a cached HTTP page using the **cache enable** keywords. The **proxy** keyword specifies a proxy-url that can be used to point to the proxy server.

(Optional) Define HTTP raw commands for a get request:

```
              (rtr) http-raw-request
              (rtr-http) http_1.0_commands
(rtr-http) exit
```

HTTP 1.0 commands can be entered to form a custom (or "raw") HTTP request to be executed. The response time of this request and the reply is measured.

g. Jitter operation:

```
(rtr) type jitter dest-ipaddr {name | ip-addr} dest-port dest-port
[source-addr {name | ip-addr}] [source-port src-port] [control  {enable |
disable}] [num-packets pkts] [interval milliseconds]
```

The round-trip time of a UDP echo is measured. In addition, packet loss and jitter are also measured in each direction. Jitter measurements must be taken between two Cisco routers—one configured with the SAA jitter operation, and the other configured as an SAA responder (see Step 5). The default data packet size for this operation is 32 bytes, but this can be changed with the **request-data-size** command.

The **dest-ipaddr** keyword specifies the remote or target router by name or IP address. The destination UDP port number and an optional source port number are given with the **dest-port** and **source-port** keywords. If desired, the source address of the request packets can be set with the **source-addr** keyword. By default, the local router sends a control message to the destination port to begin the jitter operation, as the **control enable** keywords specify. If this is not desired, use **control disable**. The number of packets sent in the jitter operation can be set with the **num-packets** keyword (the default is 10). In addition, the spacing between packets in the stream can be set with **interval** (the default is 20 milliseconds).

Note   A measurement of the one-way delay between the requesting and responding routers can also be taken. To do this, the jitter operation requires that the clocks be synchronized by configuring Network Time Protocol (NTP) on both routers. (See Section 1-4 for more information.)

h. Path Echo operation:

```
(rtr) type pathecho protocol ipicmpecho {name | ip-addr}
```

Hop-by-hop response times from the local router to an IP host are measured along a network path using a traceroute operation. The destination or target is given by name or IP address.

i. TCP Connect operation:

```
(rtr) type tcpconnect dest-ipaddr {name | ip-addr} dest-port port [source-
ipaddr {name | ip-addr} source-port port] [control {enable | disable}]
```

The response time to initiate and open a TCP connection to a remote host is measured. If the remote target is another Cisco router with an SAA responder, any TCP port number specified by the **dest-port** keyword is used. If the target is another device, the TCP port number must be available and working on the target machine.

The source address and TCP port number of the request packets can be given with the **source-ipaddr** and **source-port** keywords. By default, the SAA control protocol is enabled (**control enable**) so that the remote router will answer, even if the TCP port is not in operation.

j. UDP Echo operation.

Define the operation:

```
(rtr) type udpecho dest-ipaddr {name | ip-addr} dest-port port  [source-
ipaddr {name | ip-addr} source-port port] [control  {enable | disable}]
```

The round-trip time of a UDP echo packet sent to a remote host is measured. If the remote target is another Cisco router with an SAA responder, any UDP port number specified by the **dest-port** keyword is used. If the target is another device, the UDP port number must be available and working on the target machine. The source address and UDP port number of the request packets can be given with the **source-ipaddr** and **source-port** keywords. By default, the SAA control protocol is enabled (**control enable**) so that the remote router will answer, even if the UDP port is not in operation.

(Optional) Define a data pattern to use:

```
(rtr) data-pattern hex-value
```

The **data-pattern** command is used to ensure that data is not corrupted during the process. The default pattern is 0xABCD.

4. Define optional parameters for the operation.

a. (Optional) Set basic operation attributes.

Set the operation frequency:

```
(rtr) frequency seconds
```

The number of seconds between operations can be set to *seconds* (the default is 60).

Set the time to wait for a response:

```
(rtr) timeout milliseconds
```

The amount of time SAA waits for a response to an operation can be set to *milliseconds* (the default is 5000).

Set the rising threshold that defines a reaction:

```
(rtr) threshold milliseconds
```

A reaction event is defined by an operation's measurement rising above a threshold value. The threshold can be set to *milliseconds* (the default is 5000).

Set the size of the payload in an SAA request packet:

```
(rtr) request-data-size bytes
```

The protocol data in the request packet payload can be 0 to the maximum of the protocol (the default is 1 byte).

(SNA echo only) Set the size of the payload in an SAA response packet:

(rtr) response-data-size bytes

The response packet protocol data is 0 bytes in length for APPL protocols by default. Otherwise, the default is the same size as **request-data-size**.

Set the Type of Service (ToS) bits in the request packet IP header:

(rtr) tos value

The ToS value can be set to *value,* in decimal or hex (0x...), ranging from 0 to 255 (the default is 0).

Set the identifier tag:

(rtr) tag string

A text string tag can be assigned to an operation to identify it with a group of operations. The *string* value can be 0 to 16 characters in length.

Set the SNMP owner information:

(rtr) owner string

A text string can be used as the SAA operation owner string for SNMP. This string can contain any relevant information, such as the person issuing the operation, phone numbers, location, or the reason for the operation. The *string* value can be 0 to 255 characters and may contain embedded spaces.

Check SAA echo responses for corrupted data:

(rtr) verify-data

If data corruption is suspected, echo responses can be verified at the expense of extra overhead.

b. (Optional) Set operation statistics parameters:

(rtr) distributions-of-statistics-kept buckets

(rtr) statistics-distribution-interval milliseconds

(rtr) hours-of-statistics-kept hours

(rtr) hops-of-statistics-kept hops

(rtr) paths-of-statistics-kept paths

> **Note**   The SAA statistics commands should be used only when statistical information is needed for network modeling. Otherwise, the default values provide the correct resources for response-time operations.

Measurements from each operation are distributed into "buckets" that contain results from a distinct response-time interval. The **distributions-of-statistics-kept** command specifies how many buckets are available (the default is 1). The **statistics-distribution-interval** command sets the width of the response-time interval (the default is 20 milliseconds; this has no effect if the default, 1 distribution, is used). The **hours-of-statistics-kept** command sets the length of time that statistics are kept (the default is 2 hours). The **hops-of-statistics-kept** command sets the number of hops of a pathecho operation for which statistics are kept (the default is 16 hops for pathecho and 1 hop for echo). The **paths-of-statistics-kept** command sets the number of distinct paths for which statistics are kept, because different paths may be used over different pathecho executions (the default is 5 paths for pathecho and 1 path for echo).

c. (Optional) Set measurement history parameters:

```
(rtr) buckets-of-history-kept datapoints
```

```
(rtr) lives-of-history-kept lives
```

```
(rtr) samples-of-history-kept samples
```

(rtr) filter-for-history {none | all | overthreshold | failures}

> **Note**   You should use the SAA history commands only if you suspect a network problem. History collection records the last specified number of data points and therefore uses more router memory. By default, history collection is not performed.

The **buckets-of-history-kept** command sets the number of data points to be kept for the operation (the default is 50 buckets). The **lives-of-history-kept** command enables history collection and sets the number of lives that are collected for the operation (the default is 0). A life is how long an operation is active, from start to finish. The **samples-of-history-kept** command sets the number of history entries per bucket (the default is 16 for pathecho and 1 for all others). The **filter-for-history** command specifies the type of history information to collect. The keywords are **none** (the default; no history), **all** (keep all attempted operations), **overthreshold** (keep only results that are over the threshold), and **failures** (keep only operations that fail).

d. (Optional) Set operation thresholds.

Configure an action to perform:

```
(global) rtr reaction-configuration operation [connection-loss-enable]
```

```
  [timeout-enable] [threshold-falling milliseconds] [threshold-type
option] [action-type option]
```

A notification can be sent when a threshold or other condition is met. Notifications can be used to trigger further SAA operations or to send alerts. The reaction is configured for the numbered SAA operation. The **connection-loss-enable** keyword enables checking for loss of connections (the default is disabled). The **timeout-enable** keyword enables checking for operation timeouts based on the **timeout** command (the default is disabled). The **threshold-falling** keyword defines the falling threshold of the response-time values (the default is 3000 milliseconds). (The rising threshold is defined by the **threshold** command.)

Threshold calculations are defined by the **threshold-type** keyword, as one of **never** (no threshold violations, the default), **immediate** (immediately perform the action when the threshold is violated), **consecutive** [occurrences] (perform the action if the threshold is exceeded occurrences times; the default is 5), **xofy** [x y] (perform the action if the threshold is exceeded x times out of y; the default is 5 of 5), or **average** [attempts] (perform the action if the average of the last attempts response times exceeds the threshold; the default is 5).

The action to be taken is defined by the **action-type** keyword, as one of **none** (no action), **traponly** (send an SNMP trap), **nmvtonly** (send an SNA NMVT alert), **triggeronly** (trigger a second SAA operation), **trapandnmvt** (send a trap and an NMVT alert), **trapandtrigger** (send a trap and trigger a second operation), **nmvtandtrigger** (send an NMVT alert and trigger a second operation), or **trapnmvtandtrigger** (send a trap and an NMVT alert and trigger another operation).

Configure a second SAA operation to occur after a threshold:

```
(global) rtr reaction-trigger operation target-operation
```

The *target-operation* SAA operation number is started if a trigger is defined for the original SAA *operation*.

5. (Optional) Define an SAA responder on a remote router:

```
(global) rtr responder
```

The responder is enabled on a remote router to provide an intelligent response to various SAA operation types.

6. Schedule an SAA operation:

```
(global) rtr schedule operation [life seconds] [start-time {pending | now |
hh:mm [month day | day month]}] [ageout seconds]
```

The numbered SAA *operation* is scheduled for activity. The **life** keyword defines the total amount of time that data is collected (the default is 3600 seconds, or 1 hour). The **start-time** keyword sets how long the operation will be started: **pending** (the default; will not run until started with a time or triggered), **now** (start collecting data as soon as the command is entered), or a specific time (24-hour format) and an optional date (the default is the current date). If a date is used, at least three characters of the month name must be given. The **ageout** keyword sets how long the operation is kept while in the pending state (the default is 0 seconds—infinite).

7. Show SAA operation results.

a. (Optional) View the SAA operation configuration:

```
(exec) show rtr configuration [operation]
```

b. (Optional) View the SAA operation activity:

```
(exec) show rtr collection-statistics [operation]
```

c. (Optional) View the SAA operation results:

```
(exec) show rtr distribution-statistics [operation] [tabular | full]
```

The results of the collected distributions are displayed (only one distribution is collected by default). The **tabular** keyword displays the results in a format that can be parsed by an application. The **full** keyword displays the results in a more readable format.

Example

An operation is configured to measure ICMP echo response times to host 192.168.191.47. Measurements are to be taken every 30 seconds. The operation is scheduled for a lifetime of 8 hours, to begin immediately.

```
rtr 1
type echo protocol ipicmpecho 192.168.191.47
frequency 30


rtr schedule 1 life 28800 start-time now
```

An operation is set up to measure the HTTP response times of server 10.68.191.82. Measurements are taken once a minute for 1 hour (note that these are the defaults for frequency and life). The operation should begin at 8:00 a.m. on February 12. The URL www.swellcompany.com is used as a test page.

```
rtr 10
type http operation get url http://www.swellcompany.com


rtr schedule 10 start-time 08:00 feb 12
```

1-8: Buffer Management

Routers allocate memory into buffers to store and switch packets when routing.

Router memory is structured into *system memory* and *shared (I/O) memory*. To determine how the memory is divided, use the **show version** command. Look for "xxxK/yyyK bytes of memory," where xxx is the amount of system memory and yyy is the amount of shared memory.

Buffer space is divided into *public (system) buffers* and *interface buffers*.

Router hardware determines where the buffers are located:

Low-end models (such as the 1600, 2500, 4000, 4500, and 4700)—All buffers are located in shared memory.

Particle-based models (such as the 2600, 3600, 7200, and Catalyst 6000 MSFC)—Public buffers are used for process switching, and packets are split into particles in interface buffers for fast switching.

High-end models (such as the 7500)—Interface buffers are used for fast switching; otherwise, system buffers are used.

System buffers on a router are allocated in the following types and sizes:

Small—104 bytes

Middle—600 bytes

Big—1524 bytes

VeryBig—4520 bytes

Large—5024 bytes

Huge—18024 bytes (configurable)

Buffers are allocated for use according to buffer type and the MTU or packetsize needed.

Buffer parameters define how and when buffers are allocated:

permanent—The number of buffers allocated during router initialization.

min-free—When the number of buffers falls below this number, the router attempts to allocate more from available memory.

max-free—When the number of buffers rises above this number, as buffers are freed, the router deallocates them.

If a buffer is needed, but none are free and available, the router flags a buffer *miss* before allocating a new buffer. If an additional buffer cannot be allocated due to a lack of available memory, the router flags a buffer *failure*. In the case of interface buffers, these conditions are flagged as *fallbacks*, and the router allocates additional buffers in the public buffer space instead.

Note System buffers can be tuned to improve certain router performance conditions. However, buffer tuning should be attempted with caution. Ideally, you should open a case with Cisco TAC to obtain engineering guidance before tuning the buffers.

Configuration

This section looks at system buffers, which are used to store packets for receiving and transmitting purposes. The first subsection deals with how to monitor and view the buffer information. The second subsection deals with how to modify and tune buffer performance.

It is important to mention that although system buffers can be tuned to improve certain router performance conditions, the default buffers were designed with a great deal of study by Cisco. If you feel you need to tune the buffers, you should open a case with Cisco TAC to obtain engineering guidance before tuning the buffers.

Buffer Monitoring

1. Look for interface buffer problems:

    (exec) **show interface** [*type num*]

    If a particular interface is suspected of having buffer problems, it can be identified by *type* and *num*. Otherwise, information about all interfaces is displayed. Look for lines that list the number of "no buffer" conditions, as shown in the following example:

    ```
    Router#show interface ethernet 9/4
    Ethernet9/4 is up, line protocol is up
      Hardware is cxBus Ethernet, address is 0000.0c45.2124
        (bia 0000.0c45.2124)
      Description: Engineering department
      Internet address is 172.16.98.1/26
      MTU 1500 bytes, BW 10000 Kbit, DLY 1000 usec,
        reliability 255/255, txload 2/255, rxload 1/255
      Encapsulation ARPA, loopback not set
      Keepalive set (10 sec)
      ARP type: ARPA, ARP Timeout 04:00:00
      Last input 00:00:06, output 00:00:00, output hang never
      Last clearing of "show interface" counters never
      Queueing strategy: fifo
      Output queue 0/40, 811 drops; input queue 0/75, 36 drops
      5 minute input rate 17000 bits/sec, 18 packets/sec
      5 minute output rate 97000 bits/sec, 47 packets/sec
      247323938 packets input, 2280365753 bytes, 108 no buffer
      Received 5812644 broadcasts, 93 runts, 0 giants, 1 throttles
      199 input errors, 101 CRC, 1 frame, 4 overrun, 0 ignored
      0 input packets with dribble condition detected
      861479969 packets output, 2668694324 bytes, 0 underruns
      12 output errors, 6890760 collisions, 4 interface resets
      0 babbles, 0 late collision, 0 deferred
    0 lost carrier, 0 no carrier
    ```

    There were 108 times when packet buffers needed to be allocated, but there was not enough available memory.

2. Look for general buffer problems:

    (exec) show buffers

Each type of buffer is displayed with its size, along with counters for a variety of buffer activities. Pay close attention to the "Public buffer pools" and "Public particle pools" sections. Here are some of the more interesting counters:

total—The total number of buffers in the pool type (used and unused).

permanent—The number of buffers always in the pool.

in free list—The number of buffers currently available for use.

min—The minimum number of buffers that are maintained in the free list. If this number falls below *min*, an attempt is made to allocate more.

max allowed—The maximum number of buffers in the free list. If this number rises above the maximum, some buffers are "trimmed" or unallocated.

hits—The number of buffers allocated successfully from the free list.

misses—The number of times a buffer was needed but was unavailable in the free list.

trims—The number of buffers that have been trimmed from the free list.

created—The number of buffers that have been created to maintain the *min* number in the free list.

failures—The number of times a buffer was unavailable and could not be allocated. This reflects packets that were dropped.

no memory—The number of times an attempt was made to allocate new buffers but the router was out of memory.

The following example shows the output from the **show buffers** command. You should be suspicious of buffer problems if you see both *failures* and *no memory* numbers greater than 0.

```
Router#show buffers

Buffer elements:
     499 in free list (500 max allowed)
     140186641 hits, 0 misses, 0 created

Public buffer pools:
Small buffers, 104 bytes (total 480, permanent 480):
     467 in free list (20 min, 1000 max allowed)
     353917332 hits, 1867 misses, 402 trims, 402 created
     1347 failures (0 no memory)
Middle buffers, 600 bytes (total 360, permanent 360):
     305 in free list (20 min, 800 max allowed)
     1755872447 hits, 1660 misses, 48 trims, 48 created
     1608 failures (0 no memory)
```

```
      Big buffers, 1524 bytes (total 360, permanent 360):
           324 in free list (10 min, 1200 max allowed)
           50506313 hits, 700 misses, 11 trims, 11 created
           664 failures (0 no memory)
      VeryBig buffers, 4520 bytes (total 40, permanent 40):
           40 in free list (5 min, 1200 max allowed)
           3119206 hits, 565 misses, 6 trims, 6 created
           537 failures (0 no memory)
      Large buffers, 5024 bytes (total 40, permanent 40):
           40 in free list (3 min, 120 max allowed)
           178 hits, 363 misses, 4 trims, 4 created
           361 failures (0 no memory)
      Huge buffers, 18024 bytes (total 9, permanent 0):
           7 in free list (3 min, 52 max allowed)
           13212271 hits, 361 misses, 0 trims, 9 created
           352 failures (0 no memory)
```

Here, failures were reported, indicating that some buffers were needed but the router could not allocate them in time to route a packet. This was not necessarily due to a lack of memory, but rather to circumstances that required packets to be dropped before buffers were allocated. The 0s reported for *no memory* show that there was not a shortage of buffer memory. Also, notice that the number of failures is a very small percentage of the number of hits reported.

Buffer tuning might be required if nonzero *no memory* counters are seen. Tuning can also be appropriate if the number of failures is a noticeable percentage of the number of hits. (This percentage is a subjective one, and it might not apply in all situations. Assistance from the Cisco TAC can help determine whether buffer tuning is necessary.)

Tuning the Buffers

Use the following command to tune the buffers:

(global) buffers {small | middle | big | verybig | large | huge | *type number*}
    {permanent | max-free | min-free | initial} *value*

Parameters can be set for a specific type of public buffer pool. The type of buffer pool is given as **small, middle, big, verybig, large,** or **huge.** The pool parameter is given with the **permanent, max-free, min-free,** or **initial** keywords, along with the desired number *value.*

Note   You can also tune the interface buffer pools using the interface *type* and *number* values. You should not attempt to change the values associated with interface buffers. These values were carefully calculated by Cisco for proper operation.

Tune only the buffer type that exhibited problems in the **show buffers** command. As a general rule of thumb, a new **permanent** value should be about 20% larger than the total number of buffers in the pool. A new **min-free** value should be about 25% of the number of permanent buffers, and **max-free** should be greater than the sum of **permanent** and **min-free**.

Example

According to the **show buffers** command, the number of small buffers initially was

```
Small buffers, 104 bytes (total 480, permanent
480):
467 in free list (20 min, 1000 max allowed)
353917332 hits, 1867 misses, 402 trims, 402 created
1347 failures (0 no memory)
```

The new parameters for small buffers are set to the following values: **permanent** 576, **min-free** 144, and **max-free** 750.

```
buffers small permanent 576
buffers small min-free 144
buffers small max-free 750
```

1-9: Some Troubleshooting Tools

The **ping** (packet Internet groper) command can be used to test end-to-end connectivity from a router to a remote host or router. For IP, ping uses ICMP type 8 requests and ICMP type 0 replies.

The **traceroute** command can be used to discover the routers along the path that packets are taking to a destination. For IP, traceroute uses UDP probe packets on port 33434.

The **telnet** command can be used to open Telnet connections to other routers or hosts.

Many **debug** commands and options are available to display information about activity within the router.

If a network analyzer is unavailable, a router can be configured to present basic information about network traffic. This is called the "poor man's sniffer."

If a router crashes, information can be gathered to assist in troubleshooting the cause.

You can view information about the activity of the router CPU, memory, interfaces, and protocols.

The Cisco TAC offers a number of troubleshooting tools and technical support resources.

Note   This section does not present a complete list of troubleshooting commands. However, you should find a set of useful commands and tools here to use for a variety of situations.

IP Connectivity Tools: ping

`(exec)` **`ping`** `[protocol] {host}`

Echo requests are sent, and echo replies are expected in return. Ping can be used with a variety of protocols. The *protocol* value can be **appletalk, clns, ip** (the default), **novell, apollo, vines, decnet,** or **xns.** Some protocols require another Cisco router at the remote end to answer ping packets. The target, *host*, can be either an address or a host name.

The IP ping sends ICMP type 8 (echo request) packets to the target. The following characters are displayed each time a ping response is expected or seen:

!—A successful reply packet was received.

.—No reply was seen within the timeout period, 2 seconds.

U—A destination-unreachable error was received.

M—A could-not-fragment message was received.

C—A congestion-experienced packet was received.

I—The ping test was interrupted on the router.

?—An unknown packet type was received.

&—The packet lifetime or time-to-live was exceeded.

As soon as the test completes, the success rate is reported, along with a summary of the round-trip minimum, average, and maximum in milliseconds.

Note   For the regular **ping** command, only the destination address may be given. The source address used in the ping packets comes from the router interface that is closest to the destination. This might or might not be helpful in determining connectivity.

IP Connectivity Tools: Extended ping

`(exec)` **`ping`**

The extended ping is similar to the regular ping, except that it is typed with no options. You are prompted for all available ping options, including the source address to be used. The following options can be specified:

Protocol (the default is IP)—This can also be **appletalk, clns, novell, apollo, vines, decnet,** or **xns.**

Target IP address

Repeat count (the default is 5 packets)—The number of echo packets to send.

Datagram size (the default is 100 bytes)—The size of the echo packet. Choose a size larger than the MTU to test packet fragmentation.

Timeout (the default is 2 seconds)—The amount of time to wait for a reply to each request packet.

Extended commands

Source address or interface—Any source address can be given. The address must be the address of any active interface on the router if the reply packets are to be seen.

Type of service (the default is 0).

Set the DF bit in the IP header (the default is no)—If this is set, the packet is not fragmented for a path with a smaller MTU. This can be used to detect the smallest MTU in the path.

Validate reply data (the default is no)—The data sent in the echo request packet is compared to the data echoed in the reply packet.

Data pattern (the default is 0xABCD)—The data pattern is a 16-bit field that is repeated throughout the data portion of the packet. This can be useful for testing data integrity with CSU/DSUs and cabling.

Loose, Strict, Record, Timestamp, Verbose (the default is none)—**loose** (loose source route with hop addresses), **strict** (strict source route with hop addresses), **record** (record the route with a specified number of hops), **timestamp** (record time stamps at each router hop), or **verbose** (toggle verbose reporting). The **record** option can be useful to see a record of the router addresses traversed over the round-trip path.

Sweep range of sizes—Sends echo requests with a variety of packet sizes:

Sweep min size (the default is 36)

Sweep max size (the default is 18024)

Sweep interval (the default is 1)

IP Connectivity Tools: traceroute

```
(exec) traceroute [protocol] [destination]
```

The **traceroute** command sends successive probe packets to *destination* (either a network address or a host name). The *protocol* field can be **appletalk, clns, ip,** or **vines.**

For IP, the first set of packets (the default is 3) is sent with a Time-to-Live (TTL) of 1. The first router along the path decrements the TTL, detects that it is 0, and returns ICMP TTL-exceeded error packets. Successive sets of packets are then sent out, each one with a TTL value incremented by 1. In this fashion, each router along the path responds with an error, allowing the local router to detect successive hops.

The following fields are output as a result of traceroute probes:

Probe sequence number—The current hop count.

Host name of the current router.

IP address of the current router.

Round-trip times (in milliseconds) of each of the probes in the set.

> *—The probe timed out.

> **U**—The port unreachable message was received.

> **H**—The host unreachable message was received.

> **P**—The protocol unreachable message was received.

> **N**—The network unreachable message was received.

> **?**—An unknown packet type was received.

> **Q**—The source quench was received.

The traceroute probes continue to be sent until the maximum TTL value (30 by default for IP) is exceeded or until you interrupt the router with the escape sequence (**Ctrl-Shift-6**).

Traceroute can also be invoked with no options. This allows the router to prompt for the parameters described in the following list:

Protocol (the default is IP)—Can also be **appletalk, clns,** or **vines.**

Target IP address

Source address—An IP address of a router interface. If this isn't specified, the interface closest to the destination is used.

Numeric display (the default is no)—By default, both the host name and IP address of each hop are displayed. If this is set to yes, only the IP addresses are displayed. This is handy if DNS is unavailable.

Timeout in seconds (the default is 3)—The amount of time to wait for a responseto a probe.

Probe count (the default is 3)—The number of probes to send to each TTL(or hop) level.

Minimum Time-to-Live (the default is 1)—The default of one hop can be overridden to begin past the known router hops.

Maximum Time-to-Live (the default is 30)—The maximum number of hops to trace. Traceroute ends when this number of hops or the destination is reached.

Port number (the default is 33434)—The UDP destination port for probes.

Loose, Strict, Record, Timestamp, Verbose (the default is none)—**loose** (loose source route with hop addresses), **strict** (strict source route with hop addresses), **record** (record the route with a specified number of hops), **timestamp** (record time stamps at each router hop), or **verbose** (toggle verbose reporting). The *record* option can be useful to see a record of the router addresses traversed over the round-trip path.

> **Note**   Some routers do not respond to traceroute probes correctly. In this case, some or all of the probes sent are reported with asterisks (*) in the display.

IP Connectivity Tools: Telnet

(exec) `telnet` [*host*]

A Telnet session is opened to the target *host* (either an IP address or a host name). After it is opened, the session can be suspended using the escape sequence (**Ctrl-Shift-6 x**) so that another session can be initiated. See Section 1-1 for more information about controlling and using sessions.

> **Note**   The router initiates a Telnet connection using a source IP address taken from the interface that is "closest" to the destination. To force Telnet to use a specific active interface and IP address as a source address, use the ip telnet source-interface *interface* command in global configuration mode.

Debugging Output from the Router

1.   Choose a method to collect debug output.

(See Section 1-5 for more information about logging router messages to asyslog server.)

a.   Save debugging output in a router buffer:

(global) `logging buffered` [size]

All debugging output is stored in a circular buffer on the router itself. The size of the buffer can be given as *size*, ranging from 4096 to 4294967295 bytes. The default size is hardware-dependent. It can be verified using the **show logging** command.

b.   Send debugging output to a syslog server:

(global) `logging host`

The target, *host* (either an IP address or a host name), receives debug output as syslog messages from the router. By default, the syslog messages are at the *debugging* level.

c.   Send debugging output to a nonconsole session:

(exec) `terminal monitor`

The Telnet session that this command is executed from receives system messages and debug output. If debugging output is not seen, use the **logging monitor debugging** command to enable output at the debugging level.

d. Send debugging output to the router console:

`(global) logging console [level]`

All debugging output is sent to the router console. By default, logging is performed at the *debugging* level. If this is changed in the router configuration, you can override it by specifying the *level* option as *debugging*.

> **Note**   Use caution when sending debugging output to various destinations. Debugging commands can output a large volume of message data in a short amount of time, resulting in very sluggish router performance. Therefore, choose a destination that can collect and present the data efficiently. The logging buffered command is the most efficient method, because the messages are stored directly in a router buffer. The debug logging methods, in increasing order of system overhead, are logging buffered (the least overhead), logging *host*, terminal monitor, and logging console (the most overhead). In fact, debugging to the console can actually crash a router because of the overhead involved in large outputs. You should use *extreme caution* when using any debug command and use debug commands that focus on the information you want to look at (that is, debug events or use access lists to control the debugging actions).

2. Enable time stamps on debugging output:

`(global) service timestamp debug datetime [msec] [localtime]  [show-timezone]`

Debugging output messages are recorded with the date and time. Time is shown with millisecond resolution if the **msec** keyword is used. By default, time is displayed in the UTC format. To record time stamps using the local time zone, use the **localtime** keyword. In addition, the **show-timezone** keyword causes the local time zone name to be displayed.

> **Note**   Before time stamps are enabled, be sure that the router clock (and hardware calendar) have been set correctly. Refer to Section 1-4 for more information.

3. Enable appropriate debugging:

`(exec) debug`

There are many **debug** commands and options! Use the context-sensitive help (**debug ?**) to determine which debug options are available, or refer to the online *Debug Command Reference* at www.cisco.com/univercd/cc/td/doc/product/software/ios121/121sup/121debug/index.htm.

Use extreme caution and common sense before enabling any **debug** command. Debug messages are processed at a higher priority than other network traffic. Consider the amount and types of traffic on your network, realizing that every packet or condition matching the **debug** command causes a message to be generated. For example, enabling **debug all** generates debug output for every known debug condition. In a large IPX network, **debug ipx sap** generates messages for each SAP advertisement. Although **debug ip packet** can be very useful for determining routing problems, it also generates messages for *every* packet passing through the router.

To reduce the amount of debug information and processing, either choose a time when the traffic load is low, or fine-tune the debug parameters to further limit the activity that is being observed.

In the event that you begin to notice large amounts of debug output piling up, be ready to quickly disable the **debug** command. You can either type the **no debug** *options* form of the command, or you can use **no debug all, undebug all, or u all** to disable all possible forms of debugging. In any event, you should always disable debugging when you are finished testing so that the router doesn't continue reporting debugging output without your knowledge.

Poor Man's Sniffer

1. Use IP accounting.

    a. Enable IP accounting on an interface:

        ```
        (interface) ip accounting [access-violations]
        ```

        The router keeps records of the outbound traffic through the interface. The database consists of the source and destination addresses, the number of packets, and the number of bytes (both IP header and payload) switched for the conversation. The traffic data is gathered, regardless of the switching path through the router. This information can be useful to give you an idea of the pairs of hosts talking and the volume of data passing between them.

        If the **access-violations** keyword is included, information is gathered about outbound traffic that failed to pass an access list. This information can be used to determine whether the failed traffic is due to an attempt to breach security.

    b. Display the IP accounting information:

        ```
        (exec) show ip accounting [checkpoint] [output-packets | access-violations]
        ```

        The **checkpoint** keyword can be used to display the checkpointed database; otherwise, the active database is shown. The **output-packets** keyword causes the total number of outbound packets to be displayed (the default). The **access-violations** keyword shows the total traffic that has failed to pass access lists, along with the access list number of the last packet failure.

2. Use an extended access list to determine something about a traffic flow.

    a. Define an extended IP access list (see Section 14-1).

        A named extended IP access list is the most useful for this purpose, because you can edit it without removing and reentering the entire access list. Make **permit** conditions that break down the unknown traffic into possible categories. For example, if you need information about what protocol is being used between two hosts, use **permit** conditions that specify individual protocols. The port operators can also be useful to see into what range of port numbers a certain traffic flow falls. This can be done with the **eq, gt, lt, neq,** and **range** operators. Use as many **permit** statements as is practical, covering all possibilities for a parameter. Be sure to add a **permit all** condition at the end so that existing traffic flows are not affected by this access list. The goal here is to get the router to flag access list statements to identify traffic, not alter the traffic flow.

The following example defines an access list that helps determine whether two hosts are using TCP or UDP (or some other IP protocol) for a data connection:

```
ip access-list extended sniffer
  permit tcp host 192.168.7.15 host 12.1.6.4
  permit udp host 192.168.7.15 host 12.1.6.4
  permit icmp host 192.168.7.15 host 12.1.6.4
  permit ip any any
```

b. Apply the access list to an interface:

(interface) ip access-group acc-list {in | out}

The access list *acc-list* is used to process either inbound (**in**) or outbound (**out**) traffic on an interface.

c. Look at the access list activity:

(exec) show access-lists [acc-list]

For an extended IP access list, a count is displayed for each packet that matches a condition in the list. To see the results for a single access list, you can give an optional access list number or name as *acc-list*. If you defined the access list breakdown wisely, you should begin to see activity for the matching traffic displayed as *(xx matches)* at the end of some access list conditions.

d. (Optional) Refine the access list to uncover more detail.

If you need more information about the type of traffic, you can refine the access list. For example, you might want to know which UDP port number, TCP port number, ICMP type code, IP precedence, or ToS is in use. You can add tests for these options by editing lines in the named access list. Remember to provide access list conditions for all or groups of all possibilities so that you can locate positive results.

e. Remove the access list from the interface:

(interface) no ip access-group *acc-list* {in | out}

(global) no ip access-list extended acc-list

Don't forget to unbind the access list from the interface and to remove the access list from the configuration when you are finished with your analysis.

Troubleshooting Router Crashes

1. Collect a stack trace:

   `(exec) show stacks`

   If the router has a system failure and restarts itself, the system stack trace is saved. You can view the stack trace, along with the reason for the last router restart, using this command. The stack trace output can be copied and pasted into Cisco's Stack Decoder at www.cisco.com/stack/stackdecoder.shtml to get further diagnostic information (a Cisco.com login is required). Problem isolation and software bug IDs canbe determined through the stack decoding process.

2. Collect crashinfo data.

   When a router crashes due to data or stack corruption, a collection of useful information is saved as a file in the bootflash partition on the router. Crashinfo data is saved on the Cisco 7000, 7200, 7500, and 12000 series routers.

   a. Find the crashinfo file:

      `(exec) dir /all bootflash:`

      The files in the bootflash are listed. Crashinfo files are named.

   b. Look at the contents of the crashinfo file:

      `(exec) show file information bootflash:crashinfo`

   c. Collect a core dump.

      Choose a method to write a core dump:

      `(global) exception protocol {ftp | rcp | tftp}`

      The core dump file can be written to a server using FTP, RCP, or TFTP (the default).

      Choose a server to store the core dump:

      `(global) exception dump ip-address`

      When the router crashes, the core dump file is written to the server at *ip-address*. The file is named *hostname*-core, where *hostname* is the name of the router. If TFTP is used, only the first 16 MB of the core dump is written. If the router memory is greater than 16 MB, FTP or RCP should be used.

Monitoring Router Activity

1. Watch IP packets as they are routed.

    a. Create an extended IP access list to identify traffic to watch.

    The access list must permit only the packets that you are interested in seeing. Define the permit conditions as narrowly as you can so that only a small amount of traffic is selected to display. Any traffic that is denied will not be seen in the debugging output. (See Section 14-1 for further information.)

    b. Enable IP packet debugging:

    ```
    (global) debug ip packet detail [acc-list]
    ```

    The router displays information about IP packets as they are processed. Obviously, this command has the potential to generate great volumes of information. In all cases, you should use the optional access list field, *acc-list*, to reduce the number of packets being reported. Packets that are permitted by the extended IP access list are displayed in the debugging output. Only packets that are not fast-switched can be examined by the **debug** command. For this reason, you should use the (interface) **no ip route-cache** command to first disable fast switching on specific interfaces.

    If the debug output shows "encapsulation failed," this indicates that the packet could not be encapsulated in a lower-layer protocol. In the following example, a ping request packet was queued for the Ethernet 0 interface. Because the router could not find an ARP entry for the target address (10.5.1.5), the ping packet could not be encapsulated in a Layer 2 frame with a destination MAC address. Therefore, **debug** reported that the encapsulation failed.

    00:20:41:   ICMP type=8, code=0.

    00:20:43:   IP: s=10.5.1.1 (local), d=10.5.1.5 (Ethernet0), len 53, sending

    00:20:43:   ICMP type=8, code=0

    00:20:43:   IP: s=10.5.1.1 (local), d=10.5.1.5 (Ethernet0), len 53,encapsulation failed

2. Watch the router CPU activity:

    ```
    (exec) show processes cpu
    ```

    The average router CPU utilization is displayed for the last 5 seconds, 1 minute, and 5 minutes. The various running processes are also displayed, along with information that tells you how long each process has been running and its contribution to CPU utilization. Cisco recommends that a router CPU should stay below 70% utilization.

3. Watch the router memory:

    ```
    (exec) show memory free
    ```

Statistics regarding free router memory are displayed. This information can be useful in determining whether there is enough available memory after a router initializes, loads its IOS image, and is actively routing traffic.

4. View statistics about an interface:

```
(exec) show interface [interface]
```

If the optional *interface* is not specified, information is displayed about all interfaces on the router.

5. View information about interfaces by protocol:

```
(exec) show interface accounting
```

Each router interface is listed, along with a breakdown of the bytes and packets inbound and outbound by protocol. This information can be useful to help you see the protocols and traffic volumes that are passing through an interface.

6. View information about a specific protocol on an interface:

```
(exec) show protocol interface type num
```

For the *protocol* specified *(ip, ipx, appletalk)* on the interface, information is presented regarding how the protocol is processed. This includes any access lists that are applied, ICMP behavior, switching paths, and many more configuration parameters.

7. View summary statistics about a protocol:

```
(exec) show protocol traffic
```

Statistics are displayed about the protocol and its major components. Summary counts of the protocol traffic and router activity are shown as totals through all interfaces.

Getting Assistance from Cisco

You can find information about the router using the following command:

```
(global) show version
```

Information about the router hardware, bootstrap code, IOS software image version, router uptime, available interfaces, and router memory is displayed. This output is very useful to help you identify the version of code running on the router, as well as the amount of memory and Flash available. You can also view the contents of the router configuration register.

Information for the Cisco Technical Assistance Center (TAC)

1. Gather the information:

```
(global) show tech-support
```

Output from a large predetermined set of commands is generated. You should capture this data with a terminal emulator so that it can be sent to a TAC engineer.

2. Open a TAC case.

    If you have a service contract with Cisco for your router, you can open a TAC case either by phone or by web browser. You can contact the Cisco TAC by phone using a number listed for your location at www.cisco.com/warp/customer/687/Directory/DirTAC.shtml.

    To open a case using a browser, go to www.cisco.com/kobayashi/support/case_open.shtml and fill in the required information. This also requires a Cisco.com login with a profile that has been updated with your service contract number.

3. Cisco IOS Software bugs.

    Cisco offers information about Cisco IOS Software versions and bug reports on its web site. The Software Bug Toolkit consists of Bug Navigator II (an interactive tool that reports bug information for IOS versions and feature sets), Bug Watcher (a tool that allows you to monitor bug information and receive alerts as new bugs are reported), and a tool that allows the bug database to be searched by BugID. These tools are available at www.cisco.com/support/bugtools/.

Chapter 2

Interface Configuration

This chapter presents background and configuration information for the following router interfaces:

- 2-1: Ethernet Interfaces

- 2-2: FDDI Interfaces

- 2-3: Loopback and Null Interfaces

- 2-4: VLAN Interfaces

- 2-5: Tunnel Interfaces

- 2-6: Synchronous Serial Interfaces

- 2-7: Packet-Over-Sonet Interfaces

- 2-8: Frame Relay Interfaces

- 2-9: Frame Relay Switching

- 2-10: ATM Interfaces

2-1: Ethernet Interfaces

- All Ethernet interfaces are based on the IEEE 802.3 standard. Fast Ethernet is based on the IEEE 802.3u standard, and Gigabit Ethernet is based on the IEEE 802.3z standard.

- Ethernet interfaces support 10 Mbps media with AUI or 10BaseT connections.

- Fast Ethernet interfaces support 10/100 Mbps media with 100BaseTX or 100BaseFX (fiber) connections.

- Gigabit Ethernet interfaces support 1 Gbps media with 1000BaseSX, 1000BaseLX/LH, and 1000BaseZX GBIC modules (all fiber-optic media).

■   Fast Ethernet and Gigabit Ethernet interfaces support single subnets or can support two types of VLAN trunking. See Section 2-5 for more information.

Configuration

1. (Optional) Select an Ethernet encapsulation:

    `(interface)` **`encapsulation {arpa | sap | snap}`**

    Ethernet frames can be encapsulated as ARPA Ethernet version 2.0 (**arpa**, the default), SAP IEEE 802.3 (**sap**), or SNAP for IEEE 802.2 media (**snap**).

2. (Optional) Select the media type:

    `(interface)` *`media-type`* **`{aui | 10baset | mii | 100basex}`**

    The media type can be configured on some router platforms where more than one Ethernet or Fast Ethernet connector is provided. The connector can be **aui** (15-pin), **10baset** (RJ-45), **mii** (Media-Independent Interface), or **100basex** (RJ-45 orSC fiber).

3. (Fast Ethernet only) Specify the interface speed:

    `(interface)` **`speed {10 | 100 | auto}`**

    The speed can be locked to 10 Mbps, 100Mbps, or auto-negotiation.

4. (Fast or Gigabit Ethernet only) Specify the duplex mode:

    `(interface)` **`duplex {full | half | auto}`**

    The interface can be locked to full- or half-duplex (the default) or auto-negotiation.

5. (Optional) Configure Fast EtherChannel.

    a. Assign an interface to a channel group:

        `(interface)` **`channel-group`** *`group`*

        Up to four Fast Ethernet interfaces can be bundled under a common group number. No Layer 3 addresses should be configured on any of the bundled interfaces. All Layer 3 traffic is distributed across the individual interfaces within the bundle, and non-Layer 3 traffic is sent across the first link in the bundle.

    b. Assign network addresses to the bundle:

        `(global)` **`interface port-channel`** *`group`*
        `(interface) ...`

        Layer 3 addresses or bridge groups can be assigned to the bundle as a whole. The port channel acts as the routed interface rather than the individual physical interfaces.

Example

An Ethernet interface, two Fast Ethernet interfaces, and one Gigabit Ethernet interface are all configured for use. The Ethernet and Gigabit Ethernet interfaces are given IP addresses. The two Fast Ethernet interfaces are configured as a single Fast EtherChannel bundle (channel group 1). The bundle, as interface port channel 1, is configured with an IP address. Refer to the network diagram shown in Figure 2-1.

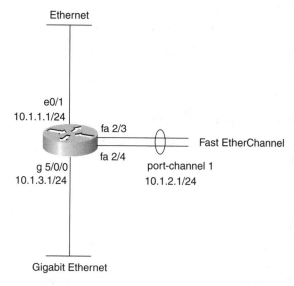

Figure 2-1 *Network Diagram for the Ethernet Interface Example*

```
interface ethernet 0/1
      ip address 10.1.1.1 255.255.255.0

interface fastethernet 2/3
      speed auto
      duplex auto
      channel-group 1
      no ip address

interface fastethernet 2/4
      speed auto
      duplex auto
      channel-group 1
      no ip address

interface port-channel 1
      ip address 10.1.2.1 255.255.255.0
```

```
interface gigabitethernet 5/0/0
      ip address 10.1.3.1 255.255.255.0
      duplex full
```

2-2: FDDI Interfaces

- FDDI supports 100 Mbps data transfer rates using a token-passing scheme.

- A dual counter-rotating fiber-optic ring makes up an FDDI network.

- The total length of the fiber ring must be less than 200 km.

- A FDDI network can have up to 500 stations, separated by no more than 2 km (MMF) or 10 km (SMF).

- FDDI frames can contain from 17 to 4500 bytes.

- FDDI interfaces can act as either Single-Attach Stations (SASs) or Dual-Attach Stations (DASs).

Configuration

1. (Optional) Configure the ring scheduling:

    ```
    (interface) fddi token-rotation-time microseconds
    ```

    To vary the token's availability, the token rotation time can be set to *microseconds* (4000 to 165000 usec; the default is 5000 usec).

2. (Optional) Set the number of frames to transmit at one time:

    ```
    (interface) fddi frames-per-token number
    ```

    Each time the token rotates and is captured, a number of queued frames are transmitted to the ring. The *number* of frames can be from 1 to 10 (the default is 3).

Example

An FDDI interface is configured with IP and IPX addresses. It transmits up to eight frames per token.

```
interface fddi 4/0
      description Server Farm FDDI ring
      ip address 10.1.1.1 255.255.255.0
      ipx network 1234
      fddi frames-per-token 8
```

2-3: Loopback and Null Interfaces

- Loopback interfaces are virtual in nature and are always up.

- Loopback interfaces can be used as termination points for protocols such as BGP, RSRB, and DLSW+. These interfaces are always available, even if other physical interfaces are down.

- Loopback interfaces can also be used to provide a known and stable ID for OSPF routers. OSPF chooses its ID from the loopback interface with the highest IP address first, if present. Otherwise, the ID is taken from the physical interface that has the highest IP address.

- Null interfaces are also virtual and are always up.

- Loopback interfaces can also be used whenever data needs an intermediate output interface, such as for address translation.

- Null interfaces never forward or receive traffic; packets routed to a null interfaceare dropped.

Configuration

1. (Optional) Define a loopback interface:

   ```
   (global) interface loopback number
   ```

   The loopback interface is created and enabled. The interface can then be given network addresses. Note that a loopback interface comes up in "no shutdown" mode as soon as it is created, unlike other types of interfaces. You can still manually shut down a loopback interface if necessary.

2. (Optional) Specify the null interface:

   ```
   (global) interface null 0
   ```

   The null interface is selected and can be configured. There is only one null interface on a router: null 0. Usually, the null interface is referenced in other commands, such as the gateway in a static route.

Example

Two loopback interfaces are configured with IP addresses. The loopbacks will be referenced by other IOS features, and each must be assigned to a unique IP network (aswith all interfaces).

```
interface loopback 0
      ip address 10.1.1.1 255.255.0.0

interface loopback 1
      ip address 192.168.17.1 255.255.255.0
```

2-4: VLAN Interfaces

■ Virtual LANs (VLANs) on a router are treated as physically separate network interfaces even though they are logical interfaces.

■ Fast Ethernet and Gigabit Ethernet interfaces can be configured with trunking encapsulations that support VLANs.

■ Encapsulation types supported are ISL and IEEE 802.1Q.

■ ISL adds a 26-byte header containing the VLAN number to the beginning of frames and a 4-byte CRC to the end. IEEE 802.1Q adds a 4-byte tag within frames just after the source address field.

■ VLANs are configured as subinterfaces on a trunking major interface.

■ All VLANs receive a tag after encapsulation, except for the IEEE 802.1Q native VLAN, which leaves frames untagged.

■ Traffic must be routed or bridged in order to cross between VLANs.

Configuration

1. Define a subinterface for a VLAN:

    ```
    (global) interface fastethernet mod/num.subinterface
    -or-
    (global) interface gigabitethernet mod/num/slot.subinterface
    ```

    A subinterface must be created to support a specific VLAN. Subinterface numbers are arbitrary and can be given to match the VLAN number if desired.

2. Configure a trunking encapsulation:

    ```
    (interface) encapsulation {isl | dot1q} vlan [native]
    ```

    The VLAN encapsulation can be either ISL (isl) or IEEE 802.1Q (dot1q). The subinterface is assigned the VLAN number, vlan. If dot1q is used, the subinterface VLAN can also be made the native VLAN with the native keyword. If the native VLAN is not specified, VLAN 1 is used. dot1q encapsulation sends data for the native VLAN without VLAN encapsulation.

3. Assign network addresses or bridging parameters.

Note   When bridging is configured, each VLAN with an ISL trunk has its own Spanning-Tree Protocol (STP) running. This is called Per-VLAN Spanning Tree (PVST). An IEEE 802.1Q trunk can have only a single instance of STP. However, Cisco supports PVST+, which allows PVST by tunneling STP instances across the dot1q domain. See Section 4-1 for more information.

Example

A Gigabit Ethernet interface is used for trunking IEEE 802.1Q VLANs. Subinterface 17 is used for VLAN 17, and subinterface 26 is used for VLAN 26. (Note that the subinterface numbers can be arbitrarily chosen and don't have to match the VLAN number. For convenience, the numbers can match, as in the example.) Figure 2-2 shows a network diagram.

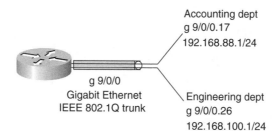

Figure 2-2   *Network Diagram for the VLAN Interface Example*

```
interface gigabitethernet 9/0/0.17
       description VLAN 17 to Accounting Dept
       encapsulation dot1q 17 native
       ip address 192.168.88.1 255.255.255.0

interface gigabitethernet 9/0/0.26
       description VLAN 26 to Engineering Dept
       encapsulation dot1q 26
       ip address 192.168.100.1 255.255.255.0
```

2-5: Tunnel Interfaces

- A tunnel can encapsulate or transport one protocol inside another.

- A tunnel is a virtual point-to-point link and must be configured at two endpoints.

- The tunnel endpoints define a source and destination address for the tunnel transport. Other network addresses can be assigned to the tunnel interfaces for the transported or passenger traffic.

- Tunneling requires CPU overhead and introduces increased latency at each end when encapsulating and decapsulating traffic.

Note   Routing protocols for the tunnel transport should not intermingle with routing protocols for the passenger or transported traffic. Otherwise, recursive routing can result, causing the tunnel interface to shut down.

Section 2-5

Configuration

1.   Create a tunnel interface on each endpoint router:

     (global) **interface tunnel** *number*

     The tunnel interface number can be arbitrarily chosen.

2.   Configure the tunnel source address:

     (interface) **tunnel source** {*ip-addr* | *type number*}

     The source address used for encapsulated or tunneled packets is defined. Either a specific IP address or a physical interface can be given.

3.   Configure the tunnel destination address:

     (interface) **tunnel destination** {*hostname* | *ip-addr*}

     The destination address used for encapsulated or tunneled packets is defined. Either a hostname or a specific IP address for the far end can be given.

Note   For a given tunnel mode, source and destination address pairs must be unique. If you need to define more than one tunnel, create a loopback interface for each tunnel, and use the loopback as the tunnel source.

4.   (Optional) Set the tunnel mode:

     (interface) **tunnel mode** {**aurp** | **cayman** | **dvmrp** | **eon** | **gre ip** | **nos** | **mpls traffic-eng**}

     The tunnel encapsulation can be set to AppleTalk Update Routing Protocol (aurp), Cayman TunnelTalk AppleTalk (cayman), Distance-Vector Multicast Routing Protocol (dvmrp), EON-compatible CLNS (eon), Generic Routing Encapsulation over IP (gre ip, the default), or KA9Q/NOS-compatible IP over IP (nos), and traffic engineering with Multiprotocol Label Switching (mpls traffic-eng).

Note   GRE encapsulation uses IP protocol number 47.

5.   (Optional) Drop out-of-order packets:

     (interface) **tunnel sequence-datagrams**

     To support transported protocols that require packets to arrive in order, the tunnel can be configured to drop packets that are out of order.

6.   (Optional) Perform end-to-end checksums:

     (interface) **tunnel checksum**

By default, no data integrity check is performed on the tunnel. Checksums can be computed for tunnel packets. If the checksum is incorrect, the packet is dropped.

7. Assign network addresses or bridging parameters to the tunnel:

```
(interface) ip address ip-address subnet-mask
```

Network addresses and other protocol parameters can be assigned to a tunnel interface. These addresses configure the tunnel for transported or passenger protocols, enabling those protocols to be routed to the tunnel interface.

Example

A tunnel interface is used to tunnel IP traffic between private address spaces in a company's internal networks over a public-service provider network. One side of the tunnel is shown in the router configuration. Internal network 10.1.0.0 connects to a Fast Ethernet interface. The serial interface connects to public service provider network 17.8.4.0. No private address space is routed over this link. However, a tunnel interface is configured for private network 10.2.0.0. The tunnel source is the serial interface, and the destination is the far-end router at 17.8.4.92. IP traffic destined for private network 10.2.0.0 is routed over the tunnel. Figure 2-3 shows a network diagram.

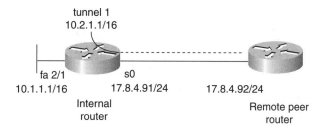

Figure 2-3   *Network Diagram for the Tunnel Interface Example*

```
interface fastethernet 2/1
       description Company's internal LAN
       ip address 10.1.1.1 255.255.0.0

interface serial 0
       description WAN link to Service Provider (public network)
       ip address 17.8.4.91 255.255.255.0

interface tunnel 1
       tunnel source serial 0
       tunnel destination 17.8.4.92
       tunnel mode gre ip
       ip address 10.2.1.1 255.255.0.0
```

```
router eigrp 101
        network 10.0.0.0
        network 17.8.4.0
        passive-interface serial 0
```

2-6: Synchronous Serial Interfaces

■ Synchronous serial interfaces transport data and a clock signal across an end-to-end connection.

■ Serial interfaces include High-Speed Serial Interface (HSSI, 45 Mbps), Channelized T3, Channelized T1, G.702, and traditional router serial interfaces up to T1 (1.544 Mbps) and E1 (2.048 Mbps) speeds.

■ Synchronous serial connections can also include CSU/DSU devices at each end. These can be external, integrated, or integrated as service modules.

■ A channelized T3 interface supports up to 28 T1 channels as a single T3 group over a single DS3.

■ Each T1 channel can be configured for a fractional or full T1 bandwidth. If it's fractional, the remaining bandwidth is filled with idle data.

Configuration

Select and configure one of the serial interfaces described in the following sections (Channelized T3, Channelized T1 or E1 Interface, Synchronous Serial Interface).

Configuring Channelized T3 Serial Interfaces

1. Select the T3 controller:

(global) **controller t3** *slot*/*port-adapter*/*port*

2. (Optional) Set the framing:

(controller) **framing {c\-bit | m23 | auto-detect}**

The T3 controller framing type can be set to C-bit, M23, or auto-detection (auto-detect, the default).

3. (Optional) Set the cable length:

(controller) **cablelength** *feet*

The length of the cable from the router to the network equipment can be given in feet (0 to 450; the default is 224).

4. (Optional) Set the clock source:

(controller) **clock source {internal | line}**

The T3 clock can be taken from the network (line) or from an internal source (internal, the default).

5. Configure each T1 channel.

After the T1 channels are configured, each can be configured further as a synchronous serial interface.

a. Set the T1 timeslot:

```
(controller) t1 channel timeslot range [speed {56 | 64}]
```

The T1 timeslot with the T3 is given as channel (0 to 27 on most T3 interfaces; 1 to 28 on the CT3IP interface). The timeslot keyword identifies the timeslots within the T1 that will be used. The range uses numbers 1 to 24. It can be a list of timeslots separated by a comma. A low to high group of timeslots gives a range separated by a dash.

The **speed** keyword can specify the data rate for the T1 channel as **56** kbps or **64** kbps (the default).

b. (Optional) Set the T1 framing:

```
(controller) t1 channel framing {esf | sf}
```

The framing for the T1 channel can be set to Extended Super Frame (**esf**, the default) or Super Frame (**sf**).

c. (Optional) Set the T1 clock source:

```
(controller) t1 channel clock source {internal | line}
```

The T1 channel clock can be set to the network clock (**line**) or the internal clock (**internal**, the default).

d. (Optional) Set the T1 line coding:

```
(controller) t1 channel linecode {ami | b8zs}
```

The T1 channel line coding can be set to AMI (**ami**) or B8ZS (**b8zs**, the default).

e. (Optional) Set the T1 yellow alarm:

```
(controller) t1 channel yellow {detection | generation}
```

The T3 interface can be set to either detect yellow alarms (detection) or generate yellow alarms (generation) for the T1 channel. By default, yellow alarms are both detected and generated.

Section 2-6

Configuring Channelized T1/E1 Serial Interfaces

1. Select the T1 or E1 controller:

    (global) **controller** {**t1** | **e1**} *number*

    The controller at slot *number* is selected for configuration.

2. Define channel groups:

    (controller) **channel-group** *channel* **timeslots** *range* [**speed** {**48** | **56** | **64**}]

    For a fractional T1 or E1, the channels can be grouped as one data stream. An arbitrary channel group numbered channel is selected, and the range of timeslots is defined. Timeslots can be given as a dash-separated range or a comma-separated list. The speed keyword specifies the speed of the timeslots in the range. It can be 48 kbps, 56 kbps (T1 default), or 64 kbps (E1 default).

3. (Optional) Define CAS signaling:

    (controller) **cas-group** *channel* **timeslots** *range* **type** *signal* **service data**

    T1 channels can be configured for Channel Associated Signaling (CAS, also called robbed-bit signaling). The channel group channel defines a group or range of timeslots as a single group. Different types of robbed-bit signaling can be assigned to each group. The timeslot range can be a comma-separated list of numbers, includingdash-separated ranges of numbers.

    The type keyword defines the type of signaling for the channel group signal: e&m-fgb (ear and mouth with feature group B), e&m-fgd (ear and mouth with feature group D), e&m-immediate-start (ear and mouth with immediate start), fxs-ground-start (Foreign Exchange Station ground start), fxs-loop-start (Foreign Exchange Station loopstart signaling), sas-ground-start (Special Access Station with ground start), or sas-loop-start (Special Access Station with loopstart).

4. (Optional) Specify the clock source:

    (controller) **clock source** {**line** {**primary** | **secondary**} | **internal**}

    The clock source can be set to the network (line) or to the free-running internal clock (internal). If the line clock is used, the T1 or E1 controller that it is applied to can be selected as the primary or secondary clock source. Choose the most reliable clock source as the primary.

5. (Optional) Select the framing type:

    (controller) **framing** {**sf** | **esf** | **crc4** | **no-crc4**} [**australia**]

    For a T1, the framing can be set to Super Frame (sf, the default) or Extended Super Frame (esf). For an E1, the framing can be CRC4 (crc4, the default), non-CRC4 (no-crc4), or Australian type (australia).

6. (Optional) Select the line coding:

```
(controller) linecode {ami | b8zs | hdb3}
```

The line coding can be set to Alternate Mark Inversion (ami, T1 default), bipolar 8 zero sequence (b8zs), or high-density bipolar 3 (hdb3, E1 default).

7. (Optional) Configure T1 cable length:

```
(controller) cablelength short {133 | 266 | 399 | 533 | 655}
(controller) cablelength long {gain26 | gain36} {-22.5 | -15 | -7.5 | 0}
```

For cable lengths shorter than 655 feet, use the cablelength short command. Use the next-highest length (in feet) than the actual cable length. If the cable length is greater than 655 feet, use the cablelength long command. Choose the receiver gain that corresponds to the cable loss, as 26 dB (gain26) or 36 dB (gain36). Then choose the decrease in transmitter gain, as −22.5 dB (-22.5), −15 dB (-15), −7.5 dB (-7.5), or 0 dB (0).

8. (Optional) Configure the E1 line termination:

```
(controller) line termination {75-ohm | 120-ohm}
```

The E1 line termination can be set to 75 ohms unbalanced or 120 ohms balanced.

Configuring Synchronous Serial Interfaces

Note   For channelized T3, E3, T1, or E1 interfaces, first configure the channelized interface and channel groups. Then you can treat the channel groups as a logical serial interface for the next configuration steps.

1. Choose an interface:

```
(global) interface serial number[:channel-group]
-or-
(global) interface hssi number
```

The serial interface *number* (or *slot/number*) is selected. If a channelized interface is being configured, add a colon and the channel group number *channel-group*. An HSSI can also be selected by using the hssi interface type.

Note   Some routers have interfaces that can operate in either asynchronous or synchronous mode. Before continuing with the synchronous serial commands, the interface should be set for synchronous mode with the (interface) **physical-layer sync** command.

2. (Optional) Choose an encapsulation:

`(interface)` **encapsulation {hdlc | ppp}**

The encapsulation can be set to HDLC (the default) or PPP. Other encapsulations can be chosen for ATM, SNA, Frame Relay, and SMDS. See the respective sections in this chapter for more information.

3. (Optional) Configure compression:

`(interface)` **compress {stac | predictor}**

HDLC frames can be compressed by a lossless Stacker (stac) LZS algorithm. PPP frames can be compressed by either a Stacker (stac) or a RAND (predictor) algorithm. Compression should be used only if the router CPU load is less than 40 to 65% and if the majority of traffic is not already compressed.

4. (Optional) Configure the serial data stream and handshaking.

  a. Configure the CRC length:

  `(interface)` **crc** *length*

  By default, the CRC length is 16 bits, but it can be set to *length* bits (16 or 32). The same CRC length must be used on both ends of a serial connection.

  b. Set the line-coding format:

  `(interface)` **nrzi-encoding** [**mark**]

  By default, serial interfaces use NRZ encoding. NRZI encoding can be used instead if it is required. If the **mark** keyword is omitted, NRZI space encoding is used.

  c. Invert the data stream:

  `(interface)` **invert data**

  The data stream can be inverted when a dedicated T1 line is used without B8ZS encoding. Don't invert the data at the router and at the CSU/DSU; invert at only one device.

  d. Set a transmit delay:

  `(interface)` **transmitter-delay** *delay*

  If packets are sent faster than a remote device can receive them, a delay can be inserted between serial packets. The FSIP, HSSI, and MIP interfaces require a *delay* value of the number of HDLC flags to send between packets. All other interfaces use a *delay* in microseconds (0 to 131071; the default is 0).

  e. Enable DTR pulsing:

  `(interface)` **pulse-time** *seconds*

By default, DTR is held down during a line failure. If a remote serial device requires the toggling or pulsing of DTR to resynchronize after a line failure, DTR can be pulsed at an interval of *seconds* (the default is 0).

f. Monitor DSR instead of DTR:

```
(interface) ignore-dcd
```

By default, the DCD signal is monitored to determine whether the line is up or down. If this is not required, DCD can be ignored, and DSR will be monitored instead.

5. (Optional) Configure the serial clock.

a. Set the clock rate for DCE mode:

```
(interface) clock rate bps
```

The serial interface is set to become a DCE device. It generates a clock signal at bps bits per second. On most routers, the rate must be set to a standard value of 1200, 2400, 4800, 9600, 19200, 38400, 56000, 64000, 72000, 125000, 148000, 250000, 500000, 800000, 1000000, 1300000, 2000000, 4000000, or 8000000. Some platforms will accept any value between 300 and 8000000 bps and will round a nonstandard value to the nearest supported rate.

Note   Be aware that higher speeds work properly only at shorter cable distances. Refer to Appendix B, "Cabling Quick Reference," for distance limitations.

b. Use the internal clock:

```
(interface) transmit-clock-internal
```

If a DTE device does not return a transmit clock, the internal clock can be used. Normally, the clock is derived from the line through the DCE device.

c. Invert the transmit clock:

```
(interface) invert txclock
```

With long cable distances and higher transmission speeds, a phase shift between the local transmit clock and the returned transmit clock can occur. If a large number of error packets are seen, you can try inverting the transmit clock to correct thephase-shift problem.

6. (Optional) Configure an integrated port adapter DSU.

a. Select the clock source:

```
(interface) clock source {line | internal}
```

The clock source can be set to the network (**line**, the default) or the internal clock.

Section 2-6

b. Set the cable length (PA-T3 only):

```
(interface) cablelength feet
```

The cable distance from the router to the network can be specified in feet (0 to 450; the default is 50).

c. Configure the CRC length (PA-T3 only):

```
(interface) crc {16 | 32}
```

The CRC length can be set to either 16 (the default) or 32 bits.

d. Set the DSU bandwidth:

```
(interface) dsu bandwidth kbps
```

The maximum bandwidth can be set as kbps (22 to 44736 kbps; the default is 34010 kbps for PA-E3 and 44736 kbps for PA-T3). Both ends of the serial connection must match, because the bandwidth is reduced to the maximum by padding frames.

e. Set the DSU mode:

```
(interface) dsu mode {0 | 1 | 2}
```

The DSU interoperability mode can be set to support a Digital Link DL3100 DSU (0, the default; also used to connect two PA-T3s or two PA-E3s), a Kentrox DSU (1), or a Larscom DSU (2).

f. Select the framing type:

```
(interface) framing {bypass | g751 | c-bit | m13}
```

The framing mode can be set to bypass (frame data is not included in the frame; scrambling must be disabled, DSU mode must be 0, and DSU bandwidth must be set to 44736), g751 (G.751 E3 framing, the default for PA-E3), c-bit (C-bit framing, the default for PA-T3), or m13 (M13 framing).

g. Invert the data stream:

```
(interface) invert data
```

The data stream can be inverted if needed. For example, if a PA-T3 does not use B8ZS encoding, the data stream should be inverted to enable one's insertion.

h. Enable scrambling:

```
(interface) scramble
```

Payload scrambling can be enabled to prevent some bit patterns from being interpreted as alarms. If it is used, scrambling should be enabled on both ends.

i. Set the national and international bits (PA-E3 only):

```
(interface) national bit {0 | 1}
(interface) international bit {0 | 1} {0 | 1}
```

The national bit in the E3 G.751 frame can be set or reset (the default is 0). The first and second international bits can also be set or reset (the default is 0 0).

7. (Optional) Configure an integrated T1/FT1 service module.

a. Select the clock source:

```
(interface) service-module t1 clock source {internal | line}
```

The clock source can be set to either the network (**line**, the default) or the internal clock.

b. Select the framing type:

```
(interface) service-module t1 framing {sf | esf}
```

The framing type can be set to D4 Super Frame (sf) or Extended Super Frame (**esf**).

c. Specify the fractional T1 timeslots:

```
(interface) service-module t1 timeslots {range | all} [speed {56 | 64}]
```

The DS0 timeslots used in the T1 are given as range, a string of one or more ranges of dash-separated values, separated by commas. To use the entire T1, use the **all** keyword. The speed of each DS0 can be given as **56** kbps or **64** kbps (the default).

d. Enable data inversion:

```
(interface) service-module t1 data-coding {inverted | normal}
```

The data stream can be inverted for alternate mark inverted (AMI) line coding (inverted). If the data stream is inverted, the CSU/DSUs on both ends must be inverted. By default, the data stream is not inverted (normal).

e. Select the line coding type:

```
(interface) service-module t1 linecode {ami | b8zs}
```

The line coding can be set to either alternate mark inverted (ami) or bipolar 8 zero sequence (b8zs, the default).

f. Set the line build-out:

```
(interface) service-module t1 lbo {-15db | -7.5db | none}
```

The outgoing signal strength can be reduced by 15 dB (-15db), 7.5 dB (-7.5db), or 0 dB (none, the default). Usually, this is needed only in back-to-back CSU/DSU scenarios.

g. Enable remote alarms:

```
(interface) service-module t1 remote-alarm-enable
```

The CSU/DSU can be configured to generate or detect remote alarms. This is disabled by default, and it should always be disabled if the line coding is set to D4 SF. Otherwise, some data bits in the SF stream will be falsely interpreted as alarms.

h. Enable remote loopback initiation:

```
(interface) service-module t1 remote-loopback {full | payload} [alternate |
v54]
```

If the service module receives a loopback test request from the far end, it can be configured to go into loopback mode. The **full** keyword (the default) allows a response to all loopback requests. The **payload** keyword enables only payload-loopback commands. The **alternate** keyword configures an inverted loopback mode, with 4-in-5 loopup and 2-in-3 loopdown patterns. The v54 keyword (the default) configures the industry standard 1-in-5 loopup and 1-in-3 loopdown patterns.

8. (Optional) Configure an integrated two- or four-wire 56 or 64 kbps service module.

a. (Optional) Select the clock source:

```
(interface) service-module 56k clock source {line | internal}
```

The clock reference can come from either the network (**line**, the default) or the **internal** clock.

b. (Optional) Set the line speed:

```
(interface) service-module 56k clock rate speed
```

The line speed can be configured to (in kbps) **2.4, 4.8, 9.6, 19.2, 38.4, 56** (the default), **64**, or **auto**. The **auto** keyword is used to detect the line speed automatically from the sealing current on the network. auto should be used only with the line clock source and a dedicated leased line.

c. (Optional) Select the mode:

```
(interface) service-module 56k network-type {dds | switched}
```

The mode can be set to dedicated leased line DDS mode (**dds**, the default for four-wire circuits) or switched dialup mode (**switched**, the default for two-wire circuits). For switched mode, the line clock source and a clock rate of **56** or **auto** must be used. Only in-band dialing is supported.

d. (Optional) Enable scrambled data for 64 kbps:

```
(interface) service-module 56k data-coding scrambled
```

On a four-wire 64 kbps DDS line, some data can be interpreted as loopback request codes. Data scrambling prevents this and should be enabled.

e. (Optional) Enable remote loopbacks:

```
(interface) service-module 56k remote-loopback
```

A service module can be configured to accept a remote loopback request. Even if remote-loopback is disabled, loopback requests can be sent to the far end.

Example

A channelized T3 interface is configured to have a T1 in channel 5, consisting of timeslots 1 through 12. The T1 framing is ESF, and the T3 cable length is about 300 feet. The line is the clock source. As soon as the controller is configured, a serial interface using T3 channel 5 can be given an IP address.

Also, a channelized T1 interface is configured. The controller is set to associate T1 time slots 1 through 8 with a single channel group. The line clock is used for the T1, with a cable length of 300 (round up to the next choice of 399) feet. As soon as the controller is configured, a serial interface with the appropriate channel group can be configured with an IP address.

```
controller t3 6/0/0
        framing auto-detect
        cablelength 300
        clock source line
        t1 5 timeslot 1-12 speed 64
        t1 5 framing esf

interface serial 6/0/0:5
        ip address 192.168.3.1 255.255.255.0

controller t1 7/0/1
        channel-group 1 timeslots 1-8 speed 56
        clock source line
        cablelength short 399

interface serial 7/0/1:1
        ip address 192.168.4.1 255.255.255.0
```

2-7: Packet-Over-SONET Interfaces

- Packet-Over-SONET is available on POSIP and POSPA router interfaces.

- POS provides an OC-3 155.520 Mbps interface that is compatible with SONET and Synchronous Digital Hierarchy (SDH) networks.

- Dynamic Packet Transport (DPT) provides IP-over-SONET on an OC-12cSRP interface.

- SRP interfaces provide fault tolerance by maintaining a topology map of all nodes on the ring. Topology discovery packets accumulate the MAC addresses of each node on the ring.

■   Automatic Protection Switching (APS) provides switchover of POS circuits, usually in a telco environment. Two SONET connections are required, both configured for APS.

Configuration

Select and configure one of the Packet-Over-SONET interfaces described in the following sections (OC-3, DPT OC-12c, APS on POS).

Configuring an OC-3 POS Interface

1.   Select the interface:

    (global) **interface pos** *slot*/*number*

2.   (Optional) Select framing:

    (interface) **pos framing-sdh**

    By default, the POS interface uses SONET STS-3c framing. The framing-sdh keyword enables SDH STM-1 framing instead.

3.   (Optional) Set the clock source:

    (interface) **clock source**

    By default, the transmit clock is derived from the recovered receive clock. The **clock source** command enables the internal clock as the transmit clock.

4.   (Optional) Enable payload scrambling:

    (interface) **pos scramble-atm**

    If necessary, payload scrambling can be enabled to provide the proper bit transition density. Scrambling must be enabled on both ends of the POS connection.

5.   (Optional) Enable loopback tests:

    (interface) **loop internal**
    -OR-
    (interface) **loop line**

    For POS testing, the interface can be looped internally (internal) or looped at the remote POS interface (line).

    Configuring a DPT OC-12c POS Interface

1.   Select the interface:

    (global) **interface srp** *slot*/*number*

2.   (Optional) Set the topology update timer:

    (interface) **srp topology-timer** *seconds*

    Topology discovery packets are sent out at intervals of seconds (1 to 600; the default is 10 seconds).

3. (Optional) Configure Intelligent Protection Switching (IPS).

   a. Set the wait-to-restore request timer:

```
(interface) srp ips wtr-timer seconds
```

The WTR timer can be set in *seconds* (10 to 600; the default is 60 seconds). This timer reduces ring oscillations by keeping a wrap condition in place for *seconds* after a wrap is removed.

   b. Set the IPS message timer:

```
(interface) srp ips timer seconds [a | b]
```

The frequency of IPS requests is set to an interval of seconds (1 to 60; the default is 1 second). The timer can be applied to either side of the ring if desired.

   c. Initiate a ring wrap:

```
(interface) srp ips request {forced-switch | manual-switch} {a | b}
```

A wrap condition is inserted on the ring. The **forced-switch** option causes the wrap to remain in effect until it is removed. The **manual-switch** option causes a wrap, but neither the command nor the wrap condition persists across a reload. The **a** keyword specifies a wrap on side A (the outer ring receive fiber), and **b** wraps on side B (the inner ring receive fiber).

Configuring APS on POS Interfaces

1. Select the working and protect interfaces.

   a. Identify the working interface:

```
(global) interface pos slot/number
(interface) aps working circuit
```

The working interface is used until a failure or a condition occurs to switch over to the protect interface. The *circuit* field is an arbitrary circuit number that links the working and protect interfaces.

   b. Identify the protect interface:

```
(global) interface pos slot/number
(interface) aps protect circuit protect-ip-address
```

The protect interface is identified and associated with the working interface that has the same arbitrary *circuit* number. The *protect-ip-address* field gives the IP address of the router with the working interface.

2. (Optional) Configure authentication:

```
(interface) aps authenticate string
```

Packets on the out-of-band POS channel are accepted if the authentication string (up to eight characters) matches *string*. Authentication must be configured on both working and protect interfaces.

3. (Optional) Set the APS timers:

```
(interface) aps timers hello hold
```

A POS interface sends a hello packet every *hello* seconds (the default is 1 second). If a hello packet is not received before the *hold* interval expires (the default is 3 seconds), the interface is declared down.

4. (Optional) Group APS interfaces:

```
(interface) aps group group-number
```

If more than one working and protect interface is used, the interfaces can be grouped. Each interface must be assigned to an arbitrary *group-number* (the default is 0).

5. (Optional) Configure APS switchover.

a. Lock out an interface:

```
(interface) aps lockout circuit
```

A protect interface can be locked out to prevent it from being used. The *circuit* number must be given to identify the working/protect pair.

b. Manually switch to a protect interface:

```
(interface) aps manual circuit
```

Normally, switchover to a protect circuit is automatic, based on interface or peer failure. However, a circuit can be manually switched from a working interface to a protect interface for the circuit number.

c. Automatically revert after a switchover:

```
(interface) aps revert minutes
```

By default, the protect circuit must be manually switched back to the working circuit as soon as the working circuit is available. If desired, the switch back to a restored working circuit can be automatic, after minutes have elapsed.

Example

A router is configured with two PoS interfaces. The first interface is the working APS interface, and the second is the protect interface. The router exchanges APS control packets with itself to determine whether the working interface is down. The router also has a Dynamic Packet Transport OC-12 SRP interface that has an IP address configured.

```
interface pos 4/0
    description PoS OC-3 connection #1
```

```
        ip address 192.168.57.1 255.255.255.0
        aps working 1
interface pos 5/0
        description PoS OC-3 connection #2
        ip address 192.168.58.1 255.255.255.0
        aps protect 1 192.168.57.1
interface srp 5/0
        description DPT OC-12c connection
        ip address 10.1.1.1 255.255.255.0
```

2-8: Frame Relay Interfaces

- A router communicates with a Frame Relay switch through Local Management Interface (LMI).

- The Frame Relay circuit is identified to the router as a Data Link Circuit Identifier (DLCI) number.

- Inverse ARP is enabled by default for protocols configured on an interface. A dynamic mapping occurs between a protocol address and a DLCI.

- Frame Relay supports either Permanent Virtual Circuits (PVCs) or Switched Virtual Circuits (SVCs) between endpoints.

- Frame Relay is supported on major interfaces (interface serial 0, for example) for fully meshed connections between routers, where each router has a circuit to every other router.

- Frame Relay is supported on subinterfaces (interface serial 0.1, for example) for partially meshed or point-to-point connections.

- Data transmission over a circuit is described and controlled by the following terms:

    - **Data Link Connection Identifier (DLCI)**—A 10-bit number (0 to 1023) that uniquely identifies a virtual circuit (VC) to the local router. DLCI numbers can be reused on the far end of a VC. In addition, DLCI numbers can be globally unique across the Frame Relay cloud if desired by the service provider. In practice, you will probably find that DLCI numbers are not globally unique but are duplicated for convenience and simplicity.

    - **Committed Information Rate (CIR)**—The throughput rate that the service provider normally supports. It is possible to exceed the CIR, but only as defined by the sampling interval (Tc) and the committed burst rate (Bc). When the CIR is defined as a 0 value (for lowest cost), attention should be paid to congestion management on the router. In general, the CIR equals Bc/Tc, as defined next.

    - **Committed Rate Measurement Interval (Tc)**—The time interval or "bandwidth interval" used to control traffic bursts on a VC.

    - **Committed Burst Rate (Bc)**—The maximum amount of traffic that the Frame Relay network will allow into the VC during the time interval Tc.

- **Excess Burst Rate (Be)**—The maximum amount of traffic on a VC that can exceed the Bc value in a time interval Tc.

- **Discard-Eligible (DE)**—A bit in the Frame Relay header that is set to indicate that the frame is more eligible than others to be discarded in case of switch congestion. The DE bit is set by the router and is passed to the Frame Relay switch for discarding if necessary.

- **Forward Explicit Congestion Notification (FECN)**—A bit in the Frame Relay header that is set to indicate Frame Relay switch congestion. The FECN bit is set in frames traveling toward the destination, or in the "forward" direction.

- **Backward Explicit Congestion Notification (BECN)**—A bit in the Frame Relay header that is set to indicate Frame Relay switch congestion. The BECN bit is set in frames traveling toward the source, or in the "backward" direction. In this manner, both FECN and BECN bits are set to notify both upstream and downstream nodes of switch congestion.

- End-to-end keepalives can be used to provide monitoring of a PVC by exchanging keepalive information between two routers. Normally, a router can only monitor a PVC based on LMI messages from its local Frame Relay switch.

- Frame Relay Inverse ARP can be used to dynamically discover the network protocol address (an IP address, for example) given a specific DLCI number. Inverse ARP is based on RFC 1293 and is enabled on Frame Relay interfaces by default.

> **Note**   DLCI 0 is used for LMI under ANSI and ITU encapsulations, whereas DLCI 1023 is used under the Cisco encapsulation.

Configuration

1. Select a major interface:

    ```
    (global) interface serial number
    ```

    Many Frame Relay circuits can be supported on a single major interface. The active DLCI numbers can be determined automatically through LMI.

2. Enable Frame Relay encapsulation:

    ```
    (interface) encapsulation frame-relay {cisco | ietf}
    ```

    The type of encapsulation can be set for the major interface. Any subinterfaces defined inherit this encapsulation unless they are overridden. The **cisco** type (the default) should be used when the router is connected to another Cisco router across the Frame Relay cloud. The **ietf** type is based on IETF RFC 1490 and provides vendor interoperability. Use this type when a Cisco router connects to non-Cisco equipment across the frame cloud.

3. Configure LMI.

   a. Configure LMI autosensing.

By default, LMI autosensing is enabled unless a specific LMI type is configured. LMI autosensing sends out full status requests in all three LMI types (ANSI T1.617 Annex D, Cisco, and ITU-T Q.933 Annex A). The LMI type is set to match the only or last reply received from the Frame Relay switch.

-or-

   b. Configure a specific LMI type.

Choose an LMI type:

```
(interface) frame-relay lmi-type {ansi | cisco | q933a}
```

The LMI type must be set to match that of the Frame Relay switch. The type can be **ansi** (ANSI T1.617 Annex D), **cisco**, or **q933a** (ITU-T Q.933 Annex A).

(Optional) Set the LMI keepalive time:

```
(interface) keepalive seconds
```

The LMI keepalive interval (the default is 10 seconds) must be set to a value less than the interval used by the Frame Relay switch.

4. (Optional) Configure subinterfaces.

   a. Define the subinterface:

```
(global) interface serial number.subinterface {multipoint | point-to-point}
```

A logical or virtual subinterface is defined as a part of the physical major interface *number*. The subinterface number can be arbitrarily chosen. The type of circuit must be identified as either **multipoint** (multiple routers connect to the local router through one virtual circuit) or **point-to-point** (one router connects to the local router).

   b. Define a DLCI for the subinterface:

```
(subinterface) frame-relay interface-dlci dlci [ietf | cisco]
```

Because multiple logical interfaces can be defined under one physical interface, each subinterface must be identified with its DLCI, *dlci*. The encapsulation type can also be set per subinterface if necessary. If the type is left off, it is inherited from the type of the major physical interface.

5. (Optional) Configure static address mappings.

   a. Map a DLCI to a protocol address:

```
(interface) frame-relay map protocol address dlci [broadcast]  [ietf |
cisco]
```

By default, Frame Relay Inverse ARP is used to resolve a next-hop protocol address given a DLCI number. If desired, static mappings can be configured instead. A *protocol* can be given as **ip, decnet, appletalk, xns, ipx, vines,** or **clns,** along with the protocol *address* and the DLCI.

The **broadcast** keyword causes broadcasts for the protocol to be forwarded on the DLCI. The Frame Relay encapsulation can also be defined for this protocol on this DLCI if desired. If not specified, the encapsulation is inherited from the major interface or subinterface.

b. Map a DLCI to a transparent bridge:

```
(interface) frame-relay map bridge dlci [broadcast | ietf]
```

The DLCI given is used to forward packets for transparent bridging. The **broadcast** keyword allows broadcasts to be forwarded on the DLCI. If desired, the encapsulation can be set to **ietf** for the bridged DLCI.

c. Map a DLCI to ISO CLNS:

```
(interface) frame-relay map clns dlci [broadcast]
```

The DLCI given is used to forward packets for CLNS routing. The **broadcast** keyword allows broadcasts to be forwarded on the DLCI.

6. (Optional) Configure Switched Virtual Circuits (SVCs).

a. Create an SVC map class.

Define the map class:

```
(global) map-class frame-relay map-class
```

A map class named *map-class* (a text string) is created. Parameters defined to the map class can be used as a template for SVC definitions, QoS, and so forth.

(Optional) Define custom queuing.

Begin by defining a custom queue list:

```
(global) queue-list list-number queue queue-number ...
```

Next, assign the custom queue list to the Frame Relay map class:

```
(map-class) frame-relay custom-queue-list custom-list
```

See Section 10-7 for more information about configuringcustom queuing.

If custom queuing is not defined, first-in-first-out (FIFO) queuing is used by default.

(Optional) Define priority queuing.

Begin by defining a priority queue list:

```
(global) priority-list list-number protocol protocol {high | medium | low |
default}
```

Next, assign the priority queue list to the Frame Relay map class:

```
(map-class) frame-relay priority-group priority-list
```

See Section 10-6 for more information about configuring priority queuing.

If priority queuing is not defined, first-in-first-out (FIFO) queuing is used by default.

(Optional) Define Frame Relay quality of service (QoS) parameters.

Begin by selecting a response to congestion:

`(map-class)` **`frame-relay adaptive-shaping {becn | foresight}`**

Two methods of congestion notification are available: Backward Explicit Congestion Notification (**becn**) and Foresight (**foresight**). BECN relies on setting a bit in a user packet to inform the router of congestion, a method that is sometimes unreliable. The Foresight method passes periodic messages between the Frame Relay switch and routers, independent of user data packets.

Next, set the CIR for an SVC:

`(map-class)` **`frame-relay cir {in | out}`** *`bps`*

The CIR for incoming and outgoing traffic on an SVC can be independently set to *bps* bits per second (the default is 56000).

Next, set the minimum acceptable CIR:

`(map-class)` **`frame-relay mincir {in | out}`** *`bps`*

The minimum acceptable CIR for incoming and outgoing traffic on an SVC can be independently set to *bps* (the default is 56000).

Next, set the committed burst size, Bc:

`(map-class)` **`frame-relay bc {in | out}`** *`bits`*

The Bc parameter for incoming and outgoing traffic on an SVC can be set independently to *bits* (the default is 7000 bits).

Next, set the excess burst size, Be:

`(map-class)` **`frame-relay be {in | out}`** *`bits`*

The Be parameter for incoming and outgoing traffic on an SVC can be set independently to *bits* (the default is 7000 bits).

Next, set the SVC idle timer:

`(map-class)` **`frame-relay idle-timer [in | out]`** *`seconds`*

An SVC is released after *seconds* (the default is 120 seconds) of time passes without sending or receiving frames. The idle timer value should be set according to the applications that are in use.

b. Create a map list to trigger SVCs.

Set the E.164 or X.121 addresses for the SVC:

```
(global) map-list map-list source-addr {e164 | x121} source-addr  dest-addr
{e164 | x121} dest-addr
```

For an SVC, a local source address and a remote destination address must be defined. A map list named *map-list* is created, containing a list of protocols that will trigger the SVC.

Addresses can be given in either E.164 (**e164**) or X.121 (**x121**) format, as they are defined on the Frame Relay switch. An E.164 address has a variable length, up to 15 digits, in the format Country Code (one, two, or three digits), National Destination Code and Subscriber Number (National ISDN number, a maximum of 12 to 14 digits), and ISDN Subaddress (a device number at the termination point). An X.121 address is 14 digits long and has the format Zone code (one digit), Country code (two digits), Public data network code (one digit), and a ten-digit number.

Set the protocol address that will trigger SVC setup:

```
(map-list) protocol protocol-address class map-class [ietf]   [broadcast
[trigger]]
```

The SVC, defined by the addresses in the map list, is triggeredfor setup by *protocol* type traffic destined for the *protocol-address*. The map class named *map-class* is used to give SVC parameters. Valid protocols include **ip, ipx, appletalk, decnet, bridge** (for transparent bridging), **dlsw, bstun, stun, cdp, arp**, and so forth. The **ietf** keyword enables RFC 1490 encapsulation rather than the Cisco default. The **broadcast** keyword causes broadcast packets for the protocol to be sent over the SVC. If the **trigger** keyword is included, broadcast traffic is allowed to trigger the SVC setup.

c. Enable SVC support on an interface.

Enable SVC on the major interface:

```
(interface) frame-relay svc
```

SVC support is inherently enabled for all subinterfaces under the major interface.

Assign a map group to an interface:

```
(interface) map-group map-list
```

A map list named *map-list* is bound to the interface (or subinterface) to define and trigger an SVC. More than one **map-group** command can be configured on an interface so that multiple SVCs can be used.

7. (Optional) Set other Frame Relay parameters.

a. Use end-to-end keepalives.

Create or add to a map class:

```
(global) map-class frame-relay map-class
```

End-to-end keepalives can be configured only from a Frame Relay map class.

Enable end-to-end keepalives:

```
(map-class) frame-relay end-to-end keepalive mode {bi-directional |
request | reply | passive-reply}
```

Under **bi-directional** mode, the router has a sender and receiver to handle keepalive messages. The **request** mode enables only the sender such that keepalive responses are requested but none are answered. The **reply** mode enables only the receiver, which waits for requests and answers them. The **passive-reply** mode operates like the **reply** mode but does not keep any timer or event states.

By default, keepalive requests are sent every 10 seconds. If requests aren't received within 15 seconds, an error counter is incremented. Only the last three keepalive events are checked for errors: If two or more requests were missed, the keepalive state moves from up to down; if two or more requests are seen again, the keepalive state moves from down to up. These values can be changed from the default with the **frame-relay end-to-end keepalive {error-threshold | event-window | success-events | timer}** command.

b. Disable Frame Relay inverse ARP:

```
(interface) [no] frame-relay inverse-arp [protocol] [dlci]
```

Frame Relay inverse ARP is enabled by default. It can be disabled if desired using the **no** form of the command. Inverse ARP can also be enabled or disabled for a particular *protocol* and/or DLCI number.

c. Create a broadcast queue:

```
(interface) frame-relay broadcast-queue size byte-rate packet-rate
```

Broadcast packets must be replicated and sent out to all DLCIs related to a protocol or bridge group. A queue can be used to hold and forward broadcasts to within a specified rate limit. The broadcast queue length is given as *size* in packets (the default is 64 packets). The size should be large enough to hold a complete routing update for each protocol over each DLCI. The maximum number of broadcast bytes to send per second is given as *byte-rate* (the default is 256000 bytes per second; this number is generally set to less than both the number of DLCIs divided by 4 and one-fourth of the local access rate in bytes per second). The maximum number of broadcast packets per second is given as *packet-rate* (the default is 36 packets per second).

d. Enable Frame Relay fragmentation.

Use end-to-end FRF.12 fragmentation:

`(map-class)` **`frame-relay fragment`** `fragment-size`

FRF.12 fragmentation is used on a per-PVC basis through a map class. The *fragment-size* is the payload size, excluding Frame Relay headers (16 to 1600 bytes; the default is 53 bytes). Use fragmentation so that time-critical packets such as voice can be interleaved with fragments of larger packets. Set the fragment size less than the MTU but not larger than a voice packet.

Use FRF.11 Annex C fragmentation.

This type of fragmentation is used when Voice over Frame Relay (VoFR) is configured, but it should not be used for Voice over IP (VoIP). See Section 12-3 for further details.

Use Cisco proprietary fragmentation.

If Voice over Frame Relay is configured and a map class is used for the PVC, Cisco proprietary fragmentation can be used. See Section 12-3 for further details.

e. Enable payload compression.

Use packet-by-packet compression:

`(interface)` **`frame-relay payload-compression packet-by-packet`**

-OR-

`(interface)` **`frame-relay map`** `protocol address dlci`   **`payload-compression packet-by-packet`**

The Stacker method is used to predict the next character in a frame, one packet at a time. This command can be used for the entire data stream on an interface or on a specified protocol and DLCI using the **frame-relay map** command.

Use FRF.9 or Cisco proprietary data-stream compression:

`(interface)` **`frame-relay payload-compression {frf9 | data-stream}  stac [distributed | ratio | software]`**

-OR-

`(interface)` **`frame-relay map`** `protocol address dlci`   **`payload-compression frf9 stac [distributed | ratio | software]`**

The standards-based FRF.9 compression can be used with the **frf9** keyword, whereas the Cisco proprietary method can be used with the **data-stream** keyword. Compression can be configured either directly on the interface or through a **frame-relay map** command. The **distributed** keyword enables compression in a VIP2 module (if available). The **ratio** keyword weighs compression against throughput: **high** (high compression, low throughput) or **low** (low compression, high throughput; this is the default). The **software** keyword enables compression in IOS software on the router CPU.

f. Enable TCP/IP header compression:

```
(interface) frame-relay ip tcp header-compression [passive]
```

TCP/IP headers can be compressed within frames. By default, this is enabled only for the Cisco Frame Relay encapsulation. Packets must arrive in order, or the packet headers will not be re-created properly. (Do not use priority queuing, which can cause packets to arrive out of order.) The **passive** keyword causes headers to be compressed only if an incoming packet had a compressed header.

g. Flag discard-eligible (DE) frames.

Identify DE frames with a DE list:

```
(global) frame-relay de-list list-number {protocol protocol |   interface
type number} characteristic
```

The DE list identifies frames that can be dropped by the Frame Relay network in case a switch is congested. Frames chosen should be those with a low time sensitivity or a low importance. The *list-number* is used to group multiple DE list commands as a single list.

The **protocol** keyword can be used to specify a protocol as discard-eligible. Possible *protocol* names are **arp, apollo, appletalk, bridge, clns, clns_es, clns_is, compressedtcp, decnet, decnet_ node, decnet_router-L1, decnet_router-L2, ip, ipx, vines,** and **xns.** For the **ip** protocol, the *characteristic* field can be given as **tcp** *port* or **udp** *port* to flag specific port numbers, or as **fragments** for fragmented IP packets. The *characteristic* field can also be used to reference an access list (**list** *access-list*, a standard or extended IP access list numbered 1 to 199 or 1300 to 2699) that can further define DE frames, or to identify frames that are less than (**lt** *bytes*) or greater than (**gt** *bytes*) a certain size.

The **interface** keyword, along with an interface *type* and *number,* can also be used to mark frames coming from that interface as discard-eligible.

Apply the DE list to an interface and DLCI:

```
(interface) frame-relay de-group list-number dlci
```

On the Frame Relay interface, the DE list numbered *list-number* is used to flag packets eligible for discarding only on the *dlci* virtual circuit.

h. Integrate priority queuing with multiple DLCIs.

Define a priority list:

```
(global) priority-list list-number protocol protocol {high | medium |  low |
default}
```

A priority list numbered *list-number* is created, grouping multiple queue definitions. A specific protocol is assigned to a priority queue level: **high, medium, low,** or **default.**

Assign DLCIs to carry traffic from priority queues:

```
(interface) frame-relay priority-dlci-group list-number high-dlci med-dlci
normal-dlci low-dlci
```

The priority queues can be applied to individual DLCIs that are carried over a single Frame Relay interface. The *list-number* given is the same number as the priority list. The priority queues are defined to DLCIs *high-dlci*, *med-dlci*, *normal-dlci*, and *low-dlci*. In this fashion, the queues can be carried over DLCIs with the appropriate CIR and quality of service characteristics.

8. (Optional) Configure Frame Relay traffic shaping.

For certain Quality of Service (QoS) needs, Frame Relay traffic can be shaped prior to transmission. See Section 10-4 for complete details.

Example

A Frame Relay connection to a remote site is configured on major interface serial 0. The interface is given an IP address and is also configured to flag all outgoing HTTP traffic (TCP port 80) as discard-eligible. Two other PVCs are defined on subinterfaces of serial 1. Each subinterface has an IP address and is configured to use map class "branches" to enable end-to-end keepalives. In addition, Frame Relay fragmentation is used to transmit data frames as 100-byte fragments. Figure 2-4 shows a network diagram.

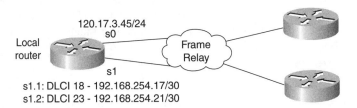

Figure 2-4 *Network Diagram for the Frame Relay Interface Example*

```
map-class frame-relay branches
        frame-relay end-to-end keepalive mode bidirectional
        frame-relay fragment 100


frame-relay de-list 1 protocol ip tcp 80


interface serial 0
        encapsulation frame-relay cisco
        ip address 120.17.3.45 255.255.255.0
        frame-relay de-group 1 5


interface serial 1
        encapsulation frame-relay cisco
        no ip address
```

```
interface serial 1.1 point-to-point
       frame-relay interface-dlci 18
       frame-relay class branches
       ip address 192.168.254.17 255.255.255.252

interface serial 1.2 point-to-point
       frame-relay interface-dlci 23
       frame-relay class branches
       ip address 192.168.254.21 255.255.255.252
```

2-9: Frame Relay Switching

- A router can perform Frame Relay switch functions.

    - Both serial (major interfaces only) and ISDN PRI/BRI interfaces (Frame Relay over ISDN) are supported.

    - An interface can act as either a DTE, DCE, or NNI (network-to-network interface) device.

    - Traffic shaping can be used to control the transmission of outgoing traffic (out of the switch).

    - Traffic policing can be used on switched PVCs to control the behavior of incoming traffic (into the switch).

- Congestion management can be used to specify how the Frame Relay switch informs other devices of congestion and how it reacts to congestion itself.

Configuration

1. Enable Frame Relay switching:

   (global) **frame-relay switching**

2. Configure the interfaces.

   a. Enable Frame Relay encapsulation:

   (interface) **encapsulation frame-relay {cisco | ietf}**

   Only major interfaces are supported for Frame Relay switching.

   b. Configure the LMI type:

   (interface) **frame-relay lmi-type {ansi | cisco | q933a}**

   The LMI type should be configured, because the router will be acting as a switch and will be providing LMI to other devices. The types are **ansi** (T1.617 Annex D), **cisco**, and **q933a** (ITU-T Q.933 Annex A).

Note   By default, LMI autosensing is enabled. For Frame Relay switching, the local router should provide one type of LMI to other devices. Therefore, you should configure a specific LMI type.

    c. Configure interface types:

        (interface) **frame-relay intf-type {dce | dte | nni}**

        By default, a Frame Relay interface operates as a DTE (Data Terminal Equipment, **dte**). The other routers and devices connected to this Frame Relay switch will likely be DTE devices. Therefore, the Frame Relay switch interface should become a DCE (Data Communications Equipment, **dce**). If the router performing switching needs to connect to another Frame Relay switch within the frame cloud, the interface should become an NNI (**nni**) type.

3. Configure the PVCs that will be switched.

    a. Configure static switching with no traffic control:

        (interface) **frame-relay route** *in-dlci out-interface out-dlci*

        The PVC is defined from the incoming DLCI *(in-dlci)* on the interface to the outgoing interface *(out-interface)* and the outgoing DLCI *(out-dlci)*.

        -or-

    b. Configure switching for traffic control or ISDN:

        (global) **connect** *name interface1 dlci1 interface2 dlci2*

        The PVC is given a text-string *name* and is defined from one endpoint *(interface1* and *dlci1)* to another endpoint *(interface2* and *dlci2)*.

4. (Optional) Use traffic shaping to control outgoing PVCs.

    Frame Relay traffic shaping can be used to characterize the parameters of a switched PVC. Traffic shaping is typically used when a router is acting as a Frame Relay switch to aggregate or concentrate multiple Frame Relay PVCs before sending a single data stream into another frame cloud. See Section 12-4 for further details.

5. (Optional) Use traffic policing to control incoming PVCs.

    a. Enable policing on an interface:

        (interface) **frame-relay policing**

    b. Use a map class to apply policing parameters.

        Configure the map class name:

        (global) **map-class frame-relay** *map-class-name*

Configure the incoming CIR:

```
(map-class) frame-relay cir in bps
```

The CIR is given as *bps* bits per second (the default is 56000). This is the CIR that the switch provides to devices on the PVC.

Configure the committed burst size, Bc:

```
(map-class) frame-relay bc in bits
```

The committed burst size is given as *bits* (the default is 7000), based on the sampling interval Tc that is defined in Step 4). The Bc value is actually Tc multiplied by the CIR.

Configure the excess burst size, Be:

```
(map-class) frame-relay be in bits
```

The excess burst size is given as *bits* (the default is 7000). It is also based on the sampling interval Tc.

Configure the 0 CIR measurement interval, Tc:

```
(map-class) frame-relay tc milliseconds
```

PVCs can be provided with a CIR of 0 bits per second, offering no guaranteed throughput. When the CIR is 0, Tc defines the time interval when the incoming traffic rate can't exceed Bc plus Be. Tc is given in *milliseconds* (10 to 10000; the default is 1000 ms).

c. Apply the map class to an interface or PVC.

Apply the map class to all PVCs on an interface:

```
(interface) frame-relay class map-class-name
```

The map class is used as a template for all PVCs on a major interface. The map class can be overridden by other map classes applied to specific PVCs on the interface.

Apply the map class to a single PVC:

```
(interface) frame-relay interface-dlci dlci switched class   map-class-
name
```

A single DLCI is defined on an interface. The **switched** keyword must be present when a map class is to be applied, along with the **class** keyword and the map class name.

6. (Optional) Use congestion management to react to traffic congestion.

a. Use congestion management for all PVCs on an interface.

Enable congestion management:

```
(interface) frame-relay congestion management
```

Configure the discard threshold:

```
(fr-congestion) threshold de percentage
```

When the interface's output queue reaches *percentage* of its maximum size, frames marked as discard-eligible are discarded.

Configure the congestion notification threshold:

```
(fr-congestion) threshold ecn {bc | be} percentage
```

The threshold for triggering the Explicit Congestion Notification (ECN) bits can be configured for the committed (**bc**) and excess (**be**) traffic rates. When the output queue reaches *percentage* of its maximum size, the ECN bits (FECN and BECN) are set in switched packets. The Bc threshold should be set equal to or less than 100%, and the Be threshold should be set equal to or less than Bc. By default, both Bc and Be are set to 100%.

b. Use congestion management for single PVCs through traffic shaping.

Define a map class:

```
(global) map-class frame-relay map-class-name
```

Configure the discard threshold:

```
(map-class) frame-relay congestion threshold de percentage
```

The threshold for beginning to discard frames is set to the *percentage* of the maximum queue size (the default is 100%).

Configure the congestion notification threshold:

```
(map-class) frame-relay congestion threshold ecn percentage
```

The threshold for beginning to set the ECN bits (FECN and BECN) is set to the *percentage* of the maximum queue size (the default is 100%).

Set the size of a traffic-shaping queue:

```
(map-class) frame-relay holdq queue-size
```

The maximum size of the shaping queue is set to *queue-size* number of packets (1 to 512; the default is 40).

Apply the map class to an interface or PVC.

To apply the map class to all PVCs on an interface, use the following command:

```
(interface) frame-relay class map-class-name
```

The map class is used as a template for all PVCs on a major interface. The map class can be overridden by other map classes applied to specific PVCs on the interface.

To apply the map class to only a single PVC, use the following command:

```
(interface) frame-relay interface-dlci dlci switched class map-class-name
```

A single DLCI is defined on an interface. The **switched** keyword must be present when a map class is to be applied, along with the **class** keyword and the map class name.

Example

A router is configured as a Frame Relay switch between two remote locations and another Frame Relay switch. The connection to remote location A is provided over interface serial 0/0, to remote location B over serial 0/1, and to the other switch over serial 0/2. DLCIs 100 and 101 at location A are switched to DLCIs 200 and 201 at the remote switch. DLCI 102 at location B is switched to DLCI 202 at the remote switch, and DLCI 103 at location A is switched to DLCI 103 at location B.

The connections to locations A and B are both configured for Cisco LMI. Serial 0/0 to location A is configured for congestion management (using FECN and BECN), a frame discard threshold of 50% of the queue size, and traffic policing using map class location A for a CIR of 128 kbps and a Bc of 144 kbps. Figure 2-5 shows a network diagram.

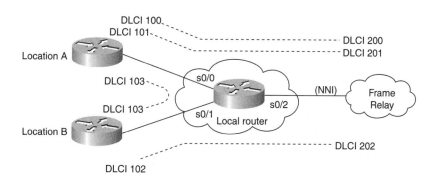

Figure 2-5   *Network Diagram for the Frame Relay Switching Example*

```
frame-relay switching
        connect vc1 serial0/0 100 serial0/2 200
        connect vc2 serial0/0 101 serial0/2 201
        connect vc3 serial0/1 102 serial0/2 202
        connect vc4 serial0/0 103 serial0/1 103
```

```
map-class frame-relay locationA
        frame-relay cir in 128000
        frame-relay bc in 144000

interface serial 0/0
        description Remote Location A
        encapsulation frame-relay cisco
        frame-relay lmi-type cisco
        frame-relay intf-type dce
        clock rate 1300000
        frame-relay policing
        frame-relay class locationA
        frame-relay congestion-management
        threshold de 50

interface serial 0/1
        description Remote Location B
        encapsulation frame-relay cisco
        frame-relay lmi-type cisco
        frame-relay intf-type dce
        clock rate 1300000

interface 0/2
        description NNI to Frame Relay switch
        encapsulation frame-relay cisco
        frame-relay lmi-type cisco
        frame-relay intf-type nni
```

2-10: ATM Interfaces

- ATM interfaces use a default MTU of 4470 bytes, a maximum of 2048 virtual circuits (VCs), and 1024 Virtual Circuit Identifiers (VCIs) per Virtual Path Identifier (VPI).

  - ATM cells are 53 bytes in length.

  - Available Bit Rate (ABR). QoS is used for best-effort service. No guarantees ofcell delay or loss are made. Transmission rates are adjusted dynamically based on congestion control messages.

  - ILMI (Integrated Local Management Interface) management. PVC can be monitored using the ILMI communication between the router and the ATM switch.

  - OAM (operation, administration, and maintenance) management. OAM loopback cells are used to monitor and manage VCs. With management, protocols in use can become aware of VC status in order to reroute packets quickly.

  - Classical IP over ATM (ClIP) emulates a logical IP subnet over SVCs. One ATM device acts as an ATM ARP server, receiving requests from ATM ARP clients (every other ClIP device) to resolve ATM NSAP addresses. Every ATM ARP client keeps an open connection to the server so that the server can keep a table of IP-to-NSAP addresses.

■ Classical IP over ATM can also use PVCs. However, PVCs inherently support ATM inverse ARP for address resolution. Therefore, no ClIP clients and server-sare necessary.

■ Inverse Multiplexing over ATM (IMA) provides a means to carry a single high-speed data stream over multiple lower-speed "bundled" physical connections. As more bandwidth is needed, additional low-speed connections can be added to the bundle.

Configuration

1. Select an ATM interface.

   a. Use a major interface:

   (global) **interface atm** *slot*/**0** (or *slot*/*port-adapter*/**0**)

   b. Use a subinterface:

   (global) **interface atm** *slot*/*0.subinterface* {**point-to-point** | **multipoint**}

   The subinterface must be defined as either a point-to-point or point-to-multipoint (**multipoint**) interface.

2. Configure a PVC.

   a. Use PVC discovery.

   Enable ILMI:

   (interface) **pvc** [*name*] **0/16 ilmi**

   A PVC is created with VPI/VCI pair 0/16 for ILMI communication. PVCs are discovered from ILMI information sent from an adjacent ATM switch.

   Enable PVC discovery:

   (interface) **atm ilmi-pvc-discovery** {**subinterface**}

   PVCs are discovered and assigned to the major ATM interface. The **subinterface** keyword causes the PVCs to be assigned to individual ATM subinterfaces, where the PVC VPI number becomes the subinterface number.

   Assign a protocol address to the interface.

   Any protocol addresses should be configured on the interface or subinterface. As soon as a PVC is discovered, it is assigned to the appropriate interface and receives the protocol address.

   -or-

   b. Manually configure a PVC on an interface:

   (interface) **pvc** [*name*] *vpi*/*vci*

The PVC can have a *name* assigned (a text string of up to 16 characters). The virtual path identifier *(vpi)* and the virtual channel identifier *(vci)* must be given.

3. Configure an SVC.

    a. Configure the ILMI PVC.

    Select the major ATM interface:

    (global) **interface atm** *slot*/0

    ILMI can be configured only on the major ATM interface, not ona subinterface.

    Define the ILMI PVC:

    (interface) **pvc** [*name*] **0/16 ilmi**

    ILMI communication with an ATM switch always occurs on VPI/VCI 0/16. This PVC can be named if desired.

    (Optional) Set the ILMI keepalive interval:

    (interface) **atm ilmi-keepalive** [*seconds*]

    ILMI keepalives are disabled by default. If enabled, keepalivesare sent to the ATM switch at *seconds* intervals (the default is 3 seconds).

    b. Define the call setup PVC:

    (interface) **pvc** [*name*] *vpi/vci* **qsaal**

    SVC call setup signaling uses QSAAL and operates over the VPI/VCI pair that is configured on the local ATM switch (usually 0/5).

    c. Define the NSAP source address.

    Use the NSAP prefix from the ATM switch:

    (interface) **atm esi-address** *esi.selector*

    The NSAP prefix (26 hexadecimal digits) is provided by the ATM switch via ILMI. The local router must then add the ESI (*esi*, 12 hexadecimal digits) and the selector (*selector*, two hexadecimal digits).

    -or-

    Define the complete NSAP address:

    (interface) **atm nsap-address** *nsap-address*

    The complete source *nsap-address* is given as a 40-digit hexadecimal string. The address should be in the dotted format pp.pppp.pp.pppppp.pppp.pppp.pppp.eeee.eeee.eeee.ss, where p is an NSAP prefix digit, e is an ESI digit, and s is a selector digit.

d. Define an SVC:

```
(interface) svc [name] nsap nsap-address
```

The NSAP destination address for the far end of the SVC is defined as *nsap-address*. The SVC can also be named with a text string (up to 16 characters).

4.   (Optional) Configure VC parameters (PVC or SVC).

a. (Optional) Create a VC class to use as a template:

```
(global) vc-class atm class-name
```

If you have several virtual circuits to define with common parameters, you can use a VC class to act as a template. The VC class receives the parameter definitions and is then applied to an ATM interface, a PVC, or an SVC.

> **Note**   Steps b through g define specific parameters for a virtual circuit. These commands can be applied to a PVC (with the **pvc** command in Step 2b), an SVC (with the **svc** command in Step 3d), or a VC class template (with the **vc-class atm** command in Step 4a). For simplicity, these commands are all shown in atm-vc configuration mode.

b. Assign a protocol address to a VC:

```
(atm-vc) protocol protocol {address | inarp} [[no] broadcast]
```

A static mapping is created for the VC and a protocol address. Available *protocol* names include **aarp** (AppleTalk ARP), **apollo**, **appletalk**, **arp** (IP ARP), **bridge**, **bstun** (Block Serial Tunnel), **cdp**, **clns**, **clns_es** (ISO CLNS end system), **clns_is** (ISO CLNS intermediate system), **compressedtcp**, **decnet**, **dlsw** (Data Link Switching), **ip**, **ipx**, **llc2** (Logical Link Control 2), **qllc** (Qualified Logical Link Control), **rsrb** (Remote Source Route Bridging), **snapshot** (snapshot routing), **stun** (Serial Tunnel), **vines**, and **xns**. A protocol *address* can be given to create a static mapping. For IP and IPX, however, the **inarp** keyword can be used instead of an address. Inverse ARP will be enabled and used on the VC to resolve protocol addresses.

The **broadcast** keyword can be used to cause broadcasts for the configured protocol to be forwarded out the VC.

c. Set the AAL and encapsulation type:

```
(atm-vc) encapsulation {aal5mux protocol | aal5snap}
```

The **aal5mux** keyword is used as a multiplex VC to support a single protocol over a VC. Available *protocol* values for aal5mux are **apollo**, **appletalk**, **decnet**, **frame** (Frame Relay-ATM), **ip**, **ipx**, **vines**, **voice** (voice over ATM), and **xns**.

The **aal5snap** keyword (the default) is used to multiplex more than one protocol over a single VC. Logical Link Control/Subnetwork Access Protocol (LLC/SNAP) is used to encode multiple protocols.

d. Enable broadcast replication:

```
(atm-vc) broadcast
```

Broadcast replication and forwarding are disabled by default. Broadcast forwarding can be configured on a per-protocol basis with the **protocol** command (in Step 4b) or for all protocols on a VC with the **broadcast** command.

e. Manage VC connectivity (PVCs and SVCs).

(PVCs and SVCs) Use end-to-end OAM loopback cells:

```
(atm-vc) {oam-pvc | oam-svc} [manage] [frequency]
```

End-to-end F5 OAM loopback cells are sent on a VC and are expected to be received from the far end. By default, loopback cells are not generated but are looped back if they are received. The **oam-pvc** keyword is used for PVCs, and **oam-svc** is used for SVCs. The **manage** keyword is used to enable OAM management. When the router sends loopback cells and doesn't receive a reply, the VC is declared down (PVC) or is torn down (SVC). The *frequency* that loopback cells are sent can be set in seconds (0 to 600; the default is 10 seconds).

Tune OAM management operation:

```
(atm-vc) oam retry up-count down-count retry-freq
```

OAM management flags a PVC as up if *up-count* loopback cell replies are received (the default is 3). A PVC is declared down or an SVC is torn down if *down-count* loopback replies are missed (the default is 5). If a loopback reply is missed, OAM management sends loopback cells at intervals of *retry-freq* (the default is 1 second) to verify the VC state.

(PVCs only) Use ILMI management:

```
(atm-vc) ilmi manage
```

f. Set the SVC idle timeout (SVC only):

```
(atm-vc) idle-timeout seconds [minimum-rate]
```

If an SVC is idle (no traffic is sent or received) for *seconds* (the default is 300 seconds), it is torn down. The SVC can also be considered idle if the *minimum-rate* is configured and the traffic flow falls below that rate (the default is 0 kbps, or no minimum rate).

g. Define an ATM quality of service (QoS).

By default, UBR QoS is used at the maximum interface line rate.

Use Available Bit Rate QoS (ABR; PVC only):

```
(atm-vc) abr output-pcr output-mcr
```

The peak cell rate (PCR) can be set to *output-pcr* (kbps), the maximum allowed cell rate (ACR). The minimum cell rate (MCR) can be set to *output-mcr* (kbps), the minimum ACR.

Use Unspecified Bit Rate QoS (UBR):

```
(atm-vc) ubr output-pcr [input-pcr]
```

The output PCR can be set to *output-pcr* (kbps). For SVCs, the input PCR can be set to *input-pcr* (kbps).

Set the UBR and peak and minimum cell rates:

```
(atm-vc) ubr+ output-pcr output-mcr [input-pcr] [input-mcr]
```

UBR is enabled, and the peak and minimum cell rates can be given as *output-pcr* and *output-mcr* (kbps). For SVCs, the input PCR and MCR can also be set to *input-pcr* and *input-mcr* (kbps).

Set the Variable Bit Rate-Non Real Time (VBR-NRT):

```
(atm-vc) vbr-nrt output-pcr output-scr output-mbs [input-pcr]    [input-scr] [input-mbs]
```

VBR-NRT QoS is enabled. The output peak cell rate (PCR), sustainable cell rate (SCR), and maximum burst cell size (MBS) are set to *output-pcr* (kbps), *output-scr* (kbps), and *output-mbs* (number of cells). For SVCs, the input PCR, SCR, and MBS can also be set.

h. Apply the VC class to a PVC or SVC:

```
(atm-vc) class vc-class-name
```

Any parameters that were set for the VC class are inherited by the interface or VC.

5. (Optional) Use Classical IP and ARP over ATM:

```
(interface) atm arp-server {self [time-out minutes] | nsap server-nsap}
```

The major interface's NSAP address must already be defined. To become an ATM ARP server, the **self** keyword is used. ARP entries are kept in the server's table for *minutes* (the default is 20 minutes) before they are verified again or aged out. To become an ATM ARP client, the **nsap** keyword is used. The NSAP address of the ATM ARP server must be specified as *server-nsap*.

6. (Optional) Use Inverse Multiplexing over ATM (IMA).

a. Configure the individual ATM links.

Select an ATM T1/E1 interface:

```
(global) interface atm slot/port
```

(Optional) Specify the clock source:

```
(controller) clock source {line | internal | loop-timed}
```

The clock source can be set to the network (**line**), to the free-running internal clock (**internal**), or from the line but decoupled from the system clock (**loop-timed**).

(Optional) Set the line build-out (T1 only):

```
(interface) lbo long dbgain dbloss
```

-or-

```
(interface) lbo short length
```

The cable characteristics and line build-out can be set using the **long** keyword for cables that are longer than 655 feet from the router to the CSU/DSU. The receiver gain, *dbgain*, is given as **gain26** (the default) or **gain36** dB. The transmit signal decrease, *dbloss*, is given as **-22.5db**, **-15db**, **-7.5db**, or **0db** (the default).

For cable lengths shorter than 655 feet, use the **short** keyword, along with the closest match length in feet: **133**, **266**, **399**, **533**, or **655**.

(Optional) Set the line impedance (E1 only):

```
(interface) line-termination {75-ohm | 120-ohm}
```

The E1 impedance can be set to either 75 ohms or 120 ohms (the default), depending on the dongle cable that is attached to the IMA interface.

b. Assign the individual links to an IMA group:

```
(interface) ima-group ima-group
```

The T1/E1 interface is assigned or bundled into an IMA group numbered *ima-group* (0 to 3).

c. Configure the IMA group.

Select the IMA group:

```
(global) interface atm slot/ima ima-group
```

The IMA group is treated as a logical interface (such as atm0/ima2). Any ATM-related parameters should be assigned tothe IMA group interface: PVCs, SVCs, IP addresses, QoStypes, and so forth.

Set the IMA clock mode:

```
(interface) ima clock-mode {common [port] | independent}
```

The transmit clock can be set to the same source for all IMA ports (**common**, where *port* is the port where the clock is derived), or to different sources on the various IMA ports (**independent**). If independent clock sources are used, the clock source must be configured for each individual ATM interface.

Set the maximum latency in an IMA group:

```
(interface) ima differential-delay-maximum milliseconds
```

The maximum latency for the slowest link in the IMA group can be set such that the slowest link can still participate in the group. The latency is given as *milliseconds* (T1: 25 to 250 msec; the default is 250; E1: 25 to 190 msec; the default is 190).

Set the minimum number of active links:

```
(interface) ima active-links-minimum links
```

An IMA group must have a minimum number of links in operation in order for the IMA interface to stay up. Individual links can drop out of service while the group stays up. The minimum number of links is given as *links* (1 to 8; the default is 1).

Example

The ATM 7/0 interface is configured with an ILMI PVC so that other PVCs can be discovered automatically from the ATM switch. Each discovered PVC is assigned to a subinterface that is numbered according to the PVC's VPI number. VPI numbers 1 and 2 are pre-configured as subinterfaces atm 7/0.1 and 7/0.2 with IP addresses. As soon as they are discovered, the IP addresses are bound to the active subinterfaces.

Interface ATM 8/0 is configured with a PVC definition for a remote site. The IP address of the interface (192.168.4.1), along with the IP address of the far-end device (192.168.4.2), are given. AAL5mux encapsulation is used to transport only the IP protocol.

Interfaces ATM 9/0, 9/1, and 9/2 are all configured as a single IMA group for inverse multiplexing. A minimum of one link must be up in order for the IMA group to be up. The IMA group is given an IP address and a mapping for the IP address of a far-end router on the PVC. Figure 2-6 shows a network diagram.

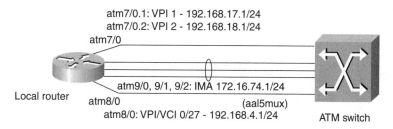

Figure 2-6   *Network Diagram for the ATM Interface Example*

```
interface atm 7/0
        pvc ILMI 0/16 ilmi
        atm ilmi-pvc-discovery subinterface
```

```
interface atm 7/0.1
        ip address 192.168.17.1 255.255.255.0
interface atm 7/0.2
        ip address 192.168.18.1 255.255.255.0

interface atm 8/0
        ip address 192.168.4.1 255.255.255.0
        pvc RemoteSite 0/27
        protocol ip 192.168.4.2 broadcast
        encapsulation aal5mux ip

interface atm 9/0
        no ip address
        ima-group 1
interface atm 9/1
        no ip address
        ima-group 1
interface atm 9/2
        no ip address
        ima-group 1

interface atm 9/ima1
        ip address 172.16.74.1 255.255.255.0
        ima clock-mode common 0
        ima active-links-minimum 1
        pvc HotsiteA 0/33
        protocol ip 172.16.74.67 255.255.255.0
```

Further Reading

Refer to the following sources for more information about the topics presented in this chapter.

Ethernet

Charles Spurgeon's Ethernet web site at ethermanage.com.

Fast Ethernet

www.cisco.com/warp/public/cc/so/neso/lnso/lnmnso/feth_tc.htm.

Gigabit Ethernet

The Gigabit Ethernet Alliance at www.gigabit-ethernet.org.

Frame Relay

The Frame Relay Forum at www.frforum.com.

Frame Relay Networks, by Uyless Black, McGraw-Hill, ISBN 0070055904.

ATM

Cisco ATM Solutions, by Galina Diker Pildush, Cisco Press, ISBN 1578702135.

The ATM Forum at www.atmforum.com.

Chapter 3

Dial Solutions

This chapter shows you how to configure and use the following network security features:

- **3-1: Modems:** Cisco routers and access servers can use internal or external modems to place and receive calls. Both digital and analog modems can be used. This section presents information on how to configure and manage all types of modems.

- **3-2: ISDN:** A router can provide dial-in or dial-out service over an ISDN PRI (23 or 30 channels) or an ISDN BRI (two channels).

- **3-3: Dial-on-Demand Routing (DDR):** Calls can be placed dynamically from a router to a dialup destination based on specific traffic. DDR provides very flexibleand scalable support for multiple dialing interfaces used to reach a destination. Connections can be made and taken down as needed, using dialup resources only when they are necessary.

- **3-4: Dial Backup:** Dialer interfaces can be used to back up other more permanent or robust interfaces on a router. When the interface goes down, DDR is used to bring up a backup connection automatically. Backup connections can also be made based on the availability of a remote IP route or IP address.

- **3-5: Routing Over Dialup Networks:** When dialup connections are used between two routers, routing protocol traffic might cause the connection to stay up indefinitely. Snapshot routing performs only periodic routing updates between routers. Routing table entries are frozen until the next periodic update, keeping the dialup connection down unless it is needed for regular traffic.

- **3-6: Point-to-Point Protocol (PPP):** PPP can be used on serial interfaces to transport other network-layer protocols over a point-to-point link. PPP offers authentication between endpoints before a connection can be established. Multilink PPP allows multiple physical links to be made, bundling the links into a logical path. Packets are fragmented and distributed over the bundled links. Fragmentation and interleaving can also be used to allow deterministic transport of time-critical data such as voice traffic.

3-1: Modems

- Internal modems include Modem ISDN Channel Aggregation (MICA) and NextPort SPE digital modems and network module analog modems.

- Internal modems can be grouped into pools such that each pool can be used for a different purpose. Users dialing into a pool receive a Dialed Number Identification System (DNIS) number and a guaranteed maximum number of simultaneous connections.

- The Call Tracker feature can be used to gather and record detailed statistics about active and disconnected calls. The statistics can be retrieved through the command-line interface, Syslog, or SNMP.

- External modems can be used when they are connected to asynchronous lines (console, Aux, or line) on routers and access servers.

Configuration

1. (Optional) Use internal digital modems.

   a. Set the country code for the modems:

   (global) **modem country {mica | microcom_hdms}** *country*

   -or-

   (global) **spe country** *country*

2. The digital modem type is given as mica (MICA), microcom_hdms (Microcom), or spe (NextPort). The country code must be one of argentina, australia, austria, belgium, brazil, canada, chile, china, columbia, czech-republic, denmark, europe, finland, france, germany, greece, hong-kong, hungary, india, indonesia, israel, italy, japan, korea, malaysia, mexico, netherlands, norway, peru, philippines, poland, portugal, saudi-arabia, singapore, south-africa, spain, sweden, switzerland, taiwan, thailand, united-kingdom, or usa. The MICA and NextPort modems also add country codes: e1-default (default E1, a-Law), russia,**t1-default** (default T1, u-Law), and **turkey**.

   a. (Optional) Group modems into a logical pool.

   Create a modem pool:

   (global) **modem-pool** *pool-name*

   By default, all internal modems are members of a system default pool. Grouping modems into a logical or virtual pool allows each pool to be used for different purposes.

   Define the range of modems in the pool:

   (modem-pool) **pool-range** *low-high*

   The range is defined as *low* (the lowest numbered modem line), a dash, and *high* (the highest numbered modem ine). To find the modem line numbers, you can use the **show modem** command.

Define one or more DNIS numbers for the pool:

```
(modem-pool) called-number dnis-number [max-conn connections]
```

When a user dials into an access server, the router uses the DNIS number (the number that was called) to find the appropriate modem pool. Each user accessing the pool can be limited to *connections* simultaneous connections.

> **Note**   You can view the Call Tracker history from the command line by using the show call calltracker active (active calls) and the show call calltracker history (disconnected calls) commands. To see detailed information about the last call on a specific modem, use the **show modem calltracker [slot/port]** command.

b. (Optional) Use Call Tracker to gather statistics from internal modems.

Enable Call Tracker:

```
(global) calltracker enable
```

Specify the Call Tracker history:

```
(global) calltracker history max-size number
(global) calltracker history retain-mins minutes
```

The maximum number of call entries that are recorded can be set to *number* (0 to 10 times the number of DS0 channels supported on the router; the default is 1 times the maximum number of supported DS0s). A value of 0 prevents call entries from being recorded. Call entries can also be retained in memory for *minutes* (0 to 26000 minutes; the default is 5000). A value of 0 prevents the call history from being saved. When increasing the history size, choose the values carefully so that Call Tracker doesn't consume too much router memory.

c. (Optional) Collect statistics on MICA modems:

```
(global) modem link-info poll time seconds
```

Call Tracker can poll MICA modems for statistics at intervals of *seconds* (10 to 65535 seconds).

■   (SNMP only) Enable the Call Tracker SNMP trap:

```
(global) snmp-server enable traps calltracker
```

If SNMP is used to gather the Call Tracker history, you must enable the **calltracker** trap. See Section 1-6 for more information about SNMP and Syslog configuration.

d. (Optional) Busy out or disable modems.

Disable a single modem:

```
(line) modem bad
```

-or-

`(line)` `modem shutdown`

You can remove an idle modem from service with the **bad** keyword. A bad active modem can be abruptly shut down with the **shutdown** keyword.

Use modem recovery to detect and recover from faults.

To detect a faulty modem, enter the following command:

`(global)` `modem recovery threshold` *number*

After *number* (1 to 1000 attempts; the default is 30 call attempts) attempts are made to use an unresponsive modem, the modem recovery process is started.

To define the amount of time before a modem is considered unresponsive, enter the following command:

`(global)` `modem recovery-time` *minutes*

A modem is considered locked and unresponsive after *minutes* (the default is 5 minutes) have passed since a call request was made.

To define the type of recovery action to take, enter the following command:

`(global)` `modem recovery action {disable | download | none}`

When modem recovery enters the maintenance window, it attempts to recover faulty modems. The recovery action can be **disable** (mark a faulty modem as bad and disable it), **download** (schedule the modem for a firmware download), or **none** (don't try to recover a faulty modem; keep using it).

To define the automatic modem recovery process, enter the following command:

`(global)` `modem recovery maintenance {action {disable | drop-call |`
  `reschedule} | max-download` *number* `| schedule {immediate | pending} |`
  `time` *hh:mm* `| window` *minutes*`}`

Every 24 hours, the router performs the modem recovery maintenance process on modems that have been marked as faulty. Faulty modems have their firmware reloaded in an attempt to bootstrap them. All modems on the same module as a faulty modem are first flagged as being in the "recovery pending" state. This prevents some modems with active calls from being reinitialized with a firmware download. The **window** keyword defines a maintenance window for *minutes* (the default is 60 minutes); as soon as the window timer expires, the pending modems are recovered.

As soon as the window is expired, an **action** is taken: **disable** (mark the faulty modems as bad and return other modems to service), **drop-call** (drop any active calls and reload the firmware), or **reschedule** (reschedule the firmware reload until the next maintenance window; this is the default). The maintenance window can be set with the **schedule** keyword, as **immediate** (attempt modem recovery now) or **pending** (wait until the next window 24 hours later; this is the default). The time of day for the regular maintenance window can be set with the **time** keyword, as *hh:mm* (a 24-hour time format; the default is 3:00 a.m.).

To prevent a large number of modems from being disabled and reloaded at one time, you can use the **max-download** keyword to place a limit on the number of modems that will be recovered, as *number* (1 to 30; the default is 20 percent of the number of modems on a system).

3. Set modem parameters (internal or external modems).

   a. Define a range of lines to use with modems:

```
(global) line start-line end-line
```

   b. Define the connection protocols that can be used over the lines:

```
(line) transport {input | output} {all | none}
```

   c. (Optional) Automatically start up an async protocol:

```
(line) autoselect {arap | ppp | slip}
```

When a connection is made to a modem line, one or more of the protocols **arap** (AppleTalk Remote Access Protocol), **ppp**, and **slip** can be started.

   d. Select the modem control mode:

```
(line) modem {dialin | inout}
```

The modem can be configured to allow incoming connections only (**dialin**) or to allow both incoming and outgoing connections (**inout**).

   e. Define the modem initialization string.

(Optional) Use an existing modem definition.

To see if the router has a preconfigured entry for your modem, enter the following command:

```
(exec) show modemcap [modem-type]
```

A list of the preconfigured modem types is shown. As soon as you find a modem type in the list, you can view all the preconfigured attributes for it by adding the *modem-type* to the command.

To edit a preconfigured modem type if needed, enter the following optional command:

```
(global) modemcap edit modem-name attribute at-command
```

The *modem-name* must be one of the types listed from **show modemcap**. The *attribute* is the name of an attribute listed in the **show modemcap** *modem-type* command. The *at-command* is a string of characters that define the "AT-style" modem command you want to use for the attribute.

To apply the modem type to the line, enter the following command:

`(line) `**`modem autoconfigure type`**` modem-name`

For internal digital modems, the type of modem can be defined as **microcom_server** (Cisco Microcom V.34/56k on an AS5200), **cisco_v110** (Cisco NEC internal V.110 TA on an AS5200), **microcom_mimic** (Cisco Microcom internal analog modem on an NM-AM), **mica** (Cisco MICA), **nextport** (Cisco NextPort CSMV/6), or **microcom_hdms** (Microcom HDMS chassis).

For external modems, the type of modem can be defined as **default** (generic Hayes-compatible), **codex_3260** (Motorola Codex 3260), **usr_courier** (US Robotics Courier), **usr_sportster** (US Robotics Sportster), **hayes_optima** (Hayes Optima), **global_village** (Global Village Teleport), **viva** (Viva Rockwell ACF with MNP), **telebit_t3000** (Telebit T3000), **nec_v34** (NEC V.34), **nec_v110** (NEC V.110 TA), or **nec_piafs** (NEC PIAFS TA).

The modem initialization string is preconfigured in the IOS software and is reapplied to the modem every time the line goes down.

(Optional) Automatically discover the modem type:

`(line) `**`modem autoconfigure discovery`**

Each time the line goes down, the router sends a string of commands to the modem in an attempt to discover the modem's type. The router can discover only modem types that are already configured (show modemcap). If the modem type can't be discovered, the router retries for 10 seconds. To see the results of the discovery, use the show line command. Be aware that discovery mode is considerably slower than using a modem type that is manually configured.

f. (Optional) Place modem lines into a rotary group:

`(line) `**`rotary`**` group`

The line is identified with the rotary group numbered *group*. It becomes part of a hunt group for outgoing calls.

4. (Optional) Create a chat script for interaction with a modem or remote system.

a. Define the chat script:

`(global) `**`chat-script`**` script-name expect-send-string`

A chat script is created with the name *script-name* (text string). You can choose a script name that corresponds to a modem vendor, type, and modulation, as in *vendor-type-modulation*. When chat scripts are used, the name of the script can be wildcarded so that a matching chat script name will be selected.

The actual chat script consists of an *expect-send-string* (text string), which consists of pairs of strings. The *expect* string is expected to be received from the modem or remote system, and the *send* string is to be sent back in response.

A chat script can contain special escape sequences, as shown in Table 3-1.

1. Here is a sample chat script:

```
chat-script DialRemote ABORT ERROR ABORT BUSY ABORT "NO ANSWER" ""
"AT H" OK "ATDT \T" TIMEOUT 45 CONNECT \c
```

Table 3-1   *Chat Script Escape Sequences*

Escape Sequence	Description
\value	Sends the ASCII character that has the value in octal (three digits of 0 to 7).
\\	Sends a backslash (\) character.
\"	Sends a double-quote (") character.
\c	Suppresses a new line at the end of the send string.
\d	Delays for 2 seconds.
\K	Inserts a BREAK.
\n	Sends a newline or linefeed character.
\N	Sends a null character.
\p	Pauses for 0.25 seconds.
\q	Reserved.
\r	Sends a return.
\s	Sends a space character.
\t	Sends a tab character.
\T	\T is replaced by the phone number from a dial string.
""	Expects a null string.
BREAK	Causes a BREAK.
EOT	Sends an end-of-transmission character.
ABORT string	Expects a string and indicates an aborted condition.
TIMEOUT time	Sets the time to wait for an expected input for time seconds (the default is 5).

2. The script is named DialRemote, and it aborts if either ERROR, BUSY, or "NO ANSWER" is received from the modem. The script expects to see nothing (two double quotes), and then it sends "AT H" to force the modem to go on-hook. As soon as OK is received from the modem, the script sends "ATDT \T" to dial the digit string that is sent in place of the \T characters. The script waits for a maximum timeout of 45 seconds, expecting to see CONNECT from the modem. The \c causes the script to suppress a newline character as the final send string.

   a. Use the chat script during a line event:

   ```
   (line) script {activation | connection | dialer | reset | startup} regexp
   ```

3. A chat script that matches the regexp regular expression is used to communicate with a modem or remote sys the line is activated with a new EXEC session), connection (when a network connection is made on the line), dialer (when DDR triggers an outbound call; used with a modem), reset (when the line is reset), or startup (when the router is started up).

Note If a chat script is not working properly, you can use the **debug chat line** *line-number* command to watch the interactive expect-send process.

3-2: ISDN

■ Primary Rate Interface (PRI) has 23 B (bearer) channels and one D (data) channel in United States, Canada, and some Caribbean islands (all places with a country code of 1). In the rest of the world, a PRI uses 30 B channels and one D channel. These are usually known as the 23B+D and 30B+D formats.

■ Each B channel carries a 64 kbps timeslot (data or voice).

■ The D channel is also a 64 kbps timeslot, carrying signaling for all the B channels. On a 23B+D PRI, the D channel is found in channel 23. On a 30B+D PRI, it is in channel 15.

■ Digital calls over a B channel are handled by the ISDN processor in the router, and analog modem calls are handled by the on-board modems in the router.

■ Basic Rate Interface (BRI) has two B channels and one D channel. Each B channel is 64 kbps, and the D channel is 16 kbps, for a total of 144 kbps. This is known as the 2B+D format.

■ BRI interfaces can use a service profile identifier (SPID) number for identification. It is assigned by the service provider.

PRI Configuration

1. Set the global ISDN switch type for all PRI interfaces:

```
(global) isdn switch-type switch-type
```

The ISDN switch-type must be set to match the switching equipment being used by the telephony provider. In North America, use basic-5ess (Lucent basic rate switches), basic-dms100 (NT DMS-100 basic rate switches), or basic-ni1 (National ISDN-1). In Australia, use basic-ts013 (TS013). In Europe, use basic-1tr6 (German 1TR6), basic-nwnet3 (Norwegian NET3 phase 1), basic-net3 (NET3), vn2 (French VN2), or vn3 (French VN3). In Japan, use ntt (NTT). In New Zealand, use basic-nznet3 (New Zealand NET3).

Note   To use QSIG signaling, use a *switch-type* of **basic-qsig**.

2. Configure the T1/E1 controller.

   a. Select the controller:

```
(global) controller {t1 | e1} slot/port
```

-or-

```
(global) card type {t1 | e1} slot
```

A T1/E1 controller is referenced by controller and slot and port number on 2600 and 3600 routers and by card type and slot number on 7200, 7500, and AS5x00 routers and access servers.

   b. (Optional) Set the ISDN switch type for this PRI:

```
(global) isdn switch-type switch-type
```

The switch type can also be set on a per-PRI basis, overriding the global switch type.

   c. Set the framing type:

```
(controller) framing {sf | esf | crc4 | no-crc4} [australia]
```

The T1 framing type can be **sf** (super frame, the default) or **esf** (extended super frame). The E1 framing type can be **crc4** (the default), **no-crc4**, and an optional **australia**.

   d. Set the clock source:

```
(controller) clock source {line [primary | secondary] | internal}
```

The controller can derive its clock from line (CO or external source) or internal (the controller's internal clock). A line clock can be designated as primary (preferred over other controllers' line clocks) or secondary (used as a backup external clock source).

e. Set the line encoding:

```
(controller) linecode {ami | b8zs | hdb3}
```

For a T1, the line coding can be set to **ami** (the default) or **b8zs** (binary 8 zero substitution). For an E1, it can be set to **ami** or **hdb3** (the default; high-densitybipolar 3).

3. Configure the PRI group:

```
(controller) pri-group [timeslots range]
```

The voice timeslots are identified as a *range* (numbers 1 to 23 or 1 to 30, separated by a dash or comma). If the **timeslots** and *range* keywords are not used, the default is a PRI with 23 B channels and one D channel.

> **Note**   To reference the serial interfaces corresponding to the PRI channels, use **interface serial** *controller:channel*, where *controller* is the T1 controller number for the physical connection and *channel* is 0 to 22 for B channels 1 to 23 and 23 for the D channel. (Interface channel numbering begins at 0, and T1/E1 channel numbering begins at 1.) For an E1 controller, the *channel* is 0 to 30 for B channels and 15 for the D channel.
>
> When you are configuring a PRI for dial-related features, always configure the features on the D channel.

4. (Optional) Set the B channel ordering for outgoing calls.

a. Select the D channel interface:

```
(global) interface serial controller:[23 | 15]
```

The D channel is identified as channel 23 for a T1 PRI and channel 15 for an E1 PRI.

b. Set the order:

```
(interface) isdn bchan-number-order {ascending | descending}
```

The first available B channel can begin with B1 in **ascending** order or B23/B30 in **descending** order (the default). Make sure the order used matches that of your service provider.

5. Set other optional parameters.

a. (Optional) Use TEI negotiation:

```
(interface) isdn tei [first-call | powerup]
```

By default, TEI negotiation occurs when the router is powered up (**powerup**). In Europe or when connecting to a DMS-100 ISDN switch, you might need to perform the negotiation during the first active call (**first-call**).

b. (Optional) Send a calling number with outbound calls:

```
(interface) isdn calling-number calling-number
```

The *calling-number* (a string of digits) represents a telephone number to be used as a billing number by the service provider.

PRI Example

A T1 controller is configured for ISDN PRI use. ESF framing and B8ZS line coding are used. The clock source is the line, and controller T1 0 is the primary source. The PRI consists of timeslots 1 to 24 (the entire T1 format), with the D channel on timeslot 24 (or interface channel 23).

```
controller T1 0

    framing esf
    clock source line primary
    linecode b8zs
    pri-group timeslots 1-24

interface serial 0:23
```

BRI Configuration

1. Set a global ISDN switch type for all BRI interfaces:

    ```
    (global) isdn switch-type switch-type
    ```

    The ISDN *switch-type* must be set to match the switching equipment being used by the telephony provider. In North America, use **basic-5ess** (Lucent basic rate switches), **basic-dms100** (NT DMS-100 basic rate switches), or **basic-ni1** (National ISDN-1). In Australia, Europe, and the UK, use **basic-1tr6** (German 1TR6), **basic-net3** (NET3), or **vn3** (French VN3). In Japan, use **ntt** (NTT). All other areas should use **none** (no specific definition).

2. Select a BRI interface:

    ```
    (global) interface bri number
    ```

    The BRI *number* is the physical location on the router.

3. (Optional) Set the ISDN switch type for the BRI:

    ```
    (global) isdn switch-type switch-type
    ```

    The selected BRI interface can have its own switch type configured, overriding the global switch type.

4. (Optional) Use SPIDs:

    ```
    (interface) isdn spid1 spid-number [ldn]
    (interface) isdn spid2 spid-number [ldn]
    ```

If your ISDN service provider assigned SPIDs to your BRI, you must configure them on the BRI interface. One or two SPIDs can be assigned as *spid-number,* usually a seven-digit telephone number with additional optional numbers. DMS-100 and NI1 ISDN switch types require SPIDs, whereas they are optional on the 5ESS type. The service provider might also assign local directory numbers *(ldn)*, to be used when answering incoming calls.

5. Set other optional parameters.

a. (Optional) Use TEI negotiation:

```
(interface) isdn tei [first-call | powerup]
```

By default, TEI negotiation occurs when the router is powered up (powerup). In Europe or when connecting to a DMS-100 ISDN switch, you might need to perform the negotiation during the first active call (first-call).

b. (Optional) Screen incoming calls for one or more numbers:

```
(interface) isdn caller number
```

If the local ISDN switch can send caller ID (CLID) information, you can specify calling numbers that will be accepted. number (up to 25 digits; X is a wildcard digit) is an accepted calling telephone number.

c. (Optional) Verify the called party number:

```
(interface) isdn answer1 [called-party-number] [:subaddress]
(interface) isdn answer1 [called-party-number] [:subaddress]
```

If more than one device is attached to a BRI, the router answers only calls that are destined for either the *called-party-number* (up to 50 digits; X is a wildcard digit) or the ISDN *:subaddress* (a colon followed by a subaddress string of up to 50 digits;X is a wildcard), or both.

d. (Optional) Send a calling number with outbound calls:

```
(interface) isdn calling-number calling-number
```

The calling-number (a string of digits) represents a telephone number to be used as a billing number by the service provider.

e. (Optional) Set a fast rollover delay to release a B channel:

```
(interface) isdn fast-rollover-delay seconds
```

If a new ISDN call fails because a previous call hasn't yet been torn down, set the delay to seconds (usually 5 seconds is sufficient).

f. (Optional) Send a disconnect cause code to the ISDN switch:

```
(interface) isdn disconnect-cause {cause-code-number | busy | not-available}
```

By default, when a BRI connection ends, the ISDN application sends a default cause code. You can override this with a specific cause-code-number (1 to 127), busy (the USER-BUSY code), or not-available (the CHANNEL-NOT-AVAILABLE code).

g. (Optional) Bind a DNIS to *an ISDN subaddress:*

```
(interface) dialer called DNIS:subaddress
```

If it is necessary to identify a DNIS number with a specific ISDN subaddress, both can be specified as DNIS:subaddress. This is sometimes required in Europe and Australia.

BRI Example

Two ISDN BRI interfaces are used on a router. A global ISDN switch type is set for a 5ESS. Interface BRI 0 uses the default switch type, with no SPID numbers. Interface BRI 1, however, has another switch type defined for a DMS-100. Two SPIDs are configured for the two B channels:

```
isdn switch-type basic-5ess
interface bri 0
      ip address 192.168.72.12 255.255.255.0
interface bri 1
      isdn switch-type basic-dms100
      isdn spid1 555123401
      isdn spid2 555123402
      ip address 192.168.71.45 255.255.255.0
```

3-3: Dial-on-Demand Routing (DDR)

- DDR allows dialed calls to be made and closed dynamically, as needed.

- Outbound calls are triggered based on configurable traffic parameters.

- DDR can be configured through two methods, depending on the level of dialing flexibility that is needed. In this section, both methods are described as a single configuration procedure to make dialer configuration more intuitive and straightforward:

  - **Dialer profiles**—Logical dialer interfaces are used to reach a destination, through dial strings and dial maps. A dialer pool can be defined to make a call from one of a group of physical interfaces. Map classes define the call's characteristics and are applied to dialer profiles based on the call destination. Dialing becomes very flexible and scalable.

  - **Hub and spoke**—Either physical or logical interfaces can be used to make calls. Logical dialer interfaces can be used to define rotary groups of physical interfaces. All dialer parameters are applied to the logical (or physical) interfaces, limiting the flexibility and scalability. Generally, the "spoke" DDR router makes calls to the centralized "hub" DDR router. The hub can both make and receive DDR calls.

Configuration

1. (Optional) Define a logical dialer interface for flexible dialing (Dialer Profiles).

    a. Select an interface for dialing out:

    (global) **interface dialer** *number*

    A dialer is a logical interface used to support rotary groups of other physical dial interfaces. The number (1 to 255) is arbitrarily chosen. If a rotary group of physical interfaces is configured, the dialer number is also used to identify the rotary group number.

    b. (Optional) Define the encapsulation for outgoing calls:

    (interface) **encapsulation ppp**

    See Section 3-6 for more configuration information on PPP encapsulation.

    c. Define any network addresses needed:

    (interface) **ip address** *ip-address subnet-mask*

    d. Define dial destinations.

    (Optional) Call only a single destination.

    Define a modem chat script. Refer to the **script dialer** command in Section 3-1 for more information.

    Define the string of digits to dial by entering the following command:

    (interface) **dialer string** *string* [**class** *class-name*]

    The *string* is sent to the modem for dialing. It can include the digits0 to 9, : (wait for a tone), < (pause), = (separator 3), > (separator 4), P (continue dialing in pulse mode), T (continue dialing with DTMF tones), and & (send a hookflash). If you are defining dialer map classes for more flexible per-destination characteristics, you can use the **class** keyword to apply the map class *class-name* (text string).

    (Optional) Define one or more destinations to call:

    (interface) **dialer map** *protocol next-hop-address* [**class** *class-name*]
      [**name** *host-name*] [**spc**] [**speed 56** | **speed 64**] [**broadcast**]
      [**modem-script** *modem-regexp*] [**system-script** *system-regexp*]
      [**dial-string**[*:isdn-subaddress*]]

    As soon as the router determines the need to make a call, both the *protocol* (**appletalk, bridge, clns, decnet, ip, ipx, novell, snapshot, vines,** or **xns**) and the destination or *next-hop-address* are compared with the **dialer map** entries to find a match. If you are defining dialer map classes for more flexible per-destination characteristics, you can use the **class** keyword to apply the map class *class-name* (text string).

If needed, the **spc** keyword causes a semi-permanent connectionto be used (Germany and Australia). If an ISDN interface is being configured, **speed 56** (56 kbps) or **speed 64** (64 kbps, the default) can be used to indicate the speed of the B channel. Use the **broadcast** keyword if broadcast packets should be forwarded to the destination.

For incoming calls, use the **name** keyword to authenticate the remote *host-name* using CHAP. See Section 3-6 for further configuration information about dial-in authentication.

For outgoing calls, the router finds a modem chat script (a **chat script** command) that matches the regular expression given by *modem-regexp* (a text string, including . and *). The chat script name can consist of the . (match a character) and * (match any characters) wildcards so that a chat script can be selected according to modem or modulation type. See Section 3-1 for more information about chat scripts. If the remote system doesn't support CHAP authentication, you can use the **system-script** keyword to select a chat script that matches the regular expression given by *system-regexp* (a text string, including . and *). The router sends and receives strings to navigate through a login procedure. A *dial-string* can also be given to define a string of digits to dial for this specific destination.

e. (Optional) Use a pool *of physical interfaces for dialing:*

```
(interface) dialer pool pool
```

> **Note** By default, the interface number of a logical dialer interface corresponds to a rotary group number. Physical interfaces can be assigned to this rotary group if desired. However, you can assign the physical interfaces to a dialer pool instead. This offers more flexibility.

Multiple physical interfaces can be assigned to a dialer pool so that they can be used for outgoing calls in a rotary fashion.

f. (Optional) Define any queuing or traffic shaping.

See Chapter 9, "Quality of Service," for more information about queuing and traffic-shaping features.

g. Identify "interesting" traffic to trigger a call.

- (Optional) Use an access list to permit specific addresses and port numbers within a protocol:

```
(global) access-list acc-list-number {permit | deny} ...
```

Dialing can be triggered by packets containing a general protocol (IP, IPX, AppleTalk, and so forth) or by packets matching a more specific criteria. Any parameter that can be matched by an access list can be used to trigger a call. See Chapter 14, "Access Lists and Regular Expressions," for further configuration information about access lists for a specific protocol.

Create a dialer list to identify the "interesting" protocol:

```
(interface) dialer-list dialer-group protocol protocol-name
  {permit | deny | list access-list-number | access-group}
```

One or more **dialer-list** statements are defined as a single arbitrary *dialer-group* (1 to 255). Each statement identifies a protocol by *protocol-name* (**appletalk, bridge, clns, clns_es, clns_is, decnet, decnet_router-L1, decnet_router-L2, decnet_node, ip, ipx, vines,** or **xns**). Dialing is triggered based on an action taken on the protocol: **permit** (trigger dialing on the protocol as a whole), **deny** (don't trigger dialing for the protocol as a whole), or **list** (trigger dialing if the access list numbered *access-list-number* permits the packet). The *access-group* parameter can be used to identify a filter list name for CLNS traffic.

Apply the dialer list to a dialer interface:

```
(interface) dialer-group group
```

The dialer list numbered *group* is used to trigger an outbound call. When traffic is destined for a dialer interface, it is first filtered through the dialer list. If the packet is permitted, the call is placed.

2. Define the dialer interface parameters.

    a. (Optional) Apply the parameter settings to a map class:

    ```
    (global) map-class dialer class-name
    ```

    A dialer map class is used to define any parameters that can be set on a dialer interface. If you are configuring flexible dialing with the logical dialer interfaces (interface dialer or "Dialer Profiles"), you can use map classes to selectively configure the dialer interface on a per-destination basis. A map class is selected according to a matching dialer-string or dialer map command.

    -or-

    b. (Optional) Apply the parameter settings to a physical interface:

    ```
    (global) interface [async | serial | bri] number
    ```

    -or-

    ```
    (global) interface serial controller/port:[23 | 15]
    ```

    If flexible dialing and logical dialer interfaces are not used, the dialer parameters can be applied directly to a physical interface. The dial interface can be async (asynchronous line), serial (synchronous serial), or bri (ISDN BRI). For a PRI interface, use serial with the T1/E1 controller number and port, followed by the D channel (23 for T1 or 15 for E1).

c. (Optional) Set the call idle timer:

`(interface)` **`dialer idle-timeout`** *`seconds`* **`[inbound | either]`**

As soon as an outbound call is made on a dialer interface, it is terminated if no traffic is detected for seconds (the default is 120 seconds) in the outbound direction. If desired, **inbound** or **either** (inbound or outbound) traffic can be used to measure the idle time.

d. (Optional) Set a fast idle timer to reuse an active interface:

`(interface)` **`dialer fast-idle`** *`seconds`*

Dialer contention occurs when a call is in progress on an interface, and the interface is then needed for another call to a different destination. To resolve the contention, the router can detect a shorter idle time and end the first call immediately. The fast idle time can be set to seconds (the default is 20 seconds).

e. (Optional) Set a line-down time before an interface can be used again:

`(interface)` **`dialer enable-timeout`** *`seconds`*

If you have problems with phone line availability, you can hold down an interface after a call is completed or fails before attempting to dial again. Set the line-down timer to seconds (the default is 15 seconds).

f. (Optional) Set the length of time to wait for a carrier signal:

`(interface)` **`dialer wait-for-carrier-time`** *`seconds`*

When an outbound call is made, the router must wait for any modem or system chat scripts to complete and for the carrier to be detected. If calls are being terminated before the remote system is successfully connected, increase the wait-for-carrier time to seconds (the default is 30 seconds).

g. (Optional) Place additional calls to increase the bandwidth on demand:

`(interface)` **`dialer load-threshold`** *`load`* **`[outbound | inbound | either]`**

When the traffic load on an interface in a rotary group reaches the load threshold (1 to 255, where 1 is unloaded and 255 is 100 percent), additional calls are placed from interfaces in the rotary group. The load threshold represents the total or cumulative load over all "up" interfaces to the destination. Links are brought up or torn down whenever the traffic load rises above or falls below the threshold. The traffic direction can be taken into account as outbound, inbound, or either.

Note   Remember that an ISDN BRI is handled as a rotary group of two B channels. Setting a load threshold lets the router bring up the second B channel if needed.

```
(interface) dialer hold-queue packets timeout seconds
```

By default, any additional packets that are destined to a call that is being established are dropped. The router can place packets in a hold queue so that they will
be sent after the call is made. The hold queue can contain up to packets (1 to 100
packets), which are held for a maximum of seconds.

h. (Optional) Redial if a call fails:

```
(interface) dialer redial interval time attempts number re-enable
disable-time
```

By default, the router makes only a single attempt to dial a destination. The router
can try to redial the destination every time (5 to 2147483 seconds) for up to number times (1 to 2147483 attempts). If all the configured redial attempts fail, the
interface is disabled for disable-time (5 to 2147483 seconds) to prevent other redial failures in the near future.

3. Define additional parameters to the physical interface.

a. Select the interface:

```
(global) interface [async | serial | bri] number
```

-or-

```
(global) interface serial controller/port:[23 | 15]
```

If flexible dialing and logical dialer interfaces are not used, the dialer parameter-
scan be applied directly to a physical interface. The dial interface can be async
(asynchronous line), serial (synchronous serial), or bri (ISDN BRI). For a PRI interface, use serial with the T1/E1 controller number and port, followed by the D
channel (23 for T1 or 15 for E1).

b. (Optional) Define the encapsulation needed for incoming calls:

```
(interface) encapsulation ppp
```

See Section 3-6 for more configuration information on PPP encapsulation.

c. (Optional) Define the authentication needed for incoming calls:

```
(interface) ppp authentication {pap | chap}
```

See Section 3-6 for more configuration information on PPP authentication.

d. (Optional) Use a group of interfaces to reach a common destination.

■ (Optional) Make the interface a member of a dialer pool:

```
(interface) dialer pool-member number [priority priority]
  [min-link minimum] [max-link maximum]
```

If the **dialer pool** command has been used on a logical dialer interface, the physical interface becomes a part of the dialer pool *number* (1 to 255). A *priority* (0 to
255; 0 is the lowest, 255 is the highest, and the default is 0) can be assigned to the

interface so that it will be chosen before other dialer pool members with lower priorities.

For ISDN, a number of B channels can be reserved for the dialer pool. You can specify the *minimum* (0 to 255; the default is 0) and *maximum* (0 to 255; the default is 255) number of channels for this purpose.

-or-

■   (Optional) Make the interface a member of a rotary group for dialing:

```
(interface) dialer rotary-group group
(interface) dialer priority priority
```

Multiple interfaces can be assigned to a rotary dialer group. As soon as a logical rotary group interface is configured with the **interface dialer** command, other physical interfaces can be assigned to it. Outbound calls are made on the first available interface in the rotary group, allowing more flexible and available calling. The *group* (0 to 255) must be the same number as the dialer interface number.

By default, a rotary group selects the next available interface in the order that they are configured. However, interfaces within a rotary group can be given a *priority* (0 to 255; 0 is the lowest and 255 is the highest) so that some interfaces are used before others.

Note   Interfaces that are members of a dialer rotary group inherit the configuration commands that were entered for the corresponding **interface dialer**. ISDN BRI interfaces are inherently part of a rotary group so that outbound calls will rotate through the B1 and B2 channels if needed.

e. (Async or sync serial only) Select the type of dialing:

```
(interface) dialer dtr
```

-or-

```
(interface) dialer in-band [no-parity | odd-parity]
```

An asynchronous or synchronous serial interface must send dialing information out-of-band (dtr; non-V.25bis modems) over the DTR signal or in-band (in-band; V.25bis modems) over the data stream.

Example

DDR is configured on a remote branch router to dial out to the Main Office router. Dialing occurs whenever there is traffic going from the 192.168.3.0 network (the remote Ethernet network) to the 192.168.209.0 network (the Main Office server farm). A static route is configured to define the next-hop address for network 192.168.209.0 as the Main Office router at 192.168.209.1. This address is matched in the **dialer map** statement, where the CHAP remote host name, the modem chat script, and the dial string are picked up.

Note that the dial string is defined in the dialer map. The modem chat scripts have an "**ATDT \T**" send string, where the dial string replaces **\T** during the dialing process. Interfaces async 1 and async 2 are members of a common dialer pool, allowing an additional call to be made if one of the lines is busy.

```
chat-script MainOffice ABORT ERROR ABORT BUSY ABORT "NO ANSWER" "" "AT H" OK
"ATDT \T"
 TIMEOUT 45 CONNECT \c TIMEOUT 30

chat-script HotSite ABORT ERROR ABORT BUSY ABORT "NO ANSWER" "" "AT H" OK "AT M0
" OK "ATDT \T" TIMEOUT 45 CONNECT \c TIMEOUT 30

username southbranch password letmein

interface async 1
        no ip address
        encapsulation ppp
        ppp authentication chap
        dialer in-band
        dialer pool-member 7
        dialer redial interval 60 attempts 10 re-enable 5

interface async 2
        no ip address
        encapsulation ppp
        ppp authentication chap
        dialer in-band
        dialer pool-member 7
        dialer redial interval 60 attempts 10 re-enable 5

interface dialer 1
        ip address 192.168.4.1 255.255.255.0
        dialer remote-name tic
        dialer idle-timeout 432000
        dialer map ip 192.168.209.1 name mainoffice modem-script MainOffice 5987572
        dialer pool 7
        dialer-group 1

interface ethernet 0
        ip address 192.168.3.1 255.255.255.0

ip route 192.168.209.0 255.255.255.0 192.168.209.1
```

```
access-list 101 permit ip 192.168.3.0 0.0.0.255 192.168.209.0 0.0.0.0

dialer-list 1 protocol ip permit list 101

line 1
        modem InOut
        transport input all
        speed 115200

line 2
        modem inout
        transport input all
        speed 115200
```

3-4: Dial Backup

- Dial backup monitors a specific router interface to determine the need for a backup connection. If the interface is down or if a traffic threshold is exceeded, the backup interface is brought up.

- Dialer Watch can be used to watch for the deletion of specific routes that correspond to a remote router interface or an advertised network. If no routes to the address are found, the backup interface is brought up, and a call is made.

- Dialer Watch is useful when the state of a local router interface does not reflect a failed connection.

Dial Backup Configuration

1. Identify the interface to be backed up:

    ```
    (global) interface type slot/port
    ```

2. Specify the backup interface:

    ```
    (interface) backup interface type slot/port
    ```

    The backup interface is a dialer interface that DDR uses to make a call.

3. (Optional) Set a traffic threshold to trigger the backup:

    ```
    (interface) backup load {enable-threshold | never}  {disable-threshold | never}
    ```

    Dial backup is triggered when the traffic load exceeds the enable-threshold percentage (1 to 100 percent) of the available link bandwidth. Dial backup is disabled when the traffic load falls under the disable-threshold percentage (1 to 100 percent) of the link bandwidth. The never keyword can be used to cause dial backup to never be enabled or never be disabled.

> **Note**   If the traffic threshold is not defined, dial backup is triggered only if the primary interface goes down.

4. (Optional) Wait until the primary interface changes state:

    (interface) **backup delay** {*enable-delay-period* | **never**}   {*disable-delay- period* | **never**}

    When the primary interface goes down, dial backup waits for enable-delay-period (the default is 0 seconds) before triggering the backup call. When the primary interface comes back up, dial backup waits for disable-delay-period (the default is 0 seconds) before disabling the backup call. The never keyword can be used to never enable or never disable dial backup based on the primary interface state.

5. Make sure DDR is configured to use the backup interface. Refer to Section 3-3 for more configuration details if needed.

Dial Backup Example

Dial backup is configured so that when interface serial 0 goes down, DDR uses interface dialer 1 to make a backup connection. Dialer 1 is a logical interface that looks to dialer pool 5 to find an available interface for a new call. Interface serial 0 identifies interface dialer 1 as the backup interface, with an enable delay of 10 seconds and a disable delay of 20 seconds. Once dial backup is triggered, DDR uses dialer list 1 to specify the "interesting" traffic to actually trigger the call. Here, the dialer list triggers by permitting any IP traffic:

```
interface dialer 1

        ip address 192.168.1.1 255.255.255.0
        encapsulation ppp
        dialer string 5551111
        dialer pool 5
        dialer-group 1

dialer-list 1 protocol ip permit
interface bri 0

        encapsulation ppp
        dialer pool-member 5

interface serial 0
        ip address 192.168.200.1 255.255.255.0
```

```
backup interface dialer 1
backup delay 10 20
```

Dialer Watch Configuration

1. Define one or more routes or IP addresses to watch:

   ```
   (global) dialer watch-list group-number [delay route-check initial  seconds]
   ip ip-address mask
   ```

   A watch list is created with an arbitrary group-number (1 to 255). Each watch-list statement in the list specifies an IP address and a subnet mask to be watched. The IP address given must exactly match a route in the routing table, as shown by the show ip route command. When the primary route to that address is removed from the routing table, the Dialer Watch feature is triggered. The delay route-check initial keywords can be used to force the router to wait for seconds (1 to 2147483 seconds) after the local router powers up and initializes before considering that the primary route is missing.

2. Select a backup interface:

   ```
   (global) interface type slot/port
   ```

   This selects the interface to be used by DDR (a logical dialer interface or a physical interface).

3. Enable Dialer Watch on the backup interface:

   ```
   (interface) dialer watch-group group-number
   ```

   Dialer Watch uses the Dialer Watch list numbered group-number (1 to 255) to determine when to trigger a DDR call.

4. (Optional) Wait to disable the backup interface:

   ```
   (interface) dialer watch-disable seconds
   ```

   After the primary route returns to the routing table, Dialer Watch can wait for seconds (the default is 0 seconds) before disabling the backup DDR call.

5. Make sure DDR is configured to use the backup interface. Refer to Section 3-3 for more configuration details if needed.

Dialer Watch Example

Dialer Watch is configured so that when the primary route to network 192.168.177.0 or network 192.168.178.0 is deleted from the routing table, DDR uses interface dialer 1 to make a backup connection. Dialer 1 is a logical interface that looks to dialer pool 5 to find an available interface for a new call. Dialer 1 also must have **dialer map** statements that exactly define the watched routes so that a call can be triggered.

```
interface dialer 1

        ip address 192.168.1.1 255.255.255.0
        encapsulation ppp

        dialer map ip 192.168.177.0 5551111
        dialer map ip 192.168.178.0 5551111

        dialer pool 5
        dialer-group 1
        dialer watch-group 10
dialer-list 1 protocol ip permit
dialer watch-list 10 ip 192.168.177.0 255.255.255.0
dialer watch-list 10 ip 192.168.178.0 255.255.255.0
interface bri 0

        encapsulation ppp
        dialer pool-member 5
interface serial 0
        ip address ...
```

3-5: Routing Over Dialup Networks

■ Snapshot routing reduces the time a DDR connection is kept up by only periodically exchanging routing updates.

■ Snapshot routing is based on the concept of active periods, when routing information can be exchanged, and quiet periods, when a snapshot of the routing information is kept frozen.

■ During a quiet period, the routing entries are frozen and cannot be changed. They also are treated as static routes and are not aged until the next active period.

■ A retry period can be defined to keep the client router from waiting another complete quiet period if a DDR interface is not available. In this case, the client router can retry the active period call after the retry period has elapsed.

■ A snapshot client router can dial remote server routers only during an active period to collect routing information.

■ Only distance vector routing protocols are supported: IP RIP.

■ On-Demand Routing (ODR) allows a centralized "hub" router to collect route advertisements from "spoke" routers on stub networks. The stub routers use only static or default routes and do not run any dynamic routing protocols.

■ ODR uses the Cisco Discovery Protocol (CDP) to dynamically learn about the stub routers and their directly connected networks. Therefore, no routing information is exchanged by routing protocols.

Snapshot Routing Configuration

1. Define snapshot routing on the client router.

    a. Select an interface to reach a server router:

    (global) **interface type** slot/port

    The interface is usually a logical interface dialer or a physical DDR interface.

    b. Enable client mode snapshot routing:

    (interface) **snapshot client** *active-time quiet-time* [**suppress-statechange-updates**] [**dialer**]

    On the client router, the active-time (5 to 100 minutes; no default; typically 5 minutes) and quiet-time (8 to 100000 minutes) intervals are defined. The suppress-statechange-updates keyword can be used to disable routing exchanges each time the DDR interface state changes from "down" to "up" or from "dialer spoofing" to "fully up." In that case, routing information is exchanged only when the active period begins, regardless of whether the DDR interface just came up. The dialer keyword is used to cause the client router to dial the server routers even if there is no active traffic to trigger a call. Otherwise, the client router waits for the call to be made from normal DDR activity.

    c. Define one or more server routers to contact:

    (interface) **dialer map snapshot** *sequence-number dial-string*

    A server router is listed with a unique sequence-number (1 to 254), specifying the order in which the routers are to be called. The dial-string (string of digits) required to reach the server router must also be given.

    d. Make sure DDR is configured on the dialer interfaces. You don't have to configure the triggers for interesting traffic, because the snapshot routing triggers DDR and provides the dial string. Refer to Section 3-3 for more configuration details if needed.

2. Define snapshot routing on the server router.

    a. Select an interface for incoming calls from the client router:

    (global) **interface** *type slot/port*

    The interface is usually a physical DDR interface that can accept incoming calls.

    b. Enable server mode snapshot routing:

    (interface) **snapshot** *active-time* [**dialer**]

    The server router must have the same active-time (5 to 100 minutes) configured as that of the client router. The dialer keyword can be used to allow the server router to accept calls from the client router, even when regular DDR traffic is not present.

Section 3-5

Snapshot Routing Example

Snapshot routing is configured on a client router at a central site. The snapshot client maintains periodic routing updates with a list of three server routers at branch sites. Snapshot routing is configured with an active period of 5 minutes and a quiet period of 480 minutes, or 8 hours. The server routers are dialed during the active period, even if a DDR call is not already in progress.

The following example shows the configuration of the client router:

```
interface dialer 1
        ip address 192.168.1.1 255.255.255.0
        encapsulation ppp
        dialer pool 5
        snapshot client 5 480 dialer

interface bri 0
        encapsulation ppp
        dialer pool-member 5

        dialer map snapshot 1 8598851234
        dialer map snapshot 2 8598855678
        dialer map snapshot 3 8598859999

router rip
        network 192.168.1.0
        network 192.168.100.0
```

The following example shows the configuration of one of the server routers:

```
interface bri 0
        encapsulation ppp
        ip address 192.168.1.2 255.255.255.0
        snapshot server 5 dialer

router rip
        network 192.168.1.0
        network 192.168.200.0
```

ODR Configuration

1. Enable ODR on the hub router:

    (global) **router odr** *process-id*

    ODR is started and is assigned a unique process number.

> **Note** Routes can be filtered as they are collected by ODR. Refer to Section 8-4 for more information. Routes can also be redistributed into or out of ODR by using the IP route redistribution commands. Refer to Section 8-3 for more information.

  2. (Optional) Tune the ODR timers.

  a. Adjust the CDP timer on the stub routers:

  `(global)` **`cdp timer`** *`seconds`*

  ODR depends on CDP advertisements to collect IP route prefixes from stub routers. By default, CDP advertisements occur every 30 seconds. Set the CDP interval to seconds for more frequent advertisements and faster route convergence.

  b. Adjust the ODR timers:

  `(router)` **`timers basic`** *`update invalid holddown flush`* `[`*`sleeptime`*`]`

  The frequency that routing updates are expected from stub routers can be adjusted to provide faster convergence. The *update* parameter (default 90 seconds) sets the rate in seconds at which updates are expected. This is the fundamental timing parameter of the ODR protocol. It should be set to match the CDP advertisement interval. The *invalid* parameter (default 270 seconds) sets the interval of time in seconds after which a route is declared invalid. It should be at least three times the value of *update*. The *holddown* parameter (default 280 seconds) sets the interval in seconds during which routing information regarding better paths is suppressed. It should be at least three times the value of *update*. The *flush* parameter (default 630 seconds) is the amount of time in seconds that must pass before the route is removed from the routing table. The interval specified must be at least the sum of *invalid* and *holddown*. If it is less than this sum, the proper holddown interval cannot elapse. This results in a new route's being accepted before the holddown interval expires. The *sleeptime* parameter (default 0 milliseconds) sets the interval in milliseconds for postponing routing updates in the event of a Flash update. The *sleeptime* value should be less than the *update* time. If the *sleeptime* is greater than the *update* time, routing tables become unsynchronized.

  c. Define a default route on the stub routers:

  `(global)` **`ip route 0.0.0.0 0.0.0.0`** *`interface-name`*

  A stub router needs only a statically defined default route pointing to an interface that connects to the hub router.

3-6: Point-to-Point Protocol (PPP)

- PPP encapsulates network layer packets for transport over point-to-point links.

- PPP is supported on DDR interfaces as well as fixed point-to-point interfaces.

- Authentication is supported over PPP using Challenge Handshake Authentication Protocol (CHAP) or Password Authentication Protocol (PAP).

- With CHAP or PAP authentication, users and other routers can be properly authenticated when they connect. In addition, a router host name is used during authentication and to prevent additional calls if it is already connected.

- CHAP offers a handshake procedure by using the local host name in a challenge to the remote user or router. The remote side responds with its host name and a hashed password. The passwords and hashing methods used must match on both ends of the connection.

- PAP requires the remote user or router to send both a username and a password to be authenticated. There is no challenge or shared secret passwords, and passwords are also sent in the clear.

- Link Quality Monitoring (LQM) compares the PPP packets exchanged between two peers. When the percentage of good packets falls below a threshold, the PPP connection is torn down.

- IP addresses can be negotiated using the IP Control Protocol (IPCP). A router can assign addresses to dial-in peers by proxying DHCP requests and replies, from a locally defined IP address pool, or from a static IP address configuration.

- Multilink PPP (MLP) uses multiple PPP links to provide load balancing and packet fragmentation. The multiple links can be brought up in succession, depending on traffic thresholds.

- PPP callback can be used to have a calling (client) router request that the destination (server) router call it back. The client router's authentication information is given to the server router. If it can be authenticated, and a dial string is found for the return call, the call is reversed.

Configuration

1. Enable PPP encapsulation on an interface:

   (interface) **encapsulation ppp**

   PPP encapsulation can be enabled on both logical and physical dialer interfaces, asynchronous, synchronous serial, HSSI, and ISDN interfaces.

2. (Async interfaces only) Select the interface mode:

   (interface) **async mode** {**dedicated** | **interactive**}

In dedicated mode, the interface uses PPP encapsulation continuously. A user connected to the interface does not receive a login prompt or an EXEC session with the router. In interactive mode, a user receives normal login and password prompting (if configured) and is presented with an EXEC session on the router. The user is free to use other router commands and must then issue the ppp command to start PPP encapsulation.

3. (Optional) Use PPP authentication:

```
(interface) ppp authentication {protocol1 [protocol2...]} [if-needed]
[list-name | default] [callin] [one-time]
```

PPP can use one or more authentication protocols (chap, pap, or ms-chap), listed in the order that they are tried. The ms-chap method can be used for CHAP between a router and a Microsoft Windows device. If you are using AAA with TACACS+ authentication, the if-needed keyword prevents PAP or CHAP from being used when the user is already authenticated. If configured, either the list-name AAA method list (aaa authentication ppp) or the default method list is used to perform AAA authentication. The callin keyword performs authentication only on incoming calls. Rather than giving the username and password separately, the one-time keyword can be used to present both at once.

Note   If AAA authentication is not used, you must configure the remote router host names and their shared secret passwords before CHAP will work. Use **username** *name* **password** *password* to define the router's host name as the username. For further information, refer to Section 1-1 for local username authentication, and refer to Section 13-1 for AAA authentication configuration.

4. (Optional) Use PPP callback to increase security or to lower toll costs.

   a. (Optional) Request a callback from a remote peer (callback client):

   ```
   (interface) ppp callback request
   ```

   As soon as a call is made to a peer router, the local router requests that it be called back to complete the PPP connection.

   b. (Optional) Accept a callback request (callback server):

   ```
   (interface) ppp callback accept
   (interface) dialer callback-server [username] [dialstring]
   (interface) dialer callback-secure
   ```

   The router accepts incoming calls that request PPP callback service. If the incoming peer router is authenticated by PPP, the call is completed. Then the local router initiates a call back to the requesting router. If authentication is successful, the PPP connection is established. The username keyword (the default) can be given to look up and authenticate the router host name in a dialer map command. The dialstring keyword is used to identify the return call during callback negotiation. The callback-secure keyword can be used to drop callback requests if the username or host name cannot be authenticated and approved for callback.

(Optional) Use LQM on the PPP interface:

```
(interface) ppp quality percentage
```

The number of PPP packets sent and received is compared to the number collected by the remote router. If the percentage of successful packet transfers falls below the *percentage* (1 to 100) threshold, the PPP link is shut down.

5.   (Optional) Assign IP addresses over PPP.

   a.   (Optional) Use DHCP proxy to relay an address.

   ■   Enable DHCP proxy:

```
(global) ip address-pool dhcp-proxy-client
```

The router accepts DHCP requests from the far end and relays them to a DHCP server.

Relay requests to one or more DHCP servers:

```
(global) ip dhcp-server [ip-address | name]
```

The router relays DHCP requests to the server identified by *ip-address* or the host name. Up to ten DHCP servers can be configured.

   ■   Assign an address over the PPP interface:

```
(interface) peer default ip address pool dhcp
```

The far-end PPP peer receives an address from the DHCP server.

   b.   (Optional) Use an address from a local pool.

   ■   Enable a local address pool:

```
(global) ip address-pool local
```

The router uses a pool of IP addresses from its own configuration.

Define the address pool:

```
(global) ip local pool {default | pool-name} low-ip-address [high-ip-
address]
```

The pool can be named either **default** or *pool-name* (a text string). The range of IP addresses starts at the lowest IP address, *low-ip-address*, and ends at the highest IP address, *high-ip-address*. If the upper limit is not given, the pool consists of a single address.

■   Assign an address over the PPP interface:

```
(interface) peer default ip address pool pool-name
```

The router assigns the PPP peer an address from the locally defined pool called *pool-name*.

c. (Optional) Assign a specific IP address over the PPP interface:

```
(interface) peer default ip address ip-address
```

Use this method if there are few IP addresses to assign to dial-in peers.

Note   If the remote dial-in PPP peer is another router, you must configure the remote PPP interface to accept a negotiated IP address. Use the (interface) **ip address negotiated** command.

d. (Optional) Permit routing protocol traffic to pass over an asynchronous interface:

```
(interface) async dynamic routing
```

By default, no dynamic routing protocol traffic is allowed to pass over an asynchronous interface. Use this command if you need to exchange routing information over an asynchronous PPP interface.

6.   (Optional) Use Multilink PPP (MLP).

a. Enable MLP on one or more interfaces:

```
(interface) ppp multilink
```

Usually, MLP is configured on a logical dialer interface so that all physical interfaces used in a rotary group or dialer pool are added to the bundle.

b. (Optional) Use MLP interleaving to fragment large packets:

```
(interface) ppp multilink interleave
(interface) ppp multilink fragment delay milliseconds
```

Packets destined for an MLP interface are fragmented and distributed across the links in the MLP bundle. The size of the fragments is governed by the required fragment transmission time milliseconds (1 to 1000 milliseconds; the default is 30). This feature is especially useful for the delivery of time-critical protocols such as voice traffic. Voice traffic requires a maximum packet serialization delay of 10 milliseconds.

Example

A router is configured for DDR using two ISDN interfaces—BRI 0 and BRI 1. A logical dialer interface is configured for PPP encapsulation, CHAP authentication, and Multilink PPP. The dialer interface uses a dialer pool that consists of both BRI interfaces. Additional B channels are brought up when the overall traffic load of the interfaces in use reaches 50 percent (or a threshold value of 255 times 50 percent, or 128). Multilink PPP fragmentation and interleaving are also configured to allow time-critical traffic, such as voice, to receive a guaranteed transmission delay of 10 milliseconds.

```
username Remote password letmein

interface dialer 1
        ip address 192.168.254.1 255.255.255.0
        encapsulation ppp
        dialer in-band
        dialer load-threshold 128
        dialer-group 10
        ppp authentication chap
        ppp multilink
        ppp multilink fragment delay 10
        dialer pool 5

interface bri 0
        encapsulation ppp
        dialer pool-member 5
        dialer load-threshold 128

interface bri 1
        encapsulation ppp
        dialer pool-member 5
        dialer load-threshold 128
```

Further Reading

Refer to the following recommended sources for further information about the topics covered in this chapter:

Cisco IOS Dial Technologies Configuration Guide:
www.cisco.com/en/US/docs/ios/dial/configuration/guide/12_4/dia_12_4_book.html

Chapter 4

IPv4 Addressing and Services

This chapter presents background and configuration information on IPv4 addressing and IPv4 services provided by the router, with a focus on the following topics:

- **4-1: IP Addressing and Resolution:** IP addresses must be assigned to an interface in order for the router to pass IP traffic. Although configuring addresses is fundamental to router operation, selections in subnet masks and address resolution methods also can be configured. This section covers configuring addressing and resolution methods, including ICMP Router Discovery Protocol (IRDP) configuration.

- **4-2: IP Broadcast Handling:** Many broadcasts exist within network environments, including those originated by the router. This section covers how the router can be configured to handle broadcasts it receives to provide appropriate handling. It also deals with how to change the address the router uses when it sends broadcast packets.

- **4-3: Hot Standby Router Protocol (HSRP):** To enhance the availability of a forwarding device, the Hot Standby Router Protocol provides a method that lets multiple routers offer a single IP gateway address so that a client can still reach that address even if one router goes down. This section discusses how to configure HSRP to operate on router interfaces to provide this IP gateway redundancy.

- **4-4: Virtual Router Redundancy Protocol (VRRP):** VRRP is an alternative to HSRP that is more widely supported across vendors and with faster default timers. This section discusses how to configure VRRP on router interfaces to provide IP gateway redundancy.

- **4-5: Dynamic Host Configuration Protocol (DHCP):** Dynamic Host Configuration Protocol is a client server protocol that allows clients to be configured with the appropriate IP configuration parameters via the DHCP server. This section discusses how to configure the router to act as a DHCP server and shows how the configurations of pools interact with one another.

- **4-6: Mobile IP:** With the introduction of more and more wireless technologies, it is becoming important to manage IP addressing for "roaming" users, who might travel to different access points in the network. This section describes how to configure mobile IP services so that mobile or "roaming" users can maintain their IP addresses wherever they are connected to the network.

■ **4-7: Network Address Translation (NAT):** Because of the exhaustion of IP addresses and the need to provide private addressing for management and security reasons, it is important to be able to provide private addressing while providing connectivity to public networks. Network address translation allows the router to provide a method to translate between private and public addresses. This section deals with the setup and configuration of NAT.

■ **4-8: Server Load Balancing (SLB):** A router can act as a virtual server on behalf of a server farm of real servers. SLB provides load balancing of connections across the servers in the server farm. SLB can also detect server failures, control access to the servers, and collect server capacity data.

4-1: IP Addressing and Resolution

The Address Resolution Protocol (ARP) is used to resolve a host's 48-bit MAC address when the IP address is known. ARP is defined in RFC 826. ARP entries are added to a router cache as requests and replies are received. The entries in the ARP cache are aged out after a configurable time.

■ To resolve a host's IP address from its MAC address, the Reverse Address Resolution Protocol (RARP) is used. RARP is defined in RFC 903. A router acts as a RARP server for addresses present in its ARP cache.

■ Proxy ARP is used to provide address resolution for hosts that reside on networks other than the ARP requester. If a router has a route to the unresolved host on another interface, it generates an ARP reply on behalf of that host. The ARP requester then receives the router's MAC address in the ARP reply.

■ Domain Name System (DNS) is used to resolve IP addresses and fully qualified domain names.

■ Router/gateway discovery methods are used to assist a router or hosts that need to locate a router. This can occur when IP routing is disabled on a router and routes to other networks need to be discovered.

Configuration

1. Assign IP addresses to interfaces.

   a. (Optional) Assign an IP address:

   ```
   (interface) ip address ip-address mask [secondary]
   ```

   One primary IP address and mask are assigned to the interface. If the optional secondary flag is added, an additional secondary IP address is assigned to the interface. Secondary addresses are useful to add support for additional logical subnets on a single interface.

-or-

b. (Optional) Allow IP over a serial or tunnel interface without an IP address:

```
(interface) ip unnumbered type number
```

The IP address of the interface specified by type and number is used for packets generated on the interface. The IP address is also used to determine whether routing updates from routing protocols should be sent over the unnumbered interface.

Note   Before an unnumbered interface can be configured, the interface that will be used to host the IP address must be configured, enabled, and active. Only the following encapsulations can be used with IP unnumbered: HDLC, PPP, LAPB, Frame Relay, SLIP, and tunnels.

2. Configure ARP features:

a. (Optional) Define a static ARP entry:

```
(global) arp {ip-address | vrf vrf-name} hardware-address encapsulation-
type [alias]
```

Normally, ARP resolution is handled dynamically. In cases where a static entry is necessary, this command enables the router to resolve the *ip-address* and *hardware-address* (MAC) values. The ARP type should be set to **arpa** for Ethernet interfaces, **snap** for FDDI and Token Ring interfaces, **sap** for Hewlett Packard interfaces, **smds** for Switched Multimegabit Data Service interfaces, **srp-a** for switch route processor side A interfaces, and **srp-b** for switch route processor side B interfaces. The **alias** keyword can be used to cause the router to answer a matching ARP request as if it were the owner of the IP address. Normally, this is done through proxy ARP (enabled by default) if the router has a route to the ARP request's destination address; however, the **alias** keyword can be used to supply a proxy ARP reply even if the destination is on an unreachable or nonexistent network.

b. (Optional) Configure the ARP cache timeout interval:

```
(interface) arp timeout seconds
```

Each ARP entry remains in the ARP cache for the specified number of seconds (the default is 14400 seconds, or 4 hours). A value of 0 keeps entries indefinitely. The timeout value is configured on a per-interface basis.

c. (Optional) Clear ARP entries manually:

```
(exec) clear arp-cache
```

All dynamic ARP cache entries are cleared when this command is executed.

3. Configure DNS features for the router.

  a. (Optional) Configure static IP host mappings (no DNS server):

     (global) **ip host** *name* [*tcp-port-number*] *address1* [*address2...address8*]

    A static mapping is defined in the router between *name* and from one to eight IP addresses. A TCP port number can also be defined to be used for Telnet sessions from the router to the host (the default is port 23).

  b. (Optional) Configure the default domain name:

     (global) **ip domain-name** *domain*

    Host names that do not include a domain name have the *domain* name appended before being used by the router.

  c. (Optional) Define a name server for the router:

     (global) **ip name-server** *address1* [*address2...address6*]

    A list of one to six name server IP addresses can be configured. These name servers are queried by the router when DNS lookups are required for executing a Cisco IOS Software command (that is, opening a Telnet session to a host name) or for command output (that is, traceroute).

  d. (Optional) Use DNS resolution for the router:

     (global) [**no**] **ip domain-lookup**

    By default, DNS lookup is enabled so that the router requests name resolution from the name servers specified with the **ip name-server** command. If DNS resolution is not needed, you can disable it with the **no** keyword.

  e. (Optional) Configure DNS round-robin:

     (global) **ip domain round-robin**

    By default, routers use the first DNS server for the entire Time-To-Live (TTL) of the cache and use other DNS servers only if the first DNS server fails. This command configures the router to use round-robin for DNS resolution when multiple DNS servers are configured.

  f. (Optional) Configure DNS spoofing:

     (global) **ip dns server**
     (global) **ip dns spoofing** [*ip-address*]

    DNS spoofing enables the router to spoof replies to a DNS query. Configuring the **ip dns server** command enables the router to act as a DNS server while the **ip dns spoofing** [*ip-address*] command configures the router to respond to DNS queries with the specified IP address. If an IP address is not configured, the IP address of the incoming interface is used in DNS replies.

g. (Optional) Configure a default gateway:

```
(global) ip default-gateway ip-address
```

When IP routing is disabled on a router, all packets destined for nonlocal networks can be forwarded to a default gateway.

4. (Optional) Configure ICMP Router Discovery Protocol (IRDP).

    a. Enable IRDP on an interface:

```
(interface) ip irdp
```

The router processes IRDP on the interface, either as a host (IRDP packets are received) or as a client (IRDP packets are sent). IRDP advertisements are sent as broadcasts.

    b. (Optional) Define the IRDP hold time:

```
(interface) ip irdp holdtime seconds
```

IRDP advertisements are considered valid for a period of *seconds*.

    c. (Optional) Set the IRDP preference:

```
(interface) ip irdp preference number
```

Advertisements from the router can be preferred over other routers, with a higher preference *number*. The preference value can be from -2^{31} to 2^{31} (the default is 0).

    d. (Optional) Enable IRDP multicast mode:

```
(interface) ip irdp multicast
```

IRDP advertisements are sent using multicast address 224.0.0.1 rather than as broadcasts. This mode makes IRDP compatible with Sun Solaris hosts.

Example

Both primary and secondary IP addresses are configured on the Ethernet 0 interface. Serial 1 is configured as an unnumbered interface, using Ethernet 0. A static ARP entry is configured for a single host. The router is also configured to look up host names using two DNS servers using round-robin:

```
interface ethernet 0
        ip address 192.168.16.1 255.255.255.0
        ip address 192.168.17.1 255.255.255.0 secondary

interface serial 1
        ip unnumbered Ethernet 0

arp 192.168.16.217 0050.0492.6e77 arpa
ip domain example.com
```

```
ip name-server 192.168.3.5 192.168.3.6
ip domain-lookup
ip domain round-robin
```

4-2: IP Broadcast Handling

■ Directed broadcasts are packets that are sent to all hosts on a specific network or subnet. By default, directed broadcasts are not forwarded on router interfaces.

■ The router can forward certain UDP broadcasts to specific "helper" IP addresses. The helper address is substituted for the broadcast destination address, and the packets are forwarded normally.

Configuration

1. (Optional) Enable directed broadcasts:

   ```
   (interface) ip directed-broadcast [access-list]
   ```

   By default, directed broadcasts are not enabled on any router interface. Packets destined for directed broadcast addresses are dropped. If necessary, they can be enabled per interface. When they are enabled, only directed broadcasts containing protocols that are defined by the **ip forward-protocol** command are actually forwarded. An optional access list can be used to permit only specific packets tobe forwarded.

2. (Optional) Define an IP broadcast address:

   ```
   (interface) ip broadcast-address [ip-address]
   ```

   By default, the broadcast address is defined as 255.255.255.255. If necessary, this address can be changed to any other IP address on a per-interface basis.

> **Note**   The "all-1s" broadcast address 255.255.255.255 is used as a function of two bits (10 and 14) in the router configuration register. These bits can be set to define the following broadcast address as a combination of 1s or 0s in the network and host portions of the address, as shown in the following table:

Bit 14	Bit 10	Broadcast Address <net>.<host>
0	0	<1s>.<1s>
0	1	<0s>.<0s>
1	0	<network>.<0s>
1	1	<network>.<1s>

3. (Optional) Configure broadcast flooding on bridged interfaces.

   a. Flood broadcasts using the spanning-tree database:

   ```
   (global) ip forward-protocol spanning-tree
   ```

Broadcast packets can be flooded or sent out all network interfaces on a router. Flooding is performed according to the spanning-tree database such that only interfaces in the forwarding STP state can actually forward the broadcast packets. These packets must be destined for broadcast addresses (either MAC or IP broadcasts), and they contain TFTP, DNS, Time, NetBIOS, Network Disk, BOOTP, or UDP protocols allowed by the **ip forward-protocol udp** command. The packet's TTL must be at least 2.

b. (Optional) Increase flooding performance:

```
(global) ip forward-protocol turbo-flood
```

Broadcast flooding occurs more rapidly on Ethernet (ARPA encapsulation), FDDI, and Serial (HDLC encapsulation) interfaces.

4. (Optional) Configure UDP broadcast forwarding.

a. Enable UDP broadcast forwarding to an IP address:

```
(interface) ip helper-address ip-address
```

By default, this command forwards BOOTP (and DHCP) packets received on an interface to the specified IP address. Additional UDP ports can be specified for forwarding with **the ip forward-protocol** command. Multiple helper addresses can be configured on a single interface.

b. (Optional) Specify UDP broadcast port numbers to forward:

```
(global) ip forward-protocol {udp [port] | nd | sdns}
```

UDP broadcast packets are identified by port number, by **nd** (the Network Disk protocol, used by diskless Sun hosts), or by **sdns** (Secure Data Network Service). If **udp** is specified without the optional *port* number, the following broadcast protocols are forwarded:

■ Trivial File Transfer Protocol (TFTP)—UDP port 69

   Domain Name System (DNS)—UDP port 53

   Time service—UDP port 37

   NetBIOS Name Server—UDP port 137

■ NetBIOS Datagram Server—UDP port 138

   —Boot protocol (BOOTP and DHCP) client and server—UDP ports 67 and 68

■ Terminal Access Controller Access Control System (TACACS)—UDP port 49

   Specific UDP ports can be given as either numbers or a protocol name. You cansee a list of common UDP broadcast protocols using the **ip forward-protocol udp ?** command.

Example

Interface ethernet 0 on a router is left at the default setting of not forwarding directed broadcasts. IP helper addresses 192.168.75.4 and 192.168.99.16 are configured to forward the default set of UDP broadcasts, including BOOTP/DHCP. However, the NetBIOS services on UDP ports 137 and 138 are not to be forwarded:

```
interface ethernet 0
        no ip directed-broadcast
        ip address 192.168.16.1 255.255.255.0
        ip helper-address 192.168.75.4
        ip helper-address 192.168.99.16


no ip forward-protocol udp netbios-dgm
no ip forward-protocol udp netbios-ns
```

4-3: Hot Standby Router Protocol (HSRP)

Hot Standby Router Protocol (HSRP) provides failover for multiple routers on a common network segment.

■   HSRP allows a group of routers to serve as a primary or standby router for hosts on a segment by letting the active HSRP router respond to requests while others monitor for failure of the active router.

■   HSRP provides a virtual MAC address that is used by the active router running the protocol.

■   Devices running HSRP send and receive multicast UDP-based hello packets to detect router failure and to designate active and standby routers.

■   HSRP uses multicast packets to choose and maintain the active HSRP router based on configuration parameters.

Note   HSRP can run multiple instances on a single interface. Each instance is given a group number and has its own MAC and IP address. Because of this, each group's configuration and setting might be different. The [*group-number*] option is a possible configuration point in each command. A common use of this is on the subinterfaces of a Fast Ethernet or Gigabit Ethernet interface, where the HSRP group number can be set to match the VLAN number. If no *group-number* is configured, the default is group 0. There are some exceptions to multiple groups: A Cisco 1000, 2500, 3000, or 4000 series router using the LANCE hardware for the Ethernet controller cannot support multiple groups. Token Ring interfaces can support only the group numbers 0, 1, and 2, and they support a maximum of three groups per interface.

Configuration

1. (Required) Configure the interface with an IP address:

    ```
    (interface) ip address ip-address subnet-mask
    ```

    In order to run HSRP, the interface must have an IP address and be an active IP interface. This address is not used when you configure the host, but it is requiredfor IP processing and therefore must be configured.

2. (Required) Configure HSRP standby groups on the router:

    ```
    (interface) standby [group-number] ip ip-address [secondary]
    ```

    HSRP is configured on the interface with the **standby** command. The standby group and IP address are configured on all the routers that participate in HSRP. The IP address configured here is the one that will be used as the default gateway by the hosts on the segment.

    The option *group-number* is added to specify multiple groups for the router. This option allows you to split the load between multiple routers on the segment while still providing redundancy for the hosts. The **secondary** option indicates that the standby IP is a secondary address. This is useful when the interface is connected to a network that provides routing for a secondary network

Note   HSRP uses the virtual MAC address of 0000.0c07.ac*XX*, where *XX* is the hexadecimal value of the group number.

3. (Optional, but recommended) Set the priority for the HSRP interface:

    ```
    (interface) standby [group-number] priority priority
    ```

    Configure the HSRP priority for the interface and group. This command lets you select which router acts as the primary router for the group. The router with the higher priority number becomes the active router. If there is a tie, the route with the higher configured primary IP address becomes the active router. The default priority is 100.

4. (Optional, but recommended) Set the interface to preempt to assume the role of active:

    ```
    (interface) standby [group-number] preempt [delay delay]
    ```

    This allows the router to preempt (take over) if it determines that it has a higher priority. During standard HSRP operation, when the routers come up, an active router is selected from the candidates. If a router with a higher priority is activated on the segment, or if it goes down and then goes up, it does not take over unless the interface is configured to preempt. The delay option causes the router to delay by the number of seconds specified before preempting the current router. The default is 0 seconds.

5. (Optional) Track an interface to determine which router should be active:

```
(interface) standby [group-number] track interfacetype interfacenumber
  [decrementvalue]
```

This command allows you to decrement the priority value for a standby group by tracking the state of an interface. If the tracked interface fails, the standby group's priority for this interface is reduced by the amount of the decrement value specified. When this occurs, any router with a higher priority and the **preempt** command configured assumes the role of active router. If no decrement value is configured, the default is 10.

6. (Optional) Change the standby timers:

```
(interface) standby [group-number] timers hellotimer holdtime
```

This configures the period of time in seconds in which the routers send out hello packets to indicate their status and the amount of time required before the router is considered down. The value for the hold time should always be greater than or equal to 3 times the hello timer. The timers configured on the active router always override those of the other routers in the group. The defaults are hello = 3 hold = 10.

7. (Optional) Specify authentication for HSRP:

```
(interface) standby [group-number] authentication string
```

This command configures an authentication for the standby group. All routers in the group must be configured with the same string. If a router does not have the appropriate string, it cannot become an active or standby router.

8. (Optional) Configure HSRP to use the burned-in address (BIA) instead of the virtual MAC address:

```
(interface) standby use-bia
```

This command allows the active router to use the BIA associated with the interface instead of the virtual group address. This is useful in Token Ring environments when devices reject ARP replies with a functional MAC address. It is also useful in preventing RIF confusion when the router is in a source route environment and runs on multiple rings. To inform all hosts on the LAN about a change in active HSRP peers, the new active HSRP router sends a gratuitous ARP so that it can answer its own request with the new MAC address.

9. (Optional) Configure the delay period before the initialization of HSRP groups:

```
(interface) standby delay minimum min-seconds reload reload-seconds
```

You can configure the time before an HSRP group is intialized when an interface comes up. The *reload-seconds* value is the time period to wait after a router is reloaded. The recommended values are 30 for *min-seconds* and 60 for *reload-seconds*.

10. (Optional) Configure HSRP MD5 authentication using a key-string:

```
(interface) standby [group-number] authentication md5 key-string [0 | 7] key
[timeout seconds]
```

You can configure MD5 authentication using a key up to 64 characters in length. Prefacing a **0** before the key leaves the key unencrypted in the configuration file; specifying a **7** encrypts the key in the configuration file. (It is also automatically encrypted if the **service password-encryption** global configuration command is configured.) You can also configure a timeout value for how long an old key string will be accepted before switching to a new key.

11. (Optional) Configure HSRP MD5 authentication using a key-chain:

a. Configure a key chain:

```
(global) key chain key-chain-name
(keychain) key key-id
(key) key-string string
```

Instead of using a single key, you can use a key-chain to allow for multiple keys.

b. Enable MD5 authentication for an HSRP group using a key-chain:

```
(interface) standby [group-number] authentication md5 key-chain key-chain-
name
```

12. (Optional) Configure HSRP plain text authentication:

```
(interface) standby [group-number] authentication text string
```

Although using MD5 keys or key-chains are the preferred means of securing HSRP, you can configure plain text authentication. The default string is **cisco**.

13. (Optional) Configure an HSRP group as a client group to improve performance:

```
(interface) standby group-number follow group-name
```

You can configure load balancing by configuring multiple HSRP groups on an interface. You can further improve performance by configuring an HSRP group as a client group that follows a master HSRP group. Client groups follow the master group with a slight, random delay so that all client groups do not change at the same time. Configuration is necessary only for client groups; no additional configuration is necessary for the master HSRP group.

14. (Optional) Enable support for ICMP redirects:

```
(interface) [no] standby redirect
```

By default, HSRP filters all ICMP redirect messages. To disable filtering, configure the **no standby redirect** command. You can also configure in global configuration mode to globally enable or disable filtering for all interfaces configured for HSRP.

15. (Optional) Change the HSRP version:

```
(interface) standby version [1 | 2]
```

HSRP uses version 1 by default. HSRP version 2 uses the multicast group 224.0.0.102; permits an expanded group number range (0 to 4095); automatically advertises and learns millisecond timer values; and has a modified packet format that aids in troubleshooting by adding an identifier field to identify the sender of HSRP messages. HSRP version 1 and version 2 are not compatible, so all routers must be configured to use the same version.

16. (Optional) Configure HSRP Bidirectional Forwarding Detection (BFD):

BFD is a protocol that detects failures in the forwarding path between two adjacent routers. It offers fast path failure detection times for all media types, encapsulations, topologies, and routing protocols.

a. Configure BFD session parameters on the interface:

```
(interface) bfd interval milliseconds min_rx milliseconds multiplier
interval-multiplier
```

This command sets the baseline BFD session parameters on an interface. The multiplier specifies the minimum number of consecutive packets that can be missed before a session is declared down.

b. Configure HSRP BFD peering:

```
(interface) standby bfd
```

c. The **standby bfd** command enables HSRP support for BFD on the interface. Alternatively, you can enable HSRP BFD on all interfaces with the global configuration command **standby bfd all-interfaces**.

Example

Figure 4-1 shows two routers configured to run HSRP. These routers are running two groups to allow the active load to be split between the two devices. If either router fails, all hosts are served by the remaining router. The routers have also been set up to track the serial interface. If the serial interface fails, the priority is lowered by 10, allowing the standby router to preempt for that group.

```
Katie


interface ethernet 0
        ip address 172.16.18.3 255.255.255.0
        standby 10 ip 172.16.18.1
        standby priority 200
```

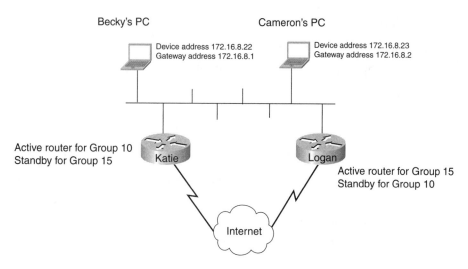

Figure 4-1 *HSRP Example*

```
        standby preempt
        standby track serial 0 10
        standby 15 ip 1.2.2.2
        standby priority 190
        standby preempt
Logan
interface ethernet 0
        ip address 172.16.18.4 255.255.255.0
        standby 10 ip 172.16.18.2
        standby priority 195 preempt
        standby 15 ip 1.2.2.2
        standby priority 200 preempt
        standby track serial 0
```

4-4: Virtual Router Redundancy Protocol

The Virtual Router Redundancy Protocol (VRRP) is an alternative to HSRP. Some of the advantages of VRRP over HSRP include the following:

- VRRP works between multiple vendors whereas HSRP was created by Cisco for Cisco equipment.(Although there are other vendors that now support HSRP.)

- VRRP has faster default timers than HSRP (a hello timer of 1 second and a hold timer of 3 seconds).

- VRRP uses an interface IP address as the group address as opposed to the virtual IP address assigned with HSRP.

Configuration

1. (Required) Configure the interface with an IP address:

   ```
   (interface) ip address ip-address subnet-mask
   ```

   Unlike HSRP, VRRP relies on the interface IP address as the group address. You must configure an IP address on an interface.

2. Enable VRRP on an interface:

   ```
   (interface) vrrp [group-number] ip ip-address
   ```

   The IP address you use should be an IP address assigned to one of the routers. All routers in the VRRP group should use the same IP address.

3. (Optional) Configure a group description for the VRRP group:

   ```
   (interface) vrrp [group-number] description description
   ```

   Adding a text description is helpful when reviewing configurations.

4. (Optional) Set the priority level of the router within a VRRP group:

   ```
   (interface) vrrp [group-number] priority priority
   ```

   The default priority of a router in a VRRP group is 100. The router with the highest priority number becomes the virtual router master.

5. (Optional) Enable VRRP preemption:

   ```
   (interface) vrrp [group-number] preempt
   ```

   By default, a router that comes online with a higher priority number will not pre-empt and become the new VRRP virtual router master. By enabling VRRP preemption, a router that comes online with a higher priority will preempt and become the new virtual router master.

Example

In the following example, two routers are configured to run VRRP. The routers use the IP address 10.0.0.1 as the virtual IP address that clients will use as their default gateway.

```
Router1
interface fastethernet0/0
  ip address 10.0.0.1 255.0.0.0
  vrrp 1 ip 10.0.0.1
  vrrp 1 priority 120
  vrrp 1 preempt

router2
  ip address 10.0.0.2 255.0.0.0
  vrrp 1 ip 10.0.0.1
  vrrp 1 priority 100
```

4-5: Dynamic Host Configuration Protocol (DHCP)

■ Cisco routers provide DHCP services for IP hosts.

■ DHCP, defined by RFC 2131, provides dynamic allocation of host IP addressing and configuration parameters for network devices.

■ DHCP is a client/server model in which the server allocates and delivers addresses to DHCP clients.

■ DHCP can be configured to assign default gateway and DNS information.

■ DHCP can be configured to assign NetBIOS mode and WINS server information.

■ There are three mechanisms for DHCP address delivery: automatic allocation (permanent assignment by the server to a client), dynamic allocation (assigns the address for a limited time), and manual allocation (the administrator manually assigns the address, and the DHCP server conveys the assignment).

■ Pool assignments are inherited by host addresses that fall within a network or subnet pool. Any direct assignments to a pool override the assignments made at a higher level.

Note   DHCP uses UDP ports 67 and 68 to convey IP assignment and parameter information.

Configuration

You must first either configure the DHCP database or disable DHCP conflict logging in order to have the router provide the DHCP addressing request.

1. Configure the DHCP database.

   a. Configure a DHCP database agent:

   `(global) ip dhcp database url [timeout seconds | write-delay seconds]`

   The DHCP database agent is a host running FTP, TFTP, or RCP that stores the DHCP bindings database. You can configure multiple DHCP database agents, and you can configure the interval between database updates and transfers for each agent.

   -OR-

   b. Disable DHCP conflict logging:

   `(global) no ip dhcp conflict logging`

   If you do not configure a DHCP database agent, you must disable the recording of DHCP address conflicts on the DHCP server. This allows the router to assign addresses without having a database agent.

   c. (Optional) Exclude IP addresses from all pools:

   `(global)ip dhcp excluded-address low-address [high-address]`

The DHCP server can exclude an address *(low-address)* or a range of addresses*(low-address* to *high-address)* when assigning addresses to clients.

d. Create a DHCP pool, and enter DHCP configuration mode:

`(global) `**`ip dhcp pool`**` name`

You must create and configure a DHCP pool. The **ip dhcp pool** command with the *name* option creates the list and then configures that pool in DHCP configuration mode. Pools can be created and attributes assigned for an entire network. Subnet-specific options can then be assigned in respective subnet pools.

e. Configure the DHCP address pool subnet and mask:

`(dhcp) `**`network`**` network-number [mask | /prefix-length]`

Set up the address pool. The *network-number* specifies the range of IP addresses that are offered for the pool, in the form of a network address. The range of pool addresses is from *network-number* plus 1 through the broadcast address minus 1. The mask can be specified in either dotted-decimal form or by the */prefix-length* (also known as CIDR or bitwise) notation. Assigning the network 172.16.18.8 with a mask of 255.255.255.248 would provide addressing from 172.16.18.9 through 172.16.18.14.

f. (Optional) Configure the domain name for the client:

`(dhcp) `**`domain-name`**` domain`

This command specifies the domain name for clients. This option places the hosts in this pool in a common domain. The domain is part of the IP configuration parameters.

g. (Optional) Specify the DNS server:

`(dhcp) `**`dns-server`**` address [address2...address8]`

This command specifies which DNS server or servers will be used by the clients.

h. (Optional) Configure the WINS server:

`(dhcp) `**`netbios-name-server`**` address [address2...address8]`

Microsoft clients use Windows Internet Naming Service (WINS) to resolve NetBIOS names to IP addresses. Configuring a WINS server is an extension of DHCP. This command specifies the IP address of the WINS server or servers that the client is configured to use.

i. (Optional) Specify the NetBIOS node type for the client:

`(dhcp) `**`netbios-node-type`**` type`

These node types can be used to specify what order or option the client is to use when resolving NetBIOS names to IP addresses: **b-node** (broadcast), **p-node** (peer-to-peer), **m-node** (mixed), or **h-node** (hybrid; recommended).

j. (Optional, but recommended) Set up the default gateway:

```
(dhcp) default-router address [address2...address3]
```

This command specifies the gateway or router to be used by the IP client when it sends packets off-net.

k. (Optional) Configure the address lease time:

```
(dhcp) lease [days [hours] [minutes] | infinite]
```

Use this command to specify in days, hours, and/or minutes how long the client can keep an address before renewing it. If you select the **infinite** option, the address will not expire, but it must be released by the client. The default lease time is one day.

2. (Optional) Configure On-Demand Address Pool Manager (ODAP). With ODAP, a subnet can be added to a pool when a configurable high utilization mark is reached. The subnet is returned to the DHCP server when the configurable low utilization mark is reached.

a. Configure an address pool as an on-demand address pool:

```
(dhcp) origin dhcp [subnet size initial size [autogrow size]
```

You must use the **autogrow** keyword to enable the pool to request additional subnets. The *size* value can be either a subnet mask (nnnn.nnnn.nnnn) or prefix size (/nn). The valid values are /0 and /4 to /30.

b. Configure the low utilization mark:

```
(dhcp) utilization mark low percentage
```

Subnets are released from the pool when the utilization is less than the low utilization mark.

c. Configure the high utilization mark:

```
(dhcp) utilization mark high percentage
```

Subnets are added to the pool when the utilization passes the high utilization mark.

3. (Optional) Configure manual bindings.

Manual bindings are used to give a specific client a particular IP address. Manual binding is typically done by the MAC address. In other words, given a specific MAC addressthe client chooses the host address that was assigned in the database. The following commands show how the router can be configured to provide manual bindings.

a. Configure the server pool, and enter DHCP pool configuration mode:

```
(global) ip dhcp pool name
```

Enter DHCP configuration mode, and create a host-specific pool. Each host-specific assignment must have a unique pool name. Because the options assigned for a major network or subnet are cumulative, the host inherits any attributes assigned to its subnet.

b. Specify the host address and mask to be used by the client:

```
(dhcp) host address [mask | /prefix-length]
```

This command specifies the IP address that the client will use. The mask is also specified in this command.

c. Identify the host:

```
(dhcp) hardware-address hardware-address type
```
-or-
```
(dhcp) client-identifier unique-identifier
```

Both commands specify the client's hardware identifier. The hardware-address command specifies the MAC address and type. The client-identifier command identifies the client and media type using dotted-hexadecimal notification.

d. (Optional) Define the client name for DNS:

```
(dhcp) client-name name
```

4. (Optional) Configure DHCP operational parameters.

a. (Optional) Control the DHCP server process:

```
(global) [no] service dhcp
```

By default, the DHCP service is configured to be on. If it has been disabled, use the command **service dhcp** to re-enable the service. If you need to stop or disable the service, use the **no** keyword.

b. (Optional) Configure the number of ping packets:

```
(global) ip dhcp ping packets number
```

This command specifies the number of ping packets the DHCP server sends to a pool address before assigning that address to a requesting client. The default is two packets.

c. (Optional) Specify the timeout value for DHCP ping packets:

```
(global) ip dhcp ping timeout milliseconds
```

Before a DHCP server sends an address to a client, it pings that address the number of times specified by the **ip dhcp ping packet** command. If a response is received, the pinged address is not used. If the ping times out, the server assumes it is safe to assign that address to a client. This command defines how long the server waits before a ping is considered unsuccessful. The default is 500 milliseconds.

5. (Optional) Configure the interface to be a DHCP relay agent:

    a. Configure the IP helper address:

```
(interface) ip helper-address ip-address
```

UDP broadcasts are not forwarded by default. If you have a DHCP server located on a different subnet than the DHCP clients, you need to configure an interface to be a DHCP relay agent. Apply this command on the interface connected to same network as the DHCP clients. The IP address is that of the DHCP server located on a different network.

    b. (Optional) Configure support for the relay agent information option:

```
(global) ip dhcp relay information option
```

DHCP address allocation is based on an IP address; however, in some environments, you might need to use the DHCP option 82 to include additional information about the DHCP client packet sent to the DHCP server. This is necessary when you want additional configurations per client such as quality of service (QoS), security policies, and some wireless implementations.

    c. (Optional) Configure DHCP smart relay:

```
(global) ip dhcp smart-relay
```

If you use secondary IP addresses on interfaces with DHCP relay configured and need the gateway address of the DHCP broadcast to use the secondary address, you need to configure DHCP smart relay. With this feature, the relay agent sets the gateway address to the secondary address after three client retries.

Example

In this example, the DHCP service is configured to use three address pools. Pool 0 sets configuration parameters that will be inherited by any device that gets an address from the 172.16.0.0 network, unless those parameters are overridden by another pool with a more specific network address. Pools 1 and 2 define the DHCP parameters for devices on networks 172.16.18.0 and 172.16.22.0, respectively. The addresses from 172.16.18.250 through 172.16.18.254 are reserved and are excluded from the DHCP pools.

All devices within 172.16.0.0 are offered the domain name example.com, DNS servers 172.16.1.250 and 172.16.2.251, a WINS address of 172.16.1.18, and p-mode NetBIOS. DHCP offers for the 172.16.18.0 network have a default gateway of 172.16.18.252 and 172.16.18.253 and a DHCP lease time of 30 days. DHCP offers for the 172.16.22.0 network also receive the DNS addresses 172.16.22.250 and 172.16.22.251—values that override the defaults configured in pool 0.

```
no ip dhcp conflict logging
ip dhcp excluded-address 172.16.18.250 172.16.18.254
```

```
ip dhcp pool 0
        network 172.16.0.0 /16
        domain-name example.com
        dns-server 172.16.1.250 172.16.2.251
        netbios-name-server 172.16.1.18
        netbios-node-type p-node

ip dhcp pool 1
        network 172.16.18.0 /24
        default-router 172.16.18.252 172.16.18.253
        lease 30

ip dhcp pool 2
        network 172.16.22.0 /24
        default-router 172.16.22.1
        netbios-name-server 172.16.22.100
dns-server 172.16.22.250 172.16.22.251
        lease 10
```

4-6: Mobile IP

- Mobile IP provides a way for users to keep a home-based IP address while roaming outside their home network. Sessions can be initiated and maintained with roaming users using their home address.

- Mobile IP builds tunnels to roaming users with generic routing encapsulation (GRE) and IP-in-IP tunneling protocols.

- Mobile IP is useful in wireless and cellular environments, where users need to maintain a single IP address while roaming between networks.

- Mobile IP must be configured as a *home agent* on a router in the "home" network, as a *foreign agent* on all routers where roaming users can be present, and also on the *mobile node*, or the user's portable host machine.

- Roaming users maintain two addresses: a static *home address*, where application connections are terminated, and a *care-of address*. The care-of address represents the user's current location and acts as a forwarding address where all connections to the home address can be sent. The care-of address is also used as one end of the Mobile IP tunnel to the roaming user.

- As a user roams, Mobile IP client software detects the local foreign agent through an extension of the ICMP Router Discovery Protocol (IRDP). Cisco's Aironet series wireless LAN products include a Mobile IP proxy agent, allowing nodes to roam without any extra Mobile IP client software.

- Mobile nodes and home agents must share Message Digest 5 (MD5) security association before the mobile node can be authenticated and registered for a tunnel.

- Mobile IP tunnels are built between the home and foreign agents as the mobile node registers itself with a newly discovered foreign agent.

Note   Mobile IP is based on the following protocols and ports:

- Mobile IP (RFC 2002), which uses TCP port 434

- IRDP (RFC 1256), which uses IP protocol number 1 (ICMP) over both broadcast address 255.255.255.255 and multicast address 224.0.0.1

- GRE tunneling (RFC 1701), which uses IP protocol number 47

- IP-in-IP tunneling (RFC 2003), which uses IP protocol number 4

Configuration

1. Configure the Home Agent.

    a. Enable Mobile IP on the Home Agent router:

    ```
    (global) router mobile
    ```

    b. Enable the Home Agent service:

    ```
    (global) ip mobile home-agent [broadcast] [care-of-access acl] [lifetime sec]
    [replay sec] [reverse-tunnel-off] [roam-access acl] [suppress-unreachable]
    ```

    The **broadcast** keyword (not enabled by default) specifies that broadcasts will be forwarded to the mobile node over the tunnel connection. Mobile node registration can be configured with a maximum **lifetime** of *sec* seconds (the default is 36000 seconds) and a replay protection time interval of **replay** *sec* seconds to prevent replay attacks. The **reverse-tunnel-off** keyword specifies that support for tunnels in the reverse direction is disabled (it is enabled by default). Normally, a tunnel is built for traffic going from the home agent network toward the mobile node, because the care-of addresses change while roaming. Traffic in the reverse direction can be forwarded without a tunnel and can reach the home destination without having to pass through the home agent. Therefore, reverse tunnels can be built, but they are optional.

    By default, any foreign agent care-of address can register itself with the home agent, and any mobile node is allowed to roam. If desired, you can restrict care-of addresses to only those permitted by the **care-of-access** *acl* standard IP access list. Mobile nodes can be permitted or denied roaming privileges by the **roam-access** *acl* standard IP access list. The IP addresses checked by the roam-access access list are the home addresses of the mobile nodes, not the dynamic foreign IP addresses.

c. (Optional) Configure one or more virtual networks:

```
(global) ip mobile virtual-network address mask
```

Mobile nodes can be assigned IP addresses that belong to a nonexistent network or that are not directly connected to the home agent router. In this case, the virtual network must be defined by *address* and network *mask* and placed in the home agent's routing table.

d. (Optional) Redistribute the virtual networks into a routing protocol:

```
(global) router routing-protocol
(global) redistribute mobile
```

All Mobile IP virtual networks are redistributed into the routing protocol specified by the **router** command. Because virtual networks are not directly connected, they are not advertised by default. Redistributing them into an existing routing protocol causes them to be advertised to other routers in the routing domain.

e. Identify the mobile nodes to be supported:

```
(global) ip mobile host lower [upper] {interface type num | virtual-network
network mask} [aaa [load-sa]] [care-of-access acl]  [lifetime seconds]
```

The range of mobile node IP addresses is between *lower* and *upper*. Mobile nodes must belong to either a physical router interface (**interface** *type num*) or a virtual network (**virtual-network** *network mask*). A limited set of foreign agents where mobile nodes are supported can be defined with the **care-of-access** keyword. A standard IP access list *acl* (either named or numbered) is used to permit only the desired foreign agent care-of addresses. The maximum mobile node lifetime can be defined with the **lifetime** keyword (3 to 65535 seconds; the default is 36000 seconds).

Mobile nodes must have security associations (SAs) for authentication during registration with the home agent. Security associations can be defined in a AAA server (either TACACS+ or RADIUS) or explicitly defined with the **ip mobile secure** command, as described next. SAs are downloaded to the home agent with the **aaa** command. The optional **load-sa** keyword causes the security associations to be stored in the router's memory after they are downloaded.

f. (Optional) Configure mobile node security associations:

```
(global) ip mobile secure host address {inbound-spi spi-in  outbound-spi spi-
out | spi spi} key {ascii | hex} string [replay   timestamp [seconds]] [algo-
rithm md5] [mode prefix-suffix]
```

The IP address of the mobile node is specified with the *address* field. Authentication for mobile node registration is defined with a security parameter index (SPI). The SPIs can be specified as a pair of inbound/outbound, using the **inbound-spi** and **outbound-spi**, or as a single bidirectional value using the **spi** keyword. The SPI is a unique 4-byte index (0x100 to 0xffffffff) that selects a security context between two endpoints.

A secret shared key is defined with the **key** keyword and either an **ascii** text string or a **hex** string of digits. The authentication exchange can be encrypted using MD5 if the **algorithm md5** keywords are used. If the **mode prefix-suffix** keywords are used, the key string is used at the beginning and end of the registration information to calculate the MD5 message digest. The **replay timestamp** keywords can be used to protect against replay attacks, because authentication exchanges are time-stamped and compared to the current time. An optional *seconds* value can be added to ensurethat the registration is received within the specified number of seconds. Both endsof the authentication must have their time clocks synchronized.

g. (Optional) Configure foreign agent security associations:

```
(global) ip mobile secure foreign-agent address {inbound-spi spi-in  outbound-
spi spi-out | spi spi} key {ascii | hex} string [replay timestamp [seconds]]
[algorithm md5] [mode prefix-suffix]
```

This command is necessary if security associations will be used between the home agent and foreign agents. A foreign agent's IP address is specified with the *address* field. Authentication for foreign agent registration is defined with an SPI, a secret shared key, and the same authentication parameters as described in Step 1f.

2. Configure a foreign agent.

a. Enable Mobile IP on the foreign agent router:

```
(global) router mobile
```

b. Enable the care-of address on the foreign agent:

```
(global) ip mobile foreign-agent [care-of type num | reg-wait seconds]
```

The care-of address on a foreign agent is defined by the **care-of** keyword and the specified interface *type* and *num*. The address of this interface is used as one endpoint of the tunnels that are built back to the home agent. The **reg-wait** keyword specifies how long the foreign agent waits for a reply from the home agent to register a mobile node (5 to 600 seconds; the default is 15 seconds).

c. Enable the foreign agent service on an interface:

```
(interface) ip mobile foreign-service [home-access acl] [limit num]
[registration-required]
```

Foreign agent service is enabled on an interface where mobile nodes can roam and connect. The care-of address defined in Step 2b is advertised on this interface. If desired, the **home-access** keyword can be used to restrict the set of home agent IP addresses with which mobile nodes can register. Only addresses permitted by the standard IP access list *acl* can be used as home agents. The **limit** keyword can be used to limit the number of visiting mobile nodes on the interface to *num* (1 to 1000; the default is unlimited). If the **registration-required** keyword is specified, all mobile nodes must register even if the care-of address is co-located.

d. (Optional) Specify network prefix lengths in foreign agent advertisements:

```
(interface) ip mobile prefix-length
```

On an interface that advertises care-of addresses of a foreign agent, this command causes the network prefix length to be added to the advertisements. Roaming mobile nodes can use the prefix to differentiate between advertisements received from more than one foreign agent.

e. (Optional) Configure home agent security associations:

```
(global) ip mobile secure home-agent address {inbound-spi spi-in outbound-spi
spi-out | spi spi} key {ascii | hex} string [replay timestamp [seconds]] [algo-
rithm md5] [mode prefix-suffix]
```

This command is necessary if security associations will be used between the home agent and foreign agents. The IP address of a home agent is specified with the *address* field. Authentication for home agent registration is defined with an SPI, a secret shared key, and the same authentication parameters as described in Step 1f.

f. (Optional) Configure roaming mobile node security associations:

```
(global) ip mobile secure visitor address {inbound-spi spi-in outbound  spi
spi-out | spi spi} key {ascii | hex} string [replay timestamp  [seconds]] [al-
gorithm md5] [mode prefix-suffix]
```

This command is necessary if security associations will be used between the foreign agent and roaming (visiting) mobile nodes. The IP address of a visiting mobile node is specified with the *address* field. Authentication for visitor registration is defined with an SPI, a secret shared key, and the same authentication parameters as described in Step 1f.

Example

A home agent router (Router 1) is configured to support Mobile IP. All roaming mobile nodes are given IP addresses on the virtual network 192.168.3.0, which does not exist inside the home agent's network. Mobile nodes are restricted such that addresses

192.168.3.17 and 192.168.3.161 are not allowed to roam beyond the home network. Mobile nodes with addresses ranging from 192.168.3.1 to 192.168.3.254 belong to the virtual network, but foreign agents with care-of addresses in the 128.10.0.0 network are not allowed to support roaming nodes. Last, security associations are set up for mobile nodes 192.168.3.1 and 192.168.3.2. SAs use MD5 encryption and the string "secret99" as a shared text key.

A foreign agent is configured on Router 2, where the ethernet 1/0 interface provides Mobile IP advertisements to mobile nodes. The care-of address becomes 17.6.3.45, or the address of the ethernet 1/0 interface. Figure 4-2 shows the network diagram for this example.

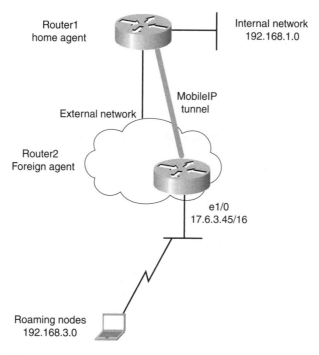

Figure 4-2   *Network Diagram for the Mobile IP Example*

```
Router 1
router mobile

ip mobile home-agent broadcast roam-access 10
ip mobile virtual-network 192.168.3.0 255.255.255.0
ip mobile host 192.168.3.1 192.168.3.254 virtual-network 192.168.3.0
255.255.255.0
  care-of-access 11
ip mobile secure host 192.168.3.1 spi 100 key ascii secret99 algorithm md5
ip mobile secure host 192.168.3.2 spi 100 key ascii secret99 algorithm md5
```

```
access-list 10 deny 192.168.3.17
access-list 10 deny 192.168.3.161
access-list 10 permit any
access-list 11 deny 128.10.0.0
access-list 11 permit any

router eigrp 101
        network 192.168.1.0
        redistribute mobile
Router 2
router mobile

interface ethernet 1/0
        ip address 17.6.3.45 255.255.0.0

        ip mobile foreign-agent care-of ethernet 1/0
        ip mobile foreign-service
```

4-7: Network Address Translation (NAT)

■   NAT can be used to interface a network of private or nonregistered IP addresses to the Internet and present them as one or more registered addresses.

■   NAT can translate one IP address space into another during an addressspace migration.

■   An entire address range can be "hidden" or translated behind a single IP address using Port Address Translation (PAT).

■   NAT can provide load balancing of a single IP address to many translated addresses, as in the case of a server farm.

■   NAT has one router interface on the "outside"and at least one interface on the "inside." (Inside refers to the local, private address space, and outside refers to the global, public address space.)

■   When NAT runs out of available address space for translation, incoming packets requiring translation are dropped, and an ICMP Host Unreachable packet is returned.

■   Cisco's EasyIP is a combination of IOS software features: NAT, DHCP server (see Section 4-5, and WAN interface IP address negotiation using PPP and IPCP (see Section 3-6).

Note   NAT is fully compatible with TCP and UDP traffic that does not contain source or destination addresses within the payload. In other words, packets that have IP addresses located within the packet header can easily be translated. These protocols include HTTP, TFTP, Telnet, finger, NTP, NFS, and rlogin/rsh/rcp.

However, many protocols do contain source and/or destination IP addresses embedded in the data portion of the packet. For these, NAT must look further into the packet payload and perform the necessary translations so that the protocols work properly after the translation occurs. Protocols that are compatible with Cisco IOS NAT include ICMP, FTP, NetBIOS over TCP/IP, RealAudio, CuSeeMe, DNS queries, NetMeeting, VDOLive, Vxtreme, IP multicast, PPTP, H.323v2, H.225/245 (except RAS), and Cisco's IP Phone Skinny Client Protocol.

Configuration

In the configuration steps, NAT is shown to translate inside source addresses. The command format is ip nat inside source. NAT can also perform other translations with the following commands:

```
(global) ip nat inside destination ...
(global) ip nat outside source ...
(global) ip nat outside destination ...
```

These commands can be used with the same options and results defined in the following configuration steps. However, the most common use of NAT is to translate inside source addresses where a private network interfaces with the Internet.

1. (Optional) Use static address translation.

    a. (Optional) Define a static translation for an IP address:

    ```
    (global) ip nat inside source static local-ip global-ip {extendable  no-alias}
    ```

    A static entry is made in the translation table such that a source address of *local-ip* is translated into *global-ip*. Two different types of translations can be configured: specific TCP or UDP port numbers associated with an IP address, and a translation for all TCP and UDP ports associated with an IP address.

    b. (Optional) Define a static translation for an IP address and a specific TCP or UDP port:

    ```
    (global) ip nat inside source static [tcp | udp] local-ip local-port  {global-
    ip | interface type num} global-port {extendable | no-alias}
    ```

    A static entry is made in the translation table such that a source address of *local-ip* and TCP or UDP port *local-port* will be translated into *global-ip* with TCP or UDP port *global-port*. Optionally, an interface type and number can be specified instead of a global IP address. The interface's IP address is then used as the global IP address for translation. This is useful when an interface's IP address is negotiated or dynamically assigned.

    The **extendable** keyword is used when several ambiguous static translations exist for the same local or global IP addresses. Full address and port NAT entries are created to resolve the ambiguity. By default, the router answers ARP requests for translations to unused global IP addresses. Use the **no-alias** keyword if this behavior is not what you want.

c. (Optional) Define a static translation for an entire network address:

(global) **ip nat inside source static network** *local-ip global-ip* {*netmask* | *prefix-length*} {**extendable** | **no-alias**}

A static entry is made in the translation table such that source addresses of the entire network *local-ip* are translated into the network *global-ip.* The network mask is specified as either a regular *netmask* in dotted notation or as a single number *prefix-length* representing the length of the subnet mask prefix.

2. (Optional) Use dynamic translation behind a pool of IP addresses.

a. Define a pool of contiguous IP addresses to use:

(global) **ip nat pool** *pool start-ip end-ip* {**netmask** *netmask* | **prefix-length** *length*}

A single range of contiguous IP addresses is identified as a pool named *pool,* beginning with *start-ip* and ending with *end-ip.* An optional mask can be specified as either a regular *netmask* in dotted notation or as a single number *length* representing the length of the subnet mask prefix.

-or-

b. Define a pool of discontiguous ranges of IP addresses:

(global) **ip nat pool** *pool* {**netmask** *netmask* | **prefix-length** *length*} [**type match-host**]
(ip-nat-pool) **address** *start-ip end-ip*
(ip-nat-pool) ...

Several ranges of IP addresses can be assigned to a NAT pool, even if they are discontiguous. In this case, only the pool name is specified, along with either the subnet mask or the prefix length. If the optional **type match-host** keyword is included, the prefix is translated, and the host number remains the same. In other words, NAT "slides" the entire range of host addresses under a new network address.

The pool's individual ranges are defined with the **address** command, along with starting and ending IP addresses.

c. Trigger the NAT operation using an access list.

- Define a standard access list that permits addresses to be translated:

(global) **access-list** *number* **permit** *source-address mask*
-or-

```
(global) ip access-list standard name
(std-nacl) permit source-address mask
```

A standard IP access list (either with a *number* 1 to 99 or a *name*) is defined. The inside address to be translated must be permitted by the access list and is defined as *source-address* and network *mask*.

■ Configure NAT to use an access list and an address pool:

```
(global) ip nat inside source list access-list pool pool
```

The numbered or named standard IP access list is used to trigger NAT to select an unused address from the pool named *pool*.

d. Trigger the NAT operation using a route map.

■ Define a route map that matches addresses to be translated:

```
(global) route-map name permit statement-num
```

A route map named *name* is defined.

■ Specify parameters to match:

```
(route-map) match ip address access-list
-or-
(route-map) match ip next-hop access-list
-or-
(route-map) match interface type num
```

One or more of the **match** statements are specified for the route map to identify the IP address, next-hop address, or outbound interface of a packet. Matching conditions flag the packet for address translation. These matching conditions are useful if translation is needed into address spaces from several service providers. The matching conditions should be selected so that a unique service provider address space or interface is chosen.

Apply a route map to a NAT address pool:

```
(global) ip nat inside source route-map map-name pool pool-name
```

Matching conditions from the route map *map-name* trigger NAT to use an IP address from the pool *pool-name*. This command can be used more than once to bind unique addressing from multiple service providers to the appropriate address pools.

3. (Optional) Define a dynamic translation to "hide" inside hosts behind a singleIP address:

```
(global) ip nat inside source list list [interface type num | pool  pool-name]
overload
```

PAT is activated using the **overload** keyword. NAT is triggered using the standard IP access list *list*. It can use a single global IP address from either an interface (specified with the **interface** keyword) or one of the NAT pool addresses (specified with the **pool** keyword).

The local or inside TCP/UDP port numbers are kept intact, and all the inside addresses are translated into the single global IP address. The global TCP/UDP port numbers are modified to create a unique translation entry. If the original source port cannot be retained in the translation, the next available port number (0 to 65535) is used. In the case of the **pool** keyword, as soon as all available ports have been used for one IP address in the pool, NAT moves to the next available pool address.

4.   (Optional) Configure load balancing for TCP traffic.

   a. Define an address pool that represents a group of real servers:

   ```
   (global) ip nat pool pool start-ip end-ip {netmask mask | prefix-length
   length} type rotary
   ```

   The IP addresses of physical servers are defined as a NAT pool named *pool* and ranging from *start-ip* to *end-ip*. An optional network mask or prefix length can be given for the range. The **type rotary** keywords must be used to enable the round-robin load balancing operation. Each new TCP connection receives a translation to the next address in the pool.

   b. Define an access list that permits the address of a virtual server:

   ```
   (global) access-list number permit source-address mask
   -or-
   (global) ip access-list standard name
   (std-nacl) permit source-address mask
   ```

   A standard IP access list (either with a *number* 1 to 99 or a *name*) is defined. Only the inside address of the virtual server must be permitted by the access list. It is defined as *source-address* and network *mask*.

   c. Apply the virtual server access list to the pool of real servers:

   ```
   (global) ip nat inside destination list access-list pool pool
   ```

   The numbered or named standard IP access list is used to trigger NAT to select the next physical server IP address from the pool. Note that the **nat** command shown here translates the **inside destination** address. This is because TCP load balancing is usually used on inbound traffic destined for a virtual server address. Therefore, the virtual server should be "located" on an outside interface, and the physical servers should be located on an inside interface.

5.   Enable NAT by identifying an "inside" interface:

   ```
   (interface) ip nat inside
   ```

The inside boundary for the NAT operation is defined on the specified interface. One or more inside interfaces can be defined so that NAT will translate selected addresses as packets cross the boundary between any inside and outside interfaces.

6. Enable NAT by identifying an "outside" interface:

```
(interface) ip nat outside
```

The outside boundary for the NAT operation is defined on the specified interface. One or more outside interfaces can be defined.

Examples

Figure 4-3 shows a network diagram for this example. A static translation is defined to map inside address 192.168.3.17 to outside address 128.3.5.64. In the second group of commands, static translations are defined to map a single outside host address to two different inside hosts—one host for SMTP (port 25) traffic, and another host for HTTP (port 80) traffic. Both SMTP and HTTP traffic can be sent to the single outside address, and NAT will sort out the traffic to the correct inside hosts.

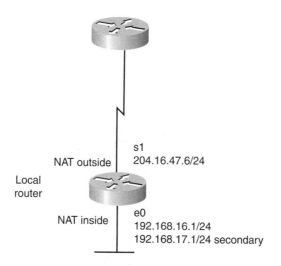

Figure 4-3 *Network Diagram for the NAT Static Translation Example*

The network 192.168.77.0 is translated into the network 128.3.77.0 by a single **static** NAT command. Two pools of dynamic addresses are created for two user groups: workgroup1 and workgroup2, each containing 128 IP addresses. Access list 101 is used to trigger NAT for addresses in the 192.168.16.0 network going out anywhere, using NAT pool workgroup1. Route map trigger2 is used to trigger NAT for addresses in the 192.168.16.0 network going anywhere except the 172.30.0.0 network, using NAT pool workgroup2. Access list 103 is used to trigger NAT with PAT or overload for addresses in the

192.168.17.0 network going anywhere. Rather than using a pool, NAT translates the inside addresses so that they are hidden behind the single IP address of interface serial 1.

```
ip nat inside source static 192.168.3.17 128.3.5.64


ip nat inside source static tcp 192.168.3.5 25 128.3.5.31 25
ip nat inside source static tcp 192.168.3.10 80 128.3.5.31 80
ip nat inside source static network 192.168.77.0 128.3.77.0 255.255.255.0


ip nat pool workgroup1 128.3.80.1 128.3.80.127 netmask 255.255.255.128
ip nat pool workgroup2 128.3.80.128 128.3.80.254 netmask 255.255.255.128
ip nat inside source list 101 pool workgroup1
ip nat inside source route-map trigger2 pool workgroup2


ip nat inside source list 103 interface serial 1 overload

access-list 101 permit ip 192.168.16.0 0.0.0.255 any
access-list 102 deny ip 192.168.16.0 0.0.0.255 172.30.0.0 0.0.255.255
access-list 102 permit ip 192.168.16.0 0.0.0.255 any
access-list 103 permit ip 192.168.17.0 0.0.0.255 any

route-map trigger2 permit 10
        match ip address 102


interface ethernet 0
        ip address 192.168.16.1 255.255.255.0
        ip address 192.168.17.1 255.255.255.0 secondary
        ip nat inside
interface serial 1
        ip address 204.16.47.6 255.255.255.0
        ip nat outside
```

NAT is used to provide TCP load balancing for a server farm. The physical servers are defined as a pool called servers, ranging from 192.168.99.10 to 192.168.99.40. A virtual server is defined as 128.100.41.5, matched by access list 1. The servers are located on inside interface ethernet 1/0, and the virtual server is located on the outside interface serial 0/3. Figure 4-4 shows a network diagram.

```
ip nat pool servers 192.168.99.10 192.168.99.40 netmask 255.255.255.0 type rotary


ip nat inside destination list 1 pool servers
access-list 1 permit 128.100.41.5 0.0.0.0
```

```
interface ethernet 1/0
        ip address 192.168.99.1 255.255.255.0
        ip nat inside

interface serial 0/3
        ip address 128.100.41.1 255.255.255.0
        ip nat outside
```

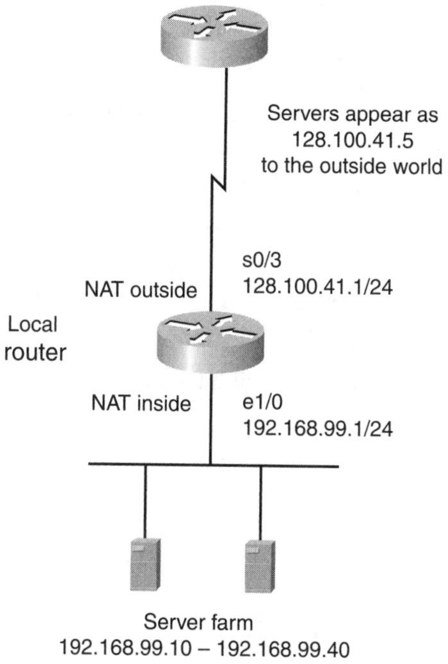

Figure 4-4 *Network Diagram for the NAT TCP Load Balancing Example*

4-8: Server Load Balancing (SLB)

- SLB is used to provide a virtual server IP address to which clients can connect, representing a group of real physical servers in a server farm.

- As clients open new connections to the virtual server, SLB decides which real server to use based on a load-balancing algorithm.

- Server load balancing is performed by one of these methods:

- **Weighted round robin**—Each real server is assigned a weight that lets it handle connections relative to th1 other servers. For a weight n, a server is assigned n new connections before SLB moves on to the next server.

- **Weighted least connections**—SLB assigns new connections to the real server with the least number of active connections. Each real server is assigned a weight m, where its capacity for active connections is m divided by the sum of all server weights. SLB assigns new connections to the real server with the number of active connections furthest below its capacity.

■   With weighted least connections, SLB controls the access to a new real server, providing a slow start function. New connections are rate-limited and are allowed to increase gradually to keep the server from becoming overloaded.

■   The virtual server can masquerade as the IP address for all TCP and UDP ports of the real server farm. In addition, the virtual server can appear as the IP address of a single port or service of a server farm.

■   Sticky connections allow SLB to assign new connections from a client to the last real server the client used.

■   SLB can detect a real server failure, take the failed server out of service, and return it to service as soon as it is working again.

■   SLB provides a control mechanism over incoming TCP SYN floods to the real servers. This can prevent certain types of denial-of-service attacks.

■   SLB can coexist with HSRP to provide a "stateless backup." If one SLB router fails, a redundant router can take over the SLB function.

■   A router performing SLB can also operate as a Dynamic Feedback Protocol (DFP) load-balancing manager. The DFP manager collects capacity information from DFP agents running on the real servers.

Configuration

1. Define a server farm.

    a. Assign a name to the server farm:

    (global) `ip slb serverfarm` serverfarm-name

    The server farm is identified by *serverfarm-name* (a text string of up to 15 characters).

    b. (Optional) Select a load-balancing algorithm for the server farm:

    (server-farm) `predictor {roundrobin | leastconns}`

    SLB selects a real server using **roundrobin** (weighted round robin, the default) or **leastconns** (weighted least connections).

    c. (Optional) Enable server NAT:

    (server-farm) `nat server`

    By default, the virtual server and real server addresses must be Layer 2-adjacent. In other words, SLB forwards packets between the virtual server and a real server by substituting the correct MAC addresses. Server NAT can be used instead, allowing the virtual and real servers to have addresses from separate IP subnets. SLB then substitutes the layer 3 IP addresses to forward packets between the virtual and real servers, allowing the servers to be separated by multiple routing hops.

d. Specify one or more real servers.

■ Identify the real server:

```
(server-farm) real ip-address
```

The real server has the IP address given by *ip-address*.

■ (Optional) Specify the maximum number of connections:

```
(real-server) maxconns number
```

At any given time, the real server is limited to *number* (1 to 4294967295; the default is 4294967295) active connections.

■ (Optional) Assign a relative capacity weight:

```
(real-server) weight weighting-value
```

■ The real server is assigned a weighting-value (1 to 155; the default is 8) that indicates its capacity relative to other real servers in the server farm. For weighted round robin, weighting-value defines the number of consecutive connections the server receives before SLB moves to the next server. For weighted least connections, the next connection is given to the server whose number of active connections is furthest below its capacity. The capacity is computed as the weighting-value divided by the sum of all real server weighting values in the server farm.

■ (Optional) Reassign connections when a server doesn't answer:

```
(real-server) reassign threshold
```

■ SLB attempts to assign a new connection to a real server by forwarding the client's initial SYN. If the server doesn't answer with an SYN handshake before the client retransmits its SYN, an unanswered SYN is recorded. After *threshold* (1 to 4; the default is 3) unanswered SYNs occur, SLB reassigns the connection to the next server.

■ (Optional) Define a failed server threshold:

```
(real-server) faildetect numconns number-conns [numclients number-
clients]
```

■ A server is determined to have failed if *number-conns* (1 to 255; the default is 8 connections) TCP connections have been reassigned to another server. You can also use the **numclients** keyword to specify the *number-clients* (1 to 8; the default is 2) of unique clients that have had connection failures.

■ (Optional) Specify the amount of time that must pass before a failed server is retried:

```
(real-server) retry retry-value
```

- After a real server is declared "failed," a new connection is assigned to it after *retry-value* (1 to 3600 seconds; the default is 60 seconds) time has elapsed. You can also use a value of 0 to indicate that new connections should not be attempted.

- Allow SLB to begin using the real server:

  ```
  (real-server) inservice
  ```

- By default, the real server is not used by SLB unless it is placed in service. To remove a server from service, use **no inservice**.

2. Define a virtual server for the server farm.

   a. Name the virtual server:

   ```
   (global) ip slb vserver virtserver-name
   ```

   The virtual server is given the name *virtserver-name* (a text string of up to 15 characters).

   b. Assign the virtual server to a server farm:

   ```
   (virtual-server) serverfarm serverfarm-name
   ```

   SLB uses the virtual server as the front end for the server farm named *serverfarm-name* (a text string of up to 15 characters).

   c. Define the virtual server capabilities:

   ```
   (virtual-server) virtual ip-address {tcp | udp} port [service service-
   name]
   ```

   The virtual server appears as IP address *ip-address*. It provides load balancing for the specified TCP or UDP *port:* **dns** or **53** (Domain Name System), **ftp** or **21** (File Transfer Protocol), **https** or **443** (HTTP over Secure Socket Layer), **www** or **80** (HTTP), **telnet** or **23** (Telnet), **smtp** or **25** (SMTP), **pop3** or **110** (POPv3), **pop2** or **109** (POPv2), **nntp** or **119** (Network News Transport Protocol), or **matip-a** or **350** (Mapping of Airline Traffic over IP, type A). A port number of 0 can be given to indicate that the virtual server will accept connections on all ports.

   The **service** keyword can be given to force SLB to assign all connections associated with a given *service-name* (**ftp**) to the same real server.

   d. (Optional) Allow only specific clients to use the virtual server:

   ```
   (virtual-server) client ip-address network-mask
   ```

   Clients having IP addresses within the range given by *ip-address* (the default is 0.0.0.0, or all addresses) and *network-mask* (the default is 0.0.0.0, or all networks)are allowed to connect to the virtual server.

e. (Optional) Assign connections from the same client to the same real server:

```
(virtual-server) sticky duration [group group-id]
```

For a given client, connections are assigned to the last-used real server for *duration* (0 to 65535 seconds). Virtual servers can be assigned to a *group-id* (0 to 255) so that related services requested by the same client are assigned to the same real server.

f. (Optional) Hold connections open after they are terminated:

```
(virtual-server) delay duration
```

After a TCP connection is terminated, SLB can maintain the connection context for *duration* (1 to 600 seconds; the default is 10 seconds). This can be useful when packets arrive out of sequence and the connection is reset before the last data packet arrives.

g. (Optional) Hold connections open after no activity:

```
(virtual-server) idle duration
```

When SLB detects an absence of packets for a connection, it keeps the connection open for *duration* (10 to 65535 seconds; the default is 3600 seconds, or 1 hour) before sending an RST.

h. (Optional) Prevent a SYN flood to the real servers:

```
(virtual-server) synguard syn-count interval
```

SLB monitors the number of SYNs that are received for the virtual server. If more than *syn-count* (0 to 4294967295; the default is 0, or no SYN monitoring) SYNs are received within the *interval* (50 to 5000 milliseconds; the default is 100 ms), any subsequent SYNs are dropped.

i. (Optional) Prevent advertisement of the virtual server:

```
(virtual-server) no advertise
```

By default, SLB creates a static route for the virtual server address to the Null0 logical interface. This static route can then be redistributed and advertised by a routing protocol. Disabling advertisement prevents the static route from being created.

j. Allow SLB to begin using the virtual server:

```
(virtual-server) inservice [standby group]
```

By default, the virtual server is not used by SLB unless it is placed in service. To remove a virtual server from service, use **no inservice**. HSRP can be used to provide virtual server redundancy. Use the **standby** keyword to associate the virtual server with the HSRP *group* that is defined on the appropriate interface. Refer to Section 6-3 for further configuration information.

3. (Optional) Use SLB Dynamic Feedback Protocol (DFP).

   a. Enable DFP:

     (global) **ip slb dfp** *[***password** *password [timeout]]*

The router can become a DFP load-balancing manager. DFP can be configured with a *password* (text string) for MD5 authentication with a host agent. The optional *timeout* (the default is 180 seconds) defines a time period when the password can be migrated from an old value to a new one. During this time, both old and new passwords are accepted.

   b. Specify a DFP agent:

     (dfp) **agent** *ip-address port [timeout [retry-count [retry-interval]]]*

A DFP agent on a real server is identified by its *ip-address* and the *port* number used. The DFP agent (the server) must contact the DFP manager (the router) at *timeout* intervals (the default is 0 seconds, no timeout period). The DFP manager attempts to reconnect to the agent *retry-count* (the default is 0 retries, infinite number) times, at intervals of *retry-interval* (the default is 180 seconds).

Example

Figure 4-5 shows a network diagram for this example. SLB is configured on a router to provide load balancing to a server farm of four Web servers. The real Web servers are grouped into a server farm called WWW, having IP addresses 192.168.254.10, 192.168.254.11, 192.168.254.12, and 192.168.254.13. SLB uses the weighted least connections algorithm for load balancing between the real servers.

Two servers are given weights of 32, one server has a weight of 16, and one server has a weight of 8. New connections will be assigned to the server with the least number of active connections, as measured by the server capacities. For example, servers 192.168.254.10and 192.168.254.11 have a weight of 32 and a capacity of 32/(32+32+16+8), or 32/88. Server 192.168.254.12 has a weight of 16 and a capacity of 16/(32+32+16+8), or 16/88. Server 192.168.254.13 has a weight of 8 and a capacity of 8/(32+32+16+8), or 8/88. Atany given time, the server with the number of active connections furthest below its capacity is given a new connection.

A virtual server named ExtranetWeb is configured as IP address 172.30.29.100 to load-balance only WWW (TCP port 80) traffic. Only clients on the 172.16.0.0 network are allowed to initiate connections to the virtual server. New connections are made sticky (passed to the real server last used by the same client) for 120 seconds. SLB also performs SYN guard to prevent SYN attacks of more than 1000 new SYN requests per 1000 milliseconds (1 second).

```
interface fastethernet 1/0
        description Server farm LAN
        ip address 192.168.254.1 255.255.255.0
```

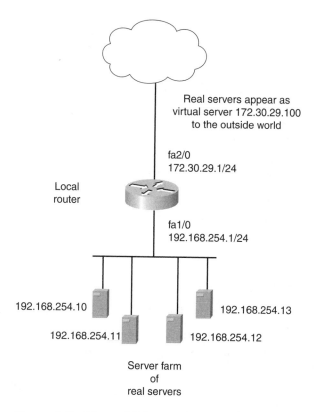

Real servers appear as
virtual server 172.30.29.100
to the outside world

fa2/0
172.30.29.1/24

Local
router

fa1/0
192.168.254.1/24

192.168.254.10

192.168.254.13

192.168.254.11

192.168.254.12

Server farm
of
real servers

Figure 4-5   *Network Diagram for the SLB Example*

```
interface fastethernet 2/0
        description Corporate network
        ip address 172.30.29.1 255.255.255.0

ip slb serverfarm WWW
        predictor leastconns
        nat server
        real 192.168.254.10
                weight 32
                inservice
        real 192.168.254.11
                weight 32
                inservice
        real 192.168.254.12
                weight 16
                inservice
        real 192.168.254.13
                weight 8
```

```
        inservice

ip slb vserver ExtranetWeb
     serverfarm WWW
     virtual 172.30.29.100 tcp www
     client 172.16.0.0 255.255.0.0
     sticky 120
     synguard 1000 1000
     inservice
```

Further Reading

Refer to the following recommended sources for further technical information about the IP addressing and services presented here.

IP Addressing and Resolution

Cisco Router Configuration, Second Edition, by Allan Leinwand and Bruce Pinsky, Cisco Press, ISBN 1578702410.

Interconnecting Cisco Network Devices, by Stephen McQuerry, Cisco Press, ISBN 1578701112.

IP Routing Fundamentals, by Mark A. Sportack, Cisco Press, ISBN 157870071X.

IP Routing Primer, by Robert Wright, Cisco Press, ISBN 1578701082.

Routing TCP/IP, Volume 1, by Jeff Doyle, Cisco Press, ISBN 1578700418.

HSRP

Advanced IP Network Design, by Alvaro Retana, Don Slice, and Russ White, Cisco Press, ISBN 1578700973.

Building Cisco Multilayer Switched Networks, by Karen Webb, Cisco Press, ISBN 1578700930.

DHCP

"The DHCP FAQ" at www.dhcp-handbook.com/dhcp_faq.html.

The DHCP Handbook: Understanding, Deploying, and Managing Automated Configuration Services, by Ralph Droms and Ted Lemon, New Riders Publishing, ISBN 1578701376.

Mobile IP

"Mobile Networking Through Mobile IP" at www.computer.org/internet/v2n1/perkins.htm.

Mobile IP: Design Principles and Practices, by Perkins, Alpert, and Woolf, Addison Wesley Longman, ISBN 0201634694.

Network Address Translation

Advanced IP Network Design, by Alvaro Retana, Don Slice, and Russ White, Cisco Press, ISBN: 1578700973.

Server Load Balancing

"Cisco IOS Server Load Balancing and the Catalyst 6000 Family of Switches," a Cisco white paper, at www.cisco.com/warp/customer/cc/pd/si/casi/ca6000/tech/ios6k_wp.htm.

"The Cisco Dynamic Feedback Protocol," a Cisco white paper, at www.cisco.com/warp/public/cc/pd/ibsw/mulb/tech/dfp_wp.htm.

Chapter 5

IPv6 Addressing and Services

This chapter presents background and configuration information on IPv6 addressing and services provided by the router, with a focus on the following topics:

- **5-1: IP Addressing:** IPv6 addresses must be assigned to an interface for the router to pass IPv6 traffic. This section covers the various types of IPv6 addresses (unicast, multicast, and anycast) and configuring IPv6 addresses.

- **5-2: Dynamic Host Configuration Protocol Version 6 (DHCPv6):** Dynamic Host Configuration Protocol (DHCP) is a client server protocol that enables clients to be configured with the appropriate IP configuration parameters via the DHCP server process. This section discusses how a router can be configured to act as a DHCP server.

- **5-3: Gateway Load Balancing Protocol Version 6 (GLBPv6):** While IPv6 routing protocols can ensure router-to-router resilience, a first-hop redundancy protocol ensures host-to-router resilience. This section discusses how to configure the Gateway Load Balancing Protocol (GLBP) for IPv6 so that network traffic can be load shared across a group of redundant routers.

- **5-4: Hot Standby Router Protocol for IPv6 (HSRP):** HSRP can be used as an alternative to GLBP. Although not enabling for the same granularity of load sharing features, HSRP does protect data traffic if a gateway failure occurs.

- **5-5: Mobile IPv6:** With the introduction of more and more wireless technologies, it is becoming important to manage IP addressing for "roaming" users, who might travel to different access points in the network. This section describes how to configure mobile IPv6 services so that mobile or "roaming" users can maintain their IPv6 addresses wherever they are connected to the network.

- **5-6: Network Address Translation-Protocol Translation (NAT-PT):** Network Address Translation-Protocol Translation (NAT-PT) is an IPv6 to IPv4 translation mechanism. With NAT-PT, devices running a single version of the Internet Protocol (IP) protocol may communicate with devices running a different version of IP.

■ **5-7: Tunneling:** Tunneling allows a host running a version of IP to communicate to across a network that is running a different version of IP. With tunneling, the end devices share the same version of IP, but the transport network runs a different version. This section discusses the common tunneling configurations, including Generic Route Encapsulation (GRE), 6to4, and Intra-Site Automatic Tunnel Addressing Protocol (ISATAP) tunnels.

IPv6 (RFC 2460) is the latest version of the Internet Protocol (IP). Some of the enhancements in IPv6 include

■ **Increased address size:** IPv6 increases the address size from 32 bits to 128 bits. This increase adds more levels of addressing hierarchy, simpler auto-configuration, and greater scalability.

■ **Simpler header format:** Some IPv4 header fields are removed or made optional with IPv6. This not only saves bandwidth but also reduces packet processing time.

■ **New flow label capability:** A new flow label capability offers greater granularity for quality of service.

■ **Authentication and privacy capabilities:** There are new options to support authentication, integrity, and confidentiality. All IPv6 nodes must now support IPsec.

■ **Support for new options:** IPv6 header options make it easier to add new features in the future.

5-1: IPv6 Addressing

While IPv4 addresses were 32 bits in length, IPv6 addresses are 128 bits. Addresses are written as a sequence of eight sets of four hexadecimal digits separated by colons. These addresses can be shortened by eliminating leading zeros in each set of four digits and by replacing a single contiguous all zero set with a double colon. For example, the address 3FFE:3700:0200:00FF:0000:0000:0000:0001 can be shorted to 3FFE:3700:200:FF::1 by removing leading zeros and replacing the contiguous sets of zeros with a double colon.

Note   The IPv6 loopback address is 0:0:0:0:0:0:0:1, or ::1 in compressed format. This address is functionally equivalent to the IPv4 127.0.0.1 loopback address.

IPv6 defines three types of addresses: unicast, multicast, and anycast. There is no broadcast address like there is with IPv4. That function in IPv6 is provided by multicast addresses. Unicast and multicast addresses serve the same function as IPv4 unicast and multicast addresses. An anycast address specifies a set of hosts or interfaces that all share the same address. For example, an organization might use a single anycast address for all internal DNS servers. A packet sent to an anycast address is delivered to the closest interface or host identified by the anycast address.

There are four types of IPv6 unicast addresses:

- Aggregatable global

- Link local

- IPv4-compatible

- Locally unique addresses

Aggregatable global addresses are addresses that are globally unique that are allocated from Internet service providers (ISP) to organizations, who in turn can further allocate the addresses among networks. The capability to aggregate many IPv6 addresses into a single address allows for the core Internet routing tables to remain small. Aggregatable global IPv6 addresses include a global routing prefix, a subnet ID, and a 64-bit interface ID. In addition, all aggregatable global addresses begin with the first three bits set to a value between 001 and 111 in binary (2000::/3 – E000::/3 in hexadecimal). Interface IDs should be in the Extended Unique Identifier (EUI-64) format. The EUI-64 format takes the 48-bit MAC address, splits it into two parts, and adds FF-FE in the middle. In addition, the seventh bit of the first octet is set to either zero, to indicate a locally administered identifier, or one to indicate a globally unique interface identifier. For example, a host on the 2001:1::/64 network with a MAC address of 01-2C-D5-00-9A-41 would have the IPv6 address 2001:1::12C:D5FF:FE00:9A41/64 in the EUI-64 format.

Note For interfaces that do not have MAC addresses (for example, serial interfaces), the MAC address used to generate the EUI-64 address is the first MAC address from a pool of MAC addresses in the router. For tunnel interfaces, the interface ID is the IPv4 address assigned to the tunnel interface with all zeros in the high-order 32 bits of the identifier.

Link-local addresses are addresses local to a particular link. In other words, routers do not forward packets that have link-local addresses as the source or destination to other links. Link-local addresses are used for the neighbor discovery protocol, stateless autoconfiguration, and some routing protocols. Link-local addresses begin with FE80::/10 and include an interface ID in the EUI-64 format (for example, FE80::93A2:99FF:FE0A:2B/10).

IPv4-compatible IPv6 addresses are used on dual-stack hosts (that is, hosts that run both the IPv4 and IPv6 protocol stacks). This transitional approach to addresses puts zeros in the high-order 96 bits and the IPv4 address in the low-order 32 bits of the address. For example, the IPv4 address 192.168.1.1 would be translated to the IPv6 address ::192.168.1.1.

Unique local addresses are globally unique but are intended for local communications. Therefore, unique local addresses are not routed on the Internet. These addresses start with a prefix of FC00::/7. The eighth bit is set to 1 to indicate that the prefix is locally assigned. (Zero is not currently used at the time of this writing.) This is then followed by a 41-bit global prefix, a 16-bit subnet ID, and finally an interface ID in the EUI-64 format (for example, FC00:912C:3301:B700:014C:33FF:FE01:3B1).

IPv6 multicast addresses work the same way as IPv4 multicast addresses. They begin with a prefix of FF00::/8. Whenever an interface is assigned an IPv6 global address, the interface automatically joins the all-nodes link-local multicast group (FF02::1), all-routers link-local multicast group (FF02::2), and solicited-node multicast group (FF02:0:0:0:0:1:FF00::/104).

Configuration

1. (Required) Configure an IPv6 address on an interface:

   ```
   (interface) ipv6 address address/prefix-length eui-64
   ```

   Only the first 64 bits of the IPv6 are required; the last 64 bits are automatically computed from the interface ID using the EUI-64 format.

2. (Optional) Configure a link-local address:

   ```
   (interface) ipv6 address address/prefix-length link-local
   ```

   Link-local addresses are automatically configured when IPv6 is enabled on an interface. IPv6 is enabled on an interface whenever an IPv6 address is configured on the interface or when the interface command **ipv6 enable** is configured. Although link-local addresses are automatically configured, you can override this and enter your own link-local address if you prefer.

3. (Optional) Configure an anycast address:

   ```
   (interface) ipv6 address address/prefix-length anycast
   ```

   Adding the keyword **anycast** designates the IPv6 address as an anycast address.

4. (Required) Enable the forwarding of IPv6 unicast packets:

   ```
   (config) ipv6 unicast-routing
   ```

   To route IPv6 packets, you must enable IPv6 unicast routing.

Example

In the following example, a router is configured with an IPv6 address. The EUI-64 interface ID is used in the low-order 64 bits. In addition, IPv6 unicast routing is enabled to allow for the forwarding of IPv6 packets.

```
interface fastethernet0/0
 ipv6 address 2001:E41:8F90:4::/64 eui-64
ipv6 unicast-routing
```

5-2: Dynamic Host Configuration Protocol (DHCP) Version 6

- Cisco routers can provide DHCPv6 services for hosts.

- DHCPv6 provides dynamic allocation of host IP addressing and configuration parameters for network devices.

- DHCPv6 is a client/server model in which the server allocates and delivers addresses to DHCP clients.

- DHCPv6 can be configured to assign default gateway and DNS information.

- DHCPv6 can deliver either stateful and stateless information. With stateful configuration, address assignment is centrally managed, and clients do not use address autoconfiguration or neighbor discovery. With stateless DHCPv6, router advertisement (RA) messages are sent from a router that include one or more IPv6 prefixes that nodes can use; the lifetime information or each prefix; whether the router sending the advertisement should be used as a default router; and additional options such as the maximum transmission unit (MTU), hop limit, DNS servers, or domain search list options.

> **Note**   DHCPv6 uses UDP ports 546 and 547 to convey IPv6 assignment and parameter information. Hosts communicate with the local DHCPv6 router using the all-DHCPv6-agents multicast address of FF02::1:2 with its link-local address (FE80::/10) as the source address.

1. (Required) Configure the DHCPv6 database and activate the service on an interface.

   a. Create a DHCPv6 pool and enter DHCP configuration mode:

   ```
   (global)ipv6 dhcp pool poolname
   ```

   You must create and configure a DHCP pool. The **ipv6 dhcp pool** command with the *poolname* option creates the list and then configures that pool in DHCP configuration mode. You can create pools and assign attributes for an entire network. Network-specific options can then be assigned in respective subnet pools.

   b. (Optional) Configure a domain name for a client:

   ```
   (dhcp) domain-name domain
   ```

   This command specifies the domain name for the client. This option places hosts in this pool in a common domain. The domain is part of the IP configuration parameters.

   c. Specify the DNS server:

   ```
   (dhcp) dns-server ipv6-address
   ```

   This command specifies which DNS server or servers will be used by clients.

d. Create a named IPv6 prefix pool:

```
(dhcp) prefix-delegation pool poolname [lifetime valid-lifetime preferred-
lifetime | infinite]
```

This command specifies a pool name and, optionally, the length of time that the prefix remains valid for the requesting client. For the *poolname*, you can use a text string or a numeric valid (such as 0). The *valid-lifetime* option specifies the time, in seconds, that the prefix remains valid (range is 60 through 4294967295). The *preferred-lifetime* specifies the time, in seconds, that the prefix remains preferred for the client. The *preferred-lifetime* value cannot exceed the *valid-lifetime* parameter. Instead of entering these values in seconds, you can also enter the **at** keyword followed by a date and time when the prefix is no longer valid and preferred. The **infinite** keyword indicates an unlimited lifetime.

e. (Optional) Configure a prefix to be delegated to a specific client:

```
(dhcp) prefix-delegation prefix/prefix-length client-DUID
```

This command manually associates a prefix (and its prefix-length) to a specified client. The client is referenced by its DHCP unique identifier (DUID).

Note   A DUID is an optional parameter to uniquely identify clients. You can read more about the DUID option, and its format, in RFC 3315. To view an example of a DUID address, you can enter the privileged EXEC **show ipv6 dhcp** command that shows the local router's DUID.

f. Associate a prefix and prefix length with the DHCPv6 pool:

```
(config) ipv6 local pool poolname prefix/prefix-length assigned-length
```

This command, done in global configuration mode, defines a prefix and prefix length for the IPv6 pool created earlier. Although the *prefix-length* indicates the number of high-order bits that comprise the prefix (network portion), the *assigned-length* is the actual length of the prefix, in bits, assigned to a client from the pool. The *assigned-length* value cannot be less than the value of the *prefix-length*.

g. Enable DHCPv6 on an interface:

```
(interface) ipv6 dhcp server [poolname | automatic] [rapid-commit]
```

This command enables the DHCPv6 service on an interface. You can either specify a *poolname* or use the **automatic** keyword to enable the router to automatically determine which pool to use when allocating addresses for a client. **The rapid-commit** option enables the rapid two-message exchange (solicit, reply) between a client and server instead of the normal four-message exchange (solicit, advertise, request, and reply).

h. Configure a DHCPv6 database agent:

```
(config) ipv6 dhcp database agent [write-delay seconds | timeout seconds]
```

By default, all bindings are maintained in RAM. To store bindings as text records on permanent storage, you need to configure a database agent. The *agent* can be flash, NVRAM, FTP, TFTP, or RCP. You can specify how often, in seconds, that the DHCPv6 service sends updates with the **write-delay** option. The **timeout** option sets how long, in seconds, that a router waits for a database transfer to complete. The default for both the **write-delay** and **timeout** timers is 300 seconds.

2. (Optional) Configure an interface to be a DHCP relay agent:

```
(interface) ipv6 dhcp relay destination address [interface]
```

By default, DHCPv6 messages are not forwarded across networks. If you have a DHCPv6 server located on a different link than the DHCP clients, you need to confirm an interface to be a DHCPv6 relay agent. Apply this command on the interface connected to the same network as the clients. The *address* parameter is the IPv6 address of the DHCPv6 server located out a different link. The *interface* option specifies which interface the router should use to reach the DHCPv6 server. (By default, the router examines the routing table to determine which interface it should use when forwarding the DHCPv6 message.)

3. (Optional) Inform the clients that they must use stateful configuration:

```
(interface) ipv6 nd managed-config-flag
```

You can inform clients that they must use stateful configuration to obtain all IPv6 information by setting the managed configuration flag. This command sets the flags in router advertisements (RA) that are sent to hosts.

4. (Optional) Configure the DHCPv6 service for stateless configuration:

```
(interface) ipv6 nd other-config-flag
```

To use stateless configuration, create the IPv6 pool, domain name, and DNS servers—the same as with stateful configuration. As before, activate the pool on an interface with **ipv6 dhcp server** *pool* interface command. Finally, to enable stateless configuration, enter the **ipv6 nd other-config-flag** command. This command sets the flags in IPv6 router advertisements (RA) that are sent to attached hosts to notify them that they can use stateless autoconfiguration to assign their IPv6 addresses. Note that other information, such as the DNS server address, still use stateful configuration.

Example

In this example, the DHCPv6 service is configured to use an address pool called *HQ-Pool* with a valid lifetime of 30 minutes (1800 seconds) and a preferred lifetime of 10 minutes (600 seconds). The prefix offered to clients is 2001:5F2:93:: with a prefix-length of /40. From this prefix, the router delegates subprefixes of /48. In addition, the pool is configured to deliver the DNS server address of 2001:5F2:93::53 and a domain name of example.com. Next, the pool is associated with interface FastEthernet0/0 and configured to use the rapid two-message exchange with clients. The router is then configured to store the bindings in a file called *dhcp-bindings* on a TFTP server, which is assigned the IPv4 address 172.16.0.69. Finally, the managed configuration flag is enabled to inform clients via RAs that they should use stateful configuration for DHCP:

```
ipv6 dhcp pool HQ-Pool
 domain-name example.com
 dns-server 2001:5F2:93::53
 prefix-delegation pool HQ-Pool lifetime 1800 600
ipv6 local pool HQ-Pool 2001:5F2:93::/40 48
ipv6 dhcp database tftp://172.16.0.69/dhcp-bindings
interface fastethernet0/0
 ipv6 address 2001:5F2:93::/64 eui-64
 ipv6 dhcp server HQ-Pool rapid-commit
 ipv6 nd managed-config-flag
```

5-3: Gateway Load Balancing Protocol Version 6 (GLBPv6)

- IPv6 Gateway Load Balancing Protocol (GLBPv6) is a first-hop redundancy feature that enables for automatic router backup for IPv6 hosts.

- Clients are configured to use a single virtual IPv6 router as their default gateway.

- Members of a GLBPv6 group elect one router to be the active virtual gateway (AVG). All other member routers are standby virtual gateways (SVG) eligible to take over as the AVG should the AVG fail. The AVG is responsible for assigning virtual MAC addresses for each of the other member routers. The AVG is also responsible for answering Address Resolution Protocol (ARP) requests for the virtual IPv6 gateway address.

- Other routers are virtual forwarders. A router can be a primary virtual forwarder (PVF) or standby virtual forwarder (SVF). Each PVF assumes responsibility for forwarding packets sent to its virtual MAC address. An SVF is available to take over as the PVF should the PVF fail.

- Routers belonging to the virtual GLBPv6 group are configured to use the same virtual IPv6 address. If the active virtual gateway fails, another router in the GLBPv6 group can take over as the AVG.

- GLBPv6 supports up to 1024 virtual router groups on each physical interface. You can have up to four virtual forwarders per group.

- You can configure preemption so that when a router with a higher configurable priority comes online, it preempts the active virtual gateway and takes over as the new active virtual gateway.

- For added security, you can configure MD5 authentication for a GLBPv6 group.

- Like HSRP, GLBPv6 supports interface tracking. If a tracked interface goes down, another router answers for the first router's MAC address.

- Routers send GLBPv6 hello messages every three seconds by default. The default holdtime is ten seconds.

- GLBPv6 supports the load balancing of traffic across routers. To accomplish load balancing, the AVG responds to ARP requests for the virtual IPv6 gateway address with different virtual MAC addresses that represent the other GLBPv6 member routers.

Note   GLBPv6 members communicate with hello messages sent every 3 seconds to the multicast group address FF02::0100:5E00:0066 using a source and destination UDP port of 3222. Virtual MAC addresses start with 0007.b4 and are derived from the virtual link-local address and the GLBPv6 group number.

Configuration

1. Enable GLBPv6 and configure options.

   a. (Required) Enable IPv6 GLBP on an interface:

   ```
   (interface) glbp [group-number] ipv6 [ipv6-address | autoconfig]
   ```

   This command activates GLBP on an interface. The group number is optional (but recommended) and can be any number between 0 and 1023. If an IPv6 address is entered, that address is used as the virtual IPv6 address for the group. The **autoconfig** option configures the router to generate an IPv6 address automatically based on the interface's MAC address. If no address is entered, or if the **autoconfig** option is not enabled, the address is learned from another router configured to be in the same GLBP group.

Caution   Be careful when enabling a GLBP group on an interface before customizing it because the router might take over as the AVG for the group before you finish customizing GLBP on the interface.

   b. (Optional) Configure the load balancing method:

   ```
   (interface) glbp group-number priority priority-value
   ```

   The router with the highest priority number becomes the AVG for the GLBPv6 group. The default value is 100. In the event of a tie, the router with the highest IPv6 address is elected as the AVG.

   c. (Optional) Enable preemption:

   ```
   (interface) glbp group-number preempt [delay minimum seconds]
   ```

By default, a router that comes online with a higher priority number will not pre-empt and take over as the new AVG. By enabling preemption, a router with a higher priority value than the current AVG takes over as AVG. The optional **delay minimum** option enables you to specify a time, in seconds, a router waits before preempting another router.

d. (Optional) Configure the hello and holdtime timers:

```
(interface) glbp group-number timers hello-interval holdtime
```

The default hello time is 3 seconds and the default holdtime is 10 seconds. The hello time defines how long a router waits between sending hello messages. The holdtime defines how long a virtual forwarder waits to hear a hello message from the AVG before considering the AVG down. If you choose to modify the default timers, best practice dictates setting the hold time to $3^{1}/_{2}$; times the hello time. This command assumes the values are in seconds; however, you can specify the time in milliseconds by preceding the *hello-interval* and *holdtime* values with the **msec** keyword.

e. (Optional) Set the desired load balancing algorithm:

```
(interface) glbp group-number load-balancing [host-dependent | weighted | round-robin]
```

The three operational modes for load balancing are the round-robin load-balancing algorithm, weighted load-balancing algorithm, and the host-dependent load-balancing algorithm. With the round-robin algorithm, each virtual forwarder MAC address takes turns being included in ARP replies. With the weighted algorithm, the amount of load directed on the active virtual forwarder is dependant upon the weighting valued advertised by the gateway. With the host-dependent algorithm, the host is guaranteed the same virtual MAC address as long as that virtual MAC address is participating in GLBP.

2. (Optional) Configure GLBP weighting and object tracking.

Weighting and object tracking can be configured to customize the election of virtual forwarders. Interfaces can be tracked so that if the interface goes down, a weight value will decrement. When the weight value is decremented below a defined value, the router will no longer be the AVF.

a. Configure an interface to be tracked:

```
(global) track object-number interface interface [line-protocol | ip routing]
```

Use this global configuration command to enable tracking of an interface. The valid range of *object-number* is between 1 and 500. The **line-protocol** option configures the router to track the line protocol status (up or down). The **ip routing** option verifies that an IPv6 address is configured and that IPv6 routing is enabled on the interface.

b. Configure the initial weighting value and the weight thresholds for an interface:

```
(interface) glbp group-number weighting maximum [lower lower-threshold |
upper upper-threshold]
```

The default weighting value is 100 and the range of possible values is between 1 and 254. The **lower** threshold option specifies a lower weighting value in the range from 1 to the specified maximum weighting value. (The default is 1.) The **upper** threshold option specifies an upper weighting value in the range from the lower weighting value to the maximum weighting value. (The default is the maximum weighting value.) If a tracked interface fails, the weighting value of the router can fall from the weighted value to below the lower threshold. When this occurs, the router ceases to be a virtual forwarder. When the weighting value of the router rises above the upper threshold, the router can take over as the active virtual forwarder again.

c. Specify the tracked interface and, optionally, the value that will be decremented from the weight if a failure occurs:

```
(interface) glbp group-number weighting track object-number [decrement
decrement-value]
```

The *object-number* is the number you specified when you entered the global configuration **track interface** command. The **decrement** parameter specifies the number that a weight decrements by if there is a failure with the tracked interface.

3. (Optional) Configure MD5 authentication using a key string:

```
(interface) glbp group-number authentication md5 key-string [0 | 7] key-string
```

By default, GLBP uses no authentication mechanism. Secure authentication protects the router against GLBP spoofing. GLBP has three authentication schemes:

- No authentication

- Plain text authentication

- MD5 authentication

Of these three schemes, MD5 authentication provides the highest level of security. You can configure MD5 using either a key string or with a key-chain. When configuring MD5 authentication using a key string, you can choose to have the *key-string* encrypted or unencrypted when stored in the configuration file. To leave the *key-string* unencrypted in the configuration file, do not enter a keyword before the *key-string* or by entering **0** before the *key-string* (unencrypted is the default). To encrypt the password in configuration file, enter the **7** keyword before the *key-string* or enter the **service password-encryption** global configuration command.

4. (Optional) Configure MD5 authentication using a key-chain.

Key-chains enable for different keys to be used at different times according to the key-chain configuration. Because brute forcing an MD5 hash takes time, rotating keys periodically makes it more challenging for an attacker to determine the key in enough time to use it when the key is active. Using a key-chain requires you to create the key-chain, add your desired key strings, and add the key-chain to your GLBP configuration on an interface.

a. Create a key-chain and enter key-chain configuration mode:

```
(config) key chain chain-name
```

b. Create a key:

```
(keychain) key key-id
```

Key-chains contain keys, which in turn contain key strings. The *key-id* is a number that identifies a key that contains the key string.

c. Specify the key string for the key:

```
(key) key-string string
```

The string can be up to 80 characters in length and can contain uppercase or lowercase alphanumeric characters; however, the first character can not be a number.

d. Apply the key-chain to the GLBP group on an interface:

```
(interface) glbp group-number authentication md5 key-chain chain-name
```

The key-chain in this command should reference the chain name you created earlier.

> **Note** Key-chains are used for other purposes beside GLBP. They are commonly found in routing protocol authentication and VPN configurations. There are other configurable parameters, such as accept-lifetime and send-lifetime, that you can use to fine-tune how the key-chain should be used. See "Chapter 6: IP Routing Protocols," "Chapter 12, "Router Security," and "Chapter 13, "Virtual Private Networks" for more information.

Example

Figure 5-1 shows two routers configured to run GLBP. The routers are configured to use weighted load balancing and are tracking their serial interfaces. Should the serial interface on the AVG go down, RouterB can assume the new role as AVG. Brett's and Chris' PCs are configured to use the virtual IP address 2001:F012::D38:C677:2925:1 as their gateway address. Finally, MD5 authentication is configured on the two routers to improve security and reliability.

```
hostname RouterA
!
track 10 interface serial0/0 line-protocol
```

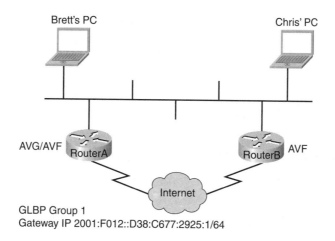

GLBP Group 1
Gateway IP 2001:F012::D38:C677:2925:1/64

Figure 5-1   *GLBP Example*

```
!
interface fastethernet0/0
 ipv6 address 2001:F012::/64 eui-64
 glbp 1 ipv6 2001:F012::D38:C677:2925:1
 glbp 1 priority 110
 glbp 1 preempt
 glbp 1 load-balancing weighted
 glbp 1 weighting 110 lower 95 upper 105
 glbp 1 weighting track 10 decrement 10
 glbp 1 authentication md5 key-string 7 S3cr3tK3y

hostname RouterB
!
track 10 interface serial0/0 line-protocol
!
interface fastethernet0/0
 ipv6 address 2001:F012::/64 eui-64
 glbp 1 ipv6 2001:F012::D38:C677:2925:1
 glbp 1 load-balancing weighted
 glbp 1 weighting 110 lower 95 upper 105
 glbp 1 weighting track 10 decrement 10
 glbp 1 authentication md5 key-string 7 S3cr3tK3y
```

5-4: Hot Standby Router Protocol for IPv6

Hot Standby Router Protocol (HSRP) provides failover for multiple routers on a common network segment.

- HSRP enables a group of routers to serve as a primary or standby router for hosts on a segment by letting the active HSRP router respond to requests whereas others monitor for failure of the active router.

- HSRP provides a virtual MAC address used by the active router running the protocol.

- Devices running HSRP send and receive multicast UDP-based hello packets to detect router failure and to designate active and standby routers.

- HSRP uses multicast packets to choose and maintain the active HSRP router based on configuration parameters.

- HSRP uses the virtual MAC address of 0000.0c07.ac*XX*, where *XX* is the hexadecimal value of the group number.

Configuration

1. (Required) Enable HSRP version 2 on the interface:

   (interface) **standby version 2**

   You must run HSRP version 2 to support IPv6. Version 2 also expands the group number range to 0 through 4095. Version 2 is not compatible with version 1.

2. (Required) Enable IPv6 unicast routing:

   (config) **ipv6 unicast-routing**

   HSRP for IPv6 requires that IPv6 unicast routing be enabled. This command enables the forwarding of IPv6 packets.

3. (Required) Activate IPv6 HSRP on the interface:

   (interface) **standby** *[group-number]* **ipv6** *[link-local-address* | **autoconfig**]

   HSRP for IPv6 uses link-local addresses. By entering the **standby ipv6** command, a link-local address is generated from the link-local prefix FE80::/10 and the interface identifier in EUI-64 format. The router advertises a RA message on the link to announce itself as a default router.

Note   IPv6 RAs are used with the Neighbor Discovery Protocol (NDP). NDP enables nodes on the same link to exchange messages to discover each other's presence, any routers on the local network, and other hosts' link-layer addresses. NDP also includes duplicate address detection that enables a host to verify that the address it wants to use is not in use by another node. Because NDP relies on a number of ICMP messages, you need to be

careful not to filter these ICMP messages when securing the nodes on your network. You
can read more about router advertisements and NDP in RFCs 5175 and 4861, respectively.

When entering the **standby ipv6** command, the *group-number* parameter is optional
(but recommended). If no group number is specified, HSRP uses a default group of 0.
You can either manually type in a link-local address or use the more common method
of entering the **autoconfig** keyword to automatically generate the link-local address.

4. (Optional, but recommended) Set the priority for the HSRP interface:

```
(interface) standby [group-number] priority priority
```

This command enables you to select which router acts as the primary router for the
group. The router with the highest priority number becomes the active router. If there
is a tie, the router with the higher primary IPv6 address becomes the active router. If a
new router is added to the group with a higher priority, it will not take over as the
active router unless the interface **standby preempt** command is configured. The
default priority is 100, and the range of possible values is between 1 and 255.

5. (Optional, but recommended) Enable preemption to force a router to assume active
the active role:

```
(interface) standby [group-number] preempt [delay {minimum seconds | reload
seconds | sync seconds}]
```

This enables the router to preempt (take over) if it determines that it has a higher priority. During standard HSRP operation, when the routers come up, an active router is
selected from the candidates. If a router with a higher priority is activated on the
segment, or if it goes down and then goes up, it does not take over unless the interface is configured to preempt.

The **delay** option specifies how long a router will wait before preempting. The
default delay is 0 seconds, causing a new router with a higher priority value to preempt immediately. The **delay** option requires you to also enter the **minimum, reload,**
or **sync** keyword. The **minimum** keyword specifies the number of seconds to wait
before a router preempts. The **reload** keyword specifies the preemption delay after a
reload. Finally, the **sync** keyword specifies the maximum synchronization period for
IP redundancy clients. In most cases, the default values are sufficient.

Note In large environments, you might have multiple HSRP groups that are all capable of
failing over to each other. You can configure an HSRP group to become an IP redundancy
client of another HSRP group by entering the interface **standby follow** command. Note
that if this command is used, you do not enter any priority or preemption commands for
the group that is followed.

Section 5-4

6. (Optional) Change the standby timers:

`(interface)` **standby** `[group-number]` **timers** `hellotime holdtime`

This command configures the period of time, in seconds, in which the routers send out hello packets to indicate their status, and the amount of time required before the router is considered down. The value for the hold time should always be greater than or equal to three times the hello timer. The timers configured on the active router always override those of the other routers in the group. By default, the hello time is 3 seconds and the dead time is 10 seconds.

7. (Optional) Track an interface to determine which router should be active:

`(interface)` **standby** `[group-number]` **track** `interface [decrement-value]`

This command enables you to decrement the priority value for a standby group by tracking the state of an interface. If the tracked interface fails, the standby group's priority for this interface is reduced by the amount of the decrement value specified. When this occurs, any router with a higher priority and the preempt command configured assume the role of active router. If no decrement value is configured, the default is 10.

8. (Optional) Specify authentication for HSRP:

`(interface)` **standby** `[group-number]` **authentication** `string`

This command configures authentication for the standby group. All routers in the group must be configured with the same string. If a router does not have the appropriate string, it cannot become an active or standby router.

Example

Figure 5-2 shows two routers configured to run HSRP. The routers are set up to track their serial interfaces. If the serial interface fails, the priority is lowered by 10, enabling the standby router to preempt for that group. To provide added security, HSRP authentication is also configured.

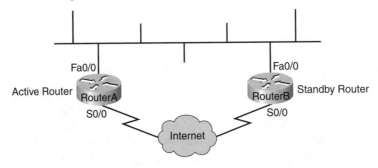

Figure 5-2 *HSRP Example*

```
hostname RouterA
!
```

```
ipv6 unicast-routing
!
interface fastethernet0/0
 ipv6 address 2001:8C1:FF01:9192::/64 eui-64
 standby version 2
 standby 10 ipv6 autoconfig
 standby 10 priority 110
 standby preempt delay minimum 30
standby track serial0/0 30
 standby 10 authentication S3cr3t

hostname RouterB
!
ipv6 unicast-routing
!
interface fastethernet0/0
 ipv6 address 2001:8C1:FF01:9192::/64 eui-64
 standby version 2
 standby 10 ipv6 autoconfig
 standby 10 priority 90
 standby preempt delay 30
 standby track serial0/0 30
 standby 10 authentication S3cr3t
```

5-5: Mobile IPv6

- Mobile IP provides a way for users to keep a home-based IP address while roaming outside their home network. Sessions can be initiated and maintained with roaming users using their home address.

- Mobile IP is useful in wireless and cellular environments, where users need to maintain a single IP address while roaming between networks.

- The three main components in mobile IPv6 are the *home agent, correspondent node*, and *mobile node*. The home agent maintains an association between the mobile node's home IPv4 or IPv6 address and its *care of address (CoA)* on the foreign network. The correspondent node is the destination IPv4 or IPv6 host in session with a mobile node. The mobile node is an IPv4 or IPv6 host that maintains network connectivity using its home IPv4 or IPv6 address regardless of the network to which it is connected. (See RFC 3573 for a comprehensive list of Mobile IP terms and their definitions.)

- Roaming users maintain two addresses: a static *home address,* where application connections are terminated, and a *care-of address*. The CoA represents the user's current location and acts as a forwarding address where all connections to the home address can be sent. The CoA is also used as one end of the Mobile IP tunnel to the roaming user.

- A binding update (BU) list is maintained by each mobile node. A home agents list is maintained by each home agent and mobile node.

- Mobile IP must be configured as a home agent on the "home" network where the mobile node's home address resides. The IPv6 home address (HA) is assigned to the mobile node. Unlike mobile IP for IPv4, no foreign agent configuration is necessary.

- The home agent acts as a proxy for the mobile node, intercepting traffic to the mobile node's home address (HA) and tunneling it to the mobile node.

- Network Mobility Support (NEMO) enables mobile IPv6 networks to attach to different points in the Internet.

- Direct routing is built into Mobile IPv6 using an IPv6 routing header and IPv6 destination options header.

Configuration

1. Enable Mobile IPv6 on the router.

   a. (Optional) Enter home agent configuration mode if you want to configure binding options:

   ```
   (config) ipv6 mobile home-agent
   ```

   This command puts you into home-agent configuration mode.

   b. (Optional) Configure binding information:

   ```
   (config-ha) binding [access access-list-name | seconds | maximum | refresh]
   ```

   If you want to configure binding options for the mobile IPv6 home agent feature, you must do so before activating mobile IPv6 on the interface. The *access-list-name* option enables you to specify an access list to limit responses. All dynamic home agent address discovery (DHAAD) requests and binding updates (Bus) are filtered by the home and destination address. The *seconds* option can be used to specify the maximum binding lifetime in seconds. The default value is 262,140. The *maximum* option defines the maximum number of binding cache entries. If this value is set to 0, no new binding requests are accepted. The default is to enable as many entries as permitted by the memory on the router. Finally, the *refresh* option configures the suggested binding refresh interval. This option is configured in seconds. The default is 300 seconds.

   c. Start mobile IPv6 on the home agent router:

   ```
   (interface) ipv6 mobile home-agent
   ```

2. (Optional) Configure NEMO on the IPv6 mobile router.

   a. Enter mobile router configuration mode:

   ```
   (config) ipv6 mobile router
   ```

This command places you at the IPv6-mobile-router prompt. It also enables NEMO functionality on the router. NEMO is an extension of mobile IP that enables a network to change its attachment point on the Internet.

b. Use the MAC address from an interface to derive the IPv6 mobile home address:

```
(ipv6-mobile-router) eui-interface interface
```

You can automatically derive the mobile home address using this command. The interface should be an interface that has a MAC address (for example, FastEthernet). Alternatively, you can manually configure the home address using the **home-address** command.

c. Configure the home network's IPv6 prefix:

```
(ipv6-mobile-router) home-network prefix
```

The prefix identifies the home network of the mobile router. You can configure up to ten home network entries. If you have multiple networks, you should use the **home-address home-network eui-64** command and not the **eui-interface** command so that the router uses a home address that matches the home network to which it registers.

d. Register IPv6 prefixes connected to the IPv6 mobile router:

```
(ipv6-mobile-router) explicit-prefix
```

This command presents a list of prefixes to the home agent as part of the binding update procedure.

3. (Optional) Configure NEMO on the IPv6 mobile router's home agent.

a. Enable the NEMO routing process on the home agent:

```
(config) ipv6 router nemo
```

This command enables the NEMO routing process and places you into the router configuration mode.

b. (Optional) Configure the administrative distance for NEMO routes:

```
(router) distance admin-distance
```

Administrative distance is a rating of trustworthiness of a routing information source. When a router receives routing information for a network from multiple routing sources (such as different routing protocols), the router chooses the routing source with the lowest administrative distance value. The default administrative distance for mobile routes is 3.

4. Enable roaming on the IPv6 mobile router interface:

```
(interface) ipv6 mobile router-service roam
```

This command enables the interface to roam.

Section 5-5

Example

In Figure 5-3, RouterA is operating as a Mobile IPv6 home agent.

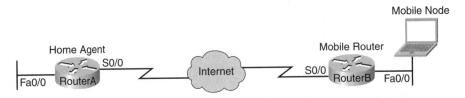

Figure 5-3   *Mobile IPv6 Example*

```
hostname RouterA
!
ipv6 unicast-routing
!
ipv6 router nemo
!
ipv6 router ospf
 router-id 1.1.1.1
 redistribute nemo
!
interface fastethernet0/0
 ipv6 address 2001:F83A:FF11:98::1/64
 ipv6 mobile home-agent


hostname RouterB
!
ipv6 unicast-routing
!
ipv6 mobile router
 home-network 2001:F83A:FF01:1::/64
 home-address home-network ::12
 explicit-prefix
!
interface fastethernet0/0
 ipv6 address autoconfig
 ipv6 mobile router-service roam
interface fastethernet0/1
 ipv6 address 2001:F83A:FF01:1::12/64
 ipv6 mobile home-agent
```

5-6: Network Address Translation-Protocol Translation

- Network Address Translation with Protocol Translation (NAT-PT) is necessary when you need to communicate between IPv6 and IPv4 networks.

- NAT-PT can be implemented as static NAT-PT, dynamic NAT-PT, NAT-PT with port address translation (PAT), or as an IPv4-mapped operation.

- Static NAT-PT is a one-to-one mapping between an IPv6 and IPv4 address. It is useful when you have a server or a few hosts that need to be accessible on a network running a different protocol stack.

- Dynamic NAT-PT enables for multiple IPv6-to-IPv4 mappings using a pool of addresses. When a host needs to send packets through a router, a temporary address is assigned to that host's traffic. The router can be configured with an IPv6 access list, prefix list, or route map to determine which packets are allowed to be translated by NAT-PT.

- Dynamic NAT-PT requires at least one static mapping to a DNS server. IPv4 host-to-name mappings use "A" records in the DNS server while IPv6 host-to-name mappings use "AAAA" records.

- Port Address Translation (PAT), or NAT-PT overload, enables a single IPv4 address to be used among multiple IPv6 sessions. When an IPv6 host sends traffic to the NAT-PT-enabled router, the router maps the IPv6 address to either the IP address on an interface or to a pool of addresses. Multiple hosts can share the same translated address because the router maintains a mapping not just of IP addresses, but of port numbers.

- With IPv4 mapped operation, a user can send traffic from an IPv6 to an IPv4 network without configuring explicit mappings. Instead, a packet arriving on an IPv6-enabled interface is checked against the configuration to see if the packet is allowed to be translated. If it is, the last 32 bits of the destination IPv6 address is used as the IPv4 destination address.

Note Just as with NAT for IPv4, NAT-PT might cause problems with certain applications. For example, problems often occur when trying to implement IPsec or Voice over IP (VoIP) through NAT-PT. Cisco provides a limited Application Layer Gateway (ALG) support for some common services (for example, ICMP, FTP, DNS) to handle services that might otherwise be problematic when translating between IPv4 and IPv6 networks. Because of these challenges, many engineers look at other tunnel approaches (see "Section 5-7: Tunneling" later in this chapter) and only use NAT-PT when tunneling is not possible. For general information on NAT-PT, see RFC 2766. For specific information about the problems you might face with using NAT-PT in your network, see RFC 4966.

Configuration

1. Configure static NAT-PT.

   a. Configure an IPv6 global prefix:

      ```
      (config) ipv6 nat prefix prefix/96
      ```

      The IPv6 NAT prefix is used to match a destination address of an IP6 packet. If the destination address is a match with the prefix, NAT-PT uses the address mapping rules to translate the address to an IPv4 packet. This command can be configured globally, or you can configure different IPv6 prefixes on individual interfaces. The prefix must be 96 bits in length.

   b. Enable NAT-PT on the incoming and outgoing interfaces:

      ```
      (interface) ipv6 nat
      ```

      Unlike IPv4 NAT, where you configure the **ip nat inside** and **ip nat outside** commands on the inside and outside interfaces respectively, here you enter only the **ipv6 nat** command on the inside and outside interfaces. The router knows how to perform the operation by looking at what protocol stack is in use on the interface (IPv4 or IPv6).

   c. Configure a static IPv6 to IPv4 mapping:

      ```
      (config) ipv6 nat v6v4 source ipv6-address ipv4-address
      ```

      This command maps the IPv6 address to an IPv4 address.

   d. Configure a static IPv4 to IPv6 mapping:

      ```
      (config) ipv6 nat v4v6 source ipv4-address ipv6-address
      ```

      This is similar to the previous command, but here you configure a static mapping of an IPv4 address to an IPv6 address.

2. Configure dynamic NAT-PT.

   a. Configure an IPv6 global prefix:

      ```
      (config) ipv6 nat prefix prefix/96
      ```

      The IPv6 NAT prefix is used to match a destination address of an IP6 packet. The destination address is a match with the prefix; NAT-PT uses the address mapping rules to translate the address to an IPv4 packet. This command can be configured globally, or you can configure different IPv6 prefixes on individual interfaces. The prefix must be 96 bits in length.

   b. Enable NAT-PT on the incoming and outgoing interfaces:

      ```
      (interface) ipv6 nat
      ```

      Unlike IPv4 NAT, where you configure the **ip nat inside** and **ip nat outside** commands on the inside and outside interfaces respectively, here you enter only the

ipv6 nat command on the inside and outside interfaces. The router knows how to perform the operation by looking at what protocol stack is in use on the interface (IPv4 or IPv6).

c. Configure dynamic NAT-PT using an access list:

```
(config) ipv6 nat source list access-list-name pool pool-name
```

Dynamic NAT-PT can be configured using an access control list, prefix-list, or route map. Using an access control list is the most common method. Any packets arriving on the IPv6-enabled NAT interface will be checked against the access control list. If the source address matches the permitted source address criteria in the IPv6 access control list, that address will be translated to the next available IPv4 address in the pool.

d. Configure the IPv6 access control list:

```
(config) ipv6 access-list access-list-name
(config-ipv6-acl) permit protocol {source-ipv6-prefix/prefix-length | any |
host source-ipv6-address} {destination-ipv6-prefix/prefix-length | any |
host destination-ipv6-address}
```

This access list defines which IPv6 addresses will be translated using the NAT pool. In the majority of installations, you use **ipv6** for the *protocol* (to represent all IPv6 traffic) and **any** as the destination.

e. Configure a pool of IPv4 addresses to be used for dynamic NAT-PT:

```
(config) ipv6 nat v6v4 pool pool-name start-ipv4-address end-ipv4-address
prefix-length prefix-length
```

The *pool-name* should match the pool name you previously specified in Step c. This pool includes the IPv4 address range to be used during NAT-PT translation. Enter the number of bits used for the subnet mask as the *prefix-length* parameter.

3. Configure dynamic NAT-PT with port address translation (overload).

a. Configure an IPv6 global prefix:

```
(config) ipv6 nat prefix prefix/96
```

The IPv6 NAT prefix is used to match a destination address of an IP6 packet. If the destination address is a match with the prefix, NAT-PT uses the address mapping rules to translate the address to an IPv4 packet. This command can be configured globally, or you can configure different IPv6 prefixes on individual interfaces. The prefix must be 96 bits in length.

b. Enable NAT-PT on the incoming and outgoing interfaces:

```
(interface) ipv6 nat
```

Unlike IPv4 NAT, where you configure the **ip nat inside** and **ip nat outside** commands on the inside and outside interfaces, respectively, here you enter only the **ipv6 nat** command on the inside and outside interfaces. The router knows how to perform the operation by looking at what protocol stack is in use on the interface (IPv4 or IPv6).

c. Configure dynamic NAT-PT with port address translation using an access list:

(config) **ipv6 nat source list** *access-list-name* **pool** *pool-name* **overload**

Dynamic NAT-PT can be configured using an access control list, prefix list, or route map. Using an access control list is the most common method. Any packets arriving on the IPv6 enabled NAT interface will be checked against the access control list. If the source address matches the permitted source address criteria in the IPv6 access control list, that address will be translated to the next available IPv4 address in the pool. Adding the **overload** keyword to the end of this command enables port address translation (PAT).

d. Configure the IPv6 access control list:

(config) **ipv6 access-list** *access-list-name*
(config-ipv6-acl) **permit** *protocol* {*source-ipv6-prefix/prefix-length* | **any** | **host** *source-ipv6-address*} {*destination-ipv6-prefix/prefix-length* | **any** | **host** *destination-ipv6-address*}

This access list defines which IPv6 addresses will be translated using the NAT pool. In the majority of installations, you use **ipv6** for the *protocol* (to represent all IPv6 traffic) and **any** as the destination.

e. Configure a pool of IPv4 addresses to be used for dynamic NAT-PT:

(config) **ipv6 nat v6v4 pool** *pool-name* *start-ipv4-address* *end-ipv4-address*
prefix-length *prefix-length*

The *pool-name* should match the pool name you previously specified in Step c. This pool includes the IPv4 address range to be used during NAT-PT translation. Enter the number of bits used for the subnet mask as the *prefix-length* parameter.

f. (Alternative to using a pool of addresses) Configure dynamic NAT-PT with port address translation using a single address assigned to an interface:

(config) **ipv6 nat v6v4 source** {**list** *access-list-name* | **route-map** *map-name*}
interface *interface* **overload**

You can use the IPv6 address assigned to the interface (specified after the **interface** keyword in this command) instead of a pool. You still need to create an access control list as in the previous steps.

4. Configure static NAT-PT.

   a. Configure an IPv6 global prefix:

```
(config) ipv6 nat prefix prefix/96
```

The IPv6 NAT prefix is used to match a destination address of an IP6 packet. If the destination address is a match with the prefix, NAT-PT uses the address mapping rules to translate the address to an IPv4 packet. This command can be configured globally, or you can configure different IPv6 prefixes on individual interfaces. The prefix must be 96 bits in length.

   b. Enable NAT-PT on the incoming and outgoing interfaces:

```
(interface) ipv6 nat
```

Unlike IPv4 NAT, where you configure the **ip nat inside** and **ip nat outside** commands on the inside and outside interfaces, respectively, here you enter only the **ipv6 nat** command on the inside and outside interfaces. The router knows how to perform the operation by looking at what protocol stack is in use on the interface (IPv4 or IPv6).

   c. Configure a static IPv6-to-IPv4 mapping:

```
(config) ipv6 nat v6v4 source ipv6-address ipv4-address
```

This command maps the IPv6 address to an IPv4 address.

   d. Configure a static IPv4-to-IPv6 mapping:

```
(config) ipv6 nat v4v6 source ipv6-address ipv4-address
```

This is similar to the previous command, but here you configure a static mapping of an IPv4 address to an IPv6 address.

5. Configure dynamic NAT-PT.

   a. Configure an IPv6 global prefix:

```
(config or interface) ipv6 nat prefix prefix/96 v4-mapped access-list-name
```

This command can be entered in either global configuration or interface configuration mode. The IPv6 NAT prefix is used to match a destination address of an IP6 packet. The destination address is a match with the prefix; NAT-PT will use the address mapping rules to translate the address to an IPv4 packet. This command can be configured globally, or you can configure different IPv6 prefixes on individual interfaces. The prefix must be 96 bits in length.

The *access-list-name* references an IPv6 access control list that you need to configure. In this access control list, permit the addresses that you want translated automatically into IPv4 addresses.

   b. Enable NAT-PT on the incoming and outgoing interfaces:

```
(interface) ipv6 nat
```

Unlike IPv4 NAT, where you configure the **ip nat inside** and **ip nat outside** commands on the inside and outside interfaces, respectively, here you only enter the **ipv6 nat** command on the inside and outside interfaces. The router knows how to perform the operation by looking at what protocol stack is in use on the interface (IPv4 or IPv6).

Example

In the following example, RouterA is configured for NAT-PT with port address translation (PAT). To allow multiple hosts to communicate between the networks, a pool is created with ten addresses (192.168.1.20–192.168.1.29) along with the **overload** option. In addition, a static IPv4 to IPv6 mapping is created to map the DNS server on the IPv4 network to an IPv6 address.

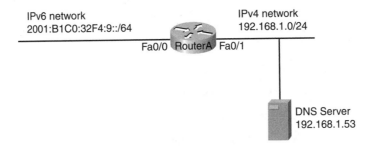

Figure 5-4 *NAT-PT Example*

```
hostname RouterA
!
ipv6 nat prefix 2001:B1C0:32F4:9::/96
ipv6 nat source list natptlist pool natptpool overload
ipv6 nat v6v4 pool natptpool 192.168.1.20 192.168.1.29 prefix-length 24
ipv6 nat v4v6 source 192.168.1.53 2001:B1C0:32F4:9::53
!
ipv6 access-list natptlist
 permit ipv6 2001:B1C0:32F4:9::/64 any
!
interface fastethernet0/0
 ipv6 address 2001:B1C0:32F4:9::/64 eui-64
 ipv6 nat
!
interface fastethernet0/1
 ip address 192.168.1.1 255.255.255.0
 ipv6 nt
```

5-7: Tunneling

■ Tunneling is a common transition approach. Tunneling enables you to carry IPv6 traffic across IPv4 networks (and vice versa). Common tunneling types include Generic Route Encapsulation (GRE), 6to4, and Intra-Site Automatic Tunnel Addressing Protocol (ISATAP) tunnels.

■ Tunnels can reduce the maximum transmission unit (MTU) of an interface by 20 octets.

■ GRE tunnels are ideal for point-to-point tunnels. Both 6to4 and ISATAP tunnels are ideal for point-to-multipoint tunnels.

■ When configuring tunnel interfaces, the tunnel source will be an IPv4 address or a reference to an IPv4 configured interface. For GRE tunnels the tunnel destination will be an IPv4 address. For 6to4 and ISATAP tunnels, which are commonly used for point-to-multipoint tunnels, you do not need to configure a tunnel destination address. The IPv4 destination address is generated on a packet-by-packet basis.

■ Tunnel interfaces should be configured with an IPv6 address. For 6to4 tunnels, the prefix starts with 2002::/16 followed by the tunnel source IPv4 address (converted into hexadecimal). ISATAP tunnel interfaces use a 64-bit link-local or global prefix followed by an interface ID in the EUI-64 format. The first 32 bits of the interface ID are 0000:5EFE followed by the 32-bit IPv4 address (converted into hexadecimal).

■ Use GRE tunnels if you need to tunnel IS-IS traffic.

Configuration

1. Configure a GRE IPv6 tunnel.

   a. Create a tunnel interface and assign an IPv6 address:

   ```
   (config) interface tunnel tunnel-number
   (interface) ipv6 address ipv6-address/prefix-length [eui-64]
   ```

   The tunnel interface must be configured with an IP address. You can use the EUI-64 keyword to automatically generate the interface ID using the EUI-64 format.

   b. Configure the tunnel source:

   ```
   (interface) tunnel source {ipv4-address | interface}
   ```

   The tunnel source must reference either an IPv4 address or an interface with a configured IPv4 address.

   c. Configure the tunnel destination:

   ```
   (interface) tunnel destination ipv4-address
   ```

   The tunnel destination should be the IPv4 address assigned to the tunnel interface on the other router to which you are tunneling. In other words, each router enters the IP address of the far router's tunnel source as the tunnel destination.

d. Enable the tunnel interface for GRE tunneling:

```
(interface) tunnel mode gre ipv6
```

This command specifies GRE as the encapsulation protocol.

Note   GRE uses IP protocol 47. You can read more about GRE in RFC 2784.

---

2. Configure a 6to4 tunnel.

a. Create a tunnel interface and assign an IPv6 address:

```
(config) interface tunnel tunnel-number
(interface) ipv6 address ipv6-address/prefix-length
```

The tunnel interface must be configured with an IP address; 6to4 tunnels have strict rules as to what you can use as the interface address. The IPv6 address must begin with the prefix 2002::/16 followed by the 32 bit IPv4 address used by the border router (converted into hexadecimal).

b. Configure the tunnel source:

```
(interface) tunnel source interface
```

The tunnel source must reference an interface with a configured IPv4 address. Note that when configuring a 6to4 tunnel, you do not configure the tunnel destination. Instead, the tunnel destination is automatically extracted from the interface IPv6 address.

c. Enable the tunnel interface for 6to4 tunneling:

```
(interface) tunnel mode ipv6ip 6to4
```

This command enables 6to4 tunneling.

d. Configure a static route for the 2002::/16 prefix to the tunnel interface:

```
(config) ipv6 route 2002::/16 tunnel tunnel-interface-number
```

You must configure a static route for the 2002::/16 prefix. The *tunnel-interface-number* must be the same as the tunnel interface you previously created.

3. Configure an ISATAP tunnel.

a. Create a tunnel interface and assign an IPv6 address:

```
(config) interface tunnel tunnel-number
(interface) ipv6 address ipv6-address/prefix-length [eui-64]
```

The tunnel interface must be configured with an IP address. You can use the EUI-64 keyword to automatically generate the interface ID using the EUI-64 format.

b. (Optional, but recommended) Enable the sending of router advertisements (RAs) to allow for client autoconfiguration:

```
(interface) no ipv6 nd ra suppress
```

RAs are used for client autoconfiguration. By default, IPv6 router advertisements are enabled on IPv6 configured physical interfaces but disabled on tunnel interfaces. ISATAP tunnels support client autoconfiguration, but you must first enter this command to not suppress neighbor discovery router advertisements. For more on neighbor discovery router advertisements, see RFC 2461.

c. Configure the tunnel source:

```
(interface) tunnel source interface
```

The tunnel source must reference an interface with a configured IPv4 address. Note that when configuring an ISATAP tunnel that you do not configure a tunnel destination.

d. Enable the tunnel interface for ISATAP tunneling:

```
(interface) tunnel mode ipv6 isatap
```

This command enables ISATAP tunneling.

Example

In Figure 5-5, a 6to4 tunnel is configured between two routers. On RouterA, the IPv4 address 192.168.1.1 is translated into the IPv6 prefix 2002:c0a8:0101::/48. This prefix is used on the tunnel interface. This prefix is also subnetted and used as 2002:c0a8:0101:1::1/64 for the IPv6 interface. Finally, a static route is configured so that any traffic destined for the IPv6 prefix 2002::/16 is forwarded to the tunnel interface.

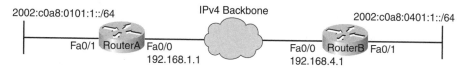

2002:c0a8:0101:1::/64   IPv4 Backbone   2002:c0a8:0401:1::/64

Fa0/1 RouterA Fa0/0   Fa0/0 RouterB Fa0/1
              192.168.1.1   192.168.4.1

Figure 5-5 *6to4 Tunnel Example*

On RouterB, the IPv4 address 192.168.4.1 is translated into the IPv6 prefix 2002:c0a8:0401::/48. This prefix is used on the tunnel interface. This prefix is also subnetted and used as 2002:c0a8:0401:1::1/64 for the IPv6 interface. Finally, a static route is configured so that any traffic destined for the IPv6 prefix 2002::/16 is forwarded to the tunnel interface.

```
hostname RouterA
!
ipv6 unicast-routing
```

Section 5-7

```
!
interface fastethernet0/0
 description ***Uplink to IPv4 backbone***
 ip address 192.168.1.1 255.255.255.0
!
interface fastethernet0/1
 ipv6 address 2002:c0a8:0101:1::1/64
!
interface tunnel0
 ipv6 address 2002:c0a8:0101::1/64
 tunnel source fastethernet0/0
 tunnel mode ipv6ip 6to4
!
ipv6 route 2002::/16 tunnel0


hostname RouterB
!
ipv6 unicast-routing
!
interface fastethernet0/0
 description ***Uplink to IPv4 Backbone***
 ip address 192.168.4.1 255.255.255.0
!
interface fasthernet0/1
 ipv6 address 2002:c0a8:0401:1::1/64
!
interface tunnel0
 ipv6 address 2002:c0a8:0401::1/64
 tunnel source fasethernet0/0
 tunnel mode ipv6ip 6to4
!
ipv6 route 2002::/16 tunnel0
```

Further Reading

Refer to the following recommended sources for further technical information about the topics in this chapter.

General IPv6 References

Cisco Self-Study: Implementing IPv6 Networks by Regis Desmeules, Cisco Press, ISBN 978-1-58705-086-2.

Deploying IPv6 Networks by Ciprian Popuviciu, Eric Levy-Abegnoi, Patrick Grossetete, Cisco Press, ISBN 978-1-58705-210-1.

IP Addressing

RFC 4291, "Internet Protocol Version 6 (IPv6) Addressing," by R. Hinden and S. Deering.

RFC 4862, "IPv6 Stateless Address Autoconfiguration," by S. Thomson, T. Narten, and T. Jinmei.

DHCP for IPv6

RFC 3315, "Dynamic Host Configuration Protocol for IPv6 (DHCPv6)," by R. Doms, J. Bound, B. Volz, T. Lemon, C. Perkins, and M. Carney.

GLBP for IPv6

Gateway Load Balancing Protocol Overview (http://tinyurl.com/y8qpz3g).

HSRP for IPv6

IPv6 Security by Scott Hogg and Eric Vyncke, Cisco Press, ISBN 978-1-58705-594-2.

Mobile IPv6

RFC 3775, "Mobility Support in IPv6," by D. Johnson, C. Perkins, and J. Arkko.

RFC 3963, "Network Mobility (NEMO) Basic Support Protocol," by V. Devarapalli, R. Wakikawa, A. Petrescu, and P. Thubert.

NAT-PT

RFC 2766, "Network Address Translation – Protocol Translation (NAT-PT)," by G. Tsirtsis and P. Srisuresh.

RFC 4966, "Reasons to Move the Network Address Translator – Protocol Translator (NAT-PT) to Historic Status," by C. Aoun and E. Davies.

Tunneling

RFC 2473, "Generic Packet Tunneling in IPv6 Specification," by A. Conta and S. Deering.

RFC 3056, "Connection of IPv6 Domains via IPv4 Clouds," by B. Carpenter and K. Moore.

RFC 4214, "Intra-Site Automatic Tunnel Addressing Protocol (ISATAP)," by F. Templin, T. Gleeson, M. Talwar, and D. Thaler.

Chapter 6

IP Routing Protocols

This chapter presents background and configuration information on the following IP routing protocols:

- 6-1: Routing Information Protocol (RIP)

- 6-2: Routing Information Protocol (RIP) for IPv6

- 6-3: Enhanced Interior Gateway Routing Protocol (EIGRP)

- 6-4: Enhanced Interior Gateway Routing Protocol (EIGRP) for IPv6

- 6-5: Open Shortest Path First (OSPF)

- 6-6: Open Shortest Path First (OSPF) Version 3 (IPv6)

- 6-7 Integrated IS-IS

- 6-8: Integrated IS-IS for IPv6

- 6-9: Border Gateway Protocol (BGP)

- 6-10: Multiprotocol Border Gateway Protocol (BGP) for IPv6

6-1: Routing Information Protocol (RIP)

- RIP is a distance vector routing protocol that uses hop count as its metric.

- RIP has two versions: RIP Version 1 (RIP-1), defined by RFC 1058, and RIP Version 2 (RIP-2), defined by RFC 2453. RIP-1 is the default version of RIP.

- RIP-1 uses broadcasts to send routing information out on all defined network interfaces. RIP-2 uses multicasts to send out routing advertisements on all defined networks.

- RIP-1 is classful and does not support variable length subnet masks (VLSM). RIP-2 is classless and supports VLSM.

- The maximum hop count for either version is 15 hops. A route with a hop count of 16 is considered unreachable.

- When redistributing, a default metric must be defined, or 15 will be used as the default, and any redistributed route will be inaccessible.

- RIP advertises a full routing table every 30 seconds. Routes are marked as unusable if no updates are received in 180 seconds. Routes are removed if no update occurs after 240 seconds.

Note   RIP uses UDP port 520 to communicate. RIP-1 broadcasts out the defined broadcast address for participating interfaces (the default defined address is 255.255.255.255). RIP-2 sends out multicast to the well-known address 224.0.0.9 on participating interfaces. If a neighbor is defined, Versions 1 and 2 send out as a unicast message to the neighbor address.

Configuration

1. Enable the RIP routing process:

    ```
    (global) router rip
    ```

    This command enables the RIP process and places the device in router configuration mode. If no networks are assigned to the process, RIP does not function.

2. Associate the network with the RIP process:

    ```
    (router) network network-number
    ```

    The **network** command associates the classful networks to be advertised with the routing process. If a subnet is entered, it is reduced to the major class address in the configuration. Therefore, any interface on the router that has an address assigned to the major class network becomes an active RIP interface unless configured otherwise.

3. (Optional) Specify the version of RIP that is used:

    ```
    (router) version { 1 | 2 }
    ```

    This configures the router to send and receive only the specified version of RIP packets.

Note   By default, when the RIP protocol is enabled, the router sends Version 1 packets but receives and processes both RIP-1 and RIP-2 packets. When you use the **version** command, the router sends and receives only the specified version. This behavior can be changed on a per-interface basis, as described in Steps 4 and 5.

4. (Optional) Change the RIP send parameters for a given interface:

    ```
    (interface) ip rip send version [ 1 | 2 | 1 2 ]
    ```

In interface configuration mode, the router can be configured to send only Version 1 updates with the **1** option, only Version 2 updates with the **2** option, or both Version 1 and Version 2 updates with the **1 2** option. This command overrides both the default behavior and the global behavior assigned with the router **version** command.

5. (Optional) Change the RIP receive parameters for a given interface:

    `(interface)` **`ip rip receive version`** `[ 1 | 2 | 1 2]`

    In interface configuration mode, the router can be configured to receive only Version 1 updates with the **1** option, only Version 2 updates with the **2** option, or both Version 1 and Version 2 updates with the **1 2** option. This command overrides both the default behavior and the global behavior assigned with the router **version** command.

6. (Optional) Specify RIP to send a unicast update:

    `(router)` **`neighbor`** `ip-address`

    This configures the router to send unicast RIP updates to the specified neighbor.

7. (Optional) Configure an interface to not send RIP updates:

    `(router)` **`passive-interface`** `type number`

    In router configuration mode, this command prevents an interface from sending any broadcast or multicast RIP updates. This does not affect the router's ability to receive or send unicast updates.

8. (Optional) Adjust routing protocol timers:

    `(router)` **`timers basic`** `update invalid holddown flush [sleeptime]`

    In router configuration mode, this controls the frequency of the routing updates and can be used to provide faster convergence. The update parameter sets the rate in seconds at which updates are sent (the default is 30 seconds). This is the fundamental timing parameter of the routing protocol. The invalid parameter, whose default is 180 seconds, sets the interval of time in seconds after which a route is declared invalid; it should be at least three times the value of update. The hold-down parameter sets the interval in seconds during which routing information regarding better paths is suppressed (the default is 180 seconds). It should be at least three times the value of update. The flush parameter, whose default is 240 seconds, is the amount of time in seconds that must pass before the route is removed from the routing table; the interval specified must be at least the sum of invalid and holddown. If it is less than this sum, the proper hold-down interval cannot elapse. This causes a new route to be accepted before the hold-down interval expires. The sleeptime parameter sets the interval in milliseconds for postponing routing updates in the event of a Flash update. The sleeptime value should be less than the update time. If the sleeptime is greater than the update time, routing tables will become unsynchronized.

9. (Optional) Add interpacket delay for RIP updates sent:

    `(router)` **`output-delay`** `delay`

The router paces the outgoing packets of multiple-packet updates by delay milliseconds. The delay can range from 8 to 50 milliseconds (the default is 0). This can be helpful when the sending router is much faster than a receiving router. If the low-speed router is dropping incoming RIP updates, the delay value can be experimentally configured. Start with a value of 10 milliseconds, and increase it until performance is acceptable.

> **Caution**   You must adjust routing timers with great care. If these timers are inconsistent between neighboring devices, route flapping could occur.

10. (Optional) Disable the validation of source IP addresses for incoming updates:

    (router) **no validate-update-source**

    Use this command to prevent the router from discarding an update received from a source address that is "off network"—a device for which the source address is not in the routing table.

11. (Optional) Disable split horizon:

    (interface) **no ip split-horizon**

    As a distance vector routing protocol, RIP implements split horizon. The no ip split-horizon command is used to disable the feature on a per-interface basis. This is useful for protocols such as X.25 or multipoint Frame Relay.

12. (Optional) Enable triggered updates:

    (interface) **ip rip triggered**

13. On low-speed connection-oriented WAN links, the overhead of periodic RIP transmissions could saturate the link and impact data transfer. Triggered extensions (RFC 2091) can be enabled on connection-oriented links to suppress periodic updates and send updates only when a change to the routing table occurs.

RIP-2-Specific Commands

1. (Optional) Disable automatic summarization:

   (router) no auto-summary

   Route summarization is enabled by default. Subnet routes are summarized into classful network routes when advertised. If contiguous subnets are separated among interfaces, route summarization should be disabled.

2. (Optional) Enable RIP authentication.

   a. Enable authentication of RIP packets:

      (interface) ip rip authentication key-chain name-of-chain

This command enables authentication on a given interface using the specified key chain. It allows updates to be validated before they are processed by the router.

b. Select the authentication mode:

```
(interface) ip rip authentication mode {text | md5}
```

This specifies the encryption mode the router process uses to send the key. Plain text is not encrypted, and md5 causes Message Digest 5 encryption to be used.

c. Define a key chain:

```
(global) key chain keychain-name
```

The key chain is defined and named. It contains one or more authentication keys that can be used. Generally, one key chain is used per interface.

d. Configure a numbered key in the key chain:

```
(keychain) key number
```

Keys can be numbered from 0 to 2147483647.

e. Define the text string for the key:

```
(keychain-key) key-string text
```

The authentication string text is used as an authentication key. The string is from 1 to 80 characters (uppercase and lowercase alphanumerics; the first character must be alphabetic).

f. Specify for how long a valid key can be received:

```
(keychain-key) accept-lifetime start-time {infinite | end-time | duration
seconds}
```

The start-time can be specified as hh:mm:ss month date year or as hh:mm:ss date month year (use the first three letters of the month and all four digits of the year). The infinite keyword allows the key to be accepted from the start-time on. Otherwise, an end-time can be specified in the same format, or a duration in seconds after the start-time.

g. Specify for how long a valid key can be sent:

```
(keychain-key) send-lifetime start-time {infinite | end-time | duration
seconds}
```

Time parameters are identical to those in Step f.

Note For proper key chain operation using **accept-lifetime** and/or **send-lifetime** parameters, the router's clock must be set and synchronized to other routers in the network. Network Time Protocol (NTP) can be used as a synchronization method, if desired. The accept and send lifetimes should also be specified with some overlap in case there is a discrepancy in router clocks or a migration in key values.

3. See the following sections for information on route-processing features:

8-3: Redistributing Routing Information

8-4: Filtering Routing Information

Example

Figure 6-1 shows the network diagram for this example. In the example, RIP has been enabled for the 1.0.0.0 network, which enables RIP on each of the interfaces shown here. For the Ethernet interface, broadcast updates are not sent due to the **passive-interface** command. Instead, unicast updates are sent to neighbor 1.2.2.2 on that segment. Globally, IP has been set to Version 1, which means that the Ethernet 0 and Serial 0 interface will send and receive RIP-1 updates only, but the Serial 1 interface has been configured to send and receive RIP-1 and RIP-2. Split horizon has been disabled for the Serial 0 interface.

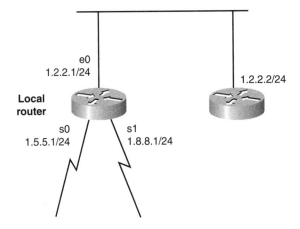

Figure 6-1   *Network Diagram for the RIP Example*

```
interface ethernet 0
      ip address 1.2.2.1 255.255.255.0

interface serial 0
      ip address 1.5.5.1 255.255.255.0
      encapsulation frame-relay

      no ip split-horizon

interface serial 1
      ip address 1.8.8.1 255.255.255.0
      ip rip send version 1 2
      ip rip receive version 1 2
```

```
router rip
      network 1.0.0.0
      version 1
      passive-interface ethernet 0
      neighbor 1.2.2.2
```

6-2: Routing Information Protocol (RIP) for IPv6

- IPv6 RIP uses the all-RIP-routers multicast group address FF02::9 as the destination address for RIP update messages.

- IPv6 RIP uses UDP port 521.

Note   The manner in which IPv6 RIP operates is not that different from RIPv2. Refer to RFC 2080, "RIPng for IPv6," for more information on IPv6 RIP.

Configuration

1.   Enable IPv6 unicast routing:

     ```
     (config) ipv6 unicast-routing
     ```

     As with all IPv6 routing protocols, you must first enable IPv6 unicast routing to allow the forwarding of IPv6 packets.

2.   Enable IPv6 RIP on all interfaces that you want to participate in the RIP process:

     ```
     (interface) ipv6 rip name enable
     ```

     Unlike RIP for IPv4, you do not enter the RIP routing process and specify the networks you want to advertise. Instead, navigate to the interfaces and activate RIP for IPv6. The *name* paramer identifies the IPv6 routing process.

Note   Most of the configuration options available for RIPv1 and RIPv2 are also available for IPv6 RIP. To customize IPv6 RIP, first navigate to the RIP process by entering the global configuration command **ipv6 router rip** *name*, where *name* is the RIP process name you entered when activating RIP on the interfaces. When in this mode, you can customize RIP as you would for RIPv1 or RIPv2 (for example, configuring the maximum paths or redistributing routing protocols).

Example

In Figure 6-2, RouterA is configured for IPv6 RIP. The RIP process is activated on both the FastEthernet0/0 and FastEthernet0/1 interfaces.

Fa0/0   Router A   Fa0/1
2001:429F:DA90:1::1/64   2001:429F:DA90:2::1/64

Figure 6-2   *IPv6 RIP*

```
hostname RouterA
!
ipv6 unicast-routing
!
interface fastethernet0/0
 ipv6 address 2001:429F:DA90:1::1/64
 ipv6 rip ripprocess enable
!
interface fastethernet0/1
 ipv6 address 2001:429F:DA90:2::1/64
 ipv6 rip ripprocess enable
```

6-3: Enhanced Interior Gateway Routing Protocol (EIGRP)

■   EIGRP is a distance vector routing protocol that computes a metric from a combination of *delay, bandwidth, reliability, load,* and *mtu.*

■   EIGRP has an increased network width: 224 hops (the transport hop count is incremented after only 15 EIGRP hops).

■   EIGRP has neighbor discovery by hello protocol (multicast to all EIGRP routers; no ACK is required).

■   EIGRP uses partial routing table updates (reliable multicast).

■   EIGRP supports variable-length subnet masking (VLSM) and route summarization.

■   When the topology changes, the DUAL algorithm tests for feasible successors. If they are found, recomputation is not performed.

Note   EIGRP uses IP protocol 88 to communicate with its neighbors over multicast address 224.0.0.10. If specific neighbors are defined, their unicast IP addresses are used instead.

Configuration

1. Enable the EIGRP routing process:

   (global) **router eigrp** *autonomous-system-number*

   The autonomous-system (AS) is a number that associates EIGRP routers with the same routing domain. Routers running EIGRP with the same AS number can exchange routes.

2. Associate the network with the EIGRP AS:

   (router) **network** *network-number*

   Updates are sent out these interfaces, and these interfaces are advertised. Network numbers are reduced to classful networks in the configuration.

Note If you are transitioning from IGRP, run both IGRP and EIGRP on the transition routers. The AS or process number must be the same in both IGRP and EIGRP to automatically redistribute routes. As soon as redistribution is complete, IGRP can be turned off.

3. (Optional) Enable the EIGRP routing process using a named configuration:

   (global) **router eigrp** *virtual-name*

   As an alternative to configuring an AS number when enabling EIGRP, you can use a named configuration. Creating a virtual name is necessary if you want to configure IPv4 or IPv6 EIGRP VPNs.

4. (Optional) Configure an address family and assign it an AS number:

   (router) **address-family** [**ipv4** | **ipv6**] **autonomous-system** *autonomous-system-number*

   When using a named configuration, you must configure address families and assign the AS number to the address family.

5. (Optional) Specify unequal-cost load balancing:

   (router) **variance** *multiplier*

   The default variance is 1 (equal-cost load balancing). The multiplier argument specifies the limit a route metric can vary from the lowest-cost metric and still be included in unequal-cost load balancing.

6. (Optional) Adjust metric weights:

   (router) **metric weights** *tos k1 k2 k3 k4 k5*

   The default is a 32-bit metric—the sum of segment delays and lowest segment bandwidth (scaled and inverted). For homogeneous networks, this reduces to hop count.

Refer to Section 8-3: Redistributing Routing Information for more information about the metric computation and weight values.

> **Note**   The **bandwidth** command can be used to alter the EIGRP route metric. However, this affects both EIGRP and OSPF, because both use the bandwidth value for metric computation. To affect only EIGRP, modify the metric using the **delay** interface configuration command.

7.   (Optional) Adjust the EIGRP link bandwidth percentage:

```
(router) ip bandwidth-percent eigrp percentage
```

EIGRP limits its updates to use no more than 50% of a link's bandwidth by default. The link bandwidth is defined by the **bandwidth** interface configuration command.

8.   (Optional) Enable EIGRP stub routing:

```
(router) eigrp stub [receive-only | connected | static | summary | receive-only
| leak-map map-name]
```

In a hub-and-spoke topology, there is little need to query spoke routers during a topology change. To limit the query range so that stub routers are not queried, you can enable EIGRP stub routing on the strub routers. Stub routers advertise only connected and summary routes by default. Optionally, you can configure the stub router to only receive routes. You can also configure a leak-map that identifies routes that are allowed to be advertised on a stub router that would normally be suppressed. The leak-map references a route map configured on the router that permits the networks you want to advertise. Ideally, you should configure the hub router to send only default routes or summary routes to the spoke routers.

9.   (Optional) Disable automatic route summarization:

```
(router) no auto-summary
```

Route summarization is enabled by default. Subnet routes are summarized into classful network routes when advertised. If contiguous subnets are separated among interfaces, route summarization should be disabled.

10.   (Optional) Apply summary aggregate addresses:

```
(interface) ip summary-address eigrp autonomous-system-number address mask
```

The aggregate route address and mask are advertised out an interface. The metric is equal to a minimum of the more-specific routes.

11.   (Optional) Adjust hello and hold-down intervals:

```
(interface) ip hello-interval eigrp autonomous-system-number seconds
```

Hello is 5 seconds by default; low-speed nonbroadcast multiaccess (NBMA) media (∂T1) is 60 seconds. The default holdtime is three times the hello interval (15 seconds or 180 seconds for NBMA).

12. (Optional) Disable split horizon:

`(interface)` **`no ip split-horizon eigrp`** `autonomous-system-number`

If split horizon is enabled, updates and queries are not sent to destinations for which the interface is the next hop. Split horizon is enabled by default and sometimes needs to be disabled for Frame Relay or SMDS.

13. (Optional) Enable EIGRP authentication.

    a. Enable Message Digest 5 (MD5) authentication of EIGRP packets:

      `(interface)` **`ip authentication mode eigrp`** `autonomous-system-number` **`md5`**

    b. Enable a key chain to use for MD5 authentication:

      `(interface)` **`ip authentication key-chain eigrp`** `autonomous-system-number`
      `key-chain`

    This enables authentication on a given interface using the specified key chain. This allows updates to be validated before they are processed by the router.

    c. Define a key chain:

      `(global)` **`key chain`** `name-of-chain`

    A key chain is defined and named. It contains one or more authentication keys that can be used. Generally, one key chain is used per interface.

    d. Configure a numbered key in the key chain:

      `(keychain)` **`key`** `number`

    Keys can be numbered from 0 to 2147483647.

    e. Define the text string for the key:

      `(keychain-key)` **`key-string`** `text`

    The authentication string *text* is used as an authentication key. The string is from1 to 80 characters (uppercase and lowercase alphanumerics; the first character must be alphabetic).

    f. Specify for how long a valid key can be received:

      `(keychain-key)` **`accept-lifetime`** `start-time` {**`infinite`** | `end-time` | **`duration`**
      `seconds`}

    The *start-time* can be specified as *hh:mm:ss month date year* or as *hh:mm:ss date month year* (use the first three letters of the month and all four digits of the year). The **infinite** keyword allows the key to be accepted from the *start-time* on. Otherwise, an *end-time* can be specified in the same format, or a **duration** in seconds after the *start-time*.

g. Specify for how long a valid key can be sent:

```
(keychain-key) send-lifetime start-time {infinite | end-time | duration
seconds}
```

Time parameters are identical to those in Step f.

> **Note**   For proper key chain operation using the **accept-lifetime** and/or **send-lifetime** parameters, the router's clock must be set and synchronized to other routers in the network. NTP can be used as a synchronization method. The accept and send lifetimes should also be specified with some overlap in case there is a discrepancy in router clocks or a migration in key values.

14. See the following sections for information on route-processing features:

8-3: Redistributing Routing Information

8-4: Filtering Routing Information

Example

Figure 6-3 shows a network diagram. A router is configured with an EIGRP routing process. All directly connected networks are advertised by EIGRP. On the Fast Ethernet interface, the router performs EIGRP authentication with its neighbors through MD5. The key chain named MyChain has two possible strings, secret123 and secret987. MD5 keys can be accepted all day on January 1, 2001, and MD5 keys will be sent for 24 hours beginning at 1:00 a.m. on January 1, 2001.

```
interface fastethernet 0/0
        ip address 10.1.1.5 255.255.255.0
        ip authentication mode eigrp 101 md5
        ip authentication key-chain eigrp 101 MyChain

key chain MyChain
        key 1
                key-string secret123
        key 2
                key-string secret987
                accept-lifetime 00:00:00 Jan 1 2001 23:59:00 Jan 1 2001
                send-lifetime 01:00:00 Jan 1 2001 01:00:00 Jan 2 2001

interface serial 0
        encapsulation frame-relay
        ip address 192.168.254.9 255.255.255.252
```

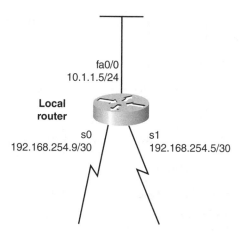

Figure 6-3 *Network Diagram for the EIGRP Example*

```
interface serial 1
        encapsulation frame-relay
        ip address 192.168.254.5 255.255.255.252

router eigrp 101
        network 10.1.1.0
        network 192.168.254.0
        no auto-summary
```

6-4: Enhanced Interior Gateway Routing Protocol (EIGRP) for IPv6

- IPv6 EIGRP requires a router ID before it can be activated.

- Like IPv6 RIP, IPv6 EIGRP is configured on the interfaces that should participate in the EIGRP process.

Configuration

1. Enable the IPv6 unicast routing:

    (config) **ipv6 unicast-routing**

    You must enable IPv6 unicast routing to forward IPv6 packets.

2. Enable the IPv6 process on interfaces:

    (interface) **ipv6 eigrp** *autonomous-system-number*

This command activates EIGRP on the interface. If EIGRP is not already running on the router, a new EIGRP process is started for the AS number.

3. Enter the EIGRP process and configure a router ID:

```
(config) ipv6 router eigrp autonomous-system-number
(router) eigrp router-id ipv4-address
```

IPv6 EIGRP requires a 32-bit router ID used in EIGRP messages to identify the source of the message. The IPv4 address you enter does not have to be an actual address assigned to any of the interfaces.

4. (Optional) Configure a summary aggregate address for an interface:

```
(interface) ipv6 summary-address eigrp autonomous-system-number ipv6-
aggregate-address/prefix-length
```

The aggregate route address and prefix length are advertised out an interface. The metric is equal to a minimum of the more specific routes.

5. (Optional) Adjust the EIGRP link bandwidth percentage:

```
(interface) ipv6 bandwidth-percent eigrp autonomous-system-number percentage
```

EIGRP limits its updates to use no more than 50 percent of a link's bandwidth by default. The link bandwidth is defined by the **bandwidth** interface configuration command.

6. (Optional) Enable EIGRP authentication.

   a. Enable Message Digest 5 (MD5) authentication of EIGRP packets:

   ```
   (interface) ipv6 authentication mode eigrp autonomous-system-number md5
   ```

   b. Enter a key chain to use for MD5 authentication:

   ```
   (interface) ipv6 authentication key-chain eigrp autonomous-system-number
   key-chain
   ```
   This enables authentication on a given interface using the specified keychain, which allows updates to be validated before they are processed by the router.

   c. Define a keychain:

   ```
   (global) key chain name-of-chain
   ```

   A keychain is defined and named. The keychain contains one or more authentication keys that can be used. Generally, one keychain is used per interface.

   d. Configure a numbered key in the keychain:

   ```
   (keychain) key number
   ```

   Keys can be numbered from 0 to 2147483647.

e. Define the text string for the key:

```
(keychain-key) key-string text
```

The authentication string *text* is used as an authentication key. The string is from1 to 80 characters (uppercase and lowercase alphanumerics; the first character must be alphabetic).

f. Specify for how long a valid key can be received:

```
(keychain-key) accept-lifetime start-time {infinite | end-time | duration
seconds}
```

The *start-time* can be specified as *hh:mm:ss month date year* or as *hh:mm:ss date month year* (Use the first three letters of the month and all four digits of the year.) The **infinite** keyword allows the key to be accepted from the *start-time* on. Otherwise, an *end-time* can be specified in the same format, or a **duration** in seconds after the *start-time*.

g. Specify for how long a valid key can be sent:

```
(keychain-key) send-lifetime start-time {infinite | end-time | duration
seconds}
```

7. (Optional) Adjust hello and hold-down intervals.

```
(interface) ipv6 hello-interval eigrp autonomous-system-number seconds
(interface) ipv6 hold-time eigrp autonomous-system-number seconds
```

Hello is 5 seconds by default; low-speed nonbroadcast multiaccess (NBMA) media (T1) is 60 seconds. The default holdtime is three times the hello interval (15 seconds or 180 seconds for NBMA).

8. (Optional) Disable split horizon:

```
(interface) no ipv6 split-horizon eigrp autonomous-system-number
```

If split horizon is enabled, updates and queries are not sent to destinations for which the interface is the next hop. Split horizon is enabled by default and sometimes needs to be disabled for Frame Relay or SMDS.

9. (Optional) Enable EIGRP stub routing:

```
(config) ipv6 router eigrp autonomous-system-number
(router) eigrp stub [receive-only | connected | static | summary | receive-only
| leak-map map-name]
```

In a hub-and-spoke, topology there is little need to query spoke routers during a topology change. To limit the query range so that stub routers are not queried, you can enable EIGRP stub routing on the stub routers. Stub routers advertise only connected and summary routes by default. Optionally, you can configure the stub router to only receive routes. You can also configure a leak-map that identifies routes allowed to be advertised on a stub router that would normally be suppressed. The leak-map references a route map configured on the router that permits the networks you want to advertise. Ideally, you should configure the hub router to send only default routes or summary routes to the spoke routers.

Example

In Figure 6-4, RouterA is configured for IPv6 EIGRP. Both FastEthernet interfaces are configured for EIGRP.

Fa0/0   Router A   Fa0/1
2001:429F:DA90:1::1/64   2001:429F:DA90:2::1/64

Figure 6-4   *IPv6 EIGRP Example*

```
hostname RouterA
!
ipv6 unicast-routing
!
ipv6 router eigrp 1
 router-id 1.1.1.1
!
interface fastethernet0/0
 ipv6 address 2001:429F:DA90:1::1/64
 ipv6 eigrp 1
!
interface fasthernet0/1
 ipv6 address 2001:429F:Da90:2::1/64
 ipv6 eigrp 1
```

6-5: Open Shortest Path First (OSPF)

■ OSPF is a link-state routing protocol that uses a cost metric that is computed using the links' bandwidth.

■ OSPF is a vendor-independent protocol defined by RFC 2328.

■ OSPF uses multicast advertisements to communicate changes in the routing topology.

■ OSPF is a classless routing protocol that supports VLSM.

■ The hierarchical routing protocol supports areas to control the distribution ofrouting updates.

■ OSPF supports routing summarization between areas to minimize routingtable entries.

> **Note** OSPF uses IP protocol 89 to communicate and uses the multicast address of 224.0.0.5 to send updates to all OSPF routers. OSPF uses the multicast address of 224.0.0.6 to send updates to OSPF-designated routers.

Configuration

1. (Optional, recommended) Configure an IP address on a loopback interface to set the OSPF router ID:

    ```
    (global) interface loopback 0
    (interface) ip address ip-address subnet mask
    ```

    All OSPF routers identify themselves and their link-state announcements. Cisco routers use the highest loopback address if one is configured; otherwise, they use the highest IP address on the active interfaces. By setting the loopback address, you control what the router ID will be. This should be done before the OSPF process is enabled. Alternatively, you can specify the router ID with the **router-id** *ip-address* OSPF process command. The IP address specified with the **router-id** command does not need to be an IP address assigned to any of the router's interfaces.

2. Enable the OSPF process:

    ```
    (global) router ospf process-id
    ```

    This places the device in router configuration mode. The process ID is router-independent and is used to identify a particular instance of OSPF for the router.

3. Activate OSPF for a network, and associate that network with an area:

    ```
    (router) network network-number wildcard-mask area area-id
    ```

    The **network** command enables the OSPF process on any interface that falls within the range specified by the wildcard mask. For example, 172.16.0.0 with a mask of 0.0.255.255 would enable OSPF on any interface that was assigned an address where the first two octets were 172.16.

    The area-id assigns those networks to an OSPF area. The area-id can be defined as a decimal area (0 to 4294967295) or as four octets written in IP address format. IP address format can be useful if you are correlating IP subnets to OSPF areas. In any event, the area-id is a 32-bit quantity that can be written in either of the two formats. For example, area 5 can also be written as area 0.0.0.5.

> **Note** An OSPF network must have a *backbone* area, defined by routers with an OSPF area of 0 or 0.0.0.0.

4. (Optional) Configure stub area:

    ```
    (router) area area-id stub [no-summary]
    ```

Specifies the stub flag for an area. If an area is defined as a stub, all routers in the area must have the stub flag set. Using the **no-summary** option for the ABR creates a totally stubby area that prevents the introduction of any external or interarea routes into the configured area.

5. (Optional) Set the cost of the default route generated in a stub area:

    `(router) **area** area-id **default-cost** cost`

    If you set a stub area or totally stubby area, area routers are sent a default route in place of any external or interarea routes. This command sets the default cost for those default routes.

6. (Optional) Configure a not-so-stubby area (NSSA):

    `(router) **area** area-id **nssa** [**no-redistribution**] [**default-information-originate**]`

    Setting an NSSA allows the transport of external routes through a stub area. The **no-redistribution** option is used on an ABR when you want the external routes to be redistributed only into normal areas and not into any NSSAs. The **default-information-originate** option is used on an Area Border Router (ABR) to generate a default route into the NSSA.

7. (Optional) Configure a virtual link to provide backbone connectivity:

    `(router) **area** area-id **virtual-link** router-id [**hello-interval** seconds]`
    `[**retransmit-interval** seconds] [**transmit-delay** seconds] [**dead-interval**`
    `seconds] [[**authentication-key** key] [**message-digest-key** keyid`
    `**md5** key]]`

    The virtual link is an extension of the backbone. It provides connectivity for the backbone for discontiguous areas. The area-id is that of the transit area—the area that must be crossed to reach the backbone. The router-id is that of the complementary router that will form the virtual link.

Note   The **virtual-link** command must be configured on each device that forms the connection from a remote area to the backbone (area 0 or 0.0.0.0). Because this is an extension of the backbone, any authentication parameters or timers must also be set for the virtual link.

8. (Optional) Summarize routes between areas:

    `(router) **area** area-id **range** summary-address mask`

    This command allows an ABR to reduce the number of routes it sends into the specified area by sending the summary address in place of any route that falls within the range specified by the mask.

9. (Optional) Set the OSPF interface priority:

    `(interface) **ip ospf priority** number`

This can be from 0 to 255; the default is 1. It is used to choose the Designated Router (DR) and Backup Designated Router (BDR) on broadcast-type networks. A priority of 0 indicates that the router cannot be a DR or BDR for the broadcast network.

Note   Beware of making the OSPF priority 0 on all routers connected to a broadcast domain. If all of them are priority 0, none of them will be able to form adjacencies. Also, there will be no elected DR.

   a. (Optional) Set the hello interval:

```
(interface) ip ospf hello-interval seconds
```

This specifies the number of seconds between hello updates (the default is 10 seconds). The hello interval must match between neighbor devices in order for the routers to form an adjacency.

   b. (Optional) Set the dead interval:

```
(interface) ip ospf dead-interval seconds
```

This specifies the number of seconds after which no hello updates are received before the neighbor is declared down (the default is four times the hello interval). The dead interval must match between neighbor devices in order for the routers to form an adjacency.

   c. (Optional) Set the retransmit interval:

```
(interface) ip ospf retransmit-interval seconds
```

This specifies the number of seconds between link-state advertisement retransmissions for a neighbor out the OSPF interface (the default is 5 seconds).

   d. (Optional) Set the transmit delay:

```
(interface) ip ospf transmit-delay seconds
```

This specifies the number of seconds it takes to transmit a link-state update packet on an OSPF interface (the default is 1 second).

10. (Optional) Configure interface parameters.

   a. Set the interface cost:

```
(interface) ip ospf cost
```

This manually sets the unitless cost of the interface (1 to 65535). This is useful when connecting to a device that does not compute cost in the same way as the Cisco router. OSPF cost is computed as 108 divided by the interface bandwidth, given by the **bandwidth** command. Default interface costs are then 56 kbps (1785), 64 kbps (1562), T1 (65), E1 (48), 4 Mbps Token Ring (25), Ethernet (10), 16 Mbps Token Ring (6), FDDI (1), ATM (1), Fast Ethernet (1), and Gigabit Ethernet (1).

b. Set the reference bandwidth:

```
(router) auto-cost reference-bandwidth ref-bw
```

OSPF cost is calculated by dividing the interface bandwidth by the *ref-bw* (1 to 4294967 Mbps; the default is 100). The default *ref-bw* is 108, or 100 Mbps, which means that a Fast Ethernet and Gigabit Ethernet link have the same cost of 1. This command allows for differentiation between the high-bandwidth links. For example, if the *ref-bw* is set to 1000, Fast Ethernet (100 Mbps) would have a cost of 1000/100, or 10, and Gigabit Ethernet would be 1000/1000, or 1.

Caution   You should choose a reference bandwidth value that is just high enough to differentiate your highest-speed interfaces. Choosing a *ref-bw* value that is too high will result in an interface cost that looks unreachable. For example, with a reference bandwidth of 5000 Mbps (5000000000 bps) and an interface bandwidth of 64 kbps (64000 bps), the resulting cost would be 5000000000/64000, or 78125—a value that is greater than the maximum OSPF cost of 65535.

A reference bandwidth of 1000 or 2000 would provide a much more reasonable cost for a 64 kbps interface, at 15625 or 31250, respectively.

c. Set the interface to support on-demand OSPF routing:

```
(interface) ip ospf demand-circuit
```

This command allows the router to suppress the routing link-state advertisements over the configured interface. This is useful for an on-demand circuit such as ISDN or a switched virtual circuit (SVC).

d. Configure OSPF network types:

```
(interface) ip ospf network { broadcast | non-broadcast | {point-to-multi-
point [non-broadcast] | point-to-point}}
```

This command allows you to configure the OSPF network type regardless of the media type. By changing the network type, you alter the way the OSPF router forms adjacencies. This command is particularly useful for Frame Relay, ISDN on-demand, and X.25 networks.

Note   A loopback interface will automatically be flagged as OSPF network type "loopback" and will be advertised as a /32 route.

11. (Required for nonbroadcast network types) Specify OSPF neighbors:

```
(router) neighbor ip-address [priority number] [poll-interval seconds] [cost
number]
```

This is used to form adjacencies for routers in nonbroadcast network environments. The **priority** option specifies the neighbor's priority for selection of the designated router for nonbroadcast or broadcast network types (the default is 0). **poll-interval** sets how often to poll the neighbor for nonbroadcast or broadcast network types (the default is 120 seconds). The **cost** option assigns a neighbor's cost. Without this command, the cost is based on the **ip ospf cost** command. On a point-to-multipoint interface, this is the only relevant option.

12. (Optional) Use authentication for an OSPF area:

a. Set up authentication:

```
(router) area area-id authentication [message-digest]
```

This sets up an area to require authentication. If authentication is enabled, it must be configured on all routers in the area. The **message-digest** option sets the authentication type for MD5 encryption.

b. Set cleartext passwords (keys) on the interfaces:

```
(interface) ip ospf authentication-key key
```

This sets the password on an interface in an area requiring plain-text authentication. The *key* argument represents the text string password.

-or-

c. Set MD5 passwords (keys) on the interfaces:

```
(interface) ip ospf message-digest-key keyid md5 key
```

This sets the password (key) for an interface participating in an area configured for MD5 authentication. The key is entered as a text string of up to 16 alphanumeric characters. The *keyid* argument, ranging from 1 to 255, represents one possible authentication key that can be shared between neighboring routers. The same *keyid* on neighbors must have the same *key* string. To change an MD5 key to a new value, configure an additional *keyid*/*key* pair. The routers will roll over to the new key by continuing to advertise and accept the old key until all neighbors have been updated.

13. (Optional) Set the administrative distance for OSPF routes:

```
(router) distance ospf {[intra-area dist] [inter-area dist2] [external dist3]}
```

This command allows you to set the administrative distances for OSPF for each route type (each defaults to 110). Using this command, the router could distinguish between choosing an external route over an interarea route without comparing the metrics.

14. (Optional) Change the route calculation timers:

```
(router) timers spf spf-delay spf-holdtime
```

This sets the delay (the default is 5 seconds) and the holdtime (the default is 10 seconds) for the SPF calculation. The delay is how long in seconds after the topology change the router starts the SPF calculation. The holdtime is how long to wait between consecutive SPF updates. This command can help alleviate the overhead associated with the SPF calculation caused by multiple quick changes in the topology for OSPF routers that might not have much processing power.

15. (Optional) Configure the OSPF process to resolve names using DNS:

`(global) ip ospf name-lookup`

This command configures the router to attempt to do a DNS lookup to resolve addresses to host names anytime a **show** OSPF command is executed.

> **Caution**   Because this command starts very much like an OSPF interface command, it is often enabled inadvertently during OSPF configuration. If this command is inadvertently turned on, OSPF displays might become very slow.

16. (Optional) Enable OSPF redistribution to handle subnetted routes:

`(router) redistribute protocol [as-number | process-id] subnets`

One particular bit of information that is handy to remember when redistributing subnetted routes into an OSPF network is the **redistribute subnets** command. If this information isn't specified, OSPF picks out only classful routes for redistribution. Redistribution is discussed in greater detail in Section 8-4.

17. (Optional) Summarize routes as they are redistributed into OSPF:

`(router) summary-address address mask`

This command allows you to send a single advertisement for all routes redistributed into OSPF that fall within the address space defined by the address and mask options. Redistribution is discussed in greater detail in Section 8-3.

18. (Optional) Force an Autonomous System Boundary Router (ASBR) to generate a default route into the OSPF domain:

`(router) default-information originate [always] [metric value]`
`  [metric-type 1 | 2] [route-map map-name]`

By enabling this command, you tell the ASBR to generate a default route into the OSPF domain. Basically, you tell all other participating OSPF routers that the ASBR is the router to send traffic to if no route exists in the routing table. The option **always** means that the ASBR should always send the route. The **metric** value specifies the metric for the default route (the default is 10). **metric-type** specifies the type of external link advertised into the OSPF domain. This field can be **1** (a type 1 external route) or **2** (a type 2 external route; this is the default). The **route-map** option specifies a route map that must permit default routes to be advertised.

19. (Optional) Prevent OSPF LSA flooding out interfaces on broadcast, nonbroadcast, and point-to-point networks:

```
(interface) ip ospf database-filter all out
```

OSPF floods new LSAs over all interfaces in the same area except for the interface on which the LSA arrives. Redundant interfaces connected to the same area might cause excessive flooding and thus waste bandwidth. To prevent excessive flooding in an area, you can block LSAs from being flooded out of the redundant interfaces.

20. (Optional) Prevent OSPF LSA flooding out interfaces on point-to-multipoint networks.

```
(router) neighbor ip-address database-filter all out
```

You can also block LSA floods out interfaces on point-to-multipoint networks, but you must specify the neighbor IP address.

21. See the following sections for information on route-processing features:

8-3: Redistributing Routing Information

8-4: Filtering Routing Information

Example

Figure 6-5 shows a network diagram. In this example, the OSPF router ID has been set to 99.99.99.99 with the loopback interface IP address. OSPF has been enabled, and interface Ethernet 0 has been placed in Area 0. Interface Serial 0 has been placed in Area 1, and interface Serial 1 has been placed in Area 2. Area 1 has been configured as a totally stubby area. Area 0 has been configured for cleartext authentication. Area 2 is also a transit area for a discontiguous area, so a virtual link has been set up. Because a virtual link is connected to the backbone, the virtual link must also be set for authentication. Interface Ethernet 0 has been set up so that it cannot become a designated router. The hello and dead timers have been altered in Serial 1.

```
interface loopback 0
      ip address 99.99.99.99 255.255.255.255

interface ethernet 0
      ip address 1.2.2.1 255.255.255.0
      ip ospf priority 0
      ip ospf authentication-key KaTiE

interface serial 0
      ip address 1.5.5.1 255.255.255.0
      encapsulation frame-relay
      ip ospf network-type point-to-multipoint
      frame-relay map ip 1.5.5.2 110 broadcast
      frame-relay map ip 1.5.5.3 111 broadcast
```

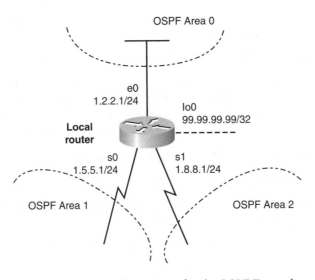

Figure 6-5   *Network Diagram for the OSPF Example*

```
interface serial 1
        ip address 1.8.8.1 255.255.255.0
        ip ospf hello-interval 20
        ip ospf dead-interval 95

router ospf 101
        network 1.2.2.1 0.0.0.0 area 0
        network 1.5.5.1 0.0.0.0 area 1
        network 1.8.8.1 0.0.0.0 area 2
        area 1 stub no-summary
        area 0 authentication
        area 2 virtual-link 100.100.100.100 authentication-key KaTiE
```

6-6: Open Shortest Path First (OSPF) Version 3 (IPv6)

■ IPv6 for OSPF (OSPFv3) is configured on interfaces instead of using network state-ments.

■ Multiple OSPF instances can run over a single link.

■ Link-local addresses can find adjacent neighbors.

■ Authentication is dependent on IPsec (a mandatory feature of IPv6) and not on OSPF.

■ The IPv6 equivalent address of 224.0.0.5 is FF02::5 and the equivalent address of 224.0.0.6 is FF02::6.

- OSPFv3 introduces two new LSA types. Type 8 is used for link-local flooding. Type 9, the intra-area prefix LSA, is generated by the area border router (ABR) and sent into backbone.

Configuration

1. Enable IPv6 unicast routing:

```
(config) ipv6 unicast-routing
```

As with any IPv6 routing protocol, you must first enable IPv6 unicast routing first to allow for the forwarding of IPv6 packets.

2. Enable OSPFv3:

```
(config) ipv6 router ospf process-id
```

3. Assign a 32-bit router ID:

```
(router) router-id ipv4-address
```

Although OSPFv3 is designed for IPv6, it still requires a 32-bit router ID. This IPv4 address does not need to be an address assigned to any interface.

4. Enable the OSPF process on interfaces:

```
(interface) ipv6 ospf process-id area area-number
```

Unlike OSPFv2, you do not configure network statements under the router process. With OSPFv3, you enable the OSPF process on the individual interfaces that you want to particpate in the routing process.

5. (Optional) Configure the OSPF interface priority:

```
(interface) ipv6 ospf priority number
```

This can be from 0 to 255; the default is 1. It is used to choose the Designated Router (DR) and Backup Designated Router (BDR) on broadcast-type networks. A priority of 0 indicates that the router cannot be a DR or BDR for the broadcast network.

6. (Optional) Set the interface cost:

```
(interface) ipv6 ospf cost cost
```

This command operates the same as with OSPFv2.

7. (Optional) Summarize routes between areas:

```
(router) area area-number range summary-address/prefix-length
```

This command enables an ABR to reduce the number of routes it sends into the specified area by sending the summary address in place of any route that falls within the range specified by the *prefix-length*.

Example

In Figure 6-6, RouterA is configured for OSPFv3. OSPF is activated on both FastEthernet interfaces. RouterA is an ABR with a link in Area 1 and a link in Area 0. In addition, FastEthernet0/1 is configured with an interface priority of 0 to prevent it from taking part in any DR/BDR election.

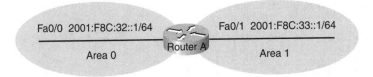

Figure 6-6   *OSPFv3 Example*

```
hostname RouterA
!
ipv6 unicast-routing
!
ipv6 router ospf 1
 router-id 1.1.1.1
!
interface fastethernet0/0
 ipv6 address 2001:F8C:32::1/64
 ipv6 ospf 1 area 0
!
interface fastethernet0/1
 ipv6 address 2001:F8C:33::1/64
 ipv6 ospf 1 area 1
 ipv6 ospf 1 priority 0
```

6-7: Integrated IS-IS

- IS-IS is a link-state routing protocol published by ISO in 1992, based on DECnet phase V.

- IS-IS is a classless routing protocol that supports VLSM.

- The hierarchical routing protocol supports areas to control the distribution of routing updates.

- IS-IS supports routing summarization between areas to minimize routing table entries.

- IS-IS supports area and domain authentication.

Configuration

1. (Required) Enable the IS-IS process:

   ```
   (global)router isis [area tag]
   ```

   This command enables the IS-IS routing protocol. If your router is in multiple IS-IS areas, you need to use the tag option to specify the area associated with the router. Areas are compared between routers to establish levels of domains and how exchanges will be performed.

2. (Required) Configure the router ID:

   ```
   (router) net network-entity-title
   ```

   This specifies the router's area and system ID. The net ID does not enable routing. It is the ID of the router within the areas defined by the **router isis** command. A net is a network service access point (NSAP) using a format such as 47.0004.004d.0001.0000.0c11.1111.00, where the last byte is always 0 (.00). The six bytes directly in front of the n-selector are the system ID (0000.0c11.1111). The system ID length is a fixed size and cannot be changed. The system ID must be unique for each device throughout each area (level 1) and throughout the backbone (level 2). All bytes in front of the system ID are the area ID (47.0004.004d.0001). When IS-IS is used to perform IP routing only, a net must still be configured to define the router system ID and area ID.

3. (Optional) Specify the IS-IS router type:

   ```
   (interface) is-type {level-1 | level-1-2 | level-2-only}
   ```

   A router can be a level 1 router only (intra-area), a level 2 router (interarea), or both level 1 and level 2.

4. (Required) Activate IS-IS routing on the interface:

   ```
   (interface) ip router isis [area tag]
   ```

   If the router has multiple areas, use the *area tag* option to specify which area the interface is operating in.

5. (Optional) Specify the IS-IS circuit type for the interface:

   ```
   (interface) isis circuit-type {level-1 | level-1-2 | level-2-only}
   ```

   Use this command to configure the type of adjacency desired for neighbors on the specified interface. Level 1 adjacencies can be established if the neighbor is configured with a common area. For the **level-1-2** option, level 1 and level 2 adjacencies can be established if the routers have a common area; otherwise, only level 2 adjacencies are established (this is the default). For the **level-2-only** option, only level 2 adjacencies are formed if the neighbors are configured with L2 or L1L2 circuit types.

6. (Optional) Set the metric on the IS-IS interface:

```
(interface) isis metric default-metric {level-1 | level-2}
```

This command specifies the IS-IS cost for this interface. The cost is used to determine the best route. The range is from 0 to 63; the default is 10.

7. (Optional) Specify the hello interval:

```
(interface) isis hello-interval seconds {level-1 | level-2}
```

This command specifies the length of time, in seconds, between hello packets the router sends on the specified interface. The options **level-1** and **level-2** allow you to set the timer individually for each type, except on a serial interface.

8. (Optional) Set the retransmit interval:

```
(interface) isis retransmit-interval seconds
```

This command specifies in seconds how long the router waits between retransmission of IS-IS Link State Packets (LSPs) for point-to-point links.

9. (Optional) Control the LSP transmission frequency:

```
(interface) isis lsp-interval seconds
```

This command allows you to control how often LSP updates are sent out the interface. By setting the *seconds* option, you specify or control how often LSP updates are sent out the interface on a point-to-point link. This can reduce the amount of overhead on the sending link. Or, if this parameter is changed, it reduces the number of LSPs received by the other side.

10. (Optional) Limit the LSP retransmission rate:

```
(interface) isis retransmit-throttle-interval milliseconds
```

This command allows you to control how often the same LSP updates are retransmitted out the interface. By setting the *milliseconds* option, you specify or control how often updates are sent out in a successive manner for the same LSP.

11. (Optional) Control adjacency update settings:

```
(interface) isis hello-multiplier multiplier {level-1 | level-2}
```

This command allows you to control how many packets are missed before the adjacency is considered down. The *multiplier* is the number of missed packets; the default is 3. The multiplier can be set for level 1 or level 2 routers.

12. (Optional) Specify the priority to control which device becomes the designated router:

```
(interface) isis priority value {level-1 | level-2}
```

This command sets the priority sent out on the interface. The device with the highest priority on a multipoint broadcast interface becomes the designated router for that network. The default setting is 64.

13. (Optional) Assign a password to the interface:

```
(interface) isis password password {level-1 | level-2}
```

By specifying the password, you can control which devices the IS-IS router communicates with. Level 1 and level 2 passwords are set independently and are plain text.

14. (Optional) Assign a password to the area:

```
(router) area password password
```

All the routers in the area have to be configured with the same password in order to exchange LSPs. The area password is exchanged between level 1 routers within the area.

15. (Optional) Assign a password to the domain:

```
(router) domain-password password
```

All the routers in the domain have to be configured with the same password in order to exchange LSPs. The domain password is exchanged between level 2 routers within the network.

16. (Optional) Summarize between areas:

```
(router) summary-address address mask {level-1 | level-1-2 | level-2}
```

This command allows you to configure summarization for IS-IS routers when performing redistribution from another routing protocol. You can set summaries for each level. By setting summaries, you control the number of entries in the routing table.

17. (Optional) Generate a default route:

```
(router) default-information originate [route-map map-name]
```

This command allows you to inject a default route into the IS-IS area. Whenever you redistribute, the router does not put in a default route automatically. This command allows the default to be generated. You can have the route created conditionally if you use the **route-map** option.

18. See the following sections for information on route-processing features:

8-3: Redistributing Routing Information

8-4: Filtering Routing Information

Example

This example configures IS-IS for the router Kiddie to be in Area 1 with a device ID of 1. Each interface is configured for integrated IS-IS routing, and a password is configured on Ethernet 0 to prevent unauthorized LSP updates. Also, the priority of the Ethernet 0 interface is set to 90 for level 1 routers so that this router will be the preferred designated router on the segment. RIP routes are redistributed from the 172.16.254.254 subnet from a router running OSPF and are redistributed into IS-IS for level 1 and are summarized on the Class B network address. Figure6-7 shows the basic layout of the router example.

Section 6-7

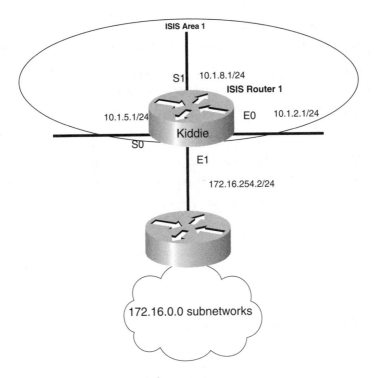

Figure 6-7   *IS-IS Example*

```
interface ethernet 0
        ip address 10.1.2.1 255.255.255.0
        ip router isis
        isis password KaTiE
        isis priority 90 level-1

interface ethernet 1
        ip address 172.16.254.2 255.255.255.0

interface serial 0
        ip address 10.1.5.1 255.255.255.0
        encapsulation ppp
        ip router isis

interface serial 1
        ip address 10.1.8.1 255.255.255.0
        ip router isis

router isis
        net 01.0000.0000.0001.00
        redistribute ospf 101 level-1 metric 40
```

```
        summary-address 172.16.0.0 255.255.0.0 level-1

router ospf 1
        network 172.16.254.2 0.0.0.0 area 0
```

6-8: Integrated IS-IS for IPv6

IPv6 IS-IS operates the same as IPv4 IS-IS. Prior to Cisco IOS Software Release 12.2(15)T, IPv6 IS-IS supported only single topologies. This meant that if you wanted to run both IPv4 and IPv6 IS-IS, the two protocols had to share a common topology, and all interfaces had to be configured for both protocols. Beginning with Cisco IOS Software Release 12.2(15)T, Cisco added multitopology. You are no longer restricted to having the same network topology, and it is no longer necessary to have all interfaces configured for both protocols.

Because IPv6 IS-IS operates almost identically to IPv4 IS-IS (including the CLI commands), only a minimal configuration is shown. Refer to the previous section on Integrated IS-IS for other commands.

Configuration

1. Enable IPv6 unicast routing:

    ```
    (config) ipv6 unicast-routing
    ```

    As with other unicast routing protocols for IPv6, you must first enable IPv6 unicast routing to allow for the forwarding of IPv6 packets.

2. Enter IS-IS configuration mode and configure the Network Entity Title (NET) address:

    ```
    (config) router isis area-tag
    (router) net network-entity-title
    ```

    These commands are the same as IPv4 IS-IS.

3. Activate IPv6 IS-IS on the interface.

    ```
    (interface) ipv6 router isis area-tag
    ```

    This command enables the routing process on the interface.

6-9: Border Gateway Protocol (BGP)

■   BGP is a path vector routing protocol. Routing updates carry a full list of transit networks (*autonomous system paths*) required to reach a remote network.

■   Routing loops are detected and prevented by looking for the local autonomous system (AS) number within the AS path.

- BGP peers are defined in relation to their local AS number. Peers within the same AS form an Interior BGP (IBGP) relationship, whereas peers in different ASs use Exterior BGP (EBGP).

- IBGP peers exchange reachability information with each other and also redistribute BGP information to Interior Gateway Protocols (IGPs) running within the common AS. (IGPs can be other routing protocols such as RIP, IGRP, EIGRP, OSPF, and IS-IS.)

- IBGP peers must synchronize BGP information with IGP information to ensure that IGP routes have propagated across the local AS.

- The Multi-Exit Discriminator (MED) is a unitless metric that can be modified with a route map.

- The local preference is assigned to control the path-selection process. Local preferences are advertised with network prefixes throughout the AS. Therefore, they are significant only within the AS.

- The weight attribute is also assigned to control the path-selection process. Weights are significant only to the local router.

- BGP selects the best path to a destination in the following order:

   1. If the next hop is inaccessible, don't consider it.

   2. Prefer the highest weight value.

   3. Prefer the highest local preference.

   4. Prefer the route that the local router originated.

   5. Prefer the shortest AS path if no route was originated.

   6. Prefer the lowest origin (igp < egp < incomplete).

   7. Prefer the lowest MED (a missing MED is a 0).

   8. Prefer an external path over an internal path.

   9. If synchronization is disabled and only internal paths remain, prefer the path with the closest IGP neighbor.

   10. Prefer the older, more stable path.

   11. Prefer the lowest BGP router ID IP address.

Note   BGP uses both UDP port 179 and TCP port 179 to form reliable transport connections between peer or neighbor routers.

Configuration

1. Enable the BGP routing process, and associate the local router with an autonomous system:

`(global) ` **`router bgp`** ` as-number`

2. Define all BGP neighbors:

`(router) ` **`neighbor`** ` {ip-address | peer-group} ` **`remote-as`** ` as-number`

Neighbors can be specified by IP address or peer group name. A peer group is a grouping of many neighbors that share a common set of attributes or update policies. Each BGP neighbor is defined with this command. For IBGP neighbors, the AS number is the same as that used in the **router bgp** command. The IBGP neighbors must be reachable by IGP routing, and they need not be on the same subnet. For EBGP neighbors, the AS number will be different. An optional text description can be added to the neighbor:

`(router) ` **`neighbor`** ` {ip-address | peer-group} ` **`description`** ` text-string`

Note   IBGP neighbors do not redistribute or forward received routes to all other IBGP neighbors within an AS. Rather, they forward that information to their EBGP neighbors. It is important to configure IBGP relationships with all other neighbors within an AS as a full mesh of connections. If this is too complex, use either BGP confederations or route reflectors.

EBGP neighbors must be directly connected to each other and must share a subnet. In some cases, this is not possible. An IGP or static route should then be configured so that the two neighbors can reach each other. Then, EBGP multihop can be configured:

`(router) ` **`neighbor`** ` ip-address ` **`ebgp-multihop`** ` ttl`

The *ttl* value specifies a time-to-live in the form of a hop count (1 to 255; the default is 255 hops).

3. (Optional) Configure an interface to use for BGP TCP connections:

`(router) ` **`neighbor`** ` {ip-address | peer-group} ` **`update-source`** ` interface`

Ordinarily, BGP uses a source address from the "best local interface" when communicating with an IBGP neighbor peer. This address might not always be optimal, especially when a loopback interface is desired. To override the default source address, you can specify an *interface*. Typically, a loopback interface is used for IBGP peers, because it is always up and available. If used, the loopback interface should be reachable from the remote IBGP neighbors.

4. Define the networks to advertise by BGP as originating from the local AS. Specify a list of up to 200 networks:

```
(router) network network-number [mask mask]
```

Specified networks must be present in the routing table, as directly connected, static routes, or learned from dynamic routing processes. The optional *mask* allows networks to be supernetted.

-or-

Redistribute routes from an IGP:

```
(router) redistribute protocol [process-id] ... [route-map map]
```

Normally, local networks (within the local AS) should be specified with the **network** command. However, IGP routes can be redistributed into BGP if necessary. A route map should be used to filter the IGP routes that are redistributed.

5. (Optional) Propagate aggregate or supernet addresses to reduce the routing table size:

```
(router) aggregate-address address mask [as-set] [summary-only]
  [suppress-map map] [advertise-map map] [attribute-map map]
```

The aggregate address specified is generated if there is at least one more-specific entry in the BGP table. Both the aggregate address and more-specific addresses are advertised unless you use the summary-only keyword. If an aggregate is composed of more-specific routes from several ASs, using **as-set** causes the set of originating AS numbers to be advertised too.

Route maps can be used to suppress more-specific routes (**suppress-map**) or to generate a certain aggregate address to advertise (**advertise-map**). If needed, you can modify BGP attributes of the aggregate (**attribute-map**). For each, you can use a route map with **match ip address** or **match as-path** to select routes. You modify attributes using **set** commands in the route map.

6. (Optional) Disable synchronization between BGP and an IGP:

```
(router) no synchronization
```

By default, BGP waits until a local IGP propagates routing information across the AS. BGP synchronization is enabled, and routes to be advertised by BGP are tested for inclusion in the IGP tables. If synchronization is not needed, you can disable it.

7. (Optional) Configure attributes and metrics for best path selection.

  a. Network weight is locally significant; it is not advertised or propagated.

   Set the weight attribute according to the BGP neighbor:

```
(router) neighbor {ip-address | peer-group} weight weight
```

The weight ranges from 0 to 65535. If the router originates a path, the weight defaults to 32768, and nonoriginated paths default to a weight of 0. A path with a higher weight value is preferred.

-or-

Set the weight attribute using a route map:

```
(route-map) set weight weight
```

(See Step 12 for more information on route map usage.)

b. Local preference is propagated within the local AS.

Set the default local preference value for updates within the AS:

```
(router) bgp default local-preference value
```

Local preference ranges from 0 to 4294967295 and defaults to 100. A path with a higher local preference is preferred.

-or-

Set the local preference using a route map:

```
(route-map) set local-preference value
```

(See Step 12 for more information on route map usage.)

c. The metric or MED is exchanged between ASs. The value is received but is reset to 0 when it is passed along to another AS.

Set the default MED of routes redistributed into BGP:

```
(router) default-metric med
```

The MED value ranges from 1 to 4294967295. A path with a *lower* MED value is preferred.

-or-

Set the MED using a route map:

```
(route-map) set metric metric
```

(See Step 12 for more information on route map usage.)

8. (Optional) Configure the community attribute of advertised routes.

Note   Normally, a router only compares metrics from neighbors in a common AS. To compare metrics for paths advertised by all neighbors, regardless of AS, use this command:

```
(router) bgp always-compare-med
```

a. Use a route map to set the community value:

```
(route-map) set community community [additive]
```

(See Step 12 for more information about route map usage.) A route map is used to match routes and set the community attribute so that routes are grouped into common communities. A community value is a number from 0 to 4294967200, arbitrarily chosen, and the community attribute is a collection of these values. A route can be a member of more than one community. The **additive** keyword adds the new value to the list of existing values. Predefined values are **internet** (advertise the route to the Internet community, or all peers), **no-export** (don't advertise the route to EBGP peers), and **no-advertise** (don't advertise the route to any peer).

b. Send the community attribute to BGP neighbors:

```
(router) neighbor {ip-address | peer-group} send-community
```

By default, the community attribute is not passed to neighbors in BGP updates. This command allows the attribute to be sent to BGP peers.

9. (Optional) Use community filtering to match incoming path advertisements.

a. Configure a community list to perform the matching:

```
(global) ip community-list community-list-number {permit | deny} community-
value
```

One or more community list statements with a common list number (1 to 99) are used in sequential order to match a community value. The value can be a single value or a string of values separated by spaces. Values range from 0 to 4294967200 and can include the predefined **internet, no-export,** and **no-advertise** values. An implicit **deny all** statement exists at the end of the community list.

b. Configure a route map to apply the community list:

```
(route-map) match community-list community-list-number [exact]
```

The route map uses the *community-list-number* argument, a value from 1 to 99, to match community values. The **exact** keyword is used to exactly match the list of community values.

10. (Optional) Use route filtering of network numbers to restrict routing information that is learned or advertised.

a. Use a prefix list to perform filtering:

```
(router) neighbor {ip-address | peer-group} prefix-list prefix-list-name

  {in | out}
```

The prefix list named *prefix-list-name* is used to permit or deny networks based on a number of leading bits (prefixes) in the network numbers. Refer to Section 14-1 for more information on prefix lists.

b. Create a numbered standard access list to perform the filtering:

```
(global) access-list list-number {deny | permit} network wildcard
```

The access list, numbered 1 to 99, either denies or permits the network number specified (with the wildcard applied). 0 matches exactly, and 1 matches anything).

Note In the case of filtering a supernet network number, an extended access list must be used to match both network number and subnet mask:

```
(global) access-list list-number {deny | permit} ip network net-wildcard
   subnet-mask mask-wildcard
```

c. Create a named standard access list to perform filtering:

```
(global) ip access-list standard name
```

```
(access-list) {permit | deny} network [wildcard]
```

d. Use a distribute list to apply the standard or extended IP access list for filtering:

```
(router) neighbor {ip-address | peer-group} distribute-list access-list
{in | out}
```

The access list (either numbered or named) is used to filter the network numbers in routing updates to or from a specific neighbor. The **in** and **out** keywords specify the filter direction.

11. (Optional) Use path filtering of AS paths to control inbound and outbound BGP updates.

a. Create an AS path access list to perform AS path filtering:

```
(global) ip as-path access-list as-path-list-number {permit | deny}
   as-regular-expression
```

The as-path-list-number argument (with values ranging from 1 to 199) either permits or denies BGP updates based on matching the as-regular-expression against the AS path contents. Refer to Section 14-5, "Regular Expressions," for complete instructions on creating an AS regular expression. For the purposes of BGP AS path matching, refer to Table 6-1, which lists common regular expressions.

b. Use a filter list to apply the AS path access list for filtering:

```
(router) neighbor {ip-address | peer-group} filter-list as-path-list-num
   {in | out}
```

The AS path access list filters the AS paths in routing updates to or from a specific neighbor. You can use the **in** and **out** keywords to specify the filter direction. Only one **in** and one **out** AS path filter can be configured.

Table 6-1 *Common Regular Expressions*

Regular Expression	Example	Result
.*	.*	Matches any path information.
^n$	^400$	Matches paths that start with AS n and end with AS n. (AS n is the only one in the path.)
^$	^$	Matches paths that originate from the local AS.
^n_ ^n_.*	^400_ ^400_.*	Matches paths that start with AS n. An update came from AS n. An alternative expression has the same results.
_n$.*_n$	_400$.*_400$	Matches paths that end with AS n. An update originated in AS n. An alternative expression has the same results.
_n_	_400_	Matches paths that pass through AS n.
_n_m_	_400_ 300_	Matches paths that pass through exactly AS n and then AS m.

Note Recall that as each BGP peer sends an update, it *prepends* its own AS number onto the AS path. This means that the AS path builds from right to left, such that the originating AS is on the rightmost end of the AS path string. The last peer to send an update has its AS on the leftmost end of the path. To test the results of a regular expression prior to using it in an AS path access list, use the **show ip bgp regexp** *regular-expression* command.

12. (Optional) Use route maps to control or modify inbound and outbound BGP updates.

a. Create a route map to match and modify BGP attributes:

```
(global) route-map map-name [permit | deny] [sequence-num]
```

The route map can be made up of one or more statements evaluated in sequential order, according to the optional sequence number. The **permit** keyword (the default) causes the **route-map** statement to be evaluated and an action taken.

You can use one or more optional **match** statements, along with optional **set** commands. If you configure more than one **match** statement, all of the conditions must be met before the **set** action is taken. If all route map statements are evaluated and no match is found, the update is not sent or received.

1. Configure a match condition. Match an AS path in the update:

```
(route-map) match as-path as-path-list
```

An *as-path-list* (numbered from 1 to 199) is used to match an AS regular expression, as in Step 11a.

Match a network number in the update:

```
(route-map) match ip address access-list [...access-list]
```

Network numbers in the update are matched against the numbered or named IP access list (either standard or extended). Refer to Step 10a or 10b.

Match a community in the update:

```
(route-map) match community-list community-list [exact]
```

A community list (1 to 99) is used to match community values. The **exact** keyword is used to match the list of community values exactly. Refer to Step 9a.

2. Configure a **set** command to modify an attribute.

Modify the AS path:

```
(route-map) set as-path prepend as-path-string
```

The *as-path-string* is prepended to the AS path attribute. By prepending the local AS multiple times, you can modify the path length to influence the path-selection process on a distant peer.

```
Modify the BGP origin:
(route-map) set origin {igp | egp as | incomplete}
```

Set the origin to **igp** (the origin is inside the local AS; it is normally seen if the BGP **network** command is used or if IGP routes are redistributed into BGP), **egp** (learned from Exterior Gateway Protocol from AS number *as*), or **incomplete** (the origin is unknown, or a static route is redistributed into BGP).

Modify the community attribute:

```
(route-map) set community {community [additive] | none}
```

The community attribute is set to one of these *community* values: a 32-bit number (1 to 4294967200), an AS number and a 2-byte community number in the form *as:nn*, **local-AS** (don't advertise the route outside the local AS), **no-export** (don't advertise to the next AS), or **no-advertise** (don't advertise to any peer). If the **additive** keyword is used, the *community* value specified is added to the existing community attribute. The **none** keyword removes all *community* values.

Modify the BGP dampening:

```
(route-map) set dampening halflife reuse suppress max-suppress-time
```

The BGP route dampening factors are set. (See Step 15 for further details.) The *halflife* ranges from 1 to 45 minutes (the default is 15 minutes), the *reuse* penalty threshold ranges from 1 to 20000 (the default is 750), the *suppress* penalty threshold ranges from 1 to 20000 (the default is 2000), and the *max-suppress-time* ranges from 1 to 20000 minutes (the default is 60 minutes). Dampening can be set only with route maps that are referenced by the **bgp dampening** command.

Modify the local preference value:

```
(route-map) set local-preference value
```

Local preference ranges from 0 to 4294967295 (the default is 100). Higher local preference values are preferred.

Modify the weight value (for the incoming route map only):

```
(route-map) set weight weight
```

The BGP weight value ranges from 0 to 65535 (the default isnot changed). Weights set with a route map override weights set with BGP **neighbor** commands. Routes with a higher weight are preferred.

Modify the MED:

```
(route-map) set metric [+ | -] metric
```

metric ranges from 0 to 4294967295. If the plus or minus signs are used with a value, the metric is adjusted by that value. Lower metric values are preferred.

a. Apply the route map to inbound or outbound updates on a per-neighbor basis:

```
(router) neighbor {ip-address | peer-group} route-map map-name {in | out}
```

The route map named *map-name* is used to modify updates to or from this BGP neighbor.

13. (Optional) Reduce internal peering by using BGP confederations.

a. Create a confederation identifier:

```
(router) bgp confederation identifier autonomous-system
```

The confederation has an identifier, *autonomous-system*, so that it will appear to the outside world to be a single AS.

b. Specify the ASs that belong to the confederation:

```
(router) bgp confederation peers autonomous-system [autonomous system]
```

EBGP neighbors within the confederation will exchange updates as if they are IBGP peers.

Note   Each AS within the confederation must have a full mesh of IBGP peers defined, through the use of BGP **neighbor** commands. Although a confederation reduces the total IBGP mesh inside the overall confederation AS, the full-mesh requirement must be kept within the smaller internal ASs.

14. (Optional) Reduce peering by using route reflectors.

a. Configure a route reflector and its clients:

```
(router) neighbor ip-address route-reflector-client
```

The local router is configured as a BGP route reflector and relays BGP updates to all IBGP clients. The peer *ip-address* is configured as a client. The route reflector and its clients form a *cluster*. Clients do not need to be fully meshed. Route reflectors must be fully meshed with each other between clusters.

b. For redundant route reflectors within a cluster, assign a specific cluster ID:

```
(router) bgp cluster-id {cluster-id | ip-address}
```

This command is used on each route reflector to assign a common 4-byte cluster ID number (1 to 4294967295, or 4 bytes in IP address format). The cluster ID is passed along with updates to other route reflectors. It is used to detect loops.

15. (Optional) Minimize route flapping with route dampening.

a. Enable BGP route dampening:

```
(global) bgp dampening
```

The effects of route flapping are minimized as follows:

If a route to an AS flaps, the dampening router assigns a cumulative penalty value. The route is flagged with a problem, in "history" state, but it is still advertised.

Further flapping incurs further penalties. If the cumulative penalty isgreater than the *suppress limit*, the route moves into "damp" state and isnot advertised

The penalty is lowered by half after a *half-life* period passes without flapping. Penalty reduction is examined every 5 seconds.

As soon as the penalty falls below the *reuse limit*, the route is unsuppressed and advertised again. Suppressed routes are examined every 10 seconds for this condition.

Routes are suppressed for only the *max-suppress* limit of time.

b. Tune route-dampening factors:

```
(global) bgp dampening half-life reuse suppress max-suppress [route-map
map]
```

The *half-life* ranges from 1 to 45 minutes (the default is 15 minutes), the *reuse* penalty threshold ranges from 1 to 20000 (the default is 750), the *suppress* penalty threshold ranges from 1 to 20000 (the default is 2000), and the *max-suppress-time* ranges from 1 to 20000 minutes (the default is 60 minutes).

16. (Optional) Configure the BGP network timers:

```
(router) timers bgp keepalive holdtime
```

The *keepalive* argument specifies the frequency, in seconds, with which the router sends BGP keepalive messages to a BGP peer. (The default is 60 seconds.) The *holdtime* argument specifies how long the router will wait, in seconds, to hear a keepalive message before declaring the BGP peer dead. (The default is 180 seconds.)

17. (Optional) Enable soft-reconfiguration:

```
(router) neighbor [ip-address | peer-group-name] soft-reconfiguration
[inbound]
```

Soft-reconfiguration allows for a faster recovery when a BGP peer is reset. With soft-reconfiguration, all the updates received from a neighbor are stored unmodified.

Example

In Figure 6-8, a router is configured for BGP in autonomous system 10000. Two IBGP peers (within AS 10000) have IP addresses 190.67.17.254 and 190.67.41.3. The local router is a BGP route reflector, and each of the IBGP peers is a BGP route reflector client. Another router, an EBGP peer (not in AS 10000), has IP address 217.6.15.1.

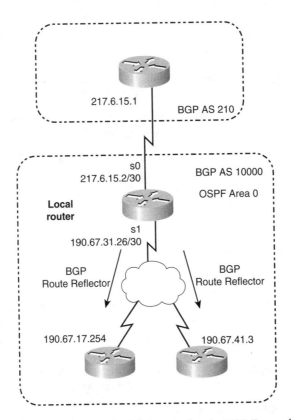

Figure 6-8   *Network Diagram for the BGP Example*

The EBGP peer receives BGP community information. Route map ispcommunity causes route advertisement to be suppressed for routes to 190.67.18.0. However, for routes to 190.67.0.0, an additional community value of 10000:1 (AS 10000 and community 1) is added to the community string.

For incoming BGP updates from the EBGP peer, route map ispfilter references AS path access list 1. Updates containing a path consisting of AS 1001 only or a path passing through AS 1002 have their local-preference values set to 40.

BGP routes (including subnets) from AS 10000 are redistributed into OSPF with a metric of 500.

```
interface serial 0
     ip address 217.6.15.2 255.255.255.252

interface serial 1
     ip address 190.67.31.26 255.255.255.252

router bgp 10000
     network 217.6.15.0
     neighbor 217.6.15.1 description ISP peer
     neighbor 217.6.15.1 remote-as 210
     neighbor 217.6.15.1 route-map ispfilter in
     neighbor 217.6.15.1 send-community
     neighbor 217.6.15.1 route-map ispcommunity out
     neighbor 190.67.17.254 remote-as 10000
     neighbor 190.67.17.254 route-reflector-client
     neighbor 190.67.41.3 remote-as 10000
     neighbor 190.67.41.3 route-reflector-client

router ospf 101
     redistribute bgp 10000 metric 500 subnets
     passive-interface serial 0
     network 217.6.15.0 0.0.0.255 area 0
     network 190.67.31.0 0.0.0.255 area 0

route-map ispfilter permit 10
     match as-path 1
     set local-preference 40
route-map ispfilter permit 20
     ip as-path access-list 1 permit ^1001$
     ip as-path access-list 1 permit _1002_

route-map ispcommunity permit 10
     match ip address 2
     set community no-advertise
route-map ispcommunity permit 20
     match ip address 1
     set community 10000:1 additive
route-map ispcommunity permit 30
```

```
access-list 1 permit 190.67.0.0 0.0.255.255
access-list 2 permit 190.67.18.0 0.0.0.255
```

6-10: Multiprotocol Border Gateway Protocol (BGP) for IPv6

■ MBGP is an extension to BGP 4 that supports routing for multiple protocol address families (for example, IPv4 multicast, IPv6 unicast, IPv6 multicast, VPNv4, and so forth).

■ MBGP is defined by RFC 2283. MBGP runs over a BGP session and uses separate address families and databases for each address family.

■ MBGP uses both UDP and TCP ports 179.

Configuration

1. Configure a BGP routing process:

    (config) **router bgp** *autonomous-system-number*

2. Configure a router ID:

    (router) **bgp router-id** *ipv4-address*

    BGP uses a 32-bit router ID for identification of packets. If the router is configured only for IPv6, you must manually configure a router ID.

3. (Optional) Disable the IPv4 unicast address family:

    (router) **no bgp default ipv4-unicast**

    If the router will be used only for IPv6, you can safely remove all routing information for IPv4 with this command.

4. Configure a BGP neighbor:

    (router) **neighbor** *ipv6-address* **remote-as** *as-number*

    You configure IPv6 BGP neighbors the same as with IPv4 BGP.

5. Specify support for the IPv6 unicast address family:

    (router) **address-family ipv6 unicast**

    MBGP supports the concept of "address families," which group common characteristics according to IP version, unicast or multicast addressing, or virtual routing and forwarding (VRF) instance. You can use this command several times to define characteristics of multiple address families. By default, if no address family is specified, IPv4 unicast is assumed and support for the neighbor. IPv6 unicast support must be explicitly configured.

6. Activate route prefix exchanges with the IPv6 neighbor:

    (router-af) **neighbor** *ipv6-address* **activate**

MBGP activations are done by address family.

> **Note** Most of the commands previously listed for BGP work with MBGP. Although the commands are the same, it is the address family configuration mode that makes the difference.

7. Define the networks to advertise by MBGP as originating from the local AS:

   a. Specify a list of up to 200 networks:

   ```
   (router-af) network network-number/prefix-length
   ```

   Specified networks must be present in the unicast routing table as directly connected, static routes, or learned from dynamic routing processes.

   -or-

   b. Redistribute routes from an IGP:

   ```
   (router-af) redistribute protocol [process-id] ... [route-map map]
   ```

   Normally, local networks (within the local AS) should be specified with the **network** command; however, IGP routes can be redistributed into BGP if necessary. A route map should be used to filter the IGP routes that are redistributed.

8. Configure other BGP attributes and operations using the commands found in Section 6-9. To apply these commands to IPv6 MBGP, first make sure that the IPv6 address family is specified and that a MBGP neighbor is activated.

Example

In Figure 6-9, RouterB is configured for MBGP. RouterB has an iBGP peering relationship with RouterA and an eBGP peering relationship with RouterC.

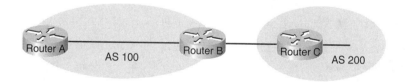

Figure 6-9 *IPv6 MBGP Example*

```
hostname RouterB
!
ipv6 unicast-routing
!
interface fastethernet 0/0
 description ***Link to RouterA***
 ipv6 address 2001:1:1:1::1/64
```

```
!
interface fastethernet0/1
 description ***Link to RouterC***
 ipv6 address 2001:2:2:2::1/64
!
router bgp 100
 bgp router-id 1.1.1.1
 no bgp default ipv4-unicast
 neighbor 2001:2:2:2::2 remote-as 200
 neighbor 2001:1:!:1::2 remote-as 100
 address-family ipv6 unicast
  neighbor 2001:2:2:2::2 activate
  neighbor 2001:1:1:1::2 activate
  network 2001:1:1:!::/64
  network 2001:2:2:2::/64
```

Further Reading

Refer to the following recommended sources for further technical information about the routing protocols presented here.

All IP Routing Protocols

Cisco Router Configuration, Second Edition, by Allan Leinwand and Bruce Pinsky, Cisco Press, ISBN 1578702410.

Interconnecting Cisco Network Devices, by Stephen McQuerry, Cisco Press, ISBN 1578701112.

IP Routing Fundamentals, by Mark A. Sportack, Cisco Press, ISBN 157870071X.

IP Routing Primer, by Robert Wright, Cisco Press, ISBN 1578701082.

Routing TCP/IP, Volume 1, by Jeff Doyle, Cisco Press, ISBN 1578700418.

Large-Scale IP Network Solutions, by Khalid Raza and Mark Turner, Cisco Press, ISBN 1578700841.

Troubleshooting IP Routing Protocols, by Faraz Shamim, Zaheer Aziz, Johnson Lui, and Abe Martey, Cisco Press, ISBN 1587050196.

EIGRP

EIGRP Network Design Solutions, by Ivan Pepelnjak, Cisco Press, ISBN 1578701651.

Building Scalable Cisco Networks, by Catherine Paquet and Diane Teare, Cisco Press, ISBN 1578702283.

Advanced IP Network Design, by Alvaro Retana, Don Slice, and Russ White, Cisco Press, ISBN 1578700973

"Enhanced Interior Gateway Routing Protocol," Cisco white paper, www.cisco.com/warp/public/103/eigrp-toc.html

"IGRP Metric," Cisco TAC Technical Note, www.cisco.com/warp/public/103/3.html

OSPF

OSPF Network Design Solutions, by Thomas M. Thomas II, Cisco Press, ISBN 1578700469.

Building Scalable Cisco Networks, by Catherine Paquet and Diane Teare, Cisco Press, ISBN 1578702283.

Advanced IP Network Design, by Alvaro Retana, Don Slice, and Russ White, Cisco Press, ISBN 1578700973.

"Initial Configurations for OSPF Over Frame Relay Subinterfaces," Cisco Sample Configuration, www.cisco.com/warp/public/104/22.html.

BGP and MBGP

"BGP Case Studies," Cisco TAC Technical Note, www.cisco.com/warp/public/459/bgp-toc.html.

"Using the Border Gateway Protocol for Interdomain Routing," Cisco TAC Case Study, www.cisco.com/univercd/cc/td/doc/cisintwk/ics/icsbgp4.htm.

"BGP Best Path Selection Algorithm," Cisco TAC Technical Note, www.cisco.com/warp/public/459/25.shtml.

Internet Routing Architectures, Second Edition, by Sam Halabi and Danny McPherson, Cisco Press, ISBN 157870233X.

Routing TCP/IP, Volume 2, by Jeff Doyle, Cisco Press, ISBN 1578700892.

BGP4 Command and Configuration Reference, by William Parkhurst, Cisco Press, ISBN 158705017x.

Building Scalable Cisco Networks, by Catherine Paquet and Diane Teare, Cisco Press, ISBN 1578702283.

Advanced IP Network Design, by Alvaro Retana, Don Slice, and Russ White, Cisco Press, ISBN 1578700973.

Chapter 7

IP Multicast Routing

This chapter presents the background and configuration on IP multicast services, with a focus on the following topics:

- **7-1: Protocol Independent Multicast (PIM)**—Cisco routers support multicast routing using the PIM routing protocol version 1 and version 2. PIM can operate in sparse mode (PIM-SM), dense mode (PIM-DM), sparse-dense mode, bidirectional PIM, and Source Specific Multicast (PIM-SSM).

- **7-2: Internet Group Management Protocol (IGMP)**—IGMP is a messaging protocol between a host and a router that is used when a host wants to join a multicast group. Routers operate as queriers and maintain a list of multicast group members. Cisco routers support IGMP versions 1, 2, and 3.

- **7-3: Multiprotocol BGP (MBGP) for Multicast**—MBGP is an extension to BGP-4 that supports routing for multiple protocols' address families (IPv4 unicast and multicast, VPNv4, and so forth). MBGP enables multicast routing over BGP.

- **7-4: Multicast Source Discovery Protocol (MSDP)**—MSDP connects multiple PIM sparse mode domains. Rendezvous Points (RP) form peering relationships with MSDPD-enabled RPs in other domains to exchange source information. Messages are sent over TCP port 639.

- **7-5: IPv6 Multicast**—Cisco routers supports IPv6 multicast routing using either PIM-SM or PIM-SSM. Routers use the Multicast Listener Discovery Protocol (MLD) to discover the presence multicast listeners. Cisco routers support both version 1 and version 2 of MLD. MLD version 1 is based on IGMP version 2 whereas MLD version 2 is based on IGMP version 3.

7-1: Protocol Independent Multicast (PIM)

IP multicast communication is a method of sending a packets to a group of multicast receivers. The Internet Group Management Protocol (IGMP) is used on a local network to map receivers (members) to an IPv4 multicast group. For IPv6 multicast groups, the Multicast Listener Discover (MLD) protocol is used instead. Multicast routing maps a multicast source to receivers across an internetwork. Routers use reverse path forwarding (RPF) to find the path to the source. Unlike unicast routing, which is based on the destination IP address, multicast routing is based on the source address. Routers build multicast trees to find the best path from the multicast receivers back to the source using either source distribution trees or shared distribution trees. With a source distribution tree, each multicast source is mapped in a tree to the group receivers. With a shared distribution tree, a Rendezvous Point (RP) is used instead. Groups are mapped to RPs, which saves memory but might introduce suboptimal routing. Cisco routers support IP multicast routing using PIM.

An IPv4 multicast address is a Class D address consisting of 1110 as the highest bit in the first octet. Class D multicast addresses are divided into three scopes (address ranges). Reserved link local addresses use 224.0.0.0 to 224.0.0.255. Globally scoped addresses use 224.0.1.0 to 238.255.255.255. Limited scope addresses use 239.0.0.0 to 239.255.255.255. IPv4 multicast addresses are converted into Ethernet Media Access Control (MAC) addresses by converting the last three octets into hexadecimal, changing the first bit of the second octet to zero, and prefacing the multicast MAC address with 01-00-5E.

An IPv6 multicast address uses the prefix ff00::/8. The first group of eight bits is the general routing prefix and is set to "FF" to specify a multicast address. The next four bits are used to set flag options. The first three are always set to zero, whereas the fourth bit is either set to zero to indicate an IANA well-known multicast address or one to indicate a transient (nonpermanently assigned) address. The next four bits define the scope value. Node-local scope addresses set the value to one, link-local to two, site-local to five, and organization-level to eight.

- Cisco routers support PIM versions 1 and 2. Both versions enable automatic discovery of RPs, but PIM version 1 uses RP mapping agents to complete this function whereas PIM version 2 uses bootstrap routers (BSR).

- PIM operates in dense mode (PIM-DM), sparse mode (PIM-SM), sparse-dense mode, bidirectional PIM, or source specific multicast (PIM-SSM).

- PIM-SM, PIM-SSM, and bidirectional PIM all support RPs (or bootstrap routers in PIM version 2). Routers map a multicast source to the RP. PIM-DM does not use RPs. PIM sparse-dense mode can operate in sparse mode when RPs are configured and as dense mode when an RP is not configured.

- PIM-SSM uses source filtering so that a receiver only receives multicast packets from a particular source that it requests. It relies on IGMPv3 for source filtering. PIM-SSM does not require the use of RPs.

- Bidirectional PIM offers performance improvements over PIM-SM. Although PIM-SM builds unidirectional shared trees rooted at RPs and optional shortest-path trees per source, bidirectional PIM builds bidirectional shared trees rooted at RPs but no shortest-path trees.

Configuration

1. Enable IP multicast routing:

    ```
    (global) ip multicast-routing
    ```

    This command enables the multicast routing capabilities on the router. If you do not enable multicast routing, none of the PIM commands have any effect.

2. Configure PIM on a participating multicast interface:

    ```
    (interface) ip pim {dense-mode | sparse-mode | sparse-dense-mode}
    ```

    Any interface that receives or forwards multicast traffic on the connected network must be configured with PIM. Which mode you choose for that network depends on the traffic requirements. Dense mode operation requires that PIM be configured on each segment that passes the multicast traffic. Sparse mode operation enables you to run multicast packets on only the segments that will have multicast servers. Which mode you choose to configure depends on the particulars of your network. The command option **sparse-dense-mode** is the most versatile. With this option, the interface operates in dense mode for some groups on the connected network and sparse mode for other groups. To have any groups operate in sparse mode, you must configure an RP. Choose **sparse-mode** if you want to configure PIM-SSM or bidirectional PIM.

3. (Required for sparse mode) Configure an RP:

    ```
    (global) ip pim rp-address ip-address [access-list-number] override
    ```

    This command specifies the RP for leaf routers so that they can register groups with the RP or determine the location of group routers from the RP. The *access-list-number* parameter enables you to configure specific groups for a given RP. By using the command with an access list specifying the group address, you can configure multiple RPs—one for each access list configured. The **override** option tells the router to use the configured group over the one that is learned with the auto RP option (discussed in the next step).

4. (Optional) Configure automatic RPs.

    a. Configure a router to be an automatic RP:

        ```
        (global) ip pim send-rp-announce type number scope ttl group-list access-
        list-number
        ```

        The router announces itself as an RP to the mapping agent for the groups defined by the **group-list** *access-list-number* option. The *type* and *number* options identify the interface address announced as the RP address; this must be a PIM interface. The **scope** option determines how far in hops the message will be propagated.

    b. Configure the RP mapping agent:

        ```
        (global) ip pim rp-announce-filter rp-list access-list-number group-list
        access-list-number
        ```

The **rp-list** option is used to filter incoming messages from a particular RP. The **group-list** option filters messages about the listed group.

5. (Optional) Configure the PIM version:

`(interface) ip pim version [1 | 2]`

Specify the version of PIM operating on an interface. Version 2 is the default version for routers using Cisco IOS Software Release 11.3(2)T or later. All routers in the same broadcast domain must be the same version of PIM. A PIM version 2 router automatically downgrades itself if it detects PIM version 1 messages.

6. (Required for PIM version 2) Configure candidate BSRs:

`(global) ip pim bsr-candidate interface hash-mask-length [priority]`

PIM version 2 is an IETF standards track protocol that uses a mechanism called a bootstrap router (BSR) to discover and announce the RP-set information. This command configures candidates to become BSRs. The *interface* specifies the PIM interface from which the BSR address is derived. The *hash-mask-length* is a value up to 32 bits that is ANDed with the group address to enable you to specify which parts of the address matter. This is used to get one RP for multiple groups. The optional *priority* setting enable you to increase the priority to determine which router will be chosen as the BSR. The priority is an integer from 0 to 255. The bootstrap router with the larger priority is preferred. If the priority values are the same, the router with the larger IP address is the bootstrap router. The default value is 0.

7. (Required for version 2) Configure candidate RPs:

`(global) ip pim rp-candidate interface {ttl} [group-list access-list-number]`

This specifies a router to be an RP for all or any portion of the multicast groups. The *interface* specifies which PIM interface address will be used to identify the RP. *ttl* describes how many hops the messages can be propagated. The **group-list** option enables you to specify which multicast groups this RP serves.

8. (Optional) Configure a PIM domain border:

`(interface) ip pim [border | bsr-border]`

This command is placed on an interface to set a border for the PIM domain. Use the **border** keyword for PIM version 1 and the **bsr-border** keyword for PIM version 2. Bootstrap messages do not cross this interface in either direction, enabling for the configuration of different BSRs on either side of the border.

9. (Optional) Define the IP multicast boundary:

`(global) ip multicast boundary access-list-number`

Use this command along with an access list specifying groups 224.0.1.39 and 224.0.1.40 to prevent auto RP messages from entering into a PIM Version 2 domain with a BSR.

10. (Optional) Configure source specific multicast (PIM-SSM).

a. Enable SSM globally:

```
(global) ip pim ssm {default | range access-list}
```

This global configuration command enables source-specific multicast on a router. Use the **default** keyword if you want to define the SSM range as 232/8. Use the **range** keyword to specify a standard IP access list number or name that defines the SSM range.

b. Enable IGMPv3 on all interfaces:

```
(interface) ip igmp version 3
```

Interfaces run IGMP version 2 by default. Because PIM-SSM requires version 3 for source filtering, you must change the IGMP version to 3. This command should be applied on all interfaces attached to hosts.

11. (Optional) Configure bidirectional PIM.

a. Globally enable bidirectional PIM:

```
(global) ip pim bidir-enable
```

This command enables bidirectional PIM on a router. Remember to also allow PIM-SM on all interfaces with the **ip pim sparse-mode** interface command.

b. Configure the PIM RP for a group to be bidirectional:

```
(global) ip pim rp-address rp-address [access-list] bidir
```

This is the same command mentioned previously in Step 3. Use this command to configure the IP address of the RP. The *access-list* parameter references an access list that permits the multicast group that you want to be bidirectional.

Example

Figure 7-1 shows a network diagram for this example. In this example, multicast routing has been enabled, and the router has been set up to use the router with the address 199.9.9.2 as an RP. Each of the interfaces has been set up to use sparse-dense mode. Because an RP is configured, they operate in sparse mode.

```
ip multicast-routing
ip pim rp-address 199.9.9.2

interface ethernet 0
       ip address 1.2.2.1 255.255.255.0
       ip pim sparse-dense-mode

interface ethernet 1
       ip address 199.9.9.1 255.255.255.0
```

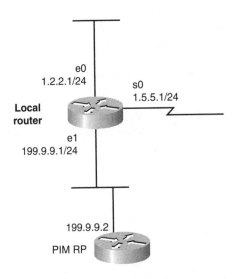

Figure 7-1   *Network Diagram for PIM Routing Example*

```
        ip pim sparse-dense-mode

interface serial 0
        ip address 1.5.5.1 255.255.255.0
        ip pim sparse-dense-mode

router eigrp 1
        network 1.0.0.0
        network 199.9.9.0
```

7-2: Internet Group Management Protocol (IGMP)

The Internet Group Management Protocol (IGMP) is a host to router protocol that informs the router if hosts are on an attached network that should receive multicast traffic. Hosts inform a router when it wants to join a multicast group by sending a host membership report. Routers send queries on an attached network to determine if any receivers should receive multicast traffic.

Routers running IGMP version 1 query all hosts every 60 seconds. The queries are sent to the multicast address 224.0.0.1. Hosts send join requests when they want to join a multicast group. Hosts do not send a leave message when they want to leave a group. When multiple routers are attached to a network, IGMP version 1 elects a router to operate as both the designated router and querier for a given network. The designated router function ensures that duplicate multicast packets are not sent onto a network. The querier function is responsible for querying hosts to determine if any members need to receive multicast traffic.

The default IGMP version on Cisco routers is version 2. With version 2, routers do not send their queriers to all hosts using the destination multicast address 224.0.0.1; instead, routers send group-specific queries by using the destination multicast address of a group. Also, hosts can now send leave group messages (sent to the all-routers multicast address 224.0.0.2). Finally, IGMP version 2 separates the designated router and querier functions. The router with the highest IP address is the designated router for a network segment whereas the router with the lowest IP address is the designated querier for a network segment.

With IGMP version 3, joining members do not wait for a query from a router but instead send join messages immediately to the destination multicast address 224.0.0.22. IGMP version 3 also adds support for source filtering, which enables a multicast receiver host to signal to a router the groups from which it wants to receive traffic and from which sources.

This section covers IGMP and some miscellaneous multicast configuration options for improving multicast forwarding in your network:

- Cisco switches and routers support the Cisco Group Management Protocol (CGMP) to provide Cisco switches with Layer 2 to Layer 3 multicast information. With this information, the switch can make intelligent forwarding decisions for multicast traffic instead of flooding the traffic out unnecessary interfaces.

- Cisco routers and switches support the proprietary Router-Port Group Management Protocol (RGMP). RGMP enables a router to communicate to a switch, which multicasts groups for which the router would like to receive or forward traffic. You cannot enable both CGMP and RGMP concurrently.

- IGMP is enabled automatically as soon as PIM is enabled on an interface. Therefore, all commands in the following configuration section are optional.

Configuration

1. Specify the IGMP version:

    ```
    (interface) ip igmp [1 | 2 | 3]
    ```

    IGMP version 2 is automatically enabled as soon as PIM is enabled on an interface. However, there are times when you might want to change the default version. If a host does not support version 2, you should configure the router for version 1. If you implement source specific multicast (PIM-SSM), you should configure the router for version 3.

2. Set the IGMP query interval:

    ```
    (interface) ip igmp query-interval seconds
    ```

    This specifies how often, in seconds, the IGMP designated router sends query messages to the hosts to determine group memberships. The default is 60 seconds.

3.   Set the maximum query response time:

`(interface) `**`ip igmp query-max-response-time`**` seconds`

This command determines how long the router waits for a response from a host about group membership. The default is 10 seconds, but you can alter it using this command. If the host does not respond quickly enough, there might be a need to lengthen this time. IGMPv1 does not support this command.

4.   Set the IGMP query timeout:

`(interface) `**`ip igmp query-timeout`**` seconds`

This specifies how long the router waits before it takes over as the querier for a particular network. By default, it is two times the query interval, but this command enables you to change the timeout to the number of seconds specified.

5.   Set the last member query interval (LMQI):

`(interface) `**`ip igmp last-member-query-interval`**` seconds`

When a router sends a leave message, the designated querier sends out another query to the multicast group to see if there are any more hosts. It waits one second (the last member query interval) for a response; however, because packets can get lost, the router repeats this process up to two more times (the last member query count). Thus, it waits 3 seconds by default. You can change the last member query interval (LMQI) with this interface command.

6.   Set the last member query count (LMQC) value:

`(interface) `**`ip igmp last-member-query-count`**` query-count-number`

This command modifies the number of times that a designated query sends out queries to a multicast group to determine if any hosts exist.

7.   Configure the TTL threshold:

`(interface) `**`ip multicast ttl-threshold`**` ttl`

This sets the maximum number of hops that a packet will be forwarded. If a multicast packet is received with a TTL greater than the TTL threshold, it is forwarded by the interface; otherwise, it is dropped.

8.   Disable fast switching for IP multicast packets:

`(interface) `**`no ip mroute-cache`**

It is useful to do this when you want to log debug messages for multicast packets.

9.   Enable CGMP support:

`(interface) `**`ip cgmp`**

This command enables CGMP support to communicate multicast forwarding information with Cisco switches.

10. Configure the router to forward multicast traffic even if there is not a directly connected IGMP host:

```
(interface) ip igmp join-group group-address
```

-or-

```
(interface) ip igmp static-group { * | group-address}
```

Sometimes you might want multicast traffic to be forwarded to a network segment even if a host cannot report its group membership using IGMP. If you use the **ip igmp join-group** interface command, the router accepts and forwards multicast packets for the group specified in the *group-address*. If you use the **ip igmp static-group** command, the router forwards only the multicast traffic and will not be a member of the group.

11. Enable the Router-Port Group Management Protocol (RGMP) on an interface:

```
(interface) ip rgmp
```

RGMP enables a router to communicate with a switch that multicast groups for which the router would like to receive or forward traffic. The switch must support IP multicast and be enabled for IGMP snooping with the global configuration **ip igmp snooping** command.

12. Configure an IGMPv3 to include a specified group and source pair:

```
(interface) ip igmp join-group group-address source source-address
```

IGMPv3 enables for source filtering. This command enables the router to include the specified source and group channel.

Example

Figure 7-2 shows a network diagram for this example. In this example, PIM-SSM is configured on RouterA. To support SSM, IGMPv3 is enabled on the interfaces. In addition, the IGMP query interval and the query timeout values are doubled from the default settings. Finally, the query timeout value is configured to be twice that of the query interval time.

```
ip multicast-routing
!
interface fastethernet0/0
 ip address 192.168.0.1 255.255.255.0
 ip pim sparse-mode
 ip igmp version 3
 ip igmp query-interval 120
 ip igmp query-max-response-time 20
 ip igmp query-timeout 240
!
interface fasthethernet0/1
 ip address 172.16.0.1 255.255.0.0
 ip pim sparse-mode
```

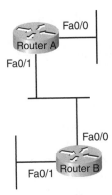

Figure 7-2 *Network Diagram for IGMP Example*

```
ip igmp version 3
ip igmp query-interval 120
ip igmp query-max-response-time 20
ip igmp query-timeout 240


!
ip pim ssm default
```

7-3: Multiprotocol BGP (MBGP)

- MBGP is an extension to BGP-4 that supports routing for multiple protocols' address families (IPv4 unicast and multicast, VPNv4, and so forth).

- Unicast and multicast network topologies can be different.

- Multicast routing information can be carried between autonomous systems, just like unicast routing.

- A full set of BGP capabilities is available for multicast routing.

- MBGP-capable routers maintain two sets of routes—unicast and multicast. Multiprotocol (or multicast) routes cannot be redistributed into regular unicast BGP.

- PIM utilizes the MBGP multicast route database. (Both PIM and MBGP must be configured.)

Note MBGP is defined by RFC 2858. Beginning with Cisco IOS Software Release 12.1, MBGP runs over a BGP session and uses separate address families and databases for unicast and multicast information. MBGP operates over BGP (both UDP port 179 and TCP port 179), with additional BGP attributes.

Configuration

1. Configure a new or existing BGP routing process:

   (global) **router bgp** *as-number*

   Multicast over MBGP is configured within a normal BGP process, using the same AS number as unicast BGP.

2. Configure a BGP neighbor for multicast:

   (router) **neighbor** *ip-address* **remote-as** *as-number*

   A BGP peer can support both unicast and multicast information exchange.

3. Specify support for the IPv4 multicast address family:

   (router) **address-family ipv4 multicast**

   MBGP supports the concept of *address families*, which group common characteristics according to IP version, unicast or multicast addressing, or virtual routing and forwarding (VRF) instance. This command can be used several times to define characteristics of multiple address families. By default, if no address family is specified, IPv4 unicast is assumed and supported for the neighbor. Multicast support must be explicitly configured.

4. Activate multicast route prefix exchanges with the neighbor:

   (router-af) **neighbor** *ip-address* **activate**

   MBGP activations are done by address family. Therefore, the IPv4 multicast address family is activated. (The unicast address family is activated by default.)

> **Note** The **neighbor activate** command must be used to enter address family configuration mode (router-af). In this mode, many of the normal BGP commands can be used and applied to multicast or MBGP. Although the following configuration steps seem identical to the BGP commands presented in Section 7-6, it is the address family configuration mode that makes the difference.

5. Define the networks to advertise by MBGP as originating from the local AS.

   a. Specify a list of up to 200 networks:

   (router-af) **network** *network-number* [**mask** *mask*]

   Specified networks must be present in the unicast routing table, as directly connected, static routes, or learned from dynamic routing processes. The optional *mask* enables networks to be supernetted.

   -or-

b. Redistribute routes from an IGP:

`(router-af)` `redistribute protocol [process-id]` ... [**route-map** `map`]

Normally, local networks (within the local AS) should be specified with the **network** command. However, IGP routes can be redistributed into BGP if necessary. A route map should be used to filter the IGP routes that are redistributed.

6. (Optional) Configure other BGP attributes and operations using the commands presented in Section 7-6. To apply these commands to multicast or MBGP, first make sure that the IPv4 multicast address family is specified and that an MBGP neighbor is activated.

Example

Figure 7-3 shows a network diagram for this example. Neighbor 192.168.24.1 supports both unicast and multicast MBGP exchanges, and neighbor 192.168.25.1 uses only unicast. In addition, neighbor 192.168.24.1 acts as both a unicast and multicast route reflector.

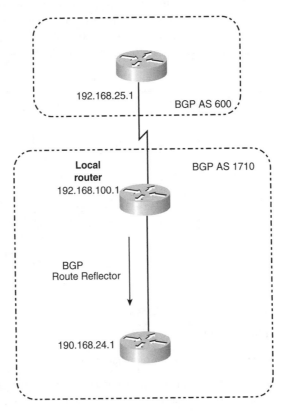

Figure 7-3 *Network Diagram for the MBGP Example*

```
router bgp 1710
        neighbor 192.168.24.1 remote-as 1710
        neighbor 192.168.25.1 remote-as 600


        address-family ipv4 unicast
        network 192.168.100.0
        neighbor 192.168.24.1 activate
        neighbor 192.168.24.1 route-reflector-client
        neighbor 192.168.24.1 filter-list 1 in
        neighbor 192.168.25.1 activate

        address-family ipv4 multicast
        network 192.168.100.0
        neighbor 192.168.24.1 activate
        neighbor 192.168.24.1 route-reflector-client
        neighbor 192.168.24.1 filter-list 1 in

ip as-path access-list 1 permit _300_
ip as-path access-list 1 deny _100_
ip as-path access-list 1 permit .*.
```

7-4: Multicast Source Discovery Protocol (MSDP)

The Multicast Source Discovery Protocol (MSDP) is a mechanism to connect multiple PIM sparse mode (PIM-SM) domains. Each PIM-SM domain has its own RP. RPs configured for MSDP form a peering relationship with RPs configured for MSDP in other PIM-SM domains. When an RP first learns of a new sender through a PIM register message, it builds a source-active (SA) message and sends is to its MSDP peers. The SA message contains the IP unicast data source address, the IP destination multicast group address, and the IP address of the RP. Each MSDP peer that receives the SA message forwards the message on to all MSDP peers (except the peer it received the message from).

- Domains with receiver only and no sources can get data globally without advertising group membership.

- MSDP messages are sent over TCP port 639. Peers are explicitly configured and rely on the underlying unicast routing system to find each other.

- Keepalives are sent every 60 seconds to keep the MSDP session active. The MSDP session is reset after 75 seconds without any keepalive or SA message.

- You can reduce the flooding of SA messages by configuring MSDP mesh groups. An MSDP mesh group is when all MSDP speakers have peering relationships with each other (that is, fully meshed). Using mesh groups also eliminates the need for reverse path forwarding (RPF) checks on arriving SA messages.

- MSDP relies on BGP or MBGP routing. The exceptions to this rule are when you have only a single MSDP peer, are using a default MSDP peer, or have MSDP mesh groups.

Configuration

1.   (Required) Configure PIM sparse mode (PIM-SM) as described in Section 7-1.

2.   (Required) Enable MSDP and configure a peer:

(global) **ip msdp peer** {*peer-name* | *peer-address*} {**connect-source** *interface*} [**remote-as** *as-number*]

MSDP is automatically enabled as soon as you begin to configure MSDP peers. You can reference the MSDP peer by an IP address or, if DNS is configured, by its DNS hostname. The MSDP peer should also be configured as a BGP neighbor. You can control what IP address is used by the router to make its MSDP TCP connection by specifying the interface with the IP address of your choice after the **connect-source** option. The **remote-as** option specifies the AS in which the MSDP peer resides. This option is only for display purposes to help when reviewing configurations and has no actual impact on MSDP operations.

3.   (Optional) Give a description for the peer:

(global) **ip msdp description** {*peer-name* | *peer-address*} *text*

You should configure a description for each MSDP peer that makes it easier to identify the peer when reviewing the configuration.

4.   (Optional) Configure MSDP MD5 authentication:

(global) **ip msdp password peer** {*peer-name* | *peer-address*} [*encryption-type*] *string*

Configuring MD5 passwords to authenticate the TCP connection between MSDP peers helps to protect against spoofing attacks. The valid options for *encryption-type* are 0 and 7. If you enter a plain text string, use an *encryption-type* of 0. If you enter a string that is already encrypted with Cisco type 7 encryption, enter 7 for the *encryption-type*. Both peers need to be configured with the same *string*.

5.   (Optional) Configure a default MSDP peer:

(global) **ip msdp default-peer** {*peer-address* | *peer-name*} [**prefix-list** *list*]

MSDP peers are typically BGP peers; however, if you have a single-homed nontransit or stub AS, you can use a static default unicast route and configure a default MSDP peer. The MSDP peer must already be configured as an MSDP peer. If the **prefix-list** option is used, the peer will be a default peer for those prefixes specified by the *list* argument. You must also configure a BGP prefix list that contains the list of prefixes for which you want the peer to be the default.

6.   (Optional) Configure an MSDP mesh group:

(global) **ip msdp mesh-group** *mesh-name* {*peer-address* | *peer-name*}

MSDP mesh groups reduce source active (SA) message flooding and eliminate the need for reverse path forwarding (RPF) checks on arriving SA messages. To use MSDP mesh groups, every MSDP peer must have a peering relationship with all other MSDP peers in the group. Repeat this command to add additional peers to the MSDP peer group.

Example

Figure 7-4 is used in this example. RouterA is configured to use RouterB as a default peer. The IP address on the loopback 0 interface is used as the peering IP address. To protect against TCP spoofing threats, the router is configured to authenticate the peering session

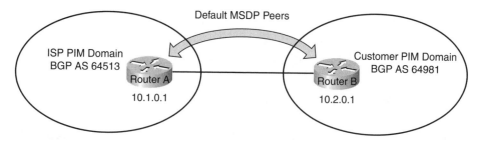

Figure 7-4   *Network Diagram for the MSDP Example*

with an MD5 password of C1sc0.

```
hostname RouterA
!
interface loopback 0
 ip address 10.1.0.1 255.255.0.0
!
ip multicast-routing
ip msdp peer 10.2.0.1 connect-source loopback0
ip msdp password peer 10.2.0.1 0 C1sc0
ip msdp default-peer 10.2.0.1
!
router bgp 64513
 neighbor 10.2.0.1 remote-as 64981
 neighbor 10.2.0.1 update-source loopback0
 address-family ipv4 unicast
  network 10.1.0.0
  network 172.16.0.0
  neighbor 10.2.0.1 activate
!
ip pim rp-address 10.1.0.1
!
interface fastethernet0/0
```

```
ip address 172.16.0.1 255.255.0.0
ip pim sparse-mode
```

7-5: IPv6 Multicast

Cisco routers support IPv6 multicast routing using either PIM-SM or PIM-SSM. Routers use the Multicast Listener Discovery Protocol (MLD) to discover the presence multicast listeners.

■ You must first enable IPv6 unicast routing on the router before enabling IPv6 multicast routing.

■ Cisco routers support both MLD protocol version 1 and version 2. MLD version 1 is based on IGMPv2; MLD version 2 is based on IGMPv3.

■ IPv6 multicast addresses use a prefix of FF00::/8. Addresses can have node, link, site, organizational, or global scopes.

■ MLD relies on the Internet Control Message Protocol (ICMP) for its messages.

■ The PIM router with the highest IPv6 address becomes the designated router (DR) for the network segment unless you force the election using the **ipv6 pim dr-priority** command.

■ IPv6 PIM provides embedded RPs support that enables routers to dynamically learn RP information using multicast group destination addresses instead of having to statically configure an RP. Routers that are the RP, however, must still be statically configured as the RP.

Configuration

1. (Required) Enable IPv6 unicast routing:

   (global) **ipv6 unicast-routing**

   You must first enable IPv6 unicast routing before you can enable IPv6 multicast routing. You also need to enable IPv6 on the interfaces that you want to use with IPv6 multicast routing. See Chapter 5, "IPv6 Addressing and Services," for more information on configuring IPv6.

2. (Required) Enable IPv6 multicast routing:

   (global) **ipv6 multicast-routing**

   This command enables IPv6 multicast routing on all IPv6-enabled interfaces.

3. (Required on the RP) Configure the IPv6 address of a PIM RP:

   (global) **ipv6 pim rp-address** *ipv6-address* [*group-access-list*]

   You need to statically configure only the RP address on the RP. Cisco routers have embedded RP support and automatically discover the RP address from the IPv6 group address. Use the optional *group-access-list* argument to reference a named IPv6 access list that specifies which multicast groups for which the router should be the RP.

4. (Optional) Set the designated router priority:

```
(interface) ipv6 pim dr-priority value
```

The router with the highest priority value for a network segment is the designated router. All interfaces have a default value of 1. If routers have the same priority value, the router with the highest IPv6 address on the interface becomes the DR.

5. (Optional) Disable PIM on interfaces for which you do not want to participate in IPv6 multicast routing:

```
(interface) no ipv6 pim
```

As soon as you enable IPv6 multicast routing by entering the global configuration **ipv6 multicast-routing** command, PIM sparse mode (PIM-SM) is automatically activated on all IPv6-enabled interface. If you have interfaces that should not participate in PIM routing, enter this command to disable PIM.

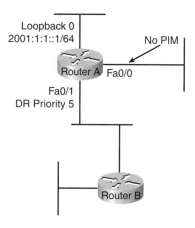

Figure 7-5   *Network Diagram for the IPv6 Multicast Example*

Example

Figure 7-5 is used in this example. RouterA is configured for IPv6 multicast routing and is the RP for the PIM multicast domain. Interface FastEthernet0/0 is not enabled for PIM. Finally, interface FastEthernet0/1 is configured with an interface priority of 5 for the PIM designated router (DR) election.

```
hostname RouterA
!
```

```
ipv6 unicast-routing
ipv6 multicast-routing
ipv6 pim rp-address 2001:1:1::1
!
interface loopback0
 ipv6 address 2001:1:1::1/64
!
interface fastethernet0/0
 ipv6 address 2001:2::/eui-64
 no ipv6 pim
!
interface fastethernet0/1
 ipv6 address 2001:3::/eui-64
 ipv6 pim dr-priority 5
```

Further Reading

See Table 7-1 for a list of Request For Comments (RFC) pertaining to the multicast topics covered in this chapter.

Table 7-1 *Multicast RFCs*

RFC #	Topic
1112	Host Extensions for IP Multicasting (IGMP version 1)
2236	IGMP version 2
2375	IPv6 Multicast Address Assignments
2858	Multiprotocol Extensions for BGP-4
3171	IANA Guidelines for IPv4 Multicast Address Assignments
3376	IGMP version 3
3569	Overview of Source-Specific Multicast (SSM)
3618	Multicast Source Discovery Protocol (MSDP)
3973	Protocol Independent Multicast Dense Mode (PIM-DM)
4291	IP Version 6 Addressing Architecture
4601	Protocol Independent Multicast Sparse Mode (PIM-SM)
5059	Bootstrap Router (BSR) Mechanisms for Protocol Independent Multicast (PIM)

Chapter 8

IP Route Processing

This chapter presents background and configuration information for processing routes to IP networks. The following topics are covered:

- **8-1: Manually Configuring Routes**—IP routes can be placed in the routing table as static or default routes. Routes can also be manually cleared. These features are used when routes are not learned through one or more dynamic routing protocols.

- **8-2: Policy Routing**—IP packets are routed or forwarded out interfaces based on flexible rules that are defined, rather than on the contents of the routing table. This can be used when routing must be performed based on criteria other than the destination network and a routing metric.

- **8-3: Redistributing Routing Information**—IP routes can be passed from one routing protocol to another. When more than one routing protocol is configured on a router, routes can be selectively or conditionally redistributed between them.

- **8-4: Filtering Routing Information**—Measures can be taken to prevent outbound routing updates and to selectively suppress routes from being advertised or processed when advertisements are received. You can also configure the router to trust one routing protocol over another by adjusting the administrative distance values.

- **8-5: Load Balancing**—IP packets can be load balanced across multiple interfaces to increase throughput.

8-1: Manually Configuring Routes

- Static routes can be manually defined for an IP network.

- Static routes should be defined if a dynamic routing protocol cannot be used or cannot build a route to a destination network.

- Static routes have a default administrative distance of 0 if defined to an interface and 1 if defined to a next hop.

- Static routes can be specified with an administrative distance as *floating static routes*.

- All unroutable packets can be sent to a *default route*, also called a *gateway of last resort*.

- Default routes can be static in nature or configured with the **default-route** command and can be redistributed into routing protocols.

- Default routes can be originated by a dynamic routing protocol.

Configuration

1. (Optional) Define a static route:

    (global) **ip route** *network mask* {*next-hop-addr* | *interface*} [*distance*] [**tag** *tag*] [**permanent**]

    A static route to the IP network defined by network and mask is added to the routing table. The path to the destination is defined by the IP address of the next-hop router or by the outbound interface on the local router. An administrative distance can be given with the distance field. By default, a static route has a distance of 1 and cannot be overridden by any dynamic routing protocol. Assigning a greater distance allows the static route to be defined and used until a routing protocol with a lesser distance defines the same route. The tag keyword can be used to assign a tag for conditionally redistributing the route. The permanent keyword causes the route to remain in the routing table even if the outbound interface shuts down.

    Table 8-1 shows the default values of administrative distance for each source of routing information. This table can be used to choose a value for a floating static route such that only desired routing protocols or sources can override the static route.

2. (Optional) Define a default route.

    a. Configure a static default route:

    (global) **ip route 0.0.0.0 0.0.0.0** {*ip-address* | *interface*}

    Note   Static routes that point to an interface are considered directly connected. When the interface is up, these routes appear in the routing table. These routes are also advertised by dynamic routing protocols as long as the interface belongs to a network specified in the routing protocol's network command.

    The static route 0.0.0.0 with a mask of 0.0.0.0 is a special route known as a default static. This route is used as the forwarding path if there is no entry in the routing table for the destination address of the packet.

    b. Configure a candidate default network:

    (global) **ip default-network** *network*

Table 8-1 *Default Administrative Distance Values*

Route Source	Default Distance
Connected or static with interface specified	0
Static next hop	1
EIGRP summary	5
EBGP	20
Internal EIGRP	90
OSPF	110
IS-IS	115
RIP	120
IBGP	200
Untrusted	255

The network specified is flagged as a candidate for the default route. This command is very similar to the default static route, except that the network specified does not have to be directly connected. To be considered, the network must already appear in the routing table. One of the candidate default routes is selected based on the lowest administrative distance and the lowest metric. The gateway of last resort can be displayed with the **show ip route** command. The candidate default routes are flagged with a * in the output.

c. (Optional) Clear routes from the routing table:

```
(exec) clear ip route {network [mask] | *}
```

Routes can be manually cleared from the routing table, if necessary, in EXEC mode. The routes defined by the network and mask combination are cleared. If the * is used, the entire routing table is cleared.

Example

A static route for 10.1.0.0 255.255.0.0 is defined such that it can be overridden by external BGP, EIGRP, and IGRP routes, but not by OSPF routes. (The default administrative distance of External BGP is 20, EIGRP is 90, IGRP is 100, and OSPF is 110.) Networks 192.168.1.0 and 192.168.22.0 are flagged as candidate default networks:

```
ip route 10.1.0.0 255.255.0.0 192.168.1.1 105


ip default-network 192.168.1.0
ip default-network 192.168.22.0
```

8-2: Policy Routing

- Routing is normally performed based on the packet destination and the lowest route metric.

- Policy routing makes routing decisions based on the actions of a *route map*.

- Policy routing is applied to an interface and processes inbound packets.

- Packets can be tested for packet size or a matching condition from a standard or extended IP access list.

- Packets can then be directed to a specific next-hop router or an outbound interface.

Configuration

1. Define a route map to use for matching and directing packets:

   (global) **route map** *map-tag* [**permit** | **deny**] [*sequence-num*]

   The route map named *map-tag* either permits or denies a certain action. If more than one action is to be defined, the sequence number must be used. Route maps with the same name are processed in sequential order. For policy routing, a matching **permit** action routes according to the route map, and a matching **deny** action routes normally.

2. (Optional) Define a matching condition for the route map. If no matching condition is defined, every packet is matched successfully.

   a. Match against the packet size:

      (route-map) **match length** *min max*

      -or-

      IP packets that are between min and max bytes in size are matched.

   b. Match against a standard or extended IP access list:

      (route-map) **match ip address** {*access-list-num* | *name*} [*access-list-num* | *name*]

      IP packets are tested against one or more numbered or named access lists. A successful match results if all specified access lists permit the packet.

3. (Optional) Set the action(s) to be taken by policy routing.

   a. Set the IP precedence value in the packet header:

      (route-map) **set ip precedence** *value*

      -or-

   b. Specify the next-hop router where the packet will be forwarded:

      (route-map) **set ip next-hop** *ip-address* [...*ip-address*]

Matching packets are forwarded to the first available router in the list. The next-hop router must be an adjacent neighbor. If it isn't adjacent, or if the next-hop router is unreachable, the packet is routed normally instead.

The IP precedence value can be set at the edge of the network, for further downstream Quality of Service processing. Valid values are a number or a name, as listed in Table 8-2.

Table 8-2 *IP Precedence Values*

Number	Name
0	Routine
1	Priority
2	Immediate
3	Flash
4	Flash-override
5	Critical
6	Internet
7	Network

-or-

c. Specify the outbound router interface:

```
(route-map) set interface type num [... type num]
```

Matching packets are forwarded out the first available interface in the list.

-or-

d. Specify the default destination to be used for the packet if no specific route for that packet exists:

```
(route-map) set ip default next-hop ip-address [... ip-address]
(route-map) set default interface type num [... type num]
```

default next-hop is the IP address of the next neighboring router; default interface is the outbound interface from which a packet is forwarded.

4. (Optional) Define more route maps using the same name, with greater sequence numbers.

5. Apply the route map to an inbound interface for policy routing:

```
(interface) ip policy route-map map-tag
```

Incoming packets on the interface are processed according to the route map named map-tag.

Example

For packets entering interface serial 0, route all POP3 and SMTP traffic out interface
serial 3:

```
route-map mailtraffic permit 10
        match ip address 101
        set interface serial 3

interface serial 0
        ip policy route-map mailtraffic

access-list 101 permit tcp any any eq pop3
access-list 101 permit tcp any any eq smtp
```

8-3: Redistributing Routing Information

- Routes can be redistributed from one IP routing protocol to another when both are
  running simultaneously on a router. Only routes present in the routing table are actually redistributed into and advertised by another routing protocol.

- Routing information can be conditionally redistributed using a *route map*.

- Route metrics do not automatically translate or scale from one routing protocol to
  another.

- A default metric can be used for redistribution, or metrics can be modified based on
  a route map.

> **Note**   Use caution when redistributing routes between different routing protocols,
> because the resulting route metrics might not be what you expect. Always use a default
> metric or a route map to assign new metrics that agree with the new routing protocol.

Configuration

1. Enable the routing process into which routes will be redistributed: RIP (see Section 6-
    1 and Section 6-2), EIGRP (see Section 6-3 and Section 6-4), OSPF (see Section 6-5
    and Section 6-6), BGP (see Section 6-9), or Integrated IS-IS (see Section 6-7):

    (global) **router** *protocol* [*process-id*]

2. (Optional) Assign a default metric for all redistributed routes:

    (router) **default-metric** *metric*

    All routes from all redistributed routing processes receive this metric value. For
    IGRP and EIGRP, the value metric is actually five values: bandwidth, delay, reliability,
    loading, and mtu.

> **Note**   Table 8-3 compares routing protocol metrics. Metrics do not automatically scale or translate when you redistribute routes between routing protocols. This table provides an idea of the range of metric values and how they are computed so that you can choose appropriate default metric values.

Table 8-3   *Routing Protocol Metric Comparisons*

Routing Protocol	Metric Components	Range
RIP	Hop count	0 to 16 (16 = unreachable)
IGRP and EIGRP	metric = k1 * bandwidth + (k2 * bandwidth)/(256–load) + k3 * delay if k5 > 0 metric = metric * (k5/(reliability * k4))	1 to 4294967295 (4294967295= a poisoned or inaccessible route)
	Defaults: k1 = 1, k2 = 0, k3 = 1, k4 = 0, k5 = 0, or metric = lowest bandwidth + sum of delays along the route bandwidth: kilobits per second delay: 10 microsecond units reliability: 0 to 255 (255 = 100% reliable) loading: 0 to 255 (255 = 100% loading) mtu: MTU of route in bytes	
	Example: Fast Ethernet bandwidth = 100000 delay = 100 reliability = 255 loading = 1 mtu = 1500	
OSPF	108 divided by interface bandwidth	1 to 65535
BGP	MED	1 to 4294967295
IS-IS	Hop count unless configured on each interface	0 to 63 per interface

3. (Optional) Create a route map to conditionally redistribute routes into a routing process.

  a. Define a route map for redistribution:

  ```
  (global) route map map-tag [permit | deny] [sequence-num]
  ```

  The route map named *map-tag* either permits or denies a certain action. If more than one action is to be defined, the sequence number must be used. Route maps with the same name are processed in sequential order. For route redistribution, a matching **permit** action redistributes routes according to the route map, whereas a matching **deny** action does not redistribute them.

b. (Optional) Define a matching condition for the route map. If no matching condition is defined, every route is successfully matched. Here are some of the matching conditions for route maps:

Match the IP address of the route itself:

```
(route-map) match ip address access-list [... access-list]
```

-or-

```
(route-map) match ip address prefix-list prefix-list-name [... prefix-
list-name]
```

A standard or extended IP access list (either named or numbered) or an IP prefix list can be used to match each route's network address. Refer to Chapter 14, "Access Lists and Expressions," for more information about either list type.

Note   Normally, a standard access list is used to match the destination network address. However, exactly matching a network address that is a summary or aggregate address (that is, 128.0.0.0) and not any of the more-specific routes contained within the summary requires the use of an extended access list. Here, both the network number and subnet mask are matched. The source address and mask portions of the access list correspond to the route's network number (that is, 128.0.0.0 0.255.255.255). The destination address and mask portions are used to match the subnet mask (that is, 255.0.0.0 0.0.0.0).

Note   Alternatively, an IP prefix list can be used to exactly match the summary address.

Match against a route's metric:

```
(route-map) match metric metric
```

The *metric* value is used to match the metric of each route. (In the case of IGRP or EIGRP, the metric value is the composite metric and not the five-part metric.)

Match against the IP address of the next-hop router:

```
(route-map) match ip next-hop access-list [...access-list]
```

Routes with next-hop router addresses that are permitted by a standard or extended IP access list are matched.

Match against a route's tag value:

```
(route-map) match tag tag [...tag]
```

The *tag* attribute of each route is compared to one or more tag values (0 to 4294967295) specified.

Match against a route's next-hop outbound interface:

```
(route-map) match interface type number [... type number]
```

Routes with their next hop located out one or more of the specified interfaces are matched.

Match against the IP address of the advertising router:

```
(route-map) match ip route-source access-list [...access-list]
```

Routes that have been advertised by a router with IP addresses permitted by a standard or extended IP access list are matched.

Match against the type of route:

```
(route-map) match route-type {local | internal | external [type-1 | type-2]
| level-1 | level-2}
```

Routes are matched according to their type: **local** (BGP locally generated), **internal** (EIGRP internal or OSPF intra-area and interarea), **external** (EIGRP external), **external type-1** (OSPF Type 1 external), **external type-2** (OSPF Type 2 external), **level-1** (IS-IS Level 1), or **level-2** (IS-IS Level 2).

(BGP only) Match against an AS path:

```
(route-map) match as-path as-path-list-number
```

An AS path access list (1 to 199) is used to match an AS regular expression. See Section 7-5 for more information about configuring an AS path access list.

(BGP only) Match against a community list:

```
(route-map) match community-list community-list [exact]
```

A community list (1 to 99) is used to match community values. The **exact** keyword is used to match the list of community values exactly. Refer to Section 7-5 for more information about configuring an IP community list.

c. (Optional) Configure attributes to be set during redistribution.

■ Set the next-hop IP address for a route:

```
(route-map) set next-hop ip-address
```

Set the route metric:

```
(route-map) set metric [+ | -]metric
```

-or-

```
(route-map) set metric bandwidth delay reliability loading mtu
```

The redistributed route is assigned the specified metric value. Use the first single-value case with all but IGRP and EIGRP. *metric* ranges from 0 to 4294967295. If the plus or minus signs are used with a value, the metric is adjusted by that value. Lower metric values are preferred.

Set the route metric type:

```
(route-map) set metric-type {internal | external | type-1 | type-2}
```

The metric types of the redistributed route are **internal** and **external** for IS-IS and **type-1** and **type-2** for OSPF.

Set the route tag value:

```
(route-map) set tag tag
```

By default, a route's tag value is redistributed as is into the new routing protocol. The tag value (0 to 4294967295) can be set if desired. Tags are arbitrary values that can be used to mark and filter routes during redistribution.

Automatically compute a route's tag value:

```
(route-map) set automatic-tag
```

By default, route tags are arbitrary values that can be set or matched with route maps. An automatic tag computation is also available, to be used where BGP interacts with OSPF on Autonomous System Boundary Routers (ASBRs). Automatic tag computation is described in RFC 1403, "BGP OSPF Interaction."

(BGP only) Set the BGP local preference value:

```
(route-map) set local-preference value
```

value can be from 0 to 4294967295 (the default is 100). Higher local preference values are preferred.

(BGP only) Set the BGP weight:

```
(route-map) set weight weight
```

The BGP *weight* value ranges from 0 to 65535 (the default is not changed). Weights set with a route map override weights set with BGP **neighbor** commands. Routes with a higher weight are preferred.

(BGP only) Set the BGP origin:

```
(route-map) set origin {igp | egp as | incomplete}
```

Set the origin to **igp** (the origin is inside the local AS; normally seen if the BGP **network** command is used or if IGP routes are redistributed into BGP), **egp** (learned from EGP from AS number *as*), or **incomplete** (the origin is unknown, or a static route is redistributed into BGP).

(BGP only) Modify the BGP AS path:

```
(route-map) set as-path {tag | prepend as-path-string}
```

as-path-string is prepended to the AS path attribute. By prepending the local AS multiple times, you can modify the path length to influence the path-selection process on a distant peer.

(BGP only) Set the BGP community attribute:

```
(route-map) set community {community [additive]} | none
```

The community attribute is set to the *community* value. If the **additive** keyword is used, the community value specified is added to the existing community attribute. The **none** keyword removes all community values.

(BGP only) Set the BGP route dampening parameters:

```
(route-map) set dampening halflife reuse suppress max-suppress-time
```

The *halflife* value ranges from 1 to 45 minutes (the default is 15 minutes). The *reuse* penalty threshold ranges from 1 to 20000 (the default is 750). The *suppress* penalty threshold ranges from 1 to 20000 (the default is 2000). *max-suppress-time* ranges from 1 to 20000 minutes (the default is 60 minutes).

d. (Optional) Define more route map commands, using the same name with greater sequence numbers.

e. Apply the route map to a redistribution process, as defined next.

4. For the corresponding routing process described next, redistribute routes from other routing protocols or sources (**connected, static, rip, igrp, eigrp, ospf, bgp,** or **isis;** connected routes result from directly connected interfaces with assigned IP addresses).

Redistribute into RIP:

```
(router) redistribute protocol [process-id] [metric metric]
  [route-mapmap]
```

Routes imported into RIP can receive a fixed metric value *metric* if desired. You can use an optional route map for conditional redistribution and attribute modification.

Redistribute into EIGRP:

```
(router) redistribute protocol [process-id] [metric bandwidth
  delay reliability loading mtu] [route-map map]
```

Routes imported into EIGRP can receive a fixed set of metric values if desired. When redistributing from IGRP, the metric values are properly preserved. You can use an optional route map for conditional redistribution and attribute modification.

Redistribute into OSPF:

```
(router) redistribute protocol [process-id] [metric metric]
  [metric-type type] [match {internal | external 1 | external 2}]
  [tag tag] [subnets] [route-map map]
```

Routes imported into OSPF can receive a fixed metric value. By default, routes imported into OSPF are flagged as Type 2 external routes unless the **metric-type** option is used. When OSPF routes are redistributed into another OSPF process, the **match** keyword can be used to filter only internal, Type 1, or Type 2 external routes. The **tag** keyword is used to assign a tag field to external routes to be exchanged between ASBRs. By default, only routes that are not subnetted are redistributed into OSPF unless the **subnets** keyword is given. An optional route map can be used for conditional redistribution and attribute modification.

Note   An OSPF router that redistributes routes from another source becomes an ASBR.

Redistribute into BGP:

```
(router) redistribute protocol [process-id] [metric metric]
  [weight weight] [route-map map]
```

Routes imported into BGP can receive a fixed metric value for the Multi-Exit Discriminator (MED) or the INTER_AS (BGP versions 2 and 3). A fixed BGP weight value can also be assigned to all redistributed routes. An optional route map can be used for conditional redistribution and attribute modification.

Redistribute into IS-IS:

```
(router) redistribute protocol [process-id] [metric metric]
  {level-1 | level-1-2 | level-2} [route-map map]
```

Routes imported into IS-IS can receive a fixed metric value. Imported routes can be redistributed at level-1 (intra-area) or at level-2 (interarea) or both. An optional route map can be used for conditional redistribution and attribute modification.

Example

Routes from EIGRP process 101 are redistributed into the RIP process and are given a default RIP metric of 5:

```
router rip
      network 192.168.1.0
      default-metric 5
      redistribute eigrp 101
```

Routes (including subnets) from the RIP process are redistributed into OSPF process 200 with a metric of 10. Routes (including subnets) from EIGRP process 200 are redistributed into OSPF process 200 with a metric of 5. For EIGRP process 200, all routes from RIP are redistributed with a bandwidth metric of 100 Mbps, a delay metric of 100, a reliability metric of 255, a loading metric of 1, and an MTU of 1500 bytes:

```
router ospf 200
        network 172.16.3.0 0.0.0.255 area 0.0.0.0
        redistribute rip metric 10 subnets
        redistribute eigrp 200 metric 5 subnets
router rip
        network 10.0.0.0
router eigrp 200
        network 192.168.1.0
        redistribute rip metric 100000 100 255 1 1500
```

A route map is used to conditionally redistribute routes from the OSPF process into BGP. Specifically, only routes with a tag number of 10 are redistributed with a metric of 10:

```
router ospf 199
        network ...


router bgp 1001
        neighbor ...
        redistribute ospf 199 route-map ospf-to-bgp


route-map ospf-to-bgp permit
        match tag 10
        set metric 10
```

8-4: Filtering Routing Information

- Routing updates from a routing protocol can be completely suppressed on an interface if desired.

- The *administrative distance* can be tuned such that one routing protocol is more trusted than another within the local router.

- The routes advertised by a routing protocol can be closely controlled so that route filtering takes place toward neighboring routers.

- The routes received and processed by a routing protocol can be closely controlled so that inbound route filtering takes place from neighboring routers.

Route filtering is useful for distance vector routing protocols, because routes are sent and received among neighbors. However, filtering is not useful for link state protocols, such as OSPF, because all routers in a domain have an identical copy of the link-state database. In this case, filtering is useful only at link state advertisement boundaries, such as an OSPF ASBR.

Route filtering is also useful when mutual route redistribution is configured between two routing protocols. In some cases, routes redistributed into another routing protocol can be redistributed again in return. Route filters can be used to prevent this from happening.

Configuration

1. Enable the routing processes: RIP (see Section 6-1 and Section 6-2), EIGRP (see Section 6-3 and Section 6-4), OSPF (see Section 6-5 and Section 6-6), BGP (see Section 6-9), or Integrated IS-IS (see Section 6-7):

    (global) **router** *protocol* [*process-id*]

2. (Optional) Prevent all outbound routing updates on an interface:

    (router) **passive-interface** *type number*

    No routes will be advertised using this routing protocol and interface. Incoming routing updates will still be listened to and processed, except in the case of EIGRP: The router will also stop sending and receiving EIGRP hello packets on the interface, resulting in the loss of neighbor adjacencies.

3. (Optional) Make a routing protocol more trusted than another, to filter the source of routing information:

    (router) distance weight [address mask [access-list-num | name]] [ip]

    Assign an administrative distance value to a routing information source. The distance or weight ranges from 0 to 255 and is significant only to the local router. Every routing information source has a default administrative distance; the lower the distance, the more trusted the source. Table 8-4 documents administrative distances for routing information sources.

    The *address* and *mask* (inverted mask: 0 = match, 1 = don't care) fields can be given to match the IP addresses of routers sending routing information and to set the administrative distance for these sources alone. Also, either a named or standard IP access list can be used to more closely match IP addresses of advertising routers.

    Note EIGRP has two forms of this command to assign independent distances to internal (intra-AS) and external (inter-AS) routes: **distance eigrp** *internal-distance external-distance*.

4. (RIP, IGRP, EIGRP only) Increase the routing metric on matching routes:

    (router) **offset-list** *access-list* {**in** | **out**} *offset* [*type number*]

    Routes are matched against the named or numbered IP access list, and a fixed *offset* (positive number) is added to the route metric. The **in** and **out** keywords are used to select an offset for incoming or outgoing routes. If desired, the offset list can be applied to a specific interface *type* and *number*.

Table 8-4 *Default Administrative Distances*

Routing Info Source	Default Admin Distance
Connected interface	0
Static route	1
EIGRP summary route	5
External BGP	20
Internal EIGRP	90
OSPF	110
IS-IS	115
RIP	120
EGP	140
Internal BGP	200
Unknown (not trusted; ignored)	255

5. (Optional) Filter routes being advertised in outbound routing updates:

```
(router) distribute-list {access-list-num | name} out [interface]
```

Routes being advertised are first passed through the standard IP or named access list. Matching routes are either permitted to be advertised or are denied, according to the access list statements. The distribute list can be applied to only a single outbound interface if desired.

6. (Optional) Filter routes received from incoming advertisements:

```
(router) distribute-list {access-list-num | name} in [interface]
```

Routes received in routing updates are passed through the standard IP or named access list before being processed by the local routing protocol. Matching routes are either permitted to be used or are denied, according to the access list statements. The distribute list can be applied to only a single inbound interface if desired.

Note Inbound route filtering does not apply to the link-state protocols OSPF or IS-IS. By definition, the entire routing topology database is kept on each router. Therefore, specific routes are not received and processed independently.

Section 8-4

Example

For EIGRP, suppress routing updates on interface serial 1. Filter incoming routing updates to include only the 192.168.1.0 route. Filter outbound updates to include all but the 10.2.0.0 route. Adjust the administrative distance for EIGRP to 100 (instead of the default 90) on updates from EIGRP neighbors with IP addresses within the range 192.168.3.x:

```
router eigrp 101
        network 10.0.0.0
        passive-interface serial 1
        distribute-list 5 in
        distribute-list 6 out
        distance 100 192.168.3.0 0.0.0.255
access-list 5 permit 192.168.1.0
access-list 6 deny 10.2.0.0
access-list 6 permit any
```

8-5: Load Balancing

- Most routing protocols install a maximum of four parallel routes in a routing table by default.

- Static routes install up to six parallel routes by default.

- BGP installs one path by default.

- EIGRP and BGP can support unequal cost load balancing.

Configuration

1. (Optional) Change the number of parallel paths a routing process load balances packets across.

   (router) **maximum-paths** *number-paths*

   Most routing protocols install a maximum of four parallel routes in a routing table by default. The exceptions to this are static routes and BGP. Static routes install up to six routes, and BGP installs one path by default. You can change the number of routes that will be injected into the routing table by a routing process with the **maximum-paths** router configuration command. The maximum number of paths supported is six.

2. (Optional) Configure the router to use as many interfaces as possible:

   (global) **traffic-share min across-interfaces**

   You can load balance across as many interfaces as possible. This command configures multi-interface load splitting across different interfaces.

Example

In the following example, a router is configured to load balance across six equal cost paths:

```
hostname RouterA
!
interface fastethernet0/0
 ip address 192.168.1.1 255.255.255.0
!
interface fastethernet0/1
 ip address 172.16.0.1 255.255.0.0
!
router ospf 1
 network 172.16.0.0 0.0.255.255 area 0
 network 192.168.1.0 0.0.0.255 area 0
 maximum-paths 6
```

Further Reading

Refer to the following recommended sources for further technical information about the topics covered in this chapter:

IP Routing Fundamentals, by Mark A. Sportack, Cisco Press, ISBN 157870071X.

IP Routing Primer, by Robert Wright, Cisco Press, ISBN 1578701082.

Routing TCP/IP, Volume 1, by Jeff Doyle, Cisco Press, ISBN 1578700418.

Section 8-5

Chapter 9

Quality of Service

This chapter discusses how to configure and use the Quality of Service (QoS) features described here:

- Comprehensive QoS Configuration

    - **9-1: Modular QoS Command-Line Interface (MQC)**—A "user-friendly" way to configure all QoS features within a single framework. This framework is based on the Diffserv model. Traffic is defined as class maps; class maps are used in policy maps; policy maps are applied to interfaces. You should consider using the modular QoS CLI rather than configuring a variety of individual QoS features, just for its intuitive and structured approach.

        Class maps perform versatile traffic classification. Policy maps define QoS policies by using traffic marking (reclassification), congestion management (WFQ and LLQ), congestion avoidance (WRED), and traffic policing and shaping.

- Packet Classification Techniques

    - **9-2: Network-Based Application Recognition (NBAR)**—Traffic can be intelligently and automatically recognized and classified based on a database of protocols. NBAR provides an easy-to-use classification of protocols—even those that use dynamic TCP and UDP port assignments.

    - **9-3: Policy-Based Routing (PBR)**—Traffic can be classified with access lists, marked with an IP Precedence, and routed to specified interfaces.

    - **9-4: Quality of Service for VPNs**—Traffic can be classified before it is encrypted or encapsulated by a VPN mechanism.

    - **9-5: QoS Policy Propagation via BGP**—Traffic classification policies can be propagated throughout a large network through the use of BGP updates.

- Congestion Management Techniques

    - **9-6: Priority Queuing (PQ)**—Traffic is assigned to four strict priority queues for transmission on an interface.

    - **9-7: Custom Queuing (CQ)**—Traffic is assigned to a set of queues that each receives a proportional amount of the interface bandwidth.

    - **9-8: Weighted Fair Queuing (WFQ)**—Traffic is automatically classified into conversations or flows, each of which receives a weight according to the type of traffic. Low-volume traffic receives priority over high-volume traffic, providing timely delivery of low-volume interactive traffic.

- Congestion Avoidance Techniques

    - **9-9: Weighted Random Early Detection (WRED)**—Traffic is randomly dropped as congestion becomes apparent, causing the traffic source to reduce its transmission rate. WRED can drop packets based on IP Precedence or DSCP so that higher-priority traffic is delivered without being dropped.

- Traffic Policing and Shaping Techniques

    - **9-10: Committed Access Rate (CAR)**—Both inbound and outbound traffic can be rate-limited according to CAR policies. Policies can identify traffic according to interface, classification, addresses, application, and access lists. Each policy is configured with a bandwidth restriction and actions to take if the policy is met or exceeded.

    - **9-11: Generic Traffic Shaping (GTS)**—Outbound traffic can be shaped to a particular rate to prevent congestion.

    - **9-12: Frame Relay Traffic Shaping (FRTS)**—Outbound traffic on a Frame Relay interface can be shaped to conform to the CIR. Congestion notification methods can be used to adapt the shaping.

- QoS Signaling Techniques

    - **9-13: Use RSVP for QoS Signaling**—RSVP provides a means for an end node or router to request a resource reservation from the source to the destination network. End-to-end guaranteed QoS is the result.

- Improving QoS on Physical Links

    - **9-14: Link Efficiency Mechanisms**—At the interface level, some additional techniques are available to improve data transmission performance. Link Fragmentation and Interleaving (LFI) can adjust the transmitted packet size and order so that time-critical packets (voice, video, ERP, and so forth) can be inserted into the data stream at a guaranteed interpacket delay. Compressed Real-Time Protocol (CRTP) performs header compression to reduce the overhead involved in transporting time-critical packets.

    - **9-15 AutoQoS for the Enterprise**—AutoQoS provides an easy means for administrators to enable quality of service (QoS). AutoQoS for the Enterprise uses Network-Based Application Recognition (NBAR) for protocol discovery and statistical analyses. After a predefined learning period that defaults to 3 days, AutoQoS generates and deploys MQC-based QoS policies automatically to the router configuration.

QoS is also built around the concept of Differentiated Services (Diffserv), in which the QoS specification is carried within each packet. IP packets have a Type of Service (ToS) byte that is formatted according to the top row of Table 9-1. Bits P2, P1, and P0 form the IP Precedence value. Bits T3, T2, T1, and T0 form the ToS value.

Table 9-1 *ToS and DSCP Byte Formats*

ToS Byte	P2	P1	P0	T3	T2	T1	T0	Zero
DS Byte	DS5	DS4	DS3	DS2	DS1	DS0	Unused	Unused
	(Class selector)			(Drop precedence)				

For Differentiated Services, the same byte is called the Differentiated Services (DS) byte. It is formatted according to the bottom row of Table 9-1. Bits DS5 through DS0 form the Differentiated Services Code Point (DSCP). The DSCP is arranged to be backward-compatible with the IP Precedence bits, because the two quantities share the same byte in the IP header.

Bits DS5, DS4, and DS3 form the DSCP Class Selector. Classes 1 through 4 are the Assured Forwarding (AF) service levels. Each AF service level has three Drop Precedence categories: Low, Medium, and High. Traffic in the AF classes can be dropped. The greatest likelihood of dropping is in the Low category, and the least is in the High category.

Class 5 is also called the Expedited Forwarding (EF) class, offering premium service and the least likelihood of packet drops. The Default class selector (DSCP 000 000) offers only best-effort forwarding.

Table 9-2 shows how the IP Precedence names and bits are mapped to DSCP values. DSCP is broken down into Per-Hop Behavior (PHB), Class Selector, and Drop Precedence. Many times, DSCP values are referred to by their Codepoint names (such as AF23); these are also listed in the table. The DSCP bits are shown, along with their decimal equivalents. In many DSCP-related commands, you need to enter a decimal DSCP value, even though it is difficult to relate the decimal numbers to the corresponding DSCP service levels and PHBs. Use this table as a convenient cross-reference.

Table 9-2 *Mapping of IP Precedence and DSCP Fields*

IP Precedence (3 bits)		DSCP (6 bits)				
Name	Value	Bits	Per-Hop Behavior	Class Selector	Drop Precedence	Codepoint Name	DSCP Bits (Decimal)
Routine	0	000	Default			Default	000 000 (0)
Priority	1	001	AF	1	1: Low	AF11	001 010 (10)
					2: Medium	AF12	001 100 (12)
					3: High	AF13	001 110 (14)
Immediate	2	010	AF	2	1: Low	AF21	010 010 (18)
					2: Medium	AF22	010 100 (20)
					3: High	AF23	010 110 (22)
Flash	3	011	AF	3	1: Low	AF31	011 010 (26)
					2: Medium	AF32	011 100 (28)
					3: High	AF33	011 110 (30)
Flash Override	4	100	AF	4	1: Low	AF41	100 010 (34)
					2: Medium	AF42	100 100 (36)
					3: High	AF43	100 110 (38)
Critical	5	101	EF			EF	101 110 (46)
Internetwork Control	6	110	—				
Network Control	7	111	—				

9-1: Modular QoS Command-Line Interface (MQC)

- QoS can be defined according to the Diffserv model:

    - Packet classification at the edge of a Diffserv region

    - Packet marking (rewriting the DSCP values)

    - Traffic conditioning, including traffic shaping, Frame Relay traffic shaping, and policing with CAR

    - Policy or PHB enforcement, including EF PHB with Low Latency Queuing (LLQ) and AF PHBs with class-based WFQ, WRED, CAR, and traffic shaping

- QoS is configured in a modular fashion:

    - Traffic is classified into one or more *class map*s.

    - Class maps are applied to *policy maps*.

    - Policy maps are applied to interfaces as *service policies*.

Configuration

1. Classify traffic into a class map.

a. Define a class map:

```
(global) class-map [match-all | match-any] class-map-name
```

The class map is given an arbitrary *class-map-name* (a text string). Traffic is tested against one or more match conditions in the class map. By default, all matches must be met (**match-all**) to classify a packet as a part of the class. The **match-any** keyword can be given so that a packet matching any of the conditions is classified into the class. Exit from class map configuration mode with the **exit** command.

b. Define one or more matching conditions for packets.

Note   Use the **match** *criteria* keywords to match against a specific parameter. To match against a negated parameter, use **match not** *criteria*.

- Match any packet:

    ```
    (class-map) match any
    ```

    Packets are matched unconditionally. This can be used to create a class map that always matches packets so that all traffic can be classified into the class. QoS policies can then be easily applied to all traffic on an interface.

- Match against another class map:

    ```
    (class-map) match class-map class-name
    ```

    To be matched, a packet must have already been classified into the class named *class-name*. This allows class maps to be nested to create more complex policy structures.

- Match against a protocol type:

    ```
    (class-map) match protocol protocol
    ```

    A packet is matched if it contains the *protocol*. Valid protocol names are referenced through Network-Based Application Recognition (NBAR). (Refer to Section 9-2 for more information.) Here are some of the accepted protocol names:

    aarp (AppleTalk ARP), **apollo**, **arp** (Address Resolution Protocol), **bridge** (transparent bridging), **bstun** (Block Serial Tunnel), **cdp** (Cisco Discovery Protocol), **clns** (ISO Connectionless Network Service), **clns_es** (CLNS End System), **clns_is**

(CLNS Intermediate System), **cmns** (ISO Connection-Mode Network Service), **compressedtcp, decnet, decnet_node, decnet_router-l1** (DECnet router L1), **decnet_router-l2** (DECnet router L2), **dlsw** (Data Link Switching), **ip, ipx, llc2** (Logical Link Control 2), **pad** (Packet Assembler/Disassembler), **qllc** (Qualified Logical Link Control), **rsrb** (Remote Source Route Bridging), **snapshot** (Snapshot routing), **stun** (Serial Tunnel), **vines**, and **xns**.

- Match against an access list:

  `(class-map)` **match access-group** `[access-group | ` **name** ` access-group-name]`

  If a packet is permitted by the access list *access-group*, it is matched.

  The **name** keyword can be used to specify a named access list.

- Match against a Layer 2 Class of Service (CoS):

  `(class-map)` **match cos** `cos [cos cos cos]`

  If a packet is marked with the given CoS value *cos* (0 to 7; 0 = low, 7 = high), it is matched. IEEE 802.1Q/ISL CoS values are usually set by Layer 2 devices at the edge of the network. Up to four CoS values can be specified in a single **match** command.

- Match against IP Precedence values:

  `(class-map)` **match ip precedence** `precedence [precedence precedence`
  ` precedence]`

  If a packet is marked with IP Precedence value *precedence* (a name or number), it is matched. Valid precedence values are **0** (routine), **1** (priority), **2** (immediate), **3** (Flash), **4** (Flash-override), **5** (critical), **6** (Internet), and **7** (network). Up to four precedence values can be given. Only one needs to match.

- Match against DSCP values:

  `(class-map)` **match ip dscp** `dscp [dscp dscp dscp dscp dscp dscp dscp]`

  Up to eight DSCP values (0 to 63) can be given to match against. Only one of the values given needs to match. The IP DSCP field is carried in the first 6 bits of the IP ToS byte.

- Match against a local QoS group:

  `(class-map)` **match qos-group** `qos-group`

  A router can mark and match traffic using locally significant QoS group numbers (0 to 99). If the packet is already marked with *qos-group*, it is matched.

- Match against the MPLS experimental value:

  `(class-map)` **match mpls experimental** `mpls-value`

  A packet is matched if it has the MPLS experimental (EXP) value *mpls-value* (0 to 7).

- Match against Real-Time Protocol (RTP):

  `(class-map)` **match ip rtp** `starting-port port-range`

  To match against RTP packets, a UDP port range is given as *starting-port* (2000 to 65535) and extends for *port-range* (0 to 16383) additional port numbers. If a packet contains a UDP port within the range, it is matched.

- Match against an inbound interface:

    ```
    (class-map) match input-interface type number
    ```

    If a packet arrives on the specified interface, it is matched.

- Match against a source MAC address:

    ```
    (class-map) match source-address mac address
    ```

    If a packet has the source MAC address given by *address* (dotted-triplet hexadecimal format), it is matched. This can be used only on an input interface that has a MAC address (not a serial or ATM interface).

- Match against a destination MAC address:

    ```
    (class-map) match destination-address mac address
    ```

If a packet has the destination MAC address given by *address* (dotted-triplet hexadecimal format), it is matched.

2. Use a policy map to perform a QoS policy.

    a. Define the policy map:

        ```
        (global) policy-map policy-name
        ```

        The policy map is named *policy-name* (an arbitrary text string).

    b. Identify one or more traffic classes using class maps (up to 64 classes):

        ```
        (pmap) class class-name
        ```

        The policy will be enacted on all traffic classified into the class *class-name* (a text string). Use the **exit** command to end the current class policy definition.

    c. (Optional) Use the default class:

        ```
        (pmap) class class-default
        ```

        The default class can be referenced to include traffic that doesn't match any other class definition.

    d. (Optional) Set various QoS parameters in the packet.

        - Set the Frame Relay Discard Eligibility (DE) bit (added in Cisco IOS Software Release 12.2(2)T):

            ```
            (pmap-class) set fr-de
            ```

            By default, packets that are converted to Frame Relay frames do not have their DE bits set. If you want to, you can set the DE bit on matching packets, indicating that the frame is eligible to be discarded during switch congestion.

        - Set the ATM cell loss priority (CLP):

            ```
            (pmap-class) set atm-clp
            ```

By default, packets that are converted to ATM cells have their CLP bits set to 0 (high priority). If you want to, you can set the CLP bit to 1 (lower priority), indicating that the cell is eligible to be discarded during congestion.

■ Set the Class of Service (CoS):

```
(pmap-class) set cos cos
```

The Layer 2 IEEE 802.1Q CoS value can be set to *cos* (0 to 7; 0 = low, 7 = high). The CoS value should be set only on packets that are being forwarded into a switched environment.

■ Set the IP DSCP:

```
(pmap-class) set ip dscp dscp
```

The IP DSCP value can be set to *dscp* (0 to 63). You also can use the keywords **EF** (expedited forwarding, decimal 46), **AF11** (assured forwarding class 11, decimal 10), and **AF12** (assured forwarding class 12, decimal 12).

■ Set the IP Precedence:

```
(pmap-class) set ip precedence precedence
```

The IP Precedence value can be set to *precedence* (0 to 7; 0 = low, 7 = high).

■ Set the MPLS experimental value:

```
(pmap-class) set mpls experimental mpls-value
```

The MPLS experimental (EXP) value can be set to *mpls-value* (0 to 7).

■ Set the QoS group number:

```
(pmap-class) set qos-group qos-group
```

The locally significant QoS group number (0 to 99) can be set.

e. (Optional) Use class-based WFQ to manage congestion.

■ Allocate the bandwidth for the class:

```
(pmap-class) bandwidth {bandwidth | percent percentage}
```

Class-based WFQ derives the weights for classes from their bandwidths and, during congestion, from their bandwidth percentages. The *bandwidth* is set in Kbps, and *percentage* is unitless (0 to 100). All classes in a policy map must use bandwidth or percentage, but not a mix of both. If an interface's bandwidth is unknown, use the **percent** keyword for a relative allocation.

Note   The available bandwidth for WFQ is the interface bandwidth minus the sum of the bandwidth reservations for RSVP, LLQ, and IP RTP priority.

- (Optional) Use LLQ for a strict priority class:

```
(pmap-class) priority {bandwidth | percent percentage} [burst]
```

The guaranteed bandwidth for a strict priority class of traffic can be given as *bandwidth* (in Kbps) or as a *percentage* of the overall bandwidth (1 to 100). The burst size can also be specified as *burst* (32 to 2000000 bytes).

Note   The strict priority queue that is used with WFQ can be assigned to a class map for traffic that matches a certain criteria. For voice traffic, the (interface) **ip rtp priority** command can be used instead to assign RTP packets to the strict priority queue. See Step 4 for details.

- (Optional) Reserve a number of queues for the class:

```
(pmap-class) fair-queue [queue-limit queues]
```

The maximum number of packets that are queued per flow can be set to *queues*. If the default class is being configured, **fair-queue** [*queues*] sets the number of dynamic queues that are available for the default class (16 to 4096, as a power of 2). The default number of queues starts at 16 for a bandwidth of 64 kbps or less and doubles as the bandwidth doubles. However, any bandwidth over 512 kbps is given 256 queues.

f. (Optional) Use congestion avoidance with tail drop:

```
(pmap-class) queue-limit packets
```

The maximum number of packets in the queue is set to *packets* (1 to 64, although the maximum might depend on the router hardware; the default is 64). When the queue threshold is reached, no further queuing is performed, causing tail drop until the queue level is lowered.

g. (Optional) Use congestion avoidance with Weighted Random Early Detection (WRED).

- Select a QoS criteria for WRED:

```
(pmap-class) random-detect [prec-based | dscp-based]
```

WRED can be based on IP Precedence (**prec-based**, the default) or on IP DSCP (**dscp-based**).

- (Optional) Set the WRED thresholds:

```
(pmap-class) random-detect {precedence precedence | dscp dscp}

  min-threshold max-threshold mark-prob-denominator
```

WRED can be based on IP Precedence (**precedence**) or IP DSCP (**dscp**). When the average queue length reaches the minimum threshold, *min-threshold* (1 to

4096 packets), some packets with the *precedence* value or the *dscp* value are dropped. Likewise, when the queue length reaches *max-threshold* (*min-threshold* to 4096 packets), all packets with the *precedence* value are dropped.

When the queue meets the threshold level, one out of every *mark-prob-denominator* packets (1 to 65536; the default is 10 packets) is dropped.

IP Precedence values are given as *precedence* (0 to 7), and DSCP values are given as *dscp* (0 to 63 or a keyword: ef, af11, af12, af13, af21, af22, af23, af31, af32, af33, af41, af42, af43, cs1, cs2, cs3, cs4, cs5, or cs7.

h. (Optional) Use traffic policing to control the rate of traffic:

```
(pmap-class) police bps burst-normal burst-max conform-action action

    exceed-action action [violate-action action]
```

The average traffic rate is given as *bps* (bits per second). Traffic can burst above the average by *burst-normal* bytes and by an excess burst of *burst-max* bytes.

Depending on the relationship between the traffic rate and the policing thresholds, certain actions can be taken. If the traffic rate conforms to the *bps* rate or rises under the normal burst or *burst-normal* size, the **conform-action** is taken. If the traffic rate rises to between the normal and excess burst sizes, the **exceed-action** is taken. Finally, if the traffic rate rises above the excessive burst or *burst-max* size, the **violate-action** can be taken if it is specified. (If it is not specified, the *burst-max* value has no effect on the traffic. A one-token bucket algorithm is then used.)

The *action* parameters can be **drop** (drop the packet), **set-prec-transmit** *new-prec* (set the IP Precedence to *new-prec* and then forward the packet), **set-qos-transmit** *new-qos* (set the QoS group to *new-qos* and then forward the packet), **set-dscp-transmit** *new-dscp* (set the DSCP to *new-dscp* and then forward the packet), or **transmit** (forward the packet as-is).

i. (Optional) Use class-based shaping to match the speed of a remote target:

```
(pmap-class) shape {average | peak} cir [bc] [be]
```

Generic traffic shaping is configured with an **average** rate or a **peak** rate as *cir* (bits per second). You can also specify a normal burst size *bc* (in bits) and an excess burst size *be* (in bits).

3. Apply a policy map to an interface:

```
(interface) service-policy {input | output} policy-map-name
```

The traffic policy named *policy-map-name* is attached to the interface in either the **input** (entering the interface) or **output** (leaving the interface) direction.

4. (Optional) Use a strict priority queue for RTP voice traffic:

```
(interface) ip rtp priority starting-rtp-port port-range bandwidth
```

IP RTP voice traffic can be assigned to a strict priority queue that is serviced before any other queue on the interface. RTP packets are identified by their UDP port numbers, given as the lowest UDP port for RTP *(starting-rtp-port)* and the number of ports used in the RTP range *(port-range)*. The guaranteed *bandwidth* is also specified, in Kbps.

Allocate enough bandwidth for all simultaneous calls that will be supported, taking traffic bursts into account. The priority queue takes RTP compression into account automatically, so you only need to consider the compressed call bandwidth and any Layer 2 headers.

MQC Example

The Modular QoS CLI is used to configure a QoS policy for outbound traffic on interface serial 0. Streaming audio traffic is classified into a class map called *streaming,* containing RealAudio, StreamWorks, and VDOlive traffic flows. Voice over IP traffic is classified into class map *voip,* containing RTP traffic. FTP traffic is classified into class map *filetransfer,* using an access list to match TCP ports 20 and 21.

A policy map called *traffic-out* is used to define the QoS policy. The following policies are configured:

- Traffic belonging to the *streaming* class map has the DSCP value set to 34 (AF41), using WFQ to manage congestion for a 128 kbps bandwidth.

- Traffic belonging to the *voip* class map has the DSCP value set to 46 (EF). LLQ is used to implement a strict priority queue alongside WFQ for up to 128 kbps of voice traffic.

- Traffic belonging to the *filetransfer* class map has the DSCP value set conditionally. A traffic policer is configured to control FTP traffic to a 128 kbps bandwidth, allowing bursts of 16000 bytes. If the FTP traffic conforms to the 128 kbps rate, the DSCP value is set to 26 (AF31), and packets are forwarded. If the FTP traffic bursts to within the burst size, the DSCP value is set to 30 (AF33, high drop precedence), and the packets are forwarded. If the FTP traffic violates the burst size, packets are simply dropped.

- The default class, *class-default,* is defined to set the DSCP value of all other packets to 0. This indicates that best-effort service is acceptable.

```
class-map match-all streaming
       match protocol realaudio
       match protocol streamwork
       match protocol vdolive
class-map voip
       match ip rtp 16384 17800
access-list 110 permit tcp any any eq ftp
access-list 110 permit tcp any any eq ftp-data
```

```
class-map filetransfer
      match access-group 110


policy-map traffic-out
      class streaming
            set ip dscp 34
            bandwidth 128
      class voip
            set ip dscp 46
            priority 128
      class filetransfer
            police 128000 16000 16000 conform-action set-dscp-transmit
26
                  exceed-action set-dscp-transmit 30 violate-action drop
      class class-default
            set ip dscp 0
interface serial 0
      service-policy output traffic-out
```

9-2: Network-Based Application Recognition (NBAR)

- NBAR can be used to recognize applications within network traffic and classify them into classes.

- NBAR classes can be used by the Modular QoS CLI to assign QoS policies to the applications.

- Applications with both dynamic and static TCP/UDP port assignments can be recognized.

- HTTP traffic can be classified by host name, URL, or MIME type.

- NBAR uses an extensible Packet Description Language (PDL) to describe application traffic. PDL Modules (PDLMs) can be loaded into Flash memory at run time to add additional protocol discovery capabilities.

- NBAR requires the use of Cisco Express Forwarding (CEF) on the router. NBAR must have access to the UDP and TCP port numbers in the packets of application data. Therefore, NBAR cannot be used on interfaces in which encryption or tunnels are in use.

Note NBAR allocates 1 MB of DRAM memory to handle up to 5000 concurrent traffic flows. If more memory is needed later, it is allocated in increments of 200 to 400 KB. Each flow uses about 150 bytes of memory.

Configuration

1. Define a traffic class name for identified traffic:

   ```
   (global) class-map [match-all | match-any] class-name
   ```

   NBAR matches all or any of a given set of protocols as part of a traffic class named *class-name* (an arbitrary text string).

2. Identify one or more protocols to include in the class:

   ```
   (class-map) match protocol protocol-name
   ```

   The *protocol-name* is the name of a recognizable protocol. These are listed in Table 9-3.

   For the **http** keyword, an additional **url** *url-string*, **host** *host-string*, or **mime** *mime-string* must be added. The *url-string* is the URL without the http://hostname. domain portion. The *host-string* is just the host name portion (www.cisco.com, for example). You can use special characters as wildcards within the strings: * (matches zero or more characters), ? (matches a character), | (matches one of a choice of characters), (|) (matches one of a choice of characters in a range, as in www.name. (com|org)), and [ ] (matches any of the characters in a range, as in [0–9] for any digit).

   The *mime-string* specifies a MIME type using an arbitrary text string. Valid MIME types are listed in the document http://www.isi.edu/in-notes/iana/assignments/media-types/media-types.

   For the **citrix** protocol, an additional [**app** *application*] can be added to specify the name of an *application* (a text string).

3. (Optional) Enable protocol statistics gathering on an interface:

   ```
   (interface) ip nbar protocol-discovery
   ```

   NBAR gathers statistics about the protocols being used on an interface, based on its PDLM database of protocols. To see the results of protocol discovery, you can use the **show ip nbar protocol-discovery** command.

4. Use the class map to assign QoS policies.

   The Modular QoS CLI is used to group class maps into policy maps (**policy-map**) and assign policies to an interface (**service-policy**). See Section 9-1 for further information.

   To add additional protocol recognition to NBAR, use the following commands:

   a. Reference a PDLM file in Flash memory:

   ```
   (global) ip nbar pdlm pdlm-file
   ```

   The PDLM file is obtained from Cisco and downloaded into the router's Flash memory.

Table 9-3 *Possible protocol-name Values*

Protocol	*protocol-name* Value	Type	Well-Known Port Number	Description
EGP	egp	IP	8	Exterior Gateway Protocol
GRE	gre	IP	47	Generic Routing Encapsulation
ICMP	icmp	IP	1	Internet Control Message Protocol
IPINIP	ipinip	IP	4	IP-in-IP
IPSec	ipsec	IP	50, 51	IP Encapsulating Security Payload/Authentication Header
EIGRP	eigrp	IP	88	Enhanced Interior Gateway Routing Protocol
BGP	bgp	TCP/UDP	179	Border Gateway Protocol
CU-SeeMe	cuseeme	TCP/UDP	7648, 7649	Desktop videoconferencing
		UDP	24032	Desktop videoconferencing
DHCP/Bootp	dhcp	UDP	67, 68	Dynamic Host Configuration Protocol/Bootstrap Protocol
DNS	dns	TCP/UDP	53	Domain Name System
Exchange	exchange	TCP	stateful	MS-RPC for Exchange
Finger	finger	TCP	79	Finger user information protocol
FTP	ftp	TCP	stateful	File Transfer Protocol
Gopher	gopher	TCP/UDP	70	Internet Gopher Protocol
HTTP	http	TCP	80	Hypertext Transfer Protocol
		TCP	stateful	HTTP with URL, MIME, or Host classification
HTTPS	secure-http	TCP	443	Secured HTTP
IMAP	imap	TCP/UDP	143, 220	Internet Message Access Protocol
IRC	Irc	TCP/UDP	194	Internet Relay Chat
Kerberos	kerberos	TCP/UDP	88, 749	Kerberos Network Authentication Service
L2TP	l2tp	UDP	1701	L2F/L2TP tunnel

Table 9-3 *Possible protocol-name Values*

Protocol	*protocol-name* Value	Type	Well-Known Port Number	Description
LDAP	ldap	TCP/UDP	389	Lightweight Directory Access Protocol
MS-PPTP	pptp	TCP	1723	Microsoft Point-to-Point Tunneling Protocol for VPN
MS-SQLserver	sqlserver	TCP	1433	Microsoft SQL Server Desktop Videoconfer-encing
NetBIOS	Netbios	TCP	137, 139	NetBIOS over IP (Microsoft Windows)
		UDP	137, 138	NetBIOS over IP (Microsoft Windows)
Netshow	Netshow	TCP/UDP	stateful	Microsoft Netshow
NFS	Nfs	TCP/UDP	2049	Network File System
NNTP	nntp	TCP/UDP	119	Network News Transfer Protocol
Notes	notes	TCP/UDP	1352	Lotus Notes
Novadigm	novadigm	TCP/UDP	3460-3465	Novadigm Enterprise Desktop Manager (EDM)
NTP	ntp	TCP/UDP	123	Network Time Protocol
PCAnywhere	pcanywhere	TCP	5631, 65301	Symantec PCAnywhere
		UDP	22, 5632	Symantec PCAnywhere
POP3	pop3	TCP/UDP	110	Post Office Protocol
Printer	printer	TCP/UDP	515	Printer
r-commands	rcmd	TCP	stateful	rsh, rlogin, rexec
Realaudio	realaudio	TCP/UDP	stateful	RealAudio Streaming Protocol
RIP	rip	UDP	520	Routing Information Protocol
RSVP	rsvp	UDP	1698, 1699	Resource Reservation Protocol
SFTP	secure-ftp	TCP	990	Secure FTP
SHTTP	secure-http	TCP	443	Secure HTTP
SIMAP	secure-imap	TCP/UDP	585, 993	Secure IMAP
SIRC	secure-irc	TCP/UDP	994	Secure IRC

Table 9-3 *Possible protocol-name Values*

Protocol	*protocol-name* Value	Type	Well-Known Port Number	Description
SLDAP	secure-ldap	TCP/UDP	636	Secure LDAP
SNNTP	secure-nntp	TCP/UDP	563	Secure NNTP
SMTP	smtp	TCP	25	Simple Mail Transfer Protocol
SNMP	snmp	TCP/UDP	161, 162	Simple Network Management Protocol
SOCKS	socks	TCP	1080	Firewall security protocol
SPOP3	secure-pop3	TCP/UDP	995	Secure POP3
SQL*NET	sqlnet	TCP/UDP	stateful	SQL*NET for Oracle
SSH	ssh	TCP	22	Secured Shell
STELNET	secure-telnet	TCP	992	Secure Telnet
StreamWorks	streamwork	UDP	stateful	Xing Technology StreamWorks audio and video
SunRPC	sunrpc	TCP/UDP	stateful	Sun Remote Procedure Call
Syslog	syslog	UDP	514	System Logging Utility
Telnet	telnet	TCP	23	Telnet Protocol
TFTP	tftp	UDP	stateful	Trivial File Transfer Protocol
VDOLive	vdolive	TCP/UDP	stateful	VDOLive Streaming Video
X Windows	xwindows	TCP	6000-6003	X11, X Windows

b. Change an application's port number:

```
(global) ip nbar port-map protocol-name {tcp | udp} port
```

If you know that an application is using a port number other than the well-known port known by NBAR, you can change NBAR's behavior. For the protocol named *protocol-name*, specify TCP or UDP and the new *port* number. If the application uses more than one static port number, you can give up to 16 different port numbers in a string. To view NBAR's current protocol-to-port mappings, use the **show ip nbar port-map** command.

NBAR Example

NBAR is used to classify traffic into two classes—one for SMTP, POP3, and Lotus Notes traffic, and another for IRC Chat and PCAnywhere traffic. These classes can then be used by other QoS functions.

```
class-map match-all class1
        match protocol smtp
        match protocol pop3
        match protocol notes
class-map match-all class2
        match protocol irc
        match protocol pcanywhere
```

NBAR can also be used to classify traffic that is associated with recent Internet worms. In the following example, NBAR is configured to identify specific text strings in the URLs of HTTP GET commands. The Code Red worm uses HTTP GET requests for file-names ending with an .ida extension. These requests are identified by class map **code-red** (using NBAR). Policy map **quench-code-red** is applied to inbound traffic on interface ethernet 1/0. The policy map uses class map **code-red** to identify the suspect traffic and a traffic policer to govern the rate of Code Red traffic. Notice that the policer is config-ured to **drop** both conforming and exceeding traffic such that all matching traffic is dropped. (The bandwidth and burst values are then meaningless.)

You could also mark the matching packets with a DSCP value that is rarely used, such as DSCP 1. The goal here is to mark the packets with some method so that they can be matched later by an access list, a route map, or a policy map.

```
class-map match-all code-red
        match protocol http url "*.ida"
policy-map quench-code-red
        class code-red
        police 256000 64000 64000 conform-action drop exceed-action drop
interface ethernet 1/0
        service-policy input quench-code-red
```

9-3: Policy-Based Routing (PBR)

■   PBR provides routing based on a policy rather than a destination address or routing protocol.

■   With PBR, packets matching a condition or policy can be classified by setting the IP Precedence bits.

■   Classified packets are then routed to the next-hop address or to an interface accord-ing to the policy.

Configuration

1. Define a route map to classify traffic.

   a. Specify one or more **route-map** statements:

   `(global)` **route-map** *map-tag* [**permit** | **deny**] [*sequence*]

   An action statement is added to the route map named *map-tag* (a text string). The statements are evaluated in sequential order, according to the *sequence* number. The action taken on the packet can be to **permit** it (process the packet through the **route-map** statement and route it according to PBR) or **deny** it (route normally).

   b. Define one or more conditions to match against (all must be met).

   ■ (Optional) Match the Layer 3 packet length:

   `(route-map)` **match length** *min max*

   If the packet length is between *min* and *max* bytes, the condition is met.

   ■ (Optional) Match the IP addresses and/or ports:

   `(route-map)` **match ip address** *access-list* [*access-list*]

   A standard IP access list *access-list* (named or numbered) can be used to match the source address of packets. An extended IP access list can be used to match source and destination addresses, as well as port numbers.

   c. Define actions to perform on the packet.

   ■ (Optional) Set the IP Precedence bits:

   `(route-map)` **set ip precedence** {*number* | *name*}

   The IP Precedence can be set to a number or name: **0** (**routine**), **1** (**priority**), **2** (**immediate**), **3** (**flash**), **4** (**flash-override**), or **5** (**critical**). Precedence numbers 6 and 7 are reserved for network control information.

   ■ (Optional) Set the next-hop address:

   `(route-map)` **set ip next-hop** *ip-address* [*ip-address* ...]

   Packets will be forwarded to one or more next-hop addresses.

   ■ (Optional) Set the output interface:

   `(route-map)` **set interface** *type number*

   Packets will be forwarded to the output interface *type* and *number*.

   d. Enable PBR.

   a. Apply the route map to an inbound interface:

   `(interface)` **ip policy route-map** *map-tag*

The route map is applied to the interface where traffic is *received*. Packets are evaluated and forwarded according to PBR.

b. (Optional) Enable fast switching for PBR:

`(interface) `**`ip route-cache policy`**

By default, PBR disables fast switching on the interfaces where it is applied. Enabling fast-switched PBR also causes the **set ip default next-hop** and **set default interface** commands to be unsupported.

PBR Example

PBR is configured to classify incoming traffic into two classes: IP Precedence *flash* for all Telnet traffic, and *routine* for all other traffic. PBR is not configured with explicit next-hop addresses or output interfaces, so the IP Precedence is set, and normal routing occurs.

```
route-map pbrmap permit 10
      match ip address 101
        set ip precedence flash
route-map pbrmap permit 20
        set ip precedence routine
access-list 101 permit tcp any any eq telnet
interface ethernet 0
        ip policy route-map pbrmap
        ip route-cache policy
```

9-4: Quality of Service for VPNs

- IP packets are classified before they are encrypted and sent over a VPN tunnel.

- QoS classification is performed based on the original source and destination addresses and port numbers.

- If a packet is fragmented after encryption, only the first fragment can be preclassified.

- GRE, IP-in-IP, L2F, L2TP, and IPSec tunnels are all supported.

Configuration

1. (GRE tunnel) Specify a VPN tunnel interface:

`(global) `**`interface`** `tunnel-name`

2. (L2F or L2TP tunnel) Specify a VPN virtual template interface:

`(global) `**`interface`** `virtual-template-name`

For a Layer 2 Forwarding (L2F) or Layer 2 Tunneling Protocol (L2TP), specify the virtual template interface.

3. (IPsec tunnel) Specify the IPsec crypto map:

(global) **crypto map** *map-name*

If an IPSec tunnel is used, specify the **crypto map** itself, rather than an interface.

4. Enable QoS preclassification on the tunnel:

(interface or crypto-map) **qos pre-classify**

QoS for VPNs Example

A crypto map is configured for an IPSec tunnel to peer 4.3.50.234. QoS preclassification is performed on traffic that matches the crypto map, before the encryption is performed.

```
access-list 102 permit ip 192.3.3.0 0.0.0.255 192.168.200.0 0.0.0.255
crypto map Clients 10 ipsec-isakmp
        match address 102
        set peer 4.3.50.234
        set transform-set basic-3des
        qos pre-classify
```

9-5: QoS Policy Propagation via BGP

- Packets can be classified through the use of a BGP community list, an autonomous system (AS) path list, or a standard IP access list.

- Traffic coming in to a network can be prioritized according to BGP attributes.

- QoS policies can be distributed to remote BGP peers in a network.

Note   CEF must be enabled on the router. BGP should also be configured in advance. See Section 7-6 for more information about BGP configuration.

Configuration

1. Define a method for policy propagation.

a. Define a community list:

(global) **ip community-list** *community-list-number* {**permit** | **deny**}

community-number

Permit the community numbers that you want to classify.

b. Define an AS path list:

(global) **ip as-path access-list** *path-list-number* {**permit** | **deny**}

as-reg-expression

Permit the matching AS paths that you want to classify.

c. Define an access list:

```
(global) access-list acc-list-number {permit | deny} source
```

Use a standard IP access list to permit the source addresses you want to classify.

2. Use a route map to match and set the IP Precedence.

a. Define the route map:

```
(global) route-map route-map-name [permit | deny] [sequence]
```

b. Specify a list type for matching:

```
(route-map) match community-list community-list-number [exact]
```

-or-

```
(route-map) match as-path path-list-number
```

-or-

```
(route-map) match ip address acc-list-number
```

The route map can match against a list you configured in Step 1: a community list, a BGP AS path list, or a standard IP access list.

3. Set the IP Precedence:

```
(route-map) set ip precedence [number | name]
```

The IP Precedence number or name can be given, to be set on matching packets.

4. Configure BGP to use the route map:

```
(global) router bgp as-number
(bgp) table-map route-map-name
```

5. Enable IP Precedence propagation on an interface:

```
(interface) bgp-policy ip-prec-map
```

Packets are classified by using the IP Precedence values.

QoS Policy Propagation via BGP Example

A router is configured with BGP in AS 22. IP Precedence *flash* is assigned to traffic with a source network of 128.77.69.0, and *critical* is assigned to routes with an AS path going through AS 101. All other traffic receives a Precedence value of *routine*.

```
access-list 10 permit 128.77.69.0
ip as-path access-list 1 permit _101_
route-map mypolicies permit 10
        match ip address 10
        set ip precedence flash
route-map mypolicies permit 20
        match as-path 1
```

```
         set ip precedence critical
route-map mypolicies permit 30
         set ip precedence routine
router bgp 22
         neighbor 17.7.1.45 remote-as 50
         table-map precedence-map
interface serial 0/1
         bgp policy ip-prec-map
```

9-6: Priority Queuing (PQ)

- Priority Queuing assigns strict priorities to types of packets so that higher-priority traffic is sent before lower-priority traffic.

- PQ can assign traffic into four queues on an interface: high, medium, normal, and low. Traffic that isn't explicitly classified falls into the normal queue.

- A queue is serviced until it is emptied before moving to the next lower-priority queue.

- Lower-priority queues can potentially be "starved," or never serviced, as long as there is data in the higher-priority queues.

Configuration

1. Define one or more queue classifications to a priority list.

> **Note**   For each packet, **priority list** commands are evaluated in sequential order (the order you enter them) until a matching condition is found. Therefore, order can be important.

    a. Queue traffic according to protocol:

      (global) **priority-list** *list-number* **protocol** *protocol-name* {**high** | **medium** | **normal** | **low**} [*queue-keyword* [*keyword-value*]]

    The priority list is assigned a *list-number* (1 to 16). Traffic matching the *protocol-name* is placed in the specified queue (**high, medium, normal,** or **low**).

    The *protocol-name* field can be **aarp, apollo, appletalk, arp, bridge, clns, clns_es, clns_is, compressedtcp, cmns, decnet, decnet_node, decnet_router-l1, decnet_router-l2, dlsw** (direct encapsulation only), **ip, ipx, pad, rsrb** (direct encapsulation only), **stun** (direct encapsulation only), **vines, xns,** or **x25.**

    The *queue-keyword* can be **fragments** (noninitial fragmented IP packets), **gt** *byte-count* (a packet size greater than *byte-count* bytes), **list** *list-number* (packets permitted by access list *list-number*; for protocols **appletalk, bridge, ip, ipx, vines,** and **xns**), **lt** *byte-count* (a packet size less than *byte-count* bytes), **tcp** *port* (to or from TCP *port*), or **udp** *port* (to or from UDP *port*).

b. Queue traffic according to the inbound interface:

(global) **priority-list** *list-number* **interface** *type* *number* {**high** | **medium** |

  normal | **low**}

The priority list is assigned a *list-number* (1 to 16). Traffic entering on the interface type and number is assigned to the specified queue.

c. Queue all other traffic by default:

(global) **priority-list** *list-number* **default** {**high** | **medium** | **normal** | **low**}

All unclassified traffic for *list-number* (1 to 16) is assigned to the specified queue.

2. (Optional) Set the maximum queue size:

(global) **priority-list** *list-number* **queue-limit** [*high-limit* [*medium-limit*

  [*normal-limit* [*low-limit*]]]]

By default, the high queue is 20 packets deep, the medium queue is 40 packets deep, the normal queue is 60 packets deep, and the low queue is 80 packets deep. If you need to change the size of any or all of the queues for a given *list-number* (1 to 16), you can set each queue's limit in packets.

3. Apply the priority queue list to an interface:

(interface) **priority-group** *list-number*

Priority Queuing Example

Priority queuing is configured so that all IP traffic from host 67.2.21.5 is assigned to the *high* queue, all Telnet traffic (tcp 23) is assigned to the *medium* queue, and all HTTP and SMTP traffic is assigned to the *low* queue. All other unspecified traffic is assigned to the *normal* queue by default.

```
priority-list 2 protocol ip high list 1
priority-list 2 protocol ip medium tcp 23
priority-list 2 protocol ip low tcp 80
priority-list 2 protocol ip low tcp 25
access-list 1 permit 67.2.21.5 0.0.0.0
interface serial 8/1
     priority-group 2
```

9-7: Custom Queuing (CQ)

- Custom Queuing assigns traffic to user-configurable queues, each with a specific size and number of bytes to be forwarded.

- CQ services 16 user queues and one system queue in a round-robin fashion. As each queue is serviced, a configured number of bytes (a byte count) is forwarded.

■   The bandwidth on an interface can be divided up proportionally, as a ratio of each queue's byte count to the sum of the byte counts.

■   The system queue (queue 0) is emptied before any other queue is serviced. It contains high-priority traffic such as keepalives and signaling packets.

■   CQ is statically configured and does not adapt to changing network conditions.

Configuration

1. Define one or more queue classifications to a custom queue list.

    a. Classify traffic according to protocol:

        (global) **queue-list** *list-number* **protocol** *protocol-name queue-number*

        [queue-keyword [keyword-value]]

        The custom queue list is assigned a *list-number* (1 to 16). Traffic matching the *protocol-name* is placed in the specified *queue-number* (1 to 16).

        The *protocol-name* field can be **aarp, apollo, appletalk, arp, bridge, clns, clns_es, clns_is, compressedtcp, cmns, decnet, decnet_node, decnet_router-l1, decnet_router-l2, dlsw** (direct encapsulation only), **ip, ipx, pad, rsrb** (direct encapsulation only), **stun** (direct encapsulation only), **vines, xns,** or **x25.**

        The *queue-keyword* can be **fragments** (noninitial fragmented IP packets), **gt** *byte-count* (a packet size greater than *byte-count* bytes), **list** *list-number* (packets permitted by access list *list-number*; for protocols **appletalk, bridge, ip, ipx, vines,** and **xns**), **lt** *byte-count* (a packet size less than *byte-count* bytes), **tcp** *port* (to or from TCP *port*), or **udp** *port* (to or from UDP *port*).

    b. Queue traffic according to the inbound interface:

        (global) **queue-list** *list-number* **interface** *type number queue-number*

        The custom queue list is assigned a *list-number* (1 to 16). Traffic entering on the interface type and number is assigned to the specified *queue-number* (1 to 16).

    c. Classify all other traffic by default:

        (global) **priority-list** *list-number* **default** *queue-number*

        All unclassified traffic for *list-number* (1 to 16) is assigned to the specified queue (1 to 16).

2. (Optional) Set the queue size parameters.

    a. Set the maximum size of the queue:

        (global) **queue-list** *list-number* **queue** *queue-number* **limit** *packets*

        The depth of custom queue *queue-number* (1 to 16) is set to *packets* (0 to 32767;

0 is unlimited size; the default is 20 packets) for the custom queue list *list-number* (1 to 16).

b. Set the byte count for queue servicing:

```
(global) queue-list list-number queue queue-number byte-count bytes
```

Each time custom queue *queue-number* (1 to 16) is serviced, the router attempts to forward the byte count number of *bytes* (the default is 1500 bytes). However, if the byte count is less than the packet size, the whole packet is forwarded instead. The byte count defines a proportional amount of the overall interface bandwidth that a particular queue will receive.

To calculate the byte count values for each queue, follow these steps:

Step 1. Find the queue that has the largest packet size.

Step 2. Calculate a ratio of packet sizes for each queue by dividing the largest packet size by the actual packet size of each queue.

Step 3. Calculate a ratio of bandwidth percentages by dividing each queue's percentage by the percentage of the queue that has the largest packet size.

Step 4. Multiply each queue's bandwidth ratio (from Step 3) by the packet ratio (from Step 2).

Step 5. Normalize the numbers by dividing each number from Step 4 by the lowest value. Round each number up to the next integer if the decimal portion is greater than 0.5. Otherwise, round the number down to the next lower integer. This is the number of whole packets serviced for each queue. It must be an integer.

Step 6. Multiply the number of packets (from Step 5) by each queue's packet size. This gives you the byte count.

The result is a byte count for each queue that is a multiple of its packet size. The actual bandwidth percentages are fairly accurate, but due to packet rounding, they don't always give you the exact desired value. To calculate the actual percentages, add up the total byte counts of all queues from Step 6 of this calculation process. For each queue, divide the byte count from Step 6 by the sum of all byte counts.

If the actual bandwidth percentages are not close enough to your target values, you can make some adjustments to the calculations as follows: Multiply each value in Step 5 (before rounding) by an integer value, such as 2. Then evaluate each number, rounding up or down as necessary. Compute the values for Step 6, and check the resulting bandwidth percentages. If the values are still not desirable, you can increase the integer used to multiply in Step 5 and repeat this procedure.

For example, suppose Queue 1 contains packets that are 800 bytes, and it should get 10% of the interface bandwidth. Queue 2 contains packets that are 1500 bytes for 30% of the bandwidth. Queue 3 contains packets that are 250 bytes for 60% of the bandwidth. Table 9-4 shows the calculations for each step.

Table 9-4   *Calculating the Byte Count Values for Each Queue*

Queue	Packet Size	% BW	Step 1	Step 2	Step 3	Step 4	Step 5	Step 6
1	800	10%		1500 / 800 = 1.875	10 / 30 = 0.33	1.875 * 0.33 = 0.61875	0.61875 / 0.61875 = 1.0	1.0 * 800 = 800
2	1500	30%	1500	1500 / 1500 = 1.0	30 / 30 = 1.0	1.0 * 1.0 = 1.0	1.0 / 0.61875 = 1.6 (round to 2.0)	2.0 * 1500 = 3000
3	250	60%		1500 / 250 = 6.0	60 / 30 = 2.0	6.0 * 2.0 = 12.0	12.0 / 0.61875 = 19.39 (round to 20.0)	20.0 * 250 = 5000

The results give the following byte counts: 800 (Queue 1), 3000 (Queue 2), and 5000 (Queue 3). The actual bandwidth percentages are 800/(800+3000+5000), 3000/(800+3000+5000), and 5000/(800+3000+5000), resulting in 9.09%, 34.09%, and 56.8%, respectively.

If these values are not close enough to the desired 10%, 30%, and 60%, you can adjust them by trying different multipliers in Step 5. Using a multiplier of 3, the values in Step 5 would be 3.0 (no rounding), 4.8 (round up to 5), and 58.17 (round down to 58). The byte counts in Step 6 would be 2400, 7500, and 14500. The actual bandwidth percentages are now 2400/24400, 7500/24400, and 14500/24400, resulting in 9.8%, 30.7%, and 59.4%.

3. Apply the custom queue list to an interface:

```
(interface) custom-queue-list list-number
```

Custom Queuing Example

Custom queuing is configured so that HTTP traffic is assigned to Queue 1, SMTP traffic is assigned to Queue 2, and all other traffic defaults to Queue 3. For the sake of this example, assume that all three queues have traffic that consists of 1500 byte packets. HTTP traffic is to get 30% of the interface bandwidth, SMTP gets 10%, and all other traffic gets 60%. Table 9-5 shows the calculations for each step of the queue size computation.

Table 9-5   *Calculating the Byte Count Values for Each Queue*

Queue	Packet Size	% BW	Step 1	Step 2	Step 3	Step 4	Step 5	Step 6
1	1500	30%	1500	1500 / 1500 = 1.0	30 / 60 = 0.5	1.0 * 0.5 = 0.5	0.5 / 0.167 = 3.0	3.0 * 1500 = 4500
2	1500	10%	1500	1500 / 1500 = 1.0	10 / 60 = 0.167	1.0 * 0.167 = 0.167	0.167 / 0.167 = 1.0	1.0 * 1500 = 1500
3	1500	60%	1500	1500 / 1500 = 1.0	60 / 60 = 1.0	1.0 * 1.0 = 1.0	1.0 / 0.167 = 5.98 (round to 6.0)	6.0 * 1500 = 9000

```
queue-list 5 protocol ip 1 tcp 80
queue-list 5 protocol ip 2 tcp 25
queue-list 5 default 3
queue-list 5 queue 1 byte-count 4500
queue-list 5 queue 2 byte-count 1500
queue-list 5 queue 3 byte-count 9000
interface serial 8/1
     priority-group 2
```

9-8: Weighted Fair Queuing (WFQ)

- Flow-based WFQ classifies traffic according to *flows*, or packets that have identical source and destination addresses, source and destination TCP or UDP ports, and protocols. In other words, a flow consists of a specific type of traffic to and from a pair of hosts.

- Class-based WFQ (CBWFQ) classifies traffic according to class map definitions. It is used with the Modular QoS CLI. This type of WFQ is described in Section 9-1.

- WFQ is enabled by default on serial interfaces with E1 (2.048 Mbps) speeds or lower, on interfaces using Multilink PPP (MLP), and on serial interfaces not running LAPB, X.25, or SDLC.

- WFQ is IP Precedence-aware. Higher Precedence values receive more efficient queuing.

- WFQ works with RSVP to prepare traffic for the reserved flows.

- WFQ works with Frame Relay congestion management and notification mechanisms (DE, BECN, and FECN) to adjust the traffic in a flow when congestion is occurring.

- Distributed WFQ (DWFQ) can be used on routers with VIP-based interface processors.

Configuration

1. Enable WFQ on an interface:

    `(interface)` **fair-queue** `[congestive-discard-threshold [dynamic-queues`

    `[reservable-queues]]]`

    WFQ can be configured using *congestive-discard-threshold*, a threshold for new packets in each queue (16 to 4096 packets; the default is 64). When a queue reaches the threshold, new packets are discarded. For "best-effort" traffic, the number of dynamic queues can be given as *dynamic-queues* (valid values are **16, 32, 64, 128, 256, 512, 1024, 2048,** and **4096**). The number of queues set aside for reserved queuing (RSVP, for example) is given by *reservable-queues* (0 to 1000; the default is 0).

2. (Optional) Use QoS group or ToS-based DWFQ.

    a. Enable DWFQ:

    `(interface)` **fair-queue** `{qos-group | tos}`

Section 9-8

Traffic is classified and queued according to QoS groups (**qos-group**), locally significant numbers, or type of service (**tos**).

b. Set the bandwidth percentage per group:

(interface) **fair-queue** {**qos-group** *group* | **tos** *tos*} **weight** *percentage*

During congestion, the QoS *group* (1 to 99) or the ToS *number* (0 to 3) is given *percentage* (1 to 100) of the available bandwidth. By default, ToS 0 is set to 10, ToS 1 is 20, ToS 2 is 30, and ToS 3 is 40.

c. (Optional) Set the total number of packets in all DWFQ queues:

(interface) **fair-queue aggregate-limit** *packets*

The *packets* variable represents the setting for the total number of packets that are queued before dropping occurs.

d. (Optional) Set the total number of packets in individual queues:

(interface) **fair-queue individual-limit** *packets*

The *packets* variable represents the setting for the maximum number of packets in individual per-flow queues.

3. (Optional) Use a strict priority queue for RTP voice traffic:

(interface) **ip rtp priority** *starting-rtp-port port-range*

   bandwidth

IP RTP voice traffic can be assigned to a strict priority queue that is serviced before any other queue on the interface. RTP packets are identified by their UDP port numbers, given as the lowest UDP port for RTP *(starting-rtp-port)* and the number of ports used in the RTP range *(port-range)*. The guaranteed *bandwidth* is also specified, in Kbps.

Allocate enough bandwidth for all simultaneous calls that will be supported. The priority queue automatically takes RTP compression into account, so you only need to consider the compressed call bandwidth and any Layer 2 headers.

4. (Optional) Use a priority queue for Frame Relay.

a. Define a Frame Relay map class:

(global) **map-class frame-relay** *map-class-name*

b. (Optional) Use a strict priority queue for RTP voice traffic:

(map-class) **frame-relay ip rtp priority** *starting-rtp-port port-range*

   bandwidth

IP RTP voice traffic can be assigned to a strict priority queue that is serviced before any other queue on the interface. RTP packets are identified by their UDP port numbers, given as the lowest UDP port for RTP *(starting-rtp-port)* and the number of ports used in the RTP range *(port-range)*. The guaranteed *bandwidth* is also specified, in Kbps.

c. (Optional) Use a strict priority queue for a single PVC:

```
(map-class) frame-relay interface-queue priority {high | medium | normal |
    low}
```

-or-

```
(interface) frame-relay interface-queue priority {high-limit medium-limit
    normal-limit low-limit}
```

The strict priority queue can be assigned to either a Frame Relay map class or an interface. For a map class, the priority queue is assigned a priority level: **high**, **medium**, **normal**, or **low**. For a PVC on an interface, the size of each queue level must be given (the defaults are high, 20 packets; medium, 40 packets; normal, 60 packets; low, 80 packets).

d. Apply the map class to an interface:

```
(interface) frame-relay class map-class-name
```

-or-

```
(interface) frame-relay interface-dlci dlci

(interface-dlci) class map-class-name
```

The map class can be applied to all PVCs on a major interface or subinterface with the **frame-relay class** command. Otherwise, the map class can be applied to a single PVC on an interface (a single data link connection identifier [DLCI]) with the **class** command.

Weighted Fair Queuing Example

WFQ is configured on serial 0 with the default thresholds and the number of queues. A strict priority queue is also configured on serial 0 to handle the IP RTP traffic. That traffic is defined as using UDP ports 16384 through 32767 (16384+16383), receiving at least 50 kbps of the bandwidth.

Interface serial 8/1/1 has ToS-based WFQ configured. The bandwidth weights or percentages for each ToS value have been specified, to override the defaults. ToS 1 gets 10% of the bandwidth, ToS 2 gets 20%, and ToS 3 gets 30%.

```
interface serial 8/0/0
        ip address 192.168.14.7 255.255.255.0
        fair-queue
        ip rtp priority 16384 16383 50
interface serial 8/1/1
```

```
ip address 192.168.15.7 255.255.255.0
fair-queue tos
fair-queue tos 1 weight 10
fair-queue tos 2 weight 20
fair-queue tos 3 weight 30
```

9-9: Weighted Random Early Detection (WRED)

- WRED monitors traffic loads and performs selective packet dropping as a way to avoid and prevent congestion.

- WRED uses weight values to differentiate between classes of service, providing better service to higher-priority traffic.

- WRED is aware of IP Precedence, delivering more higher-priority packets and discarding more lower-priority packets. RSVP flows are also preferred while dropping packets from other traffic flows.

- WRED works well with TCP/IP, causing TCP to retransmit a dropped packet at a reduced rate. By randomly dropping packets, TCP flows can be reduced in a non-global fashion.

- Flow-based WRED keeps track of traffic flows through an interface. Flows that try to monopolize the network are penalized by having more packets dropped.

- If WRED is not configured, *tail drop* congestion avoidance is used. When queues fill during congestion, packets from all flows are dropped until the congestion lessens. Traffic is treated equally, with no random or preferential packet drops being performed.

Configuration

1. Use WRED on an interface.

   a. Enable WRED on the interface:

   (interface) **random-detect** [**prec-based** | **dscp-based**]

   WRED can be based on IP Precedence (**prec-based**, the default) or on IP DSCP (**dscp-based**).

   b. (Optional) Set the WRED thresholds:

   (interface) **random-detect** {**precedence** *precedence* | **dscp** *dscp*}

   min-threshold max-threshold mark-prob-denominator

   WRED can be based on IP Precedence (**precedence**) or IP DSCP (**dscp**). When the average queue length reaches the minimum threshold, *min-threshold* (1 to 4096 packets), some packets with the *precedence* value or the *dscp* value are dropped. Likewise, when the queue length reaches *max-threshold* (*min-threshold* to 4096 packets), all packets with the *precedence* value are dropped.

When the queue meets the threshold level, one out of every *mark-prob-denominator* packets (1 to 65536; the default is 10 packets) is dropped.

IP Precedence values are given as *precedence* (0 to 7), and DSCP values are given as *dscp* (0 to 63 or a keyword: **ef, af11, af12, af13, af21, af22, af23, af31, af32, af33, af41, af42, af43, cs1, cs2, cs3, cs4, cs5,** or **cs7**).

2. Use flow-based WRED instead.

  a. Enable flow-based WRED on an interface:

```
(interface) random-detect flow
```

  b. Adjust the average depth factor for flow queues:

```
(interface) random-detect flow average-depth-factor scaling-factor
```

If a flow queue becomes nonadaptive to congestion, you can change the scaling factor that WRED uses to compute the queue depth. The *scaling-factor* (**2, 4, 8,** or **16**; the default is 4) multiplied by the average flow depth should equal the peak flow depth.

  c. Adjust the flow count for the interface:

```
(interface) random-detect flow count count
```

WRED keeps a count of the active flows through an interface. Based on this count, buffers are allocated. The *count* (16 to 32768; the default is 256) can be adjusted to tune the buffer utilization if you anticipate more flows.

Weighted Random Early Detection Example

WRED is configured on serial interface 3/1 based on IP Precedence. The default WRED thresholds are used. Serial interface 3/2 has flow-based WRED configured because there are no known criteria for IP Precedence or DSCP being used. A large number of active flows is not expected, so the WRED flow count has been reduced to 128.

```
interface serial 3/1
      ip address 192.168.204.33 255.255.255.0
      random-detect prec-based
interface serial 3/2
      ip address 192.168.205.33 255.255.255.0
      random-detect flow
      random-detect flow count 128
```

9-10: Committed Access Rate (CAR)

- CAR can be used to classify IP packets at the edge of a network.

- CAR is also used for IP traffic policing to limit the rate of transmission on an interface.

- Packets can be classified and rate-limited according to all IP traffic, IP Precedence, MAC address, or an IP access list.

- Multiple CAR policies can be configured on a single interface to deal with different types of traffic.

Configuration

1. (Optional) Define an IP access list to classify the traffic:

   `(global)` **access-list** *acc-list-number* {**permit** | **deny**} *source* [*mask*]

   -or-

   `(global)` **access-list** *acc-list-number* {**permit** | **deny**}

   protocol source mask destination mask [**precedence** *precedence*] [**tos** *tos*]

   A standard IP access list can be used to identify traffic by source address. An extended IP access list can be used to identify traffic by source and destination addresses, protocol, port number, IP Precedence (3 bits, 0 through 7), or Type of Service (ToS; whole byte) numbers.

2. (Optional) Define a rate-limit access list to classify traffic according to IP Precedence or MAC address:

   `(global)` **access-list rate-limit** *acc-list-number* {*precedence* | *mac-address*

   | **mask** *mask*}

   A rate limit access list is numbered *acc-list-number* (1 to 99 for IP Precedence and 100 to 199 for MAC addresses). IP Precedence values are given as *precedence* (0 to 7). A MAC address can be given as *mac-address* (dotted-triplet hexadecimal format). If multiple IP Precedence bits should be matched in a single policy, use the *mask* (two hex characters; a 1 bit matches and a 0 ignores). The mask should be based on the IP ToS byte: p2 p1 p0 t3 t2 t1 t0, where bits 7 to 5 are IP Precedence (p2 to p0), bits 4 to 1 are ToS (t3 to t0), and bit 0 is unused. Refer to Tables 9-1 and 9-2 for more information about the IP Precedence and ToS values.

3. Define one or more CAR policies on an interface:

   `(interface)` **rate-limit** {**input** | **output**} [**access-group** [**rate-limit**]

   acc-list-number] *bps burst-normal burst-max* **conform-action** *action*

   exceed-action *action*

   Each rate-limit policy governs **input** or **output** traffic on the interface. The **access-group** keyword specifies an IP access list (standard 1 to 99 or extended 100 to 199) that is used to identify traffic for the policy. If the **rate-limit** keyword is used, a rate-limit access list is used (IP Precedence 1 to 99 or MAC address 100 to 199) instead.

Matching traffic is rate-limited to an average *bps* (given in increments of 8000 bps), with a normal burst size of *burst-normal* (in bytes; the minimum is *bps*/2000) and a maximum burst size of *burst-max* (bytes). The **conform-action** keyword is used to define an *action* to take for traffic within the rate limit, and **exceed-action** defines an *action* to take for traffic that exceeds the rate limit. The *action* values can be **continue** (evaluate the next rate-limit command), **drop** (drop the packet), **set-prec-continue** *new-prec* (set the IP Precedence value to *new-prec* and evaluate the next rate-limit command), **set-prec-transmit** *new-prec* (set the IP Precedence value to *new-prec* and send the packet), or **transmit** (send the packet).

Committed Access Rate Example

CAR is configured to limit traffic as follows:

- WWW traffic is limited to 128000 bps, with burst sizes of 24000 to 32000 bytes. Conforming traffic is forwarded, with the IP Precedence set to 3. Nonconforming traffic is also forwarded, but its IP Precedence is set to 0.

- SMTP traffic is limited to 16000 bps, with burst sizes of 1000 to 2000 bytes. Conforming traffic is forwarded, with IP Precedence reset to 2. Nonconforming traffic is dropped to prevent large SMTP transmissions of spam e-mail.

- Traffic with IP Precedence set to 5 is limited to 32000 bps, with burst sizes of 8000 to 12000 bytes. This type of traffic is always forwarded, keeping its original IP Precedence value.

- All other traffic not identified is limited to 48000 bps, with burst sizes of 1000 to 2000 bytes. Conforming traffic is forwarded, with IP Precedence set to 0. Nonconforming traffic is dropped.

```
access-list 101 permit tcp any any eq www
access-list 102 permit tcp any any eq smtp
access-list rate-limit 1 5
interface serial 0/1
      rate-limit output access-group 101 128000 24000 32000 conform-
action
          set-prec-transmit 3 exceed-action set-prec-transmit 0
      rate-limit output access-group 102 16000 1000 2000 conform-action
        set-prec-transmit 2 exceed-action drop
      rate-limit output access-group rate-limit 1 32000 8000 12000 con-
form-action
          transmit exceed-action transmit
      rate-limit output 48000 1000 2000 conform-action set-prec-transmit 0
        exceed-action drop
```

9-11: Generic Traffic Shaping (GTS)

- GTS buffers outbound traffic and then transmits it in a regulated fashion, within the bandwidth constraints of a network.

- GTS tends to prevent the effects of traffic surges or bursts from propagating through a network.

- GTS can be used to match the transmission rate to a remote device with a differing access rate.

> **Note**   GTS can be used on a Frame Relay interface to shape traffic for all VCs on an interface or subinterface. To shape traffic on a per-DLCI basis, you can configure one DLCI per subinterface and use GTS, or you can use Frame Relay Traffic Shaping (FRTS). See Section 9-12 for more information.

Configuration

1. Enable GTS for outbound traffic on an interface:

    (interface) **traffic-shape** {**rate** | **group** *access-list*} *bit-rate*

    [*burst-size* [*excess-burst-size*]]

    Outbound traffic is held to the *bit-rate* (bits per second), with an allowed *burst-size* (in bits) of traffic over the *bit-rate* within a time interval. An *excess-burst-size* (in bits) can also be specified to allow an amount of traffic over the burst size in an interval. The time interval is *burst-size/bit-rate* (if *burst-size* > 0) or *excess-burst-size/bit-rate* (if *burst-size* = 0).

    If the **rate** keyword is used, all outbound traffic is shaped. Otherwise, the **group** keyword can be used to shape only traffic matched by the *access-list* (any access list numbered 1 to 2699).

    For Frame Relay, the *bit-rate* corresponds to the Committed Information Rate (CIR) that is contracted with the service provider. In addition, *burst-size* corresponds to the Bc parameter, and *excess-burst-size* corresponds to the Be parameter.

2. (Optional) Use GTS for Frame Relay.

    a. Adjust the bandwidth when BECNs are received:

    (interface) **traffic-shape adaptive** *bit-rate*

    When BECN signaling is received from the Frame Relay switch, indicating switch congestion, GTS uses the *bit-rate* (bits per second; the default is 0) as the lower bandwidth limit. Traffic is then shaped to within this lower *bit-rate* and the normal committed bit rate.

b. Respond to FECNs:

```
(interface) traffic-shape fecn-adapt
```

The router reflects any FECNs received from the Frame Relay switch in the reverse direction as BECNs. This informs the far-end router of a congestion situation and tells it that the local router is adapting its traffic shaping. If used, the **fecn-adapt** keyword should be configured on both ends of a Frame Relay VC so that both routers can inform each other of changes in traffic shaping.

Generic Traffic Shaping Example

GTS is configured on interface serial 2/4 to shape traffic to a 128 kbps rate. The traffic is allowed to burst 16 kb over the normal rate. Serial interface 2/5 uses GTS to shape SMTP traffic to host 10.5.17.10 to within 64 kbps. All other traffic on the interface is shaped to 128 kbps.

Interface serial 2/6 is one end of a Frame Relay PVC. The PVC has a CIR of 128 kbps but is allowed to burst to 256000. If congestion is signaled by a BECN, GTS shapes the outbound traffic to within 128 kbps and 256 kbps. FECNs is reflected as BECNs.

```
interface serial 2/4
        traffic-shape rate 128000 16000 16000
access-list 101 permit tcp any host 10.5.17.10 eq smtp
access-list 102 permit ip any any
interface serial 2/5
        traffic-shape group 101 64000
        traffic-shape group 102 128000
interface 2/6
        encapsulation frame-relay
        traffic-shape rate 256000
        traffic-shape adaptive 128000
        traffic-shape fecn-adapt
```

9-12: Frame Relay Traffic Shaping (FRTS)

- FRTS can perform traffic shaping to compensate for a mismatch in access rates at the ends of a virtual circuit.

- Traffic shaping can be performed on an interface as a whole (all DLCIs) or on a per-DLCI basis.

- FRTS is configured using Frame Relay map classes.

- FRTS can dynamically adapt traffic rates based on feedback from Frame Relay switches. Backward congestion notification causes FRTS to throttle back the traffic rate.

Configuration

1. Enable FRTS on an interface:

   `(interface)` **`frame-relay traffic-shaping`**

   FRTS is enabled for all PVCs and SVCs on the interface. Frame Relay encapsulation must be configured first.

2. (Optional) Use Enhanced LMI.

   a. Enable QoS parameter exchange:

   `(interface)` **`frame-relay qos-autosense`**

   ELMI is detected on the interface if it is being used by a Cisco Frame Relay switch (BPX, MGX, and IGX families). QoS values (CIR, Bc, and Be) are exchanged between the router and the switch. ELMI must be enabled on both the router and the switch before it can be used.

   b. Choose an IP address for ELMI management.

   - Automatically choose an address:

     `(global)` **`frame-relay address registration auto-address`**

     By default, to communicate with ELMI network management stations, the router automatically chooses an Ethernet interface's IP address. If no Ethernet interface is available, a serial interface type and then other interface types are used.

   - Manually choose an address:

     `(global)` **`frame-relay address registration ip`** *`address`*

     The IP *address* given is used as the ELMI management address.

3. Define a map class for traffic shaping.

   a. Specify a map class name:

   `(global)` **`map-class frame-relay`** *`map-class-name`*

   The map class named *map-class-name* (an arbitrary text string) is used to define any parameters related to a Frame Relay VC.

   b. Define the traffic-shaping parameters:

   `(map-class)` **`frame-relay traffic-rate`** *`average`* `[`*`peak`*`]`

   The *average* traffic rate (in bps) and the *peak* traffic rate (in bps) are both defined for a map class.

   c. (Optional) Specify the type of backward congestion notification:

   `(map-class)` **`frame-relay adaptive-shaping {becn | foresight}`**

The router responds to standard BECN congestion notification (**becn**) or Foresight backward congestion notification (**foresight**) messages. Foresight can be used on some Cisco Frame Relay switches, and BECN is used on most Frame Relay switches.

d. Apply the map class to an interface, subinterface, or DLCI:

```
(interface) frame-relay class map-class-name
```

-or-

```
(interface) frame-relay interface-dlci dlci class map-class-name
```

The map class named *map-class-name* is applied to a Frame Relay interface or subinterface. If the **interface-dlci** keyword is used, the map class is applied to the specific DLCI on the interface.

Frame Relay Traffic Shaping Example

Frame Relay traffic shaping is configured on interface serial 0 for all DLCIs, using the map class *lowspeed* with an average rate of 16 kbps and a peak rate of 32 kbps. Map classes are also applied to specific DLCIs on two subinterfaces. Subinterface serial 1.1 has DLCI 100 with a map class shaping to an average rate of 16 kbps and a peak rate of 32 kbps. Subinterface serial 1.2 has DLCI 101 and shapes to an average of 64 kbps and a peak rate of 128 kbps.

```
interface serial 0
        encapsulation frame-relay
        frame-relay traffic shaping
        frame-relay class lowspeed
interface serial 1
        encapsulation frame-relay
interface serial 1.1 point-to-point
        frame-relay interface-dlci 100 class lowspeed
interface serial 1.2 point-to-point
        frame-relay interface-dlci 101 class highspeed
map-class frame-relay lowspeed
        frame-relay traffic-rate 16000 32000
map-class frame-relay highspeed
        frame-relay traffic-rate 64000 128000
```

9-13: Use RSVP for QoS Signaling

- Resource Reservation Protocol (RSVP) is used to set up end-to-end QoS across a heterogeneous network.

- RSVP is an IP protocol that provides out-of-band signaling to request the network resources to implement a specific QoS policy. Other queuing methods are needed to implement the QoS reservations.

- RSVP can make *controlled load* (using WRED) or *guaranteed rate* (using WFQ) reservations.

- When RSVP receives a reservation request for an application, it propagates requests across the network to the destination. At each network node (router), RSVP requests the reservation so that resources across an end-to-end path are reserved.

- RSVP provides admission control such that reservation requests are set up and granted only as network resources are available.

- RSVP can work with Low Latency Queuing (LLQ) to provide strict priority queuing for time-sensitive voice traffic. Other nonvoice traffic is carried over other reservations.

- RSVP supports reservations and queuing for voice flows over Frame Relay. Admission control and resource reservations occur on a per-VC (DLCI) basis.

- RSVP can work with Common Open Policy Service (COPS) to provide centralized monitoring and management of RSVP. COPS for RSVP can work over Ethernet, Fast Ethernet, HSSI, and T1 interfaces.

- COPS Policy Decision Points (PDPs) are servers running Cisco QoS Policy Manager, for example. Policy Enforcement Points (PEPs) are routers acting as COPS clients.

Note RSVP must be used in conjunction with WFQ or WRED. RSVP performs resource reservations, and WFQ or WRED performs the actual reservation implementation.

Configuration

1. Use RSVP with LLQ.

    a. Enable RSVP to work with a strict priority queue:

    (global) **ip rsvp pq-profile** [**voice-like** | *r'* [*b'* [*p-to-r'* | **ignore-peak-value**]]

    The **voice-like** keyword indicates that the typical p-q (priority queue) profile is used for voice flows. The default *r'*, *b'*, and *p-to-r'* values are used. Voice flows are directed into the strict priority queue of WFQ.

However, specific values can be given for *r'* (maximum flow rate; 1 to 1048576 bytes/sec; the default is 12288 bytes/sec), *b'* (maximum burst; 1 to 8192 bytes; the default is 592 bytes), and *p-to-r'* (maximum ratio of peak rate to average rate; 100 to 4000 percent; the default is 110 percent). With the **ignore-peak-value** keyword, the peak-to-average rate ratio is not evaluated. A flow is directed into the priority queue as long as its parameters are less than or equal to all the parameters given.

b. Enable RSVP on an interface:

```
(interface) ip rsvp bandwidth [interface-kbps [single-flow-kbps]]
```

RSVP can be configured with *interface-kbps,* the maximum amount of bandwidth that may be allocated on the interface (1 to 10,000,000 kbps), and *single-flow-kbps,* the maximum amount of bandwidth that may be allocated to a single flow (1 to 10,000,000 kbps).

c. (Optional) Specify a burst factor for the interface:

```
(interface) ip rsvp burst policing [factor]
```

The optional *factor* (100 to 700; the default is 200 percent) gives the burst factor as a percentage of the requested burst. In other words, the burst factor tells how strict or loose traffic bursts on the interface are policed. Lower values are more strict; higher values are more loosely enforced.

d. (Optional) Enable RSVP proxy for non-RSVP hosts.

- Send and receive RSVP RESV messages:

```
(global) ip rsvp reservation session-ip-address sender-ip-address
   {tcp | udp | ip-protocol} session-dport sender-sport
   next-hop-ip-address next-hop-interface {ff | se | wf} {rate | load}
   bandwidth burst-size
```

- Send and receive RSVP PATH messages:

```
(global) ip rsvp sender session-ip-address sender-ip-address
   {tcp | udp | ip-protocol} session-dport sender-sport
 previous-hop-ip-address previous-hop-interface bandwidth burst-size
```

The router simulates receiving and forwarding RSVP reservation (**ip rsvp reservation**) and path (**ip rsvp sender**) requests in case a downstream or upstream host is not RSVP-capable. IP addresses are given for *session-ip-address* (the intended receiver or destination), *sender-ip-address* (the sender), and *next-hop-ip-address* (the router nearest the receiver) or *previous-hop-ip-address* (the router nearest the sender). The interface of the next-hop or previous-hop router is also given as *next-hop-interface* or *previous-hop-interface* (**ethernet, loopback, null,** or **serial**).

The **tcp, udp,** or *ip-protocol* (0 to 255) specify what protocol is carried over the reservation. The port numbers are given for *session-dport* (the receiver's destination port) and *sender-sport* (the sender's source port). If a destination port is set to 0, RSVP expects that either the application doesn't use port numbers or all port numbers apply to the reservation.

For RESV messages (**ip rsvp reservation**), the reservation style is given as **ff** (fixed filter, a single reservation), **se** (shared explicit, a shared reservation with limited scope), or **wf** (wildcard filter, a shared reservation with unlimited scope). The reservation is either **rate** (guaranteed rate) or **load** (controlled load). The reservation bandwidth can be given as *bandwidth* (1 to 10,000,000 kbps), the average rate, which can be up to 75 percent of the total interface bandwidth. The maximum burst size is given as *burst-size* (1 to 65535 KB).

2. (Optional) Use COPS for RSVP.

   a. Define the COPS servers:

   (global) **ip rsvp policy cops** [*acl* [*acl*]...] **servers** *server-ip*

   [*server-ip...*]

   Up to eight COPS policy servers can be specified as *server-ip*, with the first one acting as the primary server. The traffic sessions to be governed by the COPS policy can be limited with one or more standard or extended *acl* numbered IP access lists (1 to 99 or 100 to 199), separated by spaces. Servers are tried in sequential order in case a server doesn't answer.

   b. (Optional) Confine a policy to PATH and RESV messages:

   (global) **ip rsvp policy cops minimal**

   In some cases, confining the COPS servers to only PATH and RESV messages improves server performance and latency times for router requests. Other RSVP messages are not forwarded to the COPS servers for management.

   c. (Optional) Set a COPS timeout:

   (global) **ip rsvp policy cops timeout** *seconds*

   The PEP (router) retains policy information for *seconds* (1 to 10000 seconds; the default is 300 seconds, or 5 minutes) after the connection to a COPS server is lost.

   d. (Optional) Report all RSVP decisions:

   (global) **ip rsvp policy cops report-all**

   By default, the PEP (router) sends only reports of RSVP configuration decisions to the PDP (COPS server). With this command, the router can also send reports of RSVP outsourcing decisions to the PDP if required by the COPS server software.

Using RSVP for QoS Signaling Example

RSVP is configured to direct all voice flows into a strict priority queue. Interface serial 1 is a full T1 with WFQ configured. RSVP is also configured on the interface, with a maximum total reserved bandwidth of 512 kbps and 30 kbps per flow. Burst policing is set to 400 percent, relaxing the policing of traffic bursts in the reserved flows. A sample proxy reservation is configured to 10.1.1.10 (UDP port 40) from 10.2.2.20 (UDP port 50). The next-hop router is 10.1.1.1 on interface serial 0. A fixed filter reservation is requested for guaranteed rate, using a bandwidth of 20 kbps and a burst size of 80 KB.

COPS for RSVP is also configured. The two COPS servers are 192.168.66.45 and 192.168.66.46. The router reports all configuration and outsourcing decisions to the COPS server.

```
ip rsvp pq-profile voice-like
interface serial 1
        description Full-T1 1.544 Mbps
        ip address 192.168.211.1 255.255.255.0
        fair-queue
        ip rsvp bandwidth 512 30
        ip rsvp burst policing 400
ip rsvp reservation 10.1.1.10 10.2.2.20 udp 40 50 10.1.1.1 serial 0 ff rate 20 80
ip rsvp policy cops servers 192.168.66.45 192.168.66.46
ip rsvp policy cops report-all
```

9-14: Link Efficiency Mechanisms

- Link Fragmentation and Interleaving (LFI) fragments large packets, reducing the serialization times as packets are sent out a serial interface.

- LFI also allows other, smaller packets to be interleaved with fragmented packets. Time-critical protocols can be sent more predictably, because they don't have to wait for large packets to be forwarded.

- LFI can work with Multilink PPP (MLP) to send fragmented packets over multiple physical links, Frame Relay, and ATM VCs.

- Compressed Real-Time Protocol (CRTP) offers a compression that can compress the 40-byte IP/UDP/RTP header into a 2- to 5-byte value. CRTP is used on a per-link basis.

- CRTP can be used on serial links with a speed of T1 or less, over HDLC, Frame Relay, PPP, or ISDN.

- CRTP can be used with CEF for maximum efficiency.

Configuration

1. Use LFI with MLP.

    a. Enable MLP on an interface:

    `(interface) ppp multilink`

    See Section 3-6 for further information about configuring MLP.

    b. Enable packet interleaving:

    `(interface) ppp multilink interleave`

    c. Set the maximum acceptable delay between fragments:

    `(interface) ppp multilink fragment-delay milliseconds`

    MLP chooses a fragment size that gives a maximum serialization delay of *milliseconds*. Voice traffic using RTP typically requires a delay of 20 milliseconds or less.

    d. (Optional) Set up a reserved bandwidth queue for RTP voice traffic:

    `(interface) ip rtp reserve lowest-UDP-port UDP-port-range [max-bandwidth]`

    A special queue with a higher priority can be set up for RTP traffic on the interface. The range of UDP port values for RTP is given as *lowest-UDP-port* with *UDP-port-range* number of ports. A maximum reserved bandwidth can be specified to set an upper limit on the RTP bandwidth used. If the actual bandwidth used rises above *max-bandwidth* (Kbps), the RTP traffic is forwarded in a best-effort fashion.

2. Use Compressed Real-Time Protocol (CRTP) on a serial interface.

    a. (HDLC, PPP, ISDN) Enable CRTP:

    `(interface) ip rtp header-compression [passive]`

    RTP headers are compressed. Be sure to enable compression on both ends of a serial link. The **passive** keyword allows CRTP to compress outbound headers only if received inbound headers are also compressed.

    b. (Frame Relay) Enable CRTP.

    ■ Use CRTP for all VCs on the physical interface:

    `(interface) frame-relay ip rtp header-compression [passive]`

    Be sure to enable compression on both ends of the VC. The **passive** keyword allows CRTP to compress outbound headers only if received inbound headers are also compressed.

    ■ Use CRTP for a single DLCI:

    `(interface) frame-relay map ip ip-address dlci [broadcast]`

```
rtp header-compression [active | passive]
```

The IP address is mapped to a specific DLCI, and CRTP is enabled. Use **active** for unconditional RTP header compression and **passive** for compression only if the far end is sending compressed headers.

c. (Optional) Define the number of supported CRTP connections:

```
(interface) ip rtp compression-connections number
```

CRTP keeps a cache of compressed RTP connections occurring on the interface. The maximum number of connections can be changed to *number* (3 to 1000; the default is 32 connections, or 16 calls). This number specifies unidirectional RTP connections such that a voice call requires two connections (one in each direction). Also, the number of compressed RTP connections should be set to the same value on both ends of a link.

Link Efficiency Mechanism Example

A dialer interface is configured with Multilink PPP and LFI. An LFI fragment delay of 20 milliseconds is used. An IP RTP priority queue is also set up for UDP ports 32768 to 32818, using a maximum bandwidth of 512 kbps. In addition, the serial 1 interface is configured for Compressed RTP headers, with a maximum of 128 RTP connections.

```
interface dialer 1
        description Dialer template for a rotary group
        ip address 192.168.33.1 255.255.255.0
        encapsulation ppp
        dialer map ...
        dialer-group 1
        dialer-list 1 protocol ip permit
        ppp multilink
        ppp multilink interleave
        ppp multilink fragment-delay 20
        ip rtp reserve 32768 50 512
interface serial 1
        ip address 192.168.116.71 255.255.255.0
        ip rtp header-compression
        ip rtp compression-connections 128
```

9-15: AutoQoS for the Enterprise

■   AutoQoS automates the deployment of QoS by discovering traffic types and network load using NBAR. After protocol discovery and statistical analyses, the AutoQoS feature maps applications to DiffServ classes and assigns bandwidth and scheduling parameters to the router's configuration.

- Autodiscovery collects data over several days. (The default is 3 days.) Cisco Express Forwarding (CEF) must be enabled for autodiscovery to work.

- An IP address must be assigned to low-speed interfaces (less than 768 kbps). Both ends of a WAN link must be configured with the same bandwidth value for AutoQoS to generate accurate policies. AutoQoS assumes a bandwidth of 1.544 Mbps for serial interfaces unless the **bandwidth** interface command is configured. AutoQoS does not change configuration if the bandwidth is changed later; therefore, if the bandwidth changes on an interface, you need to either manually modify the QoS configuration or run AutoQoS again.

- AutoQoS cannot be configured on a DLCI if a map class is already attached to a DLCI.

- AutoQoS cannot be configured if a QoS policy is already applied to an interface.

Note   Cisco has released two types of AutoQoS: AutoQoS for VoIP and AutoQoS for the Enterprise. AutoQoS for VoIP was released first, can be configured on both switches and routers, and, as the name implies, is designed for VoIP networks. It also requires CDP to be enabled. AutoQoS for the Enterprise was introduced with Cisco IOS Software Release 12.3(7)T, and is configured on routers only, and supports a much wider range of protocols. AutoQoS for VoIP and AutoQoS for the Enterprise cannot be configured concurrently on a router.

Configuration

1. (Optional) Configure the bandwidth on an interface:

    `(interface)` **`bandwidth`** `bandwidth`

    AutoQoS assumes a bandwidth of 1.544 Mbps on serial interfaces unless the bandwidth is explicitly configured with the **bandwidth** command.

Note   On ATM PVCs, you need to either configure the variable bit rate (VBR) with the **vbr-nrt** or **vbr-rt** command or configure the constant bit rate (CBR) with the **cbr** command.

2. (Required) Enable CEF:

    `(global)` **`ip cef`**

    CEF is an advanced Layer 3 switching technology that offers improved performance over fast switching route caching. CEF is required for autodiscovery to work.

3. (Required) Enable autodiscovery:

    `(interface)` **`auto discovery qos`** `[`**`trust`**`]`

    Before policies are generated and applied to the router's configuration, the router performs protocol discovery and statistical analyses. All other policies should be removed before applying this command. The optional **trust** keyword informs the router to use the DSCP markings instead of NBAR for discovery. For optimal results, you should leave this command on your router for several days to learn about traffic passing through your router. When done, enter the **no auto discovery qos** command. Upon entering this command, the router stops learning about traffic passing through your router, but the configuration AutoQoS generated remains. You can view the results of autodiscovery with the privileged EXEC **show auto discovery** command.

4. (Required) Start the AutoQoS template generation phase:

    ```
    (interface) auto qos [voip [trust] [fr-atm]
    ```

    QoS templates are generated based on the data collected during the autodiscovery phase. This phase creates and applies class maps and policy maps for your network. Optionally, you can apply AutoQoS for VoIP with the **voip** keyword. You can add the **trust** keyword to configure the router to rely on DSCP markings instead of NBAR. The **fr-atm** option should be used on low-speed (less than 768 kbps) Frame Relay-to-ATM links.

    AutoQoS for the Enterprise defines ten classes designed to accommodate common enterprise applications. Table 9-6 lists the classes, traffic, and DSCP values defined by AutoQoS.

    Policies are created for these classes based on DiffServ best practices. The classes are associated with an egress (output) queue.

Table 9-6 *AutoQoS Class Definitions*

Class Name	Traffic Type	DSCP Value
IP Routing	Network control traffic (for example, routing protocols)	CS6
Interactive Voice	Inactive voice-bearer traffic	EF
Interactive Video	Interactive video data traffic	AF41
Streaming Video	Streaming media traffic	CS4
Telephony Signaling	Telephony signaling and control traffic	CS3
Transactional/Interactive	Database applications transactional in nature	AF21
Network Management	Network management traffic	CS2
Bulk Data	Bulk data transfers; general data service	AF11
Scavenger	Rogue traffic (traffic given less-than-best-effort treatment)	CS1
Best Effort	Default class; all noncritical traffic; miscellaneous	0

Example

AutoQoS is configured on the Serial0/0 interface. The **bandwidth** command is applied on Serial0/0 so that AutoQoS can make accurate decisions based on the correct bandwidth of the interface. Following the configuration is the output of the privileged EXEC **show auto qos** command. Several classes are automatically created and configured with a policy map. The policy is then applied on the serial0/0 interface in the outbound direction.

```
ip cef
interface serial0/0
 ip address 10.0.0.1 255.0.0.0
 bandwidth 512
 auto discovery qos


! Leave this command on the router for a few days in order for the router to
gather statistics on network traffic.
! Enter the privileged EXEC show auto qos or the show running-config command to
view the automatically generated classes and policies.
policy-map AutoQoS-Policy-Se0/0
class AutoQoS-Voice-Se0/0
 priority percent 50
 set dscp 50
class AutoQoS-Signaling-Se0/0
 bandwidth remaining percent 1
 set dscp cs3
class AutoQoS-Transactional-Se0/0
 bandwidth remaining percent 19
 random-detect dscp-based
 set dscp af21
class AutoQoS-Bulk-Se0/0
 bandwidth remaining percent 5
 random-detect dscp-based
 set dscp af11
class AutoQoS-Scavenger-Se0/0
 bandwidth remaining percent 1
 set dscp cs1
class AutoQoS-Management-Se0/0
 bandwidth remaining percent 1
 set dscp cs2
class class-default
 fair-queue
class-map match-any AutoQoS-Transactional-Se0/0
 match protocol sqlnet
class-map match-any AutoQoS-Voice-Se0/0
 match protocol rtp audio
class-map match-any AutoQoS-Signaling-Se0/0
```

```
 match protocol rtcp
 match protocol h323
class-map match-any AutoQoS-Scavenger-Se0/0
 match protocol kazaa2
class-map match-any AutoQoS-Management-Se0/0
 match protocol ldap
class-map match-any AutoQoS-Bulk-Se0/0
 match protocol ftp
!
interface serial0/0
 service-policy output AutoQoS-Policy-Se0/0
```

Further Reading

Refer to the following recommended sources for further information about the topics covered in this chapter:

IP Quality of Service, by Srinivas Vegesna, Cisco Press, ISBN 1578701163.

Enhanced IP Services for Cisco Networks, by Donald Lee, Cisco Press, ISBN 1578701066.

Inside Cisco IOS Software Architecture, by Vijay Bollapragada, Curtis Murphy, and Russ White, Cisco Press, ISBN 1578701813.

Cisco IOS Quality of Service, at www.cisco.com/warp/public/732/Tech/quality.shtml.

"DiffServ—The Scalable End-to-End QoS Model," Cisco white paper, at www.cisco.com/warp/public/cc/pd/iosw/ioft/iofwft/prodlit/difse_wp.htm.

Chapter 10

Multiprotocol Label Switching

This chapter covers the background and configuration of frame mode Multiprotocol Label Switching (MPLS). The following common configurations and features are discussed:

- **10-1: Configuring Basic MPLS**—MPLS is a high-performance packet forwarding technology that is based on Layer 2 switching instead of relying only on Layer 3 routing. Routers use labels added between the Layer 2 and Layer 3 headers for forwarding decisions.

- **10-2: MPLS Traffic Engineering**—Service providers can use traffic engineering on MPLS-enabled routers to route a customer's network traffic based on throughput and delay. Tunnels are created for label switch paths (LSP) using the Resource Reservation Protocol (RSVP).

- **10-3: MPLS Virtual Private Networks (VPN)**—MPLS VPNs have separate virtual routing and forwarding (VRF) instances for each customer in addition to a global routing table that is used to reach other routers in the provider network. Each VRF has a 64-bit route distinguisher (RD) to keep each customer's IP subnet separate from other routing and forwarding tables. BGP route target communities are used in exchanging route information between routers.

10-1: Configuring Basic MPLS

Multiprotocol Label Switching (MPLS) is a high-performance packet forwarding technology based on Layer 2 switching instead of Layer 3 routing. Routers are configured for MPLS forward frames based on labels instead of traditional Layer 3 IP unicast routing that performs Layer 3 lookups on the destination address at each hop. MPLS labels are inserted between the Layer 2 and Layer 3 headers and can be pushed (added), popped (removed), swapped, or aggregated (removing the top label and performing a Layer 3 lookup).

- MPLS is attractive to service providers because of its scalability and features. Providers can scale easier with MPLS than using Asynchronous Transfer Mode (ATM) or Frame Relay permanent virtual circuits (PVC). The traffic engineering features of MPLS enable providers to route traffic not just on a destination address but also on other factors such as bandwidth requirements and quality of service (QoS).

- A label switch router (LSR) is any router or switch that implements label distribution and can forward packets based on labels. An edge-LSR is any router that performs label imposition (push) or label disposition (pop). An ATM LSR is an ATM switch that can act as an LSR. With ATM LSRs, cell switching is used for the label forwarding table.

- MPLS-enabled routers communicate with each other using the Label Distribution Protocol (LDP). LSRs discover each other using hello packets, and peer relationships are maintained using keepalives. LSRs share label binding information with other LSRs. The label bindings build a forwarding equivalence class (FEC). A forwarding equivalence class is a group of IP packets forwarded in the same manner, over the same path, with the same forwarding treatment.

- Routers still rely on Layer 3 routing protocols for determining the path a packet should take. However, routing information, along with VPN, traffic engineering, and QoS information, is sent to the data plane to build a label forwarding information base (LFIB) for optimal forwarding performance.

Note   The commands that follow are based on the IETF Label Distribution Protocol (LDP) that uses a different syntax for commands than the older proprietary Tag Distribution Protocol (TDP). Prior to Cisco IOS Software Release 12.4(2)T, LDP-related commands were saved in the configuration in the older syntax. Starting with Cisco IOS Software Release 12.4(2)T, commands are saved in the configuration as they are entered.

Configuration

1. (Required) Enable Cisco Express Forwarding (CEF):

   (global) **ip cef [distributed]**

   CEF must be enabled on all routers running MPLS and on interfaces receiving unlabeled IP packets. Core routers do not perform CEF switching but must have CEF enabled globally to exchange labels. Enter the **distributed** keyword if your router supports distributed CEF (dCEF). Use dCEF when you want your line cards (for example, VIP cards) to perform the express forwarding so that the route processor (RP) can handle routing protocols.

Note   dCEF is not compatible with the RSVP. If you plan on configuring MPLS traffic engineering with RSVP, you must use CEF and not dCEF.

2. (Required) Start MPLS packet switching:

    `(global and interface) mpls ip`

    You must enable MPLS forwarding both globally and on the router interfaces for
    which you want to participate in MPLS forwarding. This command enables label
    switching of IPv4 packets according to normally routed paths. (Additional configura-
    tion is needed to support traffic engineering, QoS, and VPNs.) When this command
    is entered, Label Distribution Protocol (LDP) hello and keepalives are sent and
    received on the interfaces enabled for MPLS.

3. (Optional) Select the distribution protocol either globally or on a particular interface:

    `(global) mpls label protcol {ldp | tdp}`

    -or-

    `(interface) mpls label protocol {ldp | tdp | both}`

    Starting with Cisco IOS Software Release 12.4(3), the default protocol changed from
    Cisco Tag Distribution Protocol (TDP) to the IETF LDP. When changing the proto-
    col on an interface, you have the option of enabling both TDP and LDP. LSRs must
    run the same distribution protocol to establish a peer session and exchange label
    information.

4. (Optional) Manually configure the LDP identifier:

    `(global) mpls ldp router-id interface [force]`

    MPLS-enabled routers identify themselves in LDP messages using an identifier. By
    default, the identifier is the highest IP address of all loopback interfaces. If there are
    no loopback interfaces, the router uses the highest IP address of all active interfaces.
    You can manually configure the LDP identifier with this command. The router then
    uses whatever IP address is configured on the interface you specify. The IP address
    entered must be reachable by adjacent LSRs. A common symptom of having an
    unreachable LDP ID IP address is that the forwarding information base (FIB) is popu-
    lated, but there is no information in the label information forwarding base (LFIB). By
    default, a router ID is not changed until the interface currently used for the router ID
    is shut down, the IP address on that interface changes or is removed, or the router is
    rebooted. You can use the **force** keyword to force the router to change the router ID.

5. (Optional) Enable the distribution of labels associated with the IP default route:

    `(global) mpls ip default-route`

    By default, Cisco routers will not distribute labels for the IP default route. Enter this
    command to enable dynamic switching of labels for a router's default route.

6. (Optional) Enable MD5 authentication between peers:

    `(global) mpls ldp neighbor ip-address password password-string`

    MD5 authentication can be configured to verify TCP communication between two
    LDP peers. Both peers must be configured to use the same password.

7. (Optional) Enable the MPLS LDP autoconfiguration feature for OSPF interfaces:

    `(router) mpls ldp autoconfig [area area-id]`

    Normally, you must enter the **mpls ip** command both globally and on each interface for which you want to send and receive LDP packets. This process might be time-consuming and prone to human errors when configuring a router with many interfaces. The autoconfiguration feature helps with these issues by automatically enabling LDP on every interface associated with an OSPF or IS-IS instance. Note that you still need to enable LDP globally. When configuring LDP autoconfiguration for OSPF, you can choose to only enable LDP for interfaces belonging to a particular area by entering the **area** keyword followed by the area number.

8. (Optional) Enable the MPLS LDP autoconfiguration feature for IS-IS interfaces:

    `(router) mpls ldp autoconfig [level-1 | level-2]`

    Like autoconfiguration for OSPF, you must first enter the global **mpls ip** command before you can allow the autoconfiguration feature. Optionally, you can allow auto-configuration on interfaces configured for level-1 or level-2 routing by entering the **level-1** or **level-2** keywords, respectively.

Example

Figure 10-1 is used for this example. The three routers are configured for MPLS with manually configured LDP identifiers and MD5 peer authentication. Additionally, RouterB is configured for OSPF autoconfiguration for Area 0, and LDP is disabled on RouterA's FastEthernet0/0 interface.

Figure 10-1 *Basic MPLS Configuration Example*

```
RouterA
hostname RouterA
!
ip cef
mpls ip
mpls ldp router-id 1.1.1.1
mpls ldp neighbor 2.2.2.2 password C1sc0
!
interface fastethernet0/0
 ip address 172.16.0.1 255.255.0.0
 no mpls ip
!
```

```
interface fastethernet0/1
 ip address 172.17.0.1 255.255.0.0
 mpls ip
!
interface loopback 0
 ip address 10.1.1.1 255.255.255.255
!
interface loopback 1
 ip address 1.1.1.1 255.255.255.255
!
router ospf 1
 router-id 10.1.1.1
 network 172.16.0.0 0.0.255.255 area 0
 network 172.17.0.0 0.0.255.255 area 0
 network 10.1.1.1 0.0.0.0 area 0
 network 1.1.1.1 0.0.0.0 area 0


RouterB
hostname RouterB
!
mpls ip
mpls ldp router-id 2.2.2.2
mpls ldp neighbor 1.1.1.1 password C1sc0
mpls ldp neighbor 3.3.3.3 password C1sc0
!
interface fastethernet0/0
 ip address 172.17.0.2 255.255.0.0
!
interface fastethernet0/1
 ip address 172.18.0.1 255.255.0.0
!
interface loopback0
 ip address 10.2.2.2 255.255.255.255
!
interface loopback1
 ip address 2.2.2.2 255.255.255.255
!
router ospf 1
 router-id 10.2.2.2
 network 172.17.0.0 0.0.255.255 area 0
 network 172.18.0.0 0.0.255.255 area 0
 network 10.2.2.2 0.0.0.0 area 0
 network 2.2.2.2 0.0.0.0 area 0
 mpls ldp autoconfig area 0
```

```
RouterC
hostname RouterC
!
mpls ip
mpls ldp router-id 3.3.3.3
mpls ldp neighbor 2.2.2.2 password C1sc0
!
interface fastethernet0/0
 ip address 172.18.0.2 255.255.0.0
 mpls ip
!
interface fastethernet0/1
 ip address 172.19.0.1 255.255.0.0
 mpls ip
!
interface loopback0
 ip address 10.3.3.3 255.255.255.255
!
interface loopback1
 ip address 3.3.3.3 255.255.255.255
!
router ospf 1
 router-id 10.3.3.3
 network 172.18.0.0 0.0.255.255 area 0
 network 172.19.0.0 0.0.255.255 area 0
 network 10.3.3.3 0.0.0.0 area 0
 network 3.3.3.3 0.0.0.0 area 0
```

10-2: MPLS Traffic Engineering

Service providers can use traffic engineering on MPLS-enabled routers to route a customer's network traffic based on throughput and delay. Traffic engineering (TE) tunnels are created for label switch paths (LSP) using the RSVP. A tunnel interface represents the head of the LSP and is configured with a set of resource requirements (for example, bandwidth requirements, media requirements, and priority):

- Topology and resource information is flooded using either IS-IS or OSPF. Traffic engineering extensions are added to the routing process to enable MPLS traffic engineering.

- IS-IS routers must be configured to use the new style of IS-IS metric to support new type, length, and value objects (TLV) for traffic engineering. The new TLVs are 22 and 135 and have sub-TLVs that enable you to add properties to a link for purposes of traffic engineering.

■ The Shortest Path First (SPF) algorithm used by IS-IS and OSPF chooses the tunnel interface before choosing an alternative path over main interfaces.

■ Multiple tunnels might be configured to load-share traffic.

Configuration

1. (Required) Allow CEF and LDP as explained in Section 10-1.

2. (Required) Allow the MPLS traffic engineering feature:

   `(global) mpls traffic-eng tunnels`

   Before you can allow interfaces for traffic engineering, you must first allow traffic engineering globally.

3. (Required) Allow traffic engineering on interfaces:

   `(interface) mpls traffic-eng tunnels`

   When you have allowed MPLS traffic engineering globally, you can then allow it on interfaces. Configuring this command causes its resource information to be flooded into the appropriate interior gateway protocol (IGP) link-state database (either IS-IS or OSPF). This command also enables the interface to accept traffic engineering tunnel signaling requests.

4. (Required when using CAC with RSVP) Allow RSVP on an interface and specify the amount of bandwidth to reserve:

   `(interface) ip rsvp bandwidth [bandwidth]`

   This command enables the resource reservation protocol (RSVP) on the interface. You must enter this command if you use Call Admission Control (CAC) with RSVP. If you do not specify a bandwidth value, a default bandwidth value of 75 percent will be used.

5. Configure OSPF for MPLS traffic engineering.

   a. (Required) Allow traffic engineering for each area:

   `(router) mpls traffic-eng area area-number`

   b. (Required) Set the traffic engineering router identifier:

   `(router) mpls traffic-eng router-id interface`

   Unlike OSPF and MPLS router IDs, MPLS traffic engineering will not automatically set a router ID. The router ID will be the IP address on the interface you enter in this command. It is recommended that you use a loopback interface and that it match that of the interface used for the OSPF process router ID. The router ID is flooded to other routers and is used as the tunnel destination IP address.

6. Configure IS-IS for MPLS traffic engineering.

    a. (Required) Allow traffic engineering:

```
(router) mpls traffic-eng {level-1 | level-2}
```

    You can choose to flood traffic engineering into IS-IS level-1 or level-2.

    b. (Required) Set the traffic engineering router identifier:

```
(router) mpls traffic-eng router-id interface
```

    c. (Required) Configure the router to generate and accept new-style TLVs:

```
(router)metric-style wide
```

    The original metric used by IS-IS does not support traffic engineering. You must enter this command to support the new type, length, value objects (TLV), and sub-TLVs used for traffic engineering.

Note   See RFC 3784, "Intermediate System to Intermediate System (IS-IS) Extensions for Traffic Engineering (TE)," for more on the new TLVs and sub-TLVs used for traffic engineering.

7. Create a tunnel interface:

```
(global) interface tunnel number
```

This command creates a new tunnel interface.

8. Assign an IP address to the tunnel interface:

```
(interface) ip unnumbered interface
```

Tunnel interfaces should be unnumbered because the tunnel interface represents a unidirectional link. It is recommended that you use a loopback interface for the *interface* value.

9. Set the tunnel destination IP address:

```
(interface) tunnel destination ip-address
```

The tunnel destination IP address should be set to the far-end router's IP address that was configured with the **mpls traffic-eng router-id** command under the IS-IS or OSPF router process.

10. Set the tunnel type to MPLS traffic engineering:

```
(interface) tunnel mode mpls traffic-eng
```

There are many types of tunnel interfaces (for example, GRE, 6to4, and so on), so you must manually set the interface type.

11. Configure the bandwidth for the tunnel:

```
(interface) tunnel mpls traffic-eng bandwidth bandwidth
```

The range of valid *bandwidth* values is 1–4294967295.

12. Configure a dynamic or explicit path option:

```
(interface) tunnel mpls traffic-eng path-option number { dynamic | explicit
{name path-name | identifier path-number}}
```

You can configure the tunnel to be dynamic, meaning the router will rely on the IS-IS or OSPF routing information to determine the best path for the tunnel. You can also manually define the path using the **explicit** option. If you choose to explicitly map out the tunnel path, you need to enter either a name or identifier to reference the configured path. The steps for configuring an explicit path follow:

a. Configure the explicit path (if applicable).

- Enter IP explicit path configuration mode:

```
(global) ip explicit-path {name path-name | identifier path-number}
```

The *path-name* or *path-number* should match what you configured with the **tunnel mpls traffic-eng path-option** command earlier.

- Enter the IP addresses for each hop:

```
(explicit-path-configuration) next-address [loose | strict] ip-address
```

Enter the next IP addresses one at a time for the path you want the tunneled traffic to take. The **loose** and **strict** keywords are optional. The **loose** option tells the router that the previous address in the explicit path does not need to be directly connected to the next address. The router is therefore free to determine the path from the previous address to the next. The **strict** option tells the router that the previous address must be directly connected to the **next** address.

Note   The next IP address can be either the link (interface) IP address of the next-hop router or the MPLS node address (set with the **mpls traffic-eng router-id** *interface* router process command). However, for Cisco IOS releases 12.4(24)T and earlier, you cannot use a link address as the first hop followed by node addresses for subsequent hops. You do not have this restriction for releases after 12.4(24).

13. Allow the IGP (that is, IS-IS or OSPF) to use the tunnel when performing its SPF route calculation:

```
(interface) tunnel mpls traffic-eng autoroute announce
```

The only way to forward traffic onto a tunnel is to allow this feature or to configure a static route to the interface.

14. (Optional) Manually configure the metric used by the SPF calculation:

```
(interface) tunnel mpls traffic-eng autoroute metric absolute metric
```

You can allow the IGP to automatically assign the metric for the tunnel or manually configure the metric value using this command.

Example

Figure 10-2 is used for this example. RouterA is configured for MPLS traffic engineering. An explicit tunnel is configured with a backup dynamic tunnel. The tunnel is configured with a metric of 10 and announced to IS-IS so that IS-IS will consider the tunnel when it performs its SPF calculation.

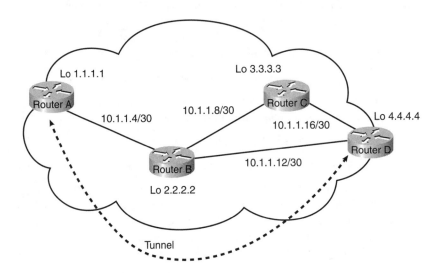

Figure 10-2   *MPLS Traffic Engineering Example*

```
hostname RouterA
!
ip cef
mpls ip
mpls ldp router-id 1.1.1.1
mpls traffic-eng tunnels
!
interface fastethernet0/0
 ip address 10.1.1.5 255.255.255.252
 mpls ip
 ip router isis
 mpls traffic-eng tunnels
 ip rsvp bandwidth 512
!
interface loopback 0
 ip address 1.1.1.1 255.255.255.255
```

```
  ip router isis
 !
router isis
  net 49.0001.0000.0000.0001.00
  is-type level-1
  metric-style wide
  mpls traffic-eng router-id loopback 0
  mpls traffic-eng level-1
 !
interface tunnel 0
  ip unnumbered loopback 0
  tunnel destination 4.4.4.4
  tunnel mpls traffic-eng bandwidth 512
  tunnel mode mpls traffic-eng
  tunnel mpls traffic-eng autoroute announce
  tunnel mpls traffic-eng autoroute metric absolute 10
  tunnel mpls traffic-eng path-option 1 explicit name TUNNEL
  tunnel mpls traffic-eng path-option 2 dynamic
 !
ip explicit-path name TUNNEL
  next-address 2.2.2.2
  next-address 4.4.4.4
```

10-3: MPLS Virtual Private Networks (VPN)

- MPLS virtual private networks (VPN) offer greater scalability than Frame Relay or ATM overlay VPN solutions.

- MPLS VPNs have a separate routing and forwarding (VRF) instance for each customer.

- Each VRF has a 64-bit route distinguisher (RD) to keep each customer's IP subnet separate from other routing and forwarding tables.

- Routers maintain a global routing table that is used to reach other routers in the provider's network.

- BGP route target communities are used to exchange route information between routers.

- There is a separate CEF and routing table for each VRF.

Configuration

1. Configure MPLS according to Section 10-1.

2. Create the VRF and enter into VRF configuration mode:

   (global) **ip vrf** *name*

   Every customer will have their own VRF.

Table 10-1 *RD Formats*

Format	Example
16-bit autonomous system number: a 32-bit number	65501:1
32-bit IP address: a 16-bit number	192.168.0.1:1

3. Create a route distinguisher for the VRF:

    `(vrf)` **rd** *route-distinguisher*

    You must configure a route distinguisher for the VRF to be functional. This command adds an 8-byte value to an IPv4 prefix to create a VPN IPv4 prefix. The RD can be entered in one of the two formats shown in Table 10-1.

4. Create a route target for import, export, or both import and export:

    `(vrf)` **route-target** {**import** | **export** | **both**} *route-target-community-number*

    This command creates a list of import and export route target extended communities for the VRF. Learned routes that carry the same extended community number as the *route-target-community-number* you configure can be either imported into the VRF or exported out of the VRF (or both). Extended communities follow the same format as RDs.

5. Associate the VRF with an interface facing a customer edge (CE) router:

    `(interface)` **ip vrf forwarding** *vrf-name*

    This command associates the VRF instance you created earlier in Step 2 with an interface. Configuring this command removes the IP address so you need to reconfigure the IP address after applying this command.

6. Configure the VRF instance under the BGP process:

    a. Enter BGP configuration mode:

        `(global)` **router bgp** *autonomous-system-number*

    b. Enter the address family configuration mode for the VRF instance:

        `(router)` **address-family ipv4 vrf** *vrf-name*

        Enter the VRF name you created earlier in Step 2.

    c. Configure the customer edge neighbor:

        `(address-family)` **neighbor** *ip-address* **remote-as** *autonomous-system-number*

        This command goes on the provider edge (PE) router and associates the VRF created in Step 2 with the BGP neighbor defined here under the VRF address family mode.

d. Activate the CE BGP neighbor:

```
(address-family) neighbor ip-address activate
```

7. Configure the provider edge (PE) to provider edge (PE) routing:

a. Enter BGP configuration mode:

```
(global) router bgp autonomous-system-number
```

b. Configure the PE BGP neighbor:

```
(router) neighbor ip-address remote-as autonomous-system-number
```

There is a separate VRF instance for each customer and a global routing table. The global routing is created here by defining the BGP peers within the provider.

c. Activate the PE BGP neighbor:

```
(router) neighbor ip-address activate
```

d. Enter the vpn4 unicast address family:

```
(router) address-family vpnv4 unicast
```

This address family configures an IPv4 unicast VPN routing instance that enables the PE routers to exchange BGP information with each other while still remaining separate from the customers' VRF instances.

e. Define and activate the PE BGP neighbors:

```
(address-family) neighbor ip-address remote-as autonomous-system-number
(address-family) neighbor ip-address activate
```

f. Allow extended communities for the PE BGP neighbor:

```
(address-family) neighbor ip-address send-community extended
```

Configuring this command activates support for extended communities. Extended communities are necessary for route targets to work with VRFs.

Note   For more on BGP configuration, see Chapter 6, "IP Routing Protocols."

Example

Figure 10-3 is used in this example. The configuration that follows shows the configuration on the PE1 router. A VRF instance is created for Customer_A and Customer_B. For Customer_A, the router is configured to both import and export all routes tagged with the extended community 100:1. For Customer_B, the router is configured to both import and export all routes tagged with the extended community 100:2:

```
hostname PE1
!
ip cef
!
```

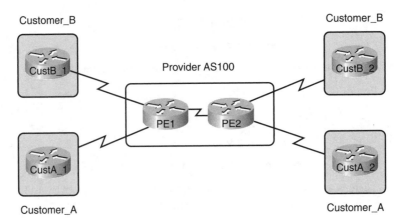

Figure 10-3   *MPLS VPN Example*

```
ip vrf Customer_A
 rd 100:1
 route-target both 100:1
!
ip vrf Customer_B
 rd 100:2
 route-target both 100:2
!
interface serial0/0
 ip address 192.168.1.5 255.255.255.252
 mpls ip
 description Link to PE
!
interface serial0/1
 ip address 192.168.1.9 255.255.255.252
 description Link to Customer_A
 ip vrf forwarding Customer_A
!
interface serial0/2
 ip address 192.168.1.13 255.255.255.252
 description Link to Customer_B
 ip vrf forwarding Customer_B
!
router bgp 100
 neighbor 192.168.1.6 remote-as 100
 neighbor 192.168.1.6 activate
 address-family vpnv4 unicast
 neighbor 192.168.1.6 remote-as 100
 neighbor 192.168.1.6 activate
 neighbor 192.168.1.6 send-community extended
```

```
address-family ipv4 unicast vrf Customer_A
redistribute connected
neighbor 192.168.1.10 remote-as 65535
neighbor 192.168.1.10 activate
address-family ipv4 unicast vrf Customer_B
redistribute connected
neighbor 192.168.1.14 remote-as 65534
neighbor 192.168.1.14 activate
```

References

Refer to the following recommended sources for further technical information about the MPLS topics covered here:

Definitive MPLS Network Designs, by Jim Guichard, Francois Le Faucheur, and Jean-Philippe Vasseur, Cisco Press, ISBN 1587051869.

MPLS Configuration on Cisco IOS Software, by Umesh Lakshman and Lancy Lobo, Cisco Press, ISBN 1587051990.

MPLS Fundamentals, by Luc DeGhein, Cisco Press, ISBN 1587051974.

MPLS and VPN Architectures, by Ivan Pepelnjak, Cisco Press, ISBN 1487050021.

MPLS and VPN Architectures, Volume II, by Ivan Pepelnjak, Jim Guichard, and Jeff Apcar, Cisco Press, ISBN 1587051125.

RFC 2547, "BGP/MPLS VPNs."

RFC 2702, "Requirements for Traffic Engineering Over MPLS."

RFC 2917, "A Core MPLS IP VPN Architecture."

RFC 3031, "Multiprotocol Label Switching Architecture."

RFC 3034, "Use of Label Switching on Frame Relay Networks Specification."

RFC 3036, "LDP Specification."

RFC 3063, "MPLS Loop Prevention Mechanism."

RFC 3032, "MPLS Label Stack Encoding."

RFC 3209, "RSVP-TE: Extensions to RSVP for LSP Tunnels."

RFC 3784, "Intermediate System to Intermediate System (IS-IS) Extensions for Traffic Engineering."

Chapter 11

Voice and Telephony

This chapter describes the functions and operations of IDS and IPS systems. This chapter will introduce you to:

- The underlying IDS and IPS technology that is embedded in the Cisco host- and network-based IDS and IPS solutions

- Cisco IOS IPS using Cisco SDM

This chapter presents several building blocks that can be used to implement a fully functional Voice over IP network. Transporting real-time, bandwidth-insensitive (or time-critical) voice traffic over a data network requires the use of many IOS features, possibly configured on many routers. You should carefully consider how to build such a network, adding a layer of complexity at a time. For example, you should approach a voice network in this fashion:

1. Build a \working IP network.

2. Add the Quality of Service (QoS) features necessary for transporting voice at the appropriate places in your network. (Although it might be tempting to get voice traffic functioning first, getting QoS configured correctly at the start ensures that all of your voice traffic will be handled efficiently from the beginning. Scaling your network into the future then becomes easy.)

3. Configure voice ports, where telephony devices will connect.

4. Plan and configure an enterprise-wide dialing plan.

5. Configure H.323 gateways in the appropriate locations.

6. If the size of the dial plan and network topologies warrant, configure H.323 gatekeepers.

7. Add additional voice functionality, such as Interactive Voice Response (IVR), Survivable Remote Site (SRS) Telephony, Media Gateway Control Protocol (MGCP), Session Initiation Protocol (SIP), debit card applications, settlement applications, and so forth.

Note   This chapter presents voice configuration for the Cisco 1700, 1800, 1900, 2600, 2800, 2900, 3600, 3700, 3800, 7200, 7300, 7500, 7600, and AS5x00 series routers and access servers. Voice configuration for the MC3810 and the 800 series routers is not covered.

This chapter discusses how to configure and use the following voice-related features:

- **11-1: Quality of Service for Voice**—Recommendations for applying the necessary QoS tools at the necessary locations in the network.

- **11-2: Voice Ports**—A router can connect to many different types of telephony devices using several types of voice ports. This section covers the many parameters that can be set or tuned on a voice port.

- **11-3: Dialing**—Dial plans must be configured in order for calls to be routed correctly. A router handles calls by creating and maintaining connections between dial peers.

- **11-4: H.323 Gateways**—The H.323 protocol is used to provide a way to send and receive voice, video, and data over an IP network. H.323 gateways provide communication between H.323 devices (VoIP nodes, Cisco CallManager, and so forth) and non-H.323 devices (POTS connections, PBXs, Cisco IP phones, and so forth). A router can be configured to function as an H.323 gateway.

- **11-5: H.323 Gatekeepers**—An H.323 gatekeeper provides address translation between standard E.164 telephone numbers and IP addresses of H.323 nodes. A gatekeeper can also control and manage the registration and admission of new calls. Gatekeepers and gateways are arranged in a hierarchical fashion to scale a voice network.

- **11-6: Interactive Voice Response (IVR)**—A router can perform IVR functions to interact with a caller when information is needed. Audio files can be played to the caller, prompting for various bits of information. Digits are then collected from the caller and can be used for authentication of the caller and authorization to make calls. Caller accounting can also be performed for statistics or billing information.

- **11-7: Survivable Remote Site (SRS) Telephony**—When Cisco CallManagers are used to provide centralized call management for a network with Cisco IP phones, a remote site becomes dependent on its WAN link for phone service. SRS Telephony allows the remote site router to take over the CallManager's function if the WAN link or the CallManager fails. Users will still be able to make calls within the remote site and to the outside via the PSTN.

11-1: Quality of Service for Voice

Many Quality of Service tools are available with the Cisco IOS software. Several of them are critical to the proper operation of a voice network. This section provides a brief overview of which QoS tools to apply at the appropriate locations in your network. For a complete description of the QoS tool configurations, refer to Chapter 9, "Quality of

Service." In particular, Section 9-1 provides a comprehensive and modular approach toward using all the QoS tools available.

1. Voice traffic should be classified as close to the edge of the network as possible.

   a. In a network with IP phones connected to Layer 2 switches, voice packets are automatically labeled with an IP Precedence value of 5 (critical) or an IP Differentiated Services Code Point (DSCP) value of EF. Because a phone is directly attached to a switch, the Precedence value can be trusted and allowed to pass into the network unchanged.

Note   For more information about IP Precedence, DSCP, Class of Service (CoS), and class-based packet marking with class maps, refer to Tables 9-1 and 9-2 and Section 9-1.

When passing voice packets between the Layer 2 and Layer 3 domains, you should use a class-based packet marking to set the DSCP, IP Precedence, and Layer 2 CoS flags. VoIP RTP packets should have IP Precedence 5, DSCP EF, and CoS 5. VoIP control packets should have IP Precedence 3, DSCP AF31, and CoS 3. Here is an example of the commands to do this:

```
class-map L3-L2-RTP
        match ip dscp ef
        match ip precedence 5
class-map L2-L3-RTP
        match cos 5
class-map L3-L2-Control
        match ip dscp af31
        match ip precedence 3
class-map L2-L3-Control
        match cos 3
policy-map output-L3-L2
        class L3-L2-RTP
                set cos 5
        class L3-L2-Control
                set cos 3
policy-map input-L2-L3
        class L2-L3-RTP
                set ip dscp ef
                set ip precedence 5
        class L2-L3-Control
                set ip dscp af31
                set ip precedence 3
interface FastEthernet 1/0
        service-policy input input-L2-L3

        service-policy output output-L3-L2
```

Note   Switches connected to IP phones can also be configured to trust the CoS values sent by the IP phone. If you trust the CoS values, configure the **mls qos trust device cisco-phone** command in the interface configuration mode on switch ports connected to IP phones.

b. For other voice IP packets entering a network through a router, the packets should be reclassified at the network edge. Any IP Precedence or DSCP values already set on incoming packets cannot be inherently trusted, because a user or application might try to set flags in all packets in order to get the best service.

Use packet classification that looks for VoIP RTP, VoIP control, MGCP, and Cisco Skinny protocols—all used for voice traffic. Voice control traffic should have the IP Precedence reset to 3 or IP DSCP reset to 26. VoIP RTP traffic should be passed unchanged, although the IP Precedence should be 5 or the IP DSCP should be 46. All other traffic can have the IP Precedence or IP DSCP reset to 0 for best-effort transport. Here is an example of the classification commands to do this:

```
ip access-list extended VoiceControl
        remark Match Skinny protocol
        permit tcp any any range 2000 2002
        remark Match H.323 protocol
        permit tcp any any eq 1720
        permit tcp any any range 11000 11999
        remark Match MGCP
        permit udp any any eq 2427


class-map voice-control
        match access-group VoiceControl
class-map rtp
        match ip rtp 16384 16383
class-map others
        match any


policy-map Classify-voice
        class voice-control
                set ip dscp 26
        class rtp
                set ip dscp 46
        class others
                set ip dscp 0


interface FastEthernet 1/0
        service-policy input Classify-voice
```

2. Use Low Latency Queuing (LLQ) with a strict priority queue for voice, where voice mixes with other traffic across a WAN link. Refer to the **priority** command described in Section 9-1 for more information. A simple example of LLQ follows in which voice traffic is put into a strict priority queue of 768 kbps:

```
clss-map match-any RTP-CLASS
   match protocol rtp audio
   match ip dscp 46
policy-map RTP-POLICY
   class RTP-CLASS
      priority 768
   class class-default
      bandwidth 256
   interface serial0/0
      service-policy output RTP-POLICY
```

3. Use Link Fragmentation and Interleaving (LFI) for efficient voice transmission over a WAN link with a bandwidth of less than 768 kbps. Voice packets must be sent out across a serial link at regular intervals, not more than every 10 milliseconds. LFI fragments large packets before transmission so that the serialization delay for each packet is minimized. Voice packets are then interleaved into the data stream. To choose the maximum fragment size for LFI, multiply the bandwidth of the WAN link (in kbps) by 10 milliseconds, and divide by 8 bits/byte. Table 11-1 lists the recommended LFI fragment sizes based on link bandwidth.

4. Provision the appropriate amount of bandwidth for voice calls.

Each type of codec uses a different sized packet, generated at a different rate. Table 11-2 provides the typical bandwidth required per call.

Table 11-1 *Recommended LFI Fragment Sizes*

Link Bandwidth	Recommended Fragment Size
56 kbps	70 bytes
64 kbps	80 bytes
128 kbps	160 bytes
256 kbps	320 bytes
512 kbps	640 bytes
768 kbps	960 bytes
Greater than 768 kbps	N/A

Table 11-2   *Typical Bandwidth Needed for Voice Calls*

Codec Type	Sampling Rate	Voice Payload (Bytes)	Packets Per Second	Bandwidth Per Call
G.711	20 ms (default)	160	50	80 kbps
	30 ms	240	33	53 kbps
G.729A	20 ms	20	50	24 kbps
	30 ms	30	33	16 kbps

Note   G.711 has a Mean Opinion Score (MOS) of 4.1 (out of 5) and is the standard for LANs. G.729 has a MOS of 3.92 and is the standard for WANs. G.729 Annex A (G.729A) is an improvement on G.729 but is a less complex codec, which decreases the load on Digital Signal Processors (DSP). Its MOS is 3.90.

When provisioning the data circuit, use a slightly greater bandwidth per simultaneous call than the table shows because of the size of additional headers (such as RTP, UDP, IP, Layer 2, and so on). The Real Time Transport Protocol (RTP) header is 12 bytes, the UDP header is 8 bytes, and the IP header is 20 bytes, totaling 40 bytes in addition to the voice payload. Using compressed RTP (cRTP), the RTP, UDP, and IP headers can be compressed to either 2 bytes without a UDP checksum or 4 bytes with a UDP checksum. You also need to consider other header overhead such as PPP, Ethernet, and IPsec. IPsec headers add an additional 50bytes to 57 bytes, GRE/L2TP headers add 24 bytes, MPLS adds 4 bytes, PPP adds 6 bytes, Ethernet adds 18 bytes, Frame Relay adds 6 bytes, and Cisco HDLC adds 7 or more bytes.

The formula to determine the amount of calls you can make on a link is as follows:

Packet size = (payload + RTP / UDP/IP + Layer 2 overhead) * 8

Bandwidth per call = packet size * packets per second (PPS)

Useable bandwidth = total bandwidth – reserved bandwidth for control / other traffic (%25 is a usual estimate if you are uncertain)

Number of calls = useable bandwidth / bandwidth per call

As an example, on a PPP T1 link, a G.729A packet using a 20-ms sampling rate (20-byte payload), with uncompressed RTP/UDP/IP headers gives a total of 66 bytes (a 528-bit packet size). Multiplying the packet size by 50 packets per second gives you 26,400 bits of bandwidth per call. A T1 link gives you 1,536,000 bits per second of available bandwidth. Subtracting a conservative 25 percent for overhead (for example, routing protocol traffic, and so on), a T1 leaves you with 1,152,000 bits per second. Finally, dividing the useable bandwidth (1,152,000) by the bandwidth per call

(26,400), gives you a maximum of 43 calls at any given time. (This assumes you are not using the bandwidth for other types of traffic.)

5. Use Frame Relay Traffic Shaping (FRTS) for Frame Relay WAN links. Chapter 9, "Quality of Service," details how to configure FRTS in Section 9-12.

6. Use Call Admission Control to protect the available WAN link bandwidth. Admission Control can be performed by a Cisco CallManager or an H.323 gatekeeper.

11-2: Voice Ports

- Voice ports on routers provide connectivity between the telephony and data networks.

- Telephony signaling is used to pass information about call status, voice port status, telephone numbers, and so forth. Signaling is configurable so that the voice port on a router can match the signaling provided by the telephony device.

- Analog voice ports connect to analog two-wire and four-wire telephony circuits:

    - *Foreign Exchange Office (FXO)* ports are used to connect to a PSTN central office (CO) or a PBX. They can function as a trunk or tie line. FXO uses a two-wire circuit.

    - *Foreign Exchange Station (FXS)* ports are used to connect to end-user equipment such as a telephone, fax machine, or modem. FXS uses a two-wire circuit.

    - *E&M (receive and transmit)* ports are used as trunk circuits to connect to a telephone switch or PBX. E&M uses a four-wire circuit, with signaling carried over separate wires from the audio.

- Digital voice ports use a single digital interface as a trunk:

    - *Channelized T1* carries 24 full-duplex voice channels (DS0) or timeslots.

    - *Channelized E1* carries 30 full-duplex voice channels (DS0) or timeslots.

    - *ISDN PRI* carries 23 B channels plus one D channel (North America and Japan) or 30 B channels plus one D channel (the rest of the world). Each B channel can carry voice or data, and the D channel is used for signaling.

- Signaling:

    - *Loop-start signaling* is usually used in residential local loops. It detects a closed circuit for going off-hook.

    - *Ground-start signaling* is usually used for PBXs and trunks. It detects a ground and current flow.

    - *Wink-start signaling* begins with the calling side's seizing the line, followed by a short off-hook "wink" by the called side.

    - *Immediate-start signaling* allows a call to begin immediately after the calling side seizes the line. It is used with E&M trunks.

- *Delay-dial signaling* begins with the calling side's seizing the line and waiting until the called side is on-hook before sending digits. It is used with E&M trunks.

- *Common-channel signaling (CCS)* is used with a channelized T1 or E1, sending signaling over a dedicated channel.

- *Channel-associated signaling (CAS)* is used with a channelized T1 or E1, sending signaling within the voice channel itself. Also known as *robbed-bit signaling,* CAS uses a bit from every sixth frame of voice data to emulate analog signaling.

- *QSIG protocol* is an ISDN signaling protocol that takes the place of D-channel signaling in some parts of the world.

- Trunk connections can be configured to provide simulated trunks between two PBXs over an IP network between two routers.

- PSTN call fallback can be used to force call rerouting over other VoIP or POTS dial peers if the network becomes too congested for good voice quality.

- Voice port busyout can be used to force a voice port into an inactive state for a variety of conditions.

Configuration

1. (Optional) Use a digital voice port.

   a. Set the Codec complexity.

   Select the Codec location:

   (global) **voice-card** *slot*

   -or-

   (global) **dspint dspfarm** *slot/port*

   Codecs are located on a **voice-card** in the Cisco 880, 2600, 3600, 3700, and MC3810 series routers. Codecs are located on a DSP interface (**dspint dspfarm**) on 3660 series routers with multiservice interchange (MIX) modules, 2600 series with advanced interchange modules (AIM), 7200 series rouers, and 7500 series routers.

   Set the complexity:

   (voicecard) codec complexity {high | med}

   -or-

   (dspfarm) **codec** {**high** | **med**}

   All voice cards on a router must use the same codec complexity. The Codec capabilities are **high** (supports G.711, G.726, G.729, G.729 Annex B, G.723.1, G.723.1

Annex A, G.728, and fax relay) or **med** (the default; supports G.711, G.726, G.729 Annex A, G.729 Annex B with Annex A, and fax relay). Medium is the default.

Note   Refer to Tables 11-2 and 11-6 for more on codecs. G.711 is the standard for LANs. G.729 is the standard for WANs. Also, low bitrate codecs such as G.729 distort tones used by faxes, modems, and dual tone multifrequency (DTMF) so you should use a high bit-rate codec for sending the tones. VoIP signaling protocols have mechanisms to handle this (for example, SIP provides in-band dtmf-relay).

Cisco 2600, 3600, and 3700 routers can support up to six voice or fax calls per voice card with **high** and up to 12 voice or fax calls with **med**. Cisco 7200 and 7500 routers can support up to two voice calls with **high** and four calls with **med**.

Note   Cisco AS5300 access servers have Codec capabilities set within the voice feature cards (VFCs). Cisco AS5800 access servers have Codec configuration performed within dial-peer configuration.

b. (ISDN PRI only) Set the ISDN switch type:

```
(global) isdn switch-type switch-type
```

The ISDN *switch-type* must be set to match the switching equipment being used by the telephony provider. In North America, use **basic-5ess** (Lucent basic rate switches), **basic-dms100** (NT DMS-100 basic rate switches), or **basic-ni1** (National ISDN-1). In Australia, use **basic-ts013** (TS013). In Europe, use **basic-1tr6** (German 1TR6), **basic-nwnet3** (Norwegian NET3 phase 1), **basic-net3** (NET3), **vn2** (French VN2), or **vn3** (French VN3). In Japan, use **ntt** (NTT). In New Zealand, use **basic-nznet3** (New Zealand NET3).

Note   To use QSIG signaling, use a *switch-type* of **basic-qsig**.

c. Configure the T1/E1 controller.

Select the controller:

```
(global) controller {t1 | e1} slot/port
```

-or-

```
(global) card type {t1 | e1} slot
```

A T1/E1 controller is referenced by **controller** and *slot* and *port* number on 2600 and 3600 routers and by **card type** and *slot* number on 7200 and 7500 routers.

Set the framing type:

```
(controller) framing {sf | esf | crc4 | no-crc4} [australia]
```

The T1 framing type can be **sf** (Super Frame, the default) or **esf** (Extended Super Frame). The E1 framing type can be **crc4** (the default), **no-crc4**, and an optional **australia**.

Set the clock source:

```
(controller) clock source {line [primary | secondary] | internal}
```

The controller can derive its clock from **line** (a CO or an external source) or **internal** (the controller's internal clock). A line clock can be designated as **primary** (preferred over other controllers' line clocks) or **secondary** (used as a backup external clock source).

Set the line encoding:

```
(controller) linecode {ami | b8zs | hdb3}
```

For a T1, the line coding can be set to **ami** (the default) or **b8zs** (binary 8 zero substitution). For an E1, it can be set to **ami** or **hdb3** (high-density bipolar 3, the default).

(T1 or E1 only) Define a DS-0 group:

```
(controller) ds0-group ds0-group-no timeslots timeslot-list type type
```

Multiple DS-0 channels can be defined as a single group that can be referenced as a logical voice port. The DS-0 group is given a number, *ds0-group-no* (T1 is 0 to 23; E1 is 0 to 30). The specific DS-0 timeslots are identified as *timeslot-list,* a comma-separated list of single DS-0s or one or more ranges of DS-0s.

The *type* field specifies an emulated signaling type and can be **e&m-delay-dial**, **e&m-fgb** (E&M type 2 feature group B), **e&m-fgd** (E&M type 2 feature group D), **e&m-immediate-start**, **e&m-melcas-delay** (E&M Mercury Exchange Limited CAS delay start), **e&m-melcas-immed** (E&M MELCAS immediate start), **e&m-melcas-wink** (E&M MELCAS wink start), **e&m-wink-start**, **ext-sig** (automatically generate off-hook state), **fgd-eana** (Feature group D Exchange Access North American), **fgd-os** (Feature group D Operator Services), **fxo-melcas**, **fxs-melcas**, **fxs-ground-start**, **fxs-loop-start**, **none** (null signaling for external call control), **p7** (the P7 switch type), **r1-itu** (R1 ITU), **sas-ground-start**, or **sas-loop-start**.

(ISDN PRI only) Configure PRI parameters.

First, configure the PRI group:

```
(controller) pri-group timeslots range
```

The voice timeslots are identified as a *range* (numbers 1 to 23 or 1 to 30, separated by a dash or comma).

Next, enable voice calls over the PRI:

```
(global) interface slot/number:[23 | 15]

(interface) isdn incoming voice-modem
```

The D-channel is selected with the **23** (PRI on T1) or **15** (PRI on E1) keyword. Voice calls will be accepted as if they were modem calls.

2. Configure a voice port.

   a. Select the voice port:

   ```
   (global) voice-port slot/subunit/port
   ```

   -or-

   ```
   (global) voice-port slot/port:ds0-group-no
   ```

   A voice port (any type) is selected according to its physical position in the router. Analog ports are referenced by *slot/subunit/port*, and digital ports are referenced by physical position and the logical DS0 group number, as in *slot/port:ds0-group-no*.

   b. (Optional) Enter a description for the port:

   ```
   (voiceport) description text-string
   ```

   c. (Analog ports only) Specify the signaling type:

   ```
   (voiceport) signal {loop-start | ground-start | wink-start |

    immediate-start | delay-dial}
   ```

   For FXS or FXO, choose **loop-start** (the default) or **ground-start**. For E&M, choose **wink-start** (the default), **immediate-start**, or **delay-dial**.

   d. (Optional) Specify the call progress tone locale:

   ```
   (voiceport) cptone locale
   ```

   The *locale* is given as a two-letter ISO3166 value (**us** is the default).

   e. (Optional) Configure the E&M interface.

   (Analog ports only) Specify the number of wires:

   ```
   (voiceport) operation {2-wire | 4-wire}
   ```

   The **2-wire** circuit is the default.

   ■ Specify the type of circuit:

   ```
   (voiceport) type {1 | 2 | 3 | 5}
   ```

   The E&M interface can be one of the types shown in Table 11-3.

Table 11-3   *E&M Interface Types*

	E-lead (Output)	M-lead (Input)	Signal Battery	Signal Ground
Type 1 (default)	Relay to ground	Referenced to ground	—	—
Type 2	Relay to signal ground	Referenced to ground	Feed for M; connected to −48V	Return for E; isolated from ground
Type 3	Relay to ground	Referenced to ground	Connected to −48V	Connected to ground
Type 5	Relay to ground	Referenced to −48V	—	—

> **f.** (Optional) Configure ringing operation.
>
> ■ (FXS only) Set the ring frequency:
>
> (voiceport) `ring frequency {25 | 50}`
>
> The ring frequency is set in hertz, to **25** (the default) or **50**.
>
> ■ (FXS only) Set the ring cadence:
>
> (voiceport) ring cadence {[pattern01 | pattern02 | ... pattern12] | [**define** *pulse interval*]}
>
> The ring pattern for incoming calls can be set to one of the 12 predefined patterns (the default is selected by the **cptone** locale) or to a user-defined pattern with the **define** keyword. The ring cycle is given by *pulse* (on-time in hundreds of milliseconds; 1 to 50) and *interval* (off-time in hundreds of milliseconds; 1 to 50).
>
> ■ (FXO only) Set the number of rings before answering:
>
> (voiceport) `ring number` *number*
>
> The router will answer an incoming call after *number* (1 to 10; the default is 1) rings.
>
> **g.** (Optional) Use disconnect supervision to detect a disconnected call.
>
> Select the disconnect supervision type.
>
> Detect battery reversal (analog ports only):
>
> (voiceport) [**no**] **battery-reversal**
>
> FXO ports reverse battery upon call connection unless the **no** keyword is used. FXS ports with loop-start detect a second battery reversal to disconnect a call (the default) unless the **no** keyword is used.

Detect supervisory disconnects (FXO only):

```
(voiceport) [no] supervisory disconnect
```

A CO switch normally drops line power for at least 350 milliseconds to signal a call disconnect. The FXO port detects this (the default) unless the **no** keyword is used.

Use disconnect acknowledgment (FXS only):

```
(voiceport) [no] disconnect-ack
```

After an FXS port detects a disconnect, it returns an acknowledgment by dropping line power (the default). Use the **no** keyword to disable the acknowledgment.

■   (Analog FXO only) Configure supervisory disconnect tones.

Create a voice class that contains the tone settings:

```
(global) voice class dualtone tag
```

The voice class is labeled as *tag* (1 to 10000). It contains the parameters for the dual disconnect tones.

Set the disconnect tone frequencies:

```
(voice-class) freq-pair tone-id frequency-1 frequency-2
(voice-class) freq-max-deviation frequency
```

With **freq-pair**, the pair of tones is given a unique *tone-id* (1 to 16) and is set to *frequency-1* and *frequency-2*, in Hz (300 to 3600 Hz). *frequency-2* can be set to 0, but random single tones can cause inadvertent disconnects. The **freq-max-deviation** keyword sets the maximum frequency deviation that will be detected (10 to 125 Hz; the default is 10 Hz).

Set the tone power:

```
(voice-class) freq-max-power dBm0
(voice-class) freq-min-power dBm0
(voice-class) freq-power-twist dBm0
```

The minimum tone power is given by **freq-min-power** (10 to 35 dBm0; the default is 30). The maximum tone power is **freq-max-power** (0 to 20 dBm0; the default is 10). The power difference between the two tones is given by **freq-power-twist** (0 to 15 dBm0; the default is 6).

Set the cadence for a complex tone:

```
(voice-class) cadence-min-on-time time
(voice-class) cadence-max-off-time time
(voice-class) cadence-variation time
(voice-class) cadence-list cadence-id cycle1-ontime cycle1-offtime
  cycle2-ontime cycle2-offtime cycle3-ontime cycle3-offtime
  cycle4-ontime cycle4-offtime
```

The tone is specified as a minimum on time (**cadence-min-on-time**; 0 to 100 milliseconds), a maximum off time (**cadence-max-off-time**; 0 to 5000 milliseconds), and a maximum variation in detectable on time (**cadence-variation**; 0 to 200 milliseconds). The cadence pattern can be specified with a unique *cadence-id* (1 to 10) and an on-off pattern of four cycle times each (0 to 1000 milliseconds; the default is 0).

Detect supervisory disconnect tones with the voice class:

```
(voiceport) supervisory disconnect dualtone {mid-call | pre-connect}
  voice-class tag
```

-or-

```
(voiceport) supervisory disconnect anytone
```

Tone detection is enabled on the voice port using the voice class *tag* for tone definitions. Disconnects can be detected during a call (**mid-call**) or only during call setup (**pre-connect**). If the PSTN or PBX cannot provide a disconnect tone, the **anytone** keyword can be used instead. Any tone used during call setup (busy or dial tone) causes the call to be disconnected.

h. (Optional) Set timeout values:

```
(voiceport) timeouts type value
```

The timeout parameters can be set with the following *type* and *value*: **call-disconnect** *seconds* (0 to 120 seconds; the default is 60), **initial** *seconds* (the maximum time between the first and next dialed digit; 0 to 120 seconds; the default is 10), **interdigit** *seconds* (the maximum time between dialed digits; 0 to 120 seconds; the default is 10), **ringing** {*seconds* | **infinity**} (the time that an outbound call is allowed to ring before disconnecting; 3 to 3600 seconds; the default is 30, or infinite with no disconnect), or **wait-release** {*seconds* | **infinity**} (the maximum time that a busy, reorder, or out-of-service tone is sent for a failed call; 3 to 3600 seconds; the default is 30, or infinite).

i. (Optional) Set timing parameters:

```
(voiceport) timing type milliseconds
```

An E&M voice port can be fine-tuned with the following timing *type*, measured in milliseconds: **clear-wait** (the minimum time between inactive seizure and call clearing; 200 to 2000 ms; the default is 400), **delay-duration** (the duration of delay-dial signaling; 100 to 5000 ms; the default is 2000), **delay-start** (the minimum time between outgoing seizure and outdial address; 20 to 2000 ms; the default is 300), **pulse** (the pulse dialing rate in pulses per seconds; 10 to 20; the default is 20), **pulse-interdigit** (pulse dialing interdigit timing; 100 to 1000 ms; the default is 500), **wink-duration** (the maximum wink signal duration; 100 to 400 ms; the default is 200), or **wink-wait** (the maximum wink wait duration; 100 to 5000 ms; the default is 200).

An FXO voice port can be tuned with the following *type*, measured in milliseconds: **guard-out** (how long to wait before seizing a remote FXS port; 300 to 3000 ms; the default is 2000), **pulse** (the pulse dialing rate in pulses per second; 10 to 20; the default is 20), **pulse-digit** (the pulse digit signal duration; 10 to 20 ms; the default is 20), or **pulse-interdigit** (the pulse dialing interdigit timing; 100 to 1000 ms; the default is 500).

Any voice port can be tuned with the following *type*, measured in milliseconds: **dial-pulse min-delay** (the time between pulse dialing pulses; 0 to 5000 ms; the default is 300), **digit** (the DTMF digit duration; 50 to 1000 ms; the default is 100), **interdigit** (the DTMF interdigit duration; 50 to 500 ms; the default is 100), or **hookflash-out** (the hookflash duration; 300 to 3000 ms; the default is 300).

j. (Optional) Use Voice Activity Detection (VAD) to reduce bandwidth.

- Set the music-on-hold threshold:

```
(voiceport) music-threshold dB
```

The minimal level of music played on hold can be set to *dB* (–70 to –30 dB; the default is –38) so that VAD is triggered to play the audio.

- Enable comfort noise generation:

```
(voiceport) comfort-noise
```

During the silent gaps when VAD doesn't detect a voice, a subtle background noise is played locally on the voice port (this is enabled by default). If this feature is disabled, the silence can make the caller think the call has been disconnected.

k. (Optional) Tune the voice quality.

- Adjust the jitter buffer.

Set the jitter buffer playout mode:

```
(voiceport) playout-delay mode {adaptive | fixed}
```

The jitter buffer can operate in two modes: **adaptive** (the buffer size and delay are adjusted dynamically; this is the default) or **fixed** (a fixed buffer size; the delay doesn't change). Adaptive mode dynamically adjusts the jitter buffer according to current or changing network conditions.

Rather than configuring the mode on the voice port (affecting all dial peers using the voice port), you can configure the mode for specific dial peers.

Set the jitter buffer parameters:

```
(voiceport) playout-delay {maximum | nominal} milliseconds
```

The jitter buffer can be set for a playout delay of **maximum** (the upper limit; the default is 160 ms) or **nominal** (the playout delay used at the beginning of a call; the default is 80 ms) for a delay of *milliseconds* (40 to 320 milliseconds).

- Adjust the echo canceler.

Enable the echo canceler:

`(voiceport) echo-cancel enable`

By default, echo cancellation is enabled on all voice interfaces. If it is disabled, the callers might hear an audible echo.

Set the maximum echo cancel duration:

`(voiceport) echo-cancel coverage { 24 | 32 | 48 | 64 | 80 | 96 | 112 | 128}`

The echo canceler covers a fixed window of the call audio. The window size can be set to **24, 32, 48, 64, 80, 96, 112,** or **128** (the default) milliseconds. The coverage window can be made larger if you hear an audible echo.

Use nonlinear echo cancellation:

`(voiceport) [no] non-linear`

By default, the echo canceler uses a nonlinear operation (residual echo suppression). The nonlinear computation attenuates the signal when a near-end speech (the end of a word) is detected. Use the **no** keyword to return to linear mode if desired.

■   Adjust the voice level.

Set the input gain:

`(voiceport) input gain value`

The voice port adjusts the amount of gain at the receiver side to *value* (–6 to 14 decibels; the default is 0). The default value is used to achieve a –6 dB attenuation between phones.

Set the output attenuation:

`(voiceport) output attenuation value`

The voice port adjusts the amount of attenuation on the transmit side to *value* (–6 to 14 decibels; the default is 0).

Set the voice port impedance (FXO only):

`(voiceport) impedance {600c | 600r | 900c | complex1 | complex2}`

An FXO voice port can be terminated with an impedance of **600c** (600 ohms complex), **600r** (600 ohms real, the default), **900c** (900 ohms complex), **complex1**, or **complex2**. Choose a value that matches the specifications of the telephony provider or equipment.

3.   (Optional) Use trunk connections with a voice port.

a. Set the trunk-conditioning signaling.

Create a voice class as a template:

`(global) voice class permanent tag`

Identify the voice class with a unique *tag* (1 to 10000).

■ Set the trunk keepalive interval:

```
(voice-class) signal keepalive seconds
```

A keepalive packet is sent at intervals of *seconds* (1 to 65535; the default is 5 seconds) to the far end of the trunk.

■ Define the signaling sequence that is sent to the PBX:

```
(voice-class) signal sequence oos {no-action | idle-only | oos-only |
   both}
```

When a keepalive packet is lost or an AIS message is received from the far end, the router sends a sequence of signaling messages: **no-action** (no signaling is sent), **idle-only** (only the idle signal pattern is sent), **oos-only** (only the out-of-service [OOS] pattern is sent), or **both** (both idle and OOS patterns are sent; this is the default).

■ Define signaling patterns for idle and OOS states:

```
(voice-class) signal pattern {idle receive | idle transmit | oos
receive |
   oos transmit} bit-pattern
```

The signaling pattern for the following conditions is defined as *bit-pattern* (ABCD, as four 0 or 1 digits): **idle receive** (an idle message from the network), **idle transmit** (an idle message from the PBX), **oos receive** (the network is out of service), or **oos transmit** (PBX is out of service). The defaults for a near-end voice port are **idle receive** (E&M: 0000 T1 or 0001 E1; FXO: 0101 loop start or 1111 ground start; FXS: 0101; MELCAS: 1101), **idle transmit** (E&M: 0000; FXO: 0101; FXS: 0101 loop start or 1111 ground start; MELCAS: 1101), **oos receive** (E&M: 1111; FXO: 1111 loop start or 0000 ground start; FXS: 1111 loop start or 0101 ground start; MELCAS: 1111), and **oos transmit** (none).

■ (Optional) Restart a permanent trunk after it has been OOS:

```
(voice-class) signal timing oos restart seconds
```

A trunk can be torn down and restarted *seconds* (0 to 65535) after it has been out of service. By default, trunks are not restarted.

■ (Optional) Return a trunk to standby state after it has been OOS:

```
(voice-class) signal timing oos slave-standby seconds
```

A trunk can be returned to its initial standby state *seconds* (0 to 65535) after it has been out of service. By default, trunks are not returned to the standby state.

■ (Optional) Stop sending packets if the PBX signals an OOS:

```
(voice-class) signal timing oos suppress-all seconds
```

If the PBX signals on OOS condition for *seconds* duration (0 to 65535), the router can stop sending voice and signaling packets. By default, the router does not stop sending.

- Apply the voice class to a voice port:

  ```
  (voice-port) voice-class permanent tag
  ```

  The trunk-conditioning signaling voice class is applied as a template to the voice port.

b. Define the type of trunk connection on a voice port:

```
(voice-port) connection {plar | tie-line | plar-opx} digits |

  {trunk digits [answer-mode]}
```

The trunk connection can be configured as **plar** (private line automatic ringdown; the caller goes off-hook and *digits* is automatically dialed), **tie-line** (a tie-line trunk to a PBX; it is automatically set up and torn down for each call when you dial *digits*), or **plar-opx** (PLAR off-premises extension; an FXO port does not answer until the remote end at *digits* answers).

The **trunk** keyword is used to create a permanent trunk between two PBXs connected by two routers. The number *digits* is dialed to reach the far end of the trunk. If the **answer-mode** keyword is given, the router waits for an incoming call before initiating the trunk connection. Otherwise, the trunk will be brought up permanently.

4. (Optional) Use PSTN fallback for call routing during network congestion.

a. Enable call fallback:

```
(global) call fallback active
```

The router samples the H.323 call requests and attempts to use alternative dial peers if the network congestion is above a threshold.

b. (Optional) Use call fallback for statistics gathering instead of true fallback:

```
(global) call fallback monitor
```

As soon as the router has gathered fallback statistics, you can display them for planning purposes. Use the **show call fallback stats** command to see the results.

c. (Optional) Use MD5 encryption keys for fallback probes:

```
(global) call fallback key-chain name-of-chain
```

Fallback uses Service Assurance Agent (SAA) probes to determine the state of the network. Use the MD5 key chain named *name-of-chain* if you are configuring the SAA responder at the far-end router to use MD5. Refer to Section 1-7 for more information about SAA and its configuration.

d. Set the jitter probe parameters.

Set the number of jitter packets:

```
(global) call fallback jitter-probe num-packets packets
```

The fallback jitter probe uses the specified number of *packets* (2 to 50; the default is 15 packets). Increase the number of packets to get a better idea of true network conditions—at the expense of additional bandwidth used for the probes.

- Set the IP Precedence to use on jitter probes:

  (global) `call fallback jitter-probe precedence` *precedence*

The router can set the IP Precedence value in each jitter probe packet to *precedence* (0 to 7; the default is 2). The IP Precedence of true VoIP packets is usually set to 5. Setting the probe packets to a more realistic Precedence value helps you measure the conditions that voice packets actually experience.

- Force the jitter probes to use a strict priority queue:

  (global) `call fallback jitter-probe priority-queue`

By default, jitter probes are sent without using a priority queue. If you have a strict priority queue configured using LLQ, the jitter probe packets are sent over the IP RTP priority queue regardless.

- Adjust the SAA probe timeout:

  (global) `call fallback probe-timeout` *seconds*

After a timeout period of *seconds* (1 to 2147483 seconds; the default is 30) elapses without a response to a probe packet, another probe is sent.

- Use an average of two probes for congestion calculations:

  (global) `call fallback instantaneous-value-weight` *weight*

Normally, network congestion is measured based on the results of one probe. You can use the weighted average of the current probe with the previous probe to get a more gradual fallback recovery during heavy congestion. The *weight* (0 to 100; the default is 66 percent) is a percentage used for the current probe so that it can be weighted more than the previous probe statistics.

- Set the fallback thresholds.

For trigger fallback based on packet delay and loss:

  (global) `call fallback threshold delay` *delay-value* `loss` *loss-value*

The fallback threshold is set if the end-to-end delay rises above *delay-value* (1 to 2,147,483,647 milliseconds; there is no default) and if the percentage of packet loss rises above *loss-value* (0 to 100 percent; there is no default). The lower you set these values, the higher your expectations for high-quality voice.

For trigger fallback based on the ICPIF threshold:

  (global) `call fallback threshold icpif` *threshold-value*

The Impairment/Calculated Planning Impairment Factor (ICPIF) threshold is calculated, producing an impairment factor for every network node along a probe's path. With fallback, the ICPIF is calculated using packet loss, delay, and the type of Codecs used. Call fallback is triggered if the ICPIF value rises above *threshold-value* (0 to 34; the default is 5). The lower the ICPIF value, the better the voice quality. Beware of setting the value to 34, because this indicates 100% packet loss.

e. Enable SAA on the far-end router:

```
(global) saa responder
```

At a minimum, you must enable the SAA responder on a far-end router so that the local router will receive SAA response packets to the jitter probes.

5. (Optional) Use local voice busyout.

a. (Optional) Busyout all voice ports on a serial interface:

```
(interface) voice-port busyout
```

If desired, you can force all voice ports that use the interface into a busyout condition—except those configured for specific busyout arrangements.

b. (Optional) Busyout a voice port based on the state of an interface:

```
(voice-port) busyout monitor {serial interface-number | ethernet

  interface-number} [in-service]
```

A voice port can be configured to monitor the up/down state of a physical interface on the router. When the interface, either **serial** or **ethernet**, is up, the voice port is usable. When the interface is down, the voice port moves to busyout so that the calls will be rerouted over another path. Also, you can configure the voice port to busyout when the interface is up by using the **in-service** keyword.

c. (Optional) Busyout with a seize condition:

```
(voice-port) busyout seize {ignore | repeat}
```

During busyout, a voice port can be configured to seize the line and either **ignore** (stay in the busyout state regardless of the reaction of the far end) or **repeat** (go into busyout; if the far end changes state, cycle back into busyout again).

d. (Optional) Force a voice port busyout:

```
(voice-port) [no] busyout forced
```

To unconditionally busyout a voice port, use **busyout forced**. The voice port will stay in the busyout state until the **no busyout forced** command is used.

e. (Optional) Busyout a voice port according to network conditions:

```
(voice-port) busyout monitor probe ip-address [codec codec-type] [icpif

  icpif | loss percent delay milliseconds]
```

SAA jitter probes are issued toward a target router at *ip-address*. The probes can mimic certain types of Codecs by using the appropriate packet size. Specify the *codec-type* as **g711a** (G.711 A-law), **g711u** (G.711 U-law, the default), **g729** (G.729), or **g729a** (G.729 Annex A). The ICPIF loss/delay threshold can be specified to trigger a busyout condition based on network congestion. The probes are used to collect active information about end-to-end packet delay and loss. The *icpif* value (0 to 30) should be chosen to reflect a threshold of poor voice quality. Lower values mean less delay and packet loss.

Otherwise, specific packet **loss** and **delay** thresholds can be specified to trigger busyout. If the packet loss measurement rises above *percent* (1 to 100) or if the end-to-end delay rises above *milliseconds* (1 to 2147483647), the voice port enters the busyout state.

11-3: Dialing

- Dial plans are used to describe the digits that must be dialed to reach a certain destination.

- Dial peers are configured to implement the dial plan. A local dial peer is used to route and terminate a call to a remote dial peer.

- The path that the call takes through the network is determined by the underlying network configuration, involving IP routing protocols and physical connectivity, including Frame Relay and ATM.

- An end-to-end call is broken into *call legs*—logical connections between any two telephony devices. Each call leg must have a dial peer associated with it.

- *POTS dial peer* is a logical definition on a router that connects to a traditional telephony network on a voice port (PSTN, PBX, telephone, or fax).

- *Voice-network dial peer* is a logical definition on a router that points to a remote dial peer. These dial peers include Voice over IP (VoIP) using an IP address, Voice over Frame Relay (VoFR) using a DLCI, Voice over ATM (VoATM) using an ATM VC, and Multimedia Mail over IP (MMoIP) using the e-mail address of an SMTP server.

- Dial peers are associated with a dial pattern. Incoming calls must match the dial pattern of a dial peer. For outgoing calls, a router collects digits from the caller and sends them to the associated voice port or remote dial peer.

- Digit manipulation can be used on a string of dialed digits to strip off digits, add prefix digits, translate digits, and expand digits into other digit strings.

- Dial numbers can be communicated through telephony signaling mechanisms:

  - *Automatic Number Identification (ANI)* identifies the calling party's telephone number.

  - *Dial Number Information Service (DNIS)* identifies the called party's telephone number.

Configuration

1. Map out your telephony network.

    a. Use a diagram to show all voice-capable routers, telephony devices, and connections to the PSTN.

    b. Divide the diagram into call legs: Identify every router voice port and logical connections to voice-network dial peers (VoIP, VoFR, and VoATM).

    c. For each voice-capable router, make a table identifying the dial peers, dial patterns, and call leg destinations. Table 11-4 shows a sample table for this purpose.

Table 11-4   *Identifying the Dial Peers, Dial Patterns, and Call Leg Destination*

Dial Peer Number	Local Type	Destination Pattern	Local Extension	Prefix to Add	Call Destination	
					Voice Port	Session Target

The Dial Peer Number uniquely identifies each dial peer that is defined on a router. The Local Type is either POTS (using a voice port) or VoIP (using a remote session target). Destination Pattern represents a shorthand notation of the digits required to reach the destination. This can be an entire ten-digit phone number to reach a single specific device, or it can include wildcard characters so that an entire remote site of multiple users can be reached.

Table 11-5 shows the destination pattern wildcard characters that can be used.

Table 11-5   *Destination Pattern Wildcards*

Wildcard	Description
.	Matches a single digit.
[ ]	Matches a range of digits, as in [1–9], or several ranges, as in [1–5,8–9].
( )	Groups digits into a pattern that can be matched with ?, %, or +.
?	Matches the preceding digit zero or one time.
%	Matches the preceding digit zero or more times.
+	Matches the preceding digit one or more times.
T	Indicates a variable-length string of digits. The string is terminated when the interdigit timeout expires or the caller enters the # (pound) digit.

The Local Extension column in Table 11-4 indicates a reduced set of digits that can be used to reach the destination. Normally, when a router matches a destination pattern string, the matching digits are discarded and the destination is sent only the remaining digits. The Prefix to Add column lists any digits that might need to be prefixed to the remaining digits to complete the call. Call Destination lists the endpoint where the router attempts to terminate the call. This can be either a voice port (a local voice port interface) or a session target (the IP address of a remote VoIP peer, the DLCI of a remote VoFR peer, or the VC of a remote VoATM peer).

2. (Optional) Use number expansion:

```
(global) num-exp extension-number expanded-number
```

The dial string *extension-number* is converted into the string *expanded-number* before being used with a dial peer. These strings consist of the digits 0 to 9 and can use a period (.) as a wildcard digit. The digits matched with periods in the *extension-number* are carried over into the corresponding period in the *expanded-number*. In this fashion, dial strings can be stripped of digits, keeping a shortened extension number, or can be expanded into a longer number.

3. Configure dial peers.

   a. Identify the dial peer:

   ```
   (global) dial-peer voice number {pots | voip | vofr | voatm}
   ```

   The dial peer is given a unique *number* (1 to 2,147,483,647). Specify the peer type as **pots** (Plain Old Telephone System; analog or digital voice port), **voip** (Voice over IP), **vofr** (Voice over Frame Relay), or **voatm** (Voice over ATM).

   b. Specify the destination pattern to reach the dial peer:

   ```
   (dial-peer) destination-pattern [+] string [T]
   ```

   The *string* is the pattern of digits or wildcard characters required to reach the destination. Digits can be 0 through 9, the letters A through D, the star (*) or pound (#) keys, or a comma (,) to indicate a pause between digits. The + can be used to indicate that a standard E.164 address follows. The optional **T** can be used to indicate that the string is of variable length. The string is terminated when the interdigit timeout expires or when the caller presses the # key.

   c. Specify the call destination.

   POTS destination:

   ```
   (dial-peer) port location
   ```

   The *location* field indicates the physical location of the voice port on the router. This can be *slot/subunit/port* for an analog voice port, *slot/port:ds0-group-no* for a channelized T1/E1, or *slot:D* for the D-channel of a PRI (also *slot:23* for a T1 PRI and *slot:15* for an E1 PRI).

- VoIP destination:

```
(dial-peer) session target {ipv4:destination-address | dns:[$s$. | $d$.
    | $e$. | $u$.] host-name | ras | settlement}
```

The VoIP session terminates at IP address *destination-address*. The target can also be specified using a DNS host name entry, *host-name*. The host name can also contain wildcard translations, to be replaced by these strings: **s.** (the source number), **d.** (the destination number), **e.** (the digits of the called number are reversed and separated by dots), and **u.** (the unmatched portion of the destination pattern). There should be no spaces between **dns:**, the wildcard pattern, and the *host-name* strings.

- VoFR destination:

```
(dial-peer) session target interface dlci [cid]
```

The session terminates on the Frame Relay *interface*, using DLCI number *dlci*. The optional *cid* field (4 to 255) identifies the DLCI subchannel to use for calls over an FRF.11 trunk. You should use values between 6 and 63 for voice traffic.

- VoATM destination:

```
(dial-peer) session target interface pvc {name | vpi/vci | vci}
```

The session terminates over the ATM PVC on *interface*. The PVC is specified by *name*, by the VPI/VCI pair *vpi/vci*, or by the *vci* alone.

d. (Optional) Select a Codec type for the dial peer.

Use a specific Codec type:

```
(dial-peer) codec type [bytes payload_size]
```

The Codec type can be set to a value from the Codec Type column of Table 11-6. You can specify the number of payload bytes in each voice frame with the **bytes** keyword and *payload_size* to override the defaults shown in the table. The table also lists the range of payload sizes for each Codec type, as a range, followed by the multiple that the size must be, and the default size.

Generally, the G.711 Codecs offer the best voice quality at the cost of higher bandwidth. The G.729 Codecs offer a good voice quality at a low bandwidth, usually deployed over serial WAN links.

- (Optional) Create a list of Codecs in order of preference.

Create a voice class for the list:

```
(global) voice class codec tag
```

The voice class is given an arbitrary number *tag* (1 to 10000).

Assign a preference to one or more Codecs that might be used:

```
(voice-class) codec preference priority codec-type [bytes size]
```

Table 11-6   *Codec Types and Characteristics*

Codec Type	Codec Standard	Data Rate (bps)	Complexity High	Complexity Medium	VoIP Payload Bytes [multiple] (default)	VoFR/VoATM Payload Bytes [multiple] (default)
g711alaw	G.711 a-Law	64000	X	X	80,160 [40](160)	40 to 240 [40](240)
g711ulaw	G.711 u-Law	64000	X	X	80,160 [40](160)	40 to 240 [40](240)
g723ar53	G.723.1 Annex A	5300	X		20 to 220 [20](20)	20 to 240 [20](20)
g723ar63	G.723.1 Annex A	6300	X		24 to 216 [24](24)	24 to 240 [24](24)
g723r53	G.723.1	5300	X		20 to 220 [20](20)	20 to 240 [20](20)
g723r63	G.723.1	6300	X		24 to 216 [24](24)	24 to 240 [24](24)
g726r16	G.726	16000	X	X	20 to 220 [20](40)	10 to 240 [10](60)
g726r24	G.726	24000	X	X	30 to 210 [30](60)	15 to 240 [15](90)
g726r32	G.726	32000	X	X	40 to 200 [40](80)	20 to 240 [20](120)
g728	G.728	16000	X		10 to 230 [10](40)	10 to 240 [10](60)
g729r8	G.729	8000	X	X	10 to 230 [10](20)	10 to 240 [10](30)
g729abr8	G.729	8000			10 to 230 [10](20)	10 to 240 [10](30)
g729ar8	G.729	8000			10 to 230 [10](20)	10 to 240 [10](30)

Table 11-6 *Codec Types and Characteristics*

Codec Type	Codec Standard	Data Rate (bps)	Complexity High	Complexity Medium	VoIP Payload Bytes [multiple] (default)	VoFR/VoATM Payload Bytes [multiple] (default)
g729br8	G.729	8000	X	X	10 to 230 [10](20)	10 to 240 [10](30)
clear-channel	Clear Channel	64000				
Gsmefr	Global System for Mobile Communications Enhanced Rate	12200				
Gsmfr	Global System for Mobile Communications Full Rate	13200				

The *codec-type* is a name from the first column of Table 11-6, assigned with a *priority* (1 to 14; lower is preferable). The payload size can be specified as *size* in case the same Codec type is defined with more than one possible payload size.

Apply the Codec preference list to a dial peer:

```
(dial-peer) voice-class codec tag
```

e. Configure parameters for all dial peer types.

(Optional) Use Voice Activity Detection (VAD) for reduced bandwidth during silence:

```
(dial-peer) [no] vad
```

With VAD (enabled by default), no voice data is transmitted during a silent audio period. An optional comfort noise can be generated instead so that the caller won't think the call has been disconnected during the silent period. VAD can be disabled with the **no** keyword so that voice data is sent continuously.

- (Optional) Limit the number of connections to the dial peer:

  (dial-peer) **max-conn** *number*

The maximum number of allowed connections to the dial peer is *number* (1 to 2147483647; the default is unlimited).

- (Optional) Match the calling number for inbound calls:

  (dial-peer) **answer-address** [+] *string* [T]

Inbound calls can be matched against the calling number (ANI) if desired. The router matches against any configured answer addresses before destination patterns are matched.

- (POTS only) Use DID to find a destination for inbound calls:

  (dial-peer) **direct-inward-dial**

The called number (DNIS) can be used on inbound calls to identify the call destination. In this case, the router accepts a DID number and matches against destination patterns to complete the call.

- (Optional) Identify the called number in a mixed modem/voice router:

  (dial-peer) **incoming called-number** *string*

When the router is handling both modem and voice calls over an interface, the voice port must be identified with the called number.

- (Optional) Match against an ITU Q.931 numbering type:

  (dial-peer) **numbering-type** *type*

The numbering type can be matched against, in addition to other dial number matching mechanisms. The Q.931 numbering *type* can be **abbreviated** (the abbreviated number as supported locally), **international** (the number to reach a subscriber in another country), **national** (the number to reach a subscriber in the same country, outside the local network), **network** (the administrative or service number), **subscriber** (the number to reach a subscriber in the local network), **unknown** (unknown to the local network), or **reserved** (reserved for extension).

- (Optional) Use digit manipulation to change a dial string.

(Optional) Add a prefix to an outbound dial peer:

  (dial-peer) **prefix** *string*

A *string* of digits can be prefixed to the telephone number associated with an outbound call to a dial peer. The string can contain digits 0 to 9 and a comma (,) to indicate a pause.

(Optional) Don't strip digits after matching:

  (dial-peer) **no digit-strip**

By default, the router strips off the leftmost digits that match a destination pattern. The remaining digits are forwarded to other telephony devices. If you need to keep and forward the matching digits, use the **no digit-strip** command.

(POTS only) Forward a specific number of digits:

```
(dial-peer) forward-digits {number | all | extra}
```

Rather than forwarding the remaining digits after matching, the router can forward a specific *number* of digits (0 to 32), **all** digits up to the length of the destination pattern string, or just the **extra** digits to the right of the matched string (if the dialed string is longer than the destination pattern).

(Optional) Use digit translation.

Step 1. Create a translation ruleset:

```
(global) translation-rule tag
```

A digit translation rule is created with an arbitrary *tag* (1 to 2147483647).

Step 2. Define a translation rule:

```
(translate) rule tag input-matched-pattern substituted-pattern
    [match-type substituted-type]
```

A rule is assigned an arbitrary *tag* (1 to 2147483647) to uniquely identify it within the ruleset. The *input-matched-pattern* is a string of digits to match against, including regular expression wildcard characters. The *substituted-pattern* is the string of digits that matches the pattern. The optional *match-type* and *substituted-type* fields specify ITU Q.931 numbering types to match and substitute, as defined earlier in the sixth bullet of Step 3e.

Step 3. (Optional) Apply the ruleset to inbound calls on a voice port:

```
(voiceport) translate {called | calling} ruleset
```

The translation ruleset numbered *ruleset* is used on the voice port to translate either the **called** or **calling** number.

Step 4. (Optional) Apply the ruleset to outbound calls on a dial peer:

```
(dial-peer) translate-outgoing {called | calling} ruleset
```

The translation ruleset numbered *ruleset* is used on the dial peer to translate either the **called** or **calling** number.

■ (Optional) Use a hunt group to rotate between multiple dial peers.

First, assign a preference value to each dial peer in the hunt group:

```
(dial-peer) preference value
```

Dial peers with identical matching destination patterns are used in a rotary fashion, according to the preference *value* (0 to 10; lower is preferable; the default is 0) given to each.

(Optional) Next, change the order in which a hunt group is searched:

```
(global) dial-peer hunt hunt-order
```

By default, hunt groups are searched according to the longest match in the destination pattern, an explicit preference value, or a random selection. If desired, the order can be changed according to the *hunt-order:* **0** (longest match, preference, random; this is the default), **1** (longest match, preference, least-used), **2** (preference, longest match, random), **3** (preference, longest match, least-used), **4** (least-used, longest match, preference), **5** (least-used, preference, longest match), **6** (random), or **7** (least-used).

(Optional) Stop hunting if a disconnect condition is reached:

```
(global) voice hunt {user-busy | invalid-number | unassigned-num-
ber}
```

Hunting through a group of outbound destination dial peers can be stopped if certain conditions occur: **user-busy** (all ports to the called party are in use), **invalid-number** (the dialed number is invalid), or **unassigned-number** (the dialed number is not assigned at the destination router).

Stop hunting if a call fails on a dial peer (optional):

```
(dial-peer) huntstop
```

If a call fails on a dial peer that is part of a hunt group, hunting will not continue.

- (Optional) Configure a transmission speed for sending faxes to the dial peer:

```
(dial-peer) fax rate {2400 | 4800 | 7200 | 9600 | 12000 | 14400 |
disable |

    voice} [bytes size]
```

Fax transmission occurs at the rate specified (in bps). The **disable** keyword disables the fax capability. Use the **voice** keyword to automatically set the fax rate to the highest value that is lower than the voice Codec in use. The fax payload size may be given as *size* (in bytes).

- (Optional) Relay DTMF tones from the caller:

```
(dial-peer) dtmf-relay [cisco-rtp] [h245-alphanumeric]

    [h245-signal]
```

-or-

```
(dial-peer) dtmf-relay
```

When keys are pressed after a call is established, DTMF tones are relayed into the VoIP network using an out-of-band method: **cisco-rtp** (RTP with a Cisco proprietary payload), **h245-alphanumeric** (H.245 "alphanumeric" messages), or **h245-signal** (H.245 "signal" messages). If more than one message type is listed, one of the methods also supported by the far end is used.

For VoFR, use the **dtmf-relay** keyword without any options. The DTMF tones are sent as FRF.11 Annex A frames.

f. Configure additional VoIP parameters.

(Optional) Change the jitter buffer playout delay.

First, choose the type of playout delay:

```
(dial-peer) playout-delay mode {adaptive | fixed}
```

The playout delay can be set according to **adaptive** (dynamically adjusted during a call; this is the default) or **fixed** (use a constant playout delay). Normally, the default adaptive method is acceptable.

Next, specify the playout delay time:

```
(dial-peer) playout-delay {nominal milliseconds | maximum milliseconds |
  minimum {default | low | high}}
```

The jitter buffer is configured to use a **nominal** playout delay (0 to 1500 milliseconds; the default is 200) at the beginning of the call. In adaptive mode, the playout delay can vary from a **maximum** (40 to 1700 milliseconds; the default is 200) to a **minimum** of **low** (10 milliseconds), **default** (40 milliseconds), or **high** (80 milliseconds).

Generally, the default playout delay settings are optimal. However, if you experience voice breakup, you can increase the playout delay. For bursty jitter conditions, increase the **minimum** playout delay for adaptive mode or the **nominal** delay for fixed mode. To get an idea of whether you are experiencing jitter problems, use the **show call active voice** command and look for nonzero values with LostPackets, EarlyPackets, or LatePackets.

■ (Optional) Use a technology prefix for a dial peer:

```
(dial-peer) tech-prefix number
```

A technology prefix *number* (a string of 1 to 11 characters, containing 0 to 9, star [*], and pound [#]) can be assigned to a dial peer, which the H.323 gateway forwards to an H.323 gatekeeper. The gatekeeper can then make call decisions based on the technology that the local router is supporting.

g. Configure additional VoFR or VoATM parameters.

(Optional) Choose a session protocol for a call:

```
(dial-peer) session protocol {cisco-switched | frf11-trunk}
```

VoFR can use **cisco-switched** (proprietary session protocol, the default) or **frf11-trunk** (FRF.11 session protocol) to transport voice data. Use the default unless you are connecting to a non-Cisco device. If **frf11-trunk** is used, you must also configure a termination string with the **called-number** *termination-string* command. The *termination-string* is the destination's E.164 number.

VoATM can use the **cisco-switched** keyword only by default. To disable it for non-Cisco trunks, precede the command with the **no** keyword.

- (Optional) Generate voice packet sequence numbers:

```
(dial-peer) sequence-numbers
```

By default, voice packets are generated for VoFR without sequence numbers. Sequence numbers can be generated to allow the far end to detect out-of-sequence, duplicate, or lost packets.

- (Optional) Select a signaling type to expect:

```
(dial-peer) signal-type {cas | cept | ext-signal | transparent}
```

A VoFR or VoATM dial peer can expect a specific signaling type from the far end: **cas** (Channel-Associated Signaling), **cept** (E1 with cept/MELCAS signaling), **ext-signal** (external signaling, out-of-band or CCS), or **transparent** (T1/E1 signaling is passed through without modification or interpretation).

11-4: H.323 Gateways

- An H.323 gateway is a device that provides communication between H.323 devices and other non-H.323 devices.

- An H.323 gatekeeper is a device that provides address translation (E.164 to IP address) and controls access to H.323 resources on the network. Gatekeepers provide Registration, Admission, and Status (RAS), registering and approving H.323 calls according to policies or available resources.

- A gateway can use AAA to authenticate callers (see Section 12-6) and generate call activity accounting records.

- A gateway can use H.235 security to provide MD5 encryption to the gatekeeper for caller authentication, RAS message exchange, call settlement (track and return accounting data for billing purposes), and call metering (prepaid call admission and control).

Configuration

1. Configure the H.323 gateway.

    a. Enable the gateway process:

        ```
        (global) gateway
        ```

    b. Enable the gateway on an interface:

        ```
        (interface) h323-gateway voip interface
        ```

        The H.323 gateway is configured once on a router, using a specific interface. Usually, a LAN interface (Ethernet, for example) or a loopback interface is used.

    c. (Optional) Bind a specific interface IP address to the gateway:

        ```
        (interface) h323-gateway voip bind srcaddr ip-address
        ```

        By default, the gateway uses a source address obtained from the interface on which it is configured. If the interface has several secondary IP addresses, one of the addresses can be bound to the gateway. In other scenarios, the gateway might be configured on a loopback interface. The IP address of a physical LAN interface can be bound to the gateway instead so that all H.323 messages use it as a source address.

    d. (Optional) Name the gateway on an interface:

        ```
        (interface) h323-gateway voip h323-id interface-id
        ```

        The gateway can be configured with a name that is used when communicating with the gatekeeper. The name, *interface-id*, can be set per interface. It is usually of the form *name@domain-name*, where *name* is the name of the gateway and *domain-name* is the domain used by the gatekeeper.

    e. (Optional) Use a technology prefix:

        ```
        (interface) h323-gateway voip tech-prefix prefix
        ```

        The technology *prefix* (up to 11 characters, containing 0 to 9, pound [#], and star [*]) can be arbitrarily chosen to flag the gatekeeper that a call needs a certain technology. Technologies are defined on the gatekeeper.

    f. (Optional) Identify the gatekeeper:

        ```
        (interface) h323-gateway voip id gatekeeper-id {ipaddr ip-address

         [port-number] | multicast} [priority number]
        ```

        The gateway uses the gatekeeper identified by name and address for H.323 functions. The gatekeeper's name is given as *gatekeeper-id*, the H.323 name that the gatekeeper is known by (usually *name.domain-name*). To find the gatekeeper, the gateway can use its *ip-address* and an optional *port-number*. Otherwise, the gateway can use a **multicast** to 224.0.1.41 to find a gatekeeper. Multiple gatekeepers (currently up to two) can be identified, each given a priority of *number* (1 to 127; the default is 127).

2. (Optional) Use RAS with a gatekeeper:

```
(interface) session-target ras
```

The gatekeeper associated with the interface will be used for all E.164-to-IP address translation and RAS functions.

3. (Optional) Use AAA accounting to record call activity.

   a. Configure AAA accounting with a RADIUS server, according to Section 11-2.

   b. Enable gateway H.323 accounting:

```
(global) gw-accounting {h323 [vsa] | syslog | voip}
```

The gateway can generate call accounting information through **h323** (standard H.323 accounting using IETF RADIUS attributes; **vsa** uses vendor-specific attributes), **syslog** (system logging facility), or **voip** (generic accounting).

   c. Specify an AAA method list for H.323 accounting:

```
(global) aaa accounting connection h323 start-stop radius
```

The gateway sends AAA accounting records for H.323 calls to the RADIUS server. Start and stop messages are sent to flag the beginning and end of a call connection.

4. (Optional) Use H.235 gateway security.

   a. Configure Network Time Protocol (NTP) on all H.323 gateways and gatekeepers for consistent time-stamping. (See Section 1-4 for further information.)

   b. Enable H.235 security on the gateway:

```
(gateway) security password password level {endpoint | per-call | all}
```

The *password* field specifies a key that is used for MD5 encryption on the gateway. The **level** keyword is used to define the level of security desired: **endpoint** (all RAS messages from the gateway will be validated), **per-call** (validation on admission messages from H.323 devices to the gateway; the caller is prompted for an account number and PIN), or **all** (a combination of **endpoint** and **per-call**).

   c. (Optional) Enable the preservation of H.323 VoIP calls:

```
(global) voice service voip
(voice-h323) call preserve
```

Call preservation for VoIP calls over WAN links is useful when signaling is handled by a remote device (for example, remote gatekeeper or call agent). This feature enables calls to remain active even if a socket failure occurs between the IP phone and a remote H.225.0 or H.245 connnection. To enable this feature, first enter VoIP service configuration mode with the **voice service voip** command. Then, enable the service with the **call preserve** command.

d. Configure Interactive Voice Response (IVR).

See Section 12-6 for further information. In particular, you need to use one of these TCL IVR scripts for account number and PIN prompting:

```
voip_auth_acct_pin_dest.tcl
```

- voip_auth_acct_pin_dest_2.tcl

> **Note**   See Appendix J, "Tool Command Language (TCL) Reference," for more on TCL scripting within Cisco IOS Software.

11-5: H.323 Gatekeepers

- An H.323 gatekeeper provides address translation between E.164 addresses and the IP addresses of endpoints and gateways.

- A gatekeeper can also control H.323 access to terminals, gateways, and multimedia control units (MCUs).

- H.323 endpoints communicate with a gatekeeper using the Registration, Admission, and Status (RAS) protocol.

- In larger H.323 networks, endpoints can be grouped into zones. Each zone is managed by a gatekeeper or a cluster of gatekeepers.

- Cisco IOS software bundles both H.323 gatekeeper and proxy functions under the feature called Multimedia Conference Manager (MCM).

- A router can use HSRP to provide a redundant IP address that is shared with other routers. A gatekeeper provides HSRP mode, moving between standby and active mode along with HSRP.

- Gatekeepers can be configured as a cluster to provide redundancy and call load balancing.

Configuration

1. Enable the gatekeeper:

   ```
   (global) gatekeeper
   ```

2. Identify one or more local zones controlled by the gatekeeper:

   ```
   (gatekeeper) zone local gatekeeper-name domain-name [ras-ip-address]
   ```

   The host name of the gatekeeper is given as *gatekeeper-name* and the *domain-name* of the domain it serves. The *ras-ip-address* can be used to specify the IP address of a router interface to use when answering gatekeeper discovery queries. This address is used for all local zones defined on the router.

3. (Optional) Create a cluster of gatekeepers in the local zone for redundancy.

a. Name the cluster:

```
(gatekeeper) zone cluster local cluster-name local-zone-name
```

The cluster named *cluster-name* is associated with the *local-zone-name* (the host name of the local gatekeeper).

b. Add an alternative gatekeeper to the cluster:

```
(gatekeeper-cluster) element alternate-gk ip-address [port port]
```

The host name of an alternative gatekeeper in the local zone is given as *alternate-gk*, along with its IP address and *port*.

c. (Optional) Use load balancing of H.323 endpoints:

```
(gatekeeper) load-balance [endpoints max-endpoints] [calls max-calls]

  [cpu max-cpu] [memory max-mem-used]
```

Load balancing occurs by defining various limits on the local gatekeeper: **endpoints** (the maximum number of endpoints served), **calls** (the maximum number of simultaneous calls), **cpu** (the maximum CPU usage, in percentage), or **memory** (the maximum percentage of available memory used). As soon as the threshold is reached, the gatekeeper moves registered H.323 endpoints to an alternative gatekeeper or rejects new registrations and calls.

4. (Optional) Limit the IP subnets associated with a gatekeeper:

```
(gatekeeper) zone subnet local-gatekeeper-name {default | subnet-address
  {/bits-in-mask | mask-address}} enable
```

By default, a gatekeeper answers requests from all subnets in its local zone. Specific subnets can be served, while others are excluded. The local gatekeeper is identified by its name, *local-gatekeeper-name*. A subnet is specified by its *subnet-address* (network address), followed by the subnet mask in */bits-in-mask* or *mask-address* (dotted string format). The **enable** keyword is used to allow the gatekeeper to respond to requests from the subnet.

If the **default** keyword is given, all subnets other than those specifically defined are used. Also, to exclude subnets from gatekeeper service, use the **no** keyword with this command. For example, **no zone subnet … default enable** excludes all subnets except those enabled in other **zone subnet** commands.

5. Communicate with other gatekeepers.

a. Use DNS to look up gatekeepers.

Set the local router's domain name:

```
(global) ip domain-name domain-name
```

- Identify one or more name servers:

    ```
    (global) ip name-server server-address [server-address2 ...
      server-address6]
    ```

Up to six DNS server addresses can be given. Each is tried in sequential order when requesting a DNS lookup.

b. Statically define gatekeepers:

```
(gatekeeper) zone remote other-gatekeeper-name other-domain-name
    other-gatekeeper-ip-address [port-number] [cost cost [priority
    priority]]
```

A remote gatekeeper can be defined with its name *(other-gatekeeper-name)*, its domain name *(other-domain-name)*, IP address *(other-gatekeeper-ip-address)*, and an optional *port-number* for RAS communication *(1 to 65535; the default is 1719)*. Least-cost call routing is used by assigning a *cost* (1 to 100; the default is 50) and a *priority* (1 to 100; the default is 50) to a remote gatekeeper.

c. (Optional) Create a cluster of gatekeepers in the remote zone for redundancy.

Name the cluster:

```
(gatekeeper) zone cluster remote remote-cluster-name domain-name

    [cost cost] [priority priority]
```

■ The remote cluster named *remote-cluster-name* is associated with the *domain-name* (remote zone name). An optional *cost* (1 to 100; the default is 50) and *priority* (1 to 100; the default is 50) can be assigned to the cluster for least-cost call routing.

■ Add an alternative gatekeeper to the cluster:

```
(gatekeeper-cluster) element alternate-gk ip-address [port port]
```

The host name of an alternative gatekeeper in the remote zone is given as *alternate-gk*, along with its IP address and *port*.

6. (Optional) Associate a technology prefix with gatekeepers:

```
(gatekeeper) gw-type-prefix type-prefix [[hopoff gkid1]
    [hopoff gkid2 ... hopoff gkidn] [seq | blast]] [default-technology]
    [[gw ipaddr ipaddr [port]]]
```

Technology prefixes are recognized before zone prefixes to find a call hop-off point with an associated gatekeeper. A technology prefix is given as *type-prefix* (an arbitrary sequence of digits, usually ending with a pound sign [#]; tech prefixes are configured in gatekeepers). Normally, gateways register technology prefixes with a gatekeeper automatically. However, one or more redundant hop-off points can be specified for the prefix with gatekeeper names *gkid1*, *gkid2*, and so forth. The gatekeepers must be identified on the router with the **zone local** or **zone remote** commands. The **default-technology** keyword can be used to route unmatched technology prefixes to the listed gatekeepers.

When resolving a prefix to a gatekeeper with multiple hop-offs (the same prefix is assigned to multiple gatekeepers), location requests (LRQs) can be sent simultaneously (**blast**) to the gatekeepers in the order they are listed. Local gatekeepers are placed at the top of the list, followed by any remote gatekeepers. Otherwise, the LRQs are sent sequentially, with a delay after each (**seq**, the default).

If a gateway is incapable of registering technology prefixes with the gatekeeper, you can add a static pointer to it with the **gw ipaddr** keywords, along with the gateway's IP address and RAS port (default 1719).

7.   (Optional) Associate an E.164 prefix with a gateway:

```
(gatekeeper) zone prefix gatekeeper-name e164-prefix [blast | seq]
  [gw-priority priority gw-alias [gw-alias, ...]]
```

A gatekeeper translates an E.164 number, *e164-prefix* (a number of digits followed by dots, each matching any digit, or a star [*], matching all digits), to the gatekeeper name *gatekeeper-name* serving that prefix. You can set priorities for specific gateways in a prefix with the **gw-priority** keyword, along with the *priority* (0 to 10; 0 excludes the gateway from a prefix) and a list of gateway names. Gateways must register with the gatekeeper before receiving a priority. If no specific priority is given for a gateway, it receives a default of 5.

When resolving a prefix to a gatekeeper with multiple hop-offs (the same prefix is assigned to multiple gatekeepers), location requests (LRQs) can be sent simultaneously (**blast**) to the gatekeepers in the order they are listed. Local gatekeepers are placed at the top of the list, followed by any remote gatekeepers. Otherwise, the LRQs are sent sequentially with a delay after each (**seq**, the default).

8.   (Optional) Statically configure nodes that are unable to register:

```
(gatekeeper) alias static ip-signaling-addr [port] gkid gatekeeper-name
  [ras ip-ras-addr port] [terminal | mcu | gateway {h320 | h323-proxy |
  voip}] [e164 e164-address] [h323id h323-id]
```

If an endpoint or node cannot register with a gatekeeper for some reason, it can be statically defined with an alias in the gatekeeper. The node's IP address and port are given as *ip-signaling-addr* [*port*]. The gatekeeper name for the node's zone is given as **gkid** *gatekeeper-name*. You can specify the RAS address and port used by the node with **ras** *ip-ras-addr port*. The type of H.323 endpoint is given by **terminal** (H.323 terminal), **mcu** (multiple control unit), or **gateway**. Gateway types are given by **h320** (H.320), **h323-proxy** (H.323 proxy), or **voip** (VoIP). One or more E.164 numbers for the node can be given as **e164** *e164-address* (up to 128 characters total). One or more H.323 identification strings can be assigned to the node with **h323id** *h323-id* (up to 256 characters total).

9.   (Optional) Use AAA authentication and accounting with H.323.

    a. Configure AAA login authentication to a RADIUS or TACACS+ server by referring to Section 12-2.

b. Enable AAA on the gatekeeper:

```
(gatekeeper) security {any | h323-id | e164} {password default password |

    password separator character}
```

Endpoints or nodes can be configured in a RADIUS or TACACS+ server, which is queried when a node registers with the gatekeeper. The type of user alias that is authenticated is given by **h323-id** (H.323 ID), **e164** (E.164 number), or **any** (uses the first alias given by the node). An alias must be accompanied by a password. A default password can be given as **password default** *password* and must also be configured in the AAA server. For H.323 ID aliases, the alias and password can be passed as a single string, separated by **password separator** *character*.

c. Configure AAA accounting to a RADIUS or TACACS+ server by referring to Section 12-2. Use the **aaa accounting connection h323** keywords for H.323 accounting.

d. Enable H.323 accounting on the gatekeeper:

```
(gatekeeper) aaa accounting
```

The gatekeeper sends registration accounting records to the configured RADIUS or TACACS+ servers.

10. (Optional) Use external applications with the gatekeeper.

a. (Optional) Define a port that the gatekeeper uses for listening:

```
(gatekeeper) server registration-port port
```

By default, the gatekeeper doesn't listen to any external sources for H.323 registration. A registration *port* (1 to 65535) can be defined to match the port used by the external application.

b. (Optional) Trigger interaction with external applications.

Define a static trigger:

```
(gatekeeper) server trigger {arq | lcf | lrj | lrq | rrq | urq}

    gkid priority server-id server-ipaddress server-port
```

A trigger is configured for one of the RAS message types shown. The local gatekeeper identifier is given as *gkid*. Each trigger is assigned a *priority* (1 to 20; 1 is highest) so that multiple triggers can be used in order. The external application server is known as *server-id* (a string or name) at IP address *server-ipaddress* and using RAS port *server-port*.

- (Optional) Generate information notifications only:

    ```
    (gatekeeper-trigger) info-only
    ```

Messages are sent as notifications without waiting for a response from the application.

- (Optional) Temporarily disable a trigger:

  `(gatekeeper-trigger) `**`shutdown`**

- (ARQ, LRQ, LCF, LRJ only) Base the trigger on a destination:

  `(gatekeeper-trigger) `**`destination-info {e164 | email-id | h323-id}`**` value`

The trigger destination can be based on *value*, of the type **e164** (an E.164 number), **email-id** (an e-mail address), or **h323-id** (an H.323-ID). More than one destination can be given by ending the *value* string with a comma and another value, or with an asterisk (*).

- (ARQ and LRQ only) Base the trigger on a specific redirect reason:

  `(gatekeeper-trigger) `**`redirect-reason`**` value`

The redirect reason is a numeric *value* (0 to 65535), with these values currently used: **0** (unknown reason), **1** (call forwarding or called DTE is busy), **2** (call forwarded; no reply), **4** (call deflection), **9** (called DTE is out of order), **10** (call forwarding by the call DTE), and **15** (call forwarding unconditionally).

- (LCF only) Base the trigger on a specific type of endpoint:

  `(gatekeeper-trigger) `**`endpoint-type`**` type`

The endpoint *type* is given as one of the following types: **gatekeeper, h320-gateway, mcu, other-gateway** (a gateway type not in this list of choices), **proxy, terminal**, or **voice-gateway**.

- (RRQ and URQ only) Base the trigger on a specific supported prefix:

  `(gatekeeper-trigger) `**`supported-prefix`**` prefix`

The prefix is given as a string of digits (0 to 9, #, *) containing the E.164 technology prefix pattern to match against.

11. (Optional) Perform H.323 proxy functions.

    a. (Optional) Act as a proxy between local and remote zones:

    `(gatekeeper) use-proxy local-zone-name {default | remote-zone`

    `  remote-zone-name}{inbound-to | outbound-from}{gateway | terminal}`

    By default, the proxy function is performed in the local zone for calls to and from local H.323 terminals only. To change this behavior, the name of the local zone or gatekeeper is given as *local-zone-name* (usually *name.domain-name*). Proxy services occur for specific remote zones identified with **remote-zone** *remote-zone-name*. Remote zones not listed can be served using the **default** keyword.

    Proxy service can be applied to calls that are **inbound-to** or **outbound-from** the local zone and to either **gateway** or **terminal** devices.

    b. (Optional) Use an H.323 proxy.

Enable the proxy:

(global) **proxy h323**

- Associate a gatekeeper with the proxy:

  (interface) h323 gatekeeper [id gatekeeper-id] {ipaddr ipaddr [port] |
      multicast}

The gatekeeper named *gatekeeper-id* (usually of the form *name.domain-name*)
using IP address *ipaddr* and *port* is used by the proxy. If the **multicast** keyword
is given, the gatekeeper is discovered through a multicast message. The IP address
of the local interface is used as the RAS source address.

- (Optional) Enable the proxy to use QoS signaling:

  (interface) h323 qos {ip-precedence value | rsvp {controlled-load |
      guaranteed-qos}}

The proxy signals QoS requirements by either setting the IP Precedence to *value*
(0 to 7) or requesting RSVP controlled load or guaranteed QoS classes of service.

- (Optional) Use Application-Specific Routing (ASR) with the proxy.

Configure ASR on the H.323 interface:

  (interface) **h323 asr** [**bandwidth** *max-bandwidth*]

The maximum bandwidth available to the proxy is *max-bandwidth* (1 to
10,000,000 kbps; the default is the bandwidth configured on the interface).

Keep the ASR interface isolated from other interfaces.

You can keep ASR traffic isolated by assigning an IP subnet to the ASR interface
that is routed by one type of routing protocol. Then, use another routing protocol for all other interfaces. Or, you can use a single routing protocol but assign
the ASR and non-ASR interfaces to two different autonomous systems.

Use an access list to ensure ASR isolation.

Create an IP access list that only permits traffic to and from the H.323 interface's
IP address (usually a loopback interface). All other traffic is denied (except for any
necessary routing protocols, and so forth). Apply the access list to both inbound
and outbound traffic on the interface at the edge of the ASR-only network. All
proxy traffic uses the H.323 interface's IP address as the source, which is permitted by the access list.

Example

An H.323 gatekeeper is configured for the local zone called *gk-myregion* at
company.com, using IP address 192.168.14.1. Another gatekeeper in the remote zone *gk-
theirregion* is also configured at 192.168.112.1. The technology prefix 2# causes calls to
hop off to the remote gatekeeper *gk-theirregion*. The default technology prefix 4# is
used to find a gateway registered with the same technology prefix. E.164 prefix 859.......

is assigned to the local zone, and 270....... is assigned to *gk-theirregion*. A proxy is configured in the local zone to provide proxy services for calls coming into the local zone to a gateway:

```
gatekeeper
        zone local gk-myregion company.com 192.168.14.1
        zone remote gk-theirregion company.com 192.168.112.1
        gw-type-prefix 2# hopoff gk-theirregion
        gw-type-prefix 4# default-technology
        zone prefix gk-myregion 859.......
        zone prefix gk-theirregion 270.......
      use-proxy gk-myregion default inbound-to gateway
```

11-6: Interactive Voice Response (IVR)

- IVR is configured on a router when an interaction with a caller is needed. IVR plays voice prompt audio files and collects digits from the caller.

- IVR can be used to authenticate a caller, use a prepaid debit card, and so forth.

- IVR uses a version of the Tool Command Language (TCL) called TCL IVR Version 2.0.

- TCL IVR scripts can be found at http://www.cisco.com/cgi-bin/tablebuild.pl/tclware.

- TCL IVR Version 2.0 documentation can be found at www.cisco.com/univercd/cc/td/doc/product/access/acs_serv/vapp_dev/tclivrv2.htm.

Note   To use IVR on VoIP call legs, you must use the G.711 u-law Codec for audio prompt playing and the call. In addition, DTMF relay must be configured so that the caller's digits can be collected.

Note   For more on TCL scripting within the Cisco IOS, see Appendix J.

Configuration

1. Download the TCL IVR scripts and audio files from cisco.com onto a TFTP server on your network.

2. The TCL and audio files can be kept on the TFTP server, moved to an anonymous FTP server, or copied into Flash memory on the router. IVR intelligently uses and requests the files as needed. Audio files are cached in memory and are requested from a server if they are not already in memory.

3. Create an IVR application:

```
(global) call application voice name url
```

The application is given an arbitrary *name* on the router. The TCL file used for the application is referenced by its *url*. It can be stored on a TFTP server (in the format *tftp://directory/file.tcl*) or FTP server (in the format *ftp://directory/file.tcl*) or in the router's Flash memory (in the format *flash:directory/file.tcl* or *slot0:directory/file.tcl*). Refer to Section 1-2 for more information about working with files on a Cisco router.

4. Set the language used in the audio files:

```
(global) call application voice name language index language
```

For the IVR application *name*, one or more audio file languages can be defined. The *index* (0 to 9) is a unique identifier for a specific *language:* **en** (English), **sp** (Spanish), **ch** (Mandarin), or **aa** (all).

5. Set the length of a PIN entry:

```
(global) call application voice name pin-length length
```

Certain IVR applications collect digits for a caller's personal identification number (PIN). For the IVR application *name*, the PIN length is set to *length* digits (0 to 10).

6. Set the PIN entry retry limit:

```
(global) call application voice name retry-count count
```

For the IVR application *name*, the caller is allowed to reenter his or her PIN up to *count* (1 to 5) times.

7. Set the user ID length:

```
(global) call application voice name uid-length length
```

For the IVR application *name*, the caller's user identification can have up to *length* characters (1 to 20).

8. Set the location of the application's audio files:

```
(global) call application voice name set-location language category
    location
```

Audio files for the IVR application name are defined by *language* (**en, sp,** or **ch**) and *category* (0 to 4; 0 means all categories). Up to four arbitrary categories can be assigned so that audio files can be stored according to some function or attribute. The *location* of the audio files is given as a URL or a TFTP directory.

9. (Optional) Define a redirect number for an application:

```
(global) call application voice name redirect-number number
```

Some IVR applications require a call to be redirected to an operator for human intervention if certain conditions apply. For the application *name*, calls can be redirected to *number* (a telephone number).

10. (Optional) Set the call-end warning time:

```
(global) call application voice name warning-time seconds
```

Some IVR applications play a warning message before the time runs out on a call and the call is ended. For the IVR application *name*, the warning is played *seconds* (10 to 600 seconds) before the calling time runs out.

11. Configure any AAA functions that are required by the IVR application. Refer to Section 12-2 for further configuration information.

12. Use the IVR application on a dial peer:

```
(dial-peer) application name
```

The IVR application *name* is run when a call is initiated on the dial peer.

11-7: Survivable Remote Site (SRS) Telephony

- SRS Telephony provides Cisco CallManager (CM) fallback support in environments using Cisco IP phones at remote sites with a central CM.

- If a WAN link to a remote site is lost, SRS Telephony configured on the remote router begins to handle calls for the IP phones.

- SRS Telephony supports the following routers and resources: Cisco 2600 and 3620 series routers (up to 24 Cisco IP phones and 48 directory numbers), the Cisco 3640 router (48 IP phones and 96 directory numbers), and the Cisco 3660 router (144 IP phones and 288 directory numbers).

- The SRS Telephony router is listed as a last resort, after the primary and other secondary CallManagers.

- It is good design practice to have both WAN (to the IP network) and PSTN connections at a remote or branch site. In the event of a WAN failure, the SRS Telephony router can still make calls over the PSTN connections.

- SRS Telephony does not support the Cisco IP Softphone, Cisco uOne, or Cisco IP Contact Center. In addition, the Cisco 3660 router is unable to support Centralized Automatic Message Accounting (CAMA) trunks for 911 emergency services.

Configuration

1. Configure DHCP server entries for IP phones.

    a. Create a DHCP pool entry for a phone:

```
(global) ip dhcp pool name
```

    The phone entry is named *name* (a text string).

    b. Define the IP phone's address:

```
(dhcp) host ip-address mask
```

The IP phone receives a reply with the *ip-address* and subnet *mask*.

c. Identify the IP phone's MAC address:

```
(dhcp) client-identifier mac-address
```

The phone's MAC address is given as *mac-address* (dotted-triplet format).

d. Define the TFTP server address:

```
(dhcp) option 150 ip tftp-address
```

The IP address of the TFTP server used to download IP phone configuration information is set to *tftp-address*.

e. Set the default router used by the IP phone:

```
(dhcp) default-router ip-address
```

The IP address of the default gateway on the IP phone's local network is given as *ip-address*.

2. Enable SRS Telephony:

```
(global) call-manager-fallback
```

3. Specify a source address when talking to IP phones:

```
(cm-fallback) ip source-address ip-address [port port] [any-match |
   strict-match]
```

The router uses the *ip-address* as the source address when communicating with IP phones. An optional *port* number (the default is 2000) can be given. The router can accept registrations from IP phones using an IP address other than the fallback source address configured here using **any-match** (the default). Otherwise, the **strict-match** keyword forces the router to accept registrations only from phones that use the specific fallback source address. Usually, the fallback source address is the same address as the Ethernet interface where the phones are connected.

4. Set the maximum number of IP phones to support:

```
(cm-fallback) max-ephones max-phones
```

The maximum number of phones is *max-phones* (0 to 24, 48, or 144, depending on router platform; the default is 0). As soon as this is set, it cannot be lowered until the router is reloaded.

5. Set the maximum number of directory numbers to support:

```
(cm-fallback) max-dn max-dn
```

The maximum number of directory numbers is *max-dn* (0 to 48, 96, or 288, depending on router platform; the default is 0). As soon as this is set, it cannot be lowered until the router is reloaded.

6. (Optional) Set the IP phone keepalive time:

```
(cm-fallback) keepalive seconds
```

The router expects to see keepalive messages from each IP phone at intervals of *seconds* (the default is 30). If keepalives are not received for three consecutive intervals, the IP phone is considered out of service.

7. (Optional) Set a default destination number for incoming calls:

```
(cm-fallback) default-destination number
```

For incoming calls from a POTS voice port, calls are normally routed according to the called number information. If this is not present, calls can be routed to *number* (a valid directory number). Otherwise, the caller receives a secondary dial tone and must enter the extension number to complete the call.

8. (Optional) Set the global prefix for the IP phone dial plan:

```
(cm-fallback) dialplan-pattern tag pattern extension-length length
```

The global prefix is used to expand the IP phone extension numbers into a full E.164 number. The *tag* value (1 to 5) is used to identify multiple dial-plan patterns. The *pattern* (a string of digits followed by dots as wildcard digits) is used to complete the E.164 number. It can contain items such as the area code, a prefix, and any missing numbers to the left of the IP phone extension range. When incoming calls are displayed on an IP phone, they can be converted back to extension numbers. This is done using an extension number *length* (number of digits).

9. (Optional) Allow call transfer to a range of non-IP phone numbers:

```
(cm-fallback) transfer-pattern pattern
```

IP phones can be allowed to transfer calls to other IP phones (the default) or to non-IP phone numbers. The *pattern* (a string of digits, along with dots as wildcard digits) is used to specify the allowed destination numbers. Up to 32 transfer patterns can be configured.

10. (Optional) Set dial codes to access outbound POTS trunks during fallback:

```
(cm-fallback) access-code {fxo | e&m | bri | pri} dial-string
```

During CallManager fallback, callers can access the POTS trunks for outbound calls by dialing a prefix *dial-string* (one or more digits). An access code can be set for each type of POTS trunk that is available. Many times, the dial string is set to 8 or 9, traditional access codes for trunks.

11. (Optional) Set a speed-dial number for voice mail:

```
(cm-fallback) voicemail number
```

By default, the "message" button on IP phones is disabled during CM fallback. To reach a voice-mail system through a fallback path (PSTN, for example), the voice-mail

Section 11-7

speed dial number can be configured. When the "message" button on an IP phone is pressed, the router dials *number* (a string of digits) to reach a voice-mail system.

Example

Figure 11-1 shows a network diagram for this example. An SRS Telephony fallback CallManager is configured to support a small branch office in the event that the WAN link to the branch is lost. The DHCP entries for two IP phones (*Joe* and *Fred*) are configured so that the phones can reboot and operate successfully. The TFTP server for the phones is at 192.168.243.100, and the default gateway is 192.168.243.1 (the SRS Telephony router).

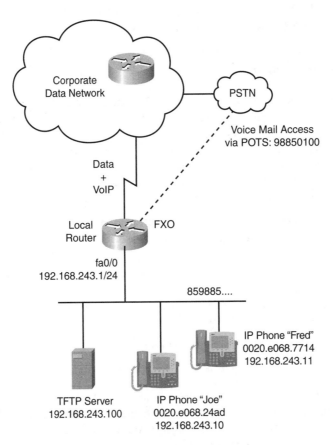

Figure 11-1 *Network Diagram for the SRS Telephony Example*

CallManager fallback uses a source address of 192.168.243.1, port 2000, and expects the IP phones to register with it using a strictly matching address of 192.168.243.1. The maximum number of supported phones is 24, with up to 48 directory numbers.

A string of "859885" is added to the four-digit extension numbers of the IP phones. The phones are allowed to transfer calls to numbers matching the range "859555....". A voice-mail system is accessible by dialing 98850100, which accesses an FXO port using a leading 9.

```
ip dhcp pool Joe
        host 192.168.243.10 255.255.255.0
        client-identifier 0020.e068.24ad
        option 150 ip 192.168.243.100
        default-router 192.168.243.1

ip dhcp pool Fred
        host 192.168.243.11 255.255.255.0
        client-identifier 0020.e068.7714
        option 150 ip 192.168.243.100
        default-router 192.168.243.1

interface fastethernet 0/0
        ip address 192.168.243.1 255.255.255.0

call-manager-fallback
        ip source-address 192.168.243.1 port 2000 strict-match
        max-ephones 24
        max-dn 48
        dialplan-pattern 1 859885.... extension-length 4
        transfer-pattern 859555....
        voicemail 98850100
        access-code fxo 9
```

Further Reading

Refer to the following recommended sources for further information about the topics covered in this chapter:

Voice Over IP Fundamentals, Second Edition, by Jonathan Davidson, James Peters, et al., Cisco Press, ISBN 15787052571.

Cisco Voice Over Frame Relay, ATM, and IP, by McQuerry, McGrew, and Foy, Cisco Press, ISBN 1578702275.

Cisco Interactive Mentor, Voice Internetworking: Basic Voice Over IP, Cisco Press, ISBN 1587200236.

Cisco CallManager Fundamentals, 2nd Edition, by Alexander, Pearce, Smith, and Whetton, Cisco Press, ISBN 1587051923.

Deploying Cisco Voice Over IP Solutions, by Jonathan Davidson, Cisco Press, ISBN 1587050307.

Integrating Voice and Data Networks, by Scott Keagy, Cisco Press, ISBN 1578701961.

Voice Over IP Security, by Patrick Park, Cisco Press, ISBN 1587054698.

Cisco Voice Gateways, by David Mallory, Ken Salhoff, and Denise Donohue, Cisco Press, ISBN: 1578701961.

Internet Phone Services Simplified (VoIP), by Jim Doherty and Neil Anderson, Cisco Press, ISBN: 1587201623.

Voice Over IP First-Step, by Kevin Wallace, Cisco Press, ISBN 1587201569.

Configuring CallManager and Unity: A Step by Step Guide, by David Bateman, Cisco Press, ISBN 1587053977.

Cisco IP Communications Express: CallManager Express with Cisco Unity Express, Cisco Press, ISBN 1587053918.

RFC 2705, "Media Gateway Control Protocol (MGCP)."

RFC 3550, "RTP: A Transport Protocol for Real-Time Applications."

RFC 3621, "Session Initiation Protocol."

Chapter 12

Router Security

This chapter discusses how to configure and use the following network security features:

- **12-1: Suggested Ways to Secure a Router**—The Cisco IOS software provides a wide range of functionality on a router. This section gives you a set of tips on how to close down unnecessary router services and control access to the router itself.

- **12-2: Authentication, Authorization, and Accounting (AAA)**—A router can interface with external servers to authenticate incoming users, grant or deny permission to specific network resources, and maintain an audit trail for billing or logging purposes.

- **12-3: Dynamically Authenticate and Authorize Users with Authentication Proxy**— A router can intercept HTTP traffic and require user authentication on behalf of external AAA servers. Authorization to network resources can also be granted per user.

- **12-4: Controlling Access with Lock and Key Security**—You can control access to a network by having a router block access until an end user authenticates. Temporary access is then granted through router security.

- **12-5: Filtering IP Sessions with Reflexive Access Lists**—Inbound traffic can be tightly controlled at a router. Outbound traffic can then trigger temporary access for returning inbound traffic.

- **12-6: Prevent DoS Attacks with TCP Intercept**—A router can monitor and intercept half-opened TCP sessions, protecting hosts on the inside of a protected network.

- **12-7: Intelligent Filtering with Context-Based Access Control (CBAC)**—A comprehensive set of firewall functions can be configured on a router. CBAC performs traffic filtering (better than access lists), traffic inspection (better than Reflexive Access Lists), and TCP Intercept. It also generates alerts and audit trails and limited intrusion detection.

- **12-8: Detect Attacks and Threats with the IOS Intrusion Detection System**—A router can monitor inbound traffic from an unprotected network. Attack signatures can be selectively enabled or disabled, according to your security requirements.

- **12-9: Control Plane Policing**—Cisco IOS Software can be configured to protect a router against infrastructure attacks that target the router.

- **12-10: AutoSecure**—The AutoSecure feature provides a means to quickly secure your router. AutoSecure can be run in interactive mode, prompting you to answer questions about how you want to secure your router, or noninteractive mode, and where recommended commands are automatically applied to your router's configuration.

12-1: Suggested Ways to Secure a Router

This section presents some ideas and suggestions that you can use to improve security on the router itself. Although a router is usually configured to provide network connectivity and services to other parts of a network, it too is subject to some types of security exploits.

User Authentication on the Router

- **Passwords (local authentication)**—Use the (global) **username** *username* **password** *password* command to define a locally authenticated user and password. By defining individual usernames, you can control user access at a finer granularity. You also can configure the router to generate an audit trail if needed.

> **Note**   You should use the (global) **service password-encryption** command so that passwords contained in the router configuration are encoded before they are displayed. This can be useful when you need to view or share a configuration with other people. However, the "encryption" algorithm is a simple one based on a Vigenere Cipher, and it should not be a substitute for proper security. Make sure you store and protect your configuration files as if they have cleartext passwords displayed.

- **The enable password**—Always use the (global) **enable secret** command to define a privileged level (enable) password. This command uses the MD5 algorithm for encryption and hashing, which is considered an irreversible encryption method.

- **AAA authentication**—For the most flexible and scalable management of user access, you should use AAA. See Section 12-2 for further information.

Control Access to the Router Lines

Interactive access is available on all router "lines," such as the Console, Aux, async, and VTY lines. The VTY lines provide a means to Telnet to the router (port 23 and other higher port numbers), whereas the other lines require a physical connection. However, other means of access exist, including rlogin, SSH, LAT, MOP, X.29, V.120, and other protocols.

Be sure to configure some form of authentication on *all* router lines. If a line is not needed for user access, disable interactive logins with the (line) **login** and (line) **no password** commands. Users can use reverse-Telnet to connect to a physical line (Aux and async lines) remotely. If this is not desired, use the (line) **transport input none** command to disable remote access.

VTY lines should be configured for the necessary access protocols only. Use the (line) **transport input telnet** command to enable reverse Telnet, or **transport input telnet ssh** to enable only Telnet and SSH access. You should also define standard IP access lists to permit only known host IP addresses to Telnet into the router. Do this with the (line) **ip access-class** *acc-list-number* command on each line.

Be aware that a router supports a limited number of VTY lines so that multiple Telnet sessions can exist. If all of these VTY lines are in use (either with successful authentications or just left at the login prompt), no other users can Telnet to the router. This might mean that you are unable to use Telnet to access a router remotely when you really need to! To prevent this from happening, set a session timeout on the VTY lines: (line) **exec-timeout** *minutes seconds*. You should also consider reserving the highest-number VTY line exclusively for management purposes. Do this by using an access list that permits only specific management station IP addresses, along with the (line) **ip access-class** command for the last VTY line.

Refer to Section 1-1 for further configuration information.

Configure Login Timing Options

Configure the quiet period for login attempts to protect against denial of service (Dos) and password attacks.

1. Configure the number of attempts to trigger a quiet period:

    (global) **login block-for** [*block-sec*] **attempts** [*att*] **within** [*attempts-sec*]

    This command specifies the number of failed login attempts (att) within a specified number of seconds (*attempts-sec*) that must occur before entering a quiet period. During the quiet period, logins are blocked for the number of seconds specified with the *block-sec* parameter.

2. Configure quiet period exemptions:

    (global) **login quiet-mode access-class** [*acl*]

    Configure an access list that permits any host that you want exempted from the quiet period rule.

3. Configure the minimum number of time between login attempts:

    (global) **login delay** [*sec*]

    This default period of time that must pass between login attempts is 1 second.

4. Configure logging for successful logins:

    (global) **login on-succcess log** [**every** *logins*]

You can configure the router to log every successful login to the router or to log after a specified number of login attempts.

5. Configure logging for failed logins:

```
(global) login on-failure log [every logins]
```

You can configure the router to log every failed login to the router or to log after a specified number of login attempts.

Use Warning Banners to Inform Users

You should configure warning banners to inform users of the legal requirements and consequences of unauthorized access to your router and your network. Use the (global) **banner login** command to define a banner message that is displayed before the username and password prompts.

To properly inform would-be users, and to be able to prosecute malicious visitors to your router, you should place additional information in the banner. Identify your company, and state that all access and actions are monitored and recorded. Also state that unauthorized actions are prohibited and might be prosecuted. You should consult your local legal counsel for help in deciding what information to place in your banner. For an example, see the "Security" section of the FBI's web site at http://www.fbi.gov/privacy.htm.

Note If you use a login banner, don't display any specific information about your router or your network. Examples of this include the router name, model, manufacturer, software, or who owns or maintains the router. Unauthorized users (crackers) can use unintentional hints as leverage to find a way to compromise your network.

Router Management

■ **SNMP**—If SNMP is used, you should try to use SNMP v2 if possible. Version 2 has support for MD5 authentication, which is much more secure than the cleartext version 1 community string. If Version 1 must be used, configure unique read-only and read-write community strings that can't be easily guessed (unlike the default "public" and "private"community strings). Also, use standard IP access lists to limit the router's SNMP access to specific management stations. See Section 1-6 for further configuration details about SNMP.

■ **HTTP**—You should carefully consider using the HTTP management interface on a router. HTTP uses cleartext passwords unless it is used in conjunction with a more secure authentication method such as AAA. Also, configure a standard access list to limit HTTP management traffic to specific management stations. See Section 1-1 for more information.

Implement Logging on the Router

A router can generate logging information for a variety of activity. Logging creates an audit trail for things such as AAA, router command usage, SNMP traps, system activity, access list violations, intrusion detection alerts, and debugging information. Logging should be disabled on the router console due to the relatively slow speed of the async line. Instead, configure logging to the router's buffer in memory (**logging buffered**) and also to one or more syslog servers. Logging is much more efficient with these methods, and a running record can be maintained in the syslog files on the servers. See Section 1-6 for more information about logging.

Control Spoofed Information

- **Address spoofing**—A malicious user can send packets to your network with "spoofed" IP addresses. These addresses either don't exist or are unreachable, so the targets of an attack can't successfully reply to or open connections that were originated by the source. Obviously, you want your router to filter out any packets with spoofed source addresses so that no internal hosts have to deal with attack traffic.

  - Use access lists to deny spoofed addresses:

    ```
    (global) access-list acc-list-number deny ip internal-network mask any
    ```

    Spoofed IP addresses are used on inbound packets from the outside, using source addresses from the inside of your network. If allowed in, the packets can reach an internal target, but replies will never find the original source.

    In addition, inbound packets can have source addresses corresponding to the RFC 1918 routes or other illegal values: 10.0.0.0 (private class A network), 127.0.0.0 (reserved for loopback), 169.254.0.0 (used by Microsoft for failed DHCP), 172.16.0.0 to 172.31.0.0 (private class B networks), 192.168.0.0 (private class C networks), and 224.0.0.0 (multicast; never used as a source address). For these, additional commands should be added to the access list:

    ```
    (global) access-list acc-list-number deny ip 10.0.0.0 0.255.255.255 any
    (global) access-list acc-list-number deny ip 127.0.0.0 0.255.255.255 any
    (global) access-list acc-list-number deny ip 169.254.0.0 0.0.255.255 any
    (global) access-list acc-list-number deny ip 172.16.0.0 0.15.255.255 any
    (global) access-list acc-list-number deny ip 192.168.0.0 0.0.255.255 any
    (global) access-list acc-list-number deny ip 224.0.0.0 31.255.255.255 any
    ```

  - **Use Reverse Path Forwarding (RPF)**—RPF can also be used to identify and drop spoofed traffic. RPF is used on the inbound interface of a router that borders a public network. When a packet is received, the router performs a reverse route lookup in the CEF database (FIB). If there is a known route back to the source, and if the route points back to the same interface that the packet was received on (or any other redundant path back to the source), the packet is routed. If no reverse lookup is found, the packet is dropped. RPF must be used with global CEF switching enabled on the router:

```
(global) ip cef
(interface) ip verify unicast reverse-path
```

- **Routing update spoofing**— Routing updates can also be spoofed and advertised into your local routing domain. You should use the various routing protocol authentication mechanisms to validate that advertisements are coming from trusted routing peers.

Control Unnecessary Router Services

- **Cisco Discovery Protocol (CDP)**—CDP should be disabled at the edges of your network so that information about your routers doesn't get propagated to untrusted recipients. CDP is forwarded only to directly connected neighbors on router interfaces. Disable CDP on an interface with the (interface) **no cdp enable** command.

- **Network Time Protocol (NTP)**—If NTP is used in your network, you should configure specific addresses for the trusted time sources. NTP authentication should also be used. If NTP is not needed, you can disable it with the (global) **no ntp enable** command.

- **UDP and TCP services**—By default, the UDP and TCP "small services" (echo, chargen, discard, and daytime services) are disabled on IOS 12.0 and greater. These services are almost never needed, and they can be abused if they are enabled. When they are disabled, the router sends ICMP port unreachable messages if the UDP services are attempted and resets the TCP connections if the TCP services are attempted. If these services are enabled, you can disable them:

```
(global) no service tcp-small-servers
(global) no service udp-small-servers
```

- **Finger**—You should disable the finger service, which provides information about users who are connected to the router. Use the (global) **no service finger** command.

- **ICMP packets**—You should be selective about the type of ICMP packets you allow into your network. Some ICMP messages can be exploited and used for attacks. As a rule of thumb, you should filter ICMP at a border router using a standard IP access list like the following:

```
(global) access-list acc-list-number permit icmp any any echo-reply
(global) access-list acc-list-number permit icmp any internal-network
  mask time-exceeded
(global) access-list acc-list-number permit icmp any internal-network
  mask packet-too-big
(global) access-list acc-list-number permit icmp any internal-network
  mask traceroute
(global) access-list acc-list-number permit icmp any internal-network
  mask unreachable
```

You should allow these ICMP messages into your network: Ping replies (echo-reply), TTL exceeded (time-exceeded), Path MTU discovery (packet-too-big), traceroute, and unreachable. All other types are implicitly denied at the end of the access list.

- **Directed broadcasts**—You should disable directed broadcasts, which send packets to a subnet's broadcast address. Obviously, if the directed broadcast were forwarded by the router, every host on the subnet would receive it and try to respond to the source address. Disable directed broadcasts on *every* interface of *every* router in your network:

  ```
  (interface) no ip directed-broadcast
  ```

  In IOS 12.0 and greater, directed broadcasts are disabled on every interface by default.

- **IP source routing**—IP packets can contain an explicit source route field that lists the exact path a packet should take through the network. In most cases, this is not needed, can be exploited, and should be disabled:

  ```
  (global) no ip source-route
  ```

- **Disable proxy ARP**—Proxy ARP can be used to set up routes dynamically. If it is not needed, you should disable it on all interfaces:

  ```
  (interface) no proxy-arp
  ```

- **Enable TCP keepalive packets for Telnet sessions**—Telnet is highly susceptible to session hijacking attacks. Enabling TCP keepalives causes the router to periodically generate TCP keepalive messages, which results in the router detecting and dropping any broken TCP sessions to and from remote systems:

  ```
  (global) service tcp-keepalives-in
  (global) service tcp-keepalives-out
  ```

12-2: Authentication, Authorization, and Accounting (AAA)

- Method lists are used to specify a sequence of methods to use for each component of AAA. If one method receives no response or an error condition, the next method in the list is tried.

- Multiple AAA servers can be defined. If the first one listed doesn't respond or generates an error, the next server is tried.

- AAA servers can be grouped so that a collection of servers can be used for a specific task.

- Authentication can use a variety of methods, including RADIUS, TACACS+, Kerberos 5, and usernames locally configured in the router.

- Authorization can use RADIUS and TACACS+ to authorize users to access available services.

- Accounting can use RADIUS and TACACS+ to track and record the services and network resources that users are using.

- Shared secret keys are configured in both the router and the RADIUS or TACACS+ server so that all interaction (including the user's password entry) is encrypted.

Configuration

1. Enable AAA functionality:

    `(global)` **`aaa new-model`**

2. Identify one or more AAA servers.

    a. Use a RADIUS server.

    - (Optional) Set global defaults for all RADIUS servers.

      Set the shared router/server key:

      `(global)` **`radius-server key {0 string | 7 string | string}`**

      The shared secret encryption key is set as *string* (a cleartext string). If **0** precedes the string, or if the string appears by itself, the string appears unencrypted in the router configuration. If **7** precedes it, the string is "hidden" and is displayed as an encrypted string in the configuration.

      Set the request timeout interval:

      `(global)` **`radius-server timeout seconds`**

      After a request, the router waits for *seconds* (1 to 1000; the default is 5) for a response from a RADIUS server.

      Set the number of request retries:

      `(global)` **`radius-server retransmit retries`**

      If no response is received from a RADIUS server, the router retries the request *retries* times (1 to 100; the default is 3).

      Set the server deadtime:

      `(global)` **`radius-server deadtime minutes`**

      If a RADIUS server doesn't respond after the retransmit retries, the router can mark it as "dead" for a period of time in *minutes* (0 to 1440; the default is 0). As soon as it is marked as dead, the router skips that server and sends requests to the next available server.

    - Specify one or more servers to use:

      `(global)` **`radius-server host`** `{hostname | ip-address}` **`[auth-port`** `port]`
        `[acct-port` `port]` **`[timeout`** `seconds]` **`[retransmit`** `retries]`
        `[alias {hostname | ip-address}]` `[key string]`

The RADIUS server is identified by host name or IP address. You can specify the UDP ports for authentication (**auth-port**; the default is 1645) and for accounting (**acct-port**; the default is 1646). You can override the defaults and set the amount of time the router waits for a RADIUS response with **timeout** (1 to 1000 seconds) and set the number of retransmitted requests with **retransmit** (1 to 100). The **alias** keyword can be used to define up to eight host names or IP addresses for a single RADIUS server name. The shared secret **key** can be set to *string* (a cleartext string). Always set the key as the last argument so that any embedded spaces will not be confused with other arguments.

- (Optional) Enable vendor-specific RADIUS attributes (VSAs):

  `(global) radius-server vsa send [accounting | authorization]`

  The router can recognize VSAs that comply with attribute 26 of the IETF draft for either **accounting** or **authorization**.

- (Optional) Enable vendor-proprietary RADIUS attributes:

  `(global) radius-server host {hostname | ip-address} non-standard`

The router can use IETF draft extensions for the most common vendor-proprietary attributes.

b. Use a TACACS+ server.

- (Optional) Set the global shared router/server key for TACACS+ servers:

  `(global) tacacs-server key key`

  The shared secret encryption key is set as *string* (a cleartext string). Embedded spaces are accepted.

- Specify one or more servers to use:

  `(global) tacacs-server host hostname [port port] [timeout seconds] [key`
  `   string]`

The TACACS+ server is identified by host name. You can specify the TCP port used with the **port** keyword (the default is 49). The amount of time the router waits for a TACACS+ response is **timeout** in seconds. The shared secret **key** can be set to *string* (a cleartext string). Always set the key as the last argument so that any embedded spaces will not be confused with other arguments.

c. Use a Kerberos server.

- Create users and SRVTAB entries on the Key Distribution Center (KDC).

  Users and SRVTAB entries are administered on the Kerberos server. Refer to your Kerberos documentation for further instructions. The SRVTAB files and the associated keys will be imported into the router in a later step.

■   Identify the Kerberos realm.

Define a default realm:

`(global) kerberos local-realm realm`

The router is located in the Kerberos *realm* (an uppercase text string), where all resources are registered to a server. This should be taken from the *default_realm* parameter on the server.

Specify the Kerberos server for the realm:

`(global) kerberos server realm {hostname | ip-address} [port]`

The server for the *realm* (an uppercase text string) is identified by its host name or IP address and also by the *port* used for the KDC (the default is 88). The host name or IP address should be taken from the *admin_server* parameter on the server itself.

(Optional) Map a DNS domain or host name to the realm:

`(global) kerberos realm {domain | hostname} realm`

A *domain* (a fully qualified domain name with a leading dot) or a *hostname* (no leading dot) can be mapped to a specific *realm* (an uppercase text string).

■   Import a SRVTAB file.

Create a DES encryption key:

`(global) key config-key 1 string`

A private DES key is created as key number **1** using *string* (up to eight alphanumeric characters). The key is used to generate DES keys for imported SRVTAB entries.

TFTP the SRVTAB file and create SRVTAB entries:

`(global) kerberos srvtab remote tftp://hostname/filename`

The SRVTAB file is identified by its URL using the server's host name (or IP address) followed by the filename. The file is retrieved via TFTP.

d. (RADIUS or TACACS+ only) Group a list of servers.

■   Define a group name:

`(global) aaa group server {radius | tacacs+} group-name`

A server group named *group-name* is created. The group can identify a subset of configured RADIUS or TACACS+ servers that can be used for a particular AAA service.

■   Add a server to the group:

`(server-group) server ip-address [auth-port port] [acct-port port]`

The server at the IP address is a member of the group. You can specify the UDP ports for authentication (**auth-port**; the default is 1645) and accounting (**acct-port**; the default is 1646).

- (Optional) Set a deadtime for the group:

```
(server-group) deadtime minutes
```

The group deadtime allows the router to skip over a group of servers that are unresponsive and declared "dead" and send requests to the next available group name. Deadtime is in *minutes* (0 to 1440; the default is 0).

3. Use AAA authentication.

   a. Create a method list for an authentication type:

```
(global) aaa authentication {login | ppp | nasi | arap | enable}
  {default | list-name} method1 [method2 ...]
```

The method list named *list-name* is created. It contains a list of login authentication methods to be tried in sequential order. The **default** keyword specifies a list of methods to be used on lines and interfaces that are configured for default authentication. The list of methods applies to the authentication type given by **login** (the login prompt on the router), **enable** (access to the privileged EXEC command level), **ppp** (dialup access through PPP), **nasi** (Netware Asynchronous Services Interface), or **arap** (AppleTalk Remote Access Protocol).

The method keywords (*method1, method2, ...*) given in the list depend on the type of authentication:

- **login**—**enable** (use the enable password), **krb5** (Kerberos 5), **krb5-telnet** (Kerberos 5 for Telnet authentication), **line** (use the line password), **local** (use the router's list of usernames and passwords), **local-case** (use the router's list of case-sensitive usernames), **none** (use no authentication; every user is successfully authenticated), **group radius** (use all listed RADIUS servers), **group tacacs+** (use all listed TACACS+ servers), and **group** *group-name* (use only the servers listed in the server group named *group-name*).

- **enable**—**enable** (use the enable password), **line** (use the line password), **none** (use no authentication; every user is successfully authenticated), **group radius** (use all listed RADIUS servers), **group tacacs+** (use all listed TACACS+ servers), and **group** *group-name* (use only the servers listed in the server group named *group-name*).

- **ppp**—**if-needed** (no authentication if the user is already logged into a TTY line), **krb5** (Kerberos 5), **local** (use the router's list of usernames and passwords), **local-case** (use the router's list of case-sensitive usernames), **none** (use no authentication; every user is successfully authenticated), **group radius** (use all listed RADIUS servers), **group tacacs+** (use all listed TACACS+ servers), and **group** *group-name* (use only the servers listed in the server group named *group-name*).

- **nasi**—**enable** (use the enable password), **line** (use the line password), **local** (use the router's list of usernames and passwords), **local-case** (use the router's list of case-sensitive usernames), **none** (use no authentication; every user is successfully authenticated), **group radius** (use all listed RADIUS servers), **group tacacs+** (use all listed TACACS+ servers), and **group** *group-name* (use only the servers listed in the server group named *group-name*).

■ **arap—auth-guest** (allow a guest login if the user has EXEC access), **guest** (allow guest logins), **line** (use the line password), **local** (use the router's list of usernames and passwords), **local-case** (use the router's list of case-sensitive usernames), **group radius** (use all listed RADIUS servers), **group tacacs+** (use all listed TACACS+ servers), and **group** *group-name* (use only the servers listed in the server group named *group-name*).

b. Apply the method list to a router line or interface.

■ (PPP only) Authenticate on an interface.

Select an interface:

`(global) interface type slot/number`

Enable PPP authentication on the interface:

`(interface) ppp authentication {protocol1 [protocol2 ...]} [if-needed]`
`  [list-name | default] [callin] [one-time]`

PPP authentication can be used with one or more protocols (*protocol1, protocol2, ...*): **chap** (CHAP), **ms-chap** (Microsoft CHAP), or **pap** (PAP). The **if-needed** keyword prevents additional authentication if TACACS or extended TACACS has already authenticated a user. The method list is specified as *list-name*, a list of methods that PPP sequentially tries. If a method list is not needed, the **default** keyword causes PPP to use the default method. The **callin** keyword authenticates only inbound users, and **one-time** allows both username and password to be presented in the username field.

■ (Login, NASI, or ARAP only) Authenticate on a line.

Select a line:

`(global) line {aux | console | tty | vty} line-number [end-line-number]`

A specific Aux, console, async, or virtual TTY line can be selected with the *line-number*. Add the *end-line-number* to select a range of line numbers.

Apply authentication to the line:

`(line) {login | nasi | arap} authentication {default | list-name}`

The authentication type is given as **login, nasi,** or **arap**. The method list named *list-name* is used to authenticate users on the line. The **default** keyword can be used instead to use the default AAA authentication methods without specifying a method list.

c. (Optional) Use the AAA banners and prompts.

- Create a login banner:

  `(global) aaa authentication banner dstringd`

  The customized banner *string* (up to 2996 characters) is displayed prior to the username login prompt. The *d* character is a delimiter (any character that doesn't appear in *string*) that must appear before and after the banner string.

- Change the password prompt:

  `(global) aaa authentication password-prompt string`

  The default password prompt string is Password:. You can change this to *string* (a text string; enclose it in double quotes if it contains spaces).

- Create a failed login banner:

  `(global) aaa authentication fail-message dstringd`

The customized banner *string* (up to 2996 characters) is displayed if the user login fails. The *d* character is a delimiter (any character that doesn't appear in *string*) that must appear before and after the banner string.

4. Use AAA authorization.

   a. Create a method list for an authorization type:

   ```
   (global) aaa authorization {auth-proxy | network | exec | commands level |
      reverse-access | configuration | ipmobile} {default | list-name}
      method1 [method2 ...]
   ```

   The method list named *list-name* is created. It contains a list of authorization methods to be tried in sequential order. The **default** keyword specifies a list of methods to be used on lines and interfaces that are configured for default authorization. The list of methods applies to the authorization type given by **auth-proxy** (use specific policies per user), **network** (network-related service requests), **exec** (permission to run a router EXEC), **commands** (permission to use all commands at privilege *level*, 0 to 15), **reverse-access** (permission to use reverse-Telnet connections), **configuration** (permission to enter router configuration mode), or **ipmobile** (permission to use IP mobility).

   The method keywords (*method1, method2, ...*) given in the list are **group** *group-name* (send requests to the servers in the group named *group-name*), **group radius** (send requests to the RADIUS server group), **group tacacs+** (send requests to the TACACS+ server group), **if-authenticated** (permission is granted if the user is already authenticated), **none** (use no authorization; every user is successfully authorized), and **local** (use the router's list of usernames and passwords).

   b. Apply the method list to a line or an interface.

      - Authorize users on a line.

        Select a line:

        `(global) line line-number [end-line-number]`

An Aux, console, async, or virtual TTY line can be selected with the *line-number*. Add the *end-line-number* to select a range of line numbers.

Apply authorization to the line:

```
(line) authorization {arap | commands level | exec | reverse-access}
  [default | list-name]
```

The authorization type is given as **arap** (AppleTalk Remote Access Protocol), **commands** *level* (permission to execute commands at privilege *level*), **exec** (permission to use a router EXEC shell), or **reverse-access** (permission to use reverse Telnet). The method list named *list-name* is used to authorize users on the line. The **default** keyword can be used instead to use the default AAA authorization methods without specifying a method list.

- (PPP only) Authorize users on an interface.

  Select an interface:

  ```
  (global) interface type slot/number
  ```
  Apply authorization to the interface:

  ```
  (interface) ppp authorization [default | list-name]
  ```

The method list named *list-name* is used to authorize PPP users on the interface. The **default** keyword can be used instead to use the default AAA authorization methods without specifying a method list.

5. Use AAA accounting (RADIUS or TACACS+ only).

a. Create a method list for an accounting type:

```
(global) aaa accounting {auth-proxy | system | network | exec |
  connection [h323] | commands level} {default | list-name} {start-stop
  stop-only | wait-start | none} [broadcast] group {radius | tacacs+ |
  group-name}
```

The method list named *list-name* is created. It contains the accounting method to be used. The **default** keyword specifies a method to be used on lines and interfaces that are configured for default accounting. The accounting type records information about **auth-proxy** (per-user events), **system** (system-level events), **network** (network-related service requests), **exec** (router EXEC sessions), **connection** (outbound connections from an access server; **h323** performs H.323 gateway accounting for Voice over IP), and **commands** (command usage at privilege *level*, 0 to 15.

The method used for accounting can be **group** *group-name* (send records to the servers in the group named *group-name*), **group radius** (send records to the RADIUS server group), or **group tacacs+** (send records to the TACACS+ server group).

The **broadcast** keyword causes records to be sent to multiple accounting servers. The type of accounting records are selected by **start-stop** ("start" when a process begins; "stop" when a process ends), **stop-only** (no "start" is sent; "stop" when the process ends), **wait-start** ("start" when a process begins; the process doesn't actually begin until "start" is received by the server; "stop" when the process ends), or **none** (no accounting is performed).

b. (Optional) Record accounting for failed authentications:

```
(global) aaa accounting send stop-request authentication failure
```

The router sends "stop" records when a user authentication or a PPP negotiation fails.

c. Apply the method list to a line or an interface.

- Perform accounting on a line.

   Select a line:

   ```
   (global) line line-number [end-line-number]
   ```

   An Aux, console, async, or virtual TTY line can be selected with the *line-number*. Add the *end-line-number* to select a range of line numbers.

   Enable accounting on the line:

   ```
   (line) accounting {arap | commands level | connection | exec}
     [default | list-name]
   ```

   The accounting type is given as **arap** (AppleTalk Remote Access Protocol), **commands** *level* (EXEC commands at privilege *level*), **connection** (PAP and CHAP authentication), or **exec** (router EXEC shell). The method list named *list-name* is used for accounting on the line. The **default** keyword can be used instead to use the default AAA accounting method without specifying a method list.

- (PPP only) Perform accounting on an interface.

   Select an interface:

   ```
   (global) interface type slot/number
   ```

   Enable accounting on the interface:

   ```
   (interface) ppp accounting default
   ```

   The default method is used for PPP accounting on the interface.

Example

The router is configured for AAA using all three authentication, authorization, and accounting functions. Two RADIUS servers are identified as 192.168.161.45 and 192.168.150.91, both having the same key. One TACACS+ server is at 192.168.44.10. One local username is also defined. It is used as a failsafe method in the event that the AAA servers are inaccessible.

Authentication is set up for PPP access on async interfaces using the RADIUS servers, followed by local authentication. Authentication is also used for login access to the router via Telnet, using the TACACS+ server, then the RADIUS servers, and then local authentication.

Authorization is configured to use the RADIUS servers and local authentication for both network and exec functions. Users entering the network via PPP and Telnet must be authorized. Accounting is configured to use the RADIUS servers for both network and exec resource reporting. The router sends accounting records for both PPP and router exec terminal sessions.

```
aaa new-model
radius-server host 192.168.161.45 key aAaUsInGrAdIuS
radius-server host 192.168.150.91 key aAaUsInGrAdIuS
tacacs-server host 192.168.44.10 key tacacs-server-1


aaa authentication login router-login group tacacs group radius local
aaa authentication ppp ppp-login group radius local
aaa authorization network default group radius local
aaa authorization exec default group radius local
aaa accounting network default start-stop group radius
aaa accounting exec default start-stop group radius


username admin password letmein


interface async 1
      encapsulation ppp
      ppp authentication pap ppp-login
      ppp authorization default
      ppp accounting default


line vty 0 4
      login authentication router-login
      authorization exec default
      accounting exec default
```

12-3: Dynamically Authenticate and Authorize Users with Authentication Proxy

■ Authentication proxy allows a router to intercept HTTP traffic from users and require an authentication if needed.

■ Security policies can be configured and applied on a per-user basis.

■ If a user is not already authenticated, the router prompts for a username and password.

■ After successful authentication, the user's authorization profile is requested from an

AAA server. A dynamic Access Control Entry (ACE) is added to an inbound access list, permitting the user's traffic to pass into the network.

■ Authentication proxy must be configured on an inbound interface at the edge of the network.

■ An access list can be used to limit what HTTP traffic can trigger authentication proxy.

Configuration

1. Configure AAA services.

   Refer to Section 13-2 for information about configuring AAA authentication.

   a. Enable login authentication:

   ```
   (global) aaa authentication login {default | list-name} method1 [method2
   ...]
   ```

   No special keywords are needed to use authentication proxy with AAA.

   b. Enable AAA authorization to import dynamic access list information:

   ```
   (global) aaa authorization auth-proxy {default | list-name} method1
   [method2
   ...]
   ```

   The **auth-proxy** keyword must be used to cause AAA authorization to interoperate with authentication proxy. Otherwise, AAA authorization can be configured normally.

   c. Enable AAA accounting to generate an audit or billing trail:

   ```
   (global) aaa accounting auth-proxy {default | list-name} {start-stop
    | stop-only | wait-start | none} [broadcast] group {radius | tacacs+
    | group-name}
   ```

   The **auth-proxy** keyword must be used to cause AAA accounting to interoperate with authentication proxy. Otherwise, AAA authorization can be configured normally. Use the **start-stop** keyword to generate both start and stop records as the user authenticates and uses the dynamic access list entry.

   d. Configure the AAA server addresses:

   ```
   (global) tacacs-server host hostname [port port] [timeout seconds] [key
     string]
   ```

   -or-

   ```
   (global) radius-server host {hostname | ip-address} [auth-port port]
     [acct-port port] [timeout seconds] [retransmit retries]
     [alias {hostname | ip-address}] [key string]
   ```

e. (Optional) Add TACACS+ or RADIUS traffic to any inbound access lists:

```
(global) access-list acc-list-number permit tcp host aaa-server eq
   {tacacs | radius} host router-address
```

Allow return (inbound) AAA traffic from the IP address of the *aaa-server* to the inbound interface IP address of the authentication proxy router interface to be permitted. Otherwise, when authentication proxy requests the user authorization information, the replies might be filtered out.

2. Use the HTTP server on the router.

a. Enable the HTTP server:

```
(global) ip http server
```

The HTTP server is used to present a username/password authentication prompt to the user.

b. Use AAA authentication for the HTTP server:

```
(global) ip http authentication aaa
```

c. Define an access list to deny all inbound traffic to the HTTP server:

```
(global) access-list acc-list-number deny ip any any
(global) ip http access-class acc-list-number
```

An IP access list (either standard or extended) is needed to make sure no outside user can initiate a connection to the router's HTTP server. The HTTP server is used only for outbound traffic, to present prompts to the user.

3. Enable authentication proxy.

a. (Optional) Define an authentication idle timeout:

```
(global) ip auth-proxy auth-cache-time minutes
```

Authentication proxy keeps a cache of authenticated users. After user traffic has been idle for *minutes* (1 to 2147483647; the default is 60), the dynamic access list entry for the user is removed, and the user must authenticate again.

b. (Optional) Display the router host name in the login banner:

```
(global) ip auth-proxy auth-proxy-banner
```

By default, the authentication proxy banner is disabled, preventing the router's name from being seen.

c. Specify an authentication proxy rule:

```
(global) ip auth-proxy name auth-proxy-name http [auth-cache-time minutes]
   [list std-access-list]
```

The rule is associated with an arbitrary ruleset named *auth-proxy-name* (up to 16 characters). The **http** keyword is used to trigger authentication proxy with HTTP traffic. The cache timeout can be overridden from the default, with **auth-cache-time** given in *minutes* (1 to 2147483647; the default comes from the **ip auth-proxy auth-cache-time** command).

A standard IP access list can be used to limit what HTTP traffic triggers authentication proxy. If used, the list is referenced as *std-access-list* (1 to 99). It must contain **permit** statements for the source addresses that trigger the authentication process. Other addresses that are denied are passed normally, without triggering authentication proxy. If no access is specified, all HTTP traffic is intercepted and is subject to authentication proxy.

d. Apply an authentication proxy rule to an inbound interface:

```
(interface) ip auth-proxy auth-proxy-name
```

The authentication proxy rule named *auth-proxy-name* is used to define whether incoming traffic requires authentication.

4. Configure user profiles in an AAA server.

a. Define an auth-proxy section in the user profile:

```
default authorization = permit
key = cisco
user = username {
login = cleartext password
service = auth-proxy
```

b. Define a privilege level for the user:

```
priv-lvl=15
```

The privilege level must be 15 for all users who are authorized through authentication proxy.

c. Define the dynamic access list entries for the user:

```
proxyacl#1="permit protocol any ..."
proxyacl#2="permit protocol any ..."
...
```

Enter the access list rules under the attribute values of the form proxyacl#n. The attributes must be entered exactly as if you were configuring access list statements on the router. Always use the source address **any** in the rules. As soon as authentication proxy imports the access list rules, it replaces **any** with the source address of the host that the user is using.

Example

Authentication proxy is configured to inspect all inbound HTTP traffic and to authenticate any users who aren't already authenticated. TACACS+ servers at 192.168.14.55 and 192.168.14.56 are used for authentication, authorization, and accounting in conjunction with authentication proxy. The authentication proxy rule named *Corporate* is defined so that all users using HTTP from any source address are required to authenticate. The AAA authorization policies configured in the TACACS+ servers are retrieved for each user to determine what resources the user is allowed to access.

```
aaa new-model
tacacs-server host 192.168.14.55
tacacs-server host 192.168.14.56
tacacs-server key mysecretkey
aaa authentication login default group tacacs+
aaa authorization auth-proxy default group tacacs+
aaa accounting auth-proxy default start-stop group tacacs+

access-list 10 deny any
ip http server
ip http authentication aaa
ip http access-class 10
ip auth-proxy auth-cache-time 120
ip auth-proxy name Corporate http

interface fastethernet 3/1
      ip address 10.14.21.10 255.255.255.0
      ip auth-proxy Corporate
```

12-4: Controlling Access with Lock and Key Security

- Lock and Key uses dynamic access lists to temporarily allow access for certain authenticated users.

- Traffic from users is normally blocked by an access list on a border router. To gain access, a user must open a Telnet session to that router and successfully authenticate.

- Access can be finely controlled, down to a per-user basis.

- After a dynamic access list entry has been created, it stays active for a preconfigured amount of time (based on an absolute or idle time) or until it is manually removed.

- New dynamic entries are added to the beginning of the dynamic access list.

Configuration

1. Create a dynamic access list.

a. Use a named extended IP access list.

- Create the access list and enable Telnet to the router:

```
(global) ip access list extended name
(named-access-list) permit tcp any host ip-address eq telnet
(named-access-list) deny ...
```

The extended IP access list named *name* is used to control inbound access through a router. You must permit Telnet access with the second command so that external users can Telnet to the router and open a dynamic entry. Use the *ip-address* of the inbound router interface. The **deny** command represents any other commands that are necessary to block inbound traffic into your router.

- Reference a named access list where dynamic entries will be put:

```
(named-access-list) dynamic name [timeout minutes] permit ...
```

The dynamic access list named *name* is used to contain dynamic or temporary entries that are added by Lock and Key. You don't need to create this list; the router creates it and adds or deletes entries to or from it as needed. The **timeout** keyword is used to set an absolute time in *minutes* (1 to 9999; the default is infinite) for the temporary entry to remain in effect.

The **permit** keyword should be used to define the conditions of the temporary access list entry. You can use a simple **permit ip any any** if you intend to trigger the temporary entries for a single host address. The temporary entry is added with one specific source address to the **any** destination address. Otherwise, you can trigger a temporary entry for an entire network address. In this case, use the **permit** keyword and define the specific protocol (if needed), the specific source network address and mask, and the specific destination network and mask. In other words, the temporary entry should open only specific access that was denied in the regular (nondynamic) access list.

b. Use a numbered extended IP access list.

- Create the access list and enable Telnet to the router:

```
(global) access-list number permit tcp any host ip-address eq telnet
(global) access-list number deny ...
```

The extended IP access list *number* (100 to 199 or 2600 to 2699) is used to control inbound access through a router. You must permit Telnet access with the second command so that external users can Telnet to the router and open a dynamic entry. Use the *ip-address* of the inbound router interface. The **deny** command represents any other commands that are necessary to block inbound traffic into your router.

- Reference a named access list where dynamic entries will be put:

  `(global) access-list number dynamic name [timeout minutes] permit ...`

  The dynamic access list named *name* is used to contain dynamic or temporary entries that are added by Lock and Key. You don't need to create this list; the router creates it and adds or deletes entries to or from it as needed. The **timeout** keyword is used to set an absolute time in *minutes* (1 to 9999; the default is infinite) for the temporary entry to remain in effect.

The **permit** keyword should be used to define the conditions of the temporary access list entry. You can use a simple **permit ip any any** if you intend to trigger the temporary entries for a single host address. The temporary entry is added with one specific source address to the **any** destination address. Otherwise, you can trigger a temporary entry for an entire network address. In this case, use the **permit** keyword and define the specific protocol (if needed), the specific source network address and mask, and the specific destination network and mask. In other words, the temporary entry should open only specific access that was denied in the regular (nondynamic) access list.

2. Apply the access list to an inbound interface:

   `(interface) ip access-group access-list in`

   The named or numbered *access-list* is used to filter inbound traffic on the interface. Filtering follows the normal access list definitions until dynamic entries are added by Lock and Key.

3. Use authentication on the VTY (Telnet) lines:

   `(line) login {local | tacacs}`

   -or-

   `(line) login authentication {default | list-name}`

   Authentication must be enabled on the VTY lines so that external users can Telnet to the router and attempt to authenticate themselves for a dynamic Lock and Key entry. If AAA is used (see Section 13-2 for more information), use the **login authentication** command. Otherwise, you can authenticate against usernames and passwords configured on the router with **login local** or against a TACACS server database with **login tacacs**.

4. Automatically add the dynamic access list entry:

   `(line) autocommand access-enable [host] [timeout minutes]`

   When a user authenticates on a VTY line, a command is automatically run to add the dynamic Lock and Key entry to allow temporary access. The **host** keyword can be used to cause a specific dynamic entry to be added for the IP address of the user's machine. If **host** is not used, the dynamic entry is created by inheriting the source and destination addresses and masks, as well as any protocol and port values, from the **dynamic** access list command. In this way, temporary access for a whole range of users or types of traffic can be granted by a single authentication. The **timeout** keyword can be used to define an idle time in *minutes* (1 to 9999; the default is infinite) that the dynamic entry remains in effect. As long as the dynamic access list entry is visited by the user's traffic within the idle time, the entry remains. Otherwise, it must time out or be manually removed.

> **Note**   The **autocommand** command can be omitted if an automatic dynamic entry is not desired. In this case, the user must Telnet to the router, be authenticated, and then manually run the EXEC command **access-enable host** to generate the dynamic entry.

5.   (Optional) Manually add an entry to the dynamic access list:

```
(global) access-template [access-list] [dynamic-name] [source]
   [destination] [timeout minutes]
```

Dynamic access list entries are usually created automatically from a template configured into a traffic filter access list containing the **dynamic** keyword. You can also manually add your own template to the dynamic access list with specific parameters. The template is associated with a named or numbered extended IP *access-list* that is acting as an inbound traffic filter. The *dynamic-name* points to the named dynamic access list where temporary entries are added. The *source* and *destination* addresses (including network addresses, the keywords **host** and **any**) can also be specified to override the original access list template. The **timeout** keyword can be used to specify an absolute time in *minutes* (1 to 9999; the default is infinite) for the temporary entries to remain in effect.

6.   (Optional) Manually remove temporary Lock and Key entries:

```
(exec) clear access-template [access-list] [dynamic-name] [source]
   [destination]
```

If a temporary Lock and Key entry is created without an absolute or idle timeout, the entry remains in effect indefinitely. You must then manually remove it with this command. With no arguments, all temporary entries are removed. You can specify the named or numbered *access-list*, the name of the dynamic access list as *dynamic-name*, and the *source* and *destination* addresses. To display the current dynamic access lists and the temporary entries, use **show access-lists** and look for lines beginning with "Dynamic."

Example

The router is configured for AAA authentication using a TACACS+ server at 192.168.4.3, followed by the router enable password (as a last resort). An access list named *mylist* is used to permit Telnet access to the inbound router interface. The list also denies any external access to the inside network 192.168.4.0. The dynamic access list *mydynlist* is referenced so that temporary Lock and Key entries can be added. The *mylist* access list is applied to the inbound Ethernet 0 interface.

After a user Telnets to the router and successfully authenticates, the autocommand is executed on the VTY line. In this case, autocommand runs **access-enable timeout 30**, which creates a temporary access list entry for the external host. The entry is a **permit** for the specific host to **any** address, matching the dynamic access list template. The user's temporary access will have a 30-minute idle timeout.

```
aaa new-model
aaa authentication login default group tacacs+ enable
tacacs-server host 192.168.4.3 key secret999

ip access list extended mylist
        permit tcp any host 172.19.7.1 eq telnet
        deny ip any 192.168.4.0 0.0.0.255
        dynamic mydynlist permit ip any any

interface ethernet 0
        ip address 172.19.7.1 255.255.255.0
        ip access-group mylist in

line vty 0 4
        login authentication default
        autocommand access-enable timeout 30
```

12-5: Filtering IP Sessions with Reflexive Access Lists

- Normally, inbound traffic is blocked on a border router by an access list. Reflexive access lists watch outbound network traffic and create temporary entries to allow the returning inbound traffic that is associated with an IP session.

- The temporary entries in a reflexive access list are removed as soon as the IP session ends.

- Reflexive access lists approximate the behavior of "stateful" firewalls, in that an outbound session triggers the permission of the inbound session traffic from the far end.

- For TCP, temporary entries are removed 5 seconds after the two FIN bits are received, or immediately after the RST bit is detected. For UDP and other connectionless protocols, the entries are removed after a timeout period from the last detected session packet.

- Reflexive access lists use extended named IP access lists only.

- Temporary entries appear as **permit** statements with the source and destination addresses and port numbers swapped in relation to the original outbound session.

Configuration

1. Create a named extended IP access list for outbound traffic:

   ```
   (global) ip access-list extended name
   (named-access-list) permit ...
   ```

   The access list named *name* filters the outbound traffic. The **permit** keyword and its arguments should be used to allow any traffic outbound from the "inside" that doesn't need the reflexive access list functionality.

2. Identify the outbound IP sessions that act as a reflexive trigger:

```
(named-access-list) permit protocol source [source-mask] destination
   [dest-mask] [operator port] reflect name [timeout seconds]
```

The **permit** command is specified as in a normal extended named IP access list. The initial session traffic that matches the protocol, source and destination addresses (can be addresses with masks, **host**, or **any**), and the optional port operator and port number is used to trigger a reflexive access list entry. The **reflect** keyword must be used, along with the *name* of a named extended IP access list that is used in the reverse direction. You don't have to configure the *name* access list. It is created automatically, and reflexive entries are added to it. If desired, a **timeout** value in *seconds* (1 to 2147483647; the default is the global timeout value) can be used to expire a reflexive entry after no session traffic is detected.

3. Apply the outbound access list to an interface:

```
(interface) ip access-group name out
```

The access list named *name* is used to filter outbound traffic on the border router. The list also triggers reflexive access list entries to be created for specific outbound sessions.

4. Create a named extended IP access list for inbound traffic:

```
(global) ip access-list extended name
(named-access-list) permit ...
```

The access list named *name* filters the inbound traffic. The **permit** keyword and its arguments should be used to allow any traffic inbound from the "outside" that is normally required and trusted. This can also include trusted traffic that is not initiated from the inside, such as routing updates.

5. Enable the addition of dynamic reflexive entries:

```
(named-access-list) evaluate name
```

The **evaluate** keyword uses any reflexive entries that have been automatically added to the *name* extended IP access list. Again, this list is created and maintained by the router according to the reflexive access list's activity. Reflexive entries are created in **permit** form, allowing inbound traffic for triggered sessions.

6. Apply the inbound access list to an interface:

```
(interface) ip access-group name in
```

The access list named *name* is used to filter inbound traffic on the border router. The interface used should be the same interface where outbound sessions triggered the reflexive access list entries. In this fashion, one border interface has both inbound and outbound access lists with reflexive functionality.

Section 12-5

Example

A reflexive access list is configured to watch outbound TCP and UDP traffic and create temporary inbound access list entries for those sessions. The extended access list *outbound* is used to trigger reflexive entries (access list *allowreplies*) for any TCP or UDP session initiated on the inside. All other IP traffic is permitted without triggering the reflexive process. The access list is applied to the external interface Ethernet 0 as an outgoing traffic filter.

Another extended access list *inbound* is used to permit any incoming HTTP traffic (because most web traffic would not be initiated from the inside). All other traffic is permitted only when the reflexive access list entries from list *allowreplies* are evaluated. The inbound list is applied to the external interface Ethernet 0 as an incoming traffic filter.

Notice that the reflexive access list keeps track of sessions by recording the source and destination addresses and the source and destination port numbers—for the returning traffic involved with both TCP and UDP sessions. This goes above and beyond what is possible with extended IP access lists, where return traffic for a session in progress can be detected only from the ACK and RST bits in the TCP headers (using the **established** keyword). Extended access lists offer no capability for detecting established or returning UDP session traffic.

```
ip access-list extended outbound
        permit tcp any any reflect allowreplies
        permit udp any any reflect allowreplies
        permit ip any any

ip access-list extended inbound
        permit tcp any any eq www
        evaluate allowreplies

interface ethernet 0
        ip access-group outbound out
        ip access-group inbound in
```

12-6: Prevent DoS Attacks with TCP Intercept

- TCP intercept watches TCP packets to determine whether connections are being requested but not completed.

- A Denial-of-Service attack can occur if TCP connections are being requested from an unreachable (or spoofed) source address. The target server is left with an abundance of half-opened connections and will eventually run out of memory.

- TCP intercept can operate in *intercept* mode, where the router actively follows these steps:

  Step 1. The router intercepts the TCP request (SYN) packet from the requester.

Step 2. The router sends a proxy reply to the requester on behalf of the target server (SYN-ACK).

Step 3. The router waits for the requester to follow with its acknowledgment (ACK).

Step 4. If the connection handshaking proceeds this far, the router sends the original request (SYN) to the target server. The router performs a proxy three-way handshake, as if the target were talking to the requester.

Step 5. The requester and the target server are allowed to carry on a normal TCP connection.

- In intercept mode, TCP intercept can become more aggressive when under a DoS attack with a large number of incoming incomplete connection requests. In aggressive mode, each new connection request causes a past incomplete connection to be deleted. The router also reduces the retransmission timeout by half and reduces the amount of time waiting for connections to be established by half.

- TCP intercept can also operate in *watch* mode, where the router passively watches to see if TCP connections become established. If connections are not established within a timeout period, the router sends a TCP reset (RST) to the target server to clear the half-open connection.

Configuration

1. Use an extended access list to identify TCP connection requests:

   (global) **access-list** *acc-list-number* **permit tcp any any**

   -or-

   (global) **access-list** *acc-list-number* **permit tcp any** *destination*
     destination-mask

   Any condition that is permitted by the access list (numbered 100 to 199) is sent to the TCP intercept software. The source address is always set to **any**, and the destination address can be **any** (watch all TCP connection attempts) or to specific destination hosts or networks with the *destination destination-mask* fields (watch only TCP connection attempts to certain targets).

2. Trigger TCP intercept with the access list:

   (global) **ip tcp intercept list** *acc-list-number*
   TCP intercept uses an extended IP access list numbered *acc-list-number*
   (100 to 199).

3. Set the TCP intercept mode:

   (global) **ip tcp intercept mode {intercept | watch}**

The **intercept** mode (the default) actively intercepts connection requests and acts as a proxy for both requester and target until the connection can be established. The **watch** mode passively watches connection requests and resets connections that don't get established.

4. (Optional) Tune TCP intercept behavior.

   a. Set the drop mode:

      `(global) ip tcp intercept drop-mode {oldest | random}`

      When TCP intercept becomes aggressive, it begins dropping the **oldest** (the default) half-open connection as each new connection request comes in. The **random** keyword can be used instead, causing half-open connections to be dropped at random.

   b. Set the timers.

      ■ (Watch mode) Set the watch mode timeout:

         `(global) ip tcp intercept watch-timeout seconds`

         If a connection is not established within *seconds* (greater than 0; the default is 30) of the request, the router sends a reset to the target server.

      ■ Set the connection reset hold time:

         `(global) ip tcp intercept finrst-timeout seconds`

         The router continues managing a connection *seconds* (greater than 0; the default is 5) after the FIN handshake or an RST occurs to close the connection.

      ■ Set the connection management time:

         `(global) ip tcp intercept connection-timeout seconds`

      The router continues managing a connection for *seconds* (greater than 0; the default is 86,400 seconds, or 24 hours) after there is no activity.

   c. Set the aggressive thresholds.

      ■ Set the connection thresholds for aggressive mode:

         `(global) ip tcp intercept max-incomplete {high | low} number`

         Aggressive mode is triggered when the number of incomplete or half-open connections rises above **high** *number* (1 to 2147483647; the default is 1100 connections). Aggressive mode ends when the number of incomplete connections falls below **low** *number* (1 to 2147483647; the default is 1100 connections).

      ■ Set the connection rates for aggressive mode:

         `(global) ip tcp intercept one-minute {high | low} number`

      Aggressive mode is triggered when the number of incomplete or half-open connections within the last minute rises above **high** *number* (1 to 2147483647; the default is 1100 connections). Aggressive mode ends when the number of incomplete connections per minute falls below **low** *number* (1 to 2147483647; the default is 1100 connections).

Example

TCP intercept is configured to manage TCP connection requests to targets in two server farm networks: 192.168.111.0 and 192.168.62.0. Intercept mode is used, and random connections are dropped.

```
access-list 140 permit tcp any 192.168.111.0 0.0.0.255
access-list 140 permit tcp any 192.168.62.0 0.0.0.255
ip tcp intercept list 140
ip tcp intercept mode intercept
ip tcp intercept drop-mode random
```

12-7: Intelligent Filtering with Context-Based Access Control (CBAC)

- CBAC acts as an intelligent traffic filter by monitoring the session states based on network, transport, and application layer information.

- CBAC supports inspection of the following protocols: TCP sessions, UDP sessions, CU-SeeMe (White Pine), FTP, H.323, HTTP (Java blocking), Microsoft NetShow, UNIX remote commands (rlogin, rexec, rsh, and so forth), RealAudio, RTSP, Sun RPC, SMTP, SQL*Net, StreamWorks, TFTP, and VDOLive.

- Outbound traffic is generally permitted through the router. CBAC creates temporary access list entries as certain outbound traffic is inspected. Return inbound traffic is permitted by these temporary entries.

- CBAC can perform intrusion detection based on SMTP traffic, sending SYSLOG messages during an attack.

Configuration

1. Choose a router interface where CBAC will operate.

   A router performing CBAC is considered a firewall, with an "inside" interface (the protected network side) and an "outside" interface (the unprotected network side). CBAC inspection can be configured on either the inside or outside interface—either is acceptable. However, you should choose the interface that gives you the greatest coverage of the network you want to protect.

   Also, you will be configuring two access lists to work with CBAC: one for outbound traffic (from the protected network) and one for inbound traffic (from the unprotected network). The access list configurations are straightforward. Pay close attention to how the access lists are applied, though. For example, if you choose to implement CBAC on an "outside" interface, be sure that the outbound traffic access list is applied going **out** and the inbound access list is applied **in**. If CBAC is used on an "inside" interface, the directions are reversed: the outbound traffic list is applied **in**, and the inbound traffic list is applied **out**. Picture yourself standing in the middle of the router, and think of the direction in which the outbound and inbound traffic travels as it arrives at or leaves the interface.

2. (Optional) Tune CBAC operation.

a. Set the time to wait for an established connection:

`(global) ip inspect tcp synwait-time seconds`

CBAC waits seconds (greater than 0; the default is 30) for a TCP connection to be established after the SYN. After that, CBAC drops the connection.

b. Set the time to manage a closed connection:

`(global) ip inspect tcp finwait-time seconds`

CBAC continues managing a TCP connection for *seconds* (greater than 0; the default is 5) after the FIN handshake closes the session.

c. Set the connection idle times:

`(global) ip inspect {tcp | udp} idle-time seconds`

CBAC continues managing a TCP session (**tcp**) for *seconds* (greater than 0; the default is 3600 seconds or 1 hour) and a UDP "session" (**udp**) for *seconds* (greater than 0; the default is 30) after no activity is detected.

d. Set the DNS idle timeout:

`(global) ip inspect dns-timeout seconds`

CBAC manages a DNS name lookup session for *seconds* (greater than 0; the default is 5) after no activity is detected.

e. Set the connection thresholds for aggressive mode:

`(global) ip inspect max-incomplete {high | low} number`

Aggressive mode is triggered when the number of incomplete or half-open TCP or UDP connections rises above **high** *number* (the default is 500 connections). Aggressive mode ends when the number of incomplete connections falls below **low** *number* (the default is 400 connections). Half-open TCP connections are not yet established, and half-open UDP connections have traffic in only one direction.

f. Set the connection rates for aggressive mode:

`(global) ip inspect one-minute {high | low} number`

Aggressive mode is triggered when the number of incomplete or half-open connections within the last minute rises above **high** *number* (the default is 500 connections). Aggressive mode ends when the number of incomplete connections per minute falls below **low** *number* (the default is 400 connections).

g. Set the thresholds for TCP connections to the same host:

```
(global) ip inspect tcp max-incomplete host number block-time minutes
```

If CBAC detects more than *number* (1 to 250; the default is 50 connections) of half-open TCP connections to the same host, it begins deleting the half-open connections. The **block-time** keyword is used to define how new connections are deleted. If *minutes* is 0 (the default), the oldest half-open connection is deleted for every new connection request received. If *minutes* is greater than 0, all half-open connections are deleted, and all new connections are blocked for *minutes*.

3. Use access lists to manage CBAC traffic inspection.

a. (Optional) Permit outbound traffic (from a protected network):

```
(global) access-list acc-list-number permit protocol source source-mask
    destination destination-mask [operator port]
```

If outbound traffic is to be filtered or limited, an access list numbered *acc-list-number* (100 to 199) can be used. You should permit all traffic that will be inspected by CBAC. If all traffic is to be permitted and inspected, the access list can be omitted, because all traffic is normally allowed to pass through an interface.

b. Filter inbound traffic (from an unprotected network).

■ Permit certain types of inbound ICMP traffic:

```
(global) access-list acc-list-number permit icmp any any echo-reply
(global) access-list acc-list-number permit icmp any internal-network
   mask time-exceeded
(global) access-list acc-list-number permit icmp any internal-network
   mask packet-too-big
(global) access-list acc-list-number permit icmp any internal-network
   mask traceroute
(global) access-list acc-list-number permit icmp any internal-network
   mask unreachable
```

CBAC doesn't inspect ICMP packets at all. Therefore, you should allow only certain types of ICMP messages into your protected network: ping replies (**echo-reply**), TTL exceeded (**time-exceeded**), path MTU discovery (**packet-too-big**), **traceroute**, and **unreachable**. All other types are implicitly denied at the end of the access list.

■ Deny spoofed IP addresses:

```
(global) access-list acc-list-number deny ip internal-network mask any
```

Spoofed IP addresses are used on inbound packets from the outside, using source addresses from the inside of your network. If allowed in, the packets can reach an internal target, but replies never find the original source.

In addition, inbound packets can have source addresses corresponding to the RFC 1918 routes or other illegal values: 10.0.0.0 (private class A network), 127.0.0.0 (reserved for loopback), 169.254.0.0 (used by Microsoft for failed DHCP), 172.16.0.0 to 172.31.0.0 (private class B networks), 192.168.0.0 (private class C networks), and 224.0.0.0 (multicast; never used as a source address). For these, additional commands should be added to the access list:

```
(global) access-list acc-list-number deny ip 10.0.0.0 0.255.255.255
any
(global) access-list acc-list-number deny ip 127.0.0.0 0.255.255.255
 any
(global) access-list acc-list-number deny ip 169.254.0.0 0.0.255.255
 any
(global) access-list acc-list-number deny ip 172.16.0.0 0.15.255.255
 any
(global) access-list acc-list-number deny ip 192.168.0.0 0.0.255.255
 any
(global) access-list acc-list-number deny ip 224.0.0.0 31.255.255.255
 any
```

■ Deny a broadcast source address:

```
(global) access-list acc-list-number deny ip host 255.255.255.255 any
```

■ Permit specific traffic not inspected by CBAC:

```
(global) access-list acc-list-number permit protocol source source-
mask
```

```
destination dest-mask [operator port]
```

For traffic that you don't intend CBAC to inspect, such as inbound routing updates, web browsing, and so forth, be sure to define **permit** commands to allow it.

■ Deny everything else:

```
(global) access-list acc-list-number deny ip any any
```

The "deny everything" command is implicit as the last statement in any access list, although it is not shown in the configuration. You can enter it manually, if desired, as a reminder of the final rule.

4. Define a CBAC inspection rule with one or more types.

a. Inspect supported application-layer protocols:

```
(global) ip inspect name inspection-name protocol [alert {on | off}]
   [audit-trail {on | off}] [timeout seconds]
```

An inspection rule named *inspection-name* is defined to inspect the *protocol:* TCP (**tcp**), UDP (**udp**), CU-SeeMe (**cuseeme**), FTP (**ftp**), H.323 (**h323**), Microsoft NetShow (**netshow**), UNIX remote commands (**rcmd**), RealAudio (**realaudio**), SMTP (**smtp**), SQL*Net (**sqlnet**), StreamWorks (**streamworks**), TFTP (**tftp**), or VDOLive (**vdolive**).

SYSLOG alert messages (**alert**) can be turned on or off to alert someone about a detected condition in real time. SYSLOG audit trail messages (**audit-trail**) can also be turned on or off to provide details about inspected sessions. The **timeout** keyword can be used to override the global TCP or UDP idle timeouts.

> **Note**   The inspection of NetMeeting 2.0 traffic requires both **h323** and **tcp** inspection. The **smtp** inspection drops any command except DATA, EXPN, HELO, HELP, MAIL, NOOP, QUIT, RCPT, RSET, SAML, SEND, SOML, and VRFY.

   b. Inspect Sun RPC:

```
(global) ip inspect name inspection-name rpc program-number number
  [wait-time minutes] [alert {on | off}] [audit-trail {on | off}]
  [timeout seconds]
```

An inspection rule named *inspection-name* is defined to inspect the Sun RPC program number given by *number*. The **wait-time** keyword can be used to keep the temporary CBAC entry in effect for subsequent connections between the same hosts for *minutes* (the default is 0).

SYSLOG alert messages (**alert**) can be turned on or off to alert someone about a detected condition in real time. SYSLOG audit trail messages (**audit-trail**) can also be turned on or off to provide details about inspected sessions. The **timeout** keyword can be used to override the global TCP or UDP idle timeouts.

   c. Inspect fragments:

```
(global) ip inspect name inspection-name fragment [max number] [timeout
  seconds]
```

An inspection rule named *inspection-name* is defined to inspect fragmented packets. Unless the initial fragmented packet passes through CBAC, all noninitial fragmented packets are dropped. The maximum number of unassembled packets kept by CBAC can be set with **max** *number* (50 to 10000; the default is 256 packets). The **timeout** keyword sets the amount of time that a fragmented packet is kept by CBAC in *seconds* (the default is 1 second).

   d. Block Java applets.

   ■   (Optional) Specify "friendly" Java sites:

```
(global) access-list acc-list-number permit ip-address
```

The standard IP access list numbered *acc-list-number* (100 to 199) permits the IP address of a trusted or friendly HTTP site with Java applets. A named standard IP access list is also acceptable for this purpose.

■ Define Java blocking:

```
(global) ip inspect name inspection-name http [java-list access-list]
   [alert {on | off}] [audit-trail {on | off}] [timeout seconds]
```

An inspection rule named *inspection-name* is defined to inspect and block Java applets. The **java-list** keyword defines a standard IP *access-list* (named or numbered) that is used to identify HTTP sites with acceptable Java applets. If the **java-list** keyword is omitted, all Java applets are blocked.

> **Note**   Only unencapsulated (not in .zip or .jar format) Java applets can be inspected and blocked. Applets loaded by FTP or gopher, as well as applets from a nonstandard HTTP port (including HTTPS or port 443), cannot be inspected.

5. Configure CBAC inspection on an interface:

```
(interface) ip inspect inspection-name {in | out}
```

The CBAC inspection rule named *inspection-name* is used on the interface to inspect traffic in either the **in** or **out** direction (relative to the interface).

6. Perform logging and audit trail functions.

a. Set up logging:

```
(global) service timestamps log datetime
(global) logging ip-address
(global) logging facility facility
(global) logging trap level
```

SYSLOG service is enabled on the router to the host at *ip-address*. SYSLOG messages are sent at *facility*, and traps are sent at *level*. See Section 1-5 for more information.

b. Enable the CBAC audit trail:

```
(global) ip inspect audit-trail
```

Example

CBAC is configured as a firewall on a router. Ethernet 0 is connected to the "inside" protected network, and Ethernet 1 is on the "outside." Access list 102 is used to filter inbound traffic from the outside network. ICMP is not inspected by CBAC, so only certain types of ICMP messages are permitted to come in. The access list also denies source addresses that are spoofed. WWW traffic is permitted inbound to the 192.168.17.0 network, because it is initiated from the outside. All other traffic is denied.

CBAC inspection is configured for inbound traffic on the inside interface, which is actually traffic destined for the outside network. As soon as CBAC inspects outgoing connections, it adds temporary entries to access list 102 that permit return traffic for those sessions. CBAC is configured to inspect FTP, RealAudio, SMTP, TCP, and UDP.

Notice that CBAC goes above and beyond the capabilities of extended IP access lists. Both TCP and UDP sessions can be tracked, allowing traffic from sessions that were initiated on the inside to return. Extended access lists are limited to detecting only whether the ACK and RST bits are set in the TCP headers of session traffic (using the "established" keyword). In addition, they cannot monitor the return traffic of UDP sessions at all.

```
ip inspect name filter ftp
ip inspect name filter realaudio
ip inspect name filter smtp
ip inspect name filter tcp
ip inspect name filter udp


interface Ethernet0
        description Internal LAN (inside)      ip address 192.168.17.3
255.255.255.0
        ip inspect filter in


interface Ethernet1
        description External LAN (outside)
        ip address 4.3.51.130 255.255.255.252
        ip access-group 102 in


access-list 102 permit icmp any any echo-reply
access-list 102 permit icmp any 192.168.17.0 0.0.0.255 time-exceeded
access-list 102 permit icmp any 192.168.17.0 0.0.0.255 packet-too-big
access-list 102 permit icmp any 192.168.17.0 0.0.0.255 traceroute
access-list 102 permit icmp any 192.168.17.0 0.0.0.255 unreachable
access-list 102 deny ip 192.168.17.0 0.0.0.255 any
access-list 102 deny ip 10.0.0.0 0.255.255.255 any
access-list 102 deny ip 127.0.0.0 0.255.255.255 any
access-list 102 deny ip 169.254.0.0 0.0.255.255 any
access-list 102 deny ip 172.16.0.0 0.15.255.255 any
access-list 102 deny ip 192.168.0.0 0.0.255.255 any
access-list 102 deny ip 224.0.0.0 31.255.255.255 any
access-list 102 deny ip host 255.255.255.255 any
access-list 102 permit tcp any 192.168.17.0 0.0.0.255 eq www
access-list 102 deny ip any any
```

12-8: Detect Attacks and Threats with the IOS Intrusion Prevention System

- The Intrusion Prevention System (IPS) is configured as an inline sensor, watching packets as they flow through a router.

- The IOS IPS comes with 100 built-in signatures of common attacks present in network traffic. The IOS IPS can support more than 1200 signatures. How many signatures a router supports is dependent on the amount of RAM installed in the router.

- When a match for an IPS signature is found, the IPS can send alerts using standard SYSLOG messages or by using the Security Device Event Exchange (SDEE) protocol.

- The IOS IPS can also take action when a threat is detected by dropping suspicious packets, resetting TCP connections, blocking traffic from the attacker for a specified period of time (DenyAttackerInline), or blocking traffic on the connection where the attack was seen for a specified period of time (DenyFlowInline).

In addition to the 100 built-in signatures, routers can be configured for additional signatures by using signature definition files (.sdf). The number of additional signatures a router can support is dependent on the amount of installed RAM. Routers with less than 128 MB of RAM come with a static file called **attack-drop.sdf** that contains 83 signatures. Routers with 128 MB to 256 MB of RAM come with the 128MB.sdf file that contains approximately 300 signatures. Routers with more than 256 MB of RAM come with the 256MB.sdf file that contains approximately 500 signatures. You should regularly check Cisco.com for the most recent signature file.

Table 12-1 lists the 83 attack signatures available in the attack-drop .sdf file. All routers with IOS IPS support these signatures at a minimum. The SME field indicates the signature microengine for the signature. Action options include A (alarm), D (drop), and R (reset).

Configuration

1. Specify the SDF location:

   ```
   (global) ip ips sdf location location
   ```

   By default, the router uses built-in signatures (enabled with the command **ip ips builtin** command). There are 100 built-in signatures (132 if you include subsignatures). To use more signatures, configure this command with the path and filename to the .sdf file.

2. Configure the failure parameter if the signature microengine (SME) is not operational:

   ```
   (global) ip ips fail [open | close]
   ```

Table 12-1 *Attack Signatures*

Signature ID: SubSig	Signature Name	Action1	SME	Signature Description
1006:0	IP options-Strict Source Route	A, D	ATOMIC.IPOPTIONS	Triggers on receipt of an IP datagram in which the IP option list for the datagram includes option 2 (Strict Source Routing).
1102:0	Impossible IP Packet	A, D	ATOMIC.L3.IP	Triggers when an IP packet arrives with source equal to destination address. This signature catches the Land Attack.
1104:0	IP Localhost Source Spoof	A, D	ATOMIC.L3.IP	Triggers when an IP packet with the address of 127.0.0.1, a local host IP address that should never be seen on the network, is detected. This signature can detect the Blaster attack.
1108:0	IP Packet with Proto 11	A, D	ATOMIC.L3.IP	Alarms upon detecting IP traffic with the protocol set to 11. There have been known "backdoors" running on IP protocol 11.
2154:0	Ping Of Death Attack	A, D	ATOMIC.L3.IP	Triggers when an IP datagram is received with the protocol field in the IP header set to 1 (Internet Control Message Protocol [ICMP]); the Last Fragment bit is set. The IP offset (which represents the starting position of this fragment in the original packet and which is in 8-byte units) plus the rest of the packet is greater than the maximum size for an IP packet.

Table 12-1 *Attack Signatures*

Signature ID: SubSig ID	Signature Name	Action1	SME	Signature Description
3038:0	Fragmented NULL TCP Packet	A, D	ATOMIC.TCP	Triggers when a single, fragmented TCP packet with none of the SYN, FIN, ACK, or RST flags set has been sent to a specific host. A reconnaissance sweep of your network might be in progress.
3039:0	Fragmented Orphaned FIN packet	A, D	ATOMIC.TCP	Triggers when a single, fragmented, orphan TCP FIN packet is sent to a privileged port (having a port number less than 1024) on a specific host. A reconnaissance sweep of your network might be in progress.
3040:0	NULL TCP Packet	A, D	ATOMIC.TCP	Triggers when a single TCP packet with none of the SYN, FIN, ACK, or RST flags set has been sent to a specific host. A reconnaissance sweep of your network might be in progress.
3041:0	SYN/FIN Packet	A, D	ATOMIC.TCP	Triggers when a single TCP packet with the SYN and FIN flags set is sent to a specific host. A reconnaissance sweep of your network might be in progress. The use of this type of packet indicates an attempt to conceal the sweep.

Table 12-1 *Attack Signatures*

Signature ID: SubSig ID	Signature Name	Action1	SME	Signature Description
3043:0	Fragmented SYN/FIN Packet	A, D	ATOMIC.TCP	Triggers when a single, fragmented TCP packet with the SYN and FIN flags set is sent to a specific host. A reconnaissance sweep of your network might be in progress. The use of this type of packet indicates an attempt to conceal the sweep.
3129:0	Mimail Virus C Variant File Attachment	A, D, R	SERVICE. SMTP	Fires when an email attachment matching the C Variant of the Mimail virus is detected. The virus sends itself to recipients as the email attachment "photos.zip" that contains the file "photos.jpg.exe" and has "our private photos" in the email subject line. If launched, the virus harvests email addresses and possible mail servers from the infected system.
3140:3	Bagle Virus Activity	A, D, R	SERVICE.HTTP	Fires when HTTP propagation using .jpeg associated with the .Q variant is detected.
3140:4	Bagle Virus Activity	A, D, R	SERVICE.HTTP	Fires when HTTP propagation using .php associated with the .Q variant is detected.
3300:0	NetBIOS OOB Data	A, D	ATOMIC.TCP	Triggers when an attempt to send Out Of Band data to port 139 is detected.

Section 12-8

Table 12-1 *Attack Signatures*

Signature ID: SubSig ID	Signature Name	Action1	SME	Signature Description
5045:0	WWW xterm display attack	A, D, R	SERVICE.HTTP	Triggers when any cgi-bin script attempts to execute the command **xterm -display**. An attempt to illegally log into your system might be in progress.
5047:0	WWW Server Side Include POST attack	A, D, R	SERVICE.HTTP	Triggers when an attempt is made to embed a server side include (SSI) in an http POST command. An attempt to illegally access system resources might be in progress.
5055:0	HTTP Basic Authenticati on Overflow	A, D	SERVICE.HTTP	A buffer overflow can occur on vulnerable web servers if a large username and password combination is used with basic authentication.
5071:0	WWW msacds.dll Attack	A, D, R	SERVICE.HTTP	An attempt has been made to execute commands or view secured files, with privileged access. Administrators are highly recommended to check the affected systems to ensure that they have not been illicitly modified.
5081:0	WWW WinNT cmd.exe Access	A, D, R	SERVICE.HTTP	Triggers when the use of the Windows NT cmd.exe is detected in a URL. This signature can detect the NIMDA attack.

Table 12-1 *Attack Signatures*

Signature ID: SubSig ID	Signature Name	Action1	SME	Signature Description
5114: 0 5114:1 5114:2	WWW IIS Unicode Attack	A, D, R	SERVICE.HTTP	Triggers when an attempt to exploit the Unicode ../ directory traversal vulnerability is detected. Looks for the commonly exploited combinations included in publicly available exploit scripts. SubSig 2 is known to detect the NIMDA attack.
5126:0	WWW IIS .ida Indexing Service Overflow	A, D, R	SERVICE.HTTP	Alarms if web traffic is detected with the ISAPI extension .ida? and a data size of greater than 200 characters.
5159:0	phpMyAdmin Cmd Exec	A, D, R	SERVICE.HTTP	Triggers when access to sql.php with the arguments' goto and btnDrop=No is detected.
5184:0	Apache Authentication Module ByPass	A, D, R	SERVICE.HTTP	Fires upon detecting a select statement on the Authorization line of an HTTP header.
5188:0	HTTP Tunneling SubSig 0: GotomyPC	A, D, R	SERVICE.HTTP	Triggers when a computer connects to gotomyPC site.
5188:1	HTTP Tunneling SubSig 1: FireThru	A, D, R	SERVICE.HTTP	Triggers when an attempt to use /cgi-bin/proxy is detected. The /cgi-bin/proxy is used to tunnel connections to other ports using web ports.

Table 12-1 *Attack Signatures*

Signature ID: SubSig ID	Signature Name	Action1	SME	Signature Description
5188:2	HTTP Tunneling SubSig 2: HTTP Port	A, D, R	SERVICE.HTTP	Triggers when a connection is made to exectech-va.com. The site runs a server, which connects to the requested resource and passes the information back to the client on web ports.
5188:3	HTTP Tunneling SubSig 3: httptunnel	A, D, R	SERVICE.HTTP	Triggers when /index/html? is detected on POST request.
5245:0	HTTP 1.1 Chunked Encoding Transfer	A, D, R	SERVICE.HTTP	Fires when HTTP 1.1 chunked encoding transfer activity is detected. This signature is known to detect the Scalper Worm.
5326:0	Root.exe access	A, D, R	SERVICE.HTTP	Alarms upon detecting an HTTP request for root.exe. This signature is known to detect the NIMDA attack.
5329:0	Apache/mod_ssl Worm Probe	A, D, R	SERVICE.HTTP	Fires when a probe by the Apache/mod_ssl worm is detected. If the worm detects a vulnerable web server, a buffer overflow attack is sent to HTTPS port (TCP 443) of the web server. The worm then attempts to propagate itself to the newly infected web server and begins scanning for new hosts to attack.

Table 12-1 *Attack Signatures*

Signature ID: SubSig ID	Signature Name	Action1	SME	Signature Description
5364:0	IIS WebDAV Overflow	A, D, R	SERVICE.HTTP	Fires when a long HTTP request (65,000+ characters) is detected with an HTTP header option "Translate:". An attack to exploit a weakness in the WebDAV component of the IIS web server might be in progress.
5390:0	Swen Worm HTTP Counter Update Attempt	A, D, R	SERVICE.HTTP	Triggers when an attempt to access the URL "/bin/counter.gif/link=bacillus" is detected. A system might be infected by the Swen worm trying the update a counter on a web page located on the server "ww2.fce.vutbr.cz."
5400:0	Beagle.B (Bagle.B) Web Beacon	A, D, R	SERVICE.HTTP	Fires when a request is made for the script 1.php or 2.php residing on the hosts "www.47df.de" or "www.strato.de," followed by the argument indicating the trojan's listening port number, p=8866.
6055:0 6055:1 6055:2	DNS Inverse Query Buffer Overflow	A, D R for sub-sig 1, 2	SERVICE.DNS	Triggers when an IQUERY request arrives with a data section greater than 255 characters.

Table 12-1 *Attack Signatures*

Signature ID: SubSig ID	Signature Name	Action1	SME	Signature Description
6056:0 6056:1 6056:2	DNS NXT Buffer Overflow	A, D R for sub-sig 1, 2	SERVICE.DNS	Triggers when a Domain Name System (DNS) server response arrives with a long NXT resource where the length of the resource data is greater than 2069 bytes or the length of the TCP stream containing the NXT resource is greater than 3000 bytes.
6057:0 6057:1 6057:2	DNS SIG Buffer Overflow	A, D R for sub-sig 1, 2	SERVICE.DNS	Triggers when a DNS server response arrives with a long SIG resource where the length of the resource data is greater than 2069 bytes or the length of the TCP stream that contains the SIG resource is greater than 3000 bytes.
6058:0 6058:1	DNS SRV DoS	A, D R for sub-sig 1	SERVICE.DNS	Alarms when a DNS query type SRV and DNS query class IN is detected with more than ten pointer jumps in the SRV resource record.
6059:0 6059:1 6059:2	DNS TSIG Overflow	A, D R for sub-sig 2	SERVICE.DNS	Alarms when a DNS query type TSIG is detected and the domain name is greater than 255 characters. This signature is known to detect the Lion work.

Table 12-1   *Attack Signatures*

Signature ID: SubSig ID	Signature Name	Action1	SME	Signature Description
6060:0 6060:1 6060:2 6060:3	DNS Complian Overflow	A, D R for subsig 2, 3	SERVICE.DNS	Alarms when a Name Server (NS) record is detected with a domain name greater than 255 characters and the IP address is 0.0.0.0, 255.255.255.255 or a multi-cast address of the form 224.x.x.x.
6100:0 6100:1	RPC Port Registration	A, D R for sub-sig 1	SERVICE.RPC	Triggers when attempts are made to register new RPC services on a target host. Port registration is the method used by new servic-es to report their presence to the portmapper and to gain access to a port. Their pres-ence is then advertised by the portmapper.
6101:0 6101:1	RPC Port Unregistratio n	A, D R for sub-sig 1	SERVICE.RPC	Triggers when attempts are made to unregister existing Remote Procedure Call (RPC) services on a target host. Port unregistration is the method used by services to report their absence to the portmapper and to remove themselves from the active port map.
6104:0 6104:1	RPC Set Spoof	A, D R for sub-sig 1	SERVICE.RPC	Triggers when an RPC set request with a source address of 127.x.x.x is detected.

Table 12-1 *Attack Signatures*

Signature ID: SubSig ID	Signature Name	Action1	SME	Signature Description
6105:0 6105:1	RPC Unset Spoof	A, D R for subsig 1	SERVICE.RPC	Triggers when an RPC unset request with a source address of 127.x.x.x is detected.
6188:0	statd dot dot	A, D	SERVICE.RPC	Alarms upon detecting a dot dot slash (../) sequence sent to the statd RPC service.
6189:0 6189:1	statd auto-mount attack	A, D R for subsig 1	SERVICE.RPC	Alarms upon detecting a statd bounce attack on the automount process. This attack targets a vulnerability in the automount process that could be exploited only via localhost.
6190:0 6190:1	statd Buffer Overflow	A, D R for subsig 1	SERVICE.RPC	Triggers when a large statd request is sent. This attack could be an attempt to over-flow a buffer and gain access to system resources.
6191:0 6191:1	RPC.tooltalk buffer over-flow	A, D R for subsig 1	SERVICE.RPC	Fires when an attempt is made to overflow an internal buffer in the tooltalk rpc program.
6192:0 6192:1	RPC mountd Buffer Overflow	A, D R for subsig 1	SERVICE.RPC	Triggers on an attempt to overflow a buffer in the RPC mountd application. This attack might result in unau-thorized access to system resources.
6193:0 6193:1	RPC CMSD Buffer Overflow	A, D R for subsig 1	SERVICE.RPC	Fires when an attempt is made to overflow an internal buffer in the Calendar Manager Service Daemon, rpc.cmsd.

Table 12-1   *Attack Signatures*

Signature ID: SubSig ID	Signature Name	Action1	SME	Signature Description
6194:0 6194:1	sadmind RPC Buffer Overflow	A, D R for subsig 1	SERVICE.RPC	Fires when a call to RPC program number 100232 procedure 1 with a UDP packet length greater than 1024 bytes is detected.
6195:0 6195:1	RPC amd Buffer Overflow	A, D R for subsig 1	SERVICE.RPC	Detects the exploitation of the RPC AMD Buffer Overflow vulnerability. The trigger for this signature is an RPC call to the berkeley automounter daemons rpc program (300019) procedure 7 that has a UDP length greater than 1024 bytes or a TCP stream length greater than 1024 bytes. The TCP stream length is defined by the contents of the two bytes preceding the RPC header in a TCP packet.
6196:0 6196:1	snmpXdmid Buffer Overflow	A, D R for subsig 1	SERVICE.RPC	Fires when an abnormally long call to the RPC program 100249 (snmpXdmid) and procedure 257 is detected.
6197:0 6197:1	rpc yppaswdd overflow	A, D R for subsig 0	SERVICE.RPC	Fires when an overflow attempt is detected. This alarm looks for an abnormally large argument in the attempt to access yppaswdd.
6276:0 6276:1	TooltalkDB overflow	A, D R for subsig 1	SERVICE.RPC	Alarms upon detecting an RPC connection to rpc program number 100083 using procedure 103 with a buffer greater than 1024.

Table 12-1 *Attack Signatures*

Signature ID: SubSig ID	Signature Name	Action1	SME	Signature Description
9200:0	Back Door Response (TCP 12345)	A, D	ATOMIC.TCP	Fires upon detecting a TCP SYN/ACK packet from port 12345, which is a known trojan port for NetBus as others.
9201:0	Back Door Response (TCP 31337)	A, D	ATOMIC.TCP	Fires upon detecting a TCP SYN/ACK packet from port 31337, which is a known trojan port for BackFire.
9202:0	Back Door Response (TCP 1524)	A, D	ATOMIC.TCP	Fires upon detecting a TCP SYN/ACK packet from port 1524, which is a common back door placed on machines by worms and hackers.
9203:0	Back Door Response (TCP 2773)	A, D	ATOMIC.TCP	Fires upon detecting a TCP SYN/ACK packet from port 2773, which is a known trojan port for SubSeven.
9204:0	Back Door Response (TCP 2774)	A, D	ATOMIC.TCP	Fires upon detecting a TCP SYN/ACK packet from port 2774, which is a known trojan port for SubSeven.

By default, a router fails to open and forward all traffic if the signature microengine is not operational. If you configure the router to fail closed, the router drops all traffic if the SME is not operational and during the time when the SME is recompiling the signatures.

3. Create an IPS rule:

```
(global) ip ips name list acl
```

An IPS rule references an access list. Traffic permitted in the access list is scanned whereas traffic denied in the access list will bypass the scanning engine.

4. Apply the IPS rule on an interface:

```
(interface) ip ips name [in | out]
```

IPS rules are typically applied inbound as the traffic enters a router, but they can also be configured in the outbound direction.

5. (Optional) Disable or delete signatures you do not want to use:

(global) **ip ips signature** *signature-number sub-signature-number* [**disable** | **delete**]

You should either disable or delete signatures you do not want to use on your router.

6. (Optional) Filter signatures to be used only for certain hosts or networks.

(global) **ip ips signature** *signature-number sub-signature-number* **list** *acl*

You can filter the IOS IPS so that it applies only the signature for certain networks or hosts. Traffic permitted in the access list will be scanned

Note You need to reapply the IPS rule on an interface anytime you make a change. To do this, remove the IPS rule with the interface **no ip ips** *name* [**in** | **out**] command; then reapply it with the **ip ips** *name* [**in** | **out**] command.

Example

In the follow example, a router is configured to use a signature file in flash called 256MB.sdf. The router is configured to drop all connections if the signature microengine is not operational. The IPS rule IPSRULE scans all traffic from the 172.16.15.128/28 sub-network to the 172.16.32.0/21 subnetwork. Traffic from a host with the IP address 172.16.15.140 will not be scanned against signature 2208. This rule is applied on the FastEthernet0/0 interface in the inbound direction.

```
ip ips sdf location flash:256MB.sdf
ip ips fail close
ip ips IPSRULE list 100
ip ips signature 2208 0 list 101
!
access-list 100 permit ip 172.16.15.128 0.0.0.15 172.16.32.0 0.0.7.255
access-list 101 permit ip host 172.16.15.140 any
!
interface fastethernet0/0
 ip ips IPSRULE in
```

12-9: Control Plane Security

Control Plane Policing (CoPP) protects both the control and management traffic on your network. Control plane traffic is any process that runs at the process level of the route processor, such as routing protocols. Management traffic includes traffic related to managing your router, such as NTP and SNMP. CoPP was first released in Cisco IOS Software Release 12.2(18)s.

With CoPP, the control plane is treated as its own entity with ingress and egress ports. Configuring CoPP helps protect your router against denial of service (DoS) attacks.

Configuration

1. Create an access list for control/management traffic. In your access list, deny traffic that you do not want policed. In other words, deny legitimate control and management traffic that you trust. Permit traffic that you want policed (untrusted traffic).

   ```
   (global) access-list acl# [permit | deny] protocol source-address wildcard-mask
   [operand value] destination-address wildcard-mask [operand value]
   ```

   See Chapter 14, "Access Lists and Expressions," for more on how to configure access lists.

2. Configure a class map and policy map to police traffic permitted in the access list:

   ```
   (global) class-map [match-any | match-all] class-map-name
   (global) policy-map policy-map-name
   ```

   See Chapter 9, "Quality of Service," for more on how to configure class maps and policy maps.

3. Apply the policy to the control plane:

   ```
   (global) control-plane
   (control-plane) service-policy input policy-name
   ```

   Enter control-plane configuration mode with the global configuration **control-plane** command. Then, apply the policy map to the control plane.

Example

Telnet traffic from 10.5.5.5.5 to the router is trusted and is not policed. All other traffic is being policed. Any traffic that exceeds 8 kbps is dropped:

```
access-list 100 deny tcp host 10.5.5.5 any eq telnet
access-list 100 permit tcp any any eq telnet
!
class-map match-any CONTROL_CLASS
 match access-group 100
!
policy-map CONTROL_POLICY
```

```
 class CONTROL_CLASS
   policy 8000 conform-action transmit exceed-action drop
 !
 control-plane
   service-poolicy input CONTROL_POLICY
```

12-10: AutoSecure

The Cisco AutoSecure option can automatically configure your router with the recommended configuration to secure your router. There are more than 80 commands applied on a typical router when this feature is enabled. AutoSecure locks down the following:

- **Management plane services**—Finger, PAD, UDP/TCP small servers, password encryptin, TCP keepalives, CDP, BOOTP, HTTP, source routing, gratuitous ARP, proxy ARP, ICMP (redirects, mask replies), directed broadcast, MOP, banner

- **Forwarding plane services**—CEF, traffic filtering with ACLs

- **Firewall services**—IOS firewall inspection for common protocols

- **Login functions**—password security

- **NTP**

- **SSH access**

- **TCP intercept services**

Starting with Cisco IOS Software Release 12.3(8)T, Cisco stores a pre-autosecure configuration snapshot in the pre_autosec.cfg file in Flash. You can roll back your configuration with the privileged EXEC **configure replace flash:pre_autosec.cfg** command.

Configuration

(exec) **auto secure [management | forwarding] [no-interact | full] [ntp | login | ssh | firewall | tcp-intercept]**

You can run **the auto secure** command in full mode, noninteractive mode, or only for a specific service you want to secure. In full mode, you are prompted with questions about how you want to secure your router. In noninteractive mode, the router automatically applies the recommended commands to secure your router. You can also choose to secure just the management plane, forwarding plane, NTP service, login access, SSH access, IOS firewall, or TCP intercept feature using the **respective** keyword.

Example

The following command executes auto secure in noninteractive mode:

```
(exec) auto secure no-interact
```

Further Reading

Refer to the following recommended sources for further information about the topics covered in this chapter:

Cisco Secure Internet Security Solutions, by Andrew Mason and Mark Newcomb, Cisco Press, ISBN 1587050161.

Designing Network Security, by Merike Kaeo, Cisco Press, ISBN 1578700434.

Managing Cisco Network Security, by Michael Wenstrom, Cisco Press, ISBN 1578701031.

Chapter 13

Virtual Private Networks

This chapter discusses how to configure and use the following virtual private networking (VPN) features:

- **13-1: Using Internet Key Exchange (IKE) for VPNs**—IKE provides a standardized means for maintaining and exchanging encryption and authentication keys between routers and other IPSec VPN devices. IKE can also integrate with certificate authorities for centralized certificate management.

- **13-2: IPSec VPN Tunnels**—IP Security (IPSec) provides a standardized way to secure data transmission over a public or unprotected network. Data can be encrypted with DES, 3DES, or AES, authenticated at the packet level to ensure data integrity, and authenticated to verify the source of the data packets.

- **13-3: High Availability Features**—Cisco routers have several features to provide high availability to your VPNs. These include Dead Peer Detection (DPD), Reverse Route Injection (RRI), Hot Standby Router Protocol (HSRP) support for IPsec VPNs, and Stateful Switchover (SSO).

- **13-4: Dynamic Multipoint VPNs (DMVPNs)**—In a hub and spoke topology, it can be daunting and error prone to configure multiple crypto maps between sites. This becomes especially challenging when public IP addresses are dynamically assigned on the spoke sites. DMVPNs address these challenges by having a single crypto profile on the hub router and having the spoke routers dynamically register their public IP addresses with the hub router. DMVPNs enable for dynamic VPNs to be created between spokes by tunneling through the hub router. DMVPNs use multipoint Generic Route Encapsulation (mGRE) tunnels and the Next Hop Resolution Protocol (NHRP) to discover endpoint IP addresses and dynamically create tunnels.

- **13-5: Secure Socket Layer VPNs**—SSL VPNs enable remote users to establish a secure VPN tunnel to a network using a web browser. Users log into an SSL-enabled web portal and, when authenticated, a secure VPN is established between them and the VPN endpoint.

13-1: Using Internet Key Exchange (IKE) for VPNs

- IPSec VPN peers must exchange some form of authentication keys in order to have a trust relationship. IKE is a standardized way to manage and exchange keys for IPSec. Although IPSec can be used without IKE, IKE provides a flexible and scalable means of managing keys.

- IKE is based on RFC 2409.

- The Internet Security Association and Key Management Protocol (ISAKMP) provides the mechanism of key exchange. It is used by both IKE and IPSec and is based on RFC 2408.

- As soon as IKE negotiations are successful between two peers, IKE creates a *security association* (SA) to the remote peer. SAs are unidirectional; two SAs actually exist between two peers.

- Preshared secret keys can be configured between VPN peers. This process is simple to set up but difficult to maintain for a large number of peers.

- A Certification Authority (CA) can be used to authenticate VPN peers on a more flexible, larger scale. The CA is a trusted source of digital certificates, each of which must be "signed" by the CA itself.

- IKE is compatible with these CAs: Baltimore unicert, Entrust VPN connector, Microsoft Windows 2000, Netscape CMS, and VeriSign onsite.

- IKE operates in two phases: phase 1, where keys are exchanged and an SA is established, and phase 2, where keys and SAs are established for IPSec. Information exchanged during both phases is secured, and the identities of the peers are usually hidden from view on the network.

- IKE supports multiple policies, such that the router searches through a list of policies to find one that matches the capabilities of a negotiating peer.

- IKE mode can be used to provide a VPN peer with a protected IP address and other network parameters during IKE negotiation. This is useful when the remote clients have dynamic IP addresses from their ISPs or corporate networks and you can't pre-configure the remote peer host names or addresses.

> **Note**   IKE uses UDP port 500 for negotiations. Be sure port 500 is not blocked.

Configuration

1. (Optional) Enable or disable IKE:

   (global) **crypto isakmp enable**

   -or-

   (global) **no crypto isakmp enable**

IKE is enabled by default on all interfaces. To disable IKE, use the **no** form of this command. If IKE is disabled, many IPSec features will become static.

2. Create an IKE policy.

   a. Define the policy:

   ```
   (global) crypto isakmp policy priority
   ```

   The policy is given a unique arbitrary *priority* number (1 to 10000, where 1 is the lowest). IKE is organized into policies that are matched in sequential order (lowest to highest).

   b. (Optional) Define the encryption algorithm:

   ```
   (isakmp) encryption {des | 3des | aes | aes 192 | aes 256}
   ```

   The encryption mode can be 56-bit DES-CBC (**des**, the default), 168-bit 3DES (**3des**), 128-bit AES (**aes**), 192-bit AES (**aes 192**), or 256-bit AES (**aes 256**).

   c. (Optional) Define the hash algorithm:

   ```
   (isakmp) hash {sha | md5}
   ```

   The hash algorithm can be **sha** (an HMAC variant of SHA-1, the default) or **md5** (an HMAC variant of MD5). MD5 has a smaller digest but is slightly slower.

   d. (Optional) Define the authentication method:

   ```
   (isakmp) authentication {rsa-sig | rsa-encr | pre-share}
   ```

   The authentication method can be **rsa-sig** (RSA signatures; requires the use of a CA and offers nonrepudiation; the default), **rsa-encr** (RSA encryption; a CA is not required; offers repudiation), or **pre-share** (keys are preshared through manual configuration). For the RSA methods, public keys must be shared between peers either by manual configuration of RSA keys or by previous use of RSA signatures.

   e. (Optional) Define the Diffie-Hellman group identifier:

   ```
   (isakmp) group {1 | 2 | 5 | 14 | 15 | 16}
   ```

   The group can be **1** (768-bit Diffie-Hellman, the default), **2** (1024-bit Diffie-Hellman), **5** (1536-bit Diffie-Hellman), **14** (2048-bit Diffie-Hellman), **15** (3072-bit Diffie-Hellman), or **16** (4096-bit Diffie-Hellman). Group 2 and Group 5 are harder to crack but are also more CPU-intensive. Generally speaking, **group 14** is good for 128-bit keys, **group 15** is good for 192-bit keys, and **group 16** is good for 256-bit keys.

   f. (Optional) Define the lifetime for security associations:

   ```
   (isakmp) lifetime seconds
   ```

   The SA lifetime is set to *seconds* (60 to 86400; the default is 86400 seconds, or 1 day).

3. ("rsa-sig" method) Use a Certification Authority (CA).

a. Make sure the router has a host name and domain name:

(global) **hostname** *hostname*

(global) **ip domain-name** *domain*

The router must have a fully qualified domain name, formed by the host name and IP domain name. This is used to generate RSA keys and is assigned to the certificates used by the router.

b. Generate RSA keys:

(global) **crypto key generate rsa** [**exportable**] [**modulus** *modulus-size*]
[**storage** *device:*] [**on** *device:*]

By default, a pair of general-purpose keys is generated for use with IKE. When prompted, enter the modulus length (up to 4096 bits). Alternatively, you can specify the modulus size when entering the command with the keyword modulus followed by the modulus-size. The larger modulus produces a more secure key but takes many times longer to generate. How long a router takes to generate the key is also dependent on the hardware. For example, a 2048-bit key takes more than 1 hour to generate on a 2500 series router but only 50 seconds to generate on a 4700 series router. The default modulus size is 1024 bits, but the recommended modulus is 2048. The **exportable** keyword enables you to export the RSA key pair to another Cisco device (for example, another router). The RSA keys are stored in the private configuration in NVRAM and are not displayed. You can store the keys in another device (such as Flash memory) by entering the **storage** keyword followed by the device name. By default the keys are generated on the router. You can use a USB token as a cyprographic device to generate the keys and securely store the keys by entering **on usbtoken0:** at the end of the command. To see the public RSA key, use the **show crypto key mypubkey rsa** command.

c. Use the CA that issued certificates to the IPSec peer.

■ Set the host name of the CA:

(global) **crypto ca identity** name

An arbitrary *name* is given to the CA definition.

■ Set the URL used to reach the CA:

(ca-identity) **enrollment url** url

To enroll with the CA, the URL given by *url* is used. The URL should be of the form *http://ca-domain-name:port/cgi-bin-location*. The port can be given, as well as any optional path to a nonstandard cgi-bin script location.

■ (Optional) Use RA mode:

(ca-identity) **enrollment mode ra**
(ca-identity) **query url** *url*

Use a Registration Authority (RA) for enrollment if one is provided by the CA. The URL used to reach the LDAP server can also be given as *url*.

■ (Optional) Set the enrollment retry parameters:

```
(ca-identity) enrollment retry period minutes
(ca-identity) enrollment retry count number
```

The router sends a request for a certificate and then waits for *minutes* (1 to 60; the default is 1) before retrying. Requests are retried for *number* times (1 to 100; the default is 0 for an infinite number).

■ (Optional) Make the Certificate Revocation List (CRL) optional:

```
(ca-identity) crl optional
```

Normally, a router downloads a CRL with a new certificate. If the certificate appears in the CRL, it is not accepted. However, the CRL can be optional so that certificates are accepted even if a CRL cannot be obtained.

d. (Optional) Use a trusted root CA.

■ Identify the trusted root CA:

```
(global) crypto ca trusted-root name
```

The trusted root is associated with an arbitrary *name*. The local router can be enrolled with the trusted root without having to enroll with the same CA that issued a certificate to the far end of an IPSec connection.

■ (Optional) Request a CRL from the trusted root:

```
(ca-root) crl query url
```

The CRL is requested via the URL.

■ Define the enrollment method:

```
(ca-root) root {CEP url | TFTP server file | PROXY url}
```

The router can enroll with the trusted root through the following methods: Simple Certificate Enrollment Protocol (**CEP**), **TFTP**, or HTTP proxy server (**PROXY**). For TFTP, the *server* IP address or host name and the *file* filename must be given.

e. Authenticate the CA:

```
(global) crypto ca authenticate name
```

The router must obtain the self-signed certificate for the CA *name*. During this process, the CA's public RSA key is also retrieved. The CA certificate is placed in the router configuration automatically after it is received.

f. Enroll the router with the CA:

```
(global) crypto ca enroll name
```

The router requests a signed certificate for itself from the CA *name*. You enter a challenge password (up to 80 characters) during this process, which will be used if you ever need to have the certificate revoked by the CA. The router's serial number can optionally be included in the certificate if the CA requires it (this isn't required by IKE or IPSec). Don't choose to have the router's IP address included in the certificate, however.

> **Note** The enrollment and certificate request process can take considerable time, especially if the CA grants certificates through a manual process. The router returns to a configuration prompt, making it seem as though the process is complete. However, the enrollment process is running in the background while waiting for the certificate to be returned. A message is posted to the console as soon as the certificate arrives. You can also use **show crypto ca certificates** to view all the router's certificates.

4. ("rsa-encr" method) Manually configure the RSA keys (no CA is used).

   a. Generate the RSA keys:

   ```
   (global) crypto key generate rsa [exportable] [modulus modulus-size]
   [storage device:] [on device:]
   ```

   By default, a pair of general-purpose keys is generated for use with IKE. When prompted, enter the modulus length (up to 4096 bits). Alternatively, you can specify the modulus size when entering the command with the keyword modulus followed by the modulus size. The larger modulus produces a more secure key but takes many times longer to generate. How long a router takes to generate the key is also dependent on the hardware. For example, a 2048 bit key takes more than one hour to generate on a 2500 series router but only 50 seconds to generate on a 4700 series router. The default modulus size is 1024 bits but the recommended modulus is 2048. The **exportable** keyword enables you to export the RSA key pair to another Cisco device (for example, another router). The RSA keys are stored in the private configuration in NVRAM and are not displayed. You can store the keys in another device (such as Flash memory) by entering the **storage** keyword followed by the device name. By default the keys are generated on the router. You can use a USB token as a cyprographic device to generate the keys and securely store the keys by entering **on usbtoken0:** at the end of the command. To see the public RSA key, use the **show crypto key mypubkey rsa** command.

   b. Specify the ISAKMP identity of this peer:

   ```
   (global) crypto isakmp identity {address | hostname}
   ```

   The router is identified to its peers either by the IP **address** of the interface used to communicate with a remote peer or by its **hostname**.

   c. Specify RSA public keys for all other peers.

   ■ Configure the public key chain:

   ```
   (global) crypto key pubkey-chain rsa
   ```

- Identify the key by name or address:

```
(pubkey-chain) named-key key-name [encryption | signature]
```

-or-

```
(pubkey-chain) addressed-key key-name [encryption | signature]
```

The key (*key-name*) from the remote peer can be identified as the fully qualified domain name (**named-key**) or as the IP address (**addressed-key**). Use the **encryption** keyword if the remote peer has a special-purpose key for encryption, or **signature** if it has a special-purpose key for signatures. If the remote peer is using general-purpose RSA keys, don't use either keyword.

- (Optional) Manually configure a remote peer's IP address:

```
(pubkey-key) address ip-address
```

Identify a remote peer's IP address only if its host name can't be resolved or if it has only one interface configured for IPSec.

- Specify the remote peer's public key:

```
(pubkey-key) key-string key-string
```

The RSA public key is *key-string* (hexadecimal format). This string is very long and can take several lines of typing to enter. You can press the Enter key at the end of a line and continue entering values after the next "pubkey" command-line prompt. It is usually more accurate to copy and paste the key string from another terminal emulator that has displayed the remote peer's public key. At the end of the key string, use the **quit** keyword to end key entry.

5. ("Preshare" method) Configure preshared keys.

   a. Enter the preshared key:

   ```
   (global) crypto isakmp key key-string {address peer-address  [mask] |
   hostname peer-hostname}
   ```

   The preshared key is entered as *key-string* (up to 128 alphanumeric characters) on both the local router and the remote peer. The key string must be identical on both peers. The key is associated with the remote peer, either by its **address** *peer-address* (if the ISAKMP identity were set to **address** in Step 4b) or by its **hostname** *peer-hostname* (if the ISAKMP identity were set to **hostname**). To have the key apply to multiple VPN endpoints on the same network, enter a network address for the *peer-address* and the subnet *mask* for that network.

Note   It is good practice to use a unique preshared key between every pair of IPSec peers. When entering the preshared key into the router configurations, use an out-of-band channel (telephone, fax, modem dialup, and so forth) so that the secret key is not revealed as cleartext on the network.

6. (Optional) Use IKE Mode:

    a. Define a pool of "internal" or protected IP addresses to hand out:

        (global) **ip local pool** *pool-name start-address end-address*

        An address pool named *pool-name* (a text string) is created, containing a range of IP addresses from *start-address* to *end-address*. These addresses should belong to an unused subnet on the protected side of the VPN tunnel. A remote peer then receives an internal network address for its tunnel endpoint.

    b. Enable IKE mode negotiation:

        (global) **crypto isakmp client configuration address-pool local** *pool-name*

        IKE uses the address pool named *pool-name* (a text string) to assign tunnel end-point addresses to peers. IKE mode can be started by the local router (also called *gateway-initiated*) or by the remote client peer (*client-initiated*).

Example

IKE is configured on the router named *hq-router* in domain *mydomain.com*. Two ISAKMP policies are defined. The first policy to be matched against required 3DES encryption and the use of a CA (rsa-sig) to authenticate a peer. The second policy requires DES encryption and can use preshared keys to authenticate a peer.

The CA is defined with a URL and is called *mydomain*. Before you use the CA for IKE, the CA must be authenticated (the CA sends a self-signed certificate to the router). Then the router must be enrolled with the CA (the CA sends a certificate for the router itself).

Finally, a preshared key is defined for a peer at address 192.168.219.1.

(For clarity, this example contains only the IKE portion of the configuration. This same configuration is built upon in Section 13-10, where the remaining IPSec commands are added.)

```
hostname hq-router
ip domain-name mydomain.com
ip name-server 4.2.2.1
ip name-server 4.2.2.2

crypto isakmp policy 10
       encryption 3des
       authentication rsa-sig
crypto isakmp policy 20
       encryption des
       authentication pre-share      lifetime 900
```

Note At this point, the **crypto key generate rsa** command should be run from the global configuration prompt:

```
crypto ca identity mydomain
       enrollment url http://ca.mydomain.com:80
       crl optional
crypto isakmp key secretvpn1 address 192.168.219.1
```

Note At this point, the **crypto ca authenticate mydomain** command should be run from the EXEC-level prompt. This requests the CA's self-signed certificate. As soon as the CA sends it, the certificate is added to the configuration as something like this:

crypto ca certificate chain mydomain

certificate ca 01

308201E5 ...

quit

After that, the **crypto ca enroll mydomain** command can be run from the EXEC-level prompt. This requests a certificate from the CA for the local router. As soon as the CA approves and returns the certificate, it too is added to the configuration as something like this:

certificate 08

308201B2 ...

quit

13-2: IPSec VPN Tunnels

- IP Security (IPSec) protects and authenticates IP packets between peers at the network layer using encryption, data integrity, origin authentication, and rejection of re-played packets.

- IPSec is useful for building intranet, extranet, and remote user access VPNs.

- IPSec supports the following standards:

  - "Security Architecture for the Internet Protocol" (RFC 2401), as well as RFCs 2402 through 2410

  - IKE (Internet Key Exchange)

  - DES (Data Encryption Standard)—56-bit DES-CBC with Explicit IV and 168-bit 3DES (RFC 1851)

- AES (Advanced Encryption Standard)–128-bit, 192-bit, and 256-bit AES (RFC 3268)

- SEAL (Software Encryption Algorithm)—160-bit SEAL

- MD5 (Message Digest 5: HMAC variant) hash algorithm (RFC 2403)

- SHA (Secure Hash Algorithm: HMAC variant) hash algorithm (RFC 4635)

- AH (Authentication Header) data authentication and anti-replay services (RFC 4302 and 4835)

- ESP (Encapsulating Security Payload) data privacy, data authentication, and anti-replay services (RFC 4303 and 4835)

- "Tunnels" or *security associations* (SAs) are set up between two peers when sensitive packets are transported. Sensitive traffic is defined by access lists, applied to interfaces through *crypto map* sets. Security protocols and settings are negotiated by *transform sets*.

Note IPSec ESP and AH protocols use protocol numbers 50 and 51, and IKE uses UDP port 500. Be sure that these protocol and port numbers are not blocked. Also, if NAT is used, use static translations so that IPSec works with global addresses.

Configuration

1. Configure IKE for key management.

   If IKE is to be used, it must be configured according to Section 13-1. If IKE is not used, it must be manually disabled with the (global) **no crypto isakmp enable** command. Otherwise, IKE is enabled on all interfaces by default and needs to be configured.

2. (Optional) Define the global lifetimes for SAs:

   (global) **crypto ipsec security-association lifetime seconds** *seconds*
   (global) **crypto ipsec security-association lifetime kilobytes** *kilobytes*

   SAs times out when one of two conditions is met: the "timed" lifetime after *seconds* has elapsed (the default is 3600 seconds, or one hour), or the "traffic volume" lifetime after *kilobytes* of traffic has passed through the tunnel (the default is 4608000 KBps or 10 MBps for one hour). These lifetimes are negotiated when an SA is established, using the smaller of the values from the two peers.

3. Define crypto access lists to define protected traffic.

   a. Create an access list:

      (global) **access-list** *access-list-number* ...

      -or-

      (global) **ip access-list extended** *name*

The extended access list (named or numbered) must define which IP traffic is to be protected by IPSec. A crypto map references this access list to identify traffic to protect at an interface. Select the outbound traffic to be protected with a **permit**. Both inbound and outbound traffic is evaluated against this "outbound" access list. Try to use only one **permit** to identify the traffic, and avoid using the **any** keyword so that protected traffic will be accurately identified.

Note   On the remote IPSec peer, you need to define a similar crypto access list. However, that access list should be a "mirror image" of this one. In other words, the source and destination addresses should be reversed in the remote peer's crypto access list.

4. Define transform sets of IPSec features.

   a. Create a transform set:

```
(global) crypto ipsec transform-set transform-set-name transform1
   [transform2 [transform3]]
```

A transform set named *transform-set-name* (a text string) is defined with up to three different transforms, defining IPSec protocols and algorithms. Transform sets are negotiated between peers when an SA initiates. Therefore, multiple transform sets can be defined within a crypto map. If IKE is not used, only one transform set can be defined.

You can choose up to three transforms, as follows:

(Optional) Pick one AH transform:

- **ah-md5-hmac**—AH with MD5 authentication

- **ah-sha-hmac**—AH with SHA authentication

(Optional) Pick one ESP encryption transform:

- **esp-des**—ESP with 56-bit DES encryption

- **esp-3des**—ESP with 168-bit 3DES encryption

- **esp-aes**—ESP with 128-bit AES encryption

- **esp-aes 192**—ESP with 192-bit AES encryption

- **esp-aes 256**—ESP with 256-bit AES encryption

- **esp-null**—Null encryption

- **esp-seal**—ESP with 160-bit SEAL encryption

and one of these authentication methods:

- **esp-md5-hmac**—ESP with MD5 authentication

■   esp-sha-hmac—ESP with SHA authentication

(Optional) Pick an IP compression transform:

■   comp-lzs—IP compression with the LZS algorithm

AH provides data authentication and anti-replay services, and ESP provides packet encryption and optional data authentication and anti-replay services.

Use an ESP encryption transform to maintain data confidentiality. Use an ESP authentication transform to maintain data integrity, or an AH authentication transform to maintain the integrity of the payload and the outer IP header. The SHA authentication algorithm is stronger than MD5 but more CPU-intensive (it is slower).

Recommended transform sets are

```
(global) crypto ipsec transform-set name esp-des esp-sha-hmac
```

-or-

```
(global) crypto ipsec transform-set name ah-sha-hmac esp-des esp-sha-hmac
```

b. (Optional) Select the mode of the transform set:

```
(crypto-transform) mode {tunnel | transport}
```

IPSec can protect data using two methods. With **tunnel** mode (the default), the original IP packet is encrypted and/or authenticated and is encapsulated in a new IP packet. Only the peers' outside addresses are seen; the protected inside addresses are hidden from view. With **transport** mode, only the payload of the original IP packet is encrypted and/or authenticated. The protected inside addresses still appear in the original IP headers.

If a router requests tunnel mode, only tunnel mode can be negotiated between the peers. However, if transport mode is requested, either transport or tunnel mode (more secure) can be negotiated.

5.   Define crypto maps with IPSec policies.

Crypto maps link a crypto access list and identify remote peers, the local address, a transform set, and a negotiation method.

a. (Optional) Use manual security associations (no IKE negotiation).

■   Create the crypto map:

```
(global) crypto map map-name sequence ipsec-manual
```

The crypto map is named *map-name* (a text string). It is assigned a priority or *sequence* number to be tried during negotiation. A lower *sequence* is tried first.

■   Reference the crypto access list to identify protected traffic:

```
(crypto-map) match address access-list
```

The access list can be a named or numbered extended IP list.

- Identify the remote IPSec peer:

  `(crypto-map) set peer {hostname | ip-address}`

- Specify the transform set to use:

  `(crypto-map) set transform-set` *transform-set-name*

  The transform set must be identical to the one used on the remote peer.

- (AH authentication only) Manually set the AH keys:

  `(crypto-map) set session-key inbound ah` *spi hex-key-data*

  `(crypto-map) set session-key outbound ah spi hex-key-data`

  The security parameter index, *spi* (256 to 4,294,967,295, or FFFF FFFF), is set to uniquely identify an SA. The *hex-key-data* field is used to enter a session key (hexadecimal; 8 bytes for DES, 16 bytes for MD5, and 20 bytes for SHA).

- (ESP only) Manually set the ESP SPIs and keys:

  `(crypto-map) set session-key inbound esp` *spi* `cipher` *hex-key-data*
      `[authenticator` *hex-key-data*`]`

  `(crypto-map) set session-key outbound esp` *spi* `cipher` *hex-key-data*
      `[authenticator hex-key-data]`

The security parameter index, *spi* (256 to 4,294,967,295, or FFFF FFFF), is set to uniquely identify an SA. The **cipher** *hex-key-data* field is used to enter a session key (hexadecimal; 8 bytes for DES, 16 bytes for MD5, and 20 bytes for SHA). The **authenticator** keyword can be used to set a *hex-key-data* string for ESP authentication.

b. (Optional) Use IKE established security associations.

- Create the crypto map:

  `(global) crypto map map-name sequence ipsec-isakmp`

  The crypto map is named *map-name* (a text string). It is assigned a priority or *sequence* number to be tried during negotiation. A lower *sequence* is tried first.

- Reference the crypto access list to identify protected traffic:

  `(crypto-map) match address access-list`

  The access list can be a named or numbered extended IP list.

- Identify the remote IPSec peer:

  `(crypto-map) set peer {hostname | ip-address}`

- Specify the transform set to use:

  `(crypto-map) set transform-set transform-set-name`

  The transform set must be identical to the one used on the remote peer.

■   (Optional) Define the SA lifetimes if they are different from the global defaults:

```
(crypto-map) set security-association lifetime seconds seconds
(crypto-map) set security-association lifetime kilobytes kilobytes
```

SAs time out when one of two conditions is met: the "timed" lifetime after *seconds* has elapsed (the default is 3600 seconds, or one hour), or the "traffic volume" lifetime after *kilobytes* of traffic has passed through the tunnel (the default is 4608000 KBps or 10 MBps for one hour). These lifetimes are negotiated when an SA is established using the smaller of the values from the two peers.

■   (Optional) Use a separate SA for each source/destination host pair:

```
(crypto-map) set security-association level per-host
```

By default, all traffic between two IPSec peers that matches a single crypto map access list **permit** entry shares one SA. In other words, SAs are defined at the granularity of the crypto access lists. Use this command to create separate SAs for each pair of hosts. Be aware that this can create too many individual SAs, overwhelming the router's resources.

■   (Optional) Use Perfect Forward Secrecy (PFS) for each new SA:

```
(crypto-map) set pfs [group1 | group2 | group5 | group14 | group15 |
group16]
```

PFS enables the router to exchange a new Diffie-Hellman key each time a new SA is negotiated. If one SA key is cracked, only that SA can be compromised. The next SA will have a different key. The PFS groups are **group1** (use the 768-bit Diffie-Hellman prime modulus group), **group2** (use the 1024-bit Diffie-Hellman prime modulus group), group5 (use the 1536-bit Diffie-Hellman prime modulus group), group14 (use the 2048-bit Diffie-Hellman prime modulus group), group15 (use the 3072-bit Diffie-Hellman prime modulus group), or group16 (use the 4096-bit Diffie-Hellman prime modolus group). Generating new Diffie-Hellman keys requires more CPU time.

c.   (Optional) Use dynamic security associations with IKE (one peer is mobile, or not fixed).

■   Create a dynamic crypto map:

```
(global) crypto dynamic-map dyn-map-name dyn-seq-num
```

Remote peers can initiate an IPSec negotiation with the local router. If it is successful, an SA and a temporary crypto map entry are created. When the SA expires, the temporary crypto map is deleted. Notice that the crypto access list and the peer identification parameters are now optional for the dynamic map. Only the transform set must be defined.

■   (Optional) Reference the crypto access list to identify protected traffic:

```
(crypto-map) match address access-list
```

The access list can be a named or numbered extended IP list.

- (Optional) Identify the remote IPSec peer:

```
(crypto-map) set peer {hostname | ip-address}
```

- Specify the transform set to use:

```
(crypto-map) set transform-set transform-set-name
```

The transform set must be identical to the one used on the remote peer.

- (Optional) Define the SA lifetimes if they are different from the global defaults:

```
(crypto-map) set security-association lifetime seconds seconds
(crypto-map) set security-association lifetime kilobytes kilobytes
```

SAs time out when one of two conditions is met: the "timed" lifetime after *seconds* has elapsed (the default is 3600 seconds, or one hour), or the "traffic volume" lifetime after *kilobytes* of traffic has passed through the tunnel (the default is 4608000 KBps or 10 MBps for one hour). These lifetimes are nego-tiated when an SA is established using the smaller of the values from the two peers.

- (Optional) Use Perfect Forward Secrecy (PFS) for each new SA:

```
(crypto-map) set pfs [group1 | group2 | group5 | group14 | group15 |
group16]
```

PFS enables the router to exchange a new Diffie-Hellman key each time a new SA is negotiated. If one SA key is cracked, only that SA can be compro-mised. The next SA will have a different key. The PFS groups are **group1** (use the 768-bit Diffie-Hellman prime modulus group), **group2** (use the 1024-bit Diffie-Hellman prime modulus group), group5 (use the 1536-bit Diffie-Hellman prime modulus group), group14 (use the 2048-bit Diffie-Hellman prime modulus group), group15 (use the 3072-bit Diffie-Hellman prime mod-ulus group), or group16 (use the 4096-bit Diffie-Hellman prime modolus group). Generating new Diffie-Hellman keys requires more CPU time.

- Add the dynamic crypto map set to a regular map set:

```
(global) crypto map map-name sequence ipsec-isakmp dynamic dyn-map-
name
  [discover]
```

The dynamic crypto map named *dyn-map-name* is used as a template for new SA requests from peers. Therefore, the dynamic map must be added to the regular crypto map named *map-name*.

The **dynamic** keyword allows Tunnel Endpoint Discovery (TED) to discover remote peers. When the dynamic crypto map permits an outbound packet, a probe is sent to the original destination to try to discover a remote IPSec peer. As soon as the probe is answered, the peers have identified each other, and normal IKE negotiation can occur.

Dynamic crypto maps should always be referenced as the last map set to try during a negotiation. The *sequence* number should be higher than any other map sets so that more-specific map sets are matched against first.

- (Optional) Use IKE mode client configuration:

  (global) crypto map map-name client configuration address [initiate | respond]

  If IKE mode is configured (see Section 13-9), the crypto map must also be configured so that the router can either set the client's address (**initiate**) or offer an address to a requesting client (**respond**).

- (Optional) Use preshared IKE keys from a AAA server:

  (global) crypto map map-name isakmp authorization list list-name

  VPN users can have secret preshared keys stored on a AAA server rather than using a CA to manage certificates for the users. The crypto map causes AAA authorization to be used to retrieve the preshared keys. The *list-name* field is the AAA authorization method list configured on the router. (See Section 13-2.)

6. Apply crypto maps to interfaces.

    a. Specify a crypto map to use:

    (interface) crypto map map-name

    The crypto map named *map-name* is applied to the interface. Traffic matching the crypto access list referenced by the crypto map triggers IPSec to initiate and negotiate an IPSec SA with a peer. Inbound traffic matching the crypto access list, but unable to trigger a successful SA, is dropped. Outbound traffic not matching the crypto access list is forwarded normally.

    b. (Optional) Share a crypto map with other interfaces:

    (global) crypto map map-name local-address interface-id

    All SAs use the same local interface IP address rather than using the addresses of each interface with a crypto map applied. This allows you to use a loopback interface as the IPSec endpoint for increased availability.

Example

The example from Section 13-9 is continued here, to add the commands necessary to implement IPSec. These commands appear below the dashed line in the configuration. Figure 13-1 shows a network diagram for this example.

Here, an IPSec tunnel is configured between the internal protected network 192.3.3.0 and a client's private network 192.168.200.0 with access list 102. This list is used for a tunnel to a specific peer with a known fixed IP address. Two other private networks at client sites are 192.168.209.0 and 192.168.219.0, identified by access list 103. This list is used to match the addresses of dynamic clients, where the peer's IP address is unknown.

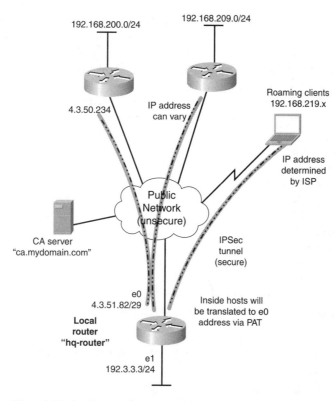

Figure 13-1   *Network Diagram for the IKE/IPSec Example*

The IPSec transform set called *basic-3des* consists of **esp-3des** (ESP with 3DES encryption) and **esp-md5-hmac** (ESP with MD5 authentication). Remote peers attempting to bring up an IPSec tunnel with this router must have an identical transform set.

A crypto map called *Clients* contains several policies so that VPN peers with varying capabilities can negotiate parameters. The first crypto map policy (10) uses access list 102 to match traffic traveling between the local and remote private networks. The policy identifies a specific IPSec peer at 4.3.50.234 and associates the *basic-3des* transform set.

For dynamic VPN peers to negotiate a tunnel, a dynamic crypto map called *ISPpeers* is used. Access list 103 is used to match the local and remote private networks at the possible tunnel endpoints. (Address matching is optional in a dynamic crypto map; it is performed here for clarity.) The *basic-3des* transform is used for peer negotiations. The dynamic crypto map is applied to the *Clients* crypto map as policy 30. It will be matched against after negotiations for all lower-numbered policies fail.

The crypto map *Clients* is applied to the outside network interface, Ethernet 0. Outbound traffic matching the addresses identified in the crypto map will cause IPSec to be triggered.

Notice that Network Address Translation (NAT) is also configured on this router. The Ethernet 0 interface IP address is used for port address translation, according to traffic permitted by access list 101. Here, access list 101 denies traffic matching the source and destination addresses that are involved in the VPN tunnel so that NAT is not used. All other outbound traffic triggers NAT. This is known as a *split tunnel,* in which both VPN and non-VPN traffic must be forwarded out the same interface. In this case, some traffic must travel over the VPN tunnel, and other traffic must be forwarded normally.

```
hostname hq-router
ip domain-name mydomain.com
ip name-server 4.2.2.1
ip name-server 4.2.2.2

crypto isakmp policy 10
        encryption 3des
        authentication rsa-sig
crypto isakmp policy 20
        encryption des
        authentication pre-share       lifetime 900
```

Note At this point, the **crypto key generate rsa** command should be run from the EXEC-level prompt.

```
crypto ca identity mydomain
        enrollment url http://ca.mydomain.com:80
        crl optional
```

Note At this point, the **crypto ca authenticate mydomain** command should be run from the EXEC-level prompt. This requests the CA's self-signed certificate. As soon as the CA sends it, the certificate is added to the configuration as something like this:

```
crypto ca certificate chain mydomain
 certificate ca 01
  308201E5 ...
  quit
```

After that, the **crypto ca enroll mydomain** command can be run from the EXEC-level prompt. This requests a certificate from the CA for the local router. As soon as the CA approves and returns the certificate, it too is added to the configuration as something like this:

```
certificate 08
  308201B2 ...
```

```
    quit
crypto isakmp key secretvpn1 address 192.168.219.1
——————————————————
access-list 102 permit ip 192.3.3.0 0.0.0.255 192.168.200.0 0.0.0.255
access-list 103 permit ip 192.3.3.0 0.0.0.255 192.168.209.0 0.0.0.255
access-list 103 permit ip 192.3.3.0 0.0.0.255 192.168.219.0 0.0.0.255


crypto ipsec transform-set basic-3des esp-3des esp-md5-hmac


crypto map Clients 10 ipsec-isakmp
        match address 102
        set peer 4.3.50.234
        set transform-set basic-3des


crypto dynamic-map ISPpeers 10
        match address 103
        set transform-set basic-3des


crypto map Clients 30 ipsec-isakmp dynamic ISPpeers


interface Ethernet0
        description Outside network
        ip address 4.3.51.82 255.255.255.248
        ip nat outside
        crypto map Clients


interface Ethernet1
        description Inside network      ip address 192.3.3.3 255.255.255.0
        ip nat inside


ip nat inside source list 101 interface Ethernet0 overload


access-list 101 deny ip 192.3.3.0 0.0.0.255 192.168.0.0 0.0.255.255
access-list 101 permit ip 192.3.3.0 0.0.0.255 any
```

13-3: High Availability Features

- High availability for VPNs can be accomplished by configuring dead peer detection (DPD), Reverse Route Injection (RRI), Hot Standby Router Protocol (HSRP) with VPNs, and Stateful Switchover (SSO).

  DPD is part of the Internet Key Exchange (IKE) protocol. Dead peer detection (DPD) relies on keepalive messages to learn if a peer is no longer accessible. The keepalives can be periodic or on-demand. When configured as on-demand, keepalives are sent only when the link is idle. A VPN endpoint can use an IPsec backup peer when DPD reports a failure.

- Reverse Route Injection (RRI) offers route stability by automatically injecting static routes into the routing process for networks protected by a remote tunnel endpoint. Protected networks and hosts are known as *remote proxy identities.*

  RRI is applied via either a static crypto map or dynamic crypto map template. When using static crypto maps, routes are created on the basis of the destination information defined in the crypto extended access list, and the next-hop IP address in the static route is the first defined peer IP address configured for that crypto map. When using dynamic crypto maps, routes are created upon a successful establishment of IPsec security associations (SA) for the remote proxies. The next-hop IP address in the static route is the IP address of the remote VPN router whose IP address is learned during the creation of the dynamic crypto map template. When designed with multiple routers and paths, RRI offers stability through route redundancy and load balancing.

- Cisco routers support HSRP with IPsec VPNs for additional high availability. HSRP is explained in Chapter 4, "IPv4 Addressing and Services." When configuring HSRP for IPsec, the standby IP address will be the local tunnel endpoint.

- Stateful Switchover (SSO) enhances HSRP with IPsec by enabling for IPsec and IKE stateful failover. When using stateful failover, both routers should be the same type of router, have the same CPU and memory, and, if installed, identical encryption accelerators. You should configure RRI with SSO so that routers can learn about the correct active device.

Configuration

1. Configure dead peer detection (DPD).

   a. Enable and configure DPD.

   (global) **crypto isakmp keepalive** *seconds* [*retries*] [**retries**] [**periodic** | **on-demand**]

   You can configure DPD to send keepalive messages either periodically or on-demand. **On-demand** is the default. (This keyword will not show in the configuration.) With on-demand, keepalives are sent only when the VPN is idle.

   b. Specify which IPsec peer will be the default:

   (crypto-map) **set peer** *peer-ip-address* **default**

   Configure a second peer and specify which peer is the default by adding the **default** keyword at the end of the **set peer** command.

2. Configure Reverse Route Injection.

   a. Enter crypto map configuration mode:

   (global) **crypto** [**dynamic-map** | **map**] *map-name* [*dsequence-number*] [**ipsec-isakmp**]

   Enter the crypto map name for which you want to add RRI.

b. Configure the source proxy IP address for your map entry:

```
(crypto-map) reverse-route [static | remote-peer ip-address [gateway]
[static]
```

Configure standard reverse-route injection with the **reverse-route** command. RRI automatically creates static routes for the protected destination network. If you add the **static** keyword, static routes will be injected based on the crypto access lists regardless if there is a flow created for the crypto access list. You can use the **reverse-route remote-peer** *ip-address* **gateway** command to create one static route to the protected subnet (via the remote tunnel endpoint) and another static route to the remote tunnel endpoint IP address (specified with the *ip-address* parameter).

c. (Optional) Change the default administrative distance value for the static route:

```
(crypto-map) set reverse-route distance administrative-distance-value
```

The default administrative distance of a static route is 1. This makes the static route preferred over routes learned via dynamic routing protocols. There are times when you might want to change the administrative distance for the RRI-generated static. For example, you might want the static route to be less preferred than a dynamic routing protocol when you use the VPN as a backup connection. If that is the case, you should configure RRI to inject a static route with a higher administrative distance than the dynamic routing protocol in use.

3. Configure HSRP for use with IPsec VPNs:

a. Name your standby group:

```
(interface) standby name standby-name
```

Standby names are required when configuring HSRP for IPsec VPNs. Both routers need to be configured to use the same standby group name.

b. Configure the standby IP address:

```
(interface) standby ip ip-address
```

Both routers should be configured to use the same standby virtual IP address. You also can configure additional HSRP options such as preemption, interface tracking, and timers. For more on configuring HSRP options, see Chapter 4.

c. Enable IPsec stateful switchover for the HSRP group:

```
(interface) crypto map map-name redundancy standby-name [stateful]
```

Stateful switchover for IKE SAs is done automatically but stateful switchover for IPSec SAs must be enabled with this command.

4. Configure stateful switchover (SSO).

a. Enter redundancy configuration mode:

```
(global) redundancy inter-device
```

Section 13-3

SSO enables routers to exchange and synchronize IKE and IPsec security associations (SA). This command both enables SSO and enters redundancy mode.

b. Define the redundancy scheme (HSRP group) that you want to use:

`(redundancy) `**`scheme`**` standby-group-name`

SSO uses HSRP for failover detection. Use the same *standby-group-name* in this command as you do with the interface **standby name** command you entered when configuring HSRP. The **scheme** command can be entered on the same line as the **redundancy inter-device** command or from within the redundancy mode.

c. Enter the Interprocess Communication (IPC) zone configuration mode.

`(global) `**`ipc zone default`**

This command enables IPC communication between the active and standby routers.

d. Enable an association between the active and standby routers:

`(ipczone) `**`association`**` association-number`

The valid range for *association-number* is 1 to 255. Entering this command puts you into IPC zone association configuration mode.

e. Enter the Stream Control Transmission Protocol (SCTP)mode:

`(ipczone-association) `**`protocol sctp`**

SSO uses SCTP, which is a streaming protocol designed to address some of the limitations in Transmission Control Protocol (TCP). SCTP sends one byte at a time and only sends a byte upon receiving an acknowledgment for the previous byte sent. You can read more about SCTP in RFC 2960.

f. Specify the local SCTP port number:

`(ipc-sctp) `**`local-port`**` port-number`

This command is required because there is no default SCTP port number. The range of valid port numbers is between 1 and 65,535. Whatever you choose for the SCTP port number needs to match the remote port number on the peer router.

g. Specify the local IP address to which the remote peer will connect:

`(ipc-local-sctp) `**`local ip`**` ip-address`

The IP address must be in the global routing table, and it must be an IP address assigned to an interface; you cannot use a virtual IP address. This IP address will be used in the **remote ip** command on the peer router.

h. (Optional) Configure the retransmit time:

`(ipc-local-sctp) `**`retransmit-timeout`**` min-time max-time`

The retransmit-timeout is the amount of time in milliseconds that SCTP waits before retransmitting data. The default minimum time is 300 milliseconds, and the maximum is 600 milliseconds.

i. (Optional) Configure the number of consecutive transmissions before considering an associated path failed:

```
(ipc-local-sctp) path-retransmit retry-value
```

By default, a router retries four times before consider a path failed. The range of possible values is between 2 and 10.

j. Define the remote SCTP port number to connect to the SCTP peer:

```
(ipc-protocol-sctp) remote-peer port-number
```

This number must match the port number defined with the **local-port** *port-number* command on the peer router.

k. Define the remote peer IP address:

```
(ipc-remote-sctp) remote-ip ip-address
```

The IP address must match the IP address configured with the **local ip** *ip-address* command on the peer router.

Example

Figure 13-2 is used in this example. The HQ-2 and HQ-3 routers peer with the Remote-1 and Remote-2 routers. IPsec tunnels are formed between the 172.16.0.0/16 and 172.17.00/16 networks to the 192.168.1.64/28 network. HSRP is configured to provide high availability for the clients on the 192.168.1.0/24 network. SSO is also configured to preserve the state of IKE and IPsec SAs if failure occurs. RRI is enabled so the HQ-1 router can learn about the correct path to the Remote-1 and Remote-2 networks. Static routes are redistributed into the EIGRP process so that HQ-1 can learn about the default route and the RRI generated route. To prevent black-hole routes, a filter is configured to block the locally originated static routes from being learned on HQ-2 and HQ-3. When a failover occurs, the new active device injects the RRI routes into the routing table and sends out routing updates to its routing peers (HQ-1 in this example).

Network address translation and split tunneling is also configured. Access-list 103 on the HQ-2 and HQ-3 router denies protected traffic with the **access-list 103 deny ip 192.168.1.64 0.0.0.63 172.16.0.0 0.0.254.255** and **access-list 103 deny ip 192.168.1.128 0.0.0.63 172.16.0.0 0.0.254.255** commands. These commands match the 192.168.1.64/26 and 192.168.1.128/26 source networks and the 172.16.0.0/16 and 172.17.0.0/16 destination networks. The **access-list 103 permit ip 192.168.1.64 0.0.0.63 any** and **access-list 103 permit ip 192.168.1.128 0.0.0.63 any** commands enable all other traffic from the 192.168.1.64/26 and 192.168.1.128/26 networks to use NAT to access the public network.

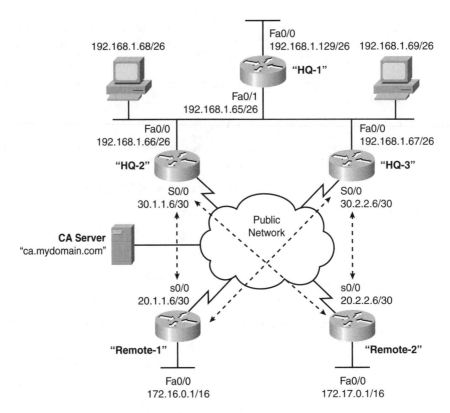

Figure 13-2   *High Availability Example*

Dead peer detection is configured on Remote-1 and Remote-2. Both routers are configured to use HQ-2 as their preferred peer.

HQ-2 Router
```
hostname HQ-2
!
crypto isakmp policy 10
 encryption 3des
 authentication pre-share
!

crypto isakmp identity address
crypto isakmp key secretvpn1 address 20.1.1.6
crypto isakmp key secretvpn1 address 20.2.2.6
!
access-list 101 permit ip 192.168.1.64 0.0.0.63 172.16.0.0 0.0.255.255
access-list 101 permit ip 192.168.1.128 0.0.0.63 172.16.0.0 0.0.255.255
access-list 102 permit ip 192.168.1.64 0.0.0.63 172.17.0.0 0.0.255.255
```

```
access-list 102 permit ip 192.168.1.128 0.0.0.63 172.17.0.0 0.0.255.255
access-list 103 deny ip 192.168.1.64 0.0.0.63 172.16.0.0 0.0.254.255
access-list 103 deny ip 192.168.1.128 0.0.0.63 172.16.0.0 0.0.254.255
access-list 103 permit ip 192.168.1.64 0.0.0.63 any
access-list 103 permit ip 192.168.1.128 0.0.0.63 any
!
ip access-list standard PREVENT-LOOP
 deny 172.16.0.0 0.0.254.255
 permit any
!
crypto ipsec transform-set VPN esp-3des esp-md5-hmac
!
crypto map REMOTE-1 10 ipsec-isakmp
 match address 101
 set peer 20.1.1.6
 set transform-set VPN
 reverse-route static
!
crypto map REMOTE-2 10 ipsec-isakmp
 match address 102
 set peer 20.2.2.6
 set transform-set VPN
 reverse-route static
!
redundancy inter-device
 scheme VPN-HSRP
!
ipc zone default
 association 1
  protocol sctp
   local-port 4444
     local ip 30.1.1.6
     retransmit-timeout 30 10000
     path-retransmit 10
   remote-port 5555
     remote ip 20.1.1.6
 association 2
  protocol sctp
   protocol sctp
    local-port 6666
     local ip 30.1.1.6
     retransmit-timeout 30 10000
     path-retransmit 10
    remote-port 7777
     remote ip 20.2.2.6
```

Section 13-3

```
!
ip nat inside source list 103 interface serial0/0 overload
!
interface fastethernet0/0
 ip address 192.168.1.66 255.255.255.192
 ip nat inside
 standby name VPN-HSRP
 standby VPN-HSRP ip 30.1.1.68
 standby VPN-HSRP priority 110
 standby VPN-HSRP preempt
 standby VPN-HSRP track serial0/0
 standby VPN-HSRP authentication hsrppass
 crypto map REMOTE-1
 crypto map REMOTE-1 redundancy VPN-HSRP
 cryto map REMOTE-2 redundancy VPN-HSRP
!
interface serial0/0
 ip address 30.1.1.6 255.255.255.252
 ip nat outside
!
ip route 0.0.0.0 0.0.0.0 serial0/0
!
router eigrp 1
 no auto-summary
 network 192.168.1.0
 network 30.0.0.0
 redistribute static
 default-metric 10000 100 255 1 1500
 distribute-list PREVENT-LOOP in interface fastethernet0/0
```

HQ-3 Router
```
hostname HQ-3
!
crypto isakmp policy 10
 encryption 3des
 authentication pre-share
!
crypto isakmp identity address
crypto isakmp key secretvpn1 address 20.1.1.6
crypto isakmp key secretvpn1 address 20.2.2.6
!
access-list 101 permit ip 192.168.1.64 0.0.0.63 172.16.0.0 0.0.255.255
access-list 101 permit ip 192.168.1.128 0.0.0.63 172.16.0.0 0.0.255.255
access-list 102 permit ip 192.168.1.64 0.0.0.63 172.17.0.0 0.0.255.255
access-list 102 permit ip 192.168.1.128 0.0.0.63 172.17.0.0 0.0.255.255
```

```
access-list 103 deny ip 192.168.1.64 0.0.0.63 172.16.0.0 0.0.254.255
access-list 103 deny ip 192.168.128 0.0.0.63 172.17.0.0 0.0.254.255
access-list 103 permit ip 192.168.1.64 0.0.63 any
access-list 103 permit ip 192.168.1.128 0.0.0.63 any
!
ip access-list standard PREVENT-LOOP
 deny 172.16.0.0 0.0.254.255
 permit any
!
crypto ipsec transform-set VPN esp-3des esp-md5-hmac
!
crypto map REMOTE-1 10 ipsec-isakmp
 match address 101
 set peer 20.1.1.6
 set transform-set VPN
 reverse-route static
!
crypto map REMOTE-2 10 ipsec-isakmp
 match address 102
 set peer 20.2.2.6
 set transform set VPN
 reverse-route static
!
redundancy inter-device
 scheme VPN-HSRP
!
ip zone default
 association 1
  protocol sctp
   local-port 4444
     local ip 30.2.2.6
     retransmit-timeout 30 10000
     path-retransmit 10
   remote-port 5555
     remote ip 20.1.1.6
 association 2
  protocol sctp
   local-port 6666
     local ip 30.2.2.6
     retransmit-timeout 30 10000
     path-retransmit 10
   remote-port 7777
     remote ip 20.2.2.6
!
ip nat inside source list 103 interface serial0/0 overload
```

```
!
interface fastethernet0/0
 ip address 192.168.1.67 255.255.255.192
 ip nat inside
 standby name VPN-HSRP
 standby VPN-HSRP ip 30.1.1.68
 standby VPN-HSRP track serial0/0
 standby VPN-HSRP authentication hsrppass
 crypto map REMOTE-1
 crypto map REMOTE-1 redundancy VPN-HSRP
 crypto map REMOTE-2 redundancy VPN-HSRP
!
interface serial0/0
 ip address 30.2.2.6 255.255.255.252
 ip nat outside
!
ip route 0.0.0.0 0.0.0.0 serial0/0
!
router eigrp 1
 no auto-summary
 network 192.168.1.0
 network 30.0.0.0
 redistribute static
 default-metric 10000 100 255 1 1500
 distribute-list PREVENT-LOOP in interface fastethernet0/0
```

Remote-1
```
hostname Remote-1
!
crypto isakmp policy 10
 encryption 3des
 authentication pre-share
!
crypto isakmp identity address
crypto isakmp key secretvpn1 address 20.1.1.6
crypto isakmp key secretvpn1 address 20.2.2.6
!
access-list 101 permit ip 172.16.0.0 0.0.255.255 192.168.1.64 0.0.0.63
access-list 101 permit ip 172.16.0.0 0.0.255.255 192.168.1.128 0.0.0.63
access-list 102 deny ip 172.16.0.0 0.0.255.255 192.168.1.64 0.0.0.63
access-list 102 deny ip 172.16.0.0 0.0.255.255 192.168.1.128 0.0.0.63
access-list 102 permit ip 172.16.0.0 0.0.255.255 any
!
crypto ipsec transform-set VPN esp-3des esp-md5-hmac
!
```

```
crypto isakmp keepalive 10 3 periodic
!
crypto map HQ-VPN 10 ipsec-isakmp
 match address 101
 set peer 30.1.1.6 default
 set peer 30.2.2.6
 set transform set VPN
!
ip nat inside source list 102 interface serial0/0 overload
!
interface fastethernet0/0
 ip address 172.16.0.1 255.255.0.0
 ip nat inside
 crypto map HQ-VPN
!
interface serial0/0
 ip address 20.1.1.6 255.255.255.252
 ip nat outside
!
ip route 0.0.0.0 0.0.0.0 serial0/0
```

Remote-2
```
hostname Remote-2
!
crypto isakmp policy 10
 encryption 3des
 authentication pre-share
!
crypto isakmp identity address
crypto isakmp key secretvpn1 address 30.1.1.6
crypto isakmp key secretvpn1 address 30.2.2.6
!
access-list 101 permit ip 172.17.0.0 0.0.255.255 192.168.1.64 0.0.0.63
access-list 101 permit ip 172.17.0.0 0.0.255.255 192.168.1.128 0.0.63
access-list 102 deny ip 172.17.0.0 0.0.255.255 192.168.1.64 0.0.0.63
access-list 102 deny ip 172.17.0.0 0.0.255.255 192.168.1.64 0.0.0.63
access-list 102 permit ip 172.17.0.0 0.0.255.255 any
!
crypto isakmp transform-set VPN esp-3des esp-md5-hmac
!
crypto isakmp keepalive 10 3 periodic
!
crypto map HQ-VPN 10 ipsec-isakmp
 match address 101
 set peer 30.1.1.6 default
```

```
   set peer 30.2.2.6
   set transform set VPN
 !
 ip nat inside source list 102 interface serial0/0 overload
 !
 interface fastethernet0/0
  ip address 172.17.0.1 255.255.0.0
  ip nat inside
  crypto map HQ-VPN
 !
 interface serial0/0
  ip address 20.2.2.6 255.255.255.252
  ip nat outside
 !
 ip route 0.0.0.0 0.0.0.0 serial0/0
```

13-4: Dynamic Multipoint VPN (DMVPN)

In a hub and spoke topology where there are many remote sites, it can be cumbersome to configure the multiple VPNs. If the remote sites are assigned their IP addresses dynamically from a provider, you would need to reconfigure the tunnels every time the IP address changed. The challenges increase if you require the remote sites to establish VPN tunnels between themselves. DMVPNs address these challenges to make configuration easier and more adaptive to the dynamic nature of adding and removing remote sites or changing IP addresses used for VPN endpoints.

- Crypto maps and crypto access lists are not used. Instead, crypto profiles are used to simplify the configurations on routers.

- DMVPN uses multipoint Generic Route Encapsulation (mGRE) tunnels to establish a VPN tunnel between spokes. GRE uses IP protocol 47. See 2784 for more on GRE encapsulation.

- Spoke routers register their public IP addresses with the hub router using the Next Hop Resolution Protocol (NHRP). You can read more about NHRP in RFC 2332 and 2333.

- You should disable split horizon when using RIP or EIGRP in a hub and spoke topology. If split horizon is left enabled, the spokes cannot learn of routes to other spoke networks.

Note If you are using OSPF as your routing protocol, it is recommended (but not required) that you configure all mGRE interfaces as point-to-multipoint. To minimize routing update traffic, unnecessssary SPF calculations, and unstable connections over public networks, it is also recommended that you configure the **ip ospf database filter-all out**

command on the hub router and configure static default routes via tunnel interface on the spoke routers.

- GRE tunnels can introduce challenges to IPv4 public networks because of the increased header size. GRE adds at least 24 bytes of overhead. The 24 bytes includes a 4-byte GRE header and a new 20-byte IP header. Adding options (such as checksums or sequence numbers) to the GRE header can increase the header size by up to an additional 12 bytes. Introducing AH and ESP headers along with GRE reduces the payload amount even further. It is therefore recommended to change the MTU size to 1400 bytes and the TCP maximum segment size (MSS) to 1360 bytes. See RFC 1191 for more on how the MTU and TCP MSS values affect IPv4 traffic.

Note   You can segment traffic with DMVPNs by using the multiprotocol Border Gateway Protocol (MBGP) and Multiprotocol Label Switching (MPLS). See Chapter 10, "Multiprotocol Label Switching," for more on configuring MPLS and mBGP.

Configuration

1. Create a transform set and IPsec profile:

   a. Create a transform set.

      ```
      (global) crypto ipsec transform-set transform-set-name transform1
      [transform2 [transform3]]
      ```

      A transform set named transform-set-name (a text string) is defined with up to three different transforms, defining IPsec protocols and algorithms. Transform sets are negotiated between peers when an SA initiates. Therefore, multiple transform sets can be defined within a crypto profile. If IKE is not used, only one transform set can be defined.

      You can choose up to three transforms, as follows:

      (Optional) Pick one AH transform:

      - **ah-md5-hmac**—AH with MD5 authentication

      - **ah-sha-hmac**—AH with SHA authentication

      (Optional) Pick one ESP encryption transform:

      - **esp-des**—ESP with 56-bit DES encryption

      - **esp-3des**—ESP with 168-bit 3DES encryption

      - **esp-aes**—ESP with 128-bit AES encryption

      - **esp-aes 192**—ESP with 192-bit AES encryption

      - **esp-aes 256**—ESP with 256-bit AES encryption

- **esp-null**—Null encryption

- **esp-seal**–ESP with 160-bit SEAL encryption

and one of these authentication methods:

- **esp-md5-hmac**—ESP with MD5 authentication

- **esp-sha-hmac**—ESP with SHA authentication

(Optional) Pick an IP compression transform:

- **comp-lzs**—IP compression with the LZS algorithm

AH provides data authentication and antireplay services, and ESP provides packet encryption and optional data authentication and antireplay services.

Use an ESP encryption transform to maintain data confidentiality. Use an ESP authentication transform to maintain data integrity or an AH authentication transform to maintain the integrity of the payload and the outer IP header. The SHA authentication algorithm is stronger than MD5 but more CPU-intensive. (It is slower.)

Recommended transform sets follow:

```
(global) crypto ipsec transform-set name esp-des esp-sha-hmac
```

-or-

```
(global) crypto ipsec transform-set name ah-sha-hmac esp-des esp-sha-hmac
```

b. (Optional) Change the transform set to transform mode:

```
(transform-set) mode transport
```

IPsec VPNs can operate in either tunnel mode or transport mode. With tunnel mode, the entire original IP packet is protect. With transport mode, only the payload of the original IP packet is protected. By default, a transform set is in tunnel mode. Use transport mode when the IP traffic has IPsec peers as both the source and destination.

c. Define the IPsec profile name and enter crypto map configuration mode:

```
(global) crypto ipsec profile profile-name
```

Crypto maps and access lists are not used with DMVPNs. Instead, IPsec profiles are used, and the configuration normally supplied through crypto maps and access lists is created automatically as VPN tunnels are established. An IPsec profile is like a crypto map but without a peer IP address or an access list to specify the protected traffic.

d. Specify the name of the transform set to be used by the profile:

```
(crypto-map) set transform-set transform-set-name
```

The transform-set name should match the name you used to create the transform set in Step 1-a.

2. Configure dynamic ISAKMP keys and Dead Peer Detection (DPD):

   a. Configure a dynamic ISAKMP key:

   ```
   (global) crypto isakmp key key-string address 0.0.0.0 0.0.0.0
   ```

   Use the IP address and mask of 0.0.0.0 0.0.0.0 to specify that the key-string should be used as the key for any dynamically created tunnel.

   b. Enable Dead Peer Detection (DPD):

   ```
   (global) crypto isakmp keepalive keepalive-value
   ```

   Dead Peer Detection is discussed in Section 13-3, "High Availability Options." DPD is required with dynamic multipoint VPNS to maintain ISKAMP peers. Without this, the tunnels cannot be established.

3. Configure the hub router:

   a. Create a tunnel interface and configure an IP address:

   ```
   (global) interface tunnel tunnel-number
   (interface) ip address ip-address mask
   ```

   All hubs and spokes must have their tunnel interfaces on the same subnet.

   b. Change the MTU size to 1400:

   ```
   (interface) ip mtu 1400
   ```

   Because of the increased overhead of IPsec and GRE headers, you should change the IP MTU size to 1400 bytes.

   c. Change the TCP maximum segment size (MSS) to 1360:

   ```
   (interface) ip tcp adjust-mss 1360
   ```

   In addition to changing the MTU size, you should also change the TCP MSS. This causes TCP sessions to quickly scale back to fit within the 1400-byte IP packet for the GRE tunnel.

   d. (Optional but recommended) Configure the bandwidth on the interface:

   ```
   (interface) bandwidth kbps
   ```

   You should configure the bandwidth of the tunnel interface so that routing protocols that use bandwidth in their path determination can make accurate decisions. The default value is 9 kbps. The recommended setting is 1000 or greater.

Note   Configuring the bandwidth to at least 1000 is especially important if you are using EIGRP. If not, EIGRP may not properly establish and maintain neighbor relationships during times of heavy traffic. It is also recommended that you change the delay to 1000 with the interface-level **delay 1000** command.

e. Specify the tunnel source address:

```
(interface) tunnel source [interface | ip-address]
```

The source should be the interface or the IP address assigned to the interface connected to the inside (protected) network.

f. (Optional but recommended) Configure NHRP authentication:

```
(interface) ip nhrp authentication string
```

You should configure NHRP authentication on all routers. NHRP authentication is an optional extension to NHRP and uses HMAC-MD5-128 as its default algorithm. All routers need to be configured with the same string.

g. Allow the hub router to automatically add the spoke router IP addresses to the multicast NHRP mappings:

```
(interface) ip nhrp map multicast dynamic
```

This command enables for dynamic NHRP mappings instead of manually configured maps. This command is only necessary on the NHRP hub router that maintains dynamic maps to all spoke routers.

h. Assign the NHRP network identifier and allow NHRP on the tunnel interface:

```
(interface) ip nhrp network-id number
```

This command enables NHRP and defines the 32-bit network identifier. The network identifier is locally significant, but it is recommended to use the same identifier on all routers to maintain consistency, which aids in deploying new routers and troubleshooting configurations. As a 32-bit number, the valid range is 1 to 4,294,967,295.

i. Configure the tunnel interface to use mGRE encapsulation:

```
(interface) tunnel mode gre multipoint
```

j. Associate the tunnel interface with an IPsec profile:

```
(interface) tunnel protection ipsec profile profile-name
```

Enter the profile name you created in Step 1 with the **crypto ipsec profile** command.

k. (Optional but recommended) Decrease the NHRP holdtime:

```
(interface) ip nhrp holdtime seconds
```

The holdtime defines the number of seconds that learned NHRP addresses are advertised to spokes as valid in authoritative NHRP responses. The default value is 7200 seconds (2 hours), but the recommended value range is between 300 to 600 seconds for NHRP Nonbroadcast Multi-access (NBMA) DMVPNs over public networks.

4. Configure the spoke routers:

a. Create a tunnel interface and configure an IP address:

```
(global) interface tunnel tunnel-number
(interface) ip address ip-address mask
```

All hubs and spokes must have their tunnel interfaces on the same subnet.

b. Change the MTU size to 1400:

```
(interface) ip mtu 1400
```

Because of the increased overhead of IPsec and GRE headers, you should change the IP MTU size to 1400 bytes.

c. Change the TCP maximum segment size (MSS) to 1360.

```
(interface) ip tcp adjust-mss 1360
```

In addition to changing the MTU size, you should also change the TCP MSS. This causes TCP sessions to quickly scale back to fit within the 1400-byte IP packet for the GRE tunnel.

d. (Optional but recommended) Configure the bandwidth on the interface:

```
(interface) bandwidth kbps
```

You should configure the bandwidth of the tunnel interface so that routing protocols that use bandwidth in their path determination can make accurate decisions. The default value is 9 kbps. The recommended setting is 1000 or greater.

Note   Configuring the bandwidth to at least 1000 is especially important if you are using EIGRP. If not, EIGRP may not properly establish and maintain neighbor relationships during times of heavy traffic. It is also recommended that you change the delay to 1000 with the interface-level **delay 1000** command.

e. Specify the tunnel source address:

```
(interface) tunnel source [interface | ip-address]
```

The source should be the interface or the IP address assigned to the interface connected to the inside (protected) network.

f. (Optional but recommended) Configure NHRP authentication:

```
(interface) ip nhrp authentication string
```

Section 13-4

You should configure NHRP authentication on all routers. NHRP authentication is an optional extension to NHRP and uses HMAC-MD5-128 as its default algorithm. All routers need to be configured with the same string.

g. Create a NHRP mapping between the IP address configured on the hub's tunnel interface and the IP address configured on the physical interface connected to the unsecure (public) network:

```
(interface) ip nhrp map hub-tunnel-ip-address hub-physical-ip-address
```

This command is required for the spoke to know the address of the NHRP server (the hub router) and the next hop IP address to reach the NHRP server (the public IP address on the hub).

h. Allow the use of dynamic routing protocols:

```
(interface) ip nhrp map multicast hub-physical-ip-address
```

Configure this command to allow multicast packets to be sent to the hub router. By default, multicast traffic is not enabled to traverse across NBMAs. Most routing protocols rely on multicast packets, so configure this command with the public IP address of the hub router for the multicast packets to reach the hub.

i. Specify the hub router as the NHRP next-hop server:

```
(interface) ip nhrp nhs hub-physical-ip-address
```

The spoke routers act as clients and register their IP addresses with the next-hop NHRP server (the hub router).

j. Assign the NHRP network identifier and allow NHRP on the tunnel interface:

```
(interface) ip nhrp network-id number
```

This command enables NHRP and defines the 32-bit network identifier. The network identifier is locally significant, but it is recommended to use the same identifier on all routers to maintain consistency, which aids in deploying new routers and troubleshooting configurations. As a 32-bit number, the valid range is 1 to 4,294,967,295.

k. Configure the tunnel interface to use mGRE encapsulation:

```
(interface) tunnel mode gre multipoint
```

Use this command to allow the automatic creation of tunnels between the spoke routers. The spoke routers establishes VPN tunnels using GRE encapsulation and routing their traffic through the hub router. If you do not need dynamic spoke-to-spoke VPNs, you can use **the tunnel destination** *hub-physical-ip-address* command instead to create only a VPN GRE tunnel to the hub router.

l. Associate the tunnel interface with an IPsec profile:

```
(interface) tunnel protection ipsec profile profile-name
```

Enter the profile name you created in Step 1 with the **crypto ipsec profile** command.

m. (Optional but recommended) Decrease the NHRP holdtime:

```
(interface) ip nhrp holdtime seconds
```

The holdtime defines the number of seconds that learned NHRP addresses are advertised to spokes as valid in authoritative NHRP responses. The default value is 7200 seconds (2 hours), but the recommended value range is between 300 to 600 seconds for NHRP NBMA DMVPNs over public networks.

Example

Figure 13-3 is used in this example. The HQ router is the hub, and Remote-1 and Remote-2 are the spokes. The spoke routers are configured to use the hub router as the NHRP next-hop server and to dynamically create VPN tunnels to each other as needed. Using NHRP, a spoke router registers its public IP address with the HQ hub router and advertises the IP address out to the other spoke router when a VPN tunnel needs to be established.

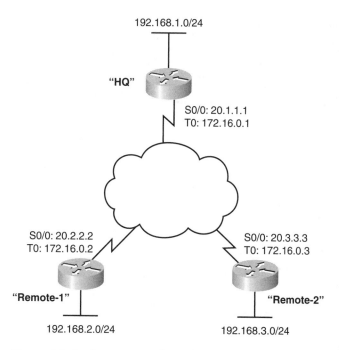

Figure 13-3 *Dynamic Multipoint VPN Example*

HQ Router
```
crypto isakmp key secretkey address 0.0.0.0 0.0.0.0
```

```
crypto isakmp keepalive 10
!
crypto ipsec transform-set VPN-SET esp-des esp-sha-hmac
 mode transport
!
crypto ipsec profile IPSEC-PROFILE
 set transform-set VPN-SET
!
interface tunnel 0
 ip address 172.16.0.1 255.255.0.0
 ip mtu 1400
 ip tcp adjust-mss 1360
 bandwidth 1000
 delay 1000
 tunnel source fastethernet0/0
 ip nhrp authentication VPNSecretKey
 ip nhrp map multicast dynamic
 ip nhrp network-id 1
 tunnel mode gre multipoint
 ip nhrp holdtime 600
 tunnel protection ipsec profile IPSEC-PROFILE
 no ip split-horizon eigrp 1
 no ip next-hop-self eigrp 1
!
interface fastethernet0/0
 ip address 192.168.1.1 255.255.255.0
!
interface serial0/0
 ip address 20.1.1.1 255.255.255.0


!
router eigrp 1
 no auto-summary
 network 20.0.0.0
 network 172.16.0.0
 network 192.168.1.0
!
ip default-network 20.0.0.0
```

Remote-1

```
crypto isakmp key secretkey address 0.0.0.0 0.0.0.0
crypto isakmp keepalive 10
!
crypto ipsec transform-set VPN-SET esp-des esp-sha-hmac
```

```
  mode transport
 !
 crypto ipsec profile IPSEC-PROFILE
   set transform-set VPN-SET
 !
 interface tunnel 0
  ip address 172.16.0.2 255.255.0.0
  ip mtu 1400
  ip tcp adjust-mss 1360
  bandwidth 1000
  delay 1000
  tunnel source fastethernet0/0
  ip nhrp authentication VPNSecretKey
  ip nhrp map 172.16.0.1 20.1.1.1
  ip nhrp multicast 20.1.1.1
  ip nhrp nhs 20.1.1.1
  ip nhrp network-id 1
  tunnel mode gre multipoint
  tunnel protection ipsec profile IPSEC-PROFILE
  ip nhrp holdtime 600
  no ip split-horizon eigrp 1

 !
 interface fastethernet0/0
  ip address 192.168.2.1 255.255.255.0
 !
 interface serial0/0
  ip address 20.2.2.2 255.255.255.0

 !
 router eigrp 1
  no auto-summary
  network 20.0.0.0
  network 172.16.0.0
  network 192.168.2.0
 !
 ip default-network 20.0.0.0
```

Remote-2

```
crypto isakmp key secretkey address 0.0.0.0 0.0.0.0
crypto isakmp keepalive 10
!
crypto ipsec transform-set VPN-SET esp-des esp-sha-hmac
 mode transport
!
```

```
crypto ipsec profile IPSEC-PROFILE
  set transform-set VPN-SET
!
interface tunnel 0
 ip address 172.16.0.3 255.255.0.0
 ip mtu 1400
 ip tcp adjust-mss 1360
 bandwidth 1000
 delay 1000
 tunnel source fastethernet0/0
 ip nhrp authentication VPNSecretKey
 ip nhrp map 172.16.0.1 20.1.1.1
 ip nhrp multicast 20.1.1.1
 ip nhrp nhs 20.1.1.1
 ip nhrp network-id 1
 tunnel mode gre multipoint
 tunnel protection ipsec profile IPSEC-PROFILE
 ip nhrp holdtime 600
 no ip split-horizon eigrp 1

!
interface fastethernet0/0
 ip address 192.168.3.1 255.255.255.0
!
interface serial0/0
 ip address 20.3.3.3 255.255.255.0

!
router eigrp 1
 no auto-summary
 network 20.0.0.0
 network 172.16.0.0
 network 192.168.3.0
!
ip default-network 20.0.0.0
```

13-5: Secure Socket Layer VPNs

- Using a web browser, remote users can establish a secure VPN tunnel over SSL.

- Tunnels can be in clientless mode, thin-client mode, or tunnel mode. Clientless mode enables for web-based applications such as file sharing (using the common Internet file system standard) and Outlook Web Access. Thin-client mode uses a Java Applet and TCP port forwarding to extend functionality. In thin-client mode, a user can access applications such as email clients, telnet, and SSH. Thin-client mode requires Java Runtime Environment (JRE) version 1.4 or later. Finally, tunnel mode enables the greatest flexibility by establishing a full VPN tunnel that enables all network traffic. Tunnel mode uses a Java or ActiveX Cisco AnyConnect VPN client that the user must download and install.

Figure 13-4 shows an example of the login screen users see.

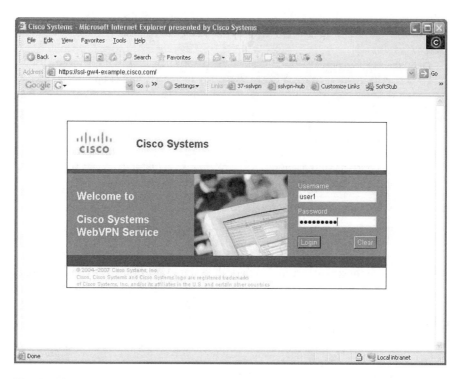

Figure 13-4 *SSL VPN Login Screen*

Configuration

There are many configurable options for SSL VPNs. This section focuses on the minimum and common configuration necessary on the router acting as the SSL VPN endpoint to establish a tunnel. The configuration given assumes a self-signed certificate and uses AAA for authentication. Refer to Cisco.com for more information on the numerous options available for SSL VPNs.

1.   Enter webvpn gateway configuration mode:

```
(global) webvpn gateway gw-name
```

This command takes you into webvpn gateway configuration mode. If you want to test only basic SSL VPN connectivity, you can enter the **webvpn enable gateway-addr** *ip-address* command from the privileged EXEC prompt. You can test connectivity by opening an SSL-compatible browser and accessing http://*ip-address*.

2. Configure a hostname for the SSL VPN gateway:

`(webvpn-gateway)` **hostname** *name*

It is also recommended that you update the records in your DNS servers with the hostname of the SSL gateway.

3. Configure the IP address for clients to use to connect to the SSL gateway:

`(webvpn-gateway)` **ip address** *ip-address* [**port** *port-number*]

The **port** *port-number* option enables you to specify a port number to be used when users connect to the VPN gateway. If you specify a port number, users need to enter the port number when typing in the address (http://*ip-address:port-number*).

4. Redirect TCP port 80 traffic to a TCP port 443:

`(webvpn-gateway)` **http-redirect**

If a user connects to the gateway using plain-text HTTP traffic over TCP port 80, this command redirects them to a secure HTTPS connection over TCP port 443.

5. Define the support encryption algorithms for the SSL VPN connections:

`(webvpn-gateway)` **ssl encryption** [**3des-sha1** | **aes-sha1** | **rc4-md5**]

You can specify more than one encryption algorithm. The gateway and the client go through the listed encryption algorithms until they find one that both support. The order in which you enter the encryption algorithms specifies the preference on the gateway.

6. Enable the gateway:

`(webvpn-gateway)` **inservice**

This command activates the SSL VPN service. You must have an IP address configured within the webvpn gateway configuration mode for this command to take effect (step 3).

7. Enable AAA, define your usernames and passwords, and configure the router to use local AAA authentication:

`(global)` **aaa new-model**
`(global)` **username** *name* **secret** *password*
`(global)` **aaa authentication login** [**default** | *list-name*] **local**

If you use the **default** keyword, AAA is automatically enabled for the console, AUX, VTY lines. As soon as the context is defined (step 8), AAA is automatically enabled for the SSL VPN. If you want to use only AAA for the SSL VPN, specify a *list-name* and apply it under the webvpn context. Refer to Chapter 12, "Router Security," for more on configuring AAA.

8. Enter webvpn context configuration mode:

`(global)` **webvpn context** *context-name*

Context configuration mode defines the virtual context that users have when connecting to the SSL VPN.

9. (Required if defined a *list-name* in step 7) Associate the context with the AAA authentication list:

```
(webvpn-context) aaa authentication list list-name
```

When this command is entered, users can use the username and password specified in the **username** global configuration command to log into the SSL VPN website.

Example

In the following example, a router is configured with AAA authentication and enabled to act as an SSL VPN gateway. Users can connect to the SSL VPN by navigating to https://www.mydomain.com and logging in with a username of user1 and password of password1. A redirect is configured so that if users enter http instead of https they will be automatically redirected to the SSL site. The gateway prefers that the client uses aes-sha1 but also supports 3des-sha1.

```
hostname SSL-Router
ip domain-name mydomain.com
!
webvpn gateway VPN_GW
 hostname www
 ip address 4.4.4.4
 http-redirect
 ssl encryption aes-sha1 3des-sha1
 inservice
!
webvpn context VPN_CONTEXT
 aaa authentication list VPN_LIST
!
aaa new-model
aaa authentication login VPN_LIST local
!
username user1 password password1
```

Further Reading

The following are some recommended resources pertaining to the topics discussed in this chapter:

Comparing, Designing, and Deploying VPNs, by Mark Lewis, Cisco Press, ISBN 1-58705-179-6.

Complete Cisco VPN Configuration Guide, by Richard Deal, Cisco Press, ISBN 1-58705-204-0.

Section 13-5

IPSec Virtual Private Network Fundamentals, by James Carmouche, Cisco Press, ISBN 1-58705-207-5.

SSL Remote Access VPNs, by Qiang Huang and Jazib Frahim, Cisco Press, ISBN 1-58705-242-3.

RFC 2332, "NBMA Next Hop Resolution Protocol (NHRP)."

RFC 2333, "NHRP Protocol Applicability Statement."

RFC 2405, "The ESP DES-CBC Cipher Algorithm with Explicit IV."

RFC 2409, "The Internet Key Exchange (IKE)."

RFC 2412, "The OAKLEY Determination Protocol."

RFC 2784, "Generic Route Encapsulation (GRE)."

RFC 4301, "Security Architecture for the Internet Protocol."

RFC 4302, "IP Authentication Header."

RFC 4303, "IP Encapsulating Security Payload (ESP)."

RFC 4309, "Using Advanced Encryption Standard (AES) CCM Mode with IPSec Encapsulation Security Payload (ESP)."

Chapter 14

Access Lists and Regular Expressions

This chapter presents background and configuration information about access lists:

- 14-1: IP Access Lists

- 14-2: MAC Address and Protocol Type Code Access Lists

- 14-3: IPv6 Access Lists

- 14-4: Regular Expressions

Cisco IOS Software uses access lists for many functions that are described throughout this book. Some of these functions include:

- Packet filtering

- Controlling access to VTY lines

- Classifying traffic for QoS

- Identifying interesting traffic for DDR

- Identifying interesting traffic for VPNs

- Identifying which addresses NAT translates

- Controlling SNMP access to the router

- Authenticating RSH and RCP requests

- Customizing PIM routing configurations

- Filtering output from a **debug** command

- Filtering IP routes

- Controlling access to NTP services

This chapter describes the configuration steps needed to create the access lists you might need to use.

Access lists can be created and referenced by number and sometimes by name. Access lists fall into several categories, depending on what type of traffic or protocol is being matched or filtered. Table 14-1 summarizes how the access list numbers correspond to the access list functions.

Table 14-1 *Access List Numbers and Functions*

Access List Type	Access List Numbers	Named Access Lists?
IP standard	1 to 99	Yes
	1300 to 1999	
IP extended	100 to 199	Yes
	2000 to 2699	
MAC address	700 to 799	
MAC address extended	1100 to 1199	
Protocol type code	200 to 299	
Extended transparent bridging vendor code	1100 to 1199	
IPX standard	800 to 899	Yes
IPX extended	900 to 999	Yes
IPX SAP	1000 to 1099	Yes
IPX summary address	1200 to 1299	Yes
AppleTalk	600 to 699	
DECnet	300 to 399	
XNS standard	400 to 499	
XNS extended	500 to 599	
IPv6 standard and extended	N/A	Yes (only named access lists are supported)

Access lists use top-down processing. Traffic is compared with the access list, and if a packet does not match, the criteria of the access list statement is passed down to the next statement. Because of the top-down processing, it is recommended that you configure your access list to match a more specific host or traffic type before more matching more general statements and to match more frequent traffic before less frequent traffic. Also, access lists have an implicit **deny all**, so every access list needs at least one **permit** statement.

Access lists use wildcard masks to inform the router how much of an address it should look at when examining the IP header of packets. A binary zero in the mask informs the router to examine a bit, whereas a binary one in the mask informs the router to not examine the bit.

Regular expressions are used to define a template that can be used to match against text strings. Regular expressions can be useful when you are matching patterns in modem chat scripts, BGP access lists, command output searching, and so forth.

14-1: IP Access Lists

- Standard IP access lists can be used to match against a specific source address or range of source addresses.

- Extended IP access lists can be used to match against source and destination addresses, protocols, source and destination port numbers, IP fields, ICMP messages, and Quality of Service (QoS) parameters.

- IP access lists can be defined by number or name. Numbered access lists cannot be edited and must be cleared and reentered if changes are needed. Named access lists can be edited by clearing specific lines.

- Dynamic IP access lists can be used to maintain a dynamic or changing list of matching conditions.

- Time range IP access lists can be used to apply matching conditions during a specified date and time period.

- IP prefix lists can be used to match against a specific number or range of address bits, as the leftmost portion of the IP address.

Configuration

1. Define a standard IP numbered access list (source address only):

    (global) **access-list** acc-list {**permit** | **deny**} source [source-mask] [**log** [word]]

    IP access lists can be referenced by number or by name. The standard access list number acc-list is in the range of 1 to 99 or 1300 to 1999. Only the source IP address source can be matched. The source-mask field is used to mask bits of the source address that do not need to be matched. A 1 bit in the mask indicates a don't-care address bit, and a 0 bit marks an address bit that must match exactly. (Think of the mask as the opposite of a subnet mask.) If all addresses are to be matched, you can replace the source and source-mask fields with the keyword **any**. If a specific host address is to be matched, you can replace the source and source-mask fields with the keyword **host** followed by its IP address.

The **log** keyword can be used to cause the router to send messages to the console or other logging facilities. (See Section 1-5 for information about system logging configuration.) A log entry is made for the first packet that matches the access list command, whether it is permitted or denied. After that, the router sends log messages every 5 minutes with the total number of matching packets for that time interval. A user-defined cookie can be appended to a log message by using the optional *word* parameter. The word must contain alphanumeric characters only.

A text-string comment can be added to a numbered access list using the **access-list** *acc-list* **remark** *remark* command.

2. Define an extended IP access list (source and destination addresses and other parameters):

```
(global) access-list acc-list [dynamic dyn-name [timeout minutes]]
  {permit | deny} protocol source source-mask [operator [port]] destination
  destination-mask [operator [port] [precedence precedence] [dscp dscp] [tos
tos [icmp-type [icmp-code] | icmp-message]][fragments] [log [word] | log-input]
[established] [time-range time-range-name] [ttl operator value]
```

IP access lists can be referenced by number or by name. The extended access list number *acc-list* is in the range of 100 to 199 or 2000 to 2699. Both the *source* and *destination* IP addresses can be matched. The *source-mask* and *destination-mask* fields are used to mask bits of the address that do not need to be matched. A 1 bit in the mask indicates a don't-care address bit, and a 0 bit marks an address bit that must match exactly. (Think of the mask as the opposite of a subnet mask.) If all addresses are to be matched, you can replace the address and mask fields with the keyword **any**. If a specific host address is to be matched, you can replace the address and mask fields with the keyword **host** followed by its IP address.

The **dynamic** and **timeout** keywords can be used to make this access list operate as a dynamic or Lock and Key access list. (See Section 13-4 for more information.)

The *protocol* field specifies which IP protocol will be used to match. The protocol can be one of **ip** (any IP protocol), **tcp**, **udp**, **eigrp** (EIGRP routing protocol), **gre** (Generic Routing Encapsulation), **icmp** (Internet Control Message Protocol), **igmp** (Internet Group Management Protocol), **igrp** (IGRP routing protocol), **ipinip** (IP-in-IP tunnel), **nos** (KA9Q Network Operating System compatible IP over IP tunnel), **ospf** (OSPF routing protocol), or an IP protocol number (0 to 255).

If the protocol is **icmp**, additional fields can be used for further filtering. One or more of *icmp-type*, *icmp-type icmp-code*, or *icmp-message* can be added to the command line. The *icmp-type* field is the ICMP message type (0 to 15), and the *icmp-code* is an optional ICMP message code (0 to 255). The *icmp-message* field is a text string name, chosen from the following: **administratively-prohibited, alternate-address, conversion-error, dod-host-prohibited, dod-net-prohibited, echo, echo-reply, general-parameter-problem, host-isolated, host-precedence-unreachable, host-redirect, host-tos-redirect, host-tos-unreachable, host-unknown, host-unreachable, information-reply, information-request, mask-reply, mask-request, mobile-redirect, net-redirect, net-tos-redirect, net-tos-unreachable, net-unreachable, network-unknown, no-room-for-option, option-missing, packet-too-big, parameter-problem, port-unreachable, precedence-unreachable, protocol-unreachable, reassembly-timeout, redirect, router-advertisement, router-solicitation, source-quench, source-route-failed, time-exceeded, timestamp-reply, timestamp-request, traceroute, ttl-exceeded,** and **unreachable.**

If the protocol is **igmp,** an additional IGMP message type field can be added for further filtering, chosen from the following: **dvmrp, host-query, host-report, pim,** and **trace.** Alternatively, you can specify an IGMP message type by its number (0 to 15). For more on IGMP messages, see Chapter 7, "IP Multicast Routing," and the RFCs mentioned in the "Further Reading" section at the end of this chapter.

The **precedence** keyword can be used to match the IP precedence value, given as a number (0 to 7) or as a text string. Available values are **critical** (5), **flash** (3), **flash-override** (4), **immediate** (2), **internet** (6), **network** (7), **priority** (1), and **routine** (0).

The **dscp** keyword can be used to match the Differentiated Services Code Point (DSCP) bits contained in the Differentiated Services (DS) byte of an IP packet. The *dscp* value can be given as a number (6 bits: 0 to 63) or as a text string name. Available names are **default** (000000), **ef** (101110), **af11** (Assured Forwarding [AF], 001010), **af12** (001100), **af13** (001110), **af21** (010010), **af22** (010100), **af23** (010110), **af31** (011010), **af32** (011100), **af33** (011110), **af41** (100010), **af42** (100100), **af43** (100110), **cs1** (Class Selector [CS], precedence 1, 001000), **cs2** (precedence 2, 010000), **cs3** (precedence 3, 011000), **cs4** (precedence 4, 100000), **cs5** (precedence 5, 101000), **cs6** (precedence 6, 110000), and **cs7** (precedence 7, 111000). See Chapter 9, "Quality of Service," and the RFCs mentioned in the "Further Reading" section at the end of this chapter for more information on DSCP bits.

The **tos** keyword matches the type of service level (0 to 15). Available values are **max-reliability, max-throughput, min-delay, min-monetary-cost,** and **normal.**

The **fragments** keyword can be used to match packets that are not initial fragments. Without the **fragments** keyword, access list entries containing only Layer 3 information (IP addresses) are applied to nonfragmented packets, initial fragments, and noninitial fragments. Access list entries containing Layer 3 (IP addresses) and Layer 4 (TCP and UDP) information without the **fragments** keyword are applied to nonfragmented packets and initial fragments. Recommended practice dictates that you use the **fragments** keyword when configuring policy routing with the **match ip address** command. (See Chapter 8, "IP Route Processing," for more information on policy routing.)

For protocol types **tcp** and **udp**, the command syntax is changed slightly to allow the matching of TCP or UDP source and destination port numbers. The syntax becomes:

```
{permit | deny} {tcp | udp} source source-mask [operator [source-port]]
destination destination-mask [operator [dest-port]] ...
```

You can specify an *operator* to determine how the source and destination port numbers are to be matched. You can use the operators **lt** (less than), **gt** (greater than), **eq** (equal to), **neq** (not equal to), or **range** (within a range given by two port number values). The source and destination ports are given as a number (0 to 65535) or as a text string port name.

Available TCP names are **bgp, chargen, daytime, discard, domain, drip, echo, finger, ftp, ftp-data, gopher, hostname, irc, klogin, kshell, lpd, nntp, pop2, pop3, smtp, sunrpc, syslog, tacacs-ds, talk, telnet, time, uucp, whois,** and **www** (actually HTTP, port 80). The **drip** keyword was added in Cisco IOS Software Release 12.4 and specifies TCP port 3949, which is used by Optimized Edge Routing (OER) for messages sent between a master controller and border router. In addition, the **established** keyword can be used to match packets from established connections, or packets that have either the RST or ACK bits set.

Available UDP names are **biff, bootpc, bootps, discard, dnsix, domain, echo, mobile-ip, nameserver, netbios-dgm, netbios-ns, non-500-isakmp, ntp, rip, snmp, snmptrap, sunrpc, syslog, tacacs-ds, talk, tftp, time, who,** and **xdmcp.**

A **permit** or **deny** statement in an extended IP access list can be applied during a time range using the **time-range** keyword. A time range must first be defined with a *time-range-name* using the following commands. The *time-range-name* must also be applied to the extended access list.

```
(global) time-range time-range-name
(time-range) periodic days-of-the-week hh:mm to [days-of-the-week] hh:mm
(time-range) absolute [start time date] [end time date]
```

Time ranges can be specified as one or more **periodic** definitions. The *days-of-the-week* field can be **daily** (Monday through Sunday), **weekdays** (Monday through Friday), **weekend** (Saturday and Sunday), **Monday, Tuesday, Wednesday, Thursday, Friday, Saturday,** or **Sunday.** The time *hh:mm* is given in 24-hour format. The router should be configured with NTP or have its clock and calendar set accurately.

Time ranges can also be specified as one **absolute** definition, with optional **start** and **end** times. The *time* is specified in *hh:mm* 24-hour format. The *date* fields must be formatted as *day month year,* as in 1 April 1963.

You can filter packets by their TTL value with the **ttl** keyword followed by an operator (**lt, gt, eq, neq**) and the TTL *value.*

Extended access lists support both the **log** and **log-input** options. The **log** keyword is the same as with a standard access list. The **log-input** records the input interface that matched the access list.

Note Only named access lists enable you to remove individual lines; however, you can treat a numbered access list as a named access list to remove a line. For example, if you have access list 100 with a line you want to remove, you can enter named configuration mode by typing **ip access-list extended 100**.

   3. Define a standard or extended IP named access list:

      a. Define a standard IP named access list:

```
(global) ip access-list standard  name
(access-list) [sequence-number] {permit | deny} source [source-mask] [log
[word]]
```

Standard IP named access lists filter source traffic just as standard IP numbered access lists. For a named access list, a text string name is given. Sequence numbers can be used to number each statement within a named access list. By using sequence numbers, you can insert lines in the middle of an access list instead of at the end. The text-string comment can be added to a named access list by using the **remark** command.

      b. Define an extended IP named access list:

```
(global) ip access-list extended  name


(access-list) [sequence-number] [dynamic dyn-name [timeout minutes]]
{permit | deny} protocol source source-mask [operator [port] destination
destination-mask
[operator [port]] [established | {match-any | match-all} {+ | -} tcp-flag] [option
option-value] [precedence precedence] [dscp dscp] [tos tos] [icmp-type
[icmp-code] | icmp-message]] [fragments] [ttl operator value] [reflect
reflect-list [timeout seconds]] [log [word]| log-input] [time-range time-
range-name]
```

Extended IP named access lists enable the same filtering as extended IP numbered access lists. Named access lists also include additional filtering options not available with numbered access lists.

The **reflect** keyword and an optional **timeout** value can be used to create a reflexive access list. (See Section 12-5, "Filtering IP Sessions with Reflexive Access Lists," for more information.)

Starting with Cisco IOS Software Release 12.2(25)S, extended IP named access lists also enable for filtering IP options, which are used for features such as loose and strict source routing, timestamps, Multiprotocol Label Switching (MPLS) traffic engineering, Resource Reservation Protocol (RSVP), and classifying packets in 1 of 16 security levels. IP options are either a single octet with an option-type value or an option-type octet followed by an option-length octet and the actual option-data octets. In the latter format, the option-type octet consists of a 1-bit copied flag (indicating if the option is to be copied for each fragment), a 2-bit option-class (indicating if the option is for traffic control or for debugging and measurement), and a 5-bit option number, to form an 8-bit value for the option-type field. (See RFC 791 for more on the format of the IP options field.) You can filter IP Options packets by either their number (0 to 255) or by name. Valid names include **add-ext, any-options, com-security, dps, encode, eool, ext-ip, ext-security, finn, imitd, lsr, mtup, mtur, no-op, nsapa, record-route, router-alert, sdb, security, ssr, stream-id, timestamp, traceroute, ump, visa,** and **zsu.**

Most Cisco routers process IP Options packets in software instead of hardware, resulting in slow processing of packets. Filtering these options helps relieve route processors (RP) and downstream routers from processing IP Options packets that they do not need to process. You can even eliminate all IP Options packets with the global **ip options drop** command or treat all IP Options packets destined for the router as if they have no options enabled with the global **ip options ignore** command.

Extended IP named access lists also enable for filtering on TCP flags. The TCP header contains a 6-bit control field that is used for setting the flags shown in Table 14-2.

Table 14-2   *TCP Flags*

Flag Name	Description
URG	Indicates that the urgent pointer is being used. The urgent pointer is a 16-bit field that points to the sequence number of the octet following the urgent data so that the host knows where nonurgent data begins. Packets flagged with the URG bit are to be processed immediately.
ACK	Indicates that the receiver is acknowledging receipt of segments and that the 32-bit acknowledge number field is being used to indicate the value of the next sequence number.
PSH	Indicates that the sender wants to push the buffered data to the receiving application layer service.
RST	Indicates that the TCP session is reset. The receiving host sets this flag to close a TCP connection.
SYN	Indicates that the host wants establish a connection and synchronize the initial sequence numbers (ISN).
FIN	Indicates that a host is finished sending data.

The following options available to you when filtering packets based on TCP flags:

- **established**
- **match-any**
- **match-all**
- **+ | -**
- *tcp-flag*

The **established** keyword is the same as when it is used with an extended IP numbered access list. Using this keyword matches packets from established connections or packets that have either the RST or ACK bits set. This keyword is considered legacy now, and you should use the **match-any** or **match-all** keywords followed by the **+** or **–** keywords and the *tcp-flag* name instead.

The **match-any** keyword matches packets with any of the TCP flags specified with the *tcp-flag* parameter. The **match-all** keyword matches packets with all of the TCP flags specified with the *tcp-flag* parameter.

The **+** or **–** keyword indicate if the router should match packets if their TCP headers have the TCP flags specified with the *tcp-flag* parameter enabled or disabled, respectively.

The *tcp-flag* parameter defines the control bits you want to match on. Valid options for this parameter include **urg**, **ack**, **psh**, **rst**, **syn**, and **fin**.

Named access lists also support noncontiguous TCP or UDP ports. You can specify up to ten port numbers on a single line following the **eq** and **neq** operators.

4. Configure Object Groups for ACLs (OGACL):

a. Create a network object group:

```
(global) object-group network object-group-name
(network-group) description text | host {host-address | host-name} |
network-address [network-mask] | range host-range-start host-range-end |
group-object group-name
```

Introduced in Cisco IOS Software Release 12.4(20)T, Object Groups for ACLs (OGACL) enable you to classify hosts, networks, or protocols into groups for use with access lists. This feature makes it easier to configure and manage large access lists. You can add, delete, or change objects without deleting the entire object group. Multiple entries can be made within a single object group. You can also nest an object group within another object group by using the **group-object** command.

Object groups can be network object groups or service object groups. Use a network object group to specify a host, a range of hosts, or a network. Use service object groups to specify ICMP messages, TCP ports, or UDP ports. Both network and service object groups enable you to enter a description of the object group using the **description** command followed by user-defined text describing the object group (up to 200 characters).

b. Create a service object group:

```
(global) object-group service object-group-name
(service-group) description text | protocol | [tcp | udp | tcp-udp] [source
{{eq | lt | gt} port | range port-range}]  | icmp {icmp-type-code | icmp-
type-name} | group-object group-name
```

Service object groups can match IP protocols, TCP ports, UDP ports, or ICMP messages. The IP *protocol* option is the same as for an IP extended list and can either be a name or the IP protocol number. You can specify a source port using the **source** keyword or specify a destination port number (the default). You can specify both TCP and UDP ports using the **tcp-udp** keyword. You can enter common application layer protocol names instead of individual port numbers and ICMP message type names just as with IP extended lists.

c. Use object groups within a named ACL:

```
{permit | deny} {tcp | udp} object-group source-network-object-group-name
[object-group service-object-group-name]
object-group destination-object-group-name object-group service-object-
group-name
```

Object Groups for ACLs work only with named access lists. Configure a named access list as normal, replacing parameters with your configured object groups as desired.

5. Configure additional access list options.

a. Enable access list syslog entry hashes:

```
(global) ip access-list logging hash-generation
```

As an alternative to appending a user-defined cookie with the **log** *word* option at the end of an access list statement, you can generate an MD5 hash for each access list statement and include the hash with each log entry. The MD5-generated hashes are stored in NVRAM.

b. Resequence a named access list:

```
(global) ip access-list resequence name start-number increment
```

By default, named access lists sequence lines in increments of 10. Sequence numbers enable you to insert lines in the middle of an access list by specifying a sequence number that falls within the sequence range of two other lines. If you need to insert 10 or more access statements, you might need to resequence your access list lines with an increment greater than 10.

Sequence numbers are not saved in the startup-configuration file stored in NVRAM. When a router is reloaded, sequence numbers revert back to the initial starting sequence number and increment.

c. Configure the threshold for the number of packets necessary to match an access list statement before generating a log message:

(global) **ip access-list log-update threshold** *number*

By default, a router generates a log message after the first matching packet and at 5-minute intervals after the first matching packet. Configure this command to change the number of packets necessary to generate a log message.

d. Enable the Turbo Access List feature:

(global) **access-list** [*number* | *name*] **compiled**

Access lists can grow to the point that searching them can require a significant amount of time and can impact the memory used when the router is forwarding packets. The search time is not consistent, and there is increased latency and higher CPU load when a packet needs to be searched against a long access list. The Turbo Access List feature processes access lists into lookup tables for greater efficiency. An access list with more than three entries can lower the CPU utilization when matching a packet and offers fixed latency times.

6. Define an IP prefix list (matches prefix address bits):

a. Create an entry in a prefix list:

(global) **ip prefix-list** *list-name* [**seq** *seq-value*] [**description** *text*] {**deny** | **permit** *network/length*} [**ge** *ge-value*] [**le** *le-value*]

A match entry is added to the prefix list named *list-name* (text string). By default, prefix list entries are automatically numbered in increments of 5, beginning with the number 5. Match entries are evaluated in sequence, starting with the lowest sequence number. You can assign a specific sequence number to the entry by specifying the **seq** keyword, along with the *seq-value* (a positive number).

The prefix list entry matches an IP address against the *network* (a valid IP network address) and *length* (the number of leftmost bits in the address) values. The **ge** (greater than or equal to a number of bits) and **le** (less than or equal to a number of bits) keywords can also be used to define a range of the number of prefix bits to match. A range can provide a more specific matching condition than the *network/length* values alone.

b. Add a text description to a prefix list:

(global) **ip prefix-list** *list-name* **description** *text*

The string *text* is added as a description line in the prefix list named *list-name*.

Examples

Standard IP access list 10 is used to permit traffic with a source address from any host on the 192.168.204.0 network. Traffic from the IP address 192.168.44.3 is also permitted.

The standard named IP access list 10 performs the same function as numbered access list 10. This is done to show the same function configured two different ways:

```
access-list 10 permit 192.168.204.0 0.0.0.255
access-list 10 permit host 192.168.44.3

ip access-list standard list10
remark This is the same as access-list 10 above
permit 192.168.204.0 0.0.0.255
permit host 192.168.44.3
```

Extended IP **access list 105** is used to deny all DNS traffic. Telnet traffic between host 192.168.14.4 and any host on the 172.17.66.0 network is permitted. All IP packets with a DSCP value of **ef** (expedited forwarding) are permitted. All other UDP traffic is permitted (remember that DNS UDP traffic was denied earlier). Lastly, HTTP traffic from hosts on the 192.168.111.0 network to anywhere is blocked on weekdays from 8:00 a.m. to 5:00 p.m. through the use of a time range. Recall that every access list has an implicit **deny all** as a hidden command at the end of the list. Every **permit** or **deny** command you enter is placed above the **deny all**:

```
access-list 105 deny udp any any eq dns
access-list 105 permit tcp host 192.168.14.4 172.17.66.0 0.0.0.255 eq telnet
access-list 105 permit ip any any dscp ef
access-list 105 permit udp any any
access-list 105 deny tcp 192.168.111.0 0.0.0.255 any eq http time-range
BlockHTTP

ip access-list extended List105
remark This does the same function as access-list 105 above
deny udp any any eq dns
permit tcp host 192.168.14.4 172.17.66.0 0.0.0.255 eq telnet
permit ip any any dscp ef
permit udp any any
deny tcp 192.168.111.0 0.0.0.255 any eq http time-range BlockHTTP

time-range BlockHTTP
periodic weekdays 8:00 to 17:00
```

Access list List110 is configured to deny FTP, POP, and SMTP traffic from any host within the range of 192.168.20.5 through 192.168.20.10 to servers srv1.example.com and srv2.example.com. All other traffic is allowed. Object groups ease administration. A log message is generated with an appended MD5 hash after five packets match an access list statement:

```
ip access-list extended List110
 remark ACL using object-groups
 deny tcp object-group source-net object-group dest-net object-group traffic-
group log
 permit ip any any

object-group network source-net
 description LAN hosts
 range 192.168.20.5 192.168.20.10

object-group network dest-net
 description Servers
 host srv1.example.com
 host srv2.example.com

object-group service traffic-group
 description FTP and E-mail
 group-object ftp
 group-object email

object-group service ftp
 description FTP traffic
 tcp eq ftp
 tcp eq ftp-data

object-group service email
 description POP and SMTP
 tcp eq 110
 tcp eq 25


ip access-list log-update threshold 5
ip access-list logging hash-generation
```

IP prefix list MyNetworks is used to deny networks (or routes) of 192.168.0.0 containing 25 or more network bits in their masks. Routes are permitted for 192.168.0.0 if they contain from 16 to 24 network bits. Routes from 172.17.0.0 are permitted if they have exactly 24 network bits:

```
ip prefix-list MyNetworks deny 192.168.0.0/16 ge 25
ip prefix-list MyNetworks permit 192.168.0.0/16 le 24
ip prefix-list MyNetworks permit 172.17.0.0/16 ge 24 le 24
```

14-2: MAC Address and Protocol Type Code Access Lists

- Standard MAC address access lists can be used to match against 48-bit source MAC addresses.

- Extended MAC address access lists can be used to match against source and destination MAC addresses, as well as a data pattern (up to 4 bytes) at an offset within the packet.

- Protocol type code access lists match against the 2-byte Ethernet protocol type codes contained in the packet header.

Note   Pay attention to the bit ordering that is used when an access list is applied to an interface. For example, an access list that is defined for Ethernet does not produce the same results on Token Ring or FDDI interfaces. This is because the bit ordering of each Token Ring and FDDI byte is reversed from Ethernet. Also, access lists for serial interfaces use Ethernet bit ordering.

Configuration

1. Define a standard MAC address access list:

    ```
    (global) access-list acc-list {permit | deny} address mask
    ```

    The access list number *acc-list* is in the range of 700 to 799. The *address* field is a 48-bit MAC address written as three groups of four hex digits separated by dots (such as 0000.1111.2222). The *mask* field specifies a mask to use for matching multiple addresses. A 1 bit in the mask causes that address bit to be ignored.

2. Define an extended MAC address access list:

    ```
    (global) access-list acc-list {permit | deny} source source-mask
        destination destination-mask [offset size operator operand]
    ```

    The access list number *acc-list* is in the range of 1100 to 1199. Both source and destination MAC addresses (*source* and *destination*) and masks (*source-mask* and *destination-mask*) are specified for matching. The addresses are 48-bit MAC addresses written as three groups of four hex digits separated by dots (such as 0000.1111.2222). The mask fields specify masks to use for matching multiple addresses. A 1 bit in the mask causes that address bit to be ignored.

    An additional matching condition can be specified based on a comparison of bytes within the packet. Values can be given as decimal numbers or hex values beginning with 0x. The *offset* field defines the location of the group of bytes to match against. The offset is given as the number of bytes offset *from the destination address* in the packet (not from the beginning of the packet). The *size* field is the number of bytes to compare (1 to 4). The comparison function is given as *operator*, and can be one of **lt** (less than), **gt** (greater than), **eq** (equal to), **neq** (not equal to), **and** (bitwise AND), **xor** (bitwise exclusive OR), or **nop** (no operation; compare addresses only). The *operand* field (decimal, hex with a leading 0x, or octal with a leading 0 format) specifies the value to compare or mask against.

3. Define a protocol type code access list:

   (global) **access-list** *acc-list* {**permit** | **deny**} *type-code mask*

   The access list number *acc-list* is in the range of 200 to 299. The *type-code* field is a 16-bit value that is specified as 0x followed by four hex digits. For Ethernet frames, this value represents the Ethernet type code; for 802.3 or 802.5 frames, it is the DSAP/SSAP pair. The *mask* is a 16-bit value used for type-code comparison, where a 1 bit indicates a type-code bit that should be ignored.

> **Note**   The Ethernet type-code values are listed in Appendix K, "Ethernet Type Codes."

Examples

Access 701 is used to filter packets based on the source MAC address. Addresses 0002.2000.3210 and 0002.2000.3211 are permitted (notice the wildcard 1 bit in the least-significant position), and all other addresses are denied.

```
access-list 701 permit 0002.2000.3210 0000.0000.0001
access-list 701 deny 0000.0000.0000 1111.1111.1111
```

Access list 1101 is used to filter packets based on extended MAC address options. Packets going from 1111.2222.3333 to 0011.0022.0033 are denied. Packets with a source address of 0101.0202.0303 going to any address are checked for a byte pattern. The pattern begins 60 bytes into the packet and is 2 bytes long. If the pattern equals the hex value 0x0f32, the packet is permitted.

```
access-list 1101 deny 1111.2222.3333 0000.0000.0000 0011.0022.0033 0000.0000.0000
access-list 1101 permit 0101.0202.0303 0000.0000.0000 0000.0000.0000
1111.1111.1111
60 2 eq 0x0f32
```

Access list 201 is used to permit IP (vendor type 0x0800) and IP ARP (0x0806) packets, while all others are denied.

```
access-list 201 permit 0x0800 0x0000
access-list 201 permit 0x0806 0x0000
```

14-3: IPv6 Access Lists

■ IPv6 neighbor discovery is permitted by default. There is an implicit **permit icmp any any nd-na**. You must enter a **deny ipv6 any any** statement within the access list to deny IPv6 neighbor discovery messages. See RFC 2461 for more on IPv6 neighbor discovery.

■ You can match TCP or UDP packets to the upper layer protocol (ULP) if an authentication header (AH) is present with the **permit icmp auth** command. See RFC 2402 for more on IPv6 authentication headers.

■ You should configure your access list to permit link-local and multicast addresses to avoid the filtering of necessary protocol packets. See RFC 4291 for more on IPv6 link-local and multicast addresses.

■ When using IPv6 access lists as packet filters on an interface, apply the access list with the interface **ipv6 traffic-filter** *ipv6-acl-name* [**in** | **out**] command.

■ Wildcard masks are not used in IPv6 access lists.

■ All IPv6 access lists are named. There is no differentiation between standard and extended access lists like there is with IPv4 access lists.

Configuration

1. Configure an access list for TCP or UDP traffic:

    a. Enter IPv6 access control list configuration mode:

    (global) **ipv6 access-list** *name*

    Unlike IPv4, there are no standard access lists with IPv6. All access lists with IPv6 are named.

    b. Configure access list statements:

    (ipv6-acl) [**permit** | **deny**] **tcp** {*source-ipv6-prefix/prefix-length* | **any** | **host** *source-ipv6-address* | **auth**} [*operator* [*port-number*]] {*destination-ipv6-prefix/prefix-length* | **any** | **host** *destination-ipv6-address* | **auth**} [*operator* [*port-number*]] [**dest-option-type** [*doh-number* | *doh-type*]] [**dscp** *value*] [**established**] [**flow-label** *value*] [**fragments**] [**log**] [**log-input**] [**mobility**] [**mobility-type** [*mh-number* | *mh-type*]] [**neq** {*port* | *protocol*}] [**range** {*port* | *protocol*}][**reflect** *name* [**timeout** *value*]] [**routing**] [**routing-type** *routing-number*] [**sequence** *value*] [**time-range** *name*] [**syn**] [**ack**] [**urg**] [**psh**] [**rst**] [**fin**]

    -or-

    (ipv6-acl) [**permit** | **deny**] **udp** {*source-ipv6-prefix/prefix-length* | **any** | **host** *source-ipv6-address* | **auth**} [*operator* [*port-number*]] {*destination-ipv6-prefix/prefix-length* | **any** | **host** *destination-ipv6-address* | **auth**} [*operator* [*port-number*]] [**dest-option-type** [*doh-number* | *doh-type*]] [**dscp** *value*] [**flow-label** *value*] [**fragments**] [**log**] [**log-input**] [**mobility**] [**mobility-type** [*mh-number*

```
| mh-type]] [neq {port | protocol}] [range {port | protocol}] [reflect name
[timeout value]] [routing] [routing-type routing-number] [sequence value]
[time-range name]
```

As with IPv4 extended access lists, both the source and destination address can be matched. You do not use a wildcard mask; instead, specify the *prefix-length* of the network or address you want to match. If you use authentication headers (AH) with TCP, you can match traffic against the AH extension header in combination with TCP by using the **auth** keyword following the source and destination address.

You can specify an **operator** to determine how the source and destination port numbers are to be matched. You can use the operators **lt** (less than), **gt** (greater than), **eq** (equal to), **neq** (not equal to), or **range** (within a range given by two port number values). The source and destination ports are given as a number (0 to 65535) or as a text string port name.

Available TCP names are **bgp, chargen, daytime, discard, domain, drip**, echo, **finger, ftp, ftp-data, gopher, hostname, irc, klogin, kshell, lpd, nntp, pop2, pop3, smtp, sunrpc, syslog, tacacs-ds, talk, telnet, time, uucp, whois**, and **www** (actually HTTP, port 80). The **drip** keyword was added in Cisco IOS Software Release 12.4 and specifies TCP port 3949, which is used by Optimized Edge Routing (OER) for messages sent between a master controller and border router.

Available UDP names are **biff, bootpc, bootps, discard, dnsix, domain, echo, mobile-ip, nameserver, netbios-dgm, netbios-ns, non-500-isakmp, ntp, rip, snmp, snmptrap, sunrpc, syslog, tacacs-ds, talk, tftp, time, who**, and **xdmcp**.

The **fragments** keyword can match packets that are not initial fragments. You cannot use the **fragments** keyword and specify a port number at the same time. The **established** keyword can match packets from established connections or packets that have either the RST or ACK bits set. You can also match one or more TCP flags with the **syn, ack, urg, psh, rst**, and **fin** keywords.

Note   IPv6 changed the way fragmentation is handled. With IPv6, fragmentation is handled by the end hosts and not by the routers.

The optional **dst-option-type** keyword can match packets against a destination option extension header. Destination option headers (Next Header type 60) define and carry additional information that must be processed by the destination host. The **dest-option-type** keyword is followed by either the number representing the option header identifier number (*doh-number*) or by the type (*doh-type*). Although the option header identifier field is between 0 to 255, currently the only supported option type is home-address (type 201), which is used for mobile IP. See Chapter 5, "IPv6 Addressing and Services," for more on mobile IP for IPv6.

The **dscp** keyword can be used to match the Differentiated Services Code Point (DSCP) bits contained in the Differentiated Services (DS) byte of an IP packet. The *dscp* value can be given as a number (6 bits: 0 to 63) or as a text string name. Available names are **default** (000000), **ef** (101110), **af11** (Assured Forwarding [AF], 001010), **af12** (001100), **af13** (001110), **af21** (010010), **af22** (010100), **af23** (010110), **af31** (011010), **af32** (011100), **af33** (011110), **af41** (100010), **af42** (100100), **af43** (100110), **cs1** (Class Selector [CS], precedence 1, 001000), **cs2** (precedence 2, 010000), **cs3** (precedence 3, 011000), **cs4** (precedence 4, 100000), **cs5** (precedence 5, 101000), **cs6** (precedence 6, 110000), and **cs7** (precedence 7, 111000). See Chapter 9 and the RFCs mentioned in the "Further Reading" section at the end of this chapter for more information on DSCP bits.

The **flow label** option can be used to match the Flow Label field in a packet. The range is 0 to 1048575.

The **log** and **log-input** options are the same as with IPv4. The **log** keyword can cause the router to send messages to the console or other logging facilities. The **log-input** keyword also records the input interface.

You can match packets containing the mobility extension header (Next Header type 135) by entering the **mobility** keyword. For a more granular configuration, configure the mobility header type using the **mobility-type** keyword followed by either the header type number (0 to 255) or the name. The supported names and type numbers include **bind-refresh** (0), **hoti** (1), **coti** (2), **hot** (3), **cot** (4), **bind-update** (5), **bind-acknowledgement** (6), and **bind-error** (7). See RFC 3775 for more on IPv6 mobility headers.

The reflect **keyword** and an optional **timeout** value can create a reflexive access list. (See Section 12-5 for more information.)

The access list can be applied for a time range using the **time-range** keyword. A time range must first be defined with a *time-range-name* using the following commands. The *time-range-name* must also be applied to the extended access list:

```
(global) time-range time-range-name
(time-range) periodic days-of-the-week hh:mm to [days-of-the-week] hh:mm
(time-range) absolute [start time date] [end time date]
```

Time ranges can be specified as one or more **periodic** definitions. The *days-of-the-week* field can be **daily** (Monday through Sunday), **weekdays** (Monday through Friday), **weekend** (Saturday and Sunday), **Monday, Tuesday, Wednesday, Thursday, Friday, Saturday,** or **Sunday**. The time *hh:mm* is given in 24-hour format. The router should be configured with NTP or have its clock and calendar set accurately.

Time ranges can also be specified as one **absolute** definition, with optional **start** and **end** times. The *time* is specified in *hh:mm* 24-hour format. The *date* fields must be formatted as *day month year,* as in 1 April 1963.

You can match packets that are source-routed using the optional routing extension header (Next Header type 43) with the **routing** keyword. You can also specify the routing header type using the **routing-type** keyword followed by the type number (0 to 255). Valid numbers are **0**, for a standard IPv6 routing header, and **2**, for a mobile IPv6 routing header.

Sequence numbers **can** be used to number each statement. By using sequence numbers, you can insert lines in the middle of an access list instead of at the end. Unlike IPv4 named access lists where the sequence number goes at the beginning of a statement, you configure the sequence number at the end of the IPv6 access list statement after entering the **sequence** keyword.

2. Configure an access list for ICMP traffic:

   a. Enter IPv6 access control list configuration mode:

   ```
   (global) ipv6 access-list name
   ```

   Unlike IPv4, there are no standard access lists with IPv6. All access lists with IPv6 are named.

   b. Configure access list statements:

   ```
   (ipv6-acl) [permit | deny] icmp {source-ipv6-prefix/prefix-length | any |
   host
   source-ipv6-address | auth} [operator [port-number]] {destination-ipv6-
   prefix/prefix-length | any | host destination-ipv6-address | auth} [operator
   [port-number]] [icmp-type [icmp-code] | icmp-message] [dest-option-type
   [doh-number | doh-type]] [dscp value] [flow-label value] [fragments] [log]
   [log-input] [mobility] [mobility-type [mh-number | mh-type]] [routing]
   [routing-type
   routing-number] [sequence value] [time-range name]
   ```

   Filtering ICMP traffic is configured much the same way as filtering TCP or UDP traffic. You can specify the *icmp-type* and *icmp-code* (both in the range of 0 to 255). You can enter a keyword for ICMP message names instead of entering the type and code number. Valid ICMP message names are **beyond-scope, destination-unreachable, echo-reply, echo-request, header, hop-limit, mid-query, mid-reduction, mid-report, nd-da, nd-ns, next-header, no-admin, no-route, packet-too-big, parameter-option, parameter-problem, port-unreachable, reassembly-timeout, renum-command, renum-result, renum-seq-number, router-advertisement, router-renumbering, router-solicitation, time-exceeded,** and **unreachable.** For more on ICMPv6 messages, see RFC 2463.

3. Configure an access list for other types of IPv6 traffic:

   a. Enter IPv6 access control list configuration mode:

   ```
   (global) ipv6 access-list name
   ```

Unlike IPv4, there are no standard access lists with IPv6. All access lists with IPv6 are named.

b. Configure access list statements:

(ipv6-acl) [**permit** | **deny**] *protocol* {*source-ipv6-prefix/prefix-length* | **any** | **host** *source-ipv6-address* | **auth**} [*operator* [*port-number*]] {*destination-ipv6-prefix/prefix-length* | **any** | **host** *destination-ipv6-address* | **auth**} [*operator*

[*port-number*]] [**dest-option-type** [*doh-number* | *doh-type*]] [**dscp** *value*] [**flow-label** *value*] [**fragments**] [**log**] [**log-input**] [**mobility**] [**mobility-type** [*mh-number*

| *mh-type*]] [**reflect** *name* [**timeout** *value*]] [**routing**] [**routing-type** *routing-number*] [**sequence** *value*] [**time-range** *name*][**undetermined-transport**]

When configuring an access list for other IPv6 protocols, specify either the protocol name or the Next Header number (0-255) for that protocol. Valid names for protocols include **ahp, esp, icmp, ipv6, pcp, sctp, tcp,** or **udp.** SCTP and PCP are new keywords not available with IPv4 access lists. SCTP (next header 132) is the Stream Control Transmission Protocol and is defined in RFC 4960. PCP (next header 108) is the Payload Compression Protocol and is defined in RFC 3173.

The **undertermined-transport** keyword option is allowed only when denying packets. Using this option matches packets from a source for which the Layer 4 protocol cannot be determined.

Examples

The following example configures an IPv6 access list named INBOUND-FILTER. This access list permits HTTP traffic from the source network 2001:1000::/64 to the host with the IP address 2001:2000::1 during the hours of 8:00 A.M. to 5:00 P.M. ICMP echo request messages are enabled from the 2001:1000::/64 network to anywhere. To support OSPFv3 (Next Header number 89), traffic destined for multicast addresses FF02::5 and FF02::6 are permitted along with all traffic sent to and from the link-local prefix FE80::/10. A final **deny** statement is added to the access list to prevent IPv6 neighbor discovery messages from traversing the router.

```
ipv6 access-list INBOUND-FILTER
 permit tcp 2001:1000::/64 host 2001:2000:1 eq 80 time-range workhours sequence 10
 permit icmp 2001:1000::/64 any echo-request log-input sequence 20
 permit 89 any host FF02::5 sequence 30
 permit 89 any host FF02::6 sequence 40
 permit 89 FE80::/10 FE80::/10 sequence 50
 deny ipv6 any any log-input sequence 60


time-range workhours
 periodic weekdays 8:00 to 17:00


interface fastethernet0/0
 ipv6 traffic-filter INBOUND-FILTER in
```

14-4: Regular Expressions

- Regular expressions are templates used to match against patterns in text strings.

- Regular expressions can be used with modem chat scripts, with BGP access lists, and to search through command output.

Configuration

You can create regular expressions by forming a template string from any of the following components:

- **Match against one or more character**—Single characters or a set of characters contained within parentheses can be explicitly given for matching.

- In addition, you can use the special characters listed in Table 14-3 to match ambiguous strings.

Table 14-3 *Regular-Expression Wildcards*

Character	Symbol	Function
Period	.	Matches any single character.
Caret	^	Matches starting at the beginning of the string.
Dollar sign	$	Matches up to the end of the string.
Underscore	_	Matches a comma (,), left brace ({), right brace (}), left parenthesis ((), right parenthesis ()), the beginning of the input string, the end of the input string, or a space.
Backslash	\char	Matches the *char* character (removes any special pattern matching meaning from the character).

- **Match against a list of characters**—You can place a list of characters within square brackets to match against a single character. For example, you can define a list as [abcxyz], where a character matches if it is a, b, c, x, y, or z.

- **Match against a range of characters**—You can place a range of characters within square brackets to match against a single character. A range is defined as two characters separated by a dash. For example, the range [A-Za-z] matches any character between A and Z or a and z (in other words, any alphabetic character).

- **Match against multiples of a pattern**—You can follow a single character or string of characters within parentheses with one of the characters listed in Table 14-4.

- **Match against alternative patterns**—Pattern strings separated by a vertical bar (|) are alternatively used for matching.

Table 14-4 *Regular-Expression Wildcards for Matching Against Pattern Multiples*

Character	Symbol	Function
Asterisk	*	Matches zero or more sequences of the pattern.
Plus sign	+	Matches one or more sequences of the pattern.
Question mark	?	Matches zero or one occurrence of the pattern.

Examples

A regular expression is used to find the appropriate modem chat scripts matching **Hayes-** followed by anything. The period matches any character, and the asterisk uses the period to match zero or more times. Therefore, any character or string after **Hayes-** is matched.

```
line 1
chat-script Hayes-.*
```

A regular expression is used to find the appropriate modem chat script for either **usrobotics** or **hayes**.

```
line 2
chat-script usrobotics | hayes
```

A regular expression is used in a BGP AS path list to permit advertisements of a path from the adjacent AS 800. Here, the caret matches the beginning of the AS path string, where 800 is the AS that is adjacent to the local router. The period and asterisk match any other AS path information past the immediately neighboring AS. Also, advertisements of a path through AS 75 are permitted. The underscore characters that surround 75 match any white space or the beginning or end of the AS path string. Refer to Section 7-6 for more information about using regular expressions to match AS paths.

```
ip as-path access-list 10 permit ^800 .*
ip as-path access-list 10 permit _75_
```

A regular expression is used to display only the lines in the running configuration that contain the word **VLAN**. This might be useful if you need to see a list of the VLAN numbers you have used.

```
show running-config | include VLAN.*_
```

Suppose you wanted to generate a quick list of interface statistics, consisting of only lines that show the interface number, followed by the line that displays the MAC address. A regular expression is used along with the **show interface** command to include only the desired information. First, the output lines containing "line protocol" are displayed, because they also begin with the interface type and number.

An alternative pattern is given to display output lines that include the word "Hardware," followed by any string, followed by the word "address." This is done to exclude the "Hardware" line for serial interfaces, which have no MAC addresses.

```
show interface | include (line protocol|Hardware.+address)
```

Further Reading

Consult the following resources for additional reading on the topics presented in this chapter:

IPv6 Security, by Scott Hogg and Eric Vyncke, Cisco Press, ISBN 1587055945.

Deploying IPv6 Networks, by Ciprian Popovich, Eric Levy-Abegnoli, and Patrick Grossetete, Cisco Press, ISBN 1587052105.

RFC 768, "User Datagram Protocol."

RFC 791, "Internet Protocol."

RFC 792, "Internet Control Message Protocol."

RFC 793, "Transmission Control Protocol."

RFC 1108, "Security Options for the Internet Protocol."

RFC 1191, "Path MTU Discovery."

RFC 1385, "EIP: The Extended Internet Protcol."

RFC 1393, "Traceroute Using an IP Option."

RFC 2236, "IGMP Version 2."

RFC 2460, "Internet Protocol, Version 6."

RFC 2463, "Internet Control Message Protocol for the Internet Protocol Version 6 Specification."

RFC 3376, "IGMP Version 3."

RFC 3775, "Mobility Support in IPv6."

RFC 4291, "IP Version 6 Addressing Architecture."

RFC 4727, "Experimental Values in IPv4, IPv6, ICMPv4, ICMPv6, UDP, and TCP Headers."

Cisco IOS Software Release and Filename Conventions

For years, network engineers were frustrated trying to keep track of the plethora of Cisco IOS Software images. When ordering IOS Software, you had to choose not only the main version number, but also select an image from as many as 44 different features sets. Cisco changed this with its Cisco IOS Packaging initiative. Beginning with Cisco IOS Software Major Release 12.3M/T, Cisco simplified the IOS selection process by using a consistent naming convention and reducing the number of feature sets down to only eight.

This appendix introduces you to these eight IOS packages. Each package is designed to address specific customer needs (such as security or voice). By understanding the differences between the packages, you can be better equipped to choose the correct IOS for your environment. There is also information about the Cisco IOS Software image filenaming convention so that you can look at the image file installed on a router and tell exactly what you have.

Cisco IOS Packaging

The Cisco IOS Packaging initiative streamlined the number of feature sets from 44 to eight. Feature sets are now called *packages*, and higher level packages inherit features from lower level packages. Figure A-1 shows a high-level overview of these eight packages.

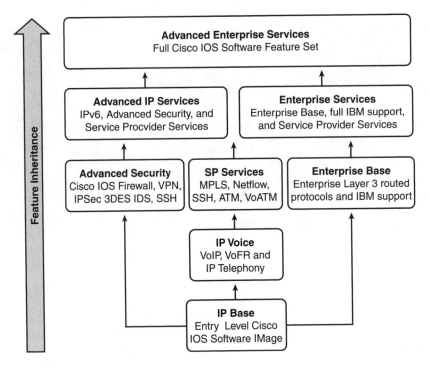

Figure A-1   *Cisco IOS Packages*

Cisco IOS Software Releases

Software images for routers and access servers were released for use in the following fashion:

- **First Commercial Shipment (FCS)**—A Cisco IOS Software version that becomes commercially available to Cisco customer

- **Major release**—A version number of Cisco IOS Software. It introduces a new set of features and functionality.

- **Maintenance release**—A revision to a major release for bug fixes. No new functionality or platforms are added. This is introduced as a periodic release and is fully regression-tested.

- **Interim build release**—A special-circumstance revision to a maintenance release. It is not regression-tested.

- **Early Deployment (ED) release**—New functionality and hardware platforms are introduced for quick delivery. ED releases also receive regular maintenance releases.

- **ED Technology ("T") release**—A train of ED releases that contains new hardware and features. It is based on a major release and regular maintenance releases. One specific "T" release becomes the next major release.

Figure A-2 shows the basic flow of Cisco IOS Software releases. The process begins with a major release (12.1 in the figure). Major releases are always numbered as a dotted-decimal number with no other suffixes. Maintenance and interim build releases occur periodically or as needed, and all are based on the major release. These releases are shown proceeding across the figure to the right.

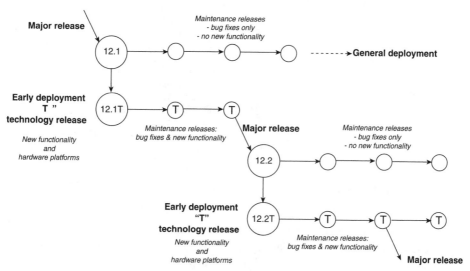

Figure A-2   *Cisco IOS Software Release Process*

At the same time, a set of new technology and hardware features are added to the technology or "T" train of releases. This set of features is added to the major release, forming a release with a "T" suffix (12.1T in Figure A-2). Maintenance and interim build releases occur as needed, just as in the major release train. New features can be added to new maintenance releases. These releases are shown proceeding across the figure to the right, parallel to the major release train.

Major and technology trains occur in parallel. New major releases are formed from the previous technology train.

Other types of early deployment releases are also possible. Many of these introduce new features or bug fixes for specific platforms on a one-time-only basis. These releases are denoted with a suffix other than "T" and are rolled into a later maintenance release in the technology train.

Release Numbering

Cisco IOS Software releases follow a standard numbering convention, as shown in Figure A-3. The major release is given as a dotted decimal number, as in "12.1." A suffix is added in parentheses to specify the maintenance release. This number begins with 1 and is incremented with each successive maintenance build. If interim builds are released, these are referenced by adding a dot and the interim build number after the maintenance release number.

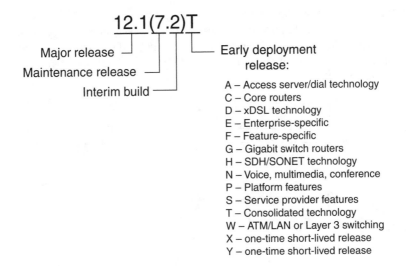

Figure A-3 *Cisco IOS Software Release Numbering*

Early Deployment releases are identified by one or two additional letters and numbers at the end of the release number. Many types of ED releases can be produced. These are categorized as shown in the figure and are identified by the letter shown. For example, all technology train releases have the letter T as the ED suffix. Other short-lived ED releases have the letter X. If more letters and numbers follow, they serve only to differentiate the release from others that have a similar ED release status.

Choosing a Cisco IOS Software Release

Cisco offers a number of Cisco IOS Software image files, each containing a specific set of features and capabilities. Each image file supports a specific router hardware platform. The following list can help you cross-reference all of these variables to choose the correct Cisco IOS Software release.

Note The URLs used in the following steps require a registered account on the Cisco Cisco.com web site. You might also need a valid service contract to gain access to the Cisco.com Software Center for downloading Cisco IOS Software images. To register for a Cisco.com account, go to www.cisco.com/register/.

1. Determine the features you need.

   a. Use the Cisco IOS Feature Navigator tool on Cisco.com:

   www.cisco.com/cgi-bin/Support/FeatureNav/FN.pl

   Select the Cisco IOS Software feature sets that are required for your network. To see the complete list of features, leave the "Search by full or partial feature name" field blank and click the Search button.

   The list of features is very detailed, because various features were introduced in specific Early Deployment releases.

   The Feature Navigator also allows you to match the list of features against a router platform and a Cisco IOS Software release if desired.

   b. Use the Cisco Hardware-Software Compatibility Matrix tool on Cisco.com:

   www.cisco.com/cgi-bin/front.x/Support/HWSWmatrix/hwswmatrix.cgi

   For a specific router platform, a table of the minimum (or earliest) software releases that offer full hardware support is shown. The platform is broken down into basic units and all possible hardware modules, referenced by Cisco part numbers. Select each module that you want to support in the platform, and click the "Display Intersection" button. The minimum supported IOS releases are listed for each hardware product.

2. Select a Cisco IOS Software release.

   This selection can be based on many factors, including reliability, maturity, new technology, bug fixes, and so forth. Consider these basic release categories and their characteristics:

   - **GD**—To reach GD status, an IOS release must be proven in the field, must be heavily tested, and must achieve a high customer satisfaction rating. You should choose a GD release if your requirements are for high reliability, maturity, and support for business-critical resources. Also remember that subsequent maintenance releases after the first GD release also retain the GD status.

   - **ED**—The technology or "T" release train provides up-to-date availability for new technologies. Maintenance releases within the "T" train also implement bug fixes and might introduce other new technologies and features. Choose a "T" release if you require support for specific new features, protocols, or technologies. The new features in the "T" release train will eventually be rolled into the next major release.

   - **ED**—The "X" or other non-"T" releases implement new features and/or bug fixes for specific router platforms. These are one-time releases, introduced for quick availability, that get rolled into a later "T" release. Choose one of these ED releases if you require early access to new functionality for a new or specific hardware platform. Then consider migrating to the next available "T" release when it becomes available.

■ **Interim**—These release builds are made available for special circumstances. Choose an interim release build if you are directed to do so by Cisco TAC or by the recommendations of a release note. Interim builds are not fully regression-tested. Therefore, you should make plans to migrate to the next maintenance release as soon as it becomes available.

3. Consider the minimum memory requirements.

Use the Cisco IOS Planner tool on Cisco.com:

www.cisco.com/cgi-bin/Software/Iosplanner/Planner-tool/iosplanner.cgi?

You can select the router platform, Cisco IOS Software release, and software feature set in any order. The remaining choices are refreshed in the tool. As soon as you have selected a specific release, the minimum memory requirements are displayed for both RAM and Flash memory.

4. Consider the caveats present in the release.

a. Consult the list of bugs.

Use the Bug Navigator tool on Cisco.com to search for known bugs:

www.cisco.com/support/bugtools/bugtool.shtml

You can search for bugs based on a description, feature set, IOS release, or general search. BugIDs are displayed, along with information about Cisco IOS Software release numbers with bug fixes.

b. Consult the release notes.

Begin by finding a specific major release number in the Cisco IOS Software Configuration section of Cisco.com:

www.cisco.com/univercd/cc/td/doc/product/software/

Then select either the Release Notes or Caveats link to read about resolved and open caveats with a Cisco IOS Software release number.

Cisco IOS Software Filenaming Convention

Cisco uses a standard convention to name all Cisco IOS Software image files. Sometimes you might have an image filename (either in Flash memory or on a TFTP server) and need to determine exactly what platform, feature sets, and Cisco IOS Software release it supports. Images follow the following naming convention:

PPPPPP-FFFF-MM-VVVV

The first group of characters, *PPPPP*, designates the image's hardware platform. The second group of characters, *FFFF*, indicates the package name. Two characters, *MM*, describe the image format. The first character specifies the type of router memory in which the image is executed. The image can be loaded in Flash (f), RAM (m), or ROM (r). The second character tells how the image is compressed. Compression types include zip compressed (z), mzip compressed (x), or stac compressed (w). The final group of characters, *VVVV*, specifies the Cisco IOS Software release number. The image filename can also have a suffix, such as .bin or .tar.

Table A-1 shows the feature sets and examples of image names. At the beginning of every image name is the platform of the router. Table A-1 uses the Cisco 2800 series platform as an example.

Tip   If you are trying to determine whether you can safely remove a Flash card from a router, look at the first M character in the Cisco IOS Software image filename. The execution area character is f if the image is executed directly from Flash. In this case, the router requires Flash to be installed so that the Cisco IOS Software image can be run. If the character is m, the router has already read the image from Flash, decompressed it, and is running it from RAM. After the router has booted, the Flash can be safely removed.

Table A-1   *Packages and Image Names*

Package	Image Name
IP Base	c2800-ipbase-mz
IP Voice	C2800-ipvoice-mz
Enterprise Base	C800-entbase-mz
Advanced Security	C800-advsecurityk9-mz
SP Services	C2800-spservicesk9-mz
Advanced IP Services	C800-advipservicesk9-mz
Enterprise Services	C2800-entservicesk9-mz
Advanced Enterprise Services	C2800-adventerprisek9-mz

To see what Cisco IOS Software image your router is running, use the **show version** or **show flash** command. The image filename is displayed, as demonstrated in Example A-1.

Example A-1 *Checking to See Which Cisco IOS Software Image Is Currently Running*

```
Router# show flash
-#- --length-- -----date/time------ path
1      13937472 Oct 04 2007 16:42:46 +00:00 c1841-ipbase-mz.124-1c.bin
...
15831040 bytes available (16101376 bytes used)
Router# show version
 Cisco IOS Software, 1841 Software (C1841-IPBASE-M), Version 12.4(1c), RELEASE
   SOFTWARE (fc1)
Technical Support: http://www.cisco.com/techsupport
Copyright (c) 1986-2005 by Cisco Systems, Inc.
Compiled Tue 25-Oct-05 17:10 by evmiller


ROM: System Bootstrap, Version 12.4(13r)T, RELEASE SOFTWARE (fc1)


Mexico uptime is 20 hours, 46 minutes
System returned to ROM by power-on
System image file is "flash:c1841-ipbase-mz.124-1c.bin"


Cisco 1841 (revision 7.0) with 114688K/16384K bytes of memory.
Processor board ID FTX1140W1C9
...
```

In this example, the router is using the c1841-ipbase-mz.14-1c.bin IOS image. It is an 1841 router with the IP Base package. The image is mzip compressed and runs from Flash memory. The IOS is version 12.4(1c).

Further Reading

Refer to the following recommended sources for further technical information about Cisco IOS Software images:

Cisco IOS Releases: The Complete Reference by Mack Coulibaly, Cisco Press, ISBN 1578701791.

Cisco IOS Packaging: Simplification, Consolidation, Consistency, www.cisco.com/en/US/products/sw/iosswrel/ps5460/prod_presentation_list.html.

Cabling Quick Reference

Network cabling is always subject to a distance limitation, depending on the medium used and the bandwidth supported. Table B-1 provides a quick reference by listing the maximum cabling distance for a variety of network media and cable types.

When using 1000BaseLX/LH GBICs with 62.5 micron MMF, a mode-conditioning patch cord must be used for distances greater than 300 m (984 ft).

Table B-1   *Cabling Distances for Network Media and Cabling*

Medium	Cable Type	Maximum Distance
10/100BaseTX Ethernet	EIA/TIA Category 5 UTP	100 m (328 ft)
100BaseFX	Multimode Fiber (MMF) 62.5/125	400 m half duplex 2000 m full duplex
	Single-Mode Fiber (SMF)	10 km
1000BaseCX	STP	25 m (82 ft)
1000BaseT	EIA/TIA Category 5 UTP (4 pair)	100 m (328 ft)
1000BaseSX	MMF 62.5 micron, 160 MHz/km	220 m (722 ft)
	MMF 62.5 micron, 200 MHz/km	275 m (902 ft)
	MMF 50.0 micron, 400 MHz/km	500 m (1640 ft)
	MMF 50.0 micron, 500 MHz/km	550 m (1804 ft)

Table B-1   *Cabling Distances for Network Media and Cabling*

Medium	Cable Type	Maximum Distance
1000BaseLX/LH	MMF 62.5 micron, 500 MHz/km	550 m (1804 ft)
	MMF 50.0 micron, 400 MHz/km	550 m (1804 ft)
	MMF 50.0 micron, 500 MHz/km	550 m (1804 ft)
	SMF 9/10	10 km (32810 ft)
1000BaseZX	SMF	70 to 100 km
SONET	MMF (62.5 or 50.0 micron)	3 km (1.5 mi)
	SMI (Single-Mode Intermediate Reach)	15 km (9 mi)
	SML (Single-Mode Long Reach)	45 km (28 mi)
FDDI	MMF	2 km (1.2 mi)
	SMF	15 km (9.3 mi)
Token Ring (IEEE 802.5)	STP (Shielded Twisted-Pair)	500 m (1640 ft)
Token Ring (IEEE 802.5)	EIA/TIA Category 5 UTP	100 m (328 ft)
ISDN BRI	UTP, RJ-45	10 m (32.8 ft)
Async EIA/TIA-232	2400 baud	60 m (200 ft)
	4800 baud	30 m (100 ft)
	9600 baud	15 m (50 ft)
	19200 baud	15 m (50 ft)
	38400 baud	15 m (50 ft)
	57600 baud	7.6 m (25 ft)
	115200 baud	3.7 m (12 ft)
Sync EIA/TIA-449 with balanced drivers, including X.21 and V.35	2400 baud	1250 m (4100 ft)
	4800 baud	625 m (2050 ft)

Table B-1   *Cabling Distances for Network Media and Cabling*

Medium	Cable Type	Maximum Distance
	9600 baud	312 m (1025 ft)
	19200 baud	156 m (513 ft)
	38400 baud	78 m (256 ft)
	56000 baud	31 m (102 ft)
	T1 (1.544 Mbps)	15 m (50 ft)

In many cases, you might find that you need to know the pinout connections for various network cables. The RJ-45 connector is commonly used across many media, but with different pinouts for each. Table B-2 shows the pinout for an RJ-45 connector when used with specific media.

Back-to-Back Router Connections

In a lab setup or in certain circumstances, you might find that you need to connect two routers to each other in a back-to-back fashion. Normally, some other active device is used to connect router interfaces. For example, an Ethernet hub or switch, a Token Ring MAU, and the Public Switched Telephone Network (PSTN) all perform an active role to interconnect routers. If these are unavailable, as in a lab environment, a special cable is needed to make the back-to-back connection.

Note   It is not possible to make a back-to-back cable to connect two Token Ring interfaces. Token Ring connections require an active device, such as an MAU or a Token Ring switch, to terminate the connection.

Table B-2 *RJ-45 Connector Pinouts Based on Media Type*

RJ-45 Pin	Router Console (DTE)	Ethernet UTP	Token Ring UTP	ISDN BRI S/ TTE	ISDN BRI U	CT1/PRI CSU	CE1/PRI	56/64k DSU/CSU (RJ-48S)	T1/E1 (RJ-48)
1	RTS	TX+	GND			Rcv Ring	TX Tip	TX Ring	RX (input)
2	DTR	TX-	GND			Rcv Tip	TX Ring	TX Tip	RX (input)
3	TxD	RX+	TX+	TX+			TX Shld		
4	GND		RX+	RX+	Tip or Ring	Ring	RX Tip		TX (output)
5	GND		RX-	RX-	Tip or Ring	Tip	RX Ring		TX (output)
6	RxD	RX-	TX-	TX-			RX Shld		
7	DSR		GND					RX Tip	
8	CTS		N/A					RX Ring	

Asynchronous Serial Connections

An asynchronous serial connection, such as the Aux port or a line on an access server, requires an RJ-45 connection. For a back-to-back link between two async ports on two different routers, a rollover cable must be used. Rollover cables are usually flat eight-conductor cables with RJ-45 connectors, fashioned so that pin 1 on one end goes to pin 8 on the other end, pin 2 goes to pin 7, and so forth. Cisco normally supplies a rollover cable with a console cable kit. Table B-3 shows the pinout connections for both ends of the rollover cable.

Table B-3 *RJ-45 Connector Pinouts for Rollover Cables*

RJ-45 Pin End A	Description End A	Description End B	RJ-45 Pin End B
1	RTS	CTS	8
2	DTR	DSR	7
3	TxD	RxD	6
4	GND	GND	5
5	GND	GND	4
6	RxD	TxD	3
7	DSR	DTR	2
8	CTS	RTS	1

Ethernet Connections

Normally, a 10BaseT or a 10/100BaseTX router interface connects to a hub or switch through a *straight-through* Category 5 UTP cable. RJ-45 pins 1 and 2 form one pair, and pins 3 and 6 form another pair. However, to connect two Ethernet router interfaces directly, without a hub or switch, a *crossover cable* is needed.

A crossover cable connects the pair containing pins 1 and 2 on one end to the pair containing pins 3 and 6 on the other end. Likewise, pins 3 and 6 are connected to pins 1 and 2. Table B-4 lists the pinout connections for both RJ-45 ends of the crossover cable.

Table B-4 *RJ-45 Connector Pinouts for Crossover Cables*

RJ-45 Pin End A	Description End A	Description End B	RJ-45 Pin End B
1	TX+	RX+	3
2	TX-	RX-	6
3	RX+	TX+	1
4			4
5			5
6	RX-	TX-	2
7			7
8			8

56/64kbps CSU/DSU Connections

Normally, if a router has an integrated or external CSU/DSU for a 56/64kbps serial interface, the CSU/DSU is connected to the service provider's termination box. The service provider or PSTN establishes the active circuit between two CSU/DSU units and routers.

Back-to-back serial connections can usually be made between the serial interfaces of two routers using one DTE serial cable and one DCE serial cable. One router becomes the DTE end, and the other becomes the DCE end and must provide the clock. However, if you have two routers with integrated CSU/DSUs, there is no way to access the physical serial interface. In this case, you can make a back-to-back 56/64 cable by crossing the transmit and receive pairs. Table B-5 shows the pinout connections for both RJ-48 (an RJ-45 will do) ends of the cable.

Table B-5   *RJ-48 Connector Pinouts for Back-to-Back 56/64kbps CSU/DSU Connections*

RJ-48 Pin End A	Description End A	Description End B	RJ-48 Pin End B
1	TX Ring	RX Ring	7
2	TX Tip	RX Tip	8
3			3
4			4
5			5
6			6
7	RX Tip	TX Tip	1
8	RX Ring	TX Ring	2

T1/E1 CSU/DSU Connections

A back-to-back connection can also be made between two routers with integrated T1/E1 CSU/DSUs using a specially made cable. Again, the transmit and receive pairs are crossed in the cable. Table B-6 lists the pinout connections of both RJ-48 (an RJ-45 will do) ends of the cable.

Table B-6   *RJ-48 Connector Pinouts for Back-to-Back T1/E1 CSU/DSU Connections*

RJ-48 Pin End A	Description End A	Description End B	RJ-48 Pin End B
1	RX (input)	TX (input)	4
2	RX (input)	TX (input)	5
3			3
4	TX (output)	RX (output)	1
5	TX (output)	RX (output)	2
6			6
7			7
8			8

Appendix C

SNMP MIB Structure

- SNMP information in a router is organized as a Management Information Base (MIB).

- A network management system can use SNMP to access data stored in the MIB.

- MIBs represent data as a hierarchical tree structure; each MIB variable is referenced by its object identifier (OID).

- OIDs are formed by concatenating the name or number of a tree branch as the tree is followed from the root to the object's location, in dotted notation.

Figure C-1 shows the top layers of the standard MIB tree. The root layer is unnamed. All MIB variables that are useful for network management are located under the *internet* subtree. Following the tree structure downward, *internet* is referenced as OID *iso.org.dod.internet*, or 1.3.6.1.

The iso.org.dod.internet.mgmt subtree (1.3.6.1.2) contains many useful objects, all organized under the mib subtree (1.3.6.1.2.1). These objects fall into the following categories:

- **system**—Descriptions of the system or router, uptime, and network services

- **interfaces**—Parameters and counters for each interface

- **at**—Address translation mappings for media- (MAC) to-IP addresses

- **ip**—IP packet counters, IP routing tables, and IP-to-MAC address mappings

- **icmp**—Counters of ICMP message types seen

- **tcp**—TCP segment counters and connection tables

- **udp**—UDP datagram counters and port tables

- **egp**—Exterior Gateway Protocol (EGP) counters

- **transmission**—Media-specific MIBs

- **snmp**—SNMP counters

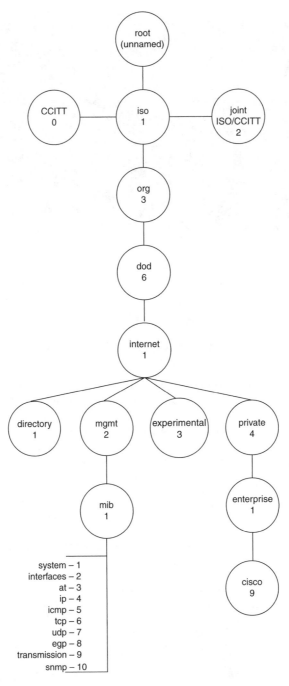

Figure C-1   *Top-Level MIB Structure*

The experimental (1.3.6.1.3) subtree can contain MIBs that are new and experimental in nature. However, experimental MIBs can also be introduced into the standard mib subtree (1.3.6.1.2).

The private (1.3.6.1.4) subtree contains one subtree, enterprise (1.3.6.1.4.1), where all network vendor-specific objects are located. The Cisco private MIB structure is contained in the cisco subtree (1.3.6.1.4.1.9). The set of specific MIBs that are included under the Cisco MIB tree varies according to the hardware platform and the IOS software release level.

A good resource for referencing and downloading MIBs is the *Cisco MIBs* page on Cisco.com:

www.cisco.com/public/sw-center/netmgmt/cmtk/mibs.shtml

Through the tools offered, you can do the following:

- **MIBs supported by product**—Browse through listings of available MIBs, based on a choice of hardware platform. The MIB listings are then broken down by IOS release level, showing MIBs that have been added to each release.

- **OID**—Find the OID (dotted decimal notation) of specific Cisco MIBs and features.

- **SNMP v1 MIBs**—Download the actual SNMP v1 MIB files.

- **SNMP v2 MIBs**—Download the actual SNMP v2 MIB files.

Tip   You can also use the undocumented **show snmp mib** command to see a list of MIB objects that are available on a router. Although this command lists the objects in a short format (without OIDs), it can be useful to find the names of specific MIB variables.

Appendix D

Password Recovery

This appendix covers the following specifications regarding password recovery for Cisco networking devices:

■ Cisco routers let you bypass the configuration file without losing the contents of that file. This allows for password recovery.

■ Two different processor types are available for Cisco routers. Each processor type has a slightly different process for password recovery.

■ You must have access to the console port to perform password recovery.

Password recovery allows you to regain administrative control of your device if you have lost or forgotten the password. The basic premise is simple—you need to get privileged access to your router without the password's taking effect. Then you need to restore the configuration and reset the password to a known value.

Password Recovery Process

There are two password recovery procedures. They involve the following basic steps:

Step 1. Configure the router to boot up without reading the configuration memory (NVRAM). This is sometimes called *test system mode*.

Step 2. Reboot the system.

Step 3. Access enable mode (this can be done without a password if you are in test system mode).

Step 4. View or change the password, or erase the configuration.

Step 5. Reconfigure the router to boot up and read the configuration in NVRAM as it normally does.

Step 6. Reboot the system.

Note   Some password recovery requires that a console terminal issue a Break signal, so you must be familiar with how your terminal or PC terminal emulator issues this signal. For example, ProComm uses the keys **Alt-B** by default to generate the Break signal. Windows HyperTerminal requires that you press **Ctrl-Break**.

The HyperTerminal program that ships on Microsoft platforms might not send a Break signal with the **Ctrl-Break** sequence for all platforms (for example, Windows NT 4 and Windows 2000). To have HyperTerminal send the proper Break sequence, you should upgrade to Private Edition. You can obtain HyperTerminal Private Edition from Hilgraeve at http://www.hilgraeve.com/htpe/index.html.

Password Recovery Procedure 1

Use this first password recovery procedure to recover lost passwords on the following Cisco routers:

- Cisco 2000 series

- Cisco 2500 series

- Cisco 3000 series

- Cisco 4000 series with 680x0 Motorola CPU

- Cisco 7000 series running Cisco IOS Software Release 10.0 or later in ROMs installed on the route processor (RP) card. The router can be booting Cisco IOS Software Release 10.0 in Flash memory, but it needs the actual ROMs on the processor card, too.

- IGS series running Cisco IOS Software Release 9.1 or later in ROMs

To recover an enable password using Procedure 1, follow these steps:

Step 1.   Attach a terminal or PC with terminal emulation software to the router's console port, and issue the command **show version.**

The configuration register value is on the last line of the display, as shown in Example D-1.

The factory default configuration register value is typically 0x2102. Copy this value. You will need it again later during the process.

Note   The bits of the configuration register are explained in greater detail in Appendix E, "Configuration Register Settings."

Turn off the router, and then turn it back on.

Example D-1   show version Command Output

```
wg_ro_a# show version
Cisco Internetwork Operating System Software
IOS (tm) 2500 Software (C2500-JS-L), Version 12.0(3), RELEASE SOFTWARE (fc1)
Copyright (c) 1986-1999 by Cisco Systems, Inc.
Compiled Mon 08-Feb-99 18:18 by phanguye
Image text-base: 0x03050C84, data-base: 0x00001000


ROM: System Bootstrap, Version 11.0(10c), SOFTWARE
BOOTFLASH: 3000 Bootstrap Software (IGS-BOOT-R),
  Version 11.0(10c), RELEASE SOFTWARE (fc1)
wg_ro_a uptime is 20 minutes
System restarted by reload
System image file is "flash:c2500-js-l_120-3.bin"

--More--


 Configuration register is 0x2102
```

Step 2. Press the **Break** key on the terminal within 60 seconds of turning on the router.

The **>** prompt with no router name appears. If the prompt does not appear, the terminal is not sending the correct Break signal. In that case, check the terminal or terminal emulation setup. To view the current configuration register, you can type in the value **e/s 2000002** or the letter **o**.

Note   The number that references the location of the configuration register might change from platform to platform. Check your specific product documentation for the exact number to be used.

Step 3. Enter **o/r 0x2142** at the **>** prompt to boot from Flash memory or **o/r0x2141** to boot an IOS subset image from the boot ROMs.

Note   The setting 0x2141 works only for devices that have boot ROM chips with an IOS subset. The Cisco 3600 series routers do not have subset images in boot ROM chips. A setting of 0x2141 on that device puts you in Rommon mode.

Note   In o/r, the first character before the slash is the letter o, not the numeral zero. If you have Flash memory and it is intact, 0x2142 is the best setting. Use 0x2141 only if the Flash memory is erased or not installed.

Step 4. At the **>** prompt, enter the **initialize** command or just **i** to initialize the router.

This causes the router to reboot but ignore its saved configuration. The system configuration display appears.

Note If you normally use the **boot network** command, or if you have multiple images in Flash memory and you boot a nondefault image, the image in Flash might be different.

Step 5. Enter **no** in response to the System Configuration dialog prompts until the following message appears:

Press RETURN to get started!

Step 6. Press Return.

The **Router>** prompt appears.

Step 7. Enter the **enable** command.

The **Router#** prompt appears.

Step 8. Choose one of the following options:

To view the password, if it is not encrypted, enter the **show startup-config** command.

To change the password (if it is encrypted, for example), enter the following commands:

```
Router # copy startup-config running-config
Router # configure terminal
Router(config)# enable secret 1234abcd
```

Step 9. Because ignoring the NVRAM and choosing to abort the setup would leave all interfaces in the shutdown state, it is important to enable all interfaces with the **no shutdown** command as follows:

```
Router(config)# interface ethernet 0
Router(config-if)# no shutdown
```

Step 10. Save your new password with the following commands:

```
Router(config-if)# ctrl-z
Router # copy running-config startup-config
```

Note The **enable secret** command provides increased security by storing the enable secret password using a nonreversible cryptographic function; however, you cannot recover a lost password that has been encrypted.

Step 11.   Enter the **configure terminal** command at the EXEC prompt to enter configuration mode.

Step 12.   Enter the **config-register** command and the original value you recorded in Step 1.

Step 13.   Press **Ctrl-Z** to quit the configuration editor.

Step 14.   Enter the **reload** command at the privileged EXEC prompt.

Note   Every time you enter configuration mode on a router, a flag is set to check and make sure configurations have been saved before the router is reloaded. When you change the configuration register, there is no need to save the configuration, but the router prompts you to do so when you issue a reload. Answer no when asked if you want to save the configuration.

Password Recovery Procedure 2

Use this second instance of the password recovery procedure to recover lost passwords on the following Cisco routers:

- Cisco 1003

- Cisco 1600 series

- Cisco 1700 series

- Cisco 1800 series

- Cisco 2600 series

- Cisco 2800 series

- Cisco 3600 series

- Cisco 3700 series

- Cisco 3800 series

- Cisco 3900 series

- Cisco 4500 series

- Cisco 7000 series Route Switch Processor (RSP7000)

- Cisco 7100 series

- Cisco 7200 series

- Cisco 7500 series

- Cisco 12000 series

- IDT Orion-based routers

- AS5200 and AS5300 platforms
- Cisco ISR G2 routers

To recover a password using Procedure 2, follow these steps:

Step 1.   Attach a terminal or PC with terminal emulation software to the router's console port, and issue the **show version** command.

The configuration register value is on the last line of the display, as shown in Example D-1.

The factory default configuration register value is 0x2102.

Step 2.   Turn off the router, and then turn it back on.

Step 3.   Press the **Break** key on the terminal within 60 seconds of turning on the router.

The **rommon>** prompt appears. If it does not appear, the terminal is not sending the correct Break signal. In that case, check the terminal or terminal emulation setup.

Step 4.   Enter the confreg command at the rommon> prompt. Record the current value of the virtual configuration register as it is output from this command.

The following prompt appears:

```
Do you wish to change configuration[y/n]?
```

Step 5.   Enter **yes** and press Return.

Step 6.   Accept the default answers to subsequent questions until the following prompt appears:

```
ignore system config info[y/n]?
```

Step 7.   Enter **yes**.

Step 8.   Enter **no** to subsequent questions until the following prompt appears:

```
change boot characteristics[y/n]?
```

Step 9.   Enter **yes**.

The following prompt appears:

```
enter to boot:
```

Step 10.   At this prompt, either enter **2** and press Return if you have Flash memory or, if Flash memory is erased, enter **1** and press **Enter**.

A configuration summary is displayed, and the following prompt appears:

```
Do you wish to change configuration[y/n]?
```

Step 11.   Answer **no** and press **Enter**.

The following prompt appears:

```
rommon>
```

Note Note that you can shorten Steps 4 through 11 by issuing the command **confreg** 0x2142 at the **rommon>** prompt.

Step 12. Enter the **reset** command at the privileged **rommon>** prompt, or power-cycle the router.

Step 13. As the router boots, enter **no** to all the setup questions until the following prompt appears:

```
Router>
```

Step 14. Enter the **enable** command to enter enable mode.

The **Router#** prompt appears.

Step 15. Choose one of the following options:

To view the password, if it is not encrypted, enter the **show startup-config** command.

To change the password (if it is encrypted, for example), enter the following commands:

```
Router # copy startup-config running-config
Router # configure terminal
Router(config)# enable secret 1234abcd
```

Step 16. Because ignoring the NVRAM and choosing to abort setup would leave all interfaces in the shutdown state, it is important to enable all interfaces with the **no shutdown** command, as demonstrated here:

```
Router(config)#interface ethernet 0/0
Router(config-if)#no shutdown
```

Step 17. Save your new password with the following commands:

```
Router(config-if)# ctrl-z
Router # copy running-config startup-config
```

Note The **enable secret** command provides increased security by storing the enable secret password using a nonreversible cryptographic function; however, you cannot recover a lost password that has been encrypted.

Step 18. Enter the **configure terminal** command at the prompt.

Step 19. Enter the **config-register** command and the original value you recorded in Step 2.

Step 20. Press **Ctrl-Z** to quit the configuration editor.

Step 21. Enter the **reload** command at the prompt.

> **Note** Every time you enter configuration mode on a router, a flag is set to check and make sure configurations have been saved before the router is reloaded. When you change the configuration register, there is no need to save the configuration, but the router prompts you to do so when you issue a reload. Answer no when asked if you want to save the configuration.

Preventing Password Recovery

Cisco IOS Software Release 12.3(8)YA introduced a security enhancement to prevent the ability of someone performing a password recovery on a Cisco router. The normal password recovery procedures enable anyone with physical console access to a router the ability to recover a password. Using the **no service password-recovery** feature prevents someone from entering ROMMON mode during a router reload to recover a password.

Enter the following command in global configuration mode to enable this feature:

```
(global) no service password-recovery
```

When this command is entered, you cannot longer perform password recovery. You can still recover a device if you forget a password, but the router resets to factory default settings, and your configuration file will be erased. Follow these steps to recover a router configured with the **no service password-recovery** command:

Step 1. Reboot the router. Press the break key sequence for your terminal application within 5 seconds after the image decompression during boot.

Step 2. Enter **Y** when you receive the following message:

```
Do You Want to Reset the Router to Factory Default Configuration and
Proceed [y/n]?
```

Remember, this erases your startup-configuration file and returns the router to its factory default settings. It is advised that you always back up your configuration file because you might need to recover a router.

Configuration Register Settings

This appendix contains an overview of the virtual configuration register used by the router during initialization. The configuration register controls many of the boot parameters, as well as the console speed. Each router has a configuration register; however, they differ slightly based on the system architecture. For example, the Cisco 2600 series configuration registers vary slightly from the 2500 series by allowing a previously unused bit (bit 5) to define more console port speeds.

Virtual Configuration Register

When a router boots, the virtual configuration register is checked to determine many boot parameters, including what mode to enter upon booting, where to get the software image, and how to deal with the configuration file in NVRAM.

The virtual configuration register is a 16-bit register stored in a special section of NVRAM separate from the startup configuration file. The parameters specified control many of the booting and low-level code functions, such as the console port baud rate, the loading operation of the software, enabling or disabling the Break key during normal operations, controlling the default broadcast address, and setting a boot source for the router. You display the configuration register by typing the command show version or show hardware.

Typically, the factory default for the configuration register is 0x2102 (hexadecimal value). Each number in the hexadecimal value represents 4 bits of the configuration register. The configuration register bits are numbered 0 to 15, inclusive, with 0 being the low-order (far-right) bit. If you translate the configuration register into binary, the value 0x2102 is as follows:

0010 0001 0000 0010

The bits are numbered 0 to 15, starting with the rightmost bit. Thus, bits 1, 8, and 13 would be on in this setting. All other bits would be off. Table E-1 lists the meaning of each of the virtual configuration register bits.

Table E-1   *Common Virtual Configuration Register Bit Meanings*

Bit Number(s)	Hexadecimal Value	Meaning
00 to 03	0x0000 to 0x000F	Boot field (see Table E-2).
04	0x0010	Undefined.
05	0x0020	Undefined or console speed. Platform-dependent; see Table E-6.
06	0x0040	Causes system software to ignore NVRAM contents.
07	0x0080	OEM bit enabled.
08	0x0100	Break disabled.
09	0x0200	Undefined.
10	0x0400	IP broadcast with all 0s if bit is on. This works with bit 14, as shown in Table E-4.
11 to 12	0x0800 to 0x1800	Console line speed. See Tables E-5 and E-6.
13	0x2000	Boots the default ROM software if the network boot fails.
14	0x4000	IP broadcasts do not have net numbers. This value works with bit 10, as shown in Table E-4.
15	0x8000	Enables diagnostic messages and ignores NVRAM contents.

Changing the Virtual Configuration Register Settings

You can change the configuration register settings through the Cisco IOS Software or in ROM monitor mode. Some common reasons to modify the value of the virtual configuration register include recovering a lost password, changing the console baud rate, and enabling or disabling the break function. Another reason for modifying the value of the virtual configuration register might be to control the boot process.

Note   If the router finds no **boot system** commands, and there are no images in Flash memory, the router uses the netboot value in the configuration register to form a filename from which to netboot a default system image stored on a network server via TFTP (see Table E-3).

To change the configuration register while running the system Cisco IOS Software, follow these steps:

Step 1. Enter the **enable** command and your password to enter the privileged level, as follows:

```
router> enable
      Password:
      router#
```

Step 2. At the privileged-level system prompt (**router#**), enter the **configure terminal** command. You are prompted as follows:

```
router# configure terminal
      Enter configuration commands, one per line.
      Edit with DELETE, CTRL/W, and CTRL/U; end with CTRL/Z
Router(config)#
```

Step 3. To set the contents of the configuration register, enter the **config-register** *value* configuration command, where *value* is a hexadecimal number preceded by 0x (see Table E-1), as in the following:

```
Router(config)# config-register 0x2102
```

Step 4. Exit configuration mode by pressing **Ctrl-Z**. The new value settings are written into the virtual configuration register; however, the new settings do not take effect until the system software is reloaded when you reboot the router.

Step 5. To display the configuration register value currently in effect and the value that will be used at the next reload, enter the show version EXEC command. The value is displayed on the last line of the screen display, as follows:

```
Configuration register is 0x2142 (will be 0x2102 at next reload)
```

Note   Although this appendix discusses the concept of the virtual configuration register, not all routers have identical settings. For example, the filenames listed in Table E-3 differ between platforms. On some routers, an additional bit (see Table E-6) is used for console speed to allow higher speeds. For more detailed information about your specific hardware, check your Documentation CD or Cisco.com.

Caution   To avoid confusion and possibly hanging the router, remember that valid configuration register settings might be combinations of settings and not just the individual settings listed in Table E-1. For example, the factory default value of 0x2102 is a combination of settings.

The lowest 4 bits of the virtual configuration register (bits 3, 2, 1, and 0) form the boot field. (See Table E-2.) The boot field specifies a number in binary. If you set the boot field value to 0, you must boot the operating system manually by entering the **b** command at the boot prompt, as follows:

```
> b [tftp] flash filename
```

Definitions of the various **b** command options follow:

- **b**—Boots the default system software from ROM.

- **b flash**—Boots the first file in Flash memory.

- **b filename** *host*—Allows you to boot using the TFTP server specified by the *host* option.

- **b flash** *filename*—Boots the file *(filename)* from Flash memory.

Table E-2   *Explanation of the Boot Field (Configuration Register Bits 00 to 03)*

Boot Field	Meaning
0x0	Upon boot, this setting directs the router to enter ROM Monitor mode.
0x1	Upon boot, this setting allows the router to boot from the image in ROM. This is also known as Boot mode.
0x2 to 0xF	Specifies a default netboot filename. May enable boot system commands that override the default netboot filename.

If you set the boot field value to be in the range of 0x2 through 0xF, and a valid **boot system** command is stored in the configuration file, the router boots using the **boot system** commands in the configuration or the first valid IOS file in Flash if there are no **boot system** commands. If you set the boot field to any other bit pattern, the router uses the resulting number to form a default boot filename for netbooting. (See Table E-3.)

The router creates a default boot filename as part of the automatic configuration processes. To form the boot filename, the router starts with Cisco and links the octal equivalent of the boot field number, a dash, and the processor-type name. Table E-3 lists the default boot filenames or actions for the 2500 series routers.

Note   A valid **boot system** configuration command in the router configuration in NVRAM overrides the default netboot filename.

Table E-3   *Default Boot Filenames*

Action/Filename	Bit 3	Bit 2	Bit 1	Bit 0
Bootstrap mode	0	0	0	0
ROM software	0	0	0	1
Cisco2-igs	0	0	1	0
Cisco3-igs	0	0	1	1
Cisco4-igs	0	1	0	0
Cisco5-igs	0	1	0	1
Cisco6-igs	0	1	1	0
cisco7-igs	0	1	1	1
cisco10-igs	1	0	0	0
cisco11-igs	1	0	0	1
cisco12-igs	1	0	1	0
cisco13-igs	1	0	1	1
cisco14-igs	1	1	0	0
cisco15-igs	1	1	0	1
cisco16-igs	1	1	1	0
cisco17-igs	1	1	1	1

In Example E-1, the virtual configuration register is set to boot the router from Flash memory and to ignore Break at the router's next reboot.

Example E-1   *Setting the Configuration Register to Boot from Flash*

```
router# configure terminal
Enter configuration commands, one per line.
Edit with DELETE, CTRL/W, and CTRL/U; end with CTRL/Z
config-register 0x2102
boot system flash [filename]
^Z
router#
```

Whereas the lower 4 bits of this register control the boot characteristics, other bits control other functions. Bit 8 controls the console Break key. Setting bit 8 (the factory default) causes the processor to ignore the console Break key. Clearing bit 8 causes the processor to interpret the Break key as a command to force the system into the ROM monitor, thereby halting normal operation. A break issued in the first 60 seconds while the system reboots affects the router, regardless of the configuration settings. After the initial 60 seconds, a break works only if bit 8 is set to 0.

Bit 10 controls the host portion of the Internet broadcast address. Setting bit 10 causes the processor to use all 0s; clearing bit 10 (the factory default) causes the processor to use all 1s. Bit 10 interacts with bit 14, which controls the network and subnet portions of the broadcast address. Table E-4 shows the combined effect of bits 10 and 14.

Bits 11 and 12 in the configuration register determine the baud rate of the console terminal.

Table E-5 shows the bit settings for the four available baud rates. (The factory-set default baud rate is 9600.)

For some devices, such as the 2600 and 3600 series routers, Bit 5 also defines the console port speed. Table E-6 shows the bit settings for the available baud rates. (The factory-set default baud rate is 9600.)

Bit 13 determines the router response to a bootload failure. Setting bit 13 causes the router to load operating software from ROM after five unsuccessful attempts to load a boot file from the network. Clearing bit 13 causes the router to keep trying to load a boot file from the network indefinitely. By factory default, bit 13 is set to 1.

Table E-4 *Configuration Register Settings for the IP Broadcast Address Destination*

Bit 14	Bit 10	Address (<net> <host>)
Off	Off	<1s> <1s>
Off	On	<0s> <0s>
On	On	<net> <0s>
On	Off	<net> <1s>

Table E-5 *System Console Terminal Baud Rate Settings*

Baud	Bit 12	Bit 11
9600	0	0
4800	0	1
1200	1	0
2400	1	1

Table E-6 *System Console Terminal Baud Rate Settings for 2600 and 3600 Series Routers*

Baud	Bit 5	Bit 12	Bit 11
115200	1	1	1
57600	1	1	0
38400	1	0	1
19200	1	0	0
9600	0	0	0
4800	0	0	1
1200	0	1	0
2400	0	1	1

Enabling Booting from Flash Memory

To enable booting from Flash memory, set configuration register bits 3, 2, 1, and 0 to a value between 2 and F in conjunction with the **boot system flash** *filename* configuration command. The actual value of 2 to F is not really relevant here; it serves only to tell the router not to boot from its ROM IOS image.

While in the system Cisco IOS Software image, enter the **configure terminal** command at the privileged-level system prompt and specify a Flash filename to boot from, as demonstrated in Example E-2.

Example E-2 *Specifying a Flash Filename*

```
router# configure terminal
Enter configuration commands, one per line.
Edit with DELETE, CTRL/W, and CTRL/U; end with CTRL/Z
Router(config)#boot system flash [filename]
```

To disable break and allow the router to boot from Flash, enter the **config-register** command with the value shown in Example E-3.

Example E-3 *Setting the Default Configuration Register*

```
router# configure terminal
Enter configuration commands, one per line.
Edit with DELETE, CTRL/W, and CTRL/U; end with CTRL/Z
Router(config)#config-reg 0x2102
^Z
router#
```

It is important to realize that the configuration register is a virtual register that is configured in a special portion of NVRAM. When you change the register, it is automatically saved into that portion of NVRAM, but it is implemented only during the next router reload. If you make this change, it is not necessary to copy the configuration to NVRAM. If you reload a router after you have entered configuration mode without a save, however, you are prompted to save the configuration. A save is necessary only if you have made other changes to the configuration.

The virtual configuration register is an integral part of a router's configuration and basic operation. Understanding how it works and what each bit does is important to the router's operation and configuration.

Well-Known IP Protocol Numbers

A higher-layer protocol is identified with an 8-bit field within an IPv4 packet called *Protocol*. Figure F-1 shows the IPv4 header format, with the Protocol field shaded. Figure F-2 shows the IPv6 header format, where the protocol number is stored in the shaded Next Header field.

Well-known or assigned IP protocols are registered with the Internet Assigned Numbers Authority (IANA). The information presented here is reproduced with permission from the IANA. For the most current IP protocol number assignment information, refer to www.iana.org/numbers.htm under the "Protocol Numbers" link.

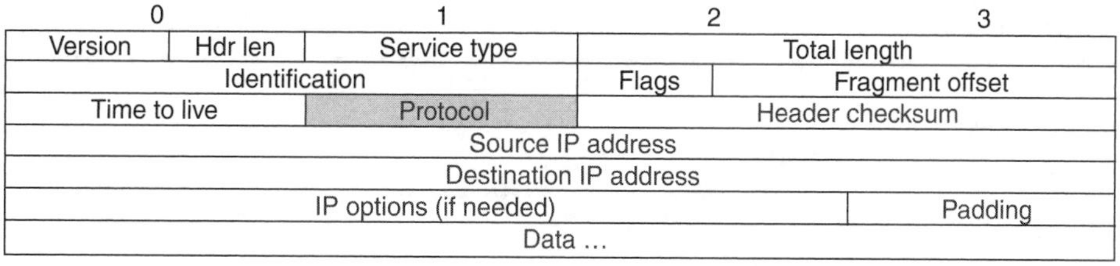

0		1		2		3
Version	Hdr len	Service type		Total length		
Identification			Flags	Fragment offset		
Time to live		Protocol		Header checksum		
Source IP address						
Destination IP address						
IP options (if needed)					Padding	
Data …						

Figure F-1 *IPv4 Header Format Showing the Protocol Field*

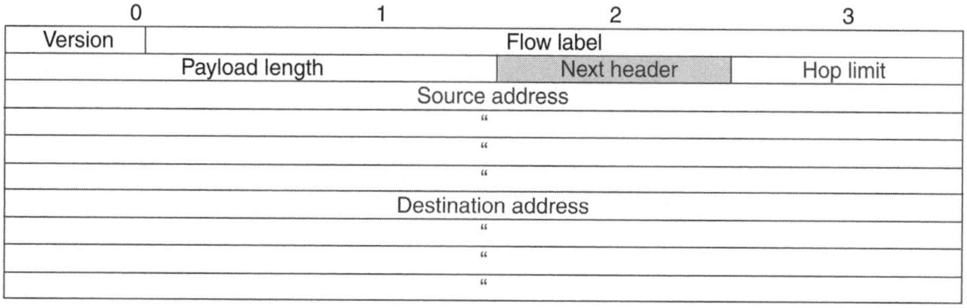

0		1		2		3
Version		Flow label				
Payload length				Next header	Hop limit	
Source address						
"						
"						
"						
Destination address						
"						
"						
"						

Figure F-2 *IPv6 Base Header Format Showing the Next Header Field*

Table F-1 shows the registered IP protocol numbers, along with the protocol keyword (or acronym), the name of the protocol, and an RFC number (if applicable).

Table F-1 *Registered IP Protocol Numbers, Keywords, Names, and Associated RFCs*

Keyword Protocol References	Number
HOPOPT IPv6 Hop-by-Hop Option RFC 1883	0
ICMP Internet Control Message RFC 792	1
IGMP Internet Group Management RFC 1112	2
GGP Gateway-to-Gateway RFC 823	3
IP IP in IP (encapsulation) RFC 2003	4
ST Stream RFC 1190, RFC 1819	5
TCP Transmission Control RFC 793	6
CBT CBT	7
EGP Exterior Gateway Protocol RFC 888	8
IGP any private interior gateway IANA (used by Cisco for IGRP)	9
BBN-RCC-MON BBN RCC Monitoring	10
NVP-II Network Voice Protocol RFC 741	11

Table F-1   *Registered IP Protocol Numbers, Keywords, Names, and Associated RFCs*

Keyword Protocol References	Number
PUP PUP	12
ARGUS ARGUS	13
EMCON EMCON	14
XNET Cross Net Debugger	15
CHAOS Chaos	16
UDP User Datagram RFC 768	17
MUX Multiplexing	18
DCN-MEAS DCN Measurement Subsystems	19
HMP Host Monitoring RFC 869	20
PRM Packet Radio Measurement	21
XNS-IDP XEROX NS IDP	22
TRUNK-1 Trunk-1	23
TRUNK-2 Trunk-2	24
LEAF-1 Leaf-1	25
LEAF-2 Leaf-2	26

Table F-1   *Registered IP Protocol Numbers, Keywords, Names, and Associated RFCs*

Keyword Protocol References	Number
RDP Reliable Data Protocol RFC 908	27
IRTP Internet Reliable Transaction RFC 938	28
ISO-TP4 ISO Transport Protocol Class 4 RFC 905	29
NETBLT Bulk Data Transfer Protocol RFC 969	30
MFE-NSP MFE Network Services Protocol	31
MERIT-INP MERIT Internodal Protocol	32
SEP Sequential Exchange Protocol	33
3PC Third-Party Connect Protocol	34
IDPR Inter-Domain Policy Routing Protocol	35
XTP XTP	36
DDP Datagram Delivery Protocol	37
IDPR-CMTP IDPR Control Message Transport Protocol	38
TP++ TP++ Transport Protocol	39
IL IL Transport Protocol	40
IPv6 Ipv6	41

Table F-1   *Registered IP Protocol Numbers, Keywords, Names, and Associated RFCs*

Keyword Protocol References	Number
SDRP Source Demand Routing Protocol	42
IPv6-Route Routing Header for IPv6	43
IPv6-Frag Fragment Header for IPv6	44
IDRP Inter-Domain Routing Protocol	45
RSVP Reservation Protocol	46
GRE General Routing Encapsulation	47
MHRP Mobile Host Routing Protocol	48
BNA BNA	49
ESP Encap Security Payload for IPv6 RFC 1827	50
AH Authentication Header for IPv6 RFC 1826	51
I-NLSP Integrated Net Layer Security TUBA	52
SWIPE IP with Encryption	53
NARP NBMA Address Resolution Protocol RFC 1735	54
MOBILE IP Mobility	55
TLSP Transport Layer Security Protocol using Kryptonet key management	56

Table F-1 *Registered IP Protocol Numbers, Keywords, Names, and Associated RFCs*

Keyword Protocol References	Number
SKIP SKIP	57
IPv6-ICMP ICMP for IPv6 RFC 1883	58
IPv6-NoNxt No Next Header for IPv6 RFC 1883	59
IPv6-Opts Destination Options for IPv6 RFC 1883	60
Any host internal protocol IANA	61
CFTP CFTP	62
Any local network IANA	63
SAT-EXPAK SATNET and Backroom EXPAK	64
KRYPTOLAN Kryptolan	65
RVD MIT Remote Virtual Disk Protocol	66
IPPC Internet Pluribus Packet Core	67
Any distributed file system IANA	68
SAT-MON SATNET Monitoring	69
VISA VISA Protocol	70
IPCV Internet Packet Core Utility	71

Table F-1 *Registered IP Protocol Numbers, Keywords, Names, and Associated RFCs*

Keyword Protocol References	Number
CPNX Computer Protocol Network Executive	72
CPHB Computer Protocol Heart Beat	73
WSN Wang Span Network	74
PVP Packet Video Protocol	75
BR-SAT-MON Backroom SATNET Monitoring	76
SUN-ND SUN ND PROTOCOL-Temporary	77
WB-MON WIDEBAND Monitoring	78
WB-EXPAK WIDEBAND EXPAK	79
ISO-IP ISO Internet Protocol	80
VMTP VMTP	81
SECURE-VMTP SECURE-VMTP	82
VINES VINES	83
TTP TTP	84
NSFNET-IGP NSFNET-IGP	85
DGP Dissimilar Gateway Protocol	86
TCF TCF	87

Table F-1   *Registered IP Protocol Numbers, Keywords, Names, and Associated RFCs*

Keyword Protocol References	Number
EIGRP EIGRP CISCO	88
OSPFIGP OSPFIGP RFC 1583	89
Sprite-RPC Sprite RPC Protocol	90
LARP Locus Address Resolution Protocol	91
MTP Multicast Transport Protocol	92
AX.25 AX.25 Frames	93
IPIP IP-within-IP Encapsulation Protocol	94
MICP Mobile Internetworking Control Pro.	95
SCC-SP Semaphore Communications Sec. Pro.	96
ETHERIP Ethernet-within-IP Encapsulation	97
ENCAP Encapsulation Header RFC 1241	98
Any private encryption scheme IANA	99
GMTP GMTP	100
IFMP Ipsilon Flow Management Protocol	101
PNNI PNNI over IP	102

Table F-1   *Registered IP Protocol Numbers, Keywords, Names, and Associated RFCs*

Keyword Protocol References	Number
PIM Protocol Independent Multicast	103
ARIS ARIS	104
SCPS SCPS	105
QNX QNX	106
A/N Active Networks	107
IPComp IP Payload Compression Protocol RFC 2393	108
SNP Sitara Networks Protocol	109
Compaq-Peer Compaq Peer Protocol	110
IPX-in-IP IPX in IP	111
VRRP Virtual Router Redundancy Protocol	112
PGM PGM Reliable Transport Protocol	113
Any 0-hop protocol IANA	114
L2TP Layer Two Tunneling Protocol	115
DDX D-II Data Exchange (DDX)	116
IATP Interactive Agent Transfer Protocol	117
STP Schedule Transfer Protocol	118

Table F-1 *Registered IP Protocol Numbers, Keywords, Names, and Associated RFCs*

Keyword Protocol References	Number
SRP SpectraLink Radio Protocol	119
UTI UTI	120
SMP Simple Message Protocol	121
SM SM	122
PTP Performance Transparency Protocol	123
ISIS over IPv4	124
FIRE	125
CRTP Combat Radio Transport Protocol	126
CRUDP Combat Radio User Datagram	127
SSCOPMCE	128
IPLT	129
SPS Secure Packet Shield	130
PIPE Private IP Encapsulation within IP	131
SCTP Stream Control Transmission Protocol	132
FC Fibre Channel	133
Unassigned IANA	134–254
Reserved IANA	255

Well-Known IP Port Numbers

Transport layer protocols identify higher-layer traffic with 16-bit fields called *port* numbers. A connection between two devices uses a source and a destination port, both contained within the protocol data unit. Figure G-1 shows the User Datagram Protocol (UDP) header format, with the source and destination port fields shaded. Figure G-2 shows the Transmission Control Protocol (TCP) header format, with the source and destination port fields shaded.

0	1	2	3
UDP source port		UDP destination port	
UDP message length		UDP checksum	
Data ...			

Figure G-1 *UDP Datagram Format Showing Port Fields*

0		1		2		3
TCP source port				TCP destination port		
Sequence number						
Acknowledgment number						
Hdr len	Reserved		Code bits	Window		
Checksum				Urgent pointer		
Options (if necessary)					Padding	
Data						
Data ...						

Figure G-2 *TCP Segment Format Showing Port Fields*

Both UDP and TCP port numbers are divided into the following ranges:

- Well-known port numbers (0 through 1023)

- Registered port numbers (1024 through 49151)

- Dynamic or Private port numbers (49152 through 65535)

Usually, a port assignment uses a common port number for both UDP and TCP. A connection from a client to a server uses the well-known port on the server as a *service contact port*, while the client is free to dynamically assign its own port number. For TCP, the connection is identified by the source and destination IP addresses, as well as the source and destination TCP port numbers.

Well-known or assigned IP protocols are registered with the Internet Assigned Numbers Authority (IANA). The information presented here is reproduced with permission from the IANA. For the most current IP protocol number assignment information, refer to http://www.iana.org/numbers.htm under the "Port Numbers" link.

Table G-1 shows some commonly used protocols, their port numbers, and a brief description. The IANA has recorded close to 3350 unique port numbers. Due to space limitations, only a small subset of these have been presented here.

Table G-1   *Commonly Used Protocols and Associated Port Numbers*

Keyword	Description	UDP/TCP Port
Echo	Echo	7
Discard	Discard	9
Systat	Active Users	11
Daytime	Daytime (RFC 867)	13
Qotd	Quote of the Day	17
Chargen	Character Generator	19
ftp-data	File Transfer [Default Data]	20
ftp	File Transfer [Control]	21
Ssh	SSH Remote Login Protocol	22
telnet	Telnet	23
Any private mail system	Any private mail system	24
Smtp	Simple Mail Transfer	25
msg-icp	MSG ICP	29
msg-auth	MSG Authentication	31
Any private printer server	Any private printer server	35
Time	Time	37
Name	Host Name Server	42
Nameserver	Host Name Server	42

Table G-1   *Commonly Used Protocols and Associated Port Numbers*

Keyword	Description	UDP/TCP Port
Nicname	Who Is	43
Tacacs	Login Host Protocol (TACACS)	49
re-mail-ck	Remote Mail Checking Protocol	50
Domain	Domain Name Server	53
Any private terminal address	Any private terminal address	57
Any private file service	Any private file service	59
whois++	whois++	63
tacacs-ds	TACACS-Database Service	65
sql*net	Oracle SQL*NET	66
Bootps	Bootstrap Protocol Server	67
Bootpc	Bootstrap Protocol Client	68
Tftp	Trivial File Transfer	69
Gopher	Gopher	70
Any private dial-out service	Any private dial-out service	75
Any private RJE service	Any private RJE service	77
Finger	Finger	79
http	World Wide Web HTTP	80
www	World Wide Web HTTP	80
www-http	World Wide Web HTTP	80
hosts2-ns	HOSTS2 Name Server	81
Xfer	XFER Utility	82
Any private terminal link	Any private terminal link	87
Kerberos	Kerberos	88
Dnsix	DNSIX Security Attribute Token Map	90
Npp	Network Printing Protocol	92
Dcp	Device Control Protocol	93
Objcall	Tivoli Object Dispatcher	94
acr-nema	ACR-NEMA Digital Imag. & Comm. 300	104

Table G-1 *Commonly Used Protocols and Associated Port Numbers*

Keyword	Description	UDP/TCP Port
Rtelnet	Remote Telnet Service	107
Snagas	SNA Gateway Access Server	108
pop2	Post Office Protocol-Version 2	109
pop3	Post Office Protocol-Version 3	110
Sunrpc	SUN Remote Procedure Call	111
ident/auth	Authentication Service	113
Audionews	Audio News Multicast	114
Sftp	Simple File Transfer Protocol	115
uucp-path	UUCP Path Service	117
Sqlserv	SQL Services	118
nntp	Network News Transfer Protocol	119
Ntp	Network Time Protocol	123
pwdgen	Password Generator Protocol	129
cisco-fna	cisco FNATIVE	130
cisco-tna	cisco TNATIVE	131
cisco-sys	cisco SYSMAINT	132
ingres-net	INGRES-NET Service	134
profile	PROFILE Naming System	136
netbios-ns	NETBIOS Name Service	137
netbios-dgm	NETBIOS Datagram Service	138
netbios-ssn	NETBIOS Session Service	139
imap	Internet Message Access Protocol	143
sql-net	SQL-NET	150
sgmp	SGMP	153
sqlsrv	SQL Service	156
pcmail-srv	PCMail Server	158
sgmp-traps	SGMP-TRAPS	160
snmp	SNMP	161

Table G-1   *Commonly Used Protocols and Associated Port Numbers*

Keyword	Description	UDP/TCP Port
snmptrap	SNMPTRAP	162
cmip-man	CMIP/TCP Manager	163
send	SEND	169
print-srv	Network PostScript	170
xyplex-mux	Xyplex	173
mailq	MAILQ	174
vmnet	VMNET	175
xdmcp	X Display Manager Control Protocol	177
bgp	Border Gateway Protocol	179
mumps	Plus Five's MUMPS	188
irc	Internet Relay Chat Protocol	194
dn6-nim-aud	DNSIX Network Level Module Audit	195
dn6-smm-red	DNSIX Session Mgt Module Audit Redir	196
dls	Directory Location Service	197
dls-mon	Directory Location Service Monitor	198
src	IBM System Resource Controller	200
at-rtmp	AppleTalk Routing Maintenance	201
at-nbp	AppleTalk Name Binding	202
at-3	AppleTalk Unused	203
at-echo	AppleTalk Echo	204
at-5	AppleTalk Unused	205
at-zis	AppleTalk Zone Information	206
at-7	AppleTalk Unused	207
at-8	AppleTalk Unused	208
qmtp	The Quick Mail Transfer Protocol	209
ipx	IPX	213
vmpwscs	VM PWSCS	214
softpc	Insignia Solutions	215

Table G-1   *Commonly Used Protocols and Associated Port Numbers*

Keyword	Description	UDP/TCP Port
dbase	dBASE Unix	217
imap3	Interactive Mail Access Protocol v3	220
http-mgmt	http-mgmt	280
asip-webadmin	AppleShare IP WebAdmin	311
ptp-event	PTP Event	319
ptp-general	PTP General	320
pdap	Prospero Data Access Protocol	344
rsvp_tunnel	RSVP Tunnel	363
rpc2portmap	rpc2portmap	369
aurp	AppleTalk Update-Based Routing Protocol	387
ldap	Lightweight Directory Access Protocol	389
netcp	NETscout Control Protocol	395
netware-ip	Novell NetWare over IP	396
ups	Uninterruptible Power Supply	401
smsp	Storage Management Services Protocol	413
mobileip-agent	MobileIP-Agent	434
mobilip-mn	MobilIP-MN	435
https	http protocol over TLS/SSL	443
snpp	Simple Network Paging Protocol	444
microsoft-ds	Microsoft-DS	445
appleqtc	apple quick time	458
ss7ns	ss7ns	477
ph	Ph service	481
isakmp	Isakmp	500
exec	remote process execution	512
login	remote login by Telnet	513
shell	Cmd	514
printer	Spooler	515

Table G-1   *Commonly Used Protocols and Associated Port Numbers*

Keyword	Description	UDP/TCP Port
ntalk	Ntalk	518
utime	unixtime	519
ncp	NCP	524
timed	timedserver	525
irc-serv	IRC-SERV	529
courier	Rpc	530
conference	Chat	531
netnews	readnews	532
netwall	For emergency broadcasts	533
iiop	Iiop	535
nmsp	Networked Media Streaming Protocol	537
uucp	Uucpd	540
uucp-rlogin	uucp-rlogin	541
klogin	Klogin	543
kshell	Krcmd	544
appleqtcsrvr	appleqtcsrvr	545
dhcpv6-client	DHCPv6 Client	546
dhcpv6-server	DHCPv6 Server	547
afpovertcp	AFC over TCP	548
rtsp	Real-Time Stream Control Protocol	554
remotefs	rfs server	556
rmonitor	rmonitord	560
monitor	Monitor	561
nntps	nntp protocol over TLS/SSL (was snntp)	563
whoami	Whoami	565
sntp-heartbeat	SNTP HEARTBEAT	580
imap4-ssl	IMAP4 + SSl (use 993 instead)	585
password-chg	Password Change	586

Table G-1 *Commonly Used Protocols and Associated Port Numbers*

Keyword	Description	UDP/TCP Port
eudora-set	Eudora Set	592
http-rpc-epmap	HTTP RPC Ep Map	593
sco-websrvrmg3	SCO Web Server Manager 3	598
ipcserver	SUN IPC server	600
sshell	SSLshell	614
sco-inetmgr	Internet Configuration Manager	615
sco-sysmgr	SCO System Administration Server	616
sco-dtmgr	SCO Desktop Administration Server	617
sco-websrvmgr	SCO WebServer manager	620
ldaps	ldap protocol over TLS/SSL (was sldap)	636
dhcp-failover	DHCP Failover	647
mac-srvr-admin	MacOS Server Admin	660
doom	doom Id Software	666
corba-iiop	CORBA IIOP	683
corba-iiop-ssl	CORBA IIOP SSL	684
nmap	NMAP	689
msexch-routing	MS Exchange Routing	691
ieee-mms-ssl	IEEE-MMS-SSL	695
cisco-tdp	Cisco TDP	711
flexlm	Flexible License Manager	744
kerberos-adm	Kerberos administration	749
phonebook	Phone	767
dhcp-failover2	dhcp-failover2	847
ftps-data	FTP protocol, data, over TLS/SSL	989
ftps	FTP protocol, control, over TLS/SSL	990
nas	Netnews Administration System	991
telnets	Telnet protocol over TLS/SSL	992
imaps	imap4 protocol over TLS/SSL	993

Table G-1 *Commonly Used Protocols and Associated Port Numbers*

Keyword	Description	UDP/TCP Port
ircs	irc protocol over TLS/SSL	994
pop3s	pop3 protocol over TLS/SSL (was spop3)	995
sunclustermgr	SUN Cluster Manager	1097
tripwire	TRIPWIRE	1169
shockwave2	Shockwave 2	1257
h323hostcallsc	H323 Host Call Secure	1300
lotusnote	Lotus Notes	1352
novell-lu6.2	Novell LU6.2	1416
ms-sql-s	Microsoft-SQL-Server	1434
ibm-cics	IBM CICS	1435
sybase-sqlany	Sybase SQL Any	1498
shivadiscovery	Shiva	1502
wins	Microsoft's Windows Internet Name Service	1512
ingreslock	Ingres	1524
orasrv	Oracle	1525
tlisrv	Oracle	1527
coauthor	Oracle	1529
rdb-dbs-disp	Oracle Remote Data Base	1571
oraclenames	oraclenames	1575
ontime	Ontime	1622
shockwave	Shockwave	1626
oraclenet8cman	Oracle Net8 Cman	1630
cert-initiator	cert-initiator	1639
cert-responder	cert-responder	1640
kermit	Kermit	1649
groupwise	groupwise	1677
rsvp-encap-1	RSVP-ENCAPSULATION-1	1698
rsvp-encap-2	RSVP-ENCAPSULATION-2	1699

Table G-1 *Commonly Used Protocols and Associated Port Numbers*

Keyword	Description	UDP/TCP Port
h323gatedisc	h323gatedisc	1718
h323gatestat	h323gatestat	1719
h323hostcall	h323hostcall	1720
cisco-net-mgmt	cisco-net-mgmt	1741
oracle-em1	oracle-em1	1748
oracle-em2	oracle-em2	1754
tftp-mcast	tftp-mcast	1758
www-ldap-gw	www-ldap-gw	1760
bmc-net-admin	bmc-net-admin	1769
bmc-net-svc	bmc-net-svc	1770
oracle-vp2	Oracle-VP2	1808
oracle-vp1	Oracle-VP1	1809
radius	RADIUS	1812
radius-acct	RADIUS Accounting	1813
hsrp	Hot Standby Router Protocol	1985
licensedaemon	Cisco license management	1986
tr-rsrb-p1	Cisco RSRP Priority 1 port	1987
tr-rsrb-p2	Cisco RSRP Priority 2 port	1988
tr-rsrb-p3	Cisco RSRP Priority 3 port	1989
stun-p1	Cisco STUN Priority 1 port	1990
stun-p2	Cisco STUN Priority 2 port	1991
stun-p3	Cisco STUN Priority 3 port	1992
snmp-tcp-port	Cisco SNMP TCP port	1993
stun-port	Cisco serial tunnel port	1994
perf-port	Cisco perf port	1995
tr-rsrb-port	Cisco Remote SRB port	1996
gdp-port	Cicso Gateway Discovery Protocol	1997
x25-svc-port	Cisco X.25 service (XOT)	1998

Table G-1 *Commonly Used Protocols and Associated Port Numbers*

Keyword	Description	UDP/TCP Port
tcp-id-port	Cisco identification port	1999
dlsrpn	Data Link Switch Read Port Number	2065
dlswpn	Data Link Switch Write Port Number	2067
ah-esp-encap	AH and ESP Encapsulated in UDP packet	2070
h2250-annex-g	H.225.0 Annex G	2099
ms-olap3	Microsoft OLAP	2382
ovsessionmgr	OpenView Session Mgr	2389
ms-olap1	MS OLAP 1	2393
ms-olap2	MS OLAP 2	2394
mgcp-gateway	Media Gateway Control Protocol Gateway	2427
ovwdb	OpenView NNM daemon	2447
giop	Oracle GIOP	2481
giop-ssl	Oracle GIOP SSL	2482
ttc	Oracle TTC	2483
ttc-ssl	Oracle TTC SSL	2484
citrixima	Citrix IMA	2512
citrixadmin	Citrix ADMIN	2513
call-sig-trans	H.323 Annex E call signaling transport	2517
windb	WinDb	2522
novell-zen	Novell ZEN	2544
clp	Cisco Line Protocol	2567
hl7	HL7	2575
citrixmaclient	Citrix MA Client	2598
sybaseanywhere	Sybase Anywhere	2638
novell-ipx-cmd	Novell IPX CMD	2645
sms-rcinfo	SMS RCINFO	2701
sms-xfer	SMS XFER	2702
sms-chat	SMS CHAT	2703

Table G-1   *Commonly Used Protocols and Associated Port Numbers*

Keyword	Description	UDP/TCP Port
sms-remctrl	SMS REMCTRL	2704
mgcp-callagent	Media Gateway Control Protocol Call Agent	2727
dicom-iscl	DICOM ISCL	2761
dicom-tls	DICOM TLS	2762
citrix-rtmp	Citrix RTMP	2897
wap-push	WAP Push	2948
wap-pushsecure	WAP Push Secure	2949
h263-video	H.263 Video Streaming	2979
lotusmtap	Lotus Mail Tracking Agent Protocol	3007
njfss	NetWare sync services	3092
bmcpatrolagent	BMC Patrol Agent	3181
bmcpatrolrnvu	BMC Patrol Rendezvous	3182
ccmail	cc:mail/lotus	3264
msft-gc	Microsoft Global Catalog	3268
msft-gc-ssl	Microsoft Global Catalog with LDAP/SSL	3269
Unauthorized Use by SAP R/3	Unauthorized Use by SAP R/3	3300–3301
mysql	MySQL	3306
ms-cluster-net	MS Cluster Net	3343
ssql	SSQL	3352
ms-wbt-server	MS WBT Server	3389
mira	Apple Remote Access Protocol	3454
prsvp	RSVP Port	3455
patrolview	Patrol View	4097
vrml-multi-use	VRML Multi-User Systems	4200–4299
rwhois	Remote Who Is	4321
bmc-reporting	BMC Reporting	4568
sip	SIP	5060
sip-tls	SIP-TLS	5061

Table G-1 *Commonly Used Protocols and Associated Port Numbers*

Keyword	Description	UDP/TCP Port
pcanywheredata	pcANYWHEREdata	5631
pcaywherestat	pcANYWHEREstat	5632
x11	X Window System	6000–6063
bmc-grx	BMC GRX	6300
bmc-perf-agent	BMC PERFORM AGENT	6767
bmc-perf-mgrd	BMC PERFORM MGRD	6768
sun-lm	SUN License Manager	7588
http-alt	HTTP Alternate (see port 80)	8080
cp-cluster	Check Point Clustering	8116
patrol	Patrol	8160
patrol-snmp	Patrol SNMP	8161
wap-wsp	WAP connectionless session service	9200
wap-wsp-wtp	WAP session service	9201
wap-wsp-s	WAP secure connectionless session service	9202
wap-wsp-wtp-s	WAP secure session service	9203
wap-vcard	WAP vCard	9204
wap-vcal	WAP vCal	9205
wap-vcard-s	WAP vCard Secure	9206
wap-vcal-s	WAP vCal Secure	9207
bmc-perf-sd	BMC-PERFORM-SERVICE DAEMON	10128
h323callsigalt	h323 Call Signal Alternate	11720
vofr-gateway	VoFR Gateway	21590
quake	quake	26000
flex-lm	FLEX LM (1–10)	27000–27009
traceroute	traceroute use	33434
reachout	REACHOUT	43188

Appendix H

ICMP Type and Code Numbers

The Internet Control Message Protocol (ICMP) is used to transport error or control messages between routers and other devices. An ICMP message is encapsulated as the payload in an IP packet. Figure H-1 shows the ICMP message format. Notice that in the case of an error condition, the first 8 bytes (64 bits) of the original datagram causing the error are included in the ICMP message. This provides the protocol and port numbers of the original message to be seen, making troubleshooting easier.

0	1	2	3
ICMP type	ICMP code	ICMP checksum	
(ICMP messages that report errors only)			
Header & first 8 bytes of datagram that caused an error ...			

Figure H-1 *ICMP Message Format*

ICMP type codes are registered with the Internet Assigned Numbers Authority (IANA). The information presented here is reproduced with permission from the IANA. For the most current ICMP type code number assignment information, refer to www.iana.org/numbers.htm under the "ICMP Type" link.

Table H-1 shows the assigned ICMP type numbers, ICMP codes (where applicable), a brief description, and a reference to an RFC.

Table H-1   *Assigned ICMP Type Numbers, Codes, Descriptions, and Associated RFCs*

Type	Code	Name	Reference
0		Echo Reply	[RFC 792]
1		Unassigned	
2		Unassigned	
3		Destination Unreachable	[RFC 792]
	0	Net Unreachable	
	1	Host Unreachable	
	2	Protocol Unreachable	
	3	Port Unreachable	
	4	Fragmentation Needed and Don't Fragment Was Set	
	5	Source Route Failed	
	6	Destination Network Unknown	
	7	Destination Host Unknown	
	8	Source Host Isolated	
	9	Destination Network Is Administratively Prohibited	
	10	Destination Host Is Administratively Prohibited	
	11	Destination Network Unreachable for Type of Service	
	12	Destination Host Unreachable for Type of Service	
	13	Communication Administratively Prohibited	[RFC 1812]
	14	Host Precedence Violation	[RFC 1812]
	15	Precedence Cutoff in Effect	[RFC 1812]
4		Source Quench	[RFC 792]
5		Redirect	[RFC 792]
	0	Redirect Datagram for the Network (or Subnet)	
	1	Redirect Datagram for the Host	
	2	Redirect Datagram for the Type of Service and Network	
	3	Redirect Datagram for the Type of Service and Host	
6		Alternate Host Address	
	0	Alternate Address for Host	

Table H-1 *Assigned ICMP Type Numbers, Codes, Descriptions, and Associated RFCs*

Type	Code	Name	Reference
7		Unassigned	
8		Echo	[RFC 792]
9		Router Advertisement	[RFC 1256]
10		Router Solicitation	[RFC 1256]
11		Time Exceeded	[RFC 792]
	0	Time to Live Exceeded in Transit	
	1	Fragment Reassembly Time Exceeded	
12		Parameter Problem	[RFC 792]
	0	Pointer Indicates the Error	
	1	Missing a Required Option	[RFC 1108]
	2	Bad Length	
13		Timestamp	[RFC 792]
14		Timestamp Reply	[RFC 792]
15		Information Request	[RFC 792]
16		Information Reply	[RFC 792]
17		Address Mask Request	[RFC 950]
18		Address Mask Reply	[RFC 950]
19		Reserved (for Security)	
20–29		Reserved (for Robustness Experiment)	
30		Traceroute	[RFC 1393]
31		Datagram Conversion Error	[RFC 1475]
32		Mobile Host Redirect	
33		IPv6 Where-Are-You	
34		IPv6 I-Am-Here	
35		Mobile Registration Request	
36		Mobile Registration Reply	
37		Domain Name Request	
38		Domain Name Reply	

Table H-1   *Assigned ICMP Type Numbers, Codes, Descriptions, and Associated RFCs*

Type	Code	Name	Reference
39		SKIP	
40		Photuris	
	0	Reserved	
	1	Unknown security Parameters Index	
	2	Valid Security Parameters, but Authentication Failed	
	3	Valid Security Parameters, but Decryption Failed	
41–255		Reserved	

Well-Known IP Multicast Addresses

Some client server applications use a multicast packet in order to send large streams of data to many hosts with a single transmission. The multicast packet uses special addressing at Layer 3 and Layer 2 to communicate with clients that have been configured to receive these packets. The multicast packet contains a Class D IP address to specify the group of devices that are to receive the packet. This group is known as the *multicast group* and the IP address translates directly to an Ethernet multicast address. The Ethernet multicast address has the first 24 bits set to 01-00-5E, the next bit is set to 0, and the last 23 bits set to match the low 23 bits of the IP multicast address. Figure I-1 shows how Layer 3 multicast addresses translate to Layer 2 Ethernet addresses.

Multicast group address Layer 3

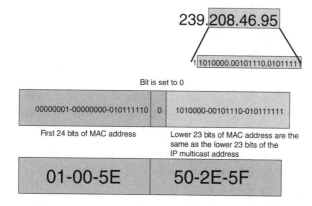

Translates into Layer 2 MAC address

Figure I-1 *Layer 3-to-Layer 2 Multicast Translation*

Well-known or assigned IP protocols are registered with the Internet Assigned Numbers Authority (IANA). The information presented here is reproduced with permission from the IANA. For the most current IP protocol number assignment information, refer to http://www.iana.org/numbers.htm under the "Multicast Addresses" link.

"Host Extensions for IP Multicasting" [RFC 1112] specifies the extensions required for a host implementation of the Internet Protocol (IP) to support multicasting. The multicast addresses are in the range 224.0.0.0–239.255.255.255. Table I-1 lists the current addresses.

The range of addresses between 224.0.0.0 and 224.0.0.255 inclusive is reserved for the use of routing protocols and other low-level topology discovery or maintenance protocols, such as gateway discovery and group membership reporting. Multicast routers should not forward any multicast datagram with destination addresses in this range, regardless of its TTL.

Table I-1 shows the registered multicast addresses, along with the application, and the RFC number (if applicable) or other reference.

Table I-1 *Registered Multicast Addresses and Associated Applications, RFCs, and References*

Group, Application, and References	Address
Base Address (Reserved) RFC 1112	224.0.0.0
All Systems on this Subnet RFC 1112	224.0.0.1
All Routers on this Subnet	224.0.0.2
Unassigned	224.0.0.3
DVMRP Routers RFC 1075	224.0.0.4
OSPFIGP OSPFIGP All Routers RFC 2328	224.0.0.5
OSPFIGP OSPFIGP Designated Routers RFC 2328	224.0.0.6
ST Routers RFC 1190	224.0.0.7
ST Hosts RFC 1190	224.0.0.8

Table I-1 *Registered Multicast Addresses and Associated Applications, RFCs, and References*

Group, Application, and References	Address
RIP-2 Routers RFC 1723	224.0.0.9
EIGRP Routers	224.0.0.10
Mobile-Agents	224.0.0.11
DHCP Server/Relay Agent RFC 1884	224.0.0.12
All PIM Routers	224.0.0.13
RSVP-ENCAPSULATION	224.0.0.14
all-cbt-routers	224.0.0.15
designated-sbm	224.0.0.16
all-sbms	224.0.0.17
VRRP	224.0.0.18
IPAllL1ISs	224.0.0.19
IPAllL2ISs	224.0.0.20
IPAllIntermediate Systems	224.0.0.21
IGMP	224.0.0.22
GLOBECAST-ID	224.0.0.23
Unassigned	224.0.0.24
router-to-switch	224.0.0.25
Unassigned	224.0.0.26
Al MPP Hello	224.0.0.27
ETC Control	224.0.0.28
GE-FANUC	224.0.0.29
indigo-vhdp	224.0.0.30
shinbroadband	224.0.0.31
digistar	224.0.0.32
ff-system-management	224.0.0.33
pt2-discover	224.0.0.34

Table I-1 *Registered Multicast Addresses and Associated Applications, RFCs, and References*

Group, Application, and References	Address
DXCLUSTER	224.0.0.35
DTCP Announcement	224.0.0.36
Unassigned	224.0.0.37–224.0.0.250
MDNS	224.0.0.251
Unassigned	224.0.0.252–224.0.0.255
VMTP Managers Group RFC 1045	224.0.1.0
NTP (Network Time Protocol) RFC 1119	224.0.1.1
SGI-Dogfight	224.0.1.2
Rwhod	224.0.1.3
VNP	224.0.1.4
Artificial Horizons – Aviator	224.0.1.5
NSS – Name Service Server	224.0.1.6
AUDIONEWS – Audio News Multicast	224.0.1.7
SUN NIS+ Information Service	224.0.1.8
MTP (Multicast Transport Protocol)	224.0.1.9
IETF-1-LOW-AUDIO	224.0.1.10
IETF-1-AUDIO	224.0.1.11
IETF-1-VIDEO	224.0.1.12
IETF-2-LOW-AUDIO	224.0.1.13
IETF-2-AUDIO	224.0.1.14
IETF-2-VIDEO	224.0.1.15
MUSIC-SERVICE	224.0.1.16
SEANET-TELEMETRY	224.0.1.17
SEANET-IMAGE	224.0.1.18
MLOADD	224.0.1.19
Any private experiment	224.0.1.20

Table I-1   *Registered Multicast Addresses and Associated Applications, RFCs, and References*

Group, Application, and References	Address
DVMRP on MOSPF	224.0.1.21
SVRLOC	224.0.1.22
XINGTV	224.0.1.23
microsoft-ds	224.0.1.24
nbc-pro	224.0.1.25
nbc-pfn	224.0.1.26
lmsc-calren-1	224.0.1.27
lmsc-calren-2	224.0.1.28
lmsc-calren-3	224.0.1.29
lmsc-calren-4	224.0.1.30
ampr-info	224.0.1.31
Mtrace	224.0.1.32
RSVP-encap-1	224.0.1.33
RSVP-encap-2	224.0.1.34
SVRLOC-DA	224.0.1.35
rln-server	224.0.1.36
proshare-mc	224.0.1.37
Dantz	224.0.1.38
cisco-rp-announce	224.0.1.39
cisco-rp-discovery	224.0.1.40
Gatekeeper	224.0.1.41
Iberiagames	224.0.1.42
nwn-discovery	224.0.1.43
nwn-adaptor	224.0.1.44
isma-1	224.0.1.45
isma-2	224.0.1.46
telerate	224.0.1.47

Table I-1   *Registered Multicast Addresses and Associated Applications, RFCs, and References*

Group, Application, and References	Address
Ciena	224.0.1.48
dcap-servers RFC 2114	224.0.1.49
dcap-clients RFC 2114	224.0.1.50
Mcntp-directory	224.0.1.51
Mbone-vcr-directory	224.0.1.52
Heartbeat	224.0.1.53
sun-mc-grp	224.0.1.54
extended-sys	224.0.1.55
pdrncs	224.0.1.56
tns-adv-multi	224.0.1.57
Vcals-dmu	224.0.1.58
Zuba	224.0.1.59
hp-device-disc	224.0.1.60
tms-production	224.0.1.61
Sunscalar	224.0.1.62
mmtp-poll	224.0.1.63
compaq-peer	224.0.1.64
Iapp	224.0.1.65
multihasc-com	224.0.1.66
serv-discovery	224.0.1.67
Mdhcpdisover RFC 2730	224.0.1.68
MMP-bundle-discovery1	224.0.1.69
MMP-bundle-discovery2	224.0.1.70
XYPOINT DGPS Data Feed	224.0.1.71
GilatSkySurfer	224.0.1.72

Table I-1   *Registered Multicast Addresses and Associated Applications, RFCs, and References*

Group, Application, and References	Address
SharesLive	224.0.1.73
NorthernData	224.0.1.74
SIP	224.0.1.75
IAPP	224.0.1.76
AGENTVIEW	224.0.1.77
Tibco Multicast1	224.0.1.78
Tibco Multicast2	224.0.1.79
MSP	224.0.1.80
OTT (One-way Trip Time)	224.0.1.81
TRACKTICKER	224.0.1.82
dtn-mc	224.0.1.83
jini-announcement	224.0.1.84
jini-request	224.0.1.85
sde-discovery	224.0.1.86
DirecPC-SI	224.0.1.87
B1Rmonitor	224.0.1.88
3Com-AMP3 Drmon	224.0.1.89
ImFtmSvc	224.0.1.90
NQDS4	224.0.1.91
NQDS5	224.0.1.92
NQDS6	224.0.1.93
NLVL12	224.0.1.94
NTDS1	224.0.1.95
NTDS2	224.0.1.96
NODSA	224.0.1.97
NODSB	224.0.1.98
NODSC	224.0.1.99

Table I-1 *Registered Multicast Addresses and Associated Applications, RFCs, and References*

Group, Application, and References	Address
NODSD	224.0.1.100
NQDS4R	224.0.1.101
NQDS5R	224.0.1.102
NQDS6R	224.0.1.103
NLVL12R	224.0.1.104
NODS1R	224.0.1.105
NODS2R	224.0.1.106
NODSAR	224.0.1.107
NODSBR	224.0.1.108
NODSCR	224.0.1.109
NODSDR	224.0.1.110
MRM	224.0.1.111
TVE-FILE	224.0.1.112
TVE-ANNOUNCE	224.0.1.113
Mac Srv Loc	224.0.1.114
Simple Multicast	224.0.1.115
SpectraLinkGW	224.0.1.116
Dieboldmcast	224.0.1.117
Tivoli Systems	224.0.1.118
pq-lic-mcast	224.0.1.119
HYPERFEED	224.0.1.120
Pipesplatform	224.0.1.121
LiebDevMgmg-DM	224.0.1.122
TRIBALVOICE	224.0.1.123
Unassigned (Retracted 1/29/01)	224.0.1.124
PolyCom Relay1	224.0.1.125
Infront Multi1	224.0.1.126

Table I-1 *Registered Multicast Addresses and Associated Applications, RFCs, and References*

Group, Application, and References	Address
XRX DEVICE DISC	224.0.1.127
CNN	224.0.1.128
PTP-primary	224.0.1.129
PTP-alternate1	224.0.1.130
PTP-alternate2	224.0.1.131
PTP-alternate3	224.0.1.132
ProCast	224.0.1.133
3Com Discp	224.0.1.134
CS-Multicasting	224.0.1.135
TS-MC-1	224.0.1.136
Make Source	224.0.1.137
Teleborsa	224.0.1.138
SUMAConfig	224.0.1.139
Unassigned	224.0.1.140
DHCP-SERVERS	224.0.1.141
CN Router-LL	224.0.1.142
EMWIN	224.0.1.143
Alchemy Cluster	224.0.1.144
Satcast One	224.0.1.145
Satcast Two	224.0.1.146
Satcast Three	224.0.1.147
Intline	224.0.1.148
8x8 Multicast	224.0.1.149
Unassigned	224.0.1.150
Intline-1	224.0.1.151
Intline-2	224.0.1.152
Intline-3	224.0.1.153

Table I-1   *Registered Multicast Addresses and Associated Applications, RFCs, and References*

Group, Application, and References	Address
Intline-4	224.0.1.154
Intline-5	224.0.1.155
Intline-6	224.0.1.156
Intline-7	224.0.1.157
Intline-8	224.0.1.158
Intline-9	224.0.1.159
Intline-10	224.0.1.160
Intline-11	224.0.1.161
Intline-12	224.0.1.162
Intline-13	224.0.1.163
Intline-14	224.0.1.164
Intline-15	224.0.1.165
marratech-cc	224.0.1.166
EMS-InterDev	224.0.1.167
itb301	224.0.1.168
rtv-audio	224.0.1.169
rtv-video	224.0.1.170
HAVI-Sim	224.0.1.171
Nokia Cluster	224.0.1.172
Unassigned	224.0.1.173–224.0.0.255
"rwho" Group (BSD) (unofficial)	224.0.2.1
SUN RPC PMAPPROC_CALLIT	224.0.2.2
SIAC MDD Service	224.0.2.64–224.0.2.95
CoolCast	224.0.2.96–224.0.2.127
WOZ-Garage	224.0.2.128–224.0.2.191
SIAC MDD Market Service	224.0.2.192–224.0.2.255
RFE Generic Service	224.0.3.0–224.0.3.255

Table I-1   *Registered Multicast Addresses and Associated Applications, RFCs, and References*

Group, Application, and References	Address
RFE Individual Conferences	224.0.4.0–224.0.4.255
CDPD Groups	224.0.5.0–224.0.5.127
SIAC Market Service	224.0.5.128–224.0.5.191
Unassigned IANA	224.0.5.192–224.0.5.255
Cornell ISIS Project	224.0.6.0–224.0.6.127
Unassigned IANA	224.0.6.128–224.0.6.255
Where-Are-You	224.0.7.0–224.0.7.255
INTV	224.0.8.0–224.0.8.255
Invisible Worlds	224.0.9.0–224.0.9.255
DLSw Groups	224.0.10.0–224.0.10.255
NCC.NET Audio	224.0.11.0–224.0.11.255
Microsoft and MSNBC	224.0.12.0–224.0.12.63
UUNET PIPEX Net News	224.0.13.0–223.0.13.255
NLANR	224.0.14.0–224.0.14.255
Hewlett Packard	224.0.15.0–224.0.15.255
XingNet	224.0.16.0–224.0.16.255
Mercantile & Commodity Exchange	224.0.17.0–224.0.17.31
NDQMD1	224.0.17.32–224.0.17.63
ODN-DTV	224.0.17.64–224.0.17.127
Dow Jones	224.0.18.0–224.0.18.255
Walt Disney Company	224.0.19.0–224.0.19.63
Cal Multicast	224.0.19.64–224.0.19.95
SIAC Market Service	224.0.19.96–224.0.19.127
IIG Multicast	224.0.19.128–224.0.19.191
Metropol	224.0.18.192–224.0.19.207
Xenoscience, Inc.	224.0.19.208–224.0.19.239

Table I-1   *Registered Multicast Addresses and Associated Applications, RFCs, and References*

Group, Application, and References	Address
HYPERFEED	224.0.19.240–224.0.19.255
MS-IP/TV	224.0.20.0–224.0.20.63
Reliable Network Solutions	224.0.20.64–224.0.20.127
TRACKTICKER Group	224.0.20.128–224.0.20.143
CNR Rebroadcast MCA	224.0.20.144–224.0.20.207
Talarian MCAST	224.0.21.0–224.0.21.127
WORLD MCAST	224.0.22.0–224.0.22.255
Domain Scoped Group	224.0.252.0–224.0.252.255
Report Group	224.0.253.0–224.0.253.255
Query Group	224.0.254.0–224.0.254.255
Border Routers	224.0.255.0–224.0.255.255
ST Multicast Groups RFC 1190	224.1.0.0–224.1.255.255
Multimedia Conference Calls	224.2.0.0–224.2.127.253
SAPv1 Announcements	224.2.127.254
SAPv0 Announcements (deprecated)	224.2.127.255
SAP Dynamic Assignments	224.2.128.0–224.2.255.255
DIS transient groups	224.252.0.0–224.255.255.255
MALLOC (temp – renew 1/01)	225.0.0.0–225.255.255.255
VMTP transient groups	232.0.0.0–232.255.255.255
Static Allocations (temp - renew 03/02)	233.0.0.0–233.255.255.255
Administratively Scoped IANA, RFC 2365	239.0.0.0–239.255.255.255
Reserved IANA	239.0.0.0–239.63.255.255
Reserved IANA	239.64.0.0–239.127.255.255
Reserved IANA	239.128.0.0–239.191.255.255

Table I-1 *Registered Multicast Addresses and Associated Applications, RFCs, and References*

Group, Application, and References	Address
Organization-Local Scope RFC 2365	239.192.0.0–239.251.255.255
Site-Local Scope (reserved) RFC 2365	239.252.0.0–239.252.255.255
Site-Local Scope (reserved) RFC 2365	239.253.0.0–239.253.255.255
Site-Local Scope (reserved) RFC 2365	239.254.0.0–239.254.255.255
Site-Local Scope RFC 2365	239.255.0.0–239.255.255.255
Rasadv	239.255.2.2

Appendix J

Tool Command Language (TCL) Reference

Cisco IOS Software supports the Tool Command Language (Tcl) for writing scripts within the IOS command-line interface (CLI). Scripts are a helpful way to automate tasks, verify configurations, and troubleshoot problems. Cisco IOS Software also has Tcl subsystems for their Embedded Syslog Manager (ESM) and Interactive Voice Response (IVR).

This appendix serves as a quick reference for Tcl scripting. Specifically, this appendix covers the following topics:

- Cisco IOS commands related to Tcl

- Custom command extensions for the IOS Tcl shell

- Tcl script example

- References for learning more about Tcl scripting

Table J-1 summarizes the Cisco IOS commands related to Tcl scripting.

Table J-2 summarizes the Cisco IOS command extensions related to Tcl scripting.

Table J-1   *Tcl-Related IOS Commands*

Command	Description
(global) scripting tcl encdir *location*	This command specifies the default location of external encoding files (*.enc). The *location* path can point to flash memory, TFTP, FTP, or RCP.
(global) scripting tcl init *location*	This command specifies the path to a Tcl script that is to be ran whenever the Tcl shell is enabled. The *location* path can point to flash memory, TFTP, FTP, or RCP.
(global) scripting tcl low-memory *number-of-bytes*	This command sets the minimum memory threshold for running Tcl scripts. If the minimum free RAM drops below this threshold, the script will stop.
(exec) tclsh	This command enables the interactive Tcl shell.
(tcl) source *path-to-tcl-script*	This command specifies the path and filename of a predefined Tcl script. This is an alternative to typing in the commands directly in the Tcl shell. The path can point to flash memory, TFTP, FTP, or RCP.
(tcl) exit	Exits the Tcl shell. You can also use the **tclquit** command.

Table J-2   *IOS Tcl Command Extensions*

Command	Description
ios_config	Runs a Cisco IOS CLI configuration command.
log_user	Toggles Tcl command output under Tcl configuration mode.
typeahead	Writes text to the router standard input buffer file.
snmp_getbulk	Retrieves a large section of the MIB table.
snmp_getid	Retrieves these SNMP variables: sysDescr.0 sysObjectID.0 sysUpTime.0 sysContact.0 sysName.0 sysLocation.0
snmp_getnext	Retrieves individual SNMP variables (similar to the SNMP **getnext** command).
snmp_getone	Retrieves individual SNMP variables (similar to the SNMP **getone** command).
snmp_setany	Retrieves the current values of a variable and performs a set request on the variable.

Tcl Example

The following example shows a simple Tcl script for testing IP reachability between devices. The **foreach** command invokes a loop that pings each IP address. A regular expression test is performed and, if the **ping** is successful (indicated by a **!** in the IOS output), the IP address is listed along with the word **success**. If the **ping** fails, the IP address is listed with the word **failed**.

```
Router(tcl)#foreach i {
+>1.1.1.1
+>2.2.2.2
+>3.3.3.3
+>4.4.4.4
+>} {if {[regexp "!" [exec "ping $i"]]} {
+>puts "$i - success"
+>} else {
+>puts "$i - failed"
+>}
+>}
1.1.1.1 - success
2.2.2.2 - success
3.3.3.3 - success
4.4.4.4 - failed
```

References

Tcl and the TK Toolkit, Second Edition by John Ousterhout and Ken Jones, ISBN 032133633X (Addison-Wesley).

Cisco IOS Scripting with Tcl, www.cisco.com/en/US/docs/ios/netmgmt/configuration/guide/nm_script_tcl_ps10591_TSD_Products_Configuration_Guide_Chapter.html.

Tcl IVR API Programming Guide, www.cisco.com/en/US/docs/ios/voice/tcl/developer/guide/tclivrv2.html.

Embedded Syslog Manager (ESM), www.cisco.com/en/US/docs/ios/12_3t/12_3t2/feature/guide/gt_esm.html.

Appendix K

Ethernet Type Codes

A listing of commonly used Ethernet type codes is maintained by the Internet Assigned Numbers Authority (IANA). The information presented here is reproduced with permission from the IANA. For the most current Ethernet type code number assignment information, refer to http://www.iana.org/numbers.htm under the "Ethernet Numbers" link. Table K-1 shows the Ethernet type code numbers in hexadecimal format, along with a description.

Table K-1 *Ethernet Type Codes*

Hex Value	Description
0000-05DC	IEEE 802.3 Length Field
0101-01FF	Experimental
200	XEROX PUP (see 0A00)
201	PUP Addr Trans (see 0A01)
400	Nixdorf
600	XEROX NS IDP
660	DLOG
661	DLOG
800	Internet IP (IPv4)
801	X.75 Internet
802	NBS Internet
803	ECMA Internet

Table K-1   *Ethernet Type Codes*

Hex Value	Description
804	Chaosnet
805	X.25 Level 3
806	ARP
807	XNS Compatibility
808	Frame Relay ARP (RFC 1701)
081C	Symbolics Private
0888-088A	Xyplex
900	Ungermann-Bass net debug
0A00	Xerox IEEE802.3 PUP
0A01	PUP Address Translation
0BAD	Banyan VINES
0BAE	VINES Loopback (RFC 1701)
0BAF	VINES Echo (RFC 1701)
1000	Berkeley Trailer negotiation
1001-100F	Berkeley Trailer encapsulation/IP
1600	Valid Systems
4242	PCS Basic Block Protocol
5208	BBN Simnet
6000	DEC Unassigned (experimental)
6001	DEC MOP Dump/Load
6002	DEC MOP Remote Console
6003	DEC DECNET Phase IV Route
6004	DEC LAT
6005	DEC Diagnostic Protocol
6006	DEC Customer Protocol
6007	DEC LAVC, SCA
6008-6009	DEC Unassigned
6010-6014	3Com Corporation

Table K-1 *Ethernet Type Codes*

Hex Value	Description
6558	Trans Ether Bridging (RFC 1701)
6559	Raw Frame Relay (RFC 1701)
7000	Ungermann-Bass download
7002	Ungermann-Bass dia/loop
7020-7029	LRT
7030	Proteon
7034	Cabletron
8003	Cronus VLN
8004	Cronus Direct
8005	HP Probe
8006	Nestar
8008	AT&T
8010	Excelan
8013	SGI diagnostics
8014	SGI network games
8015	SGI reserved
8016	SGI bounce server
8019	Apollo Domain
802E	Tymshare
802F	Tigan, Inc.
8035	Reverse ARP
8036	Aeonic Systems
8038	DEC LANBridge
8039-803C	DEC Unassigned
803D	DEC Ethernet Encryption
803E	DEC Unassigned
803F	DEC LAN Traffic Monitor
8040-8042	DEC Unassigned

Table K-1   *Ethernet Type Codes*

Hex Value	Description
8044	Planning Research Corp.
8046	AT&T
8047	AT&T
8049	ExperData
805B	Stanford V Kernel exp.
805C	Stanford V Kernel prod.
805D	Evans & Sutherland
8060	Little Machines
8062	Counterpoint Computers
8065	Univ. of Mass. @ Amherst
8066	Univ. of Mass. @ Amherst
8067	Veeco Integrated Auto.
8068	General Dynamics
8069	AT&T
806A	Autophon
806C	ComDesign
806D	Computgraphic Corp.
806E-8077	Landmark Graphics Corp.
807A	Matra
807B	Dansk Data Elektronik
807C	Merit Internodal
807D-807F	Vitalink Communications
8080	Vitalink TransLAN III
8081-8083	Counterpoint Computers
809B	Appletalk
809C-809E	Datability
809F	Spider Systems Ltd.
80A3	Nixdorf Computers

Table K-1   *Ethernet Type Codes*

Hex Value	Description
80A4-80B3	Siemens Gammasonics Inc.
80C0-80C3	DCA Data Exchange Cluster
80C4	Banyan Systems
80C5	Banyan Systems
80C6	Pacer Software
80C7	Applitek Corporation
80C8-80CC	Intergraph Corporation
80CD-80CE	Harris Corporation
80CF-80D2	Taylor Instrument
80D3-80D4	Rosemount Corporation
80D5	IBM SNA Service on Ether
80DD	Varian Associates
80DE-80DF	Integrated Solutions TRFS
80E0-80E3	Allen-Bradley
80E4-80F0	Datability
80F2	Retix
80F3	AppleTalk AARP (Kinetics)
80F4-80F5	Kinetics
80F7	Apollo Computer
80FF-8103	Wellfleet Communications
8107-8109	Symbolics Private
8130	Hayes Microcomputers
8131	VG Laboratory Systems
8132-8136	Bridge Communications
8137-8138	Novell, Inc.
8139-813D	KTI
8148	Logicraft
8149	Network Computing Devices

Table K-1   *Ethernet Type Codes*

Hex Value	Description
814A	Alpha Micro
814C	SNMP
814D	BIIN
814E	BIIN
814F	Technically Elite Concept
8150	Rational Corp
8151-8153	Qualcomm
815C-815E	Computer Protocol Pty Ltd
8164-8166	Charles River Data System
817D	XTP
817E	SGI/Time Warner prop.
8180	HIPPI-FP encapsulation
8181	STP, HIPPI-ST
8182	Reserved for HIPPI-6400
8183	Reserved for HIPPI-6400
8184-818C	Silicon Graphics prop.
818D	Motorola Computer
819A-81A3	Qualcomm
81A4	ARAI Bunkichi
81A5-81AE	RAD Network Devices
81B7-81B9	Xyplex
81CC-81D5	Apricot Computers
81D6-81DD	Artisoft
81E6-81EF	Polygon
81F0-81F2	Comsat Labs
81F3-81F5	SAIC
81F6-81F8	VG Analytical
8203-8205	Quantum Software

Table K-1   *Ethernet Type Codes*

Hex Value	Description
8221-8222	Ascom Banking Systems
823E-8240	Advanced Encryption System
827F-8282	Athena Programming
8263-826A	Charles River Data System
829A-829B	Inst Ind Info Tech
829C-82AB	Taurus Controls
82AC-8693	Walker Richer & Quinn
8694-869D	Idea Courier
869E-86A1	Computer Network Tech
86A3-86AC	Gateway Communications
86DB	SECTRA
86DE	Delta Controls
86DD	IPv6
86DF	ATOMIC
86E0-86EF	Landis & Gyr Powers
8700-8710	Motorola
876B	TCP/IP Compression (RFC 1144)
876C	IP Autonomous Systems (RFC 1701)
876D	Secure Data (RFC1701)
880B	PPP
8847	MPLS Unicast
8848	MPLS Multicast
8A96-8A97	Invisible Software
9000	Loopback
9001	3Com(Bridge) XNS Sys Mgmt
9002	3Com(Bridge) TCP-IP Sys
9003	3Com(Bridge) loop detect
FF00	BBN VITAL-LanBridge cache

Table K-1   *Ethernet Type Codes*

Hex Value	Description
FF00-FF0F	ISC Bunker Ramo
FFFF	Reserved (RFC 1701)

Index

Numerics

D

R

S

W

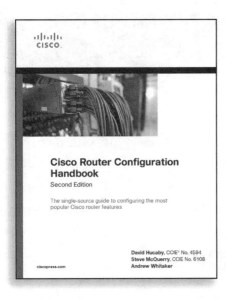

FREE Online Edition

Your purchase of **Cisco Router Configuration Handbook** includes access to a free online edition for 45 days through the Safari Books Online subscription service. Nearly every Cisco Press book is available online through Safari Books Online, along with more than 5,000 other technical books and videos from publishers such as Addison-Wesley Professional, Exam Cram, IBM Press, O'Reilly, Prentice Hall, Que, and Sams.

SAFARI BOOKS ONLINE allows you to search for a specific answer, cut and paste code, download chapters, and stay current with emerging technologies.

Activate your FREE Online Edition at
www.informit.com/safarifree

> **STEP 1:** Enter the coupon code: GNEPFDB.

> **STEP 2:** New Safari users, complete the brief registration form.
> Safari subscribers, just log in.

If you have difficulty registering on Safari or accessing the online edition, please e-mail customer-service@safaribooksonline.com

 Addison Wesley    AdobePress   ALPHA   Cisco Press   FT Press   IBM Press   lynda.com   Microsoft Press   New Riders

 O'REILLY   Peachpit Press   PRENTICE HALL   que   Redbooks   SAMS   SAS Publishing   Sun telemetrysystems   WILEY